PANEL LAYOUT
for competition²

First Edition Published	March 2012
Compiler	DAMDI Publishing Co.
Publisher	Suh, Kyong won
Editor	Pyo, Mi young
Design	Choi, Ye ji
Photograph	Roh, Kyung young
Intern	Lee, Chang wook
Translator	Lee, Ji eun
Publishing	RHED Publishing
Address	50 Playfair Road # 07-02
	Noel Building, Singapore 367995
TEL	+ 65 62899208
FAX	+ 65 62899108
E-mail	info@rhedpublishing.com
webpage	www.rhedpublishing.com

March 2012 by Damdi Publishing Co, Seoul
August 2012 by RHED Publishing, Singapore

Printing: Tiger Printing (Hongkong) Co., Ltd.
ISBN 978-981-07-3145-8 (set)

PANEL
LAYOUT
for competition[2]

CONTENTS

CONTENTS

CONTENTS

173

Cricket | *StudioNOWA*

Classification : Institutional, Kindergarten
Client : Comune di Prato
Designer : Marco Navarra_NOWA
Project Team : Maria Giacoma Marino_NOWA, Antonio Rizzo_NOWA, Salvatore

Interlandi_NOWA, Fortunato Dario Pappalardo_NOWA
Collaborators : Fabrizio Agnello, Salvatore Binanti, Andrea Moschetto, Christian Vindigni

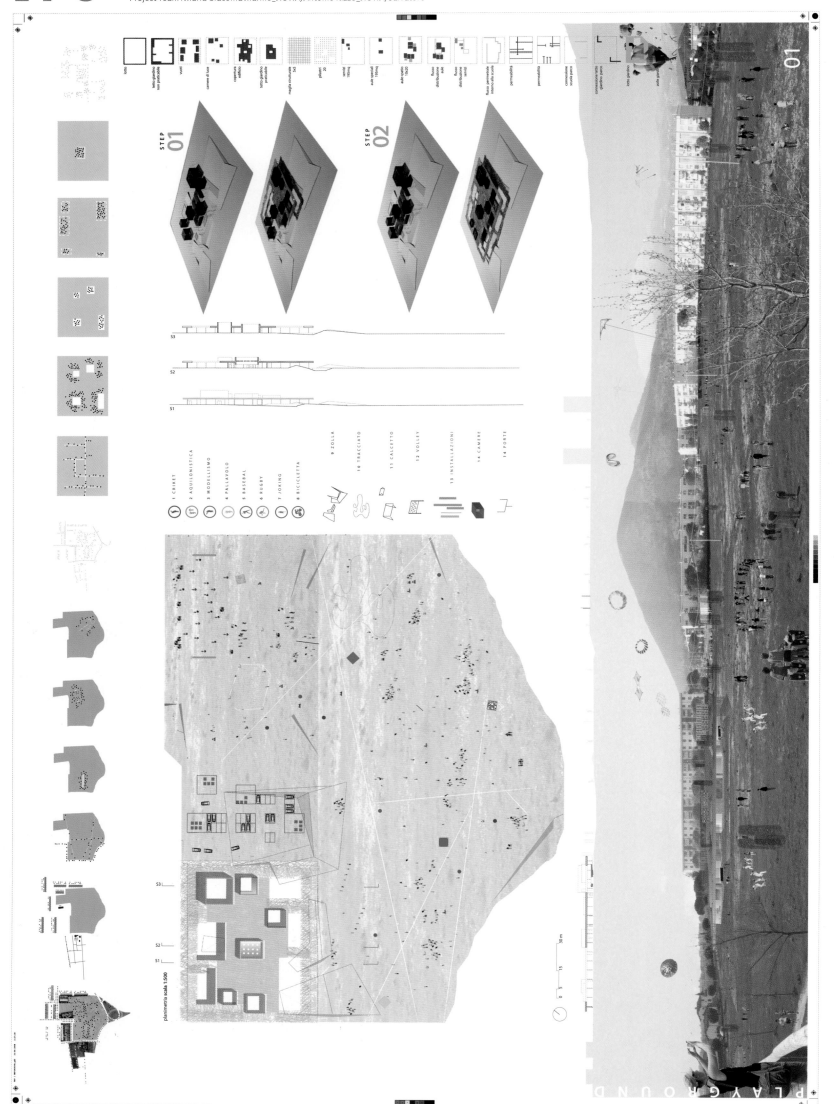

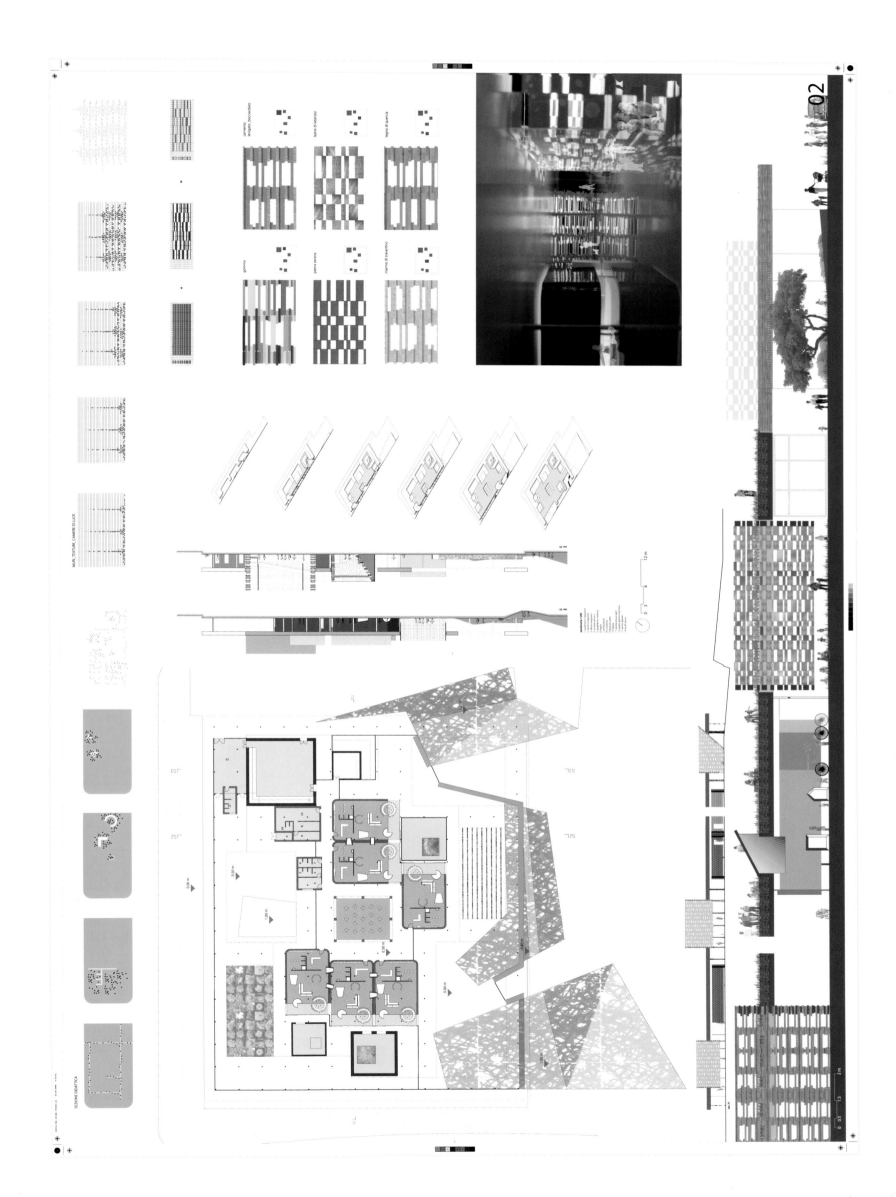

174

Kindergarten Ribnica | *OFIS arhitekti*

Location : Ribnica, Slovenia
Type : Kindergarten
Client : Community of Ribnica
Project Team : Rok Oman, Spela Videcnik, Andrej Gregoric, Janez Martincic, Janja del Linz, Katja Aljaz

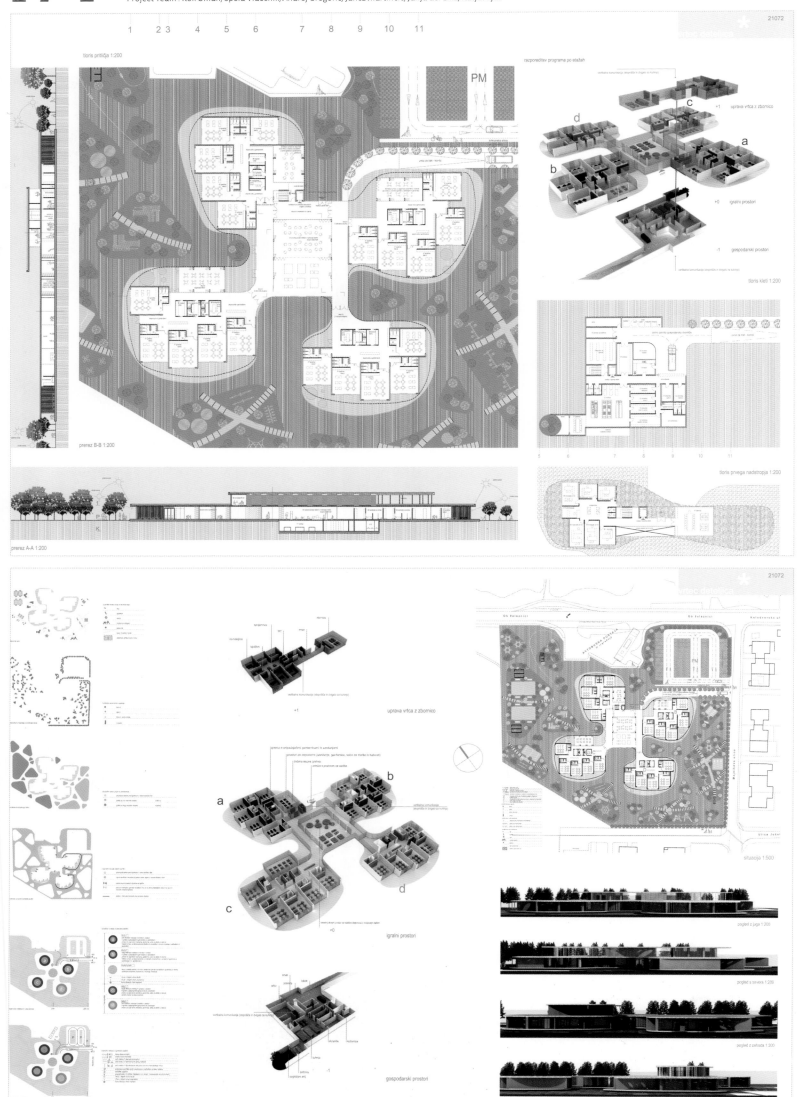

21072

PERSPEKTIVNI PROSTORSKI PRIKAZ

IZ UČILNICE V ATRIJ

21072

POGLED IZ SKUPNIH PROSTOROV NA NOTRANJI ATRIJ

POGLED NA ZUNANJO UČNO TERASO TRIJADE

SKUPNI PROSTORI

POT DO GLAVNEGA VHODA V VRTEC

175

Courbevoi | *Marchi_Architectes*

500

Title : Ville de Coubevoie - child care center
Team : Architecture project (Adelaïde et Nicola Marchi[Marchi_Architectes]), 3D images (Ryuta Amae[Japan])

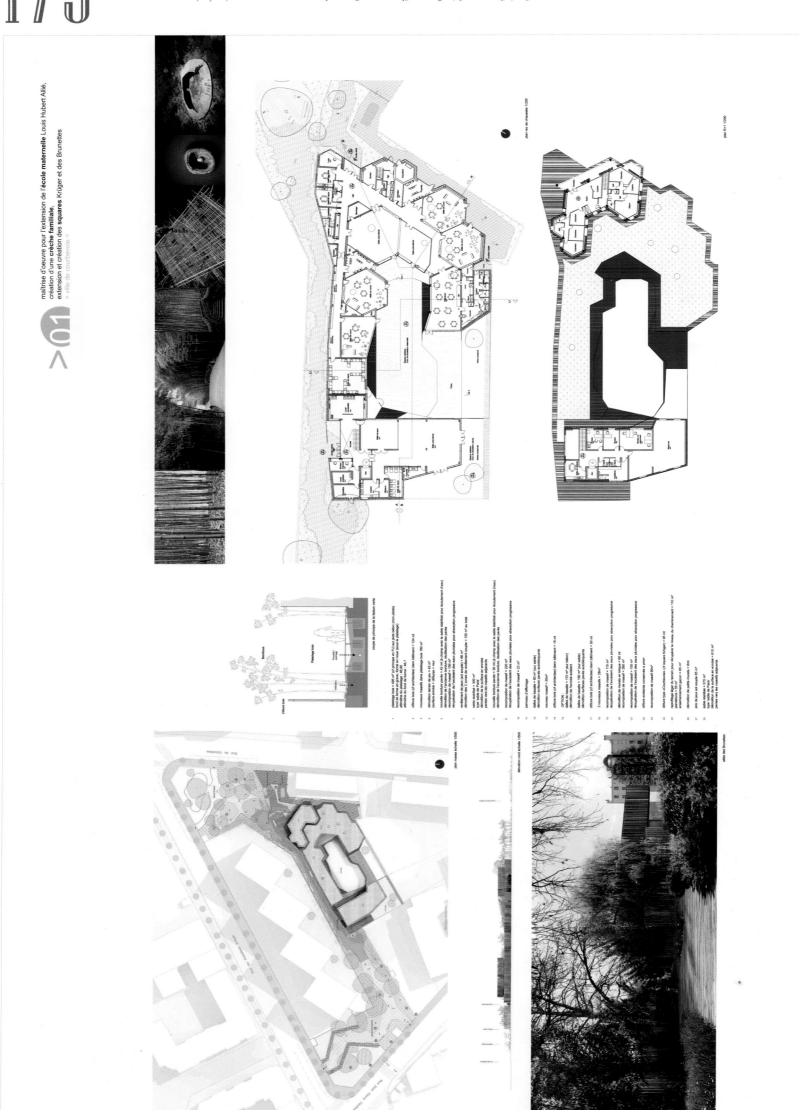

> 02   maîtrise d'oeuvre pour l'extension de l'**école maternelle** Louis Hubert Allié,
création d'une **crèche familiale**,
extension et création des **squares** Krüger et des Brunettes

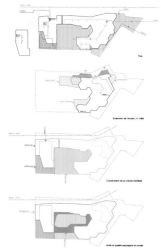

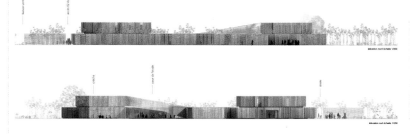

> 03   maîtrise d'oeuvre pour l'extension de l'**école maternelle** Louis Hubert Allié,
création d'une **crèche familiale**,
extension et création des **squares** Krüger et des Brunettes

176

Prêmio Masisa de Arquitetura | *Figura Arquitetos office*

Architects : Felipe Campolina, Lucas Leite, Vinícius Amaral
Location : Brazil
Use : Institutional
Dimension : 35m²

502

CENTRO TECNOLÓGICO DIGITAL

O governo de vários estados brasileiros, contando também com recursos do governo federal, municipal e da iniciativa privada, estão promovendo a criação de centros de treinamento voltados para a qualificação e profissionalização do cidadão, capacitando e preparando, gratuitamente, a comunidade para o mercado de trabalho.

Nossa proposta se insere nesse modelo de projeto, na forma de um Centro Tecnológico Digital (CTD), visando capacitar a população de regiões carentes dessa tecnologia, através de instalação de unidades de treinamento em cidades de pequeno, médio e grande porte, ou mesmo em comunidades rurais.

Os objetivos específicos do CTD são: disponibilizar cursos de capacitação em tecnologia digital, utilizando inclusive ensino à distância, para treinar e qualificar mão de obra; elaborar projetos e apoiar a implantação de pequenas empresas de base tecnológicas e tradicionais; difundir as tecnologias gerados ou adaptadas para solução de problemas regionais.

Uma unidade mínima de treinamento do CTD totaliza 210m2, feita a partir de um módulo base medindo internamente 4,88m x 4,88m (em função da chapa de OSB), com uma circulação externa de 1,83m de largura (uma e meia chapa), concebida em estrutura seca, com montagem fácil e rápida, através do sistema "steel framing" associado à chapa de OSB. A dimensão reduzida do módulo base possibilita a implantação de uma unidade de treinamento do CTD em locais distintos e em topografias as mais variados.

Externamente, o módulo pode receber vários revestimentos, entre eles PVC, cerâmica, pintura acrílica, telha.

MÓDULO ACESSO

LAB. INFORMÁTICA

SALA MULTIMEROS

MÓDULO ESCADA

CONJUNTO 2 PAVIMENTOS

TIPOLOGIAS DE IMPLANTAÇÃO

MÓDULOS UNIDOS OU SEPARADOS

ADAPTAÇÃO A DIFERENTES TOPOGRAFIAS

MÚLTIPLAS POSSIBILIDADES DE COMPOSIÇÃO

ENSAIO REVESTIMENTO EXTERNO

PREMIAÇÃO PÚBLICA NACIONAL - 1º PRÊMIO MASISA DE ARQUITETURA

MASISA DO BRASIL LTDA - IAB/PR - INSTITUTO DE ARQUITETOS DO BRASIL / DEPARTAMENTO DO PARANÁ

1/4

MÓDULO - BASE (35m2)

SISTEMA CONSTRUTIVO

O sistema construtivo parte de um módulo base, a partir do qual é possível elaborar diversas configurações, tornando o projeto flexível e passível de adaptação em qualquer terreno.

A estrutura do módulo base é a do sistema "steel framing" com chapas de OSB, em uma associação harmônica. As chapas de OSB revestem interno e externamente o aço, com preenchimento em lã de vidro, visando maior conforto ambiental e acústico.

A base da edificação é em radier, solução adotada na maioria das obras em "steel framing", já que se trata de estrutura leve. A cobertura, estrutura independente do restante da edificação, possui caibros para fixação das telhas, que ficam no interior de um "sanduíche" de telha e forro (OSB), também preenchidos com lã de vidro. Ela se apoia em quatro pilares circulares e é erguida previamente, facilitando o travamento dos painéis laterais e a execução do restante da obra, protegendo-a durante os períodos de chuva.

Toda a modulação adotada (pisos, paredes, forro) partiu da dimensão das chapas de OSB, evitando desperdício de material, viabilizando o empreendimento.

Para a instalação dos esquadrias da janela, tomou-se o partido da modulação da estrutura, usando vãos de 61cm, possibilitando aberturas em paredes inteiros, sem que o sistema construtivo ficasse prejudicado.

BRISE

Brises venezianados acompanham toda circulação afim de reduzir o impacto negativo da incidência direta da luz solar sobre os módulos, além de atribuir uma aparência esteticamente agradável ao conjunto.

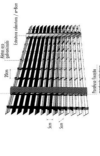

Estrutura cobertura / e=10cm
Aletas aço galvanizado 5 cm
Montante chapa metálica

ESC:1/7,5   0   10   20 cm

ENCONTRO PAINEIS x PILAR

Painéis de Steel Frame com 4,88 metros por 3,66 de altura serão montados no canteiro de obras e, em seguida, fixados na estrutura do telhado previamente executado. Uma chapa metálica irá compor o acabamento, fechando a lateral oca das paredes.

ESC:1/7,5   0   10   20 cm

MÓDULO - BASE

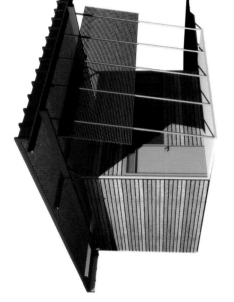

AA

Brise metálico / pingadeira termoacústica
Estrutura cobertura / e=6cm
Guarda-corpo h=90cm
Piso / OSB "Home" MF 18mm

Telha metálica galvanizada
Viga metálica 15x10cm
Viga metálica 20x10cm
Viga b=30
Fechamento externo / OSB "Home" 9mm
Estrutura cobertura / e=10cm
Grelha metálica / a.p.

Estrutura cobertura / e=10cm
Isolamento termo-acústico
Steel frame / 10cm
Montante / perfil "U" em aço galvanizado (8x3cm)
Fechamento externo / interno OSB "Home" 9mm
Montante duplo / perfil "U" em aço galvanizado (8x3cm)
Piso / placa seca / OSB "Home" MF 18mm
Estrutura cobertura / e=6cm
Proj. cobertura

A
MÓDULO BÁSICO
área = 35 m2
A

122
61 61
488
10   183
488

ESC:1/100   0   2   5 M

ESQUEMA DE COMPONENTES

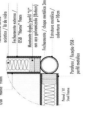
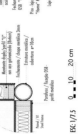

TELHAS
ESTRUTURA TELHADO
VIGAS / FORRO
BRISE
FECHAMENTO INTERNO
PAINEL STEEL FRAME
FECHAMENTO EXTERNO

ESQUEMA DE MONTAGEM

ESC:1/100   0   2   5 M

MÓDULO FINALIZADO

ISOLAMENTO TERMO-ACÚSTICO +
FECHAMENTO INTERNO

FECHAMENTO EXTERNO

INSTALAÇÃO DO BRISE

INSTALAÇÃO DOS PAINÉIS LATERAIS

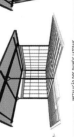
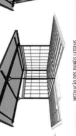

ACABAMENTO DA COBERTURA /
MONTAGEM DOS PAINÉIS LATERAIS

INSTALAÇÃO DOS PERFIS GUIAS

SUB-ESTRUTURAS

VIGAS

RADIER + ESTRUTURA TELHADO

C.T.D MÍNIMO (210m2)

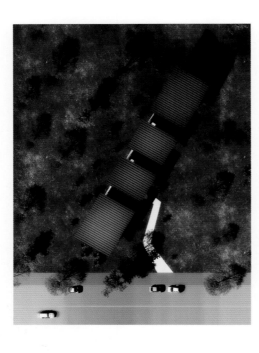

0 5 10 M

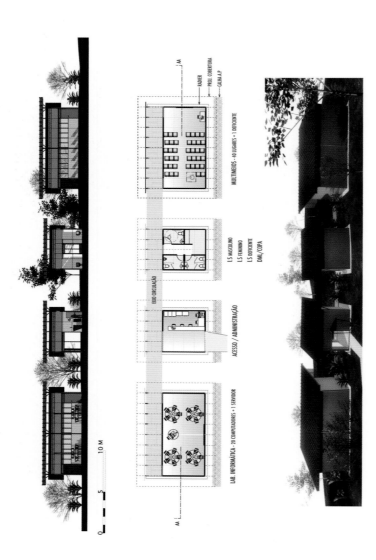

ACESSO / ADMINISTRAÇÃO

EIXO CIRCULAÇÃO

L.S MASCULINO
L.S FEMININO
L.S DEFICIENTE
DML/COPA

MULTIMEIOS - 40 LUGARES + 1 DEFICIENTE

LAB. INFORMÁTICA - 20 COMPUTADORES + 1 SERVIDOR

RADIER
PROJ. COBERTURA
CAIXA A.P
AA

Uma unidade mínima do CTD tem 210m2 e capacidade para atender até 60 alunos por dia, utilizando-se de 6 módulos base (4,88m x 4,88m). Cada módulo tem função diversificada, a saber:

1. Acesso / administração, ocupando um módulo
2. Banheiros masculino, feminino e deficiente e uma copa/d.m.l ocupando um módulo
3. Laboratório de informática com 20 estações de trabalho e um servidor ligado à internet por conexão banda larga e impressora, ocupando dois módulos
4. Sala Multimeios com capacidade para 40 lugares, com infraestrutura completa para vídeo conferências e ensino a distância, ocupando dois módulos.

A implantação linear, com os módulos independentes, conforme sugerido, facilita a execução e a acomodação dos blocos no terreno. O centro está adaptado para receber deficientes físicos.

LAB. INFORMÁTICA

CIRCULAÇÃO

MÓDULO ACESSO

MÓDULO SALA

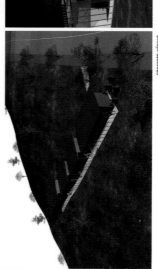

CONJUNTO MÍNIMO

PREMIAÇÃO PÚBLICA NACIONAL - 1º PRÊMIO MASISA DE ARQUITETURA

MASISA DO BRASIL LTDA - IAB/PR - INSTITUTO DE ARQUITETOS DO BRASIL / DEPARTAMENTO DO PARANÁ

3/4

C.T.D - 2 PAVIMENTOS (450m2)

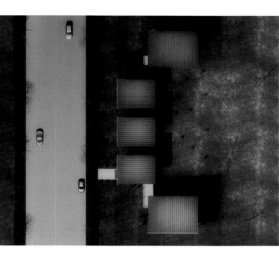

Utilizando-se doze módulos base (4,88m x 4,88m) e um módulo-escada, poderá ser implantada uma unidade CTD com 450m2, com capacidade para atender até 180 alunos por dia, em solução com dois pavimentos.

Nesse caso, os módulos têm as seguintes funções:

1. Acesso / administração / escritório, ocupando um módulo por pavimento
2. Banheiros masculino, feminino e deficiente e uma copa/d.m.l ocupando um módulo por pavimento.
3. Três salas de inclusão, cada uma ocupando dois módulos, com capacidade para 60 alunos no total
4. Sala Multimeios, com 40 lugares, ocupando dois módulos

O módulo-escada tem espaço previsto para instalação de plataforma hidráulica para atendimento de deficientes.

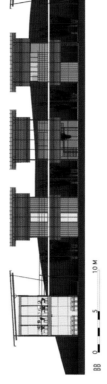

AA   0   5   10 M

BB   0   5   10 M

1º PAV

MULTIMEIOS
40 LUGARES + 1 DEFICIENTE

LS MASCULINO
LS FEMININO
LS DEFICIENTE
DML/COPA

CIRCULAÇÃO VERTICAL

ACESSO / ADMINISTRAÇÃO

LAB. INFORMÁTICA
20 COMPUTADORES
+ 1 SERVIDOR

GREIHA A.P
PROL. COBERTURA
RADIER

2º PAV

ESCRITÓRIO

0   5   10 M

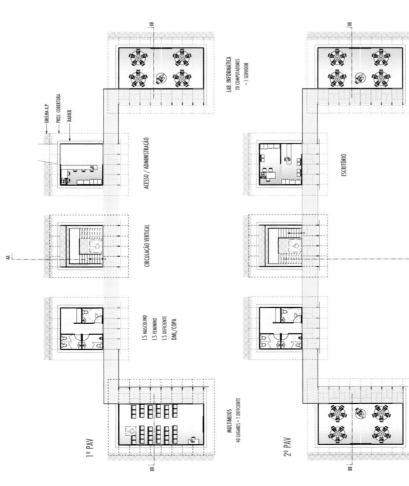

CONJUNTO 2 PAVIMENTOS

VISTA RUA

DETALHE DO CONJUNTO

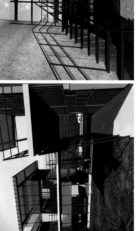

MÓDULO ESCADA

CORREDOR 2º PAVIMENTO

PREMIAÇÃO PÚBLICA NACIONAL - 1º PRÊMIO MASISA DE ARQUITETURA

MASISA DO BRASIL LTDA - IAB/PR - INSTITUTO DE ARQUITETOS DO BRASIL / DEPARTAMENTO DO PARANÁ

4/4

177

Sede do TRT Go | *Figura Arquitetos office*

Architects : Felipe Araújo, Felipe Campolina, Lucas Leite,
Tiago Viegas
Location : Brazil

Use : Institutional
Dimension : 30,000m²

506

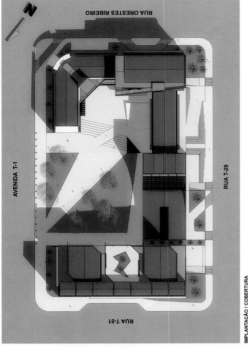

IMPLANTAÇÃO / COBERTURA
Esc.: 1/750

Como premissa, foi considerada a necessidade do projeto apresentar um caráter público e de ser um marco arquitetônico para a cidade de Goiânia. A solução adotada define volumetrias distintas para cada edifício, formando porém um conjunto uniforme. A proposta apresenta uma cota altimétrica regular e caracteriza-se por não ter definida uma fachada principal, o que confere ao complexo uma relação harmônica com seu entorno. Essa integração ao ambiente urbano é reforçada pelo espaço público criado no interior do complexo que permite uma circulação transversal permeável a todos edifícios do conjunto. A implantação no perímetro do quarteirão trouxe o espaço público para o seu interior, solução adequada a uma arquitetura pública que se distingue das soluções comerciais que pouco acrescentam ao espaço urbano.

O desenvolvimento da proposta deu-se a partir da demanda da construção a ser realizada em etapas, definindo-se, portanto, a implantação do edifício Sede do Fórum Trabalhista em uma faixa a ser demolida de 36 metros de largura paralela à rua T-51, na primeira etapa, mantendo o restante dos edifícios, a premissa assim, que o TRT continue realizando suas atividades concomitantemente com a execução da obra. A segunda etapa deve contemplar a demolição do restante e a construção dos edifícios do Centro Médico e Sede da Presidência, transferindo a operacionalidade do Tribunal para a nova sede do Fórum. Na terceira e última etapa foi previsto o rearranjo do edifício a ser preservado para acomodação da administração do complexo e tratamento do restante do terreno como espaço público agregado ao projeto.

O sistema construtivo adotado foi o de estrutura pré-fabricada de concreto. Essa decisão permitirá a realização da obra em períodos diferentes conferindo mais agilidade, praticidade e limpeza à construção. As conexões funcionais dos edifícios ocorrem no subsolo do complexo que acomoda também os dois auditórios, um com capacidade para 400 pessoas sob o edifício do Fórum e outro para 600 pessoas sob o vão livre do edifício da Presidência. A locação desses auditórios no subsolo possibilitou a concepção de pavimentos térreos mais generosos em suas circulações e que contemplam entradas voltadas para a praça tanto quanto para as vias públicas, enfatizando a característica pública da arquitetura.

		ÁREA LÍQUIDA	ÁREA CONSTRUÍDA
ETAPA 01	ED. SEDE FÓRUM TRABALHISTA	13.554,47m2	29.837,14m2
ETAPA 02	ED. CENTRO MÉDICO	4.849,81m2	9.909,27m2
	ED. SEDE PRESIDÊNCIA	8.222,21m2	16.750,25m2
ETAPA 03	ED. ADMINISTRATIVO	5.187,20m2	7.942,09m2
	TOTAL	31.813,70m2	64.238,80m2

PRIMEIRA ETAPA

SEGUNDA ETAPA

TERCEIRA ETAPA

-INSOLAÇÃO

A localização do complexo arquitetônico e a maior escala em relação ao entorno imediato proporcionam maior incidência de luz, o que levou à adoção de elementos de controle de luz nas fachadas.

-VENTOS

A implantação favorece os ventos dominantes nas direções norte e nordeste.

CAPTAÇÃO DE ÁGUA

A água captada nas coberturas é conduzida por rígencalha à plena pré-fabricada até reservatórios para reutilização nos sanitários e na irrigação das áreas verdes.

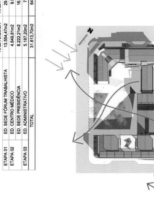

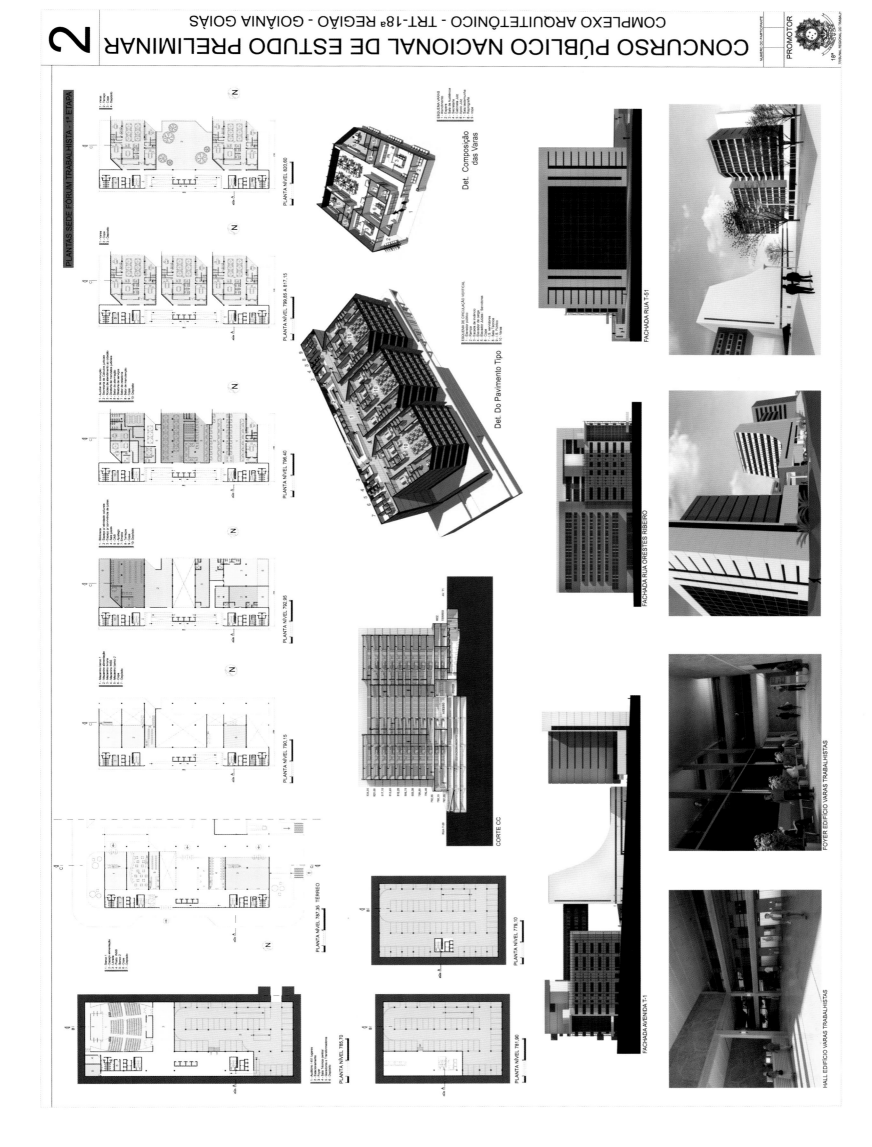

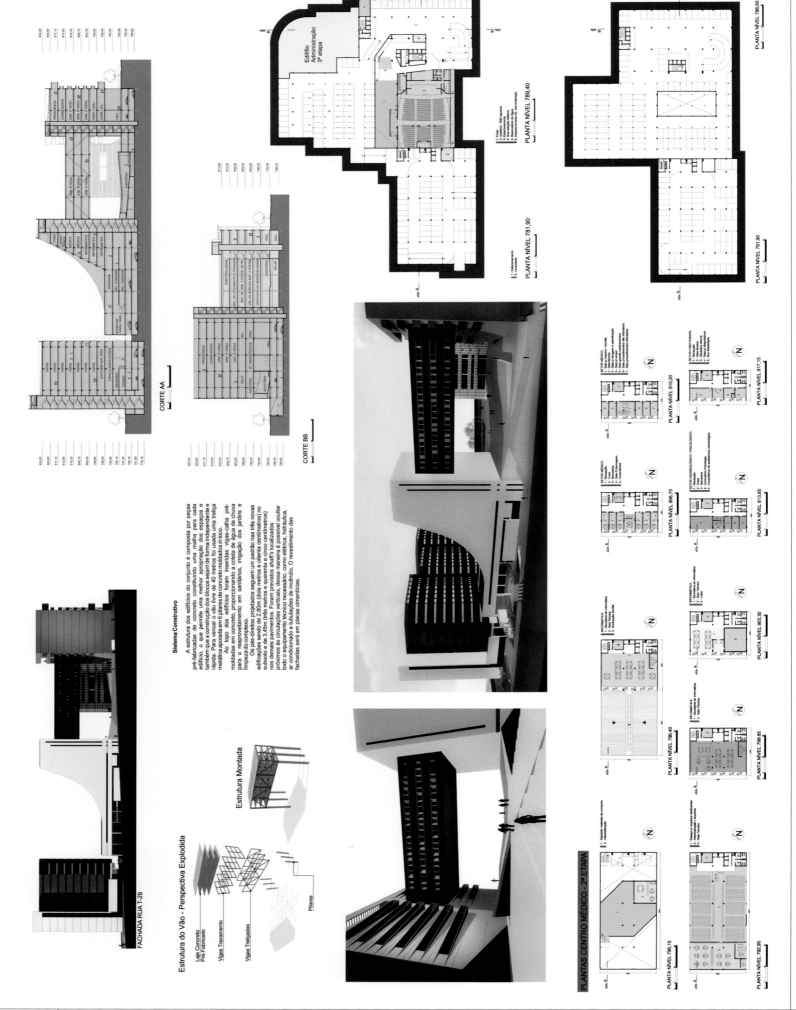

509

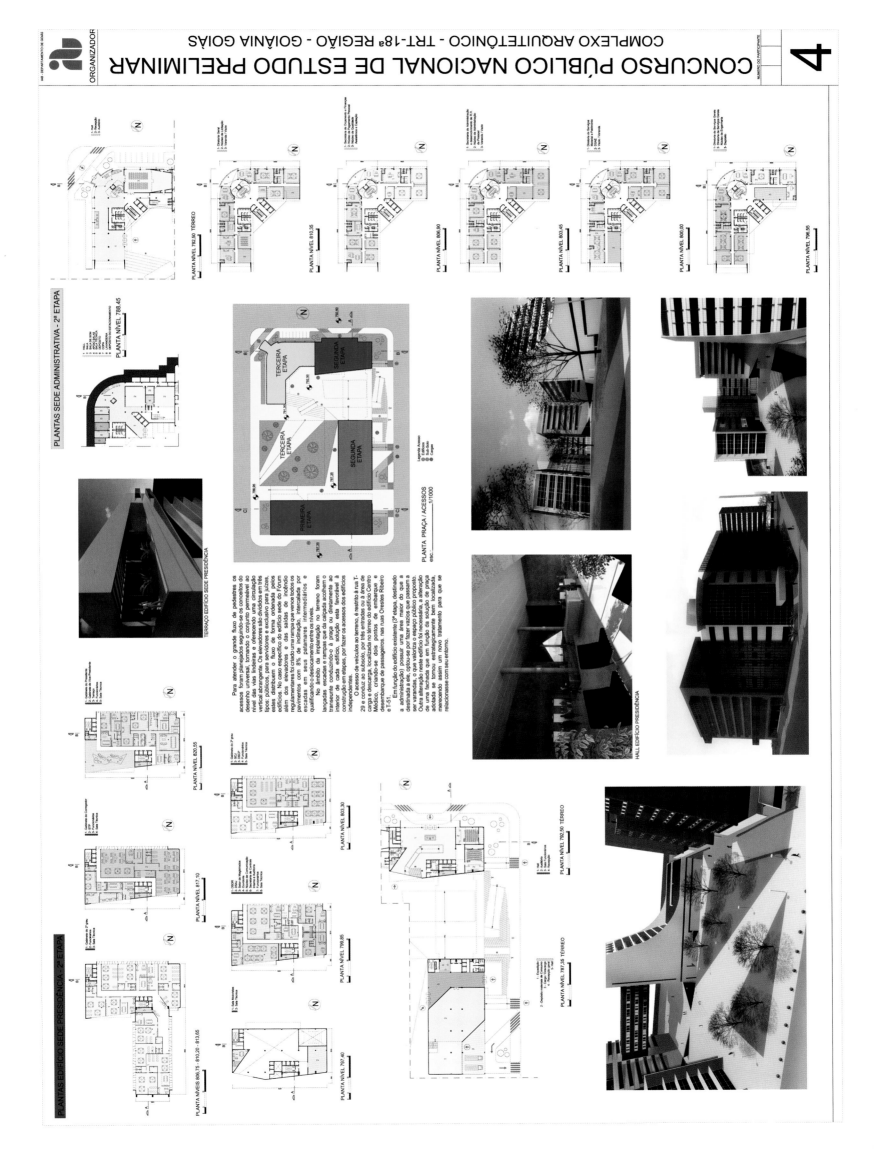

178

New School Campus and Primary School | *Donner Sorcinelli Architecture*

Location : Carbonera, Italy
Competition : 3rd Prize
Area : 154.373 sq.m.
Built surface : 3577 sq.m.

School Budget : € 4.997.708
Client : Carbonera Municipality

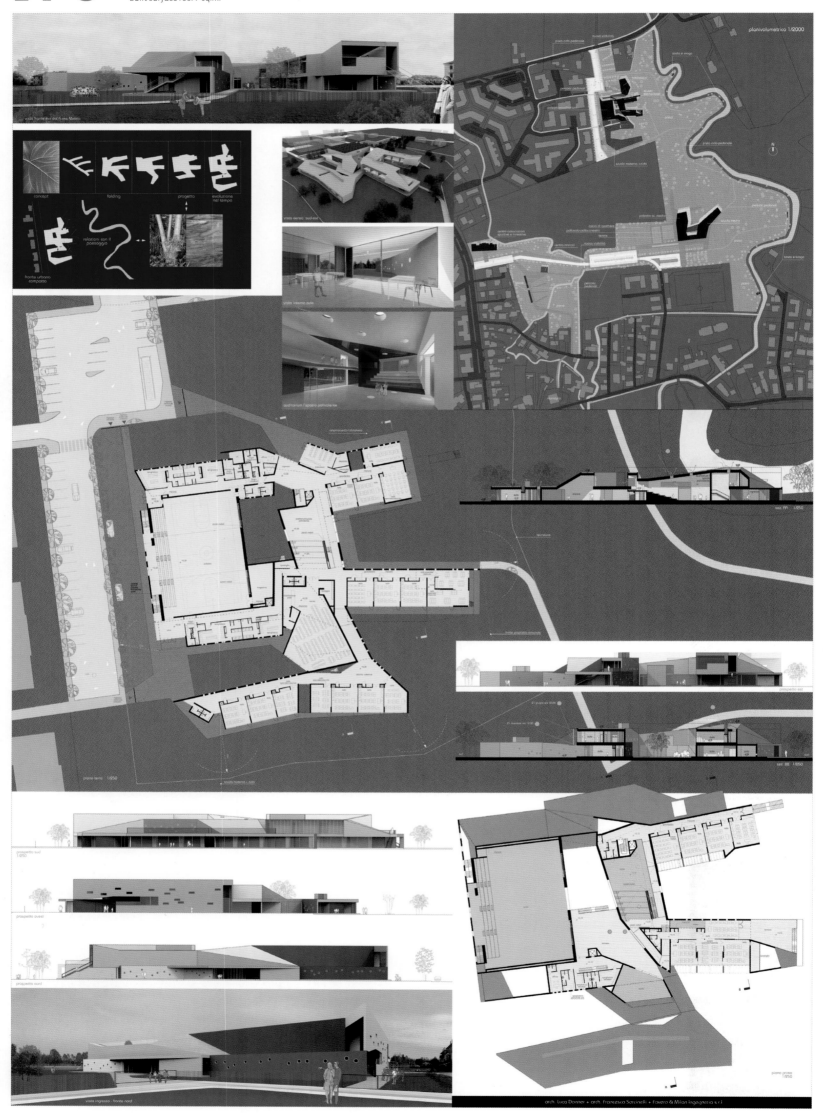

Escuela de Ciencias de la Salud | *modostudio*

Team : Design team - Modostudio (Fabio Cibinel, Roberto Laurenti, Giorgio Martocchia, Cristina Carmona Botana) with Luis Carmona Pla + Garcia Ruiz & Carmona Botana Arquitectos

Location : Badajoz – Spain
Client : Junta de Extremadura - Consejeria de Sanidad y Dependencia
Phase : Architectural Competition | 3rd Place
Area : 21.506 sqm / Construction Budget : € 18,447,000,00

179

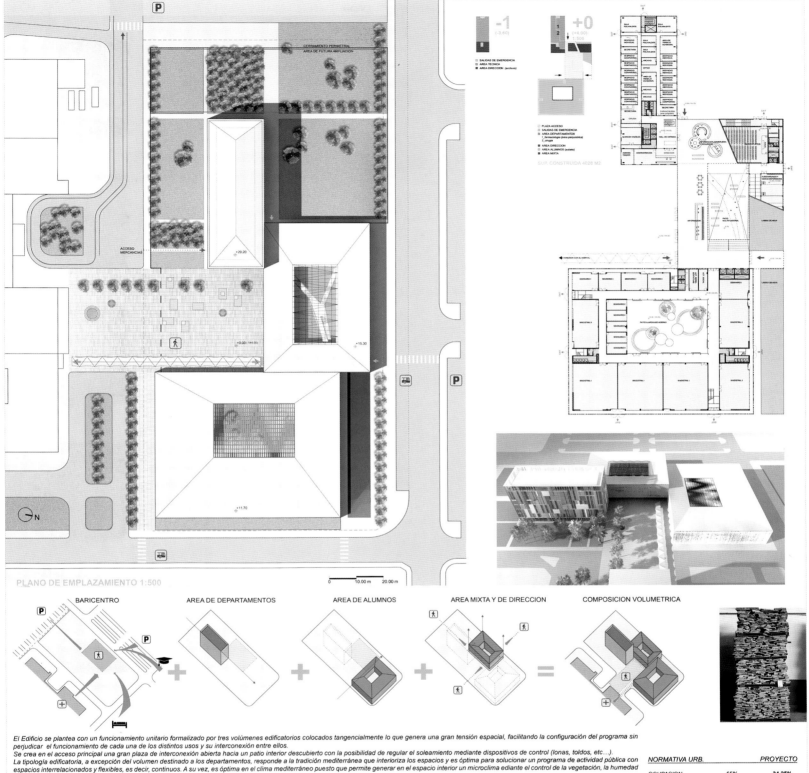

PLANO DE EMPLAZAMIENTO 1:500

0   10.00 m   20.00 m

BARICENTRO   AREA DE DEPARTAMENTOS   AREA DE ALUMNOS   AREA MIXTA Y DE DIRECCION   COMPOSICION VOLUMETRICA

El Edificio se plantea con un funcionamiento unitario formalizado por tres volúmenes edificatorios colocados tangencialmente lo que genera una gran tensión espacial, facilitando la configuración del programa sin perjudicar el funcionamiento de cada una de los distintos usos y su interconexión entre ellos.

Se crea en el acceso principal una gran plaza de interconexión abierta hacia un patio interior descubierto con la posibilidad de regular el soleamiento mediante dispositivos de control (lonas, toldos, etc...).

La tipología edificatoria, a excepción del volumen destinado a los departamentos, responde a la tradición mediterránea que interioriza los espacios y es óptima para solucionar un programa de actividad pública con espacios interrelacionados y flexibles, es decir, continuos. A su vez, es óptima en el clima mediterráneo puesto que permite generar en el espacio interior un microclima mediante el control de la vegetación, la humedad y la umbría.

Estos patios apoyan los espacios internos y sirve de fondo visual a todo el conjunto a través del hall y al que están ligados los espacios de representación.

Esta solución arquitectónica de volcar los distintos usos y circulaciones hacia un patio interior se mantiene en el volumen de usos mixtos y generales y en el volumen de aulario.

La imagen exterior del volumen de aularios de la edificación se ha conformado mediante la formación de una piel exterior de elementos prefabricados de hormigón que asemejan a las pilas de corcho como homenaje virtual a este producto propio de nuestra tierra.

El diseño del edificio se ha realizado de forma que su geometría y construcción favorezca con estrategias comprobadas, su eficiencia energética.

NORMATIVA URB.		PROYECTO
OCUPACION	65%	**34.25%**
EDIFICABILIDAD	2.5m2/m2	**1.3m2/m2**
N° MAXIMO PLANTAS	9 plantas	**7 plantas**

ESCUELA DE CIENCIAS DE LA SALUD Y AULARIO COMPLEMENTARIO

01

PILAR CARMONA BOTANA, LUIS CARMONA PLA, LUIS GARCIA RUIZ Y CIBINEL-LAURENTI-MATOCCHIA ARQUIETCTOS ASOCIADOS   UTE PIL2-MODOSTUDIO

512

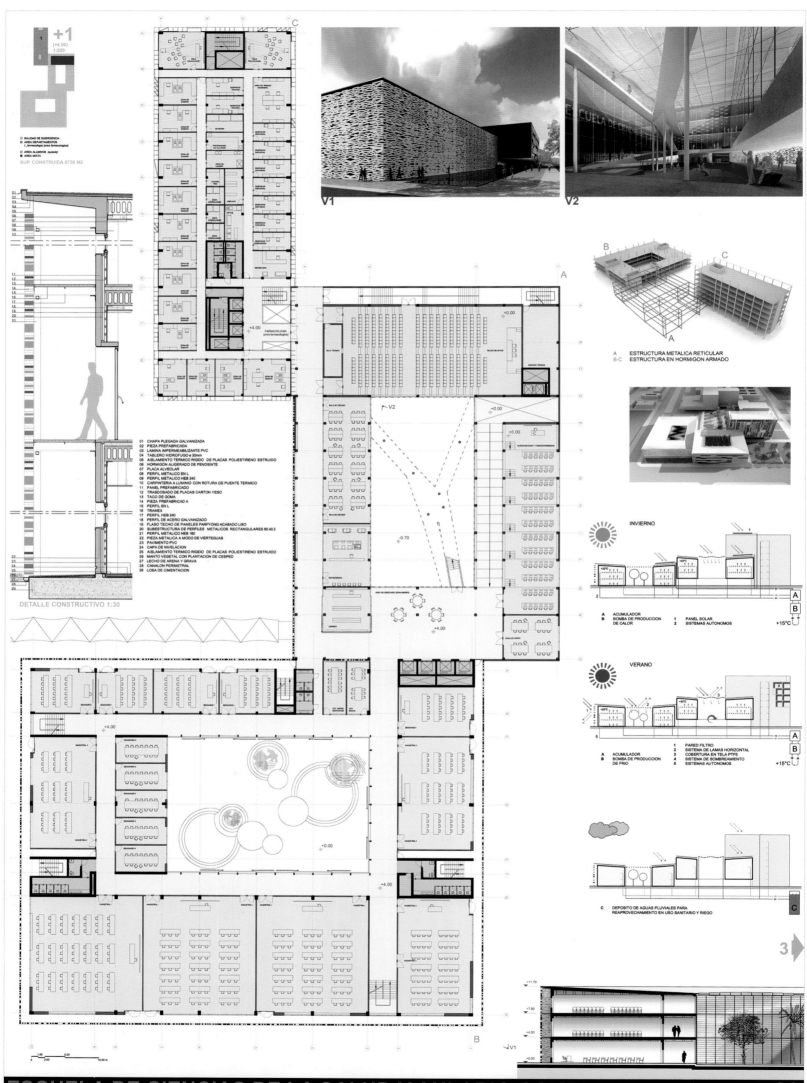

V1

V2

A   ESTRUCTURA METALICA RETICULAR
B-C ESTRUCTURA EN HORMIGON ARMADO

INVIERNO

A   ACUMULADOR
B   BOMBA DE PRODUCCION
    DE CALOR
1   PANEL SOLAR
2   SISTEMAS AUTONOMOS

VERANO

A   ACUMULADOR
B   BOMBA DE PRODUCCION
    DE FRIO
1   PARED FILTRO
2   SISTEMA DE LAMAS HORIZONTAL
3   COBERTURA EN TELA PTFE
4   SISTEMA DE SOMBREAMIENTO
5   SISTEMAS AUTONOMOS

C   DEPOSITO DE AGUAS PLUVIALES PARA
    REAPROVECHAMIENTO EN USO SANITARIO Y RIEGO

01 CHAPA PLEGADA GALVANIZADA
02 PIEZA PREFABRICADA
03 LAMINA IMPERMEABILIZANTE PVC
04 TABLERO HIDROFUGO x 30mm
05 AISLAMIENTO TERMICO RIGIDO DE PLACAS POLIESTIRENO EXTRUIDO
06 HORMIGON ALIGERADO DE PENDIENTE
07 PLACA ALVEOLAR
08 PERFIL METALICO EN L
09 PERFIL METALICO HEB 240
10 CARPINTERIA A LUMINIO CON ROTURA DE PUENTE TERMICO
11 PANEL PREFABRICADO
12 TRASDOSADO DE PLACAS CARTON YESO
13 TACO DE GOMA
14 PIEZA PREFABRICADA A
15 PERFIL EN L
16 TRAMEX
17 PERFIL HEB 240
18 PERFIL DE ACERO GALVANIZADO
19 FLASO TECHO DE PANELES PARPYONG ACABADO LISO
20 SUBESTRUCTURA DE PERFILES METALICOS RECTANGULARES 60.40.3
21 PERFIL METALICO HEB 180
22 PIEZA METALICA A MODO DE VIERTEAGUAS
23 PAVIMENTO PVC
24 CAPA DE NIVELACION
25 AISLAMIENTO TERMICO RIGIDO DE PLACAS POLIESTIRENO EXTRUIDO
26 MANTO VEGETAL CON PLANTACION DE CESPED
27 LECHO DE ARENA Y GRAVA
28 CANALON PERIMETRAL
29 LOSA DE CIMENTACION

DETALLE CONSTRUCTIVO 1:30

ESCUELA DE CIENCIAS DE LA SALUD Y AULARIO COMPLEMENTARIO   **02**
PILAR CARMONA BOTANA, LUIS CARMONA PLA, LUIS GARCIA RUIZ Y CIBINEL-LAURENTI MATOCCHIA ARQUIETCTOS ASOCIADOS   UTE PIL2-MODOSTUDIO

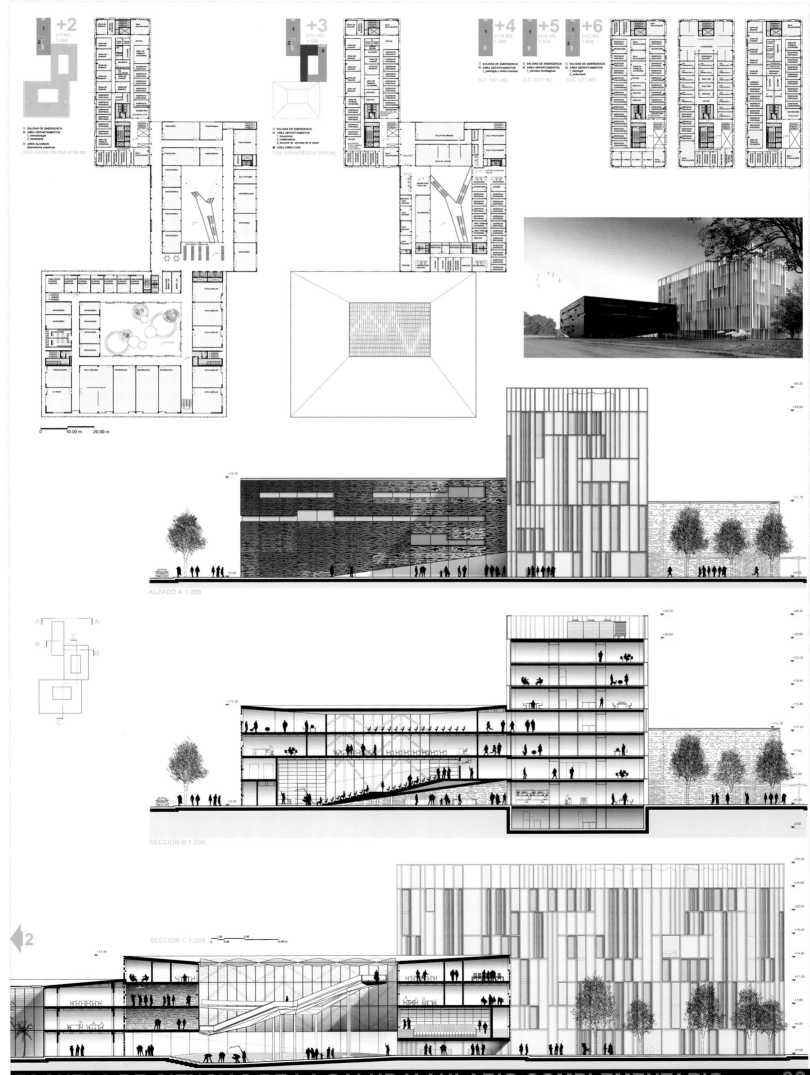

ESCUELA DE CIENCIAS DE LA SALUD Y AULARIO COMPLEMENTARIO 03

PILAR CARMONA BOTANA, LUIS CARMONA PLA, LUIS GARCIA RUIZ Y CIBINEL LAURENTI-MATOCCHIA ARQUIETCTOS ASOCIADOS

UTE PIL2-MODOSTUDIO

180

Silesian University of Technology | ZALEWSKI ARCHITECTURE GROUP

Participants : Krzysztof Zalewski, Adam Gil, Paweł Zalewski, Zbigniew Banaszkiewicz
Project : Lecture halls A, B, C at Silesian University of Technology, Faculty of Automatic Control, Electronics and Computer Science
Typology : Interiors, Public Use Building / Location : Gliwice, Poland

Construction Volume : 470 m²
Client : Silesian University of Technology

P1

110338

**Koncepcja architektoniczna
Wnętrz sal audytoryjnych
Wydziału Automatyki, Elektroniki
i Informatyki Politechniki Śląskiej**

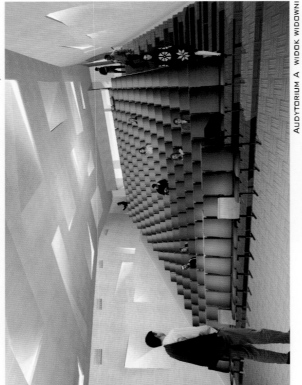

AUDYTORIUM A WIDOK WIDOWNI

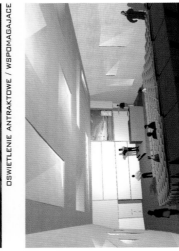

OŚWIETLENIE ANTRAKTOWE / WSPOMAGAJĄCE

PEŁNE OŚWIETLENIE (WYKŁADOWE)

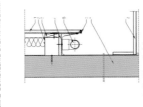

DETAL A SKALA 1 : 5
MODOWANIE OKŁADZINY ŚCIENNEJ
ORAZ OŚWIETLENIE STOPNI WIDOWNI

1. Panel typu Gustafs
2. Profil ES – podkonstrukcja
3. Listwa podkonstrukcji
4. Płyta Fermacell /25 cm
5. Belka świetlikowana do zabudowy
6. Profil aluminiowy Cupax
7. Ściana
8. Wykładzina obiektowa z cokołem

SCHEMAT IDEOWY

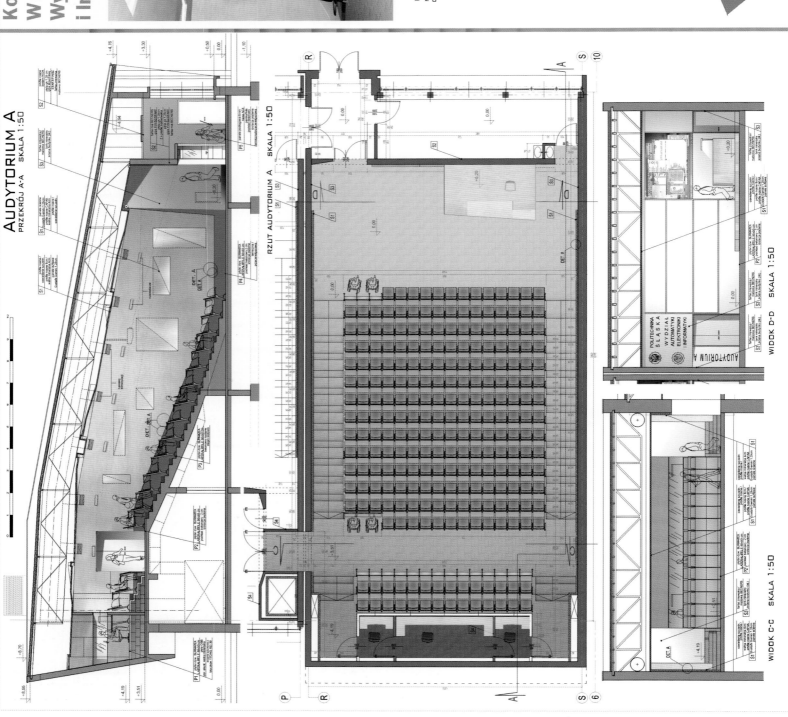

AUDYTORIUM A
PRZEKRÓJ A-A SKALA 1:50

RZUT AUDYTORIUM A SKALA 1:50

WIDOK D-D SKALA 1:50

WIDOK C-C SKALA 1:50

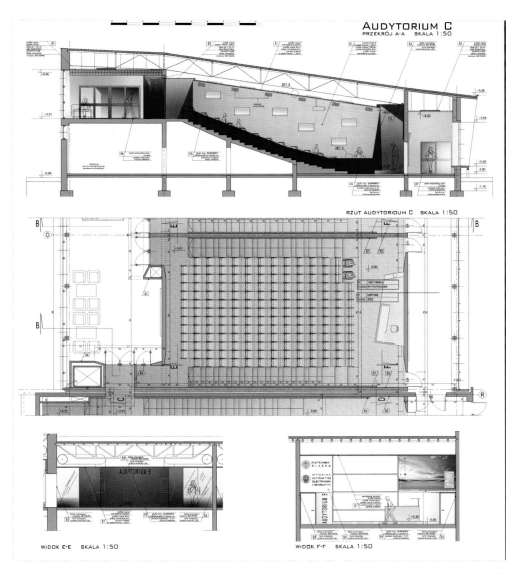

AUDYTORIUM C
PRZEKRÓJ A-A SKALA 1:50

RZUT AUDYTORIUM C SKALA 1:50

WIDOK E-E SKALA 1:50

WIDOK F-F SKALA 1:50

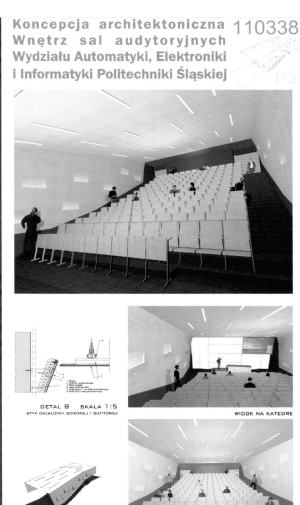

Koncepcja architektoniczna 110338
Wnętrz sal audytoryjnych
Wydziału Automatyki, Elektroniki
i Informatyki Politechniki Śląskiej

P3

DETAL B SKALA 1:5
STYK OKŁADZINY ŚCIENNEJ I SUFITOWEJ

WIDOK NA KATEDRE

SCHEMAT IDEOWY AULA C

WIDOK NA WIDOWNIE

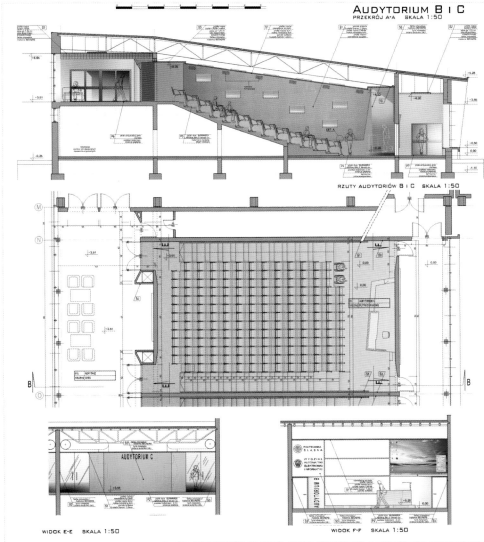

AUDYTORIUM B I C
PRZEKRÓJ A-A SKALA 1:50

RZUTY AUDYTORIÓW B I C SKALA 1:50

WIDOK E-E SKALA 1:50

WIDOK F-F SKALA 1:50

Koncepcja architektoniczna 110338
Wnętrz sal audytoryjnych
Wydziału Automatyki, Elektroniki
i Informatyki Politechniki Śląskiej

P2

SCHEMAT IDEOWY AULA B

WIDOK NA KATEDRE

DETAL B SKALA 1:5
STYK OKŁADZINY ŚCIENNEJ I SUFITOWEJ

WIDOK NA WIDOWNIE

181

Wu University of Economics | *franz zt gmbh*

Location : Vienna, Austria
Function : University of Economics And Business Admisistration
Collaboration : Ena Lloret Kristensen, Charlotte Lieske

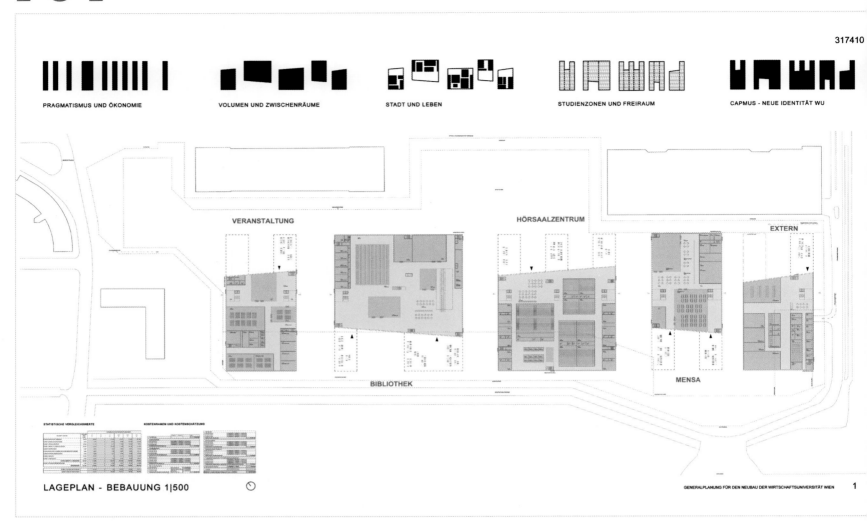

PRAGMATISMUS UND ÖKONOMIE   VOLUMEN UND ZWISCHENRÄUME   STADT UND LEBEN   STUDIENZONEN UND FREIRAUM   CAPMUS - NEUE IDENTITÄT WU

VERANSTALTUNG   HÖRSAALZENTRUM   EXTERN

BIBLIOTHEK   MENSA

LAGEPLAN - BEBAUUNG 1|500

317410

GENERALPLANUNG FÜR DEN NEUBAU DER WIRTSCHAFTSUNIVERSITÄT WIEN   1

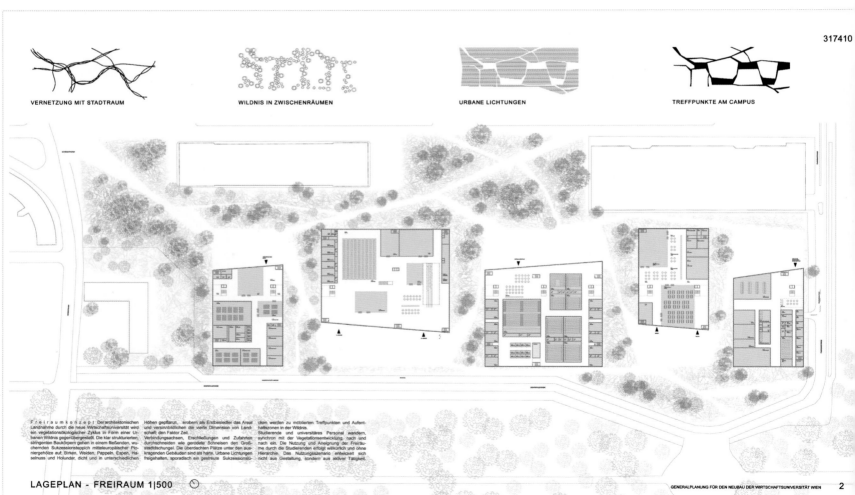

VERNETZUNG MIT STADTRAUM   WILDNIS IN ZWISCHENRÄUMEN   URBANE LICHTUNGEN   TREFFPUNKTE AM CAMPUS

LAGEPLAN - FREIRAUM 1|500

317410

GENERALPLANUNG FÜR DEN NEUBAU DER WIRTSCHAFTSUNIVERSITÄT WIEN   2

317410

NORDANSICHT

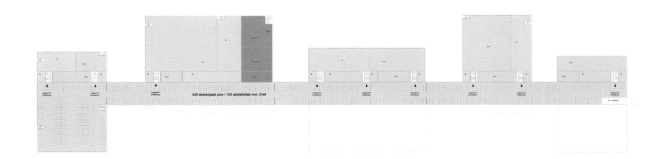

425 abstellplatz pkw / 102 abstellplatz mot. 2rad

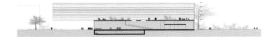

ANSICHTEN - QUERSCHNITT - TIEFGARAGE 1|500 ◔

GENERALPLANUNG FÜR DEN NEUBAU DER WIRTSCHAFTSUNIVERSITÄT WIEN   3

SÜDANSICHT

VERANSTALTUNG   **HÖRSAALZENTRUM**   **EXTERN**

BIBLIOTHEK   **MENSA**

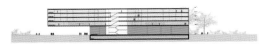

ANSICHT - ERDGESCHOSS 1|500 ◔

GENERALPLANUNG FÜR DEN NEUBAU DER WIRTSCHAFTSUNIVERSITÄT WIEN   4

LÄNGSSCHNITT

UNITS 1-6   UNITS 7-11   DEPART.   BIBLIOTHEK.   DEPART.   DEPART.   DEPART.   DEPART.   DEPART.   EXECUTIVE.

REGELGESCHOSS 3-5

EBENE 2 - SELBSTSTUDIENZONEN

REGELGESCHOSS - SELBSTSTUDIENZONE - SCHNITT   1|500

HAUPTEINGANG

KRIEAU

PERSPEKTIVEN

RIESENRAD

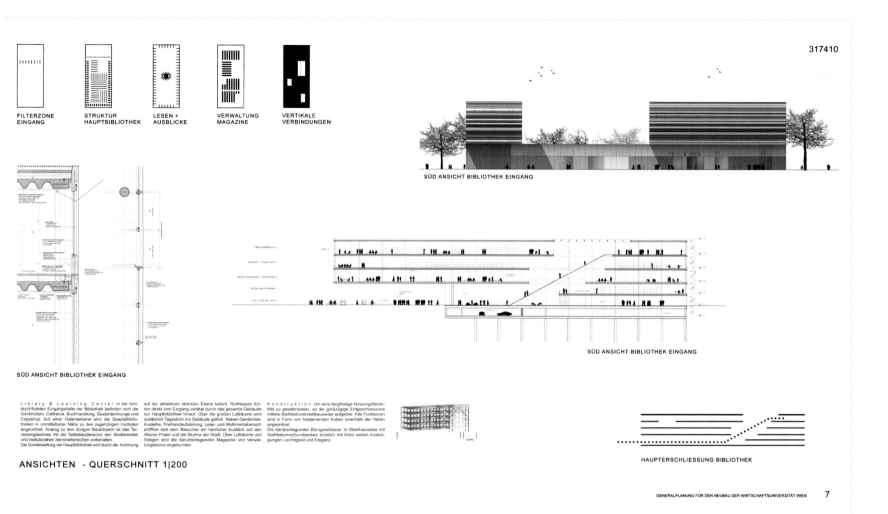

FILTERZONE
EINGANG

STRUKTUR
HAUPTBIBLIOTHEK

LESEN +
AUSBLICKE

VERWALTUNG
MAGAZINE

VERTIKALE
VERBINDUNGEN

317410

SÜD ANSICHT BIBLIOTHEK EINGANG

SÜD ANSICHT BIBLIOTHEK EINGANG

SÜD ANSICHT BIBLIOTHEK EINGANG

Library & Learning Center In der lichtdurchfluteten Eingangshalle der Bibliothek befinden sich die Garderoben, Cafeteria, Buchhandlung, Studentenlounge und Copyshop. Auf einer Galerieebene sind die Spezialbibliotheken in unmittelbarer Nähe zu den zugehörigen Instituten angeordnet. Analog zu den übrigen Baukörpern ist das Terrassengeschoss mit der Selbststudienzone den Studierenden und institutsnahen Seminarbereichen vorbehalten.
Die Sonderstellung der Hauptbibliothek wird durch die Aordnung

auf der attraktiven obersten Ebene betont. Rolltreppen führen direkt vom Eingang vertikal durch das gesamte Gebäude zur Hauptbibliothek hinauf. Über die großen Lufträume wird zusätzlich Tageslicht ins Gebäude geholt. Neben Garderobe, Ausleihe, Freihandaufstellung, Lese- und Multimediabereich eröffnet sich dem Besucher ein herrlicher Ausblick auf den Wiener Prater und die Skyline der Stadt. Über Lufträume und Stiegen sind die darunterliegenden Magazine und Verwaltungsbüros eingebunden.

Konstruktion Um eine langfristige Nutzungsflexibilität zu gewährleisten, ist die großzügige Erdgeschoszone mittels Stahlbetonskelettbauweise aufgelöst. Alle Funktionen sind in Form von freistehenden Kuben innerhalb der Hallen angeordnet.
Die darüberliegenden Bürogeschosse in Stahlbauweise mit Stahlbetonverbunddecken erzielen mit ihren weiten Auskragungen Leichtigkeit und Eleganz.

HAUPTERSCHLIESSUNG BIBLIOTHEK

ANSICHTEN - QUERSCHNITT 1|200

317410

EBENE 0.00

EBENE + 1

LL- GRUNDRISSE 1|200

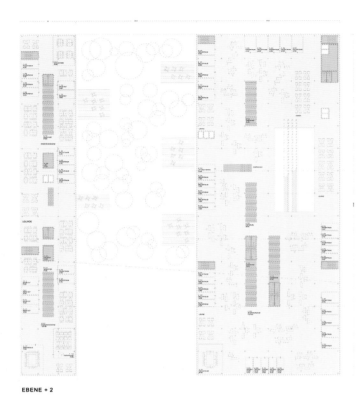

EBENE + 2

EBENE +3

EBENE +4

LL 1|200

Campus Folcara | *ZO_loft*

Architect : Filomena Acquaviva, Paolo Emilio Bellisario, Andrea Cingoli,
Francesca Fontana, Michele Manigrasso, Roberto Potenza.
Client : Università degli Studi di Cassino
Location : Cassino (FR) Italy

GREENHALL

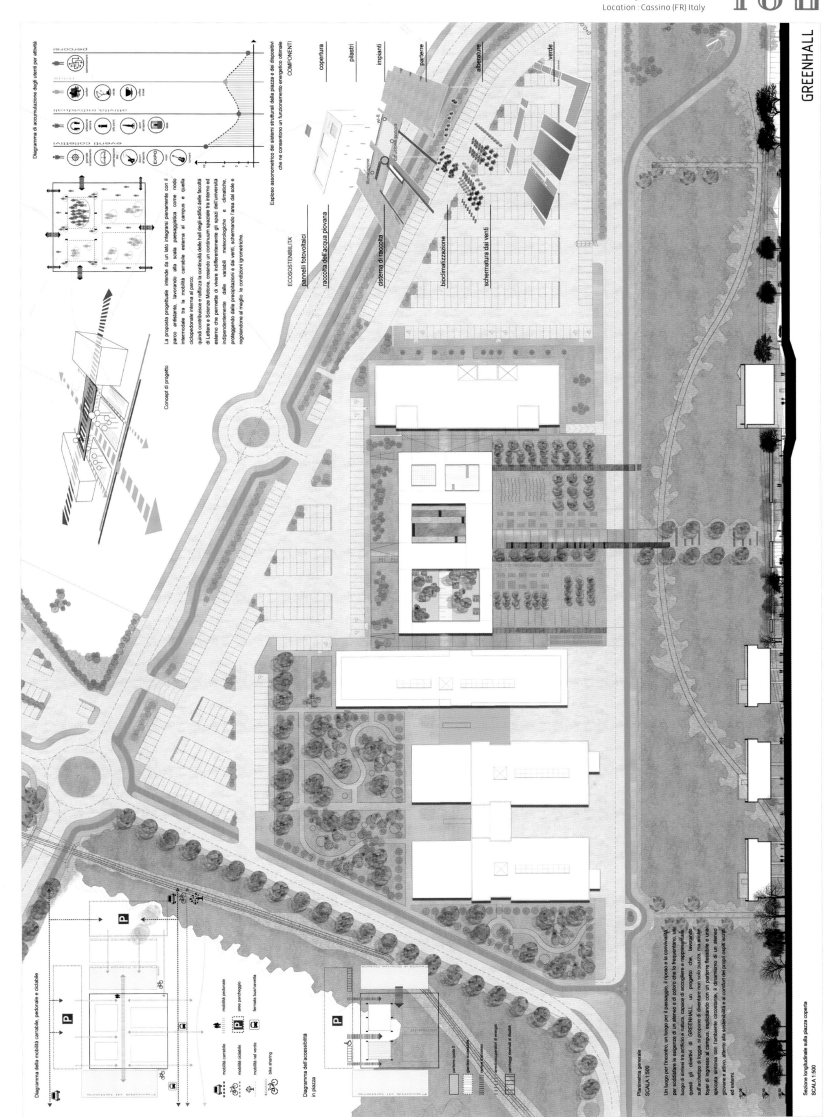

Diagramma di accumulazione degli utenti per attività

Concept di progetto

La proposta progettuale intende di un lato integrarsi pienamente con il parco antistante, lavorando alla scala paesaggistica come nodo intermodale tra la mobilità carrabile esterna al campus e quella ciclopedonale interna al parco; quindi contribuisce e rafforza la continuità delle hall degli edifici delle facoltà di Lettere e Scienze Motorie, creando un continuum spaziale tra interno ed esterno che permette di vivere indifferentemente gli spazi dell'università indipendentemente dalle variabili meteorologiche e climatiche, proteggendo dalle precipitazioni e dai venti, schermando l'area dal sole e regolandone al meglio le condizioni igrometriche.

Esploso assonometrico dei sistemi strutturali della piazza e di dispositivi che ne consentono un funzionamento energetico ottimale

COMPONENTI

copertura
pilastri
impianti
parterre
alberature
verde

ECOSOSTENIBILITÀ

pannelli fotovoltaici
raccolta dell'acqua piovana
sistema di raccolta
biocimatizzazione
schermatura dai venti

Diagramma della mobilità carrabile, pedonale e ciclabile

mobilità carrabile
mobilità ciclabile
mobilità pedonale
verde
bike sharing
aree parcheggio
fermata bus/navetta

Diagramma dell'accessibilità in piazza

Planimetria generale
SCALA 1:500

Un luogo per l'incontro, un luogo per il passaggio, il riposo e la convivialità, per soddisfare le esigenze di un ateneo e di coloro che lo frequentano, un luogo di sintesi tra artificio e natura, capace di accogliere e rappresentarli: questi gli obiettivi di GREENHALL, un progetto che, lavorando sull'archetipo di logge, si propone di diventare non solo piazza, ma anche foyer di ingresso al campus, esplicitando con un parterre flessibile e uno spazio antoma con l'ambiente circostante, il dinamismo di un ateneo giovane e attivo, attento alla sostenibilità e al comfort dei propri ospiti ricetti ed esterni.

Sezione longitudinale sulla piazza coperta
SCALA 1:500

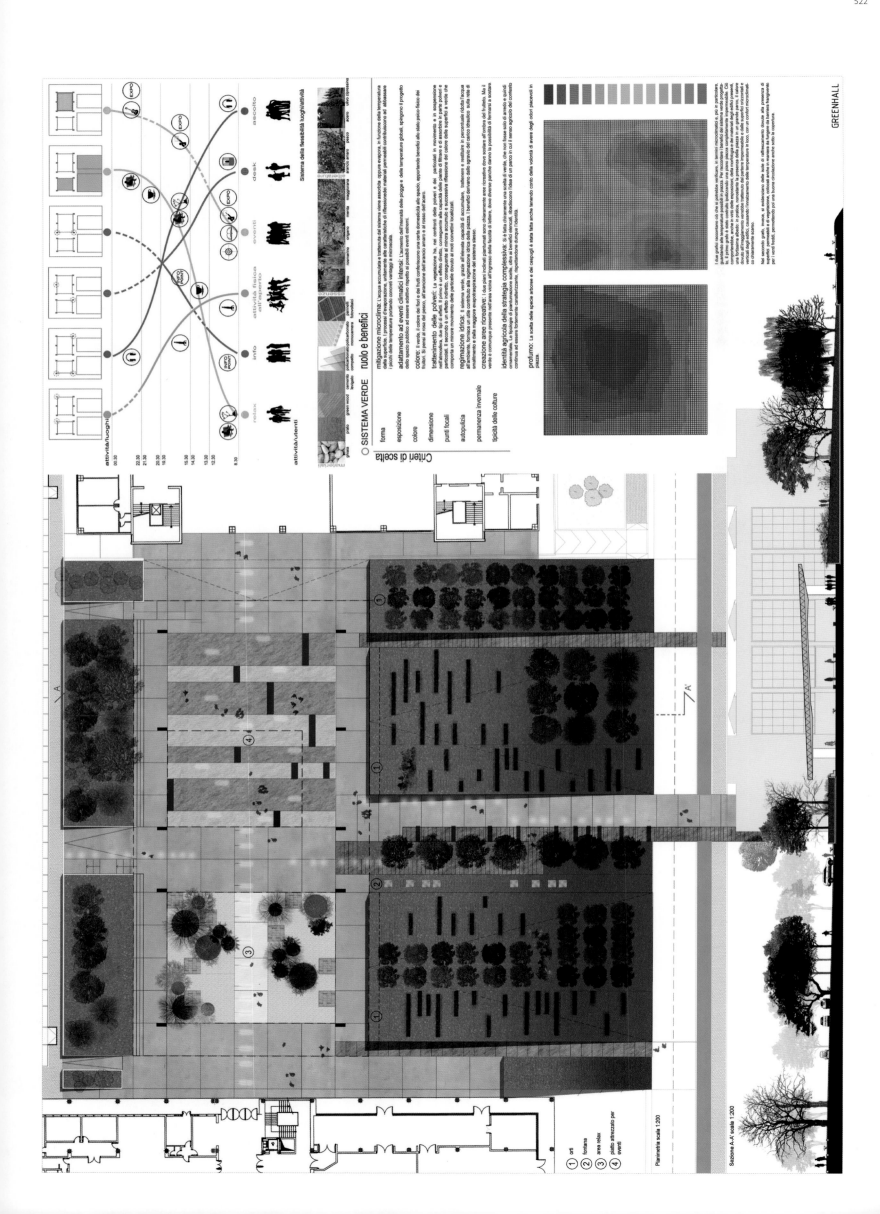

GREENHALL

SISTEMA VERDE ruolo e benefici

mitigazione microclima: L'acqua accumulata e trattenuta dal sistema evapora, in funzione della temperatura della superficie. I processi d'evaporazione, unitamente alle caratteristiche di inflessionabili materiali permeabili contribuiscono ad abbassare i picchi delle temperature portando concreti vantaggi a microscala.

adattamento ad eventi climatici intensi: L'aumento dell'intensità delle piogge e delle temperature globali, spingono il progetto dello spazio pubblico ad essere additivo rispetto ai possibili eventi estremi.

colore: Il verde, il colore dei fiori e dei frutti conferiscono una certa domesticità allo spazio, apportando benefici allo stato psico-fisico dei fruitori. Si pensi al rosa dei peschi, all'arancione dell'arancio amaro e al rosso dell'acero.

trattenimento delle polveri: La vegetazione ha, nei confronti delle polveri e dei particolati in movimento e in sospensione nell'atmosfera, due tipi di effetti: Il primo è un effetto diretto, conseguente alle capacità delle piante di filtrare e di assorbire in parte polveri e particolati; il secondo è un effetto indiretto, conseguente di minore accumulo e successiva riflessione del calore delle superficie a verde che comporta un minore movimento delle particolle dovuto ai moti convettivi localizzati.

regimazione idrica: Il sistema verde, grazie all'elevata capacità di accumulare, trattenere e restituire in percentuale ridotta l'acqua all'ambiente, formisce un utile contributo alla regimazione idrica della piazza. I benefici derivano dallo sgravio del carico idraulico sulla rete di smaltimento e dalla maggiore evapotraspirazione del sistema stesso.

creazione aree ricreative: I due piani inclinati plantumali trovano chiaramente una scala di verde, che non fossa solo di verde ornamentale. Le tipologie di piantumazione scelte, oltre ai benefici elencati, richiedono l'idea di un parco in cui il senso agricolo del contesto continua ad essere fortemente caratterizzante, rispettandone dunque l'identità.

identità agricola della strategia complessiva: Si è fatta chiaramente una scala di verde dove sostare all'ombra del frutteto. Ma il verde e comunque presente nell'area vicina all'ingresso della facciata di lettere, dove diverse panche danno la possibilità di fermarsi e sostare.

profumo: La scelta delle specie arboree e dei cespugli è stata fatta anche tenendo conto della volontà di avere degli odori piacevoli in piazza.

Criteri di scelta

- forma
- esposizione
- colore
- dimensione
- punti focali
- autopulizia
- permanenza invernale
- tipicità delle colture

Planimetria scala 1:200

① orti
② fontana
③ area relax
④ piatto attrezzato per eventi

Sezione A-A' scala 1:200

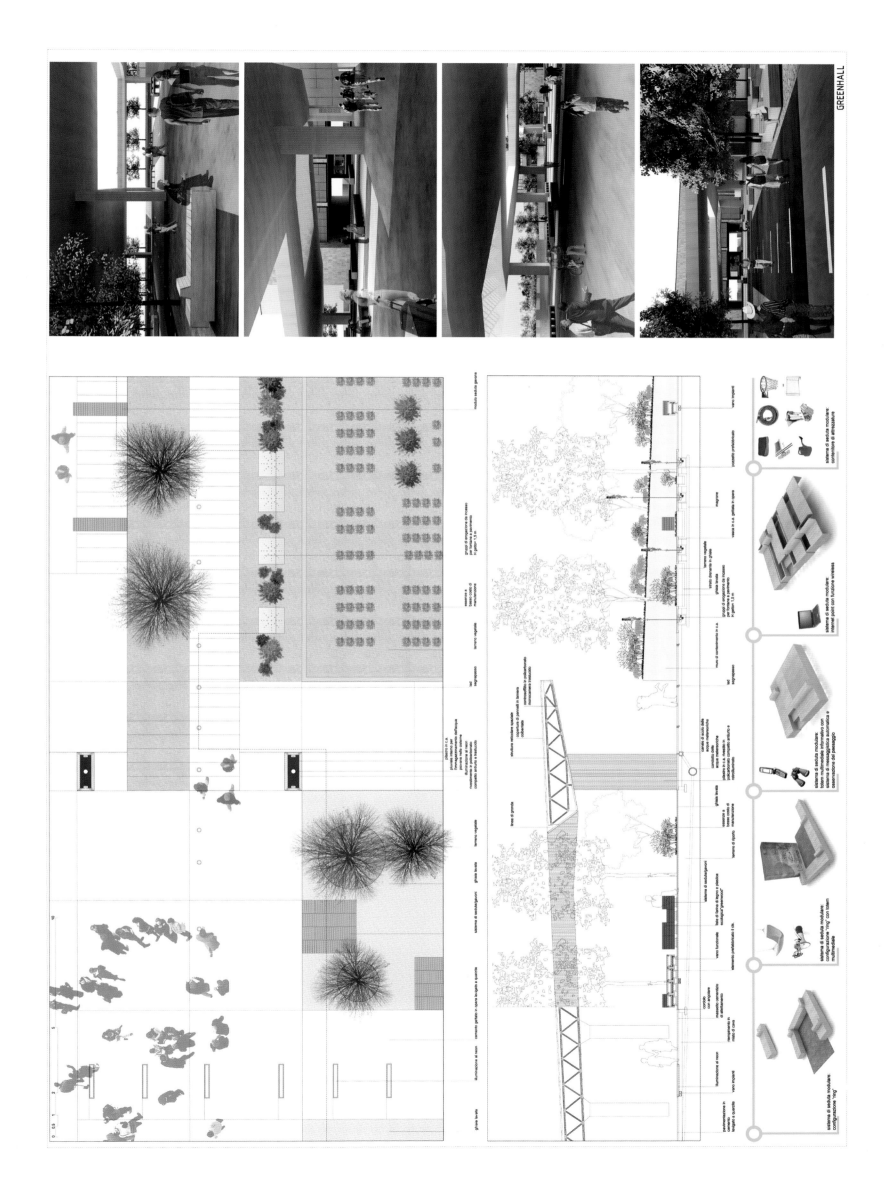

GREENHALL

183 Wifi Technology-Centre | *franz zt gmbh*

Location : St. Poelten, Lower Austria
Function : Technology Centre and new Design University
Collaboration : Anna Gruber, Wolfgang Fischer

technikzentrum wifi st. pölten   031060

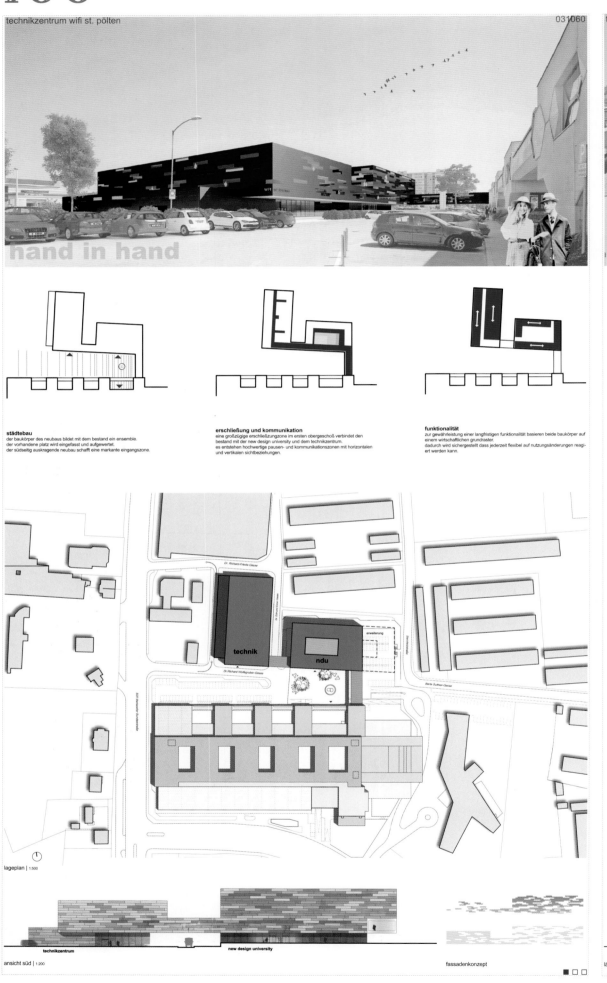

hand in hand

städtebau
der baukörper des neubaus bildet mit dem bestand ein ensemble.
der vorhandene platz wird eingefasst und aufgewertet.
der südseitig auskragende neubau schafft eine markante eingangszone.

erschließung und kommunikation
eine großzügige erschließungzone im ersten obergeschoß verbindet den
bestand mit der new design university und dem technikzentrum.
es entstehen hochwertige pausen- und kommunikationszonen mit horizontalen
und vertikalen sichtbeziehungen.

funktionalität
zur gewährleistung einer langfristigen funktionalität basieren beide baukörper auf
einem wirtschaftlichen grundraster.
dadurch wird sichergestellt dass jederzeit flexibel auf nutzungsänderungen reagiert werden kann.

lageplan | 1:500

technikzentrum   new design university

ansicht süd | 1:200   fassadenkonzept

technikzentrum wifi st. pölten

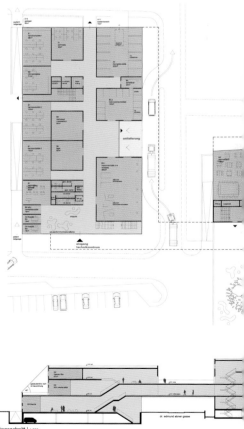

längsschnitt | 1:200

525

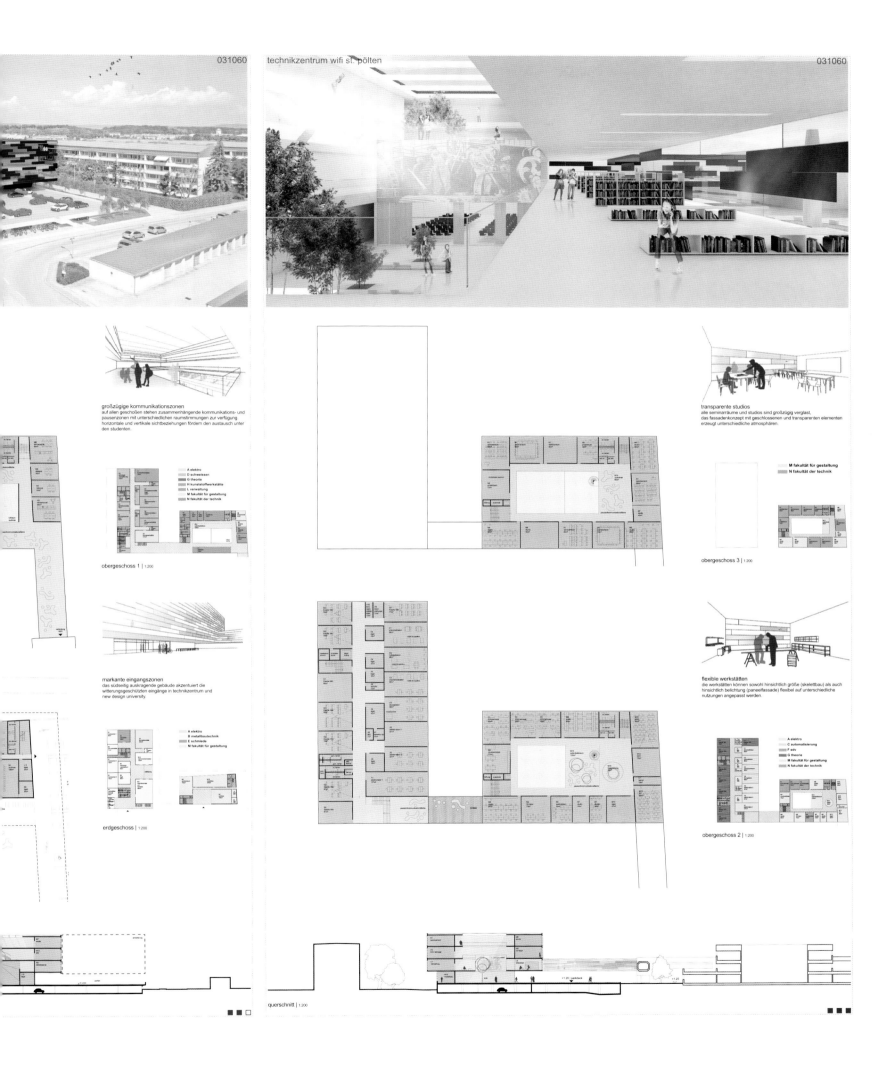

031060

031060

großzügige kommunikationszonen
auf allen geschoßen stehen zusammenhängende kommunikations- und
pausenzonen mit unterschiedlichen raumstimmungen zur verfügung.
horizontale und vertikale sichtbeziehungen fördern den austausch unter
den studenten.

transparente studios
alle seminarräume und studios sind großzügig verglast,
das fassadenkonzept mit geschlossenen und transparenten elementen
erzeugt unterschiedliche atmosphären.

A elektro
D schweissen
G theorie
H kunststoffwerkstätte
L verwaltung
M fakultät für gestaltung
N fakultät der technik

M fakultät für gestaltung
N fakultät der technik

obergeschoss 1 | 1:200

obergeschoss 3 | 1:200

markante eingangszonen
das südseitig auskragende gebäude akzentuiert die
witterungsgeschützten eingänge in technikzentrum und
new design university.

flexible werkstätten
die werkstätten können sowohl hinsichtlich größe (skelettbau) als auch
hinsichtlich belichtung (paneelfassade) flexibel auf unterschiedliche
nutzungen angepasst werden.

A elektro
B metallbautechnik
E schmiede
M fakultät für gestaltung

A elektro
C automatisierung
F edv
G theorie
M fakultät für gestaltung
N fakultät der technik

erdgeschoss | 1:200

obergeschoss 2 | 1:200

querschnitt | 1:200

184

Campus USI / SUPSI Lugano | *ZO_loft*

Architect : Filomena Acquaviva, Paolo Emilio Bellisario, Andrea Cingoli, Giorgio Giurdanella, Michele Manigrasso.
Collaborators : Giuseppe Bandieramonte, Ivea Butkute, Francesca Fontana, Gabriele Martinelli, Roberto Potenza, Emanuela Spiotta.
Client : Università USI / SUPSI Lugano Viganello

Location : Lugano Viganello (CH) Switzerland
Design : 2011

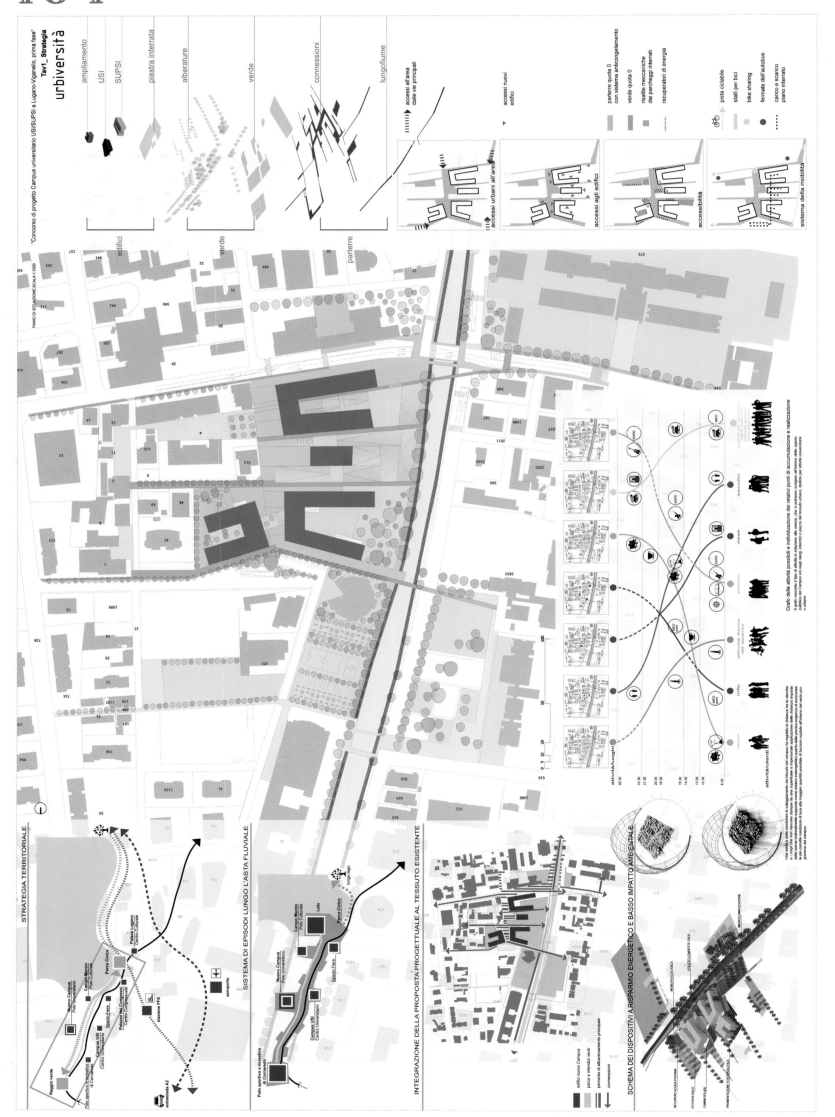

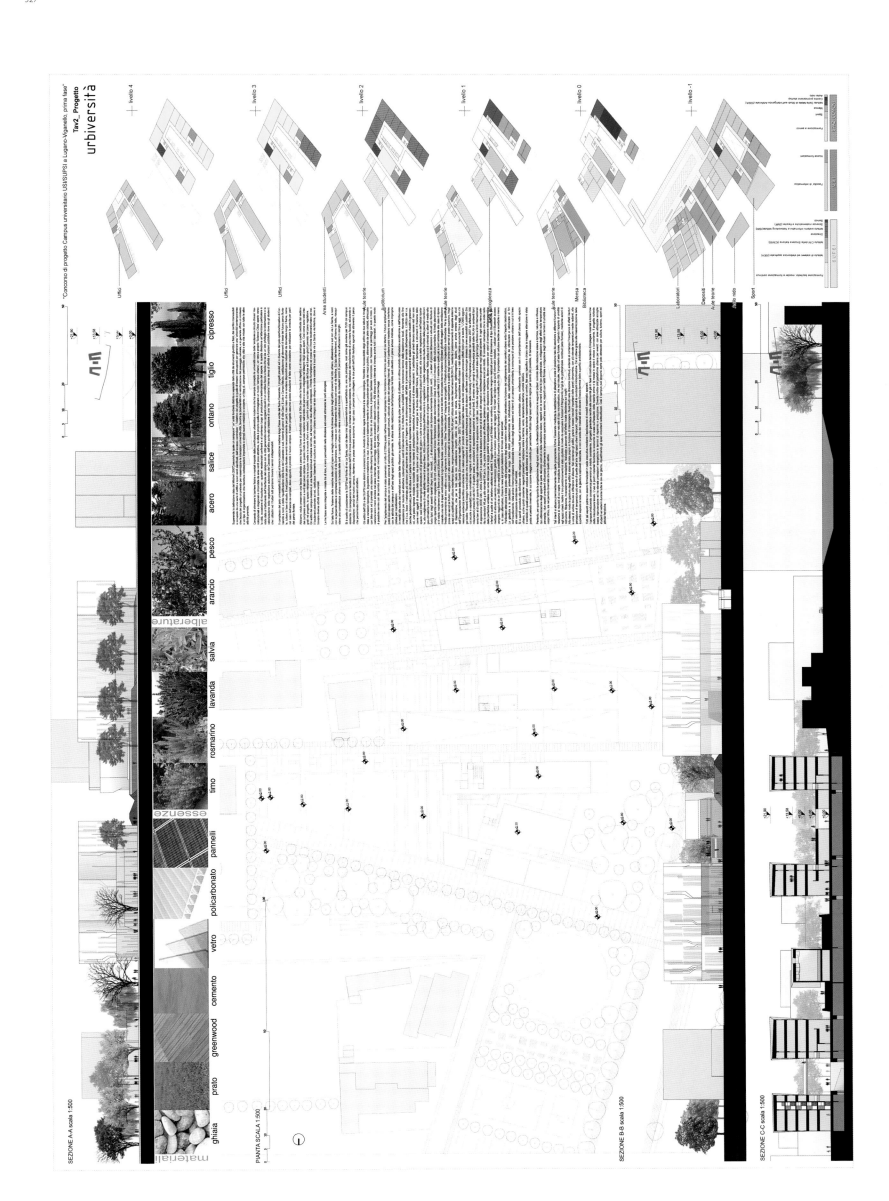

527

"Concorso di progetto Campus universitario USI/SUPSI a Lugano-Viganello, rendering"

Tav3_Prefigurazioni

urbiversità

VISTA DALL'INTERNO DEL CAMPUS

VISTA DEL SUPSI E DELL'USI DA VIA LA SANTA

VISTA DA NORD DEL LUNGO FIUME

SEZIONE LONGITUDINALE SUPSI scala 1:500

ABACO DEGLI ARREDI

sistema di seduta modulare: contenitore di attrezzature

sistema di seduta modulare: internet point con funzione wireless

sistema di seduta modulare: totem multimediale informativo con sistema di messaggistica automatica e osservazione del paesaggio

sistema di seduta modulare: configurazione "ring" con totem multimediale

sistema di seduta modulare: configurazione "ring"

PROSPETTO SU VIA LA SANTA scala 1:500

PROSPETTO LONGITUDINALE SUPSI E AUDITORIO scala 1:500

Continuitat Ritmica | *LUIS ARREDONDO_ARCHITECT*

Location : Ciutadella de Menorca, Spain
Client : Ciutadella Goberment

Project : Dance and Music School
Participants : Luis Arredondo
Typology : Educational

CONCURS D'AVANTPROJECTES PER A LA CONSTRUCCIÓ DE LA ESCOLA MUNICIPAL DE MÚSICA I DANSA
LEMA_CONTINUÏTAT RÍTMICA
PLAÇA DE LA PAU DE CIUTADELLA DE MENORCA 1/3

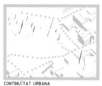

CONTINUÏTAT URBANA
Necessitat d'unir la plaça de la Pau al sistema d'espais lliures de la ciutat

ADAPTACIÓ DE LA MALLA FUNCIONAL
Esquema funcional basat en la flexibilitat de l'espai exterior i la xarxa d'aules continua.

CINTA DE MOEBIUS
Continuïtat de l'espai públic dins i fora de l'edifici com a prolongació del programa

ESPIRAL
Edifici organitzat com una gran rampa contínua que uneix tots els espais. Moviment i recorregut. La mateixa rampa és sol i coberta

La parcel.la assignada al nou centre de música i dansa de Ciutadella és un punt de gran potencial urbà, ja que la seva obertura cap a la Plaça de la Pau afegiria aquest espai a la xarxa de verds públics que per mitjà de concatenacions de zones urbanes qualificades, millora la qualitat del casc urbà.
La necessitat del pas de vianants és el primer punt determinant del projecte, ja que cedim tota la planta baixa per afavorir la continuïtat entre espais, aportant a la xarxa un nou espai amb zones d'ombra i un petit auditori a l'aire lliure.

A partir d'una malla funcional ortogonal adaptada a la parcel • la, que ocupa tot el front de la Plaça de la Pau, alineant-se a la mitgera nord i es separa en la mitgera sud, s'aconsegueix un edifici amb unes entrades clares que permet l'entrada de sol a l'espai públic i atén a una relació visual amb la Plaça, atenent a una relació necessària. Aprofitant el canvi topogràfic, l'edifici, s'organitza en mitges plantes..

El sistema funcional de l'edifici està basat en la trobada dels usuaris, la flexibilitat funcional i la continuïtat espacial. S'organitza a partir d'una rampa contínua en espiral que connecta totes les parts del programa. Aquesta espiral salva el desnivell en planta baixa, i es plega per a generar una graderia coberta com a extensió de la sala d'audicions, obrint d'aquesta manera l'ús de l'edifici al carrer i transformant el tipus de relacions que se situen en aquest punt, convertint la plaça pública en part de l'edifici. A la part ascendent de l'espiral se situa el programa d'aules, que es distribueix en les parts centrals, deixant els extrems a les aules de major dimensió.
Una segona rampa, superposada a la primera, realitza una doble funció, d'una banda cobreix el programa i el complementa, permetent la possibilitat d'estendre l'interior de les aules a la coberta, de l'altra funciona com una nova plaça d'ús intern, multiplicant les possibilitats del centre, que es converteix així en un punt de trobada d'estudiants i professors, dins i fora dels horaris de classes.

situació

emplaçament 1/5oo +37.25

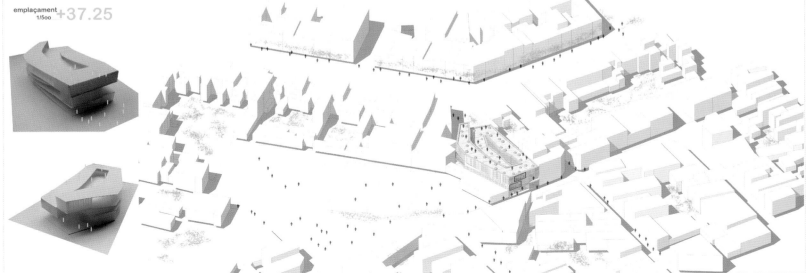

CONCURS D'AVANTPROJECTES PER A LA CONSTRUCCIÓ DE LA
LEMA_CONTINUÏTAT RÍTMICA

ESCOLA MUNICIPAL DE MÚSICA I DANSA
PLAÇA DE LA PAU DE CIUTADELLA DE MENORCA 2/3

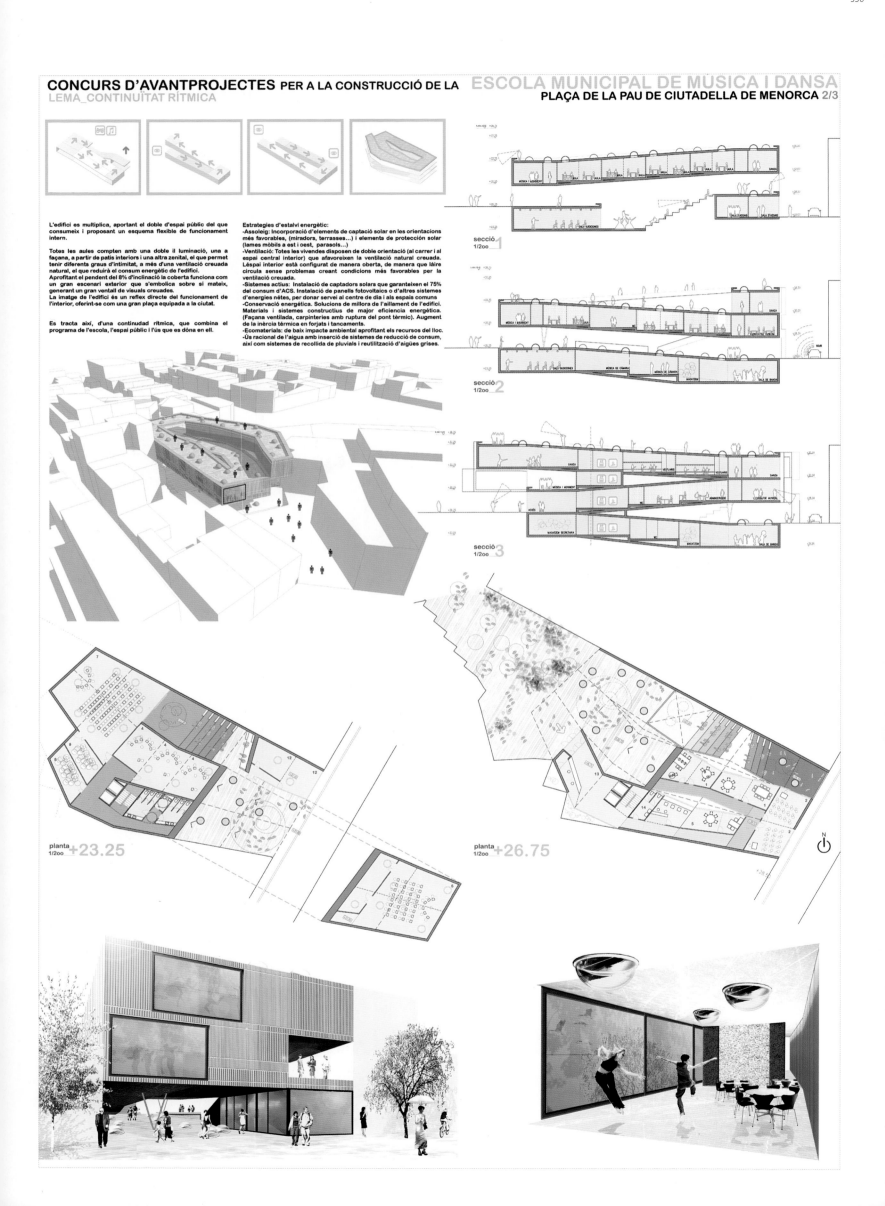

L'edifici es multiplica, aportant el doble d'espai públic del que consumeix i proposant un esquema flexible de funcionament intern.

Totes les aules compten amb una doble il·luminació, una a façana, a partir de patis interiors i una altra zenital, el que permet tenir diferents graus d'intimitat, a més d'una ventilació creuada natural, el que reduirà el consum energètic de l'edifici.
Aprofitant el pendent del 8% d'inclinació la coberta funciona com un gran escenari exterior que s'embolica sobre si mateix, generant un gran ventall de visuals creuades.
La imatge de l'edifici és un reflex directe del funcionament de l'interior, oferint-se com una gran plaça equipada a la ciutat.

Es tracta així, d'una continuitad rítmica, que combina el programa de l'escola, l'espai públic i l'ús que es dóna en ell.

Estrategies d'estalvi energètic:
-Assoleig: Incorporació d'elements de captació solar en les orientacions més favorables, (miradors, terrasses...) i elements de protecció solar (lames mòbils a est i oest, parasols...)
-Ventilació: Totes les vivendes disposen de doble orientació (al carrer i al espai central interior) que afavoreixen la ventilació natural creuada. L'espai interior està configurat de manera oberta, de manera que l'aire circula sense problemas creant condicions més favorables per la ventilació creuada.
-Sistemes actius: Instalació de captadors solars que garanteixen el 75% del consum d'ACS. Instalació de panells fotovoltaics o d'altres sistemes d'energies nétes, per donar servei al centre de dia i als espais comuns
-Conservació energètica. Solucions de millora de l'aillament de l'edifici.
-Ecomaterials: de baix impacte ambiental aprofitant els recursos del lloc.
Materials i sistemes constructius de major eficiencia energètica. (Façana ventilada, carpinteries amb ruptura del pont tèrmic). Augment de la inèrcia térmica en forjats i tancaments.
-Ús racional de l'aigua amb inserció de sistemes de reducció de consum, així com sistemes de recollida de pluvials i reutilització d'aigües grises.

secció 1
1/2oo

secció 2
1/2oo

secció 3
1/2oo

planta +23.25
1/2oo

planta +26.75
1/2oo

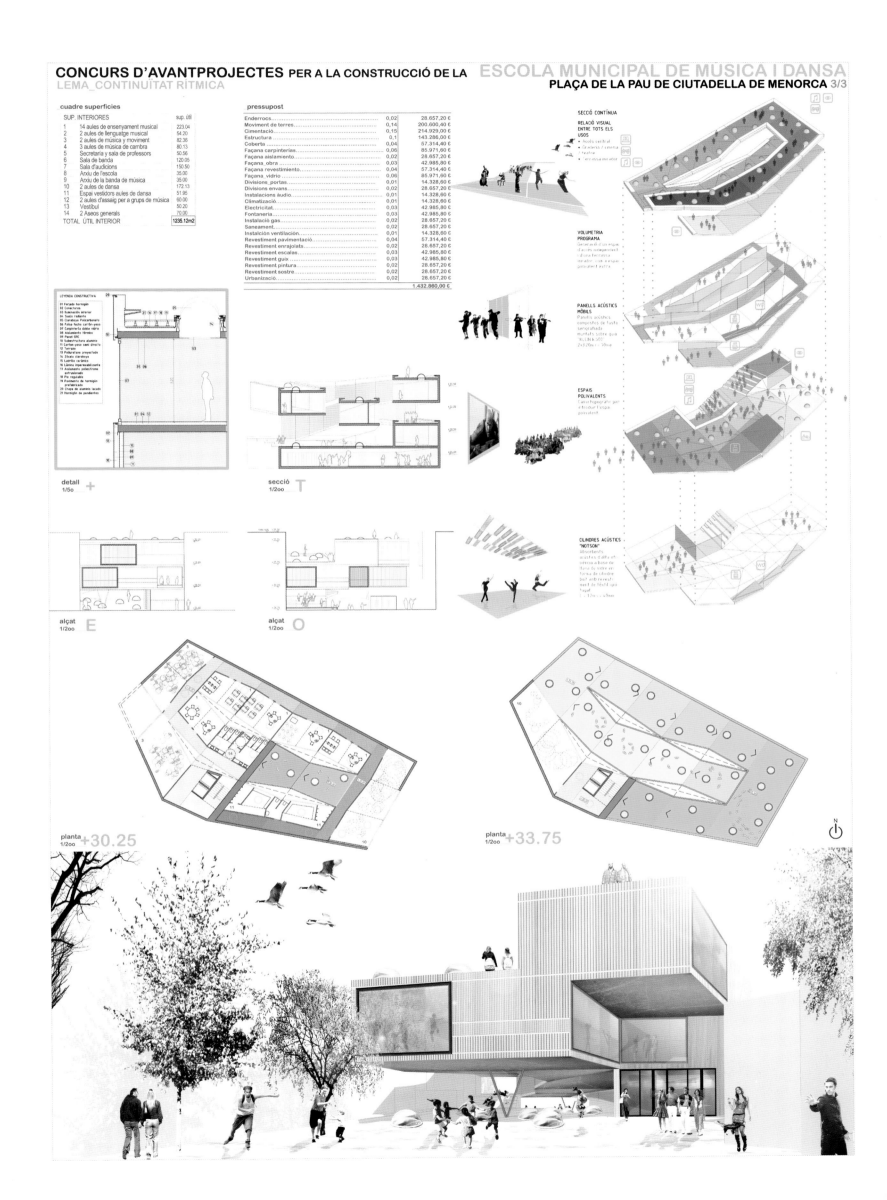

CONCURS D'AVANTPROJECTES PER A LA CONSTRUCCIÓ DE LA
LEMA_CONTINUÏTAT RÍTMICA

ESCOLA MUNICIPAL DE MÚSICA I DANSA
PLAÇA DE LA PAU DE CIUTADELLA DE MENORCA 3/3

cuadre superficies

SUP. INTERIORES

		sup. útil
1	14 aules de ensenyament musical	223.04
2	2 aules de llenguatge musical	54.20
3	2 aules de música y moviment	82.36
4	3 aules de música de cambra	80.13
5	Secretaria y sala de professors	50.56
6	Sala de banda	120.05
7	Sala d'audicions	150.50
8	Arxiu de l'escola	35.00
9	Arxiu de la banda de música	35.00
10	2 aules de dansa	172.13
11	Espai vestidors aules de dansa	51.95
12	2 aules d'assaig per a grups de música	60.00
13	Vestíbul	50.20
14	2 Aseos generals	70.00
	TOTAL ÚTIL INTERIOR	1235.12m2

pressupost

Enderrocs	0,02	28.657,20 €
Moviment de terres	0,14	200.600,40 €
Cimentació	0,15	214.929,00 €
Estructura	0,1	143.286,00 €
Coberta	0,04	57.314,40 €
Façana carpinteries	0,06	85.971,60 €
Façana aislamiento	0,02	28.657,20 €
Façana_obra	0,03	42.985,80 €
Façana revestimiento	0,04	57.314,40 €
Façana_vidrio	0,06	85.971,60 €
Divisions_portas	0,01	14.328,60 €
Divisions envans	0,02	28.657,20 €
Instalacions àudio	0,01	14.328,60 €
Climatizació	0,01	14.328,60 €
Electricitat	0,03	42.985,80 €
Fontaneria	0,03	42.985,80 €
Instalació gas	0,02	28.657,20 €
Sanejament	0,02	28.657,20 €
Instalación ventilación	0,01	14.328,60 €
Revestiment pavimentació	0,04	57.314,40 €
Revestiment enrajolats	0,02	28.657,20 €
Revestiment escalas	0,03	42.985,80 €
Revestiment guix	0,03	42.985,80 €
Revestiment pintura	0,02	28.657,20 €
Revestiment sostre	0,02	28.657,20 €
Urbanizació	0,02	28.657,20 €
		1.432.860,00 €

LEYENDA CONSTRUCTIVA
01 Forçado hormigón
02 Conectores
03 Iluminación interior
04 Suelo radiante
05 Claraboya Policarbonato
06 Falsa techo cartón-yeso
07 Carpintería doble vidrio
08 Aislamiento térmico
09 Panel GRC
10 Subestructura aluminio
11 Cartón-yeso semi directo
12 Terrazo
13 Poliuretano proyectado
14 Zócalo claraboya
15 Ladrillo cerámico
16 Lámina impermeabilizante
17 Aislamiento poliestireno extrusionado
18 Pie regulable
19 Pavimento de hormigón prefabricado
20 Chapa de aluminio lacado
21 Hormigón de pendientes

detall 1/5o +

secció 1/2oo T

alçat 1/2oo E

alçat 1/2oo O

SECCIÓ CONTÍNUA
RELACIÓ VISUAL ENTRE TOTS ELS USOS

VOLUMETRIA PROGRAMA

PANELLS ACÚSTICS MÒBILS

ESPAIS POLIVALENTS

CILINDRES ACÚSTICS "NOTSON"

planta 1/2oo +30.25

planta 1/2oo +33.75

186 Lucia | *arenas basabe palacios arquitectos*

University development in Valladolid (Spain)
Authors : Enrique Arenas Laorga, Luis Basabe Montalvo
Collaborators : Eva Miguel

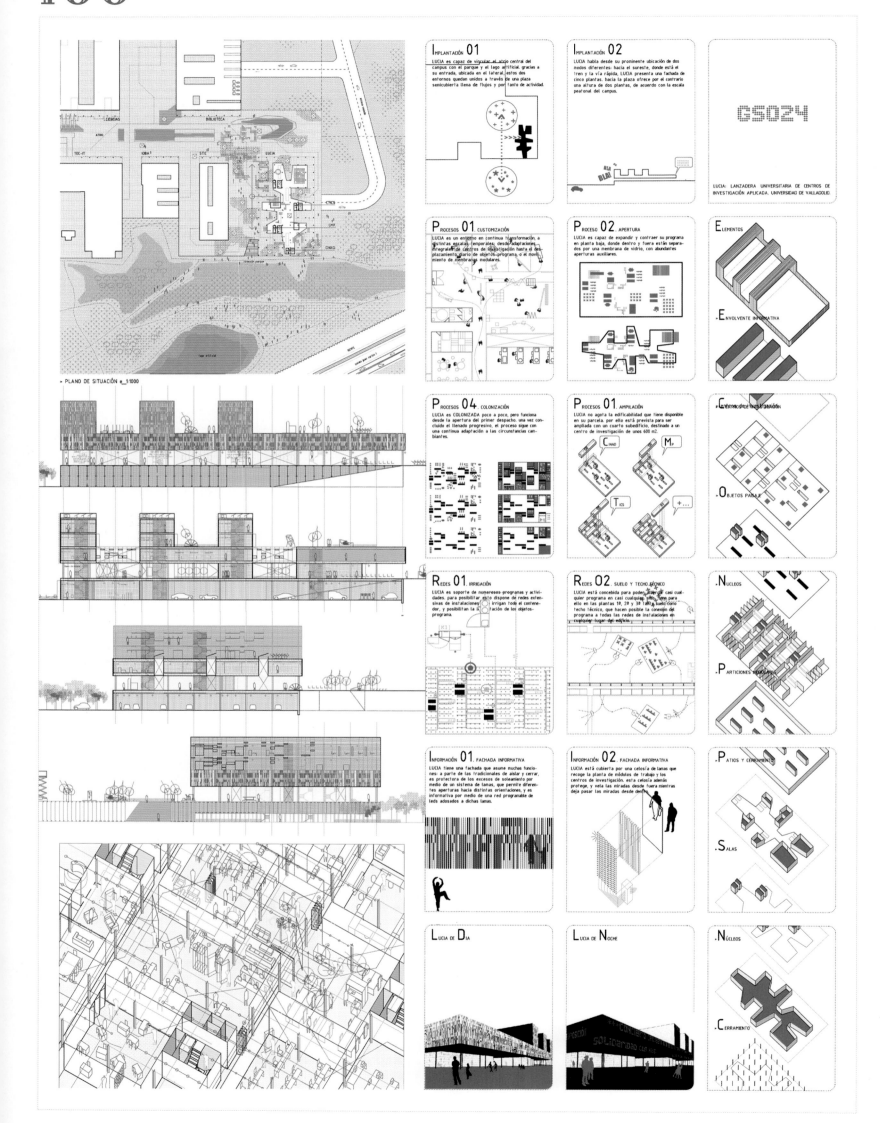

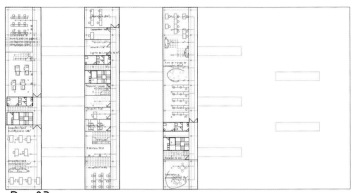

.P LANTA 03 e_1:300 [CINAD / centro de metabolopatías / CTICS / jardines reconfigurables]

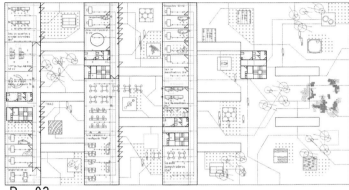

.P LANTA 02 e_1:300 [CINAD / centro de metabolopatías / CTICS / jardines reconfigurables]

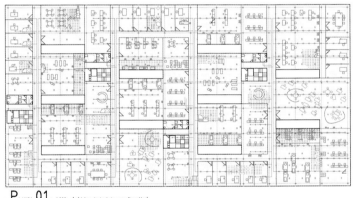

.P LANTA 01 e_1:300 [módulos de trabajo reconfigurables]

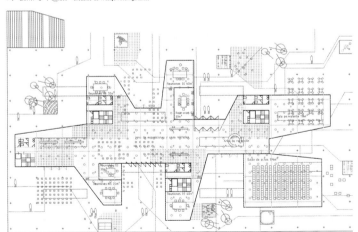

.P LANTA B AJA e_1:300 [control / accesos independientes / salón de actos / aula polivalente / salas de reunión / plaza cubierta]

.P LANTA S ÓTANO e_1:300 [aulas / parking / instalaciones]

Implantación

LUCIA se ubica en el extremo noroeste del campus miguel delibes. desde dentro el nuevo edificio supone una pieza importante para la finalización de la gran plaza central que articula el campus. desde fuera, el edificio tiene una especial visibilidad, tanto desde la calle Xy cono sobre todo desde el tren. se aprovecha su estrategica instalación para concluir el gran anillo relacionador de papel parque, y darle una fachada hacia el noreste.

Estrategia. soporte de procesos

LUCIA está destinado a albergar un programa muy complejo, en cuanto a su diversidad y sobre todo en cuanto a su variabilidad. deberá estar abierto a continuas reprogramaciones, y comportarse por tanto más como SOPORTE DE PROCESOS que como un edificio convencional. LUCIA no es por tanto sólo un contenedor de programa, sino todo un sistema que incluye además varias series de objetos y de espacios libres.

GS024

LUCIA: LANZADERA UNIVERSITARIA DE CENTROS DE INVESTIGACIÓN APLICADA. UNIVERSIDAD DE VALLADOLID.

Programa 01. estratificación

LUCIA alberga programas de diferentes naturalezas, con diferentes grados de privacidad, de predefinición, de visibilidad, etc., que se ESTRATIFICAN para dejar los usos públicos en la planta baja, vinculados a la plaza, los espacios de trabajo alquilables por módulos en una gran primera planta muy flexible, y los tres centros de investigación en las plantas segunda y tercera.

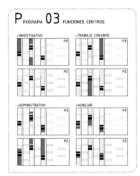

Programa 02. centros independientes

LUCIA alberga los tres centros de investigación (CINAD, CMP y C-TICS) en tres sub-edificios independientes en las plantas superiores. se accede a ellos desde el gran vestíbulo-sala de exposiciones, que les dota de un acceso controlado y representativo. los sub-bloques se manifiestan además como entidades independientes hacia el exterior.

Programa 03. funciones centros

Mutaciones 01. zonas de uso común

LUCIA es un sistema abierto al cambio en sus diferentes escalas, desde profundas reestructuraciones de programa hasta modificaciones provisionales o puntuales. de este modo, la planta de usos públicos, incluyendo la gran plaza cubierta, se plantea como espacio altamente variable y permeable para la realización de exposiciones, actos, eventos, etc.

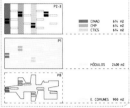

Mutaciones 02. módulos de trabajo

LUCIA es capaz de albergar las formas de trabajo más diversas para los futuros usuarios del sistema laboratorios, salas y aulas, despachos, etc. además puede compartimentarse en mayor o menor medida para albergar diferentes escalas de proyectos.

Mutaciones 03. centros independientes

LUCIA ofrece independencia a sus centros de investigación, y les dota de una estructura altamente flexible, fácilmente variable. con un único elemento no modificable, el núcleo, los subedificios lineares son capaces de adaptarse a cualquier configuración que exija el programa.

Catálogos 01. programas

LUCIA no es sólo un contenedor de programa, sino un sistema completo. en este sistema el OBJETO asume un papel fundamental como cualificador de los diferentes espacios abstractos. de este modo es esencial a lucia la existencia de todo un repertorio de objetos destinados a dotar a los espacios de trabajo -siempre de un modo fácilmente modificable- de almacenaje, instalaciones específicas, núcleos húmedos, etc.

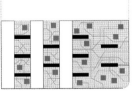

Catálogos 02. membranas

LUCIA contiene un catálogo de PARTICIONES MODULARES, destinados a compartimentar la planta primera, y a adaptar los recintos a diferentes necesidades: muros técnicos, paneles móviles, particiones traslúcidas, desmontables, etc.

Catálogos 03. paisajes

LUCIA es un sistema fluido, gracias al carácter intercambiable del objeto. también los espacios libres son cualificados gracias a objetos: 'paisajes' reducidos a una dimensión de 3x3, que contienen los elementos necesarios para programar los exteriores: desde parterres para cultivos experimentales hasta generadores de energía, mobiliario urbano y vegetación.

Paisajes 01. plazas

LUCIA diluye su interior en el espacio exterior, y en general con el campus entero, a través de la gran cubierta que rodea la planta baja. este peculiar espacio puede considerarse por un lado una extensión de las zonas públicas de LUCIA, y por otro una zona especialmente valiosa de los espacios abiertos de la universidad.

Paisajes 02. cubiertas

LUCIA tiene una gran cubierta transitable, que hace que los tres centros de investigación puedan considerarse 'a pie de calle'. esta cubierta contiene toda una serie de objetos-paisaje que la dotan, y que son fácilmente cambiables por otros para adaptar su uso a las circunstancias variables.

Paisajes 03. colonización

LUCIA es un sistema abierto al resto del campus, y sus elementos objetuales pueden colonizar la gran plaza central, o incluso otros edificios, intensificando así las relaciones, cualificando el espacio público y amplificando su presencia. el edificio no es más que una parte de LUCIA.

Interface 01. identidades

LUCIA se presenta como intermediario entre la producción científica y sus destinatarios finales, los ciudadanos. la presencia prominente del edificio con respecto a la ronda y al tren es potenciada con una gran fachada que puede ser usada para fines informativos, y que dota de visibilidad e identidad a los diferentes centros y proyectos.

Interface 02. información

LUCIA se comunica intensamente con el resto de la comunidad universitaria y con la ciudadanía, a través de su fachada informativa. con un mantenimiento escaso, una malla de leds permite usar el edificio como tablón informativo modificable en tiempo real.

Interface 03. escaparates

LUCIA ofrece a sus ocupantes un espacio para interaccionar con el público, en el gran vestíbulo de la planta baja. un gran escaparate para exponer, celebrar eventos, y que dota a los centros de un importante espacio de relación, y de un portal corporativo.

187 Un Cadavre Exquis | *arenas basabe palacios arquitectos*

University development in Peje (Kosovo)
Team : arenas basabe palacios arquitectos
Authors : Enrique Arenas Laorga, Luis Basabe Montalvo, Luis Palacios Labrador
Collaborators : Almudena Cano, Helena de Sebastian

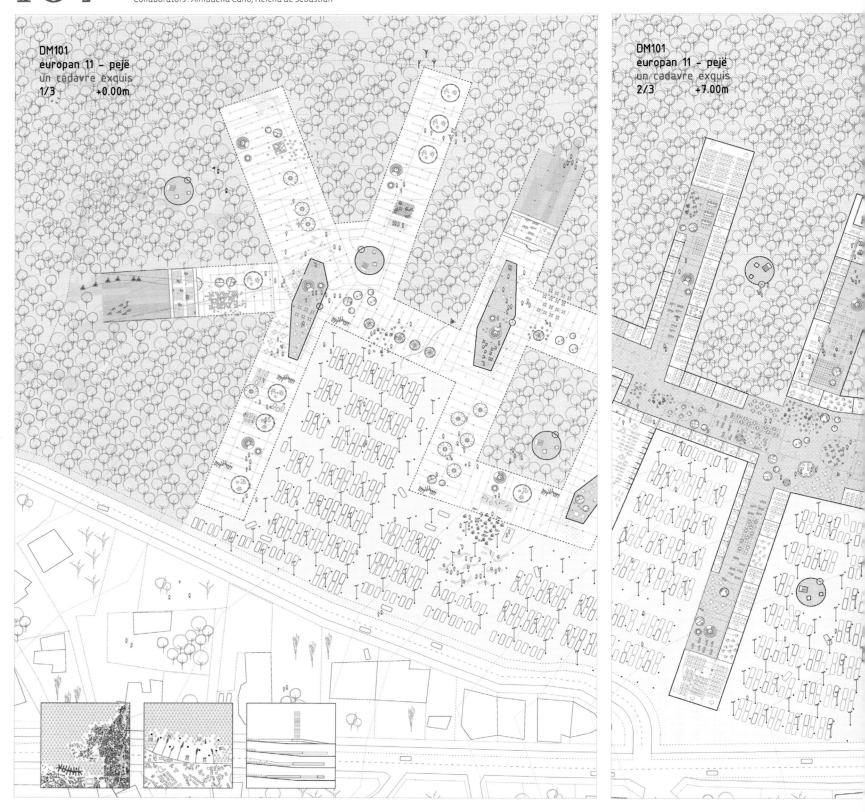

DM101
europan 11 – pejë
un cadavre exquis
1/3   +0.00m

DM101
europan 11 – pejë
un cadavre exquis
2/3   +7.00m

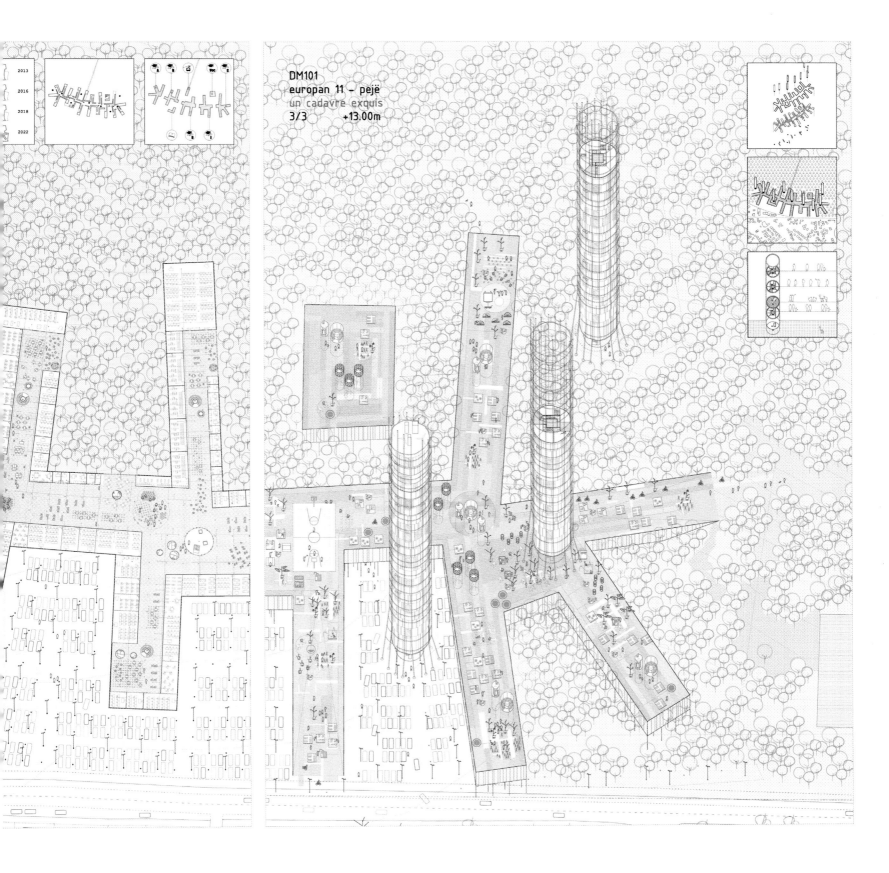

DM101
europan 11 – pejë
un cadavre exquis
3/3   +13.00m

2013
2016
2018
2022

188

Student Service Center | *kadawittfeldarchitektur*

Participants : Gerhard Wittfeld, Klaus Kada, Kilian Kada, Dirk Zweering, Julika Metz, Tim Danner, Simon Kortemeier, Johannes Münting
Partner : Tragwerkplanung (Hegger + Partner Ingenieure), TGA | Elektrotechnik (VIKA Ingenieur GmbH), Bauphysik (TOHR Bauphysik),

Freianlagen-Planung (greenbox Landschaftsarchitekten)
Construction Volume : Gfa 4,700 m², gross interior volume 13,800 m³
Project : Student Service Center
Typology : Education

Location : Düsseldorf, Germany
Client : BLB NRW Düsseldorf

NEUBAU STUDIERENDEN SERVICE CENTER _ Universität Düsseldorf

Aussen-Perspektive

Lageplan _ M 1:500

kada**wittfeld**architektur

Die Heinrich-Heine Universität Düsseldorf stellt sich städtebaulich als aus der Mitte heraus gewachsene Campus-Struktur dar, die sich mit verschiedenen Schwerpunkten und kurzen Wegen entlang einer zentralen Magistrale organisiert. Zur Universitätsstraße ist die HHU auf angenehme Weise in einen umlaufenden Grünraum eingebettet, der im Osten vom Botanischen Garten komplettiert wird.
Die Wahrnehmung dieser Parklandschaft und einer Campus-Universität im Grünen prägt auf positive Weise den ersten Eindruck der Besucher und neuen Studenten.
Dem entgegen gelingt es, abgesehen vom neuen „Oeconomicum", den bestehenden und sich zur Magistrale orientierenden Gebäuden der HHU kaum, der Universität nach Außen ein signifikantes und prägnantes Gesicht zu verleihen. Insofern ist die Zielsetzung nachvollziehbar, mit dem neuen SSC am Kreuzungspunkt von Magistrale und Universitätsstrasse eine adäquate und wiedererkennbare Adresse zu formulieren.

Neue Adresse und Tor zum Campus
Unser Entwurf für das neue SSC entwickelt sich daher aus der Prämisse, die bestehenden und besonderen Qualitäten der vorhandenen parkähnlichen Grünanlage beizubehalten und architektonisch neu zu interpretieren. Statt ein weiteres Volumen als Fremdkörper der baulichen Struktur hinzuzufügen, übersetzt unser Entwurf des SSC die Offenheit, Durchwegbarkeit und die räumliche Tiefe des Grünraums in eine leichte und lichte Architektur. Mittels eines von filigranen Stützen getragenen, umlaufenden Daches definiert sich das SSC nicht über eine austauschbar gestaltete Bürofassade, sondern fungiert vielmehr als offene und nahbare Willkommensgeste der Universität und auf diese Weise gleichzeitig als Tor zum Campus.

Helle Piazza
Zu diesem Zweck definiert das Dach des SSC eine von filigranen Stützen gesäumte Piazza, die sich auf dem belebten und stark frequentierten Niveau der zentralen Magistrale befindet. Eine breite Treppe verbindet die Piazza mit dem Niveau der Universitätsstraße und bildet so eine gut erkennbare Eingangsgeste mit Aufenthaltsqualität.
Ein Lift im Außenraum gewährleistet zudem eine barrierefreie Erschließung der Piazza und Magistralenebene.
Der eigentliche Eingang des SSC liegt zentral an der Piazza und stellt sich sowohl zum unteren Niveau der Universitätsstraße als auch zur Magistrale gleichermaßen einladend und repräsentativ dar. Eine großflächige verglaste Öffnung im Dach sorgt für eine helle und angenehme Atmosphäre.

Kommunikatives Foyer mit Ausblick
Die helle und offene Atmosphäre setzt sich auch im Inneren des Gebäudes fort. Die großzügig verglaste Eingangshalle mit Ausblick in den Park dient als zentraler Kommunikationsraum und Verteiler mit hoher Aufenthaltsqualität.
Das zweigeschossige Foyer ermöglicht auch Erstbesuchern jederzeit eine gute Orientierung im Haus.

Neben dem Infopoint als Anlaufstelle sind hier die Frontoffices als erste Beratungsplätze positioniert. Der seitliche angegliederte Mehrzweckraum kann flexibel zugeschaltet werden und steht sowohl als Event- und Ausstellungsfläche, als auch für Studentenarbeitsplätze in Lounge-artiger Atmosphäre zur Verfügung. Gegenüber befindet sich der Zugang zur Studienakademie, sowie der Eingang zum Studentensekretariat und zur Verwaltung. Entsprechend dem gewünschten Service-Konzept erfolgt die weitergehende und spezifischere Beratung der Studenten und Besucher in den anderen Geschossen, die von der Foyer-Ebene über Aufzüge oder eine großzügige Wendeltreppe erreicht werden. Durch die Mittellage der Foyer-Ebene sind diese auf kurzem Weg optimal zu erreichen, da jeweils nur ein Geschoss nach oben oder unten überwunden werden muss.

Im Obergeschoss ist eine lounge-artige Wartezone für die Bereiche mit stärkerem Publikumsverkehr an einer offenen Terrasse in der Halle positioniert. Von hier werden die Beratungsräume und Backoffices ebenfalls auf kurzem Weg erreicht. Seitlich wird die Halle von den weiteren Büroflächen flankiert. Die Abteilungen mit geringem bzw. ohne Publikumsverkehr befinden sich auf der unteren Ebene, die sich auf dem Niveau des Parks befindet. Eine vorgelagerte umlaufende Veranda als Pendant zum Dach vermittelt den Übergang von Haus und Grünraum und generiert so auch hier eine angenehme räumliche Qualität.
Die unbelichteten Flächen dieses Geschosses dienen als Lager und Technikräume.

Filigrane Zeichenhaftigkeit
Das äußere Erscheinungsbild des SSC wird von dem sich zwischen Dach und Piazza aufspannenden Raum bestimmt.
Durch die rhythmisch gestellten filigranen Stützen entwickelt sich eine elegante selbstbewusste Zeichenhaftigkeit, die das weltoffene akademische Leben an der HHU und ihren fünf Fakultäten adäquat repräsentiert.

Strasse | Grüngürtel | Universitätsgebäude

Strasse | Studierenden Service Center hat besonderen Standort im Grüngürtel | Universitätsgebäude

Vorplatz des neuen Studierenden Service Center wird zum ‚Eingang' für den Campus und verbindet Einrichtungen an der Universitätsstraße mit Einrichtungen auf der Magistrale

Haupteingang
Nebeneingang MFZ
zum Parkplatz

Mensa | Studentenwohnh. | Universitätsstraße | Studierenden Service Center | Hörsäle

Grundriss Sondergeschoss (Zugangsebene) _ M 1:200

Längsschnitt A-A _ M 1:200

kadawittfeldarchitektur

Innen-Perspektive

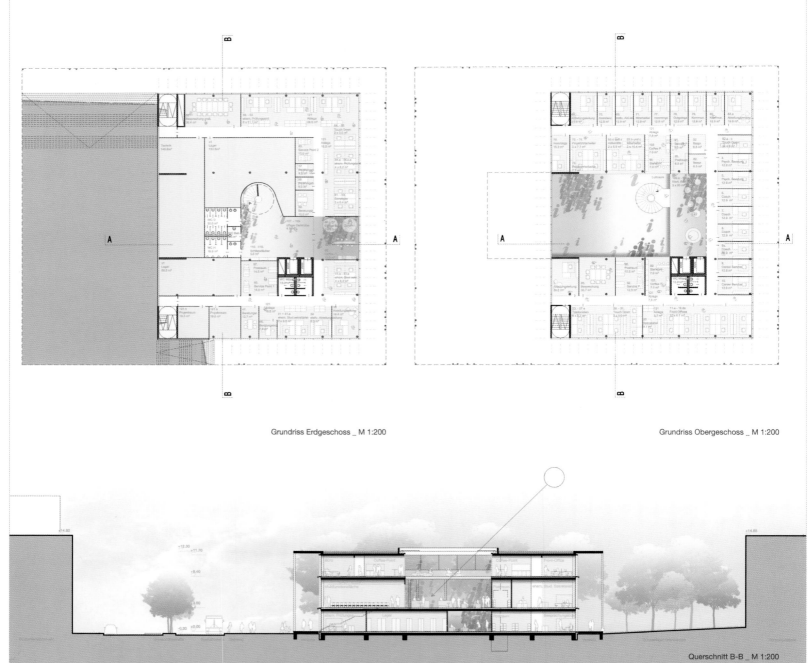

Grundriss Erdgeschoss _ M 1:200

Grundriss Obergeschoss _ M 1:200

Querschnitt B-B _ M 1:200

kadawittfeldarchitektur

Möblierungsvarianten Multifunktionsfläche

Die seitlich an die Eingangshalle angegliederte Multifunktionsfläche kann flexibel zugeschaltet werden und steht sowohl als Event- und Ausstellungsfläche, als auch als Studentenarbeits-plätze in lounge-artiger Atmo-sphäre zur Verfügung.

OG

- International Office
- Studierendenservice
- Wartezone / Foyer

OG

Zugangsebene

- Multifunktionsflächen
- Foyer / Infopoint
- Front-Office
- Dezernat
- Studierendenverwaltung
- Studierendenakademie

Zugangsebene

UG

- Studierendenverwaltung
- Lager / Technik / WC

EG

Funktionsbereiche

Brandabschnitte

Brandschutz Konzept

Das Gebäude bleibt sowohl mit seiner Fläche als auch mit seinen maximalen Abmessungen unter der Grenze von 40 x 40 m und bildet somit einen Brandabschnitt. Im Obergeschoss wird eine Bürofläche ausgebildet, die als Nutzungseinheit im Sinne des §38 BauO NRW zu bewerten ist, so dass keine notwendigen Flure ausgebildet werden. Die Entrauchung der Bürofläche erfolgt über zwei Treppenräume, die an der Kopfseite des Gebäudes liegen. Zwar wird die zulässige Größe für eine Nutzungseinheit (400m²) überschritten, jedoch kann eine Überschreitung der Fläche unter Berücksichtigung der vorzusehenden Brandmeldeanlage akzeptiert werden. Alternativ kann auch problemlos eine Unterteilung der Fläche erfolgen. Die zusätzliche Erschließung über die interne Treppe (Foyer/ Atrium) stellt keinen Rettungsweg dar, die Nutzungseinheit wird zum Atrium brandschutztechnisch abgetrennt.

Im Erdgeschoss befindet sich ein Foyer, in dem ein Info-Point und Beratungsplätze angeordnet sind. Über eine Freitreppe werden das Obergeschoss und die Besucher WC's im Untergeschoss erschlossen. Die an das Foyer angrenzenden Back-Offices und die Multifunktionsfläche (Versammlungsraum) werden brandschutztechnisch in geeigneter Weise / Vorhangsystem) abgetrennt. Die Rettungswege für den Multifunktionsraum führen im wesentlichen über einen direkten Ausgang ins Freie. Ein weiterer Rettungsweg kann bei Bedarf über das Foyer geführt werden. Mit der für das Foyer vorgesehenen Rauchableitung und der vorgesehenen Brandmeldeanlage bestehen keine Bedenken gegen die Rettungswegführung. Auf eine Sprinkleranlage kann unter Berücksichtigung der sich einstellenden raucharmen Schicht im Foyer aus brandschutztechnischer Sicht verzichtet werden. Die Büroflächen des Studierendensekretariats bilden eine Nutzungseinheit deren Rettungswege über den Treppenraum und eine für die Feuerwehr anleiterbare Stelle sichergestellt werden.

Im Untergeschoss werden der zum Foyer zugehörige Teil mit Garderobe und Besucher-WC's ebenso wie das Lager und Technikbereiche brandschutztechnisch abgetrennt. Der übrige Bereich bildet eine Nutzungseinheit. Die Rettungswege werden analog zum Obergeschoss über die beiden Treppenräume geführt.

Für das Gebäude ist neben der schon beschriebenen flächendeckenden Brandmeldeanlage und den Rauchabzugsanlagen für das Foyer auch eine Sicherheitsbeleuchtungsanlage vorzusehen. Weitere brandschutztechnische Einrichtungen (wie Wandhydranten oder Sprinkleranlagen) sind aus brandschutztechnischer Sicht nicht erforderlich.

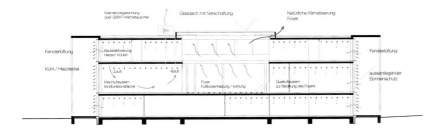

TGA Konzept

Hohe Behaglichkeit bei niedrigen Energiekosten durch

- Bedarfsorientierte hygienische Lüftung für das Foyer, den Multifunktionsbereich und die an das Foyer angrenzenden innen liegenden Räume
- Die an der äußeren Fassade liegenden Räume werden natürlich über Fenster belüftet
- Das zweigeschossige Foyer wirkt als Klimapuffer und Abluftzone für Foyer und Mehrzweckbereich
- Im oberen Bereich des Atriums kann die Luft je nach Energiegehalt in die Wärmerückgewinnung der Lüftungsanlage gespeist oder als natürliche Lüftung direkt nach außen geführt werden
- Über eine hocheffiziente Lüftungsanlage mit Wärmerückgewinnung wird über 80% der Wärme der Abluft zurück gewonnen
- Nachtauskühlung durch Aktivierung der Speichermassen über die Lüftungsanlage
- Das Atrium kann in Abhängigkeit der Temperaturverhältnisse im innen- und Außenbereich natürlich belüftet werden
- Bauteilaktivierung, die die Speichermassen des Gebäudes nutzt und über den hohen Strahlungsanteil ein sehr behagliches Raumklima schafft
- Für die Multifunktionsfläche wird über die Abhangdecke mit einer Heiz- und Kühldecke in Verbindung mit einer hygienischen Lüftung agiert
- Im Foyer wird die Temperierung mit einem Klimaboden realisiert, der sowohl für die Beheizung als auch für die Kühlung im Sommer genutzt werden kann
- Eine äußere Verschattung mit lichtlenkenden Jalousien schafft eine hohe Tageslichtausnutzung

- Energiekennwerte liegen unterhalb der aktuellen EnEV-Anforderungen

Ansicht Nord _ M 1:200

189

Encapsulated Fields | *Horhizon consortium*

Type : Education
Design : Tobias Klein, Sarah Shafiei, Johan Vordouw

The Encapsulated Field, a building that takes the Dutch horizon and vertically weaves it to enclose space, retaining the iconographic, quintessential Dutch image of field and narrow water channels and abstractly folds them to assert volumetric form.

Building Concept

The new Faculty of Architecture Building for the T.U. Delft was designed to express a revived start while retaining the values, developed at T.U. Delft prior to the fire. The faculty generates a new interpretation for the architecture school, re-working the horizontal street into a volumetric extension of space moving around the building along meandering paths and through programmatic voids. These interwoven spaces are constructed to facilitate interaction and participation by the students, to learn the practice of architecture through engaging in the act of re-build the lost faculty. The ethos for the building is one of exploration, a pedagogy of experimentation for both cognitive and physical way finding. Its spaces are linked through sinuously wandering promenades connecting individual spaces to unify the students, faculty and staff to form a new sense of community. These paths form the flexible meeting places, studios and exhibition areas visible from multiple points along the buildings circulation routes. This building is meant to not only to facilitate, but generate a dialogue, promoting divergent ideas and the expression of new cultural ideals. The programmatic voids throughout the building are large flexible spaces adjacent to studio and workshops left open for re-appropriation and inhabitation. These void areas are places in which to construct, demolish, collect and work out of, crossing multiple levels within the school to connect students and academia, studios and facilities. This continual sense of openness reveals an integrated, shifting connectedness that revels in its diversity and in its open-ended potentials, mapping a new spirit of innovation while re-building the poetic heart of the building.

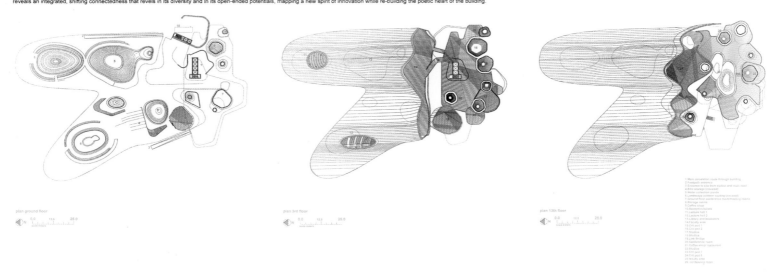

plan ground floor

plan 2nd floor

plan 13th floor

The faculty is devised to promote the ad hoc experimentation that defines and strengthens a school, to deliver the diversity of space that a faculty requires and develop the appropriated work clusters that build-up and devolve over time. The cyclical notion of making, of re-interpreting and of re-defining sets up the on-going evolution of the school to take what it has lost and re-insert it into a new paradigm for a faculty. Within this open built-scape are the necessary spaces that serve as a counterpoint to the openness found in the meandering circulation and programmatic void spaces of the studios, workshops, meeting spaces and exhibition areas, offices, administrative requirements, lecture theatres, canteens and faculty operations such as the library, book store and mechanical / storage areas form the required backbone to the faculty operations and offers a sense of permanence and stability in contrast to the playfulness of other areas within the faculty building

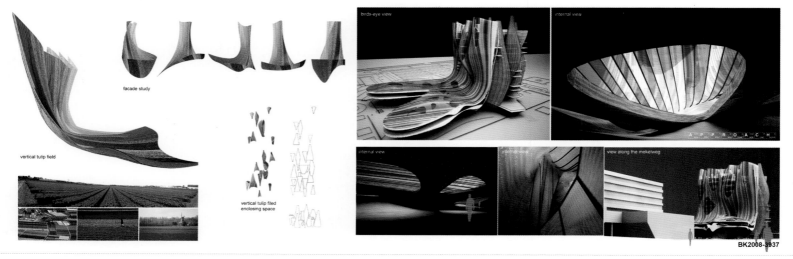

facade study

vertical tulip field

vertical tulip filed enclosing space

birds-eye view

internal view

internal view

internal view

view along the mekelweg

BK2008-3937

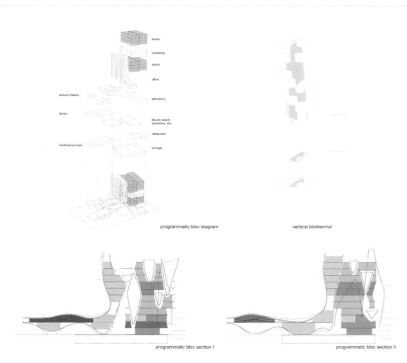

programmatic bloc diagram   vertical blokkenhal

programmatic bloc section I   programmatic bloc section II

north elevation from Berlageweg

topview north   view under theater plinth

Sustainability
The building focuses on environmental sustainability as a new mode of making and building practice but also social sustainability, creating spaces that form a sociable, responsible environment open to light and air.

Heating & Cooling
The building is orientated to prevent high solar gains with smaller inflexible spaces facing north to prevent excessive warming from solar heat gain. The rear façade forms large 'winter gardens', volumetric spaces that regulate and diffuse large temperature gradients between the internal and external environment through increased air movement. Due to the campus nature of the T.U. Delft additional mechanical heating and cooling will be provided using a geothermal system with integrated heat recovery to ensure a constant and comfortable environment.

Natural Ventilation
The flexible programmatic voids within the internal spaces of the Faculty connect at each level to outdoor spaces for user control. These large volumes are intended to promote air movement and natural ventilation opening vertically through the roof of the building to form a stack effect.

Water Retention
Water collected off the roof and main façade are channeled along the edifice to the retention ponds at ground level, water being used in a grey water system, for small scale irrigation systems for external landscapes that surround the faculty building for and building cooling.

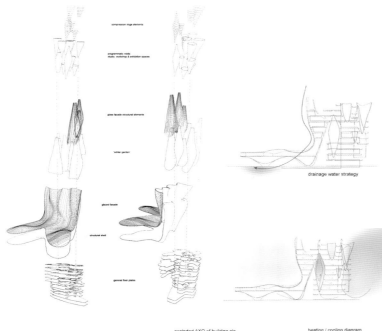

compression strut elements
programmatic voids studio, workshop & exhibition spaces
glass facade structural elements
'winter garden'
glazed facade
structural shell
general floor plates

exploded AXO of building elements

drainage water strategy

heating / cooling diagram

view void space - infrastructure   internal studio space

BSC studio   main stair

main entry space   canteen area

Social Sustainability
Further to promoting physical sustainability the flexibility of student and faculty space is to increase a notion of social sustainability, creating spaces that allow the development of social connections and create a sense of inclusion and community. The meandering of circulation continually form multiple vantage points of viewing and opportunities for communicating. Balconies and terraces link a strong connection to the outside for fresh air and natural light. All these elements are considered and used to promote a design that response to the complex nuances and requirements for each individual within the group that forms the new Faculty of Architecture.

Urbanism
The building moves beyond the notion of an object in space in how it connects to the urban fabric beyond. The 'V' shaped form of the lower floors projects the building towards the adjacent buildings across the Berlageweg & Van der Burghweg. The western extension of the building is lifted to facilitate the future tram extension along the Mekelweg and provide cover for bike stores and people entering the School of Architecture. The tower serves as a strong formal point of reference for the T.U. and surrounding community. The design continues a lengthy tradition at the T.U. as a generator of expressive architectural thought and the expression of divergent theoretical ideals.

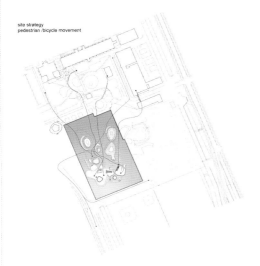

site strategy
pedestrian /bicycle movement

vertical street diagram
inverse urbanism

east elevation - context

BK2008-3937

190

Istanbul Disaster Prevention | *Horhizon consortium*

Type : Civic
Design : Tobias Klein

Overview - 01
Istanbul Disaster Prevention and Education Center

41278TK

41278TK

Istanbul Disaster Prevention and Education Centre
URBAN STRATEGY

Our design responds to a brief that, in our eyes, did not only asked for a Disaster Prevention and Education Centre but is interested in an integrated architectural and urban regeneration of the area. The centre acts a catalyst, is a place of culture, a meeting point and becomes a new attraction for Istanbul. We deliberately chose to design the entirety of the proposed area 27.000 sqm instead of just a building, providing a more holistic design approach which consequently allowed for a more interwoven public scheme.

On an urban level, by positioning the building in the far East of the site next to the topological formation , we seek to establish a connection to the public transport (bus and metro). This positioning next to the 7.00m hill allowed us to direct visitors travelling via public transport onto the publicly accessible roof through the building and into the lobby, allowing them for a hint of what is to come. Subsequently our design fluctuates between public, semi-public and private, these areas are in a fluid visual relation, similar to tectonic plates, interlocked with each other. Furthermore this positioning allowed us to design a large open plaza, adjacent to the shopping mall, inviting visitors from the university or the mall, to permeate into the Centers site. The Planetarium has been positioned on the main axis of the site which allows for its integration into the building despite it being a separate element.

The combination of a multicultural and religious background coupled with the dynamism of a city that straddles two continents, is all incorporated in the design. By a translation into various interdependent, interlocked elements and their related program and space articulations. Similar to a single part of the city the elements of the building can be read alone - on their own sculptural, but only in a composition coming to a full conclusive whole as Istanbul does. The building is made up out of the main elevated exhibition space interlinked and penetrated by the conference building, adjacent to the cinema and water simulation space and joined the office tract. The entire building is lifted by 4 meters, allowing the ground floor to act as a public area with cafes, shops and meeting points. The entrance is situated to the north and accompanied by a 18m tall sculptural tower that acts as the main vertical circulation into the exhibition area on the one hand, and as an entrance from the public roof to overlook the old city of Istanbul - a place to reflect understand and contemplate on the difficulties such a city would face in the case of a disaster. The exhibition is planned as a free and open space that allows the visitor to discover the various programmatically grouped stations, interact and meander through the building.

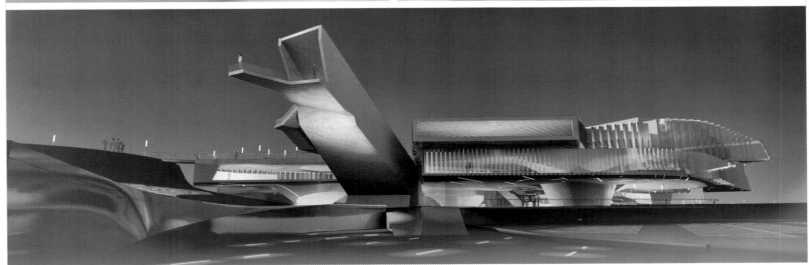

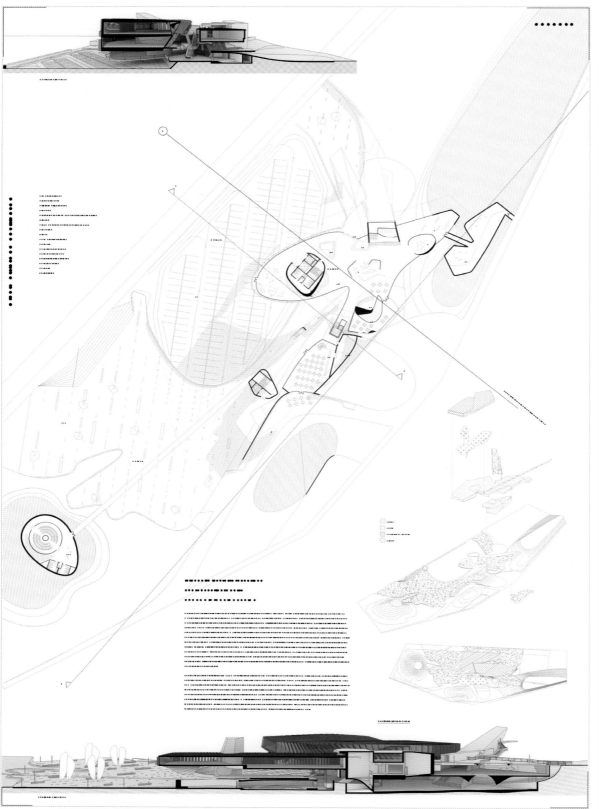

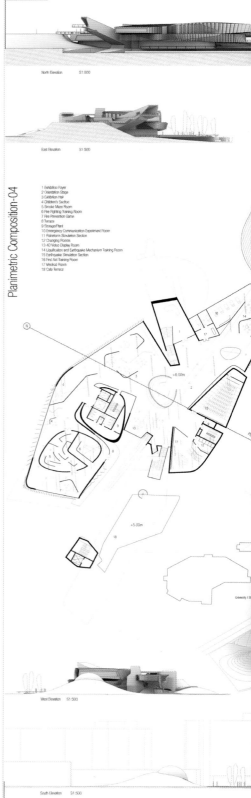

Planimetric Composition-04

1 Exhibition Foyer
2 Orientation Stage
3 Exhibition Hall
4 Children's Section
5 Smoke Maze Room
6 Fire Fighting Training Room
7 Fire Prevention Game
8 Terrace
9 Storage/Plant
10 Emergency Communication Experiment Room
11 Rainstorm Simulation Section
12 Changing Rooms
13 4D Video Display Room
14 Liquefaction and Earthquake Mechanism Training Room
15 Earthquake Simulation Section
16 First Aid Training Room
17 Medical Room
18 Cafe Terrace

North Elevation   S1:500

East Elevation   S1:500

West Elevation   S1:500

South Elevation   S1:500

41278TK

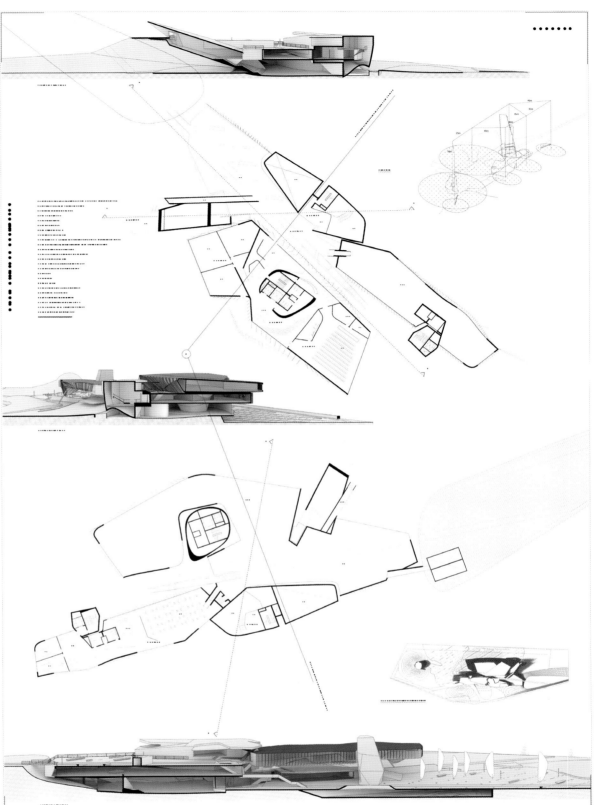

191

Youth Burgos | *gutiérrez-delafuente arquitectos*

Project : National Competition for a new Youth Centre in the inner city of Burgos
Program : New Youth Centre and Design of the Cathedral "rear" Public Space
Location : Burgos, Spain

Client : City of Burgos
Architects : Natalia Gutiérrez & Julio de la Fuente

IMAGEN DIURNA
IMAGEN NOCTURNA

IDENTIDAD URBANA:
LA PRIMERA DECISIÓN DEL PROYECTO ES ASUMIR EL CARÁCTER RESIDUAL Y DE "TRASERA" QUE TIENE EL ÁREA DE ACTUACIÓN. NO ES UNA ZONA DE PASO. MEJOR. LAS SITUACIONES PROGRAMÁTICAS ABIERTAS Y FLEXIBLES NECESITAN DE ESPACIOS DESPROGRAMADOS A PRIORI, COMO ESTE, PARA PODER EXISTIR. A TRAVÉS DE DOS ACCIONES MUY BÁSICAS, DADO EL ESPECIAL CONTEXTO, SE DOTARÁ DE IDENTIDAD Y USO A ESTA ZONA. SE ACTIVARÁ.

DOS ACCIONES:
LA PRIMERA ACCIÓN PARA CONVERTIR LA "PLAZA" EN UN SITIO DONDE OCURREN "COSAS", DONDE SE REUNE LA GENTE PARA VER Y SER VISTO, ES UNA ACCIÓN TOPOGRÁFICA DE CREAR UNA ESCALERA-GRADERÍO VOLCADA SOBRE EL ESPACIO ABIERTO , QUE ADEMÁS FACILITA LAS CIRCULACIONES PEATONALES.
LA SEGUNDA ACCIÓN ES DOTAR DE IDENTIDAD AL LUGAR, CREAR UN ESPACIO SINGULAR A TRAVÉS DE UNA ACCIÓN MÍNIMA Y VIABLE, A TRAVÉS DE LA ILUMINACIÓN URBANA COMO HERRAMIENTA DE TRANSFORMACIÓN Y CUALIFICACIÓN DEL ESPACIO URBANO. SE TRATA DE UNA GALAXIA ARTIFICIAL A BASE DE NODOS LUMINOSOS DE LED'S, QUE EMPIEZAN A FUNCIONAR PRECISAMENTE CUANDO ESA ZONA DE LA CIUDAD SE ACTIVA, POR LA NOCHE.

EL CONSULADO JOVEN:
EL EDIFICIO DE LOS SERVICIOS DE LA JUVENTUD SE PROYECTA COMO UN VOLUMEN NEUTRO, QUE TRÁS UN PROCESO DE GENERACIÓN INFORMADO POR LA NORMATIVA, EL CONTEXTO HISTÓRICO, LAS VISTAS, EL CLIMA, EL PROGRAMA Y LA MATERIALIDAD, TOMA SU FORMA DEFINITIVA. SIGUIENDO CON LA CARACTERIZACIÓN DEL ESPACIO URBANO A TRAVÉS DE LA ILUMINACIÓN, SE PROPONE UN EDIFICIO DUAL, CON UNA PIEL CAPAZ DE ABSORBER LOS REFLEJOS DEL ENTORNO DURANTE EL DÍA Y DURANTE NOCHE CONVERTIRSE EN UNA LÁMPARA A ESCALA URBANA, UNA ESCULTURA LUMÍNICA.

POSIBLES SITUACIONES PROGRAMÁTICAS URBANAS

INAGURACIÓN EXPOSICIÓN — PROYECCIONES / CINE VERANO
ACTUACIONES EXPONTÁNEAS — "COLA" INSCRIPCIÓN ACTIVIDAD
PLAZA ENTORNO WIFI — QUEDADA JOVEN POR SMS

LEMA: BURGOS

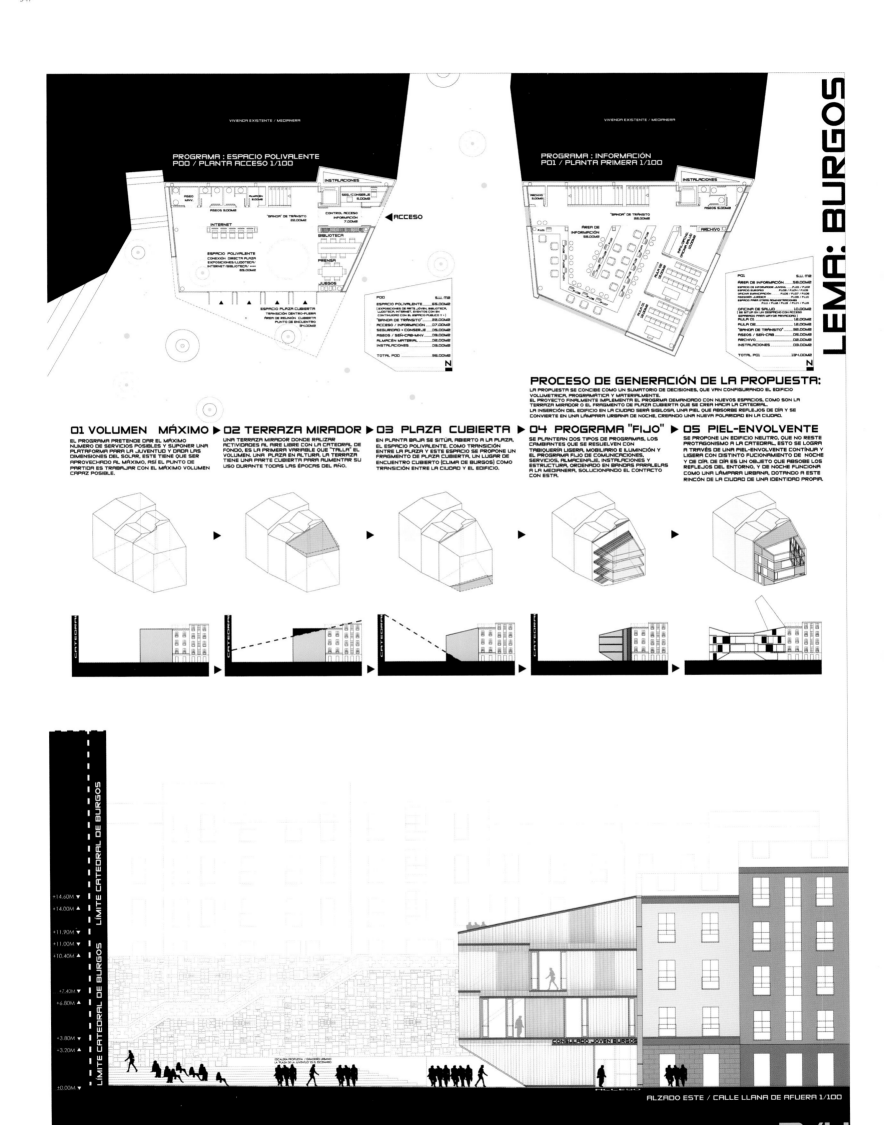

LEMA: BURGOS

PROGRAMA : ESPACIO POLIVALENTE
P00 / PLANTA ACCESO 1/100

PROGRAMA : INFORMACIÓN
P01 / PLANTA PRIMERA 1/100

PROCESO DE GENERACIÓN DE LA PROPUESTA:

01 VOLUMEN MÁXIMO ▶ 02 TERRAZA MIRADOR ▶ 03 PLAZA CUBIERTA ▶ 04 PROGRAMA "FIJO" ▶ 05 PIEL-ENVOLVENTE

ALZADO ESTE / CALLE LLANA DE AFUERA 1/100

2/4

CONCURSO DE IDEAS PARA EL EDIFICIO DE LOS SERVICIOS DE JUVENTUD DEL AYUNTAMIENTO DE BURGOS

LEMA: BURGOS

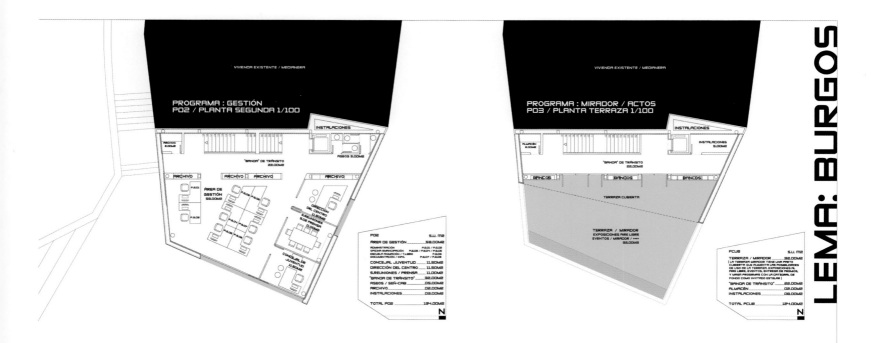

PROGRAMA : GESTIÓN
P02 / PLANTA SEGUNDA 1/100

VIVIENDA EXISTENTE / MEDIANERA

PROGRAMA : MIRADOR / ACTOS
P03 / PLANTA TERRAZA 1/100

VIVIENDA EXISTENTE / MEDIANERA

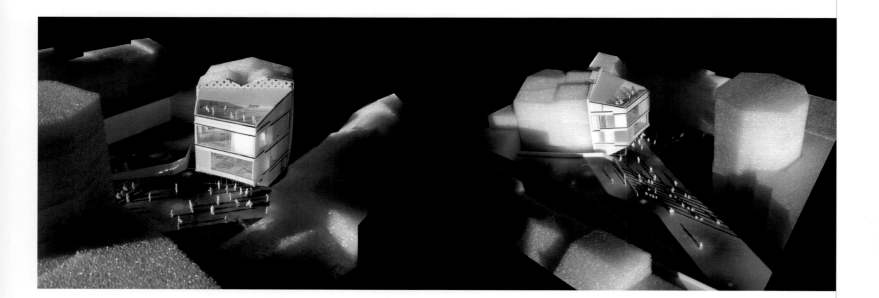

ALZADO SUR / "HACIA LA CATEDRAL" 1/100

3/4

CONCURSO DE IDEAS PARA EL EDIFICIO DE LOS SERVICIOS DE JUVENTUD DEL AYUNTAMIENTO DE BURGOS

DESARROLLO DE LA PIEL DE CERRAMIENTO Y CUBIERTA
GRADO DE OPACIDAD / 100% - 50% - 0%

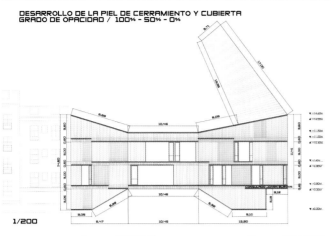

1/200

OPACO 100%
-100% OPACIDAD: FACHADA VENTILADA DE VIDRIO TRATADO AL CHORRO DE ARENA Y UN TRASDOSADO INTERIOR DE PANELES FENÓLICOS BLANCOS.

TRASLÚCIDO 50%
-50% OPACIDAD: FACHADA VENTILADA DE VIDRIO TRATADO AL CHORRO DE ARENA Y UN TRASDOSADO INTERIOR DE POLICARBONATO SEMI-TRASLÚCIDO.

VIDRIO 00%
-0% OPACIDAD: GRANDES HUECOS DESDE LOS QUE CONTEMPLAR LAS VISTAS DE LA CATEDRAL, SE TRATA DE HUECOS DE VIDRIO FIJO Y HUECOS VERTICALES PRACTICABLES PARA VENTILACIÓN.

EFICIENCIA ENERGÉTICA

EL 70% DEL CERRAMIENTO ESTA COMPUESTO POR UNA DOBLE PIEL QUE TIENE UN COMPORTAMIENTO ENERGÉTICO QUE OPTIMIZA LOS RECURSOS EN TODAS LAS ESTACIONES DEL AÑO.
EN INVIERNO LAS REJILLAS DE VENTILACIÓN EN LOS REMATES DE ZÓCALO Y DE CORNISA PERMANECEN CERRADAS, DE MANERA QUE SE CREA UN COLCHÓN TÉRMICO. EN VERANO ESTAS REJILLAS SE ABREN PROVOCANDO UN BARRIDO DE AIRE A TRAVÉS DE LA CÁMARA.

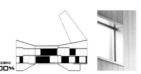

DET. 1/50

AVANCE DE PRESUPUESTO

01. movimiento de tierras	80.500 €
02. saneamiento horizontal	29.100 €
03. cimentación y c. tierras	86.000 €
04. estructura	156.400 €
05. albañilería	71.000 €
06. solados y alicatados	34.600 €
07. divisiones	99.000 €
08. suelos técnicos	12.000 €
09. cubiertas	16.500 €
10. carpintería exterior	55.000 €
11. carpintería interior	28.300 €
12. vidrios	25.100 €
13. aislamiento e imperm.	14.700 €
14. pinturas y acabado	55.000 €
15. fontanería	32.000 €
16. electricidad	85.900 €
17. instalaciones especiales	44.000 €
18. climatización	102.000 €
19. ascensores	18.000 €
20. comunicaciones	17.000 €
21. instalaciones de protección	37.200 €
22. varios	25.000 €
23. seguridad y salud	12.000 €

TOTAL P.E.M. 1.070.300 €

24. urbanización del entorno 452.600 €

TOTAL P.E.M. 452.600 €

EQUIPO REDACTOR < 40 AÑOS
el equipo redactor está compuesto por: 2 ARQUITECTOS Y 1 ARQUITECTO TÉCNICO, todos menores de 40 años.

ESTIMACIÓN DE HONORARIOS
LA OFERTA ECONÓMICA CORRESPONDIENTE A LOS HONORARIOS ES DE:
44.000,00€ (IVA NO INCLUIDO)

RESUMEN DE SUPERFICIES

RESUMEN POR PROGRAMAS — sup. útiles
espacio polivalente — 66,00m2
área de información — 68,00m2
área de gestión — 81,00m2
aulas de formación — 24,00m2
reuniones / prensa — 11,00m2
acceso / control — 12,00m2
terraza / mirador — 99,00m2
"banda de tránsito" — 108,00m2
aseos — 19,00m2
almacén / archivo — 08,00m2
instalaciones — 17,00m2

RESUMEN POR PLANTAS — sup. constr.
p00 — 128,00m2
p01 — 161,00m2
p02 — 161,00m2
pcub — 50,00m2
SUPERFICIE CONSTRUIDA TOTAL — 500,00m2

INSTALACIONES / ESTRUCTURA

LAS INSTALACIONES SON RESUELTAS DE MANERA SENCILLA AL SITUAR UN GRAN PATINILLO DE INSTALACIONES EN LA IRREGULARIDAD QUE PRESENTA EL CONTACTO CON LA MEDIANERA EXISTENTE. LUEGO, LAS INSTALACIONES DISCURRIRÁN POR FALSO TECHO A TRAVÉS DE LA BANDA DE SERVICIOS Y SE DISTRIBUIRÁN HASTA LAS ZONAS DE TRABAJO Y ZONAS PÚBLICAS.

LA ESTRUCTURA ES METÁLICA, LOS FORJADOS SON MIXTOS. PARA LIBERAR LAS ZONAS DE TRABAJO Y DE EXPOSICIONES SE CONCENTRAN LA ESTRUCTURA EN LAS BANDAS DE SERVICIOS E INSTALACIONES Y PUNTUALMENTE EN EL PERÍMETRO DEL EDIFICIO. PARA SALVAR EL VUELO QUE CONFORMA EL PORCHE DE ENTRADA ("LA PLAZA CUBIERTA"), SE USA UN PERFIL METÁLICO A TRACCIÓN COMO SE PUEDE VER EN EL ESQUEMA ESTRUCTURAL. LA OTRA SINGULARIDAD SE PRODUCE EN LAS CIMENTACIONES PARA RESOLVER EL CONTACTO CON EL EDIFICIO MEDIANERO.

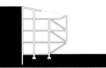

LEMA: BURGOS

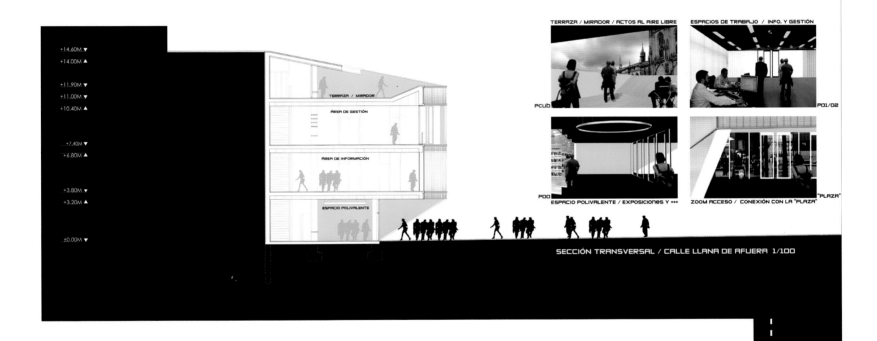

TERRAZA / MIRADOR / ACTOS AL AIRE LIBRE
ESPACIOS DE TRABAJO / INFO. Y GESTIÓN
pcub
P01/02
P00
ESPACIO POLIVALENTE / EXPOSICIONES Y •••
ZOOM ACCESO / CONEXIÓN CON LA "PLAZA"
"PLAZA"

TERRAZA / MIRADOR
ÁREA DE GESTIÓN
ÁREA DE INFORMACIÓN
ESPACIO POLIVALENTE

SECCIÓN TRANSVERSAL / CALLE LLANA DE AFUERA 1/100

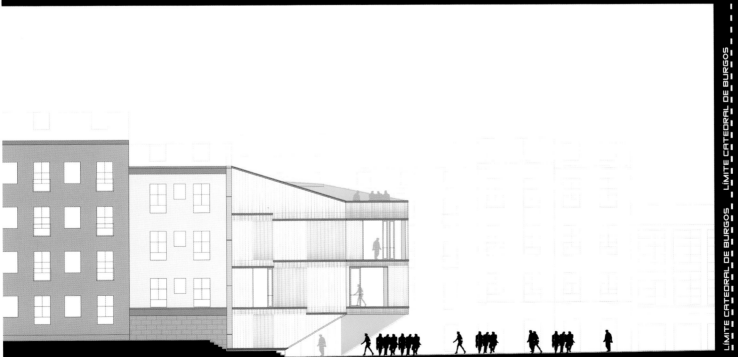

ALZADO OESTE / CALLE LLANA DE AFUERA 1/100

LÍMITE CATEDRAL DE BURGOS

4/4

CONCURSO DE IDEAS PARA EL EDIFICIO DE LOS SERVICIOS DE JUVENTUD DEL AYUNTAMIENTO DE BURGOS

192

BHW Education Campus | *franz zt gmbh*

Location : Vienna, Austria
Function : Education Campus with Kindergarten
Collaboration : Corinna Toell, Wolfgang Fischer, Christian Szalay

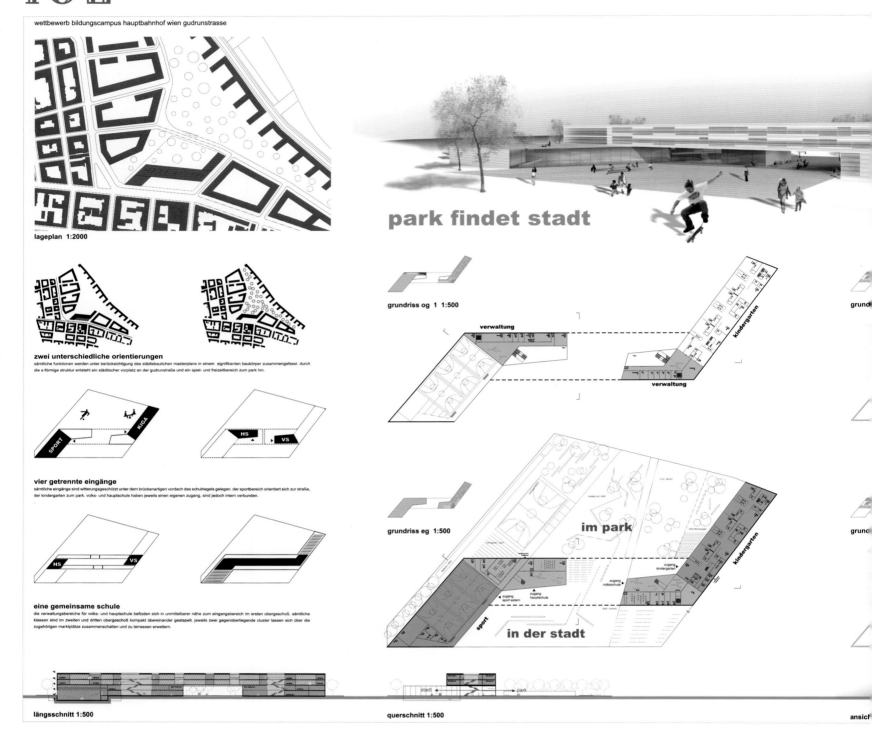

wettbewerb bildungscampus hauptbahnhof wien gudrunstrasse

lageplan 1:2000

zwei unterschiedliche orientierungen
sämtliche funktionen werden unter berücksichtigung des städtebaulichen masterplans in einem signifikanten baukörper zusammengefasst. durch die s-förmige struktur entsteht ein städtischer vorplatz an der gudrunstraße und ein spiel- und freizeitbereich zum park hin.

vier getrennte eingänge
sämtliche eingänge sind witterungsgeschützt unter dem brückenartigen vordach des schulriegels gelegen. der sportbereich orientiert sich zur straße, der kindergarten zum park. volks- und hauptschule haben jeweils einen eigenen zugang, sind jedoch intern verbunden.

eine gemeinsame schule
die verwaltungsbereiche für volks- und hauptschule befinden sich in unmittelbarer nähe zum eingangsbereich im ersten obergeschoß. sämtliche klassen sind im zweiten und dritten obergeschoß kompakt übereinander gestapelt. jeweils zwei gegenüberliegende cluster lassen sich über die zugehörigen marktplätze zusammenschalten und zu terrassen erweitern.

park findet stadt

grundriss og 1 1:500

verwaltung

kindergarten

verwaltung

grundriss eg 1:500

im park

in der stadt

sport

kindergarten

längsschnitt 1:500

querschnitt 1:500

stadt park

ansich

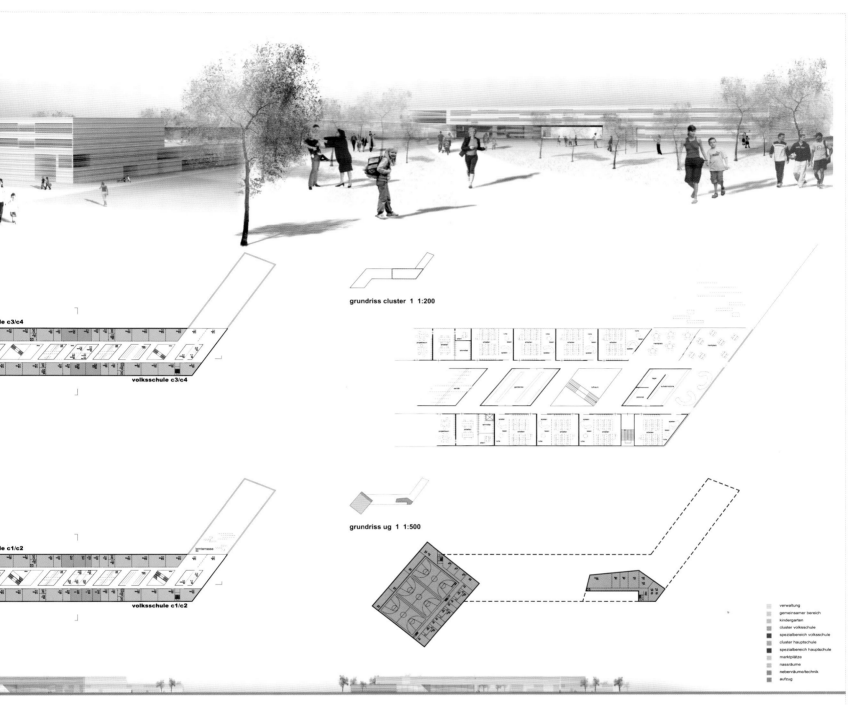

le c3/c4

volksschule c3/c4

grundriss cluster 1 1:200

le c1/c2

volksschule c1/c2

grundriss ug 1 1:500

verwaltung
gemeinsamer bereich
kindergarten
cluster volksschule
spezialbereich volksschule
cluster hauptschule
spezialbereich hauptschule
marktplätze
nassräume
nebenräume/technik
aufzug

ansicht süd 1:500

193
LPS Liese Prokop Secondary School | *franz zt gmbh*

552

Location : Maria Enzersdorf, Lower Austria
Function : Highschool Focused on Sports
Collaboration : Lucie Vencelidesova, Wolfgang Fischer, Michael Hasslacher

wettbewerb neubau liese prokop schule maria enzersdorf

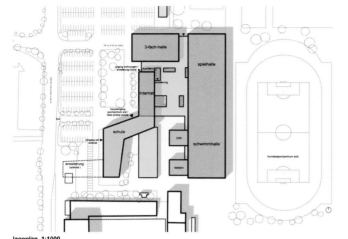

lageplan 1:1000

eingang neu definiert

> die neue schule tritt als eigenständiger baukörper in den vordergrund und verschmilzt gleichzeitig mit dem altbau zu einer städtebaulichen einheit.

> die beiden bauteile definieren durch den offenen winkel den schulvorplatz.

> die eingangsfassade springt hinter der baukörperkante zurück und markiert den gemeinsamen haupteingang.

> zugleich entsteht dadurch ein großzügiger, gedeckter eingangsbereich.

ensemble neu strukturiert

> ordnung der baumassen durch gezieltes verteilen der neuen baukörper

> es entsteht eine gemeinsame anlage: schule - sport - internat.

> schule, internat, 3-fach halle, schwimm- und spielhalle, judo und klettern werden als eigenständige baukörper in unterschiedlichen höhen definiert.

> die 1-geschoßigen funktionen verbinden diese körper. ausgeschnittene höfe ermöglichen die belichtung und zufahrt der einzelnen bereiche.

neu im tea

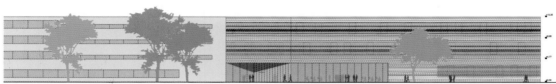

ansicht 1 1:200

funktionen eg

- aula / eingang
- sonderunterricht
- bibliothek
- verwaltung
- nebenräume / sanitär
- WC / sonderbereich
- stiegen, gänge
- technik

nachmittagsbetreuung

gezielte verteilung der funktionen im eingangsbereich mit synergieeffekten für die nachmittagsbetreuung

> großer zusammenschaltbarer bereich zwischen schule, sport und internat

> die aula ist zentraler verteiler und erweiterter aufenthaltsbereich

> kurze verbindung zum internat und den sportbereichen

> bibliothek und edv räume in direkter nähe zum aufenthaltsraum

> vorgelagerte terrasse richtung süden

ansicht 2 1:200

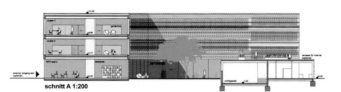

schnitt A 1:200

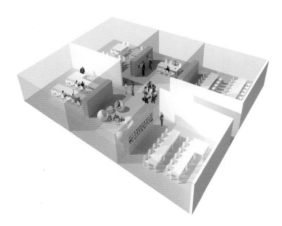

cluster 1 innenraum

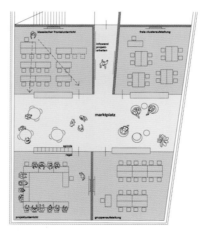

cluster 1 1:100

erdgeschoss 1:200

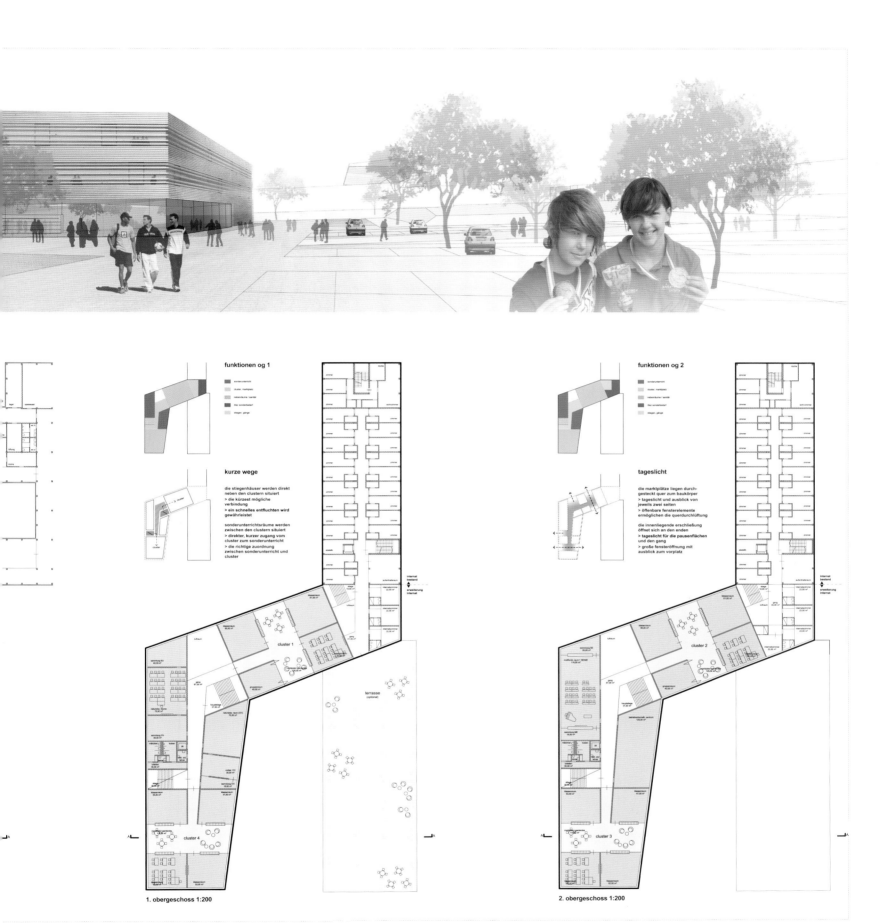

funktionen og 1

sonderunterricht
cluster / marktplatz
nebenräume / sanitär
blau: sonderbedarf
stiegen / gänge

kurze wege

die stiegenhäuser werden direkt
neben den clustern situiert
> die kürzest mögliche
verbindung
> ein schnelles entfluchten wird
gewährleistet

sonderunterrichtsräume werden
zwischen den clustern situiert
> direkter, kurzer zugang vom
cluster zum sonderunterricht
> die richtige zuordnung
zwischen sonderunterricht und
cluster

cluster 1

terrasse
(optional)

cluster 4

internat
bestand
erweiterung
internat

1. obergeschoss 1:200

funktionen og 2

sonderunterricht
cluster / marktplatz
nebenräume / sanitär
blau: sonderbedarf
stiegen / gänge

tageslicht

die marktplätze liegen durch-
gesteckt quer zum baukörper
> tageslicht und ausblick von
jeweils zwei seiten
> öffenbare fensterelemente
ermöglichen die querdurchlüftung

die innenliegende erschließung
öffnet sich an den enden
> tageslicht für die pausenflächen
und den gang
> große fensteröffnung mit
ausblick zum vorplatz

cluster 2

cluster 3

internat
bestand
erweiterung
internat

2. obergeschoss 1:200

194

PHY Technical School | *franz zt gmbh*

Location : Phyra, Lower Austria
Function : Technical School
Collaboration : Ena Lloret Kristensen

554

PARK TRIBÜNE

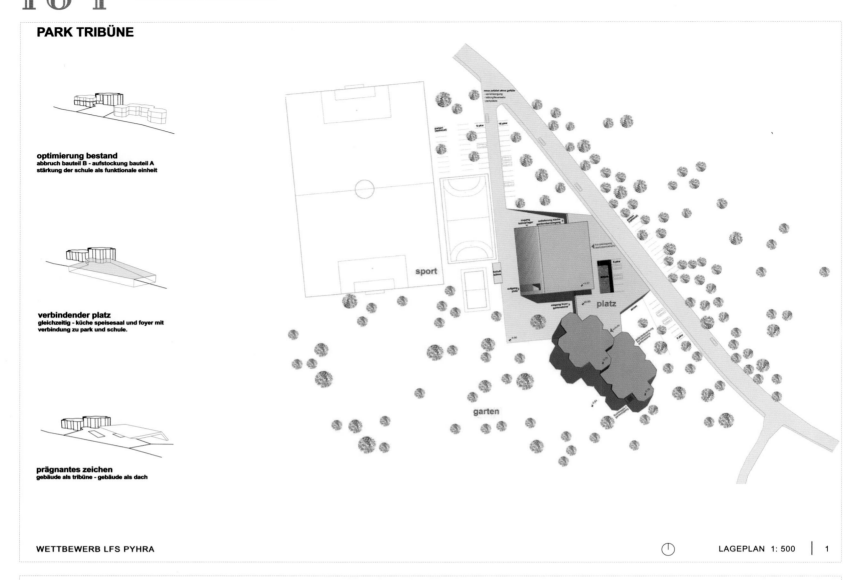

optimierung bestand
abbruch bauteil B - aufstockung bauteil A
stärkung der schule als funktionale einheit

verbindender platz
gleichzeitig - küche speisesaal und foyer mit
verbindung zu park und schule.

prägnantes zeichen
gebäude als tribüne - gebäude als dach

WETTBEWERB LFS PYHRA

LAGEPLAN 1: 500 | 1

SCHULPLATZ

zentraler platz
verbindet der eignständigen baukörper schule
und mehrzweckhalle

platzkante
eine galerie entlang platz und
foyer orientiert sich zu halle und park

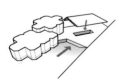

räumlichen qualitäten
geländeeinschnitte sorgen für eine optimale belichtung
und spannende blickbeziehungen

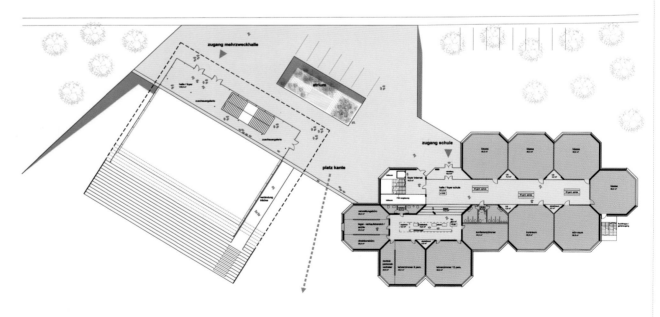

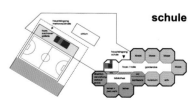

schule

WETTBEWERB LFS PYHRA

PLATZEBENE - 4.00 1: 200 | 2

VERANSTALTUNGSEBENE

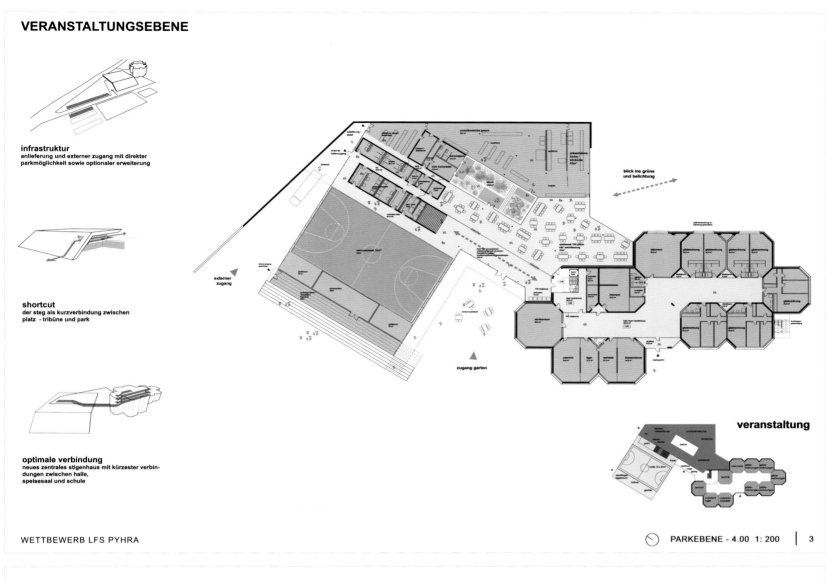

infrastruktur
anlieferung und externer zugang mit direkter
parkmöglichkeit sowie optionaler erweiterung

shortcut
der steg als kurzverbindung zwischen
platz - tribüne und park

optimale verbindung
neues zentrales stigenhaus mit kürzester verbindungen zwischen halle,
speisesaal und schule

veranstaltung

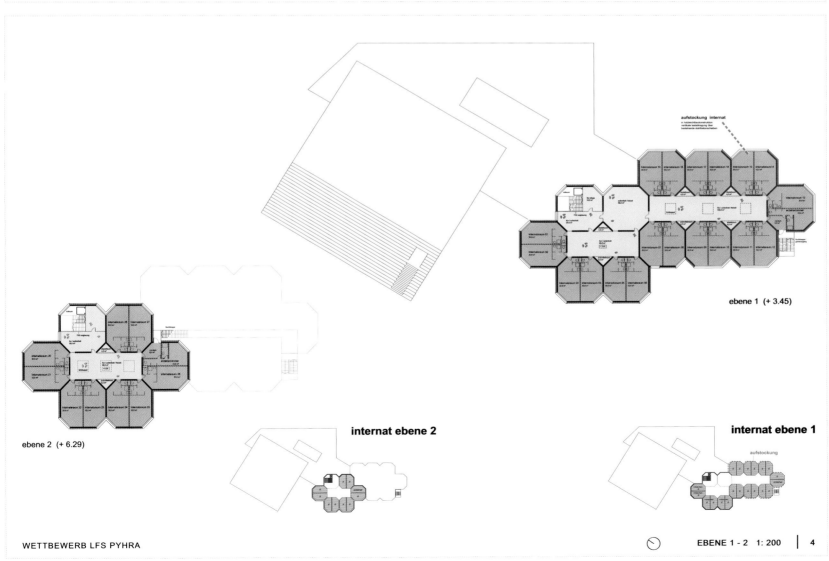

aufstockung internat

ebene 1 (+ 3.45)

ebene 2 (+ 6.29)

internat ebene 2

internat ebene 1

aufstockung

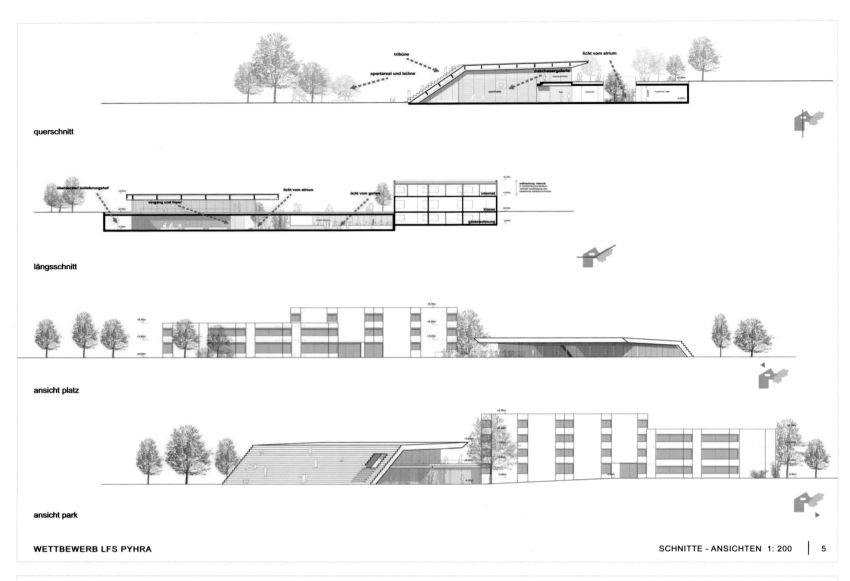

querschnitt

längsschnitt

ansicht platz

ansicht park

WETTBEWERB LFS PYHRA

SCHNITTE - ANSICHTEN 1: 200 | 5

WETTBEWERB LFS PYHRA

| 6

SZI Center for Special Pedagogics | *franz zt gmbh*

Location : Innsbruck, Tyrol, Austria
Function : Junior High School and Center for Special Pedagogics
Collaboration : Michael Hasslacher, Lucie Vencelidesova, Joe Suntinger

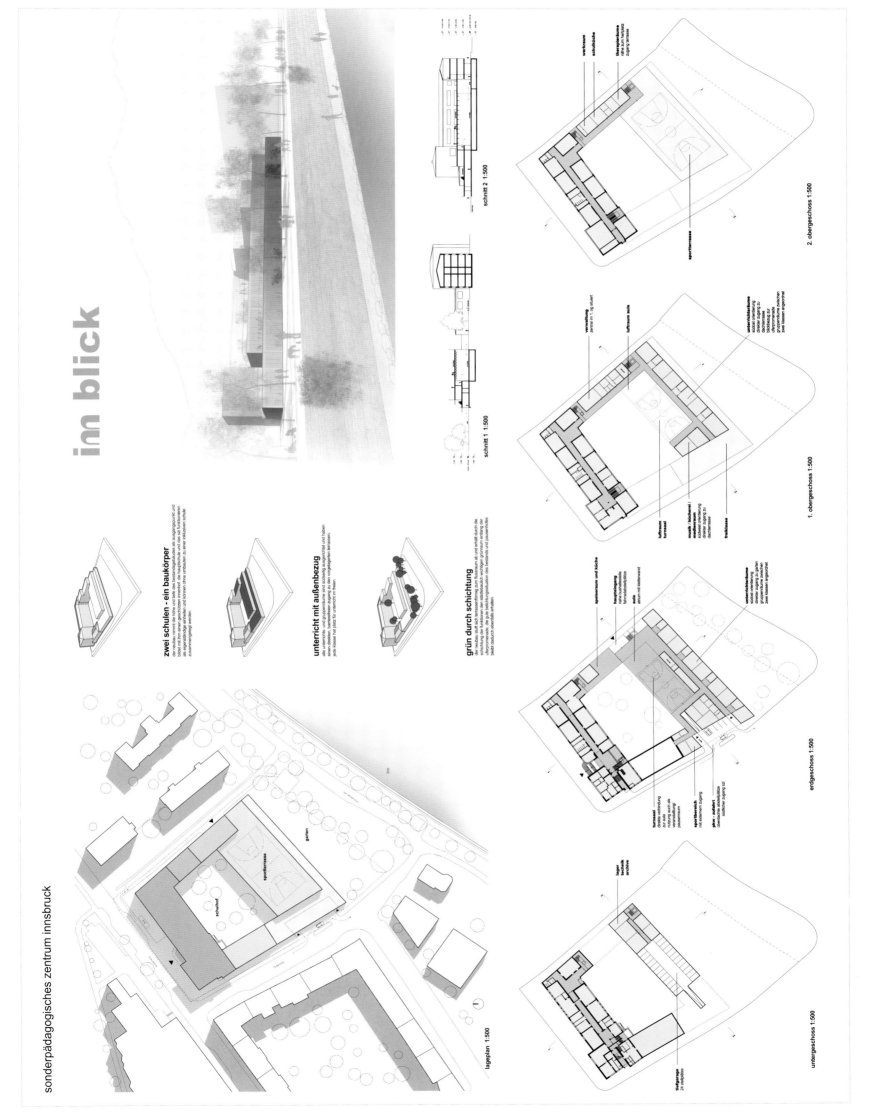

196

Architecture Faculty | *Slot.*

Location : The Netherlands, Delft
Program : Auditoriums, Workshops, Studios, Laboratories, Exhibition Areas, Library
Project Type : Open International Competition, Nominated Project

Client : Faculty of Architecture Delft together with NAI
Construction Area : 67,500m²

558

ANIMAL ARCHITECTURE

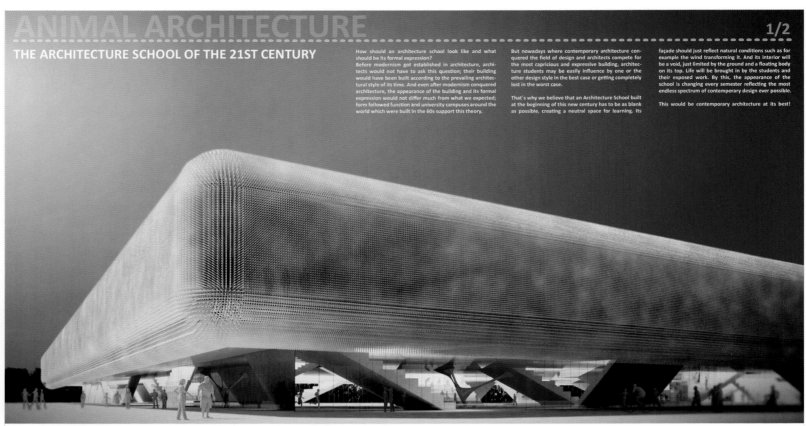

THE ARCHITECTURE SCHOOL OF THE 21ST CENTURY

1/2

How should an architecture school look like and what should be its formal expression?

Before modernism got established in architecture, architects would not have to ask this question; their building would have been built according to the prevailing architectural style of its time. And even after modernism conquered architecture, the appearance of the building and its formal expression would not differ much from what we expected; form followed function and university campuses around the world which were built in the 60s support this theory.

But nowadays where contemporary architecture conquered the field of design and architects compete for the most capricious and expressive building, architecture students may be easily influence by one or the other design style in the best case or getting completely lost in the worst case.

That´s why we believe that an Architecture School built at the beginning of this new century has to be as blank as possible, creating a neutral space for learning. Its

façade should just reflect natural conditions such as for example the wind transforming it. And its interior will be a void, just limited by the ground and a floating body on its top. Life will be brought in by the students and their exposed work. By this, the appearance of the school is changing every semester reflecting the most endless spectrum of contemporary design ever possible.

This would be contemporary architecture at its best!

CONCEPT OF SUSTAINABILITY

NATURAL SKIN

POLAR BEAR IN THE ARCTIC

Why not **learning from nature**? In our search for a sustainable building, we were inspired by **polar bears** that survive in the harsh climate of the Arctic. Their whole body, but most important their skin is highly efficient in terms of reducing heat loss. **White dense guard hair** is forming the first layer and their **black skin underneath** warms their body up because dark surfaces absorb more sun and produce energy than white surfaces do.

Although the Netherlands are not comparable with the extreme climate a polar bear is made for, **our building skin could take advantage of those principles**. First, the building is covered all over by **a dense layer of thin sticks** which by their wind-driven movement **generate energy** for the building. And second, the inner layer of the façade is basically made of glass, **with fine dark dots** on their exterior surface helping to regulate natural lightening in the building. This second layer of the façade **produces energy** because the dark dots are working as micro solar cells.

SCHEMATIC 3D SECTION

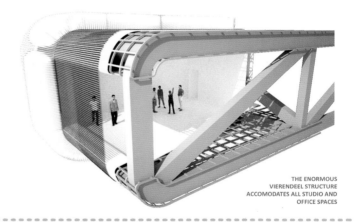

THE ENORMOUS VIERENDEEL STRUCTURE ACCOMODATES ALL STUDIO AND OFFICE SPACES

ARTIFICIAL SKIN

MICRO SOLAR CELLS with a diameter of 3 centimeters are glued on the exterior side of the glass/ reflective transparent surface and do not just help to regulate natural lightening in the building but also PRODUCE ENERGY.

Bundles of FIBER-REINFORCED POLYMER are covering the entire building facade and are connected to the glass over the small dark micro solar cells.

Those fiber-reinforced polymer sticks are IN CONSTANT MOVEMENT because of prevailing winds. This movement GENERATES ENERGY.

FROM BOUWKUNDE STREET TO BOUWKUNDE PLAZA

1 STUDIOS AND OFFICES
2 BOUWKUNDE PLAZA
3 SEE PROGRAM ON THE RIGHT (A-I)

A CONFERENCE ROOMS
B COMPUTER ROOMS
C FACULTY CLUB
D LECTURE HALLS
E FACULTY LABORATORIES

F SKETCHING AND MODELLING
G BOOKSHOP
H LIBRARY
I RESTAURANT

SUSTAINABLE BUILDING SKIN

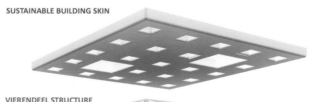

POLAR BEAR SKIN   MIRCO SOLAR CELLS

VIERENDEEL STRUCTURE

VIERENDEEL BRIDGE

STAIR COLUMNS

PROGRAMATIC STAIRS

BOUWKUNDE PLAZA

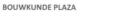

PUBLIC PLAZA IN GROUND LEVEL

BASEMENT

The Bouwkunde Street of the old building converts into the **Bouwkunde Plaza** in the new building. This plaza is the **intermediate space of a simple 3-part volumetric distribution**: studios and offices on the top and workshops for model making, the library and lecture halls in the ground. **The intermediate space connects between all parts of the school**, converting itself into **an active social plaza** and living exhibition, witnessing what´s produced and discussed in the school at every single moment.

This extremely **open and friendly plaza** invites everybody to come in and opens the school up for **a wider audience** which goes beyond activities of teachers or students; it also attends **institutes, companies and the business community**, which every day become more important for an international competitive architecture school at the beginning of this new century.

BK2008-3452

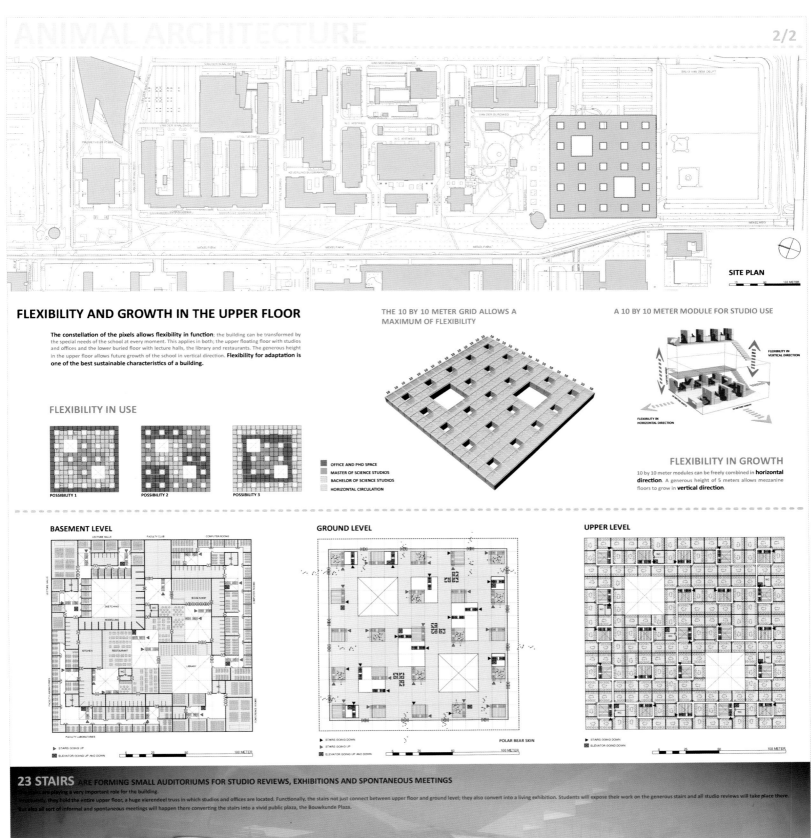

SITE PLAN

FLEXIBILITY AND GROWTH IN THE UPPER FLOOR

The constellation of the pixels allows flexibility in function; the building can be transformed by the special needs of the school at every moment. This applies in both; the upper floating floor with studios and offices and the lower buried floor with lecture halls, the library and restaurants. The generous height in the upper floor allows future growth of the school in vertical direction. **Flexibility for adaptation is one of the best sustainable characteristics of a building.**

THE 10 BY 10 METER GRID ALLOWS A MAXIMUM OF FLEXIBILITY

A 10 BY 10 METER MODULE FOR STUDIO USE

FLEXIBILITY IN VERTICAL DIRECTION

FLEXIBILITY IN HORIZONTAL DIRECTION

FLEXIBILITY IN USE

POSSIBILITY 1

POSSIBILITY 2

POSSIBILITY 3

- OFFICE AND PHD SPACE
- MASTER OF SCIENCE STUDIOS
- BACHELOR OF SCIENCE STUDIOS
- HORIZONTAL CIRCULATION

FLEXIBILITY IN GROWTH

10 by 10 meter modules can be freely combined in **horizontal direction**. A generous height of 5 meters allows mezzanine floors to grow in **vertical direction**.

BASEMENT LEVEL

▶ STAIRS GOING UP
■ ELEVATOR GOING UP AND DOWN

100 METER

GROUND LEVEL

POLAR BEAR SKIN

▶ STAIRS GOING DOWN
▶ STAIRS GOING UP
■ ELEVATOR GOING UP AND DOWN

100 METER

UPPER LEVEL

▶ STAIRS GOING DOWN
■ ELEVATOR GOING DOWN

100 METER

23 STAIRS ARE FORMING SMALL AUDITORIUMS FOR STUDIO REVIEWS, EXHIBITIONS AND SPONTANEOUS MEETINGS

The stairs are playing a very important role for the building.

Structurally, they hold the entire upper floor, a huge vierendeel truss in which studios and offices are located. Functionally, the stairs not just connect between upper floor and ground level; they also convert into a living exhibition. Students will expose their work on the generous stairs and all studio reviews will take place there.

But also all sort of informal and spontaneous meetings will happen there converting the stairs into a vivid public plaza, the Bouwkunde Plaza.

BK2008-3452

197

Extension of Serlachius Museum Gösta | *PRAUD*

Program : Exhibition
Location : Mänttä, Finland
Area : 5181m²

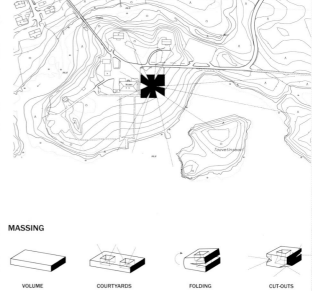

MASSING

VOLUME   COURTYARDS   FOLDING   CUT-OUTS

The site has a strong advantage of having a very fabulous landscape view towards the lake and forest.

Hence, the big idea in massing is to create a museum that is self-reflecting as well as reflecting towards the landscape, creating a counter position for visitors to reflect on the arts and its context.

The view points towards these scenarios becomes an architectural logic for forming the building.

A typical typology for a self-reflecting building is a courtyard building, which generates a void within the building creating a vertical relationship to the sky and outdoor exhibition spaces as well.

Because of the massive surface we need to deal with, we elaborated a topological mass which also folds within itself. By folding it, we generate cracks and cuts out that enhances the relation between the art and the landscape.

In terms of anchoring, the mass sits right next to the existing Manor building so that it creates smooth circulation between new extension exhibition halls and existing exhibitions.

For offices and collection facilities, they are located on the lower level so that they can be separated from visitor circulation and have protection from natural sun light. They are connected easily to loading, foyer, and collection exhibition halls with direct vertical circulation.

A light lumber structure is proposed as structural system not only to have tectonic gestures in the building but also architectural aesthetics out of it.

Series of lumber frames are manipulated to create the shape the roof grading and interior space. And the vertical walls of each programs will work as lateral member to hold the lumber frames.

In the new extension museum, we tried to create spaces for art works not only through exhibition halls but also through temporary exhibitions at the entry halls, large installations in the courtyard, and balcony level views.

Therefore, with the existing museum, the new extension will provide a variety of experiences to visitors between old and new, and nature and art.

PROGRAM

Program		Area (m2)	Program		Area (m2)
Exhibition Facilities	Traveling Exhibition 01	335	**Conference and Representation Facilities**	Assembly Hall	85
	Traveling Exhibition 02	337		Conference Hall	420
	Collection Exhibition	336		Total	505
	Total	1008			
Collection Facilities	Handling Room	87	**Restaurant Facilities**	Dining Area	180
	Conservation Room	115		Kitchen	50
	Terminal Archive	150		Total	230
	Common Space	150	**Other Facilities**	Cleaning Room	26
	Total	502		Waste Room	23
Offices	Office Conference Room	68		Servicing Room	30
	Living/Kitchen	120		Toilet	57
	Library	45		Total	136
	Archival Research	32	**Foyer Services**	Ticket Box	20
	Office (4 offices)	80		Coat Room	20
	Common Space	75		Foyer	240
	Total	420		Total	280
			Usable Net Space Area		**3081**
			Common Space		1850
			Mechanical Room		250
			Total Gross Area		**5181**

SITE PLAN (1:500)

LOADING

MUSEUM ENT.

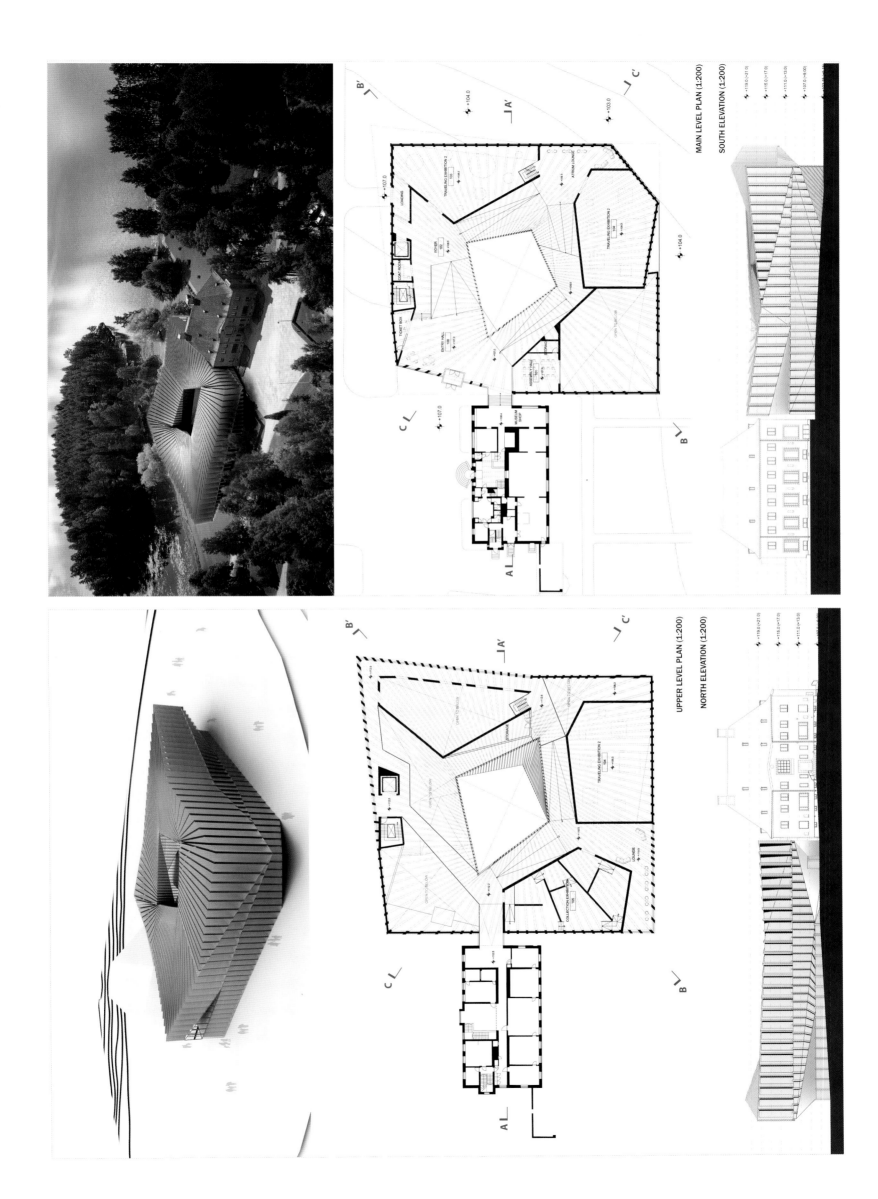

MAIN LEVEL PLAN (1:200)

SOUTH ELEVATION (1:200)

UPPER LEVEL PLAN (1:200)

NORTH ELEVATION (1:200)

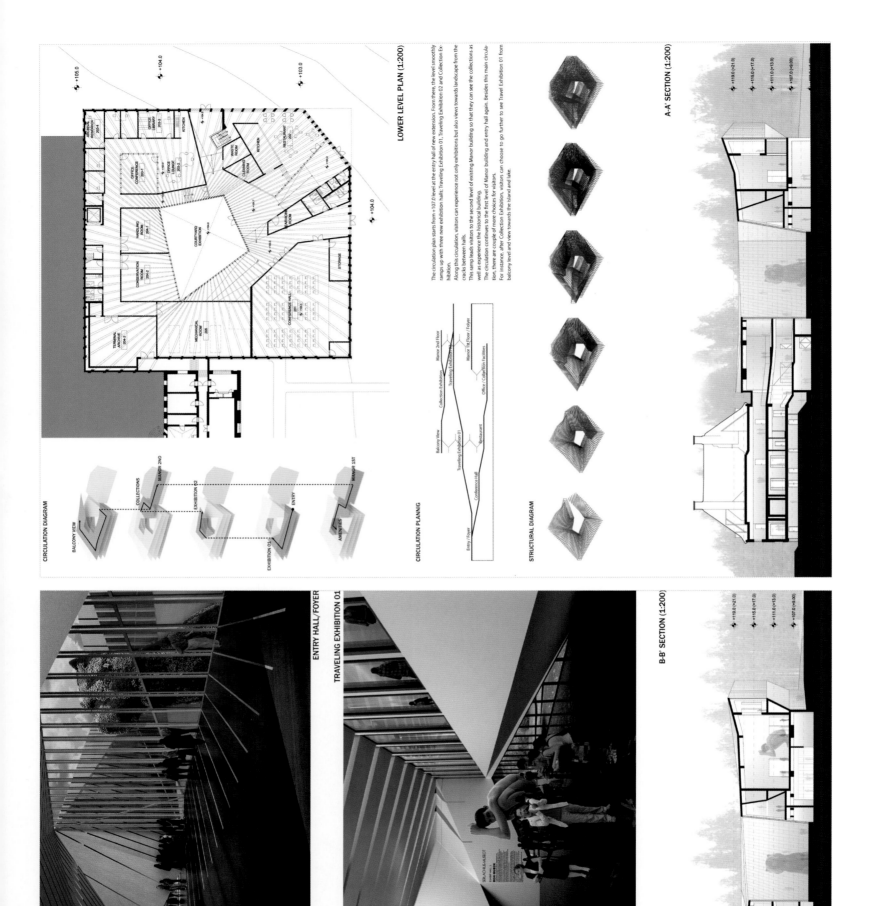

CIRCULATION DIAGRAM

LOWER LEVEL PLAN (1:200)

The circulation plan starts from +107.0 level at the entry hall of new extension. From there, the level smoothly ramps up with three new exhibition halls; Traveling Exhibition 01, Traveling Exhibition 02 and Collection Exhibition.

Along this circulation, visitors can experience not only exhibitions but also views towards landscape from the cracks between halls.

This ramp leads visitors to the second level of existing Manor building so that they can see the collections as well as experience the historical building.

The circulation continues to the first level of Manor building and entry hall again. Besides this main circulation, there are couple of more choices for visitors.

For instance, after Collection Exhibition, visitors can choose to go further to see Travel Exhibition 01 from balcony level and view towards the island and lake.

CIRCULATION PLANNIG

STRUCTURAL DIAGRAM

A-A' SECTION (1:200)

ENTRY HALL/FOYER

TRAVELING EXHIBITION 01

B-B' SECTION (1:200)

COMPUTATION

GUIDE LINES   FRAMEWORK   PANELING   COMPOSITE

C-C' SECTION (1:200)

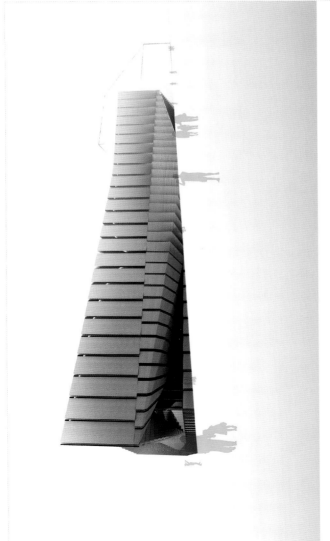

Design Team : CJ Lim/Studio 8 Architects with Dean Walker
Consultants : Techniker(Structural Engineers)

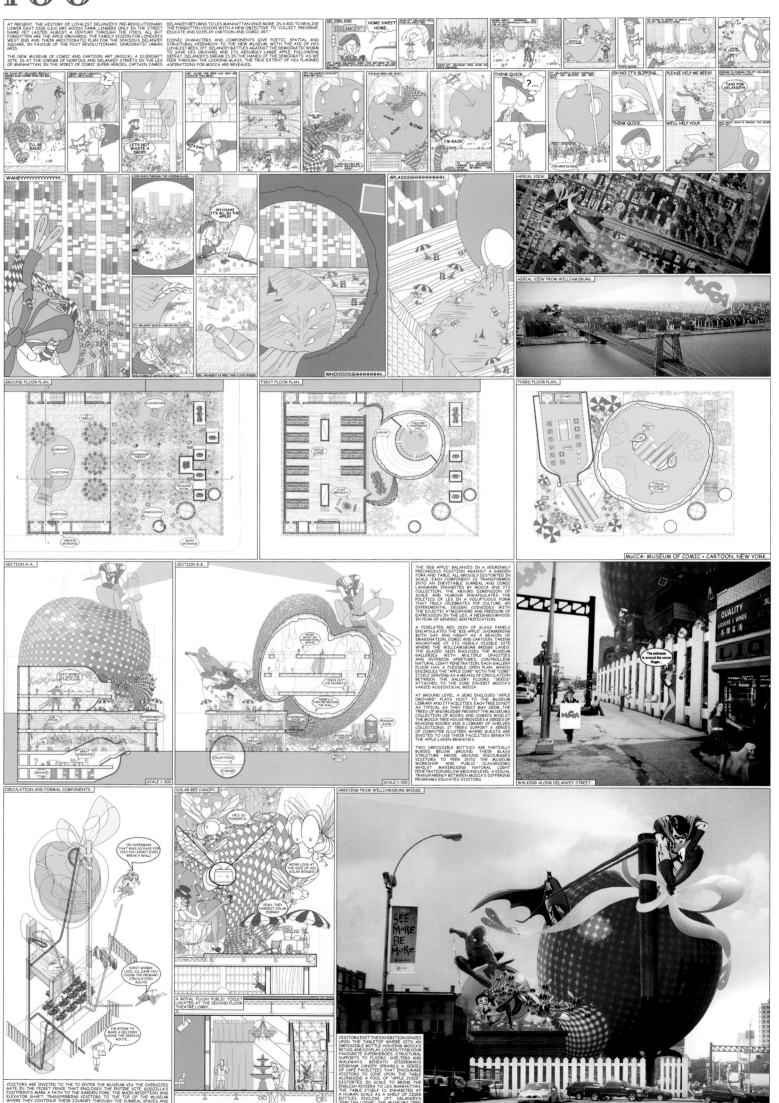

Art Gallery Maribor | *Slot.*

Year of Design : 2010 / Construction Area : 14,810m²
Credits : Slot. in Collaboration withTomaž Krištof

Location : Maribor, Slovenia, between Ribiska Street and Pristaniska Street
Program : Museum, Architecture Museum, Library, Restaurants
Project Type : Open International Competition
Client : Municipality of Maribor

199

41205/3

1

THE MARIBOR ART GALLERY AS AN ICON

THE CITY OF MARIBOR HAS UNDERGONE GREAT CHANGES OVER THE LAST DECADES FROM A CITY CHARACTERIZED BY HEAVY INDUSTRY TO A CULTURAL CITY, WHICH IS HONORED BY THE EUROPEAN UNION'S DECISION TO BECOME EUROPEAN CAPITAL OF CULTURE 2012.

THE PROJECT BRINGS ALONG MANY CHANCES AND OPPORTUNITIES TO BE RECOGNIZED AS THE ICON OF THIS IMPORTANT CULTURAL EVENT. IT NOT ONLY STANDS FOR THE URBAN CHANGE OF MARIBOR BUT ALSO OPENS UP CHANCES TO MARK THE BEGINNING OF THE NEW MILLENNIUM.

THE URBAN LAYOUT

THE BUILDING IS LOCATED RIGHT AT THE EDGE OF THE HISTORIC CITY CENTER OF MARIBOR ON THE RIVERBANKS. BY REDUCING THE BUILDING'S FOOTPRINT AS MUCH AS POSSIBLE, A MAXIMUM OF OPEN AREAS IS ACHIEVED.

AREA B IS PLANNED AS A PARK, WHICH MARKS A GAP IN THE URBAN PATTERN, SEPARATING THE HISTORIC CENTER FROM THE RESIDENTIAL AREAS IN THE WEST. THIS NEW PARK COMPLEMENTS THE CITY'S ALREADY EXISTING PARK SYSTEM (THREE PONDS – CITY PARK – MAISTER PARK – SLOMSEK PARK), LEADING VISITORS FROM THE HILLS AROUND THE CITY TO THE RIVER.

THE NEW PARK OPENS UP VIEWS FROM THE UPPER STREET TO THE RIVER WITH A NEW INCLINED PLAZA ALONG ITS VERTICAL AXIS AND CONVERTS INTO A GENEROUS PLATFORM FOR PUBLIC EVENTS OF ALL SORTS. UNINTERRUPTED VIEWS NOT ONLY TO THE RIVER DRAVA BUT ALSO TO POHORJE HILL REINFORCE THE VISUAL QUALITIES.

THE ROW OF EXISTING BUILDINGS IN THE EAST WILL BE GIVEN ADDITIONAL QUALITIES. THOSE BUILDINGS DO ALREADY HAVE A PUBLIC USE, WHICH WILL BE REINFORCED BY A SECOND FAÇADE FACING THE NEW PLAZA.

WEST OF THE PARK THE RESIDENTIAL AREA STARTS AND EAST OF THE PARK THE CITY CENTRE STARTS. THE PARK IS A FILTER BETWEEN BOTH AREAS

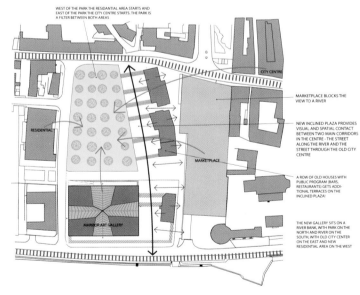

MARKETPLACE BLOCKS THE VIEW TO A RIVER

NEW INCLINED PLAZA PROVIDES VISUAL AND SPATIAL CONTACT BETWEEN TWO MAIN CORRIDORS IN THE CENTRE - THE STREET ALONG THE RIVER AND THE STREET THROUGH THE OLD CITY CENTRE

A ROW OF OLD HOUSES WITH PUBLIC PROGRAM (BARS, RESTAURANTS) GETS ADDITIONAL TERRACES ON THE INCLINED PLAZA!

THE NEW GALLERY SITS ON A RIVER BANK, WITH PARK ON THE NORTH AND RIVER ON THE SOUTH, WITH OLD CITY CENTER ON THE EAST AND NEW RESIDENTIAL AREA ON THE WEST

THE NEW GALLERY WITH AN AMBITION TO BUILD AN IMAGE OF NEW MARIBOR

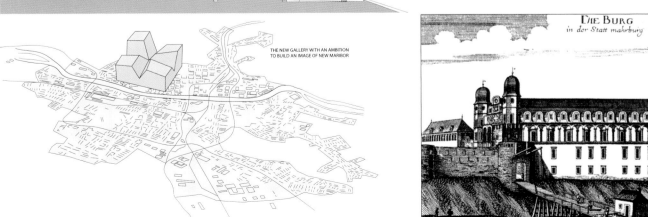

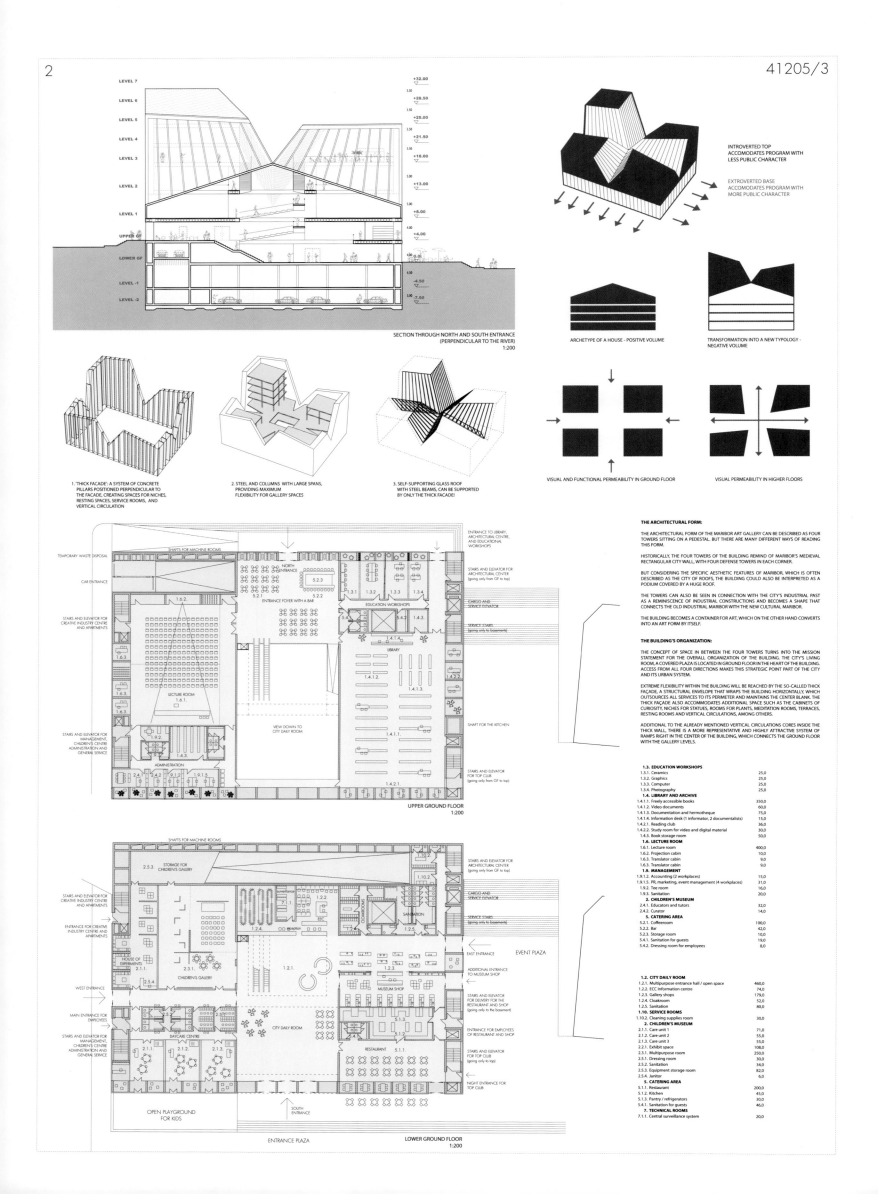

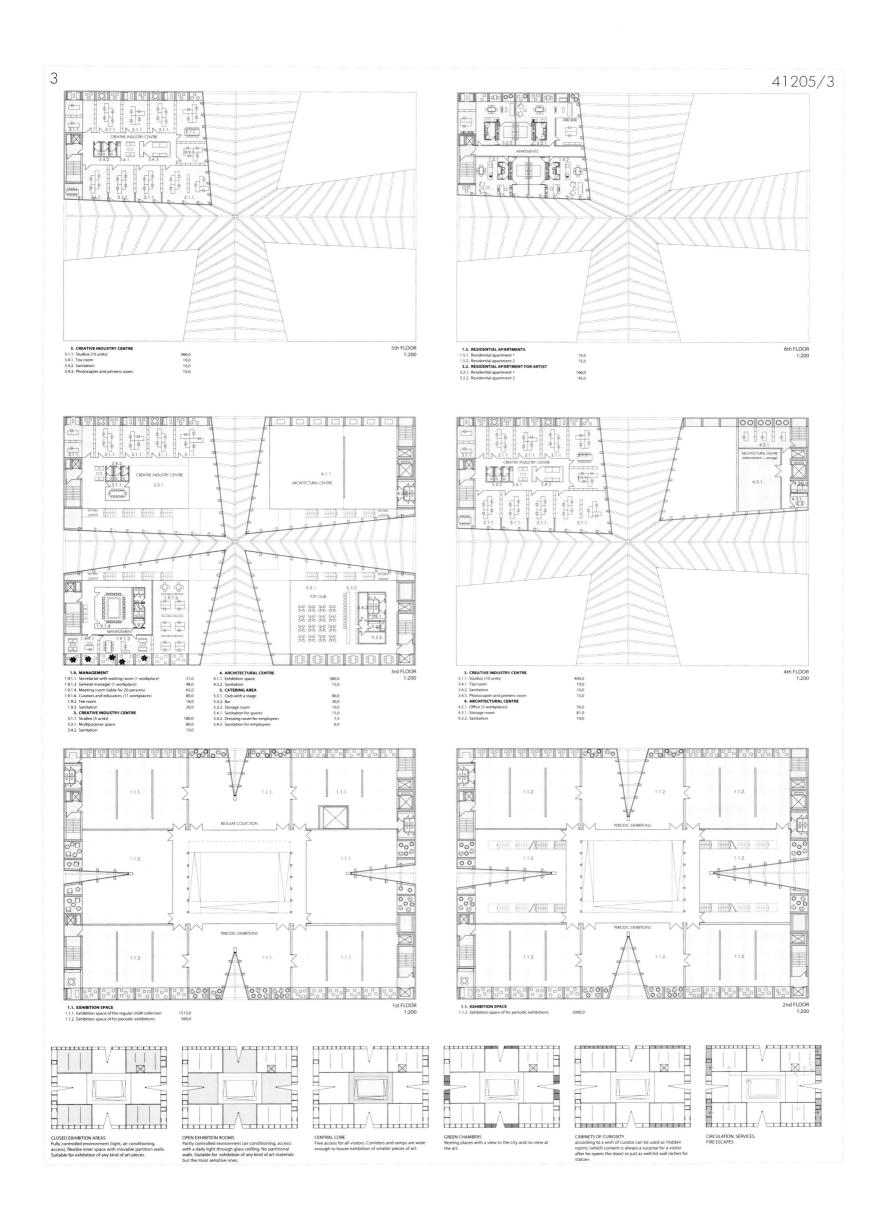

3. CREATIVE INDUSTRY CENTRE
5th FLOOR 1:200
3.1.1. Studios (10 units)   360,0
3.4.1. Tea room   10,0
3.4.2. Sanitation   10,0
3.4.3. Photocopier and printers room 15,0

1.5. RESIDENTIAL APARTMENTS
6th FLOOR 1:200
1.5.1. Residential apartment 1   75,0
1.5.2. Residential apartment 2   75,0
3.2. RESIDENTIAL APARTMENT FOR ARTIST
3.2.1. Residential apartment 1   106,0
3.2.2. Residential apartment 2   95,0

1.9. MANAGEMENT
3rd FLOOR 1:200
1.9.1.1. Secretariat with waiting room (1 workplace) 31,0
1.9.1.3. General manager (1 workplace)   48,0
1.9.1.4. Meeting room (table for 20 persons)   65,0
1.9.1.6. Curators and educators (11 workplaces)   80,0
1.9.2. Tee room   16,0
1.9.3. Sanitation   20,0
3. CREATIVE INDUSTRY CENTRE
3.1.1. Studios (5 units)   180,0
3.3.1. Multipurpose space   80,0
3.4.2. Sanitation   10,0

4. ARCHITECTURAL CENTRE
4.1.1. Exhibition space   380,0
4.3.2. Sanitation   15,0
5. CATERING AREA
5.3.1. Club with a stage   90,0
5.3.2. Bar   30,0
5.3.3. Storage room   10,0
5.4.1. Sanitation for guests   15,0
5.4.2. Dressing room for employees   7,5
5.4.3. Sanitation for employees   6,0

3. CREATIVE INDUSTRY CENTRE
4th FLOOR 1:200
3.1.1. Studios (10 units)   400,0
3.4.1. Tea room   10,0
3.4.2. Sanitation   10,0
3.4.3. Photocopier and printers room 15,0
4. ARCHITECTURAL CENTRE
4.2.1. Office (3 workplaces)   50,0
4.3.1. Storage room   81,0
4.3.2. Sanitation   19,0

1.1. EXHIBITION SPACE
1st FLOOR 1:200
1.1.1. Exhibition space of the regular UGM collection 1513,0
1.1.2. Exhibition space of for periodic exhibitions   560,0

1.1. EXHIBITION SPACE
2nd FLOOR 1:200
1.1.2. Exhibition space of for periodic exhibitions   2000,0

CLOSED EXHIBITION AREAS
Fully controlled environment (light, air conditioning, access), flexible inner space with movable partition walls. Suitable for exhibition of any kind of art pieces.

OPEN EXHIBITION ROOMS
Partly controlled invironment (air conditioning, access) with a daily light through glass ceilling. No partitional walls. Siutable for exhibition of any kind of art materials but the most sensitive ones.

CENTRAL CORE
Free access for all visitors. Corridors and ramps are wide enough to house exhibition of smaller pieces of art.

GREEN CHAMBERS
Resting places with a view to the city and no view at the art.

CABINETS OF CURIOSITY
according to a wish of curator can be used as 'Hidden rooms' (which content is always a surprise for a visitor after he opens the door) or just as well-lid wall niches for statues

CIRCULATION, SERVICES, FIRE ESCAPES

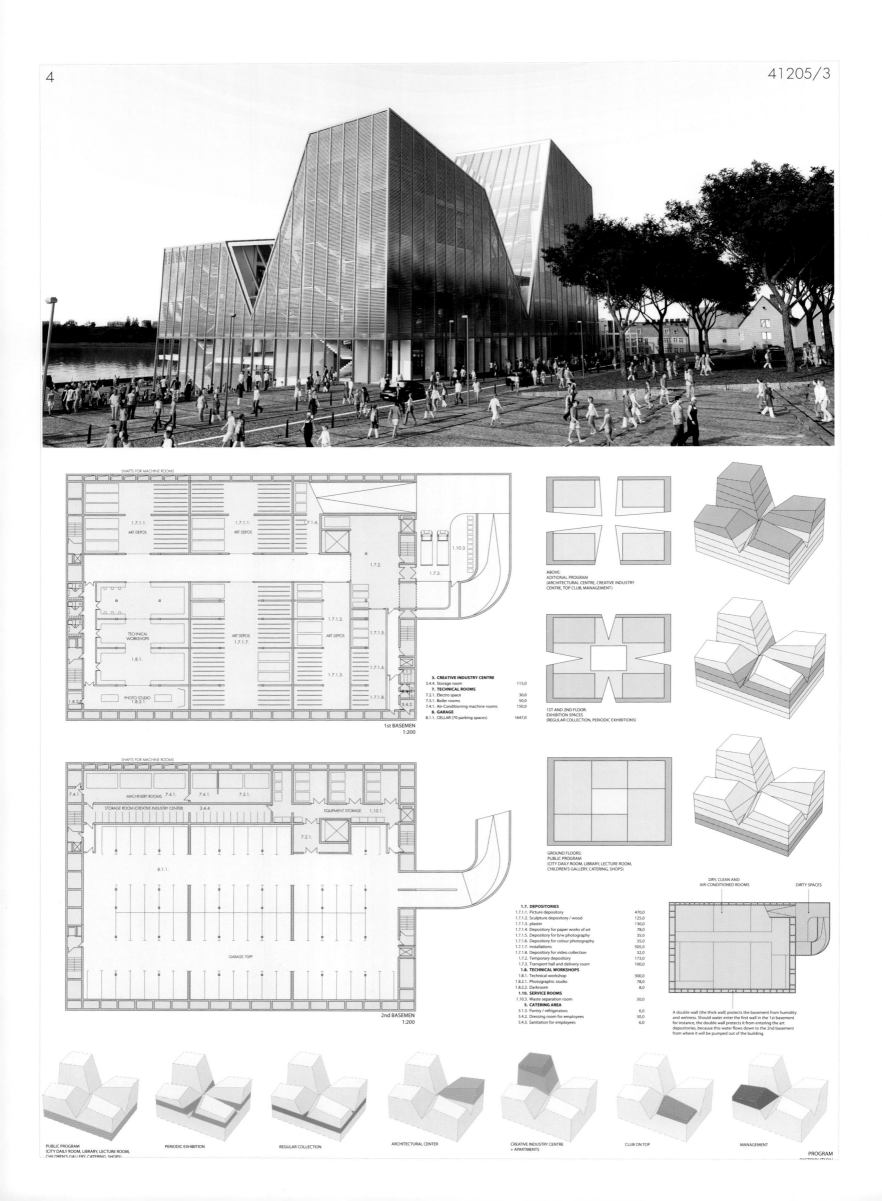

SHAFTS FOR MACHINE ROOMS

1.7.1.1. ART DEPOS
1.7.1.1. ART DEPOS
1.7.4.
1.10.3.
1.7.2.
1.7.3.
1.7.1.2.
ART DEPOS
1.7.1.7.
ART DEPOS
1.7.1.5.
TECHNICAL WORKSHOPS
1.8.1.
1.7.1.6.
1.7.1.3.
1.1.3.
PHOTO STUDIO 1.8.2.1.
1.7.1.8.
1.8.2.2.
5.4.2.

3. CREATIVE INDUSTRY CENTRE
3.4.4. Storage room — 115,0
7. TECHNICAL ROOMS
7.2.1. Electro space — 30,0
7.3.1. Boiler rooms — 50,0
7.4.1. Air-Conditioning machine rooms — 150,0
8. GARAGE
8.1.1. CELLAR (70 parking spaces) — 1647,0

1st BASEMEN
1:200

SHAFTS FOR MACHINE ROOMS

7.4.1.
MACHINERY ROOMS 7.4.1. 7.4.1. 7.3.1.
STORAGE ROOM (CREATIVE INDUSTRY CENTER) 3.4.4.
EQUIPMENT STORAGE 1.10.1.
7.2.1.
8.1.1.

GARAGE 70PP

2nd BASEMEN
1:200

1.7. DEPOSITORIES
1.7.1.1. Picture depository — 470,0
1.7.1.2. Sculpture depository / wood — 125,0
1.7.1.3. plaster — 130,0
1.7.1.4. Depository for paper works of art — 78,0
1.7.1.5. Depository for b/w photography — 35,0
1.7.1.6. Depository for colour photography — 35,0
1.7.1.7. installations — 505,0
1.7.1.8. Depository for video collection — 32,0
1.7.2. Temporary depository — 173,0
1.7.3. Transport hall and delivery room — 100,0
1.8. TECHNICAL WORKSHOPS
1.8.1. Technical workshop — 300,0
1.8.2.1. Photographic studio — 78,0
1.8.2.2. Darkroom — 8,0
1.10. SERVICE ROOMS
1.10.3. Waste separation room — 50,0
5. CATERING AREA
5.1.3. Pantry / refrigerators — 6,0
5.4.2. Dressing room for employees — 30,0
5.4.3. Sanitation for employees — 6,0

ABOVE:
ADITIONAL PROGRAM
(ARCHITECTURAL CENTRE, CREATIVE INDUSTRY
CENTRE, TOP CLUB, MANAGEMENT)

1ST AND 2ND FLOOR:
EXHIBITION SPACES
(REGULAR COLLECTION, PERIODIC EXHIBITIONS)

GROUND FLOORS:
PUBLIC PROGRAM
(CITY DAILY ROOM, LIBRARY, LECTURE ROOM,
CHILDREN'S GALLERY, CATERING, SHOPS)

DRY, CLEAN AND
AIR-CONDITIONED ROOMS
DIRTY SPACES

A double wall (the thick wall) protects the basement from humidity
and wetness. Should water enter the first wall in the 1st basement
for instance, the double wall protects it from entering the art
depositories, because this water flows down to the 2nd basement
from where it will be pumped out of the building.

PUBLIC PROGRAM
(CITY DAILY ROOM, LIBRARY, LECTURE ROOM,
CHILDREN'S GALLERY, CATERING, SHOPS)

PERIODIC EXHIBITION

REGULAR COLLECTION

ARCHITECTURAL CENTER

CREATIVE INDUSTRY CENTRE
+ APARTMENTS

CLUB ON TOP

MANAGEMENT

PROGRAM

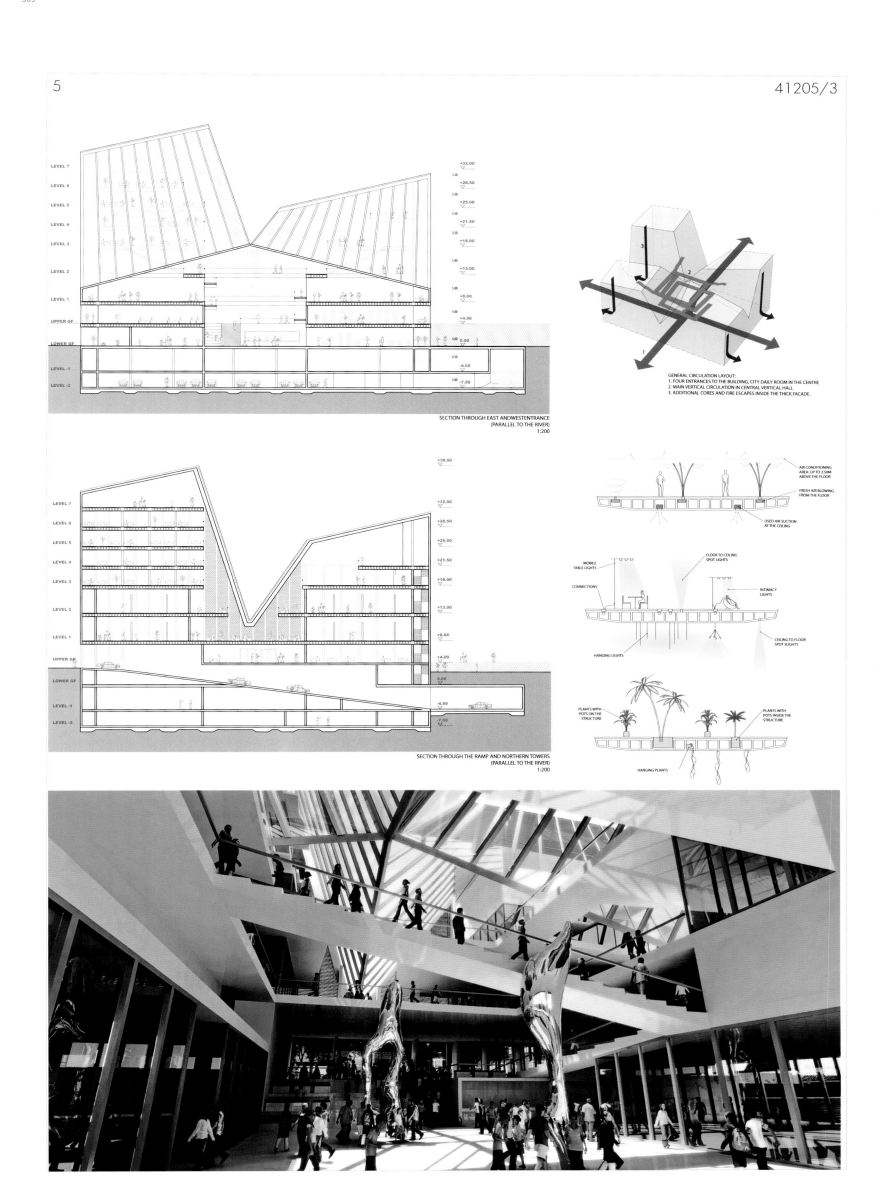

SECTION THROUGH EAST ANDWESTENTRANCE
(PARALLEL TO THE RIVER)
1:200

GENERAL CIRCULATION LAYOUT:
1. FOUR ENTRANCES TO THE BUILDING, CITY DAILY ROOM IN THE CENTRE
2. MAIN VERTICAL CIRCULATION IN CENTRAL VERTICAL HALL
3. ADDITIONAL CORES AND FIRE ESCAPES INSIDE THE THICK FACADE.

SECTION THROUGH THE RAMP AND NORTHERN TOWERS
(PARALLEL TO THE RIVER)
1:200

AIR CONDITIONING
AREA: UP TO 2.50M
ABOVE THE FLOOR

FRESH AIR BLOWING
FROM THE FLOOR

USED AIR SUCTION
AT THE CEILING

MOBILE
TABLE LIGHTS

FLOOR TO CEILING
SPOT LIGHTS

CONNECTIONS

INTIMACY
LIGHTS

CEILING TO FLOOR
SPOT SLIGHTS

HANGING LIGHTS

PLANTS WITH
POTS ON THE
STRUCTURE

PLANTS WITH
POTS INSIDE THE
STRUCTURE

HANGING PLANTS

Museum of Polish History | *Paul Preissner*

Location : Warsaw, Poland
Client : Museum of Polish History in Warsaw / Ministry of Culture and National Heritage of Poland
Program : Cultural History Museum / Site Design

Area : 10,000 SM
Cost : Euro87 million(US\$130 million)

MUSEUM OF POLISH HISTORY
LOCATION Warsaw, Poland
CLIENT Museum of Polish History in Warsaw/Ministry of Culture
and National Heritage of Poland
PROGRAM Cultural History Museum / Site Design
AREA 10,000 SM
COST Euro87 million (US\$130 million)
STATUS Design 2009 (Competition)

DESIGN INTENTIONS

For this project for a country and historic culture of nearly 40 million citizens, we have put forth a design solution that understands the significant role of history in the development of a country, but more importantly, recognizes the intricate and directional relationship to its future. The Museum of Polish History and its surrounding development site stands not just to signify and remember the path to the present, but also provides a literal platform for the continued progressive development of Polish culture.

Using a policy to promote cultural and educational activities, our proposal performs as an central character in the play of Polish culture, not only for the users of the facility and its surrounding park, but also for the entire culture of Poland; becoming a new Center for the discovery and empathetic learning of history.

SITE DESIGN

The site is holistically looked at as both a territory to preservations, natural management of resources, contemporary intervention, and radical cultural and commercial development. Conceptually turning the site into both a museum of landscape and artifactual history and a model of progressive cultural and environmental development simultaneously. The site is divided into sections that range from complete replacement of existing conditions to utmost preservation of its historic shape and allowing the site to exist as both park and narrator.

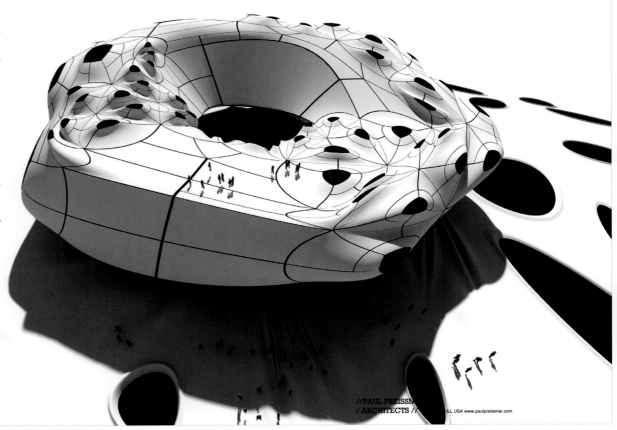

//PAUL PREISSN
/ ARCHITECTS //   ILL USA www.paulpreissner.com

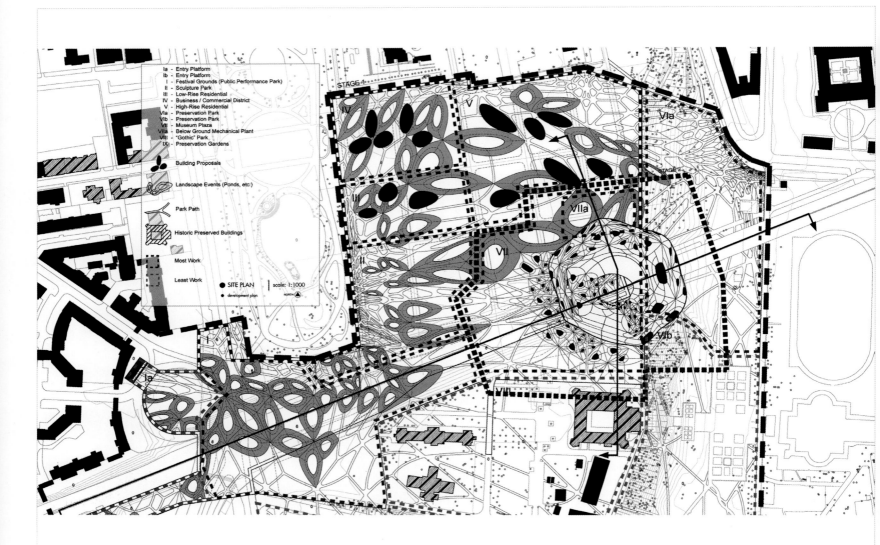

Ia - Entry Platform
Ib - Entry Platform
I - Festival Grounds (Public Performance Park)
II - Sculpture Park
III - Low-Rise Residential
IV - Business / Commercial District
V - High-Rise Residential
VIa - Preservation Park
VIb - Preservation Park
VII - Museum Plaza
VIIa - Below Ground Mechanical Plant
VIII - "Gothic" Park
IX - Preservation Gardens

Building Proposals

Landscape Events (Ponds, etc.)

Park Path

Historic Preserved Buildings

Most Work

Least Work

● SITE PLAN   scale: 1:1000
● development plan

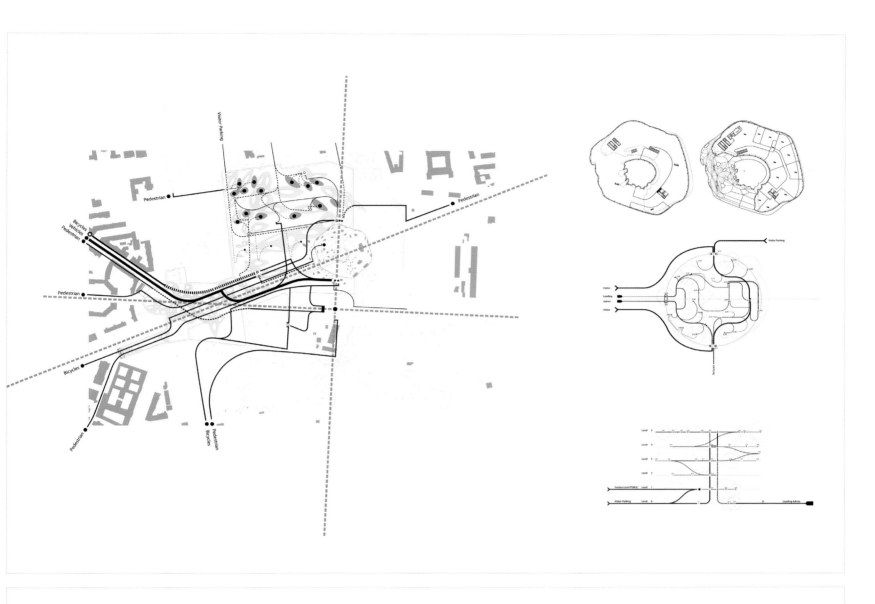

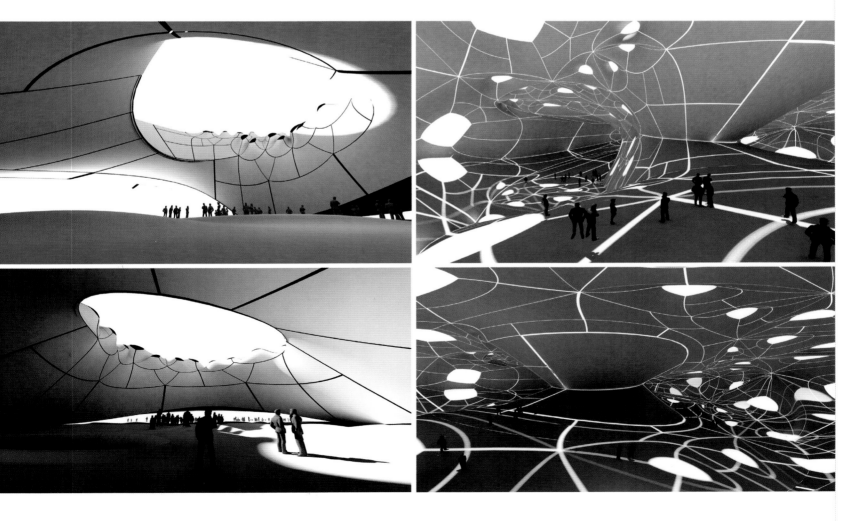

201

The 3Spheres Museum | *Geotectura*

Typology : Art Museum
Location : Taipei
Realization : Conceptual

The NTCArt is a visionary and iconic museum yet practical, flexible, sustainable and economical. Taking into account the amazing location of the museum the typology and topology of the museum are unique and site specific. The three spheres function together and independently with their surrounding as a place for education, exhibition, tourism and recreation.

The mythical spheres are like a magnet to people from the city, the mountains around, the island and the whole world. They are floating like ceramic vessels in a spatial landscape and a shallow water pond making the entire structure approachable and natural.

The site is located near the Yingge Railway Station and the Yingge Ceramics Museum and near the Art Theme Park that blends into the new museum. The circulation is straightforward in all the spheres. One can use the elevator to go all the way up and go down from there or to use the escalators to move up and down between floors. Emergency stairways are always nearby.

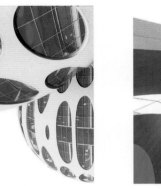

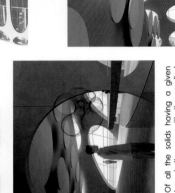

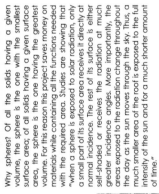

Why spheres? Of all the solids having a given volume, the sphere is the one with the smallest surface area; of all solids having a given surface area, the sphere is the one having the greatest volume. For this reason this project saves money on materials while containing all the functions needed with the required area. Studies are showing that "when a sphere is exposed to solar radiation, only a small part of its surface area receives it directly at normal incidence. The rest of its surface is either self-shaded or receives the radiation at much greater incidence angles. More importantly, the areas exposed to the radiation change throughout the day as the sun moves through the sky. Thus, a much smaller area of the roof is exposed to the full intensity of the sun and for a much shorter amount of time."

The outcome of the NTCArt is a unique structure with minimal footprint on the ground and with great environmental qualities and an amazing panoramic view.

New Taipei City Museum of Art
Geotectura – Sustainable Architecture
www.geotectura.com

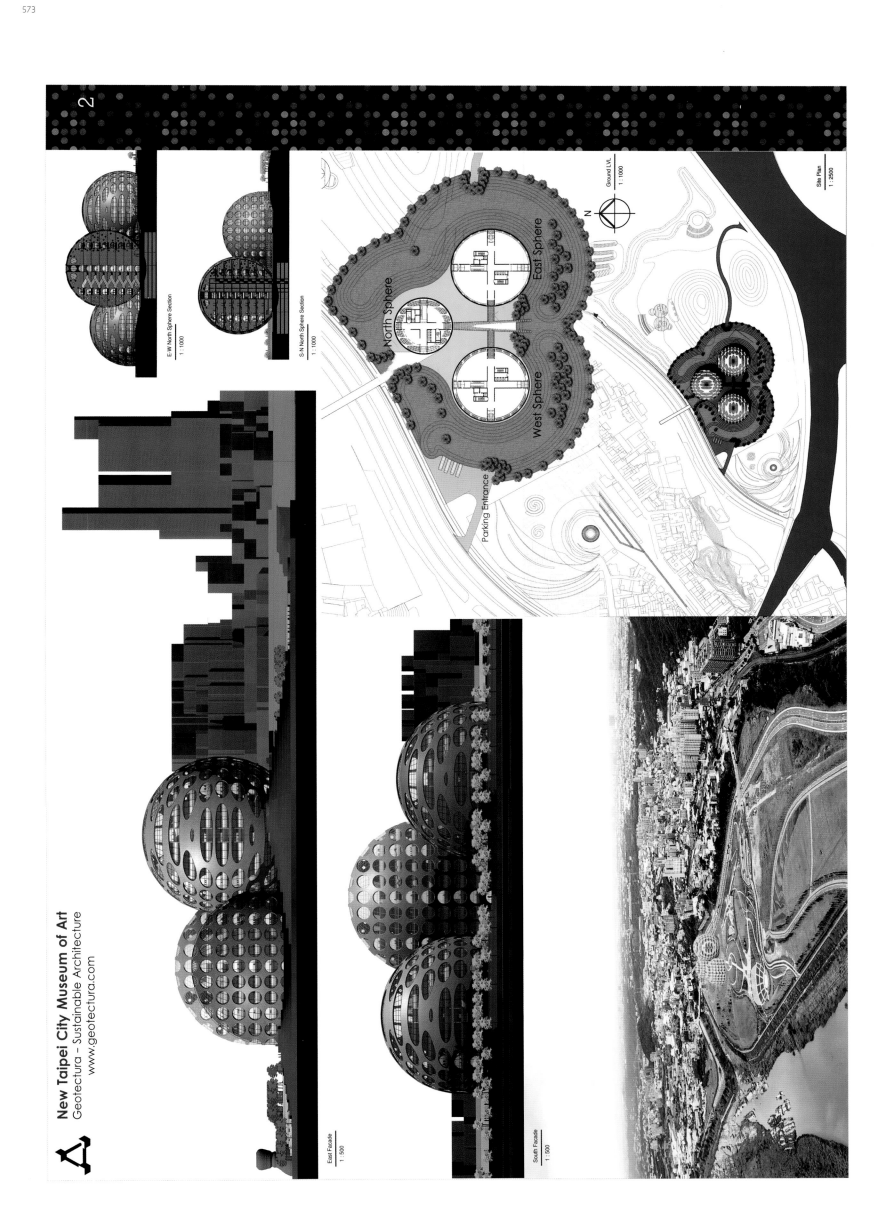

New Taipei City Museum of Art
Geotectura – Sustainable Architecture
www.geotectura.com

E-W North Sphere Section
1 : 1000

S-N North Sphere Section
1 : 1000

North Sphere

East Sphere

West Sphere

Parking Entrance

N

Ground LVL.
1 : 1000

Site Plan
1 : 2500

East Facade
1 : 500

South Facade
1 : 500

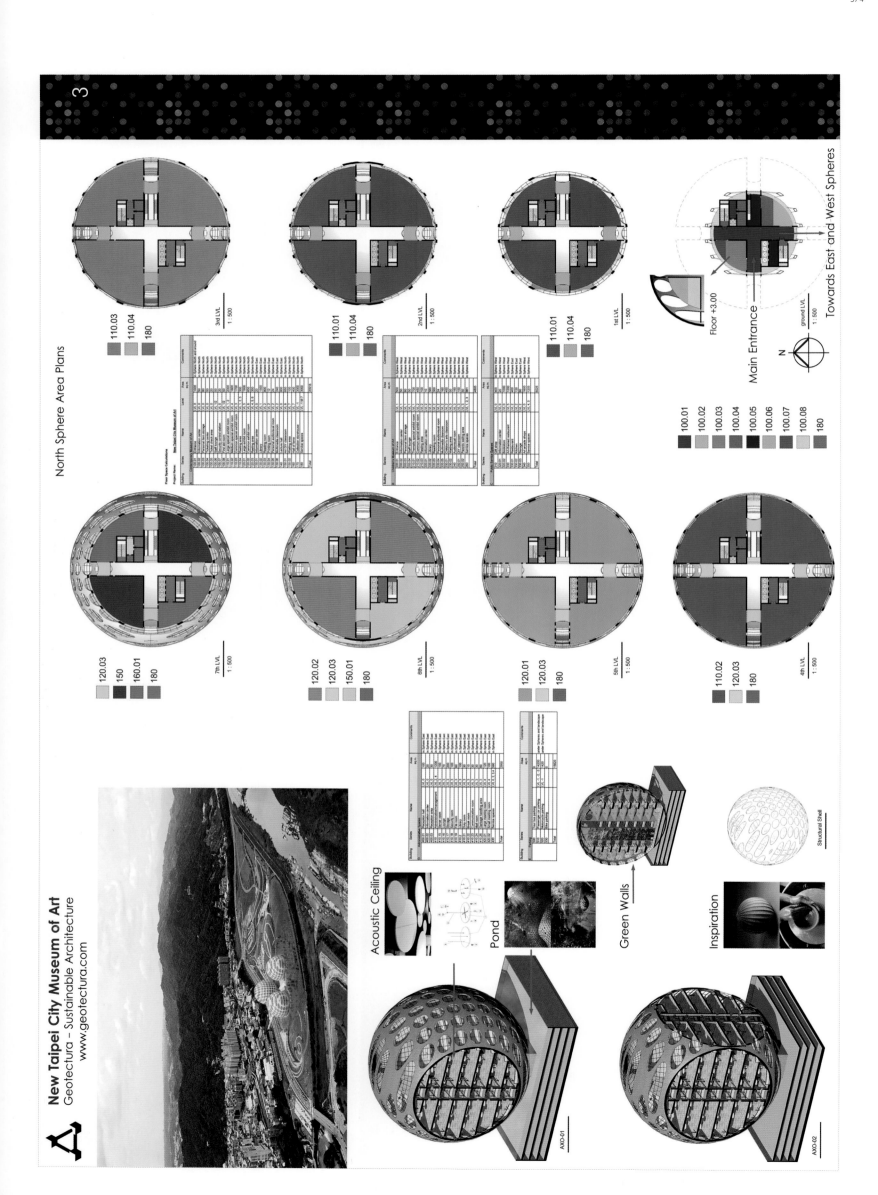

North Sphere Area Plans

New Taipei City Museum of Art
Geotectura – Sustainable Architecture
www.geotectura.com

Acoustic Ceiling

Pond

Green Walls

Inspiration

Structural Shell

AXO-01

AXO-02

Towards East and West Spheres

Main Entrance

Floor +3.00

ground LVL.
1 : 500

N

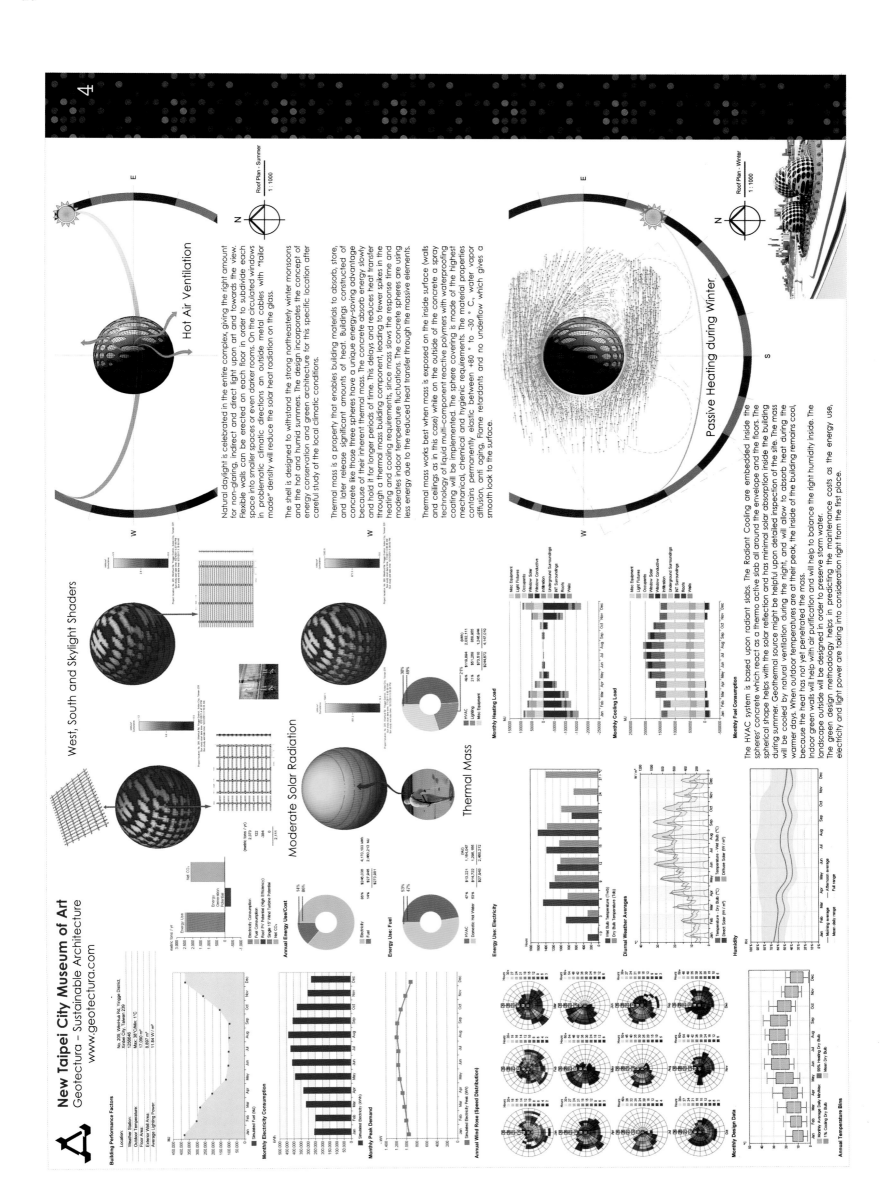

New Taipei City Museum of Art

Geotectura – Sustainable Architecture
www.geotectura.com

Building Performance Factors

Location	No. 200, Waihuai Rd, Yingge District, Xinben City, Taiwan 239
Weather Station	725646
Outdoor Temperature	Max: 38°C Min: 1°C
Floor Area	17,090 m²
Exterior Wall Area	8,897 m²
Average Lighting Power	11.84 W/m²

West, South and Skylight Shaders

Moderate Solar Radiation

Thermal Mass

Hot Air Ventilation

Passive Heating during Winter

Roof Plan - Summer 1:1000

Roof Plan - Winter 1:1000

Natural daylight is celebrated in the entire complex, giving the right amount for non-glaring, indirect and direct light upon art and towards the view. Flexible walls can be erected on each floor in order to subdivide each space into smaller spaces or even darker rooms. On the circulated windows in problematic climatic directions an outside metal cables with "tailor made" density will reduce the solar heat radiation on the glass.

The shell is designed to withstand the strong northeasterly winter monsoons and the hot and humid summers. The design incorporates the concept of energy conservation and green architecture for this specific location after careful study of the local climatic conditions.

Thermal mass is a property that enables building materials to absorb, store, and later release significant amounts of heat. Buildings constructed of concrete like those three spheres have a unique energy-saving advantage because of their inherent thermal mass. The concrete absorb energy slowly and hold it for longer periods of time. This delays and reduces heat transfer through a thermal mass building component, leading to fewer spikes in the heating and cooling requirements, since mass slows the response time and moderates indoor temperature fluctuations. The concrete spheres are using less energy due to the reduced heat transfer through the massive elements.

Thermal mass works best when mass is exposed on the inside surface (walls and ceilings as in this case) while on the outside of the concrete a spray technology of liquid multi-component reactive polymers with waterproofing coating will be implemented. The sphere covering is made of the highest mechanical, chemical and hygienic requirements. The material properties contains permanently elastic between +80 ° to -30 ° C, water vapor diffusion, anti aging. Flame retardants and no underflow which gives a smooth look to the surface.

The HVAC system is based upon radiant slabs. The Radiant Cooling are embedded inside the spheres' concrete which react as a thermo active slab all around the envelope and the floors. The spherical shape helps with the solar reflection and has minimal solar absorption inside the building during summer. Geothermal source might be helpful upon detailed inspection of the site. The mass will be cooled by natural ventilation during the night, and will allow to absorb heat during the warmer days. When outdoor temperatures are at their peak, the inside of the building remains cool, because the heat has not yet penetrated the mass.
Indoor green walls will help with air purification and will help to balance the right humidity inside. The landscape outside will be designed in order to preserve storm water.
The green design methodology helps in predicting the maintenance costs as the energy use, electricity and light power are taking into consideration right from the first place.

Monthly Electricity Consumption

Monthly Peak Demand

Annual Wind Roses (Speed Distribution)

Annual Energy Use/Cost

Energy Use: Fuel

Energy Use: Electricity

Diurnal Weather Averages

Humidity

Monthly Design Data

Annual Temperature Bins

Monthly Heating Load

Monthly Cooling Load

Monthly Fuel Consumption

202

Elisabeth and Helmut UHL Foundation | *Modostudio*

Location : Laives, Italy
Client : Elisabeth and Helmut Uhl Foundation
Phase : architectural restricted competition | winning project
Area : 1.150 sqm

Design Team : Fabio Cibinel, Roberto Laurenti, Giorgio Martocchia
Structural Engineer : KHing Knippers Helbig Beratende Ingenieure Consulting Engineers

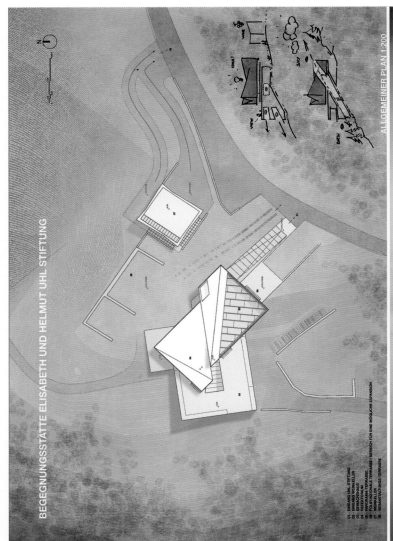

BEGEGNUNGSSTÄTTE ELISABETH UND HELMUT UHL STIFTUNG

ALLGEMEINER PLAN 1:200

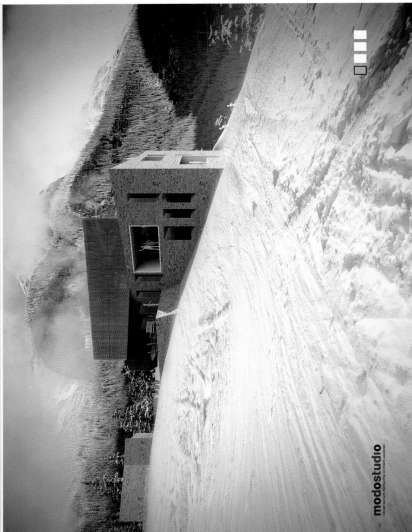

modostudio

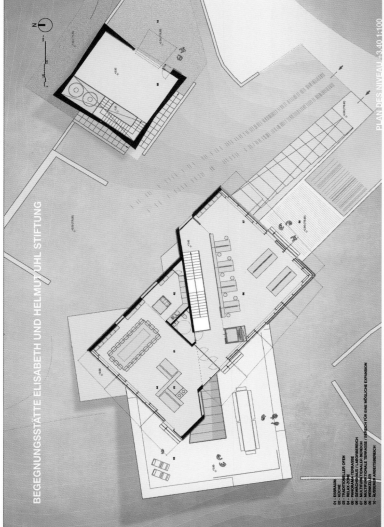

BEGEGNUNGSSTÄTTE ELISABETH UND HELMUT UHL STIFTUNG

PLAN DES NIVEAU -3.40 1:100

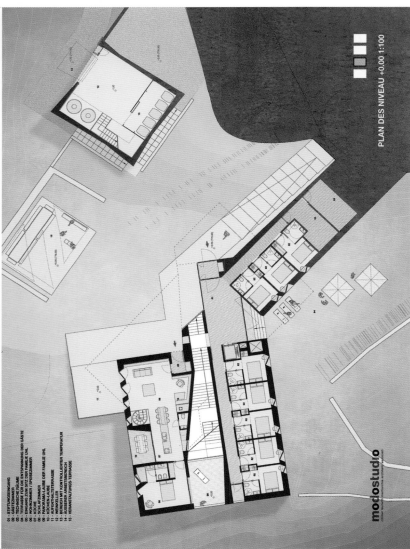

PLAN DES NIVEAU +0.00 1:100

modostudio

BEGEGNUNGSSTÄTTE ELISABETH UND HELMUT UHL STIFTUNG

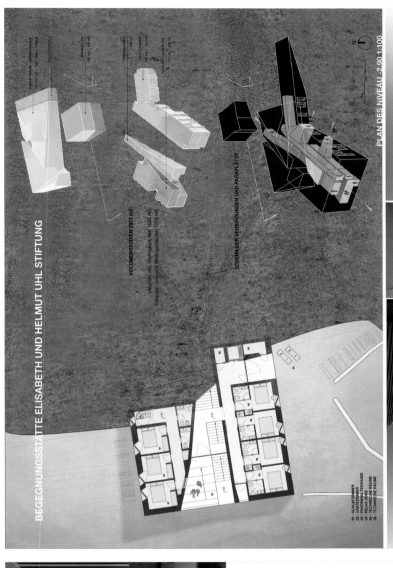

PLAN DES NIVEAU -2.90 1:100

VOLUMENSTUDIEN 2973 m3

Volumen von Wohngebäuden 1695 m3
Volumen verplant Wohngebäuden 1218 m3

SCHEMA DER VERBINDUNGEN UND PARKPLÄTZE

01 SCHLAFZIMMER
02 GÄSTEZIMMER
03 PANORAMA-TERRASSE
05 TECHNISCHE RÄUME
06 TECHNISCHE RÄUME

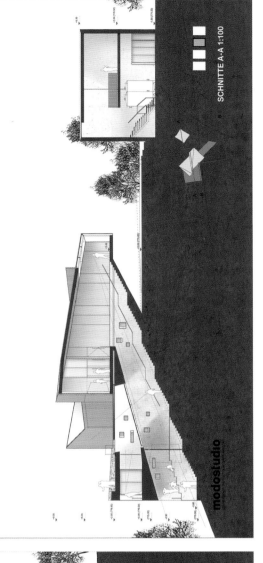

SCHNITTE A-A 1:100

modostudio

BEGEGNUNGSSTÄTTE ELISABETH UND HELMUT UHL STIFTUNG

ENERGIENACHHALTIGKEITSCHEMA

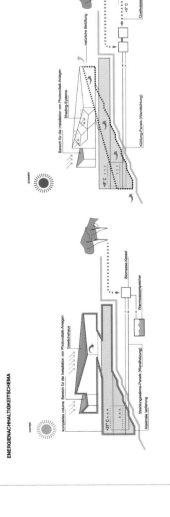

SOMMERSONNENWENDE

WINTERSONNENWENDE

ZUSAMMENHANGSSCHEMA VORHERBESTAND-PROJEKT

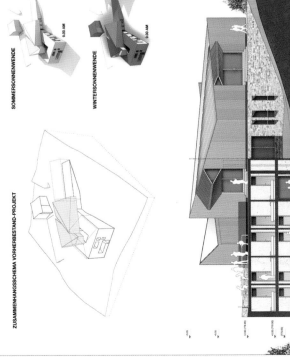

SCHNITTE B-B 1:100

modostudio

203

Walk(in) the Line | *Alessandro Console Studio*

578

Competition : International Architecture Competition MIAMI 2009. Pier Museum in South Beach, Florida
Promoter : Arquitectum
Location : Miami, Florida - USA

Typology : Immigration Museum
Project Team : Alessandro Console, Gina Oliva

106955

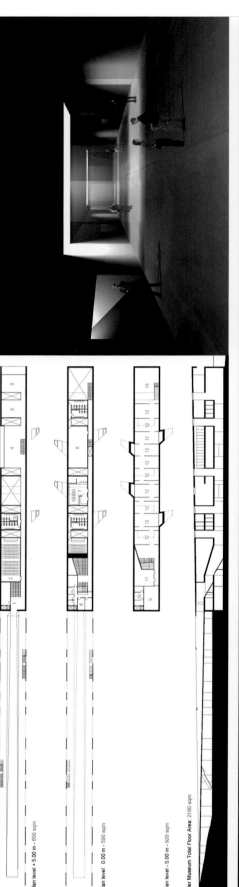

plan level + 5.00 m - 650 sqm

plan level - 0.00 m - 590 sqm

plan level - 5.00 m - 920 sqm

Pier Museum Total Floor Area: 2160 sqm

0 5 10 m

The Pier Museum is a representation of the idea of boundary. It means to create a space that suggests the idea of a walk constrained within a wall.

The museum access is located on the upper level of the building, which configuration is conceived as a progressive and descending route from the open and clear spaces of Miami Beach to the dark spaces of exhibition rooms.

The lower level of the museum is characterized by a linear and continuous sequence of Commemorative Spaces separated each other only by glass walls that allow to perceive all the following spaces but prevent from reaching and crossing them immediately. Beyond Commemorative Spaces, the route finally opens in the Permanent Exhibition Room. From here, it is possible to start rising again to the other areas on higher levels.

All spaces of the museum are illuminated by zenithal light coming from cutting edges on the roof: on the upper two levels the various spaces are located in a way to create vertical hollows that let light come into the lower rooms of the museum. Lower rooms receive also light by *cannon lumière*, located on lateral sides of external walls, that arise from water sea level.

Seen from outside, the museum is perceived as a unitary block stood out the South Beach sea without attempting a *mimesis* to the context. The museum, then, is closely related to the territorial dimension of Atlantic Ocean: it seems to be an ancient wreck run aground the shore, like a monument/memento (from Latin *moneo*: to remind - to admonish) for the users of Miami Beach Area (and in general for people all around the world).

The external walls of the museum are characterized by a peculiar treatment that reproduces the silhouette of American continent. This treatment seems to create an *erosion* of the walls by highlighting on them the geographic boundaries of each American countries.

FUNCTIONAL SPACES OF THE MUSEUM

01. Entrance Hall
02. Auditorium
03. Restrooms
04. Cafeteria
05. Temporary exhibition room
06. Administration
07. Library
08. MUR
09. General storage
10. Maintenance storage
11. Conservation documents
12. Commemorative spaces
13. Permanent exhibition room

WALK (in) THE LINE

Today, almost in all world's countries, the inside/outside moving of population has a great part from a political, economic and cultural point of view.

In USA this matter is crucial, considering that, since the beginning, the American social and cultural models have been characterized by the co-existence of communities coming from faraway geographical settings and belonging to different social and cultural backgrounds.

The proximity among different communities has been always conceived as a positive aspect within the American culture itself.

Nevertheless, the common idea of a multiethnic society based on the optimistic concept of melting-pot, is no longer able to represent now the real condition of immigrants' communities because it does not consider an important feature related to this condition: the *feeling of belonging*.

The writer Amin Maalouf states that in contemporary society the feeling of belonging is often intended in an erroneous and simplistic way as an *exclusive* choice: you belong to a specific and recognized reality, so that you can have no more than one cultural identity. And usually belonging to a specific community means to give up, as a consequence, the possibility to become a part of all the others.

The immigrant, then, lives an ambiguous and a really hard condition. On the one hand, he has been forced to leave his own country for finding better living condition abroad by giving up to belong completely to his original land. On the other hand, he never feels as a part of the new host country where he often continues to be considered (still after a completely process of integration) as part of a certain ethnic community.

The immigrant lives like a *limbo*: he is not able to conceive a multiple and complex identity and, at the same time, he feels like he had lost forever his own original roots.

Then it is possible to state that contemporary society is only apparently characterized by open boundaries and lack of separation, but rather it forces the immigrant to live within invisible and virtual *barriers* by preventing him to belong to neither one side nor the other side of the boundary.

The immigrant lives within a boundary, the same boundary that physically he has already passed but that really it could become his own *prison*.

JVC | *REC ARQUITECTURA*

Competition : Arquine –JVC, Guadalajara/México
Team : Eduardo Resendiz, Gerardo Recoder Déciga

204

Tumbling Showroom JVC

Brüder Grimm Museum | *kadawittfeldarchitektur*

Participants : Gerhard Wittfeld, Klaus Kada, Kilian Kada, Johannes Müntinga,
Simon Kortemeier, Martin van Laack, Andreas Horsky, Andrea Blaschke
Partner : Landschaftsarchitektur (Greenbox Landschaftsarchitekten, Köln),
Gebäudetechnik (PGS Ingenieurbüro, Aachen), Brandschutz(BFT Cognos GmbH, Aachen),

Lichtplanung (Lichttransfer, Büro für Lichtplanung, Berlin)
Statik: Arup Düsseldorf
Project : Grimm-Welt Kassel
Typology : Museum / Client : Stadt Kassel

Location : Kassel, Am Weinberg
Construction Volume : Gfa: 3.70
Year : 09. 2011 - 02. 2012 – 2.Prize

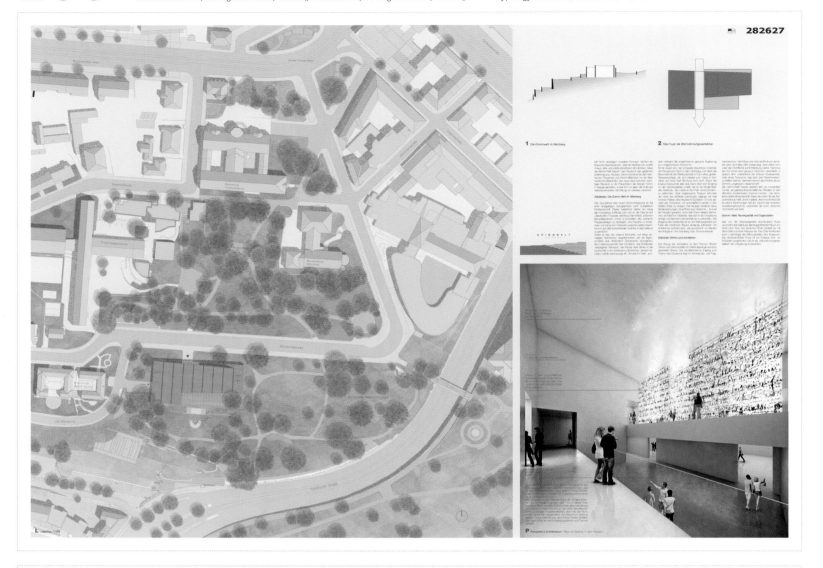

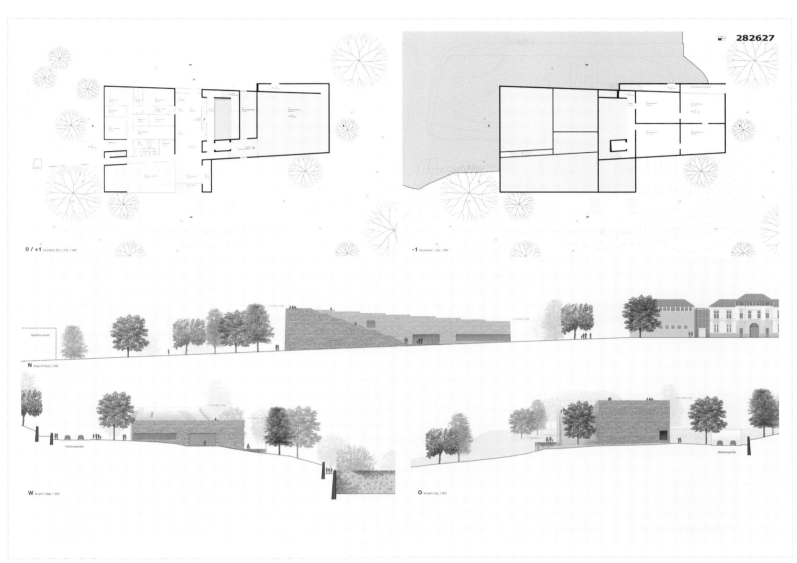

282627

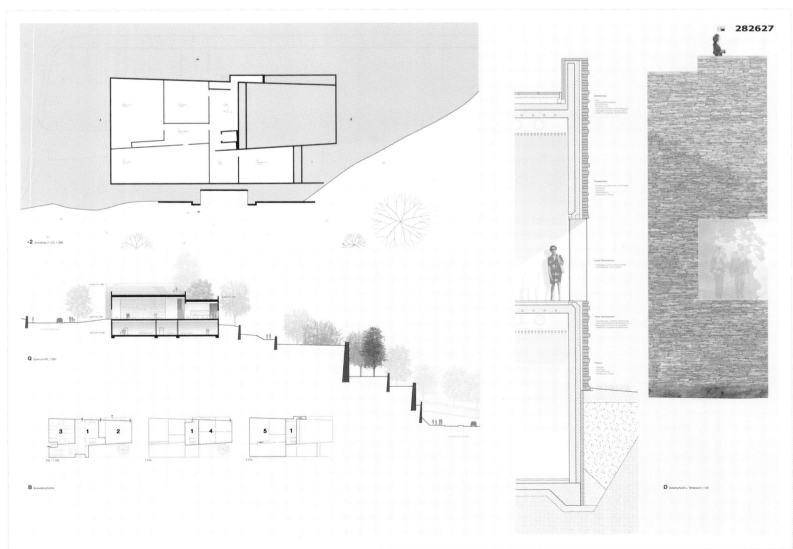

282627

206

Water and Sculpture Hills ICHIHARA | *Katsuhiro Miyamoto & Associates*

582

Result : 2nd prize (unbuilt)
Location : Ichihara-city, Chiba
Principal use : Museum

Total Floor Area : 1,740
Structure : Wood, 3 stories

■「木造」によるリノベーション

□ コスト削減
・既存施設の全体を隅々まで使い切る。
・折り畳まれたような既存プランの特性を最大限に生かした計画とする。
・全体を簡易な工法によりコンパクトに納めることで、
建設工事費、ランニングコストを押さえる。

□ ファサード
・外観の印象を大胆に
木製ルーバーのつくる
複雑なRC造ヴォリュ

□ エンガワ
・既存建築物の外周に半屋外の「エンガワ」空間を設けることによって、
豊かな屋外空間と閉鎖的な屋内展示空間を緩やかに結びつける。

'WOODEN'

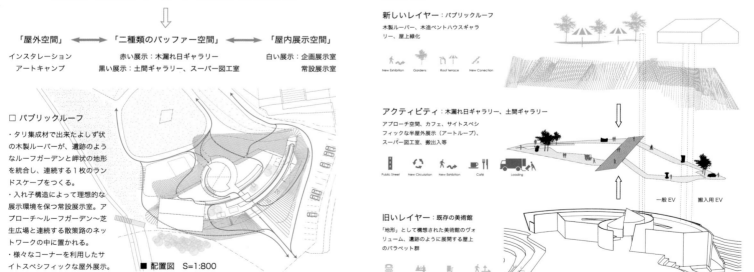

開放的な「屋外空間」 ——✕—— 閉鎖的な「屋内展示空間」

⇩

「屋外空間」 ⟷ 「二種類のバッファー空間」 ⟷ 「屋内展示空間」

インスタレーション
アートキャンプ

赤い展示：木漏れ日ギャラリー
黒い展示：土間ギャラリー、スーパー図工室

白い展示：企画展示室
常設展示室

□ パブリックルーフ
・タリ集成材で出来たよしず状
の木製ルーバーが、遺跡のよう
なルーフガーデンと岬状の地形
を統合し、連続する1枚のランド
スケープをつくる。
・入れ子構造によって理想的な
展示環境を保つ常設展示室。アプ
ローチ～ルーフガーデン～芝
生広場と連続する散策路のネッ
トワークの中に置かれる。
・様々なコーナーを利用したサ
イトスペシフィックな屋外展示。

■ 配置図　S=1:800

■ 全体構成

新しいレイヤー：パブリックルーフ
木製ルーバー、木造ペントハウスギャラ
リー、屋上緑化

アクティビティ：木漏れ日ギャラリー、土間ギャラリー
アプローチ空間、カフェ、サイトスペ
シフィックな半屋外展示（アートループ）、
スーパー図工室、搬出入等

旧いレイヤー：既存の美術館
「地形」として構想された美術館のヴォ
リューム、遺跡のように展開する屋上
のパラペット群

一般EV　　搬入用EV

■ 3つ

□ A.
公園のよ

・日射、
る環境の
・アート
クエンシ
悩ましで
・既存建
用したサ
ープを形
・時には
入自体が

□ 連続断面図　S=1:350

a-a'　　b-b'　　c-c'　　d-d'　　e-e'　　f-f'

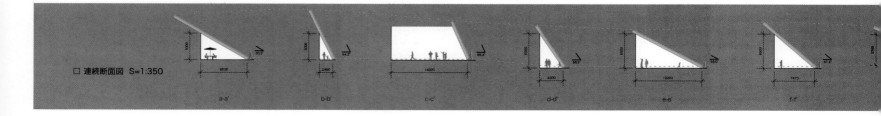

□ プログラム
・新旧2つのレイヤーの間に、新しいアクティビティをつくる。

□ 環境調整
・新しいファサードが環境のバッファーとなって、展示作品にも来館者にも優しい室内環境をつくる。

□ ペントハウスギャラリー
・常設展示のために理想的に計画された、サイトスペシフィックな閉じた箱。

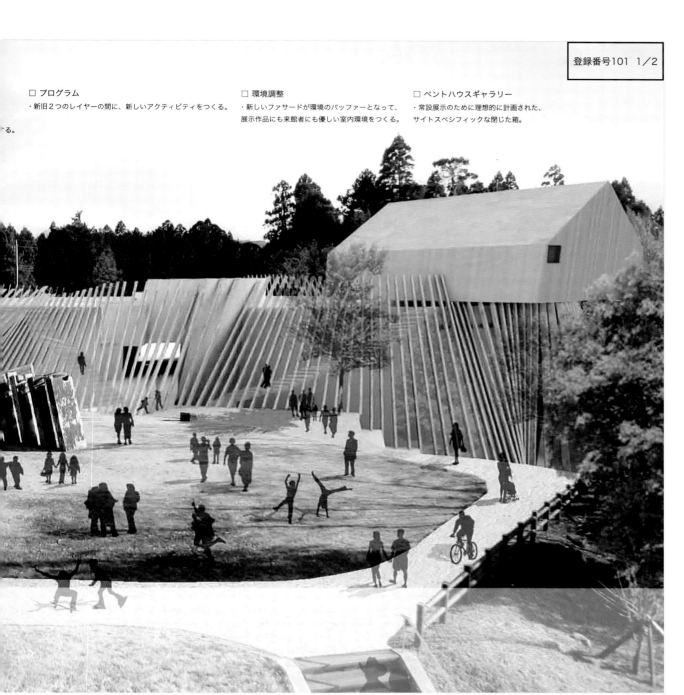

□ B. 土間ギャラリー
商店街のような展示空間→「黒い展示」

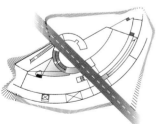

・内外を貫通する公道のような場所。展示室への前室であると同時に、カジュアルな展示空間ともなる。
・土間ギャラリーの延長である多目的ホールは、市民が気軽に立ち寄れる自然採光中心の空間。ワークショップ、アーティストトークの他、周辺小中学校のための「スーパー図工室」や美術教師の研修等に利用される。

□ C. ホワイトキューブ
オーソドックスな展示室 →「白い展示」

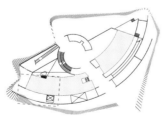

・理想的に室内環境がコントロールされたニュートラルな展示空間。
・入れ子状の二重の調湿ゾーニングを基本とする。

X, 収蔵等
・地下倉庫を改修して一時保管庫とする。
・搬入用 EV の設置によって地下、1階、屋上の一体的運用が可能になる。

■ 運営のイメージ

□アートプロジェクトの拠点として
・白い展示空間を活用したアーティスト・イン・レジデンス
・屋外や赤い展示空間を活用したインスタレーション
・カフェにおけるワークショップや交流イベント
・屋外を活用したアートキャンプ

□美術教育の秘密基地として
・黒い展示空間や赤い展示空間を活用した優秀作品展示
・スーパー図工室として小中学校に貸し出される地下の多目的ホール
・白い展示空間でのスリープオーバー
・カフェを使ったワークショップや研修会

□地域コミュニティの憩いの場として
・ぶらりと立ち寄れる木漏れ日ギャラリー
・屋外や赤い展示空間でのイベント
 ex. 地域即売所（農産物×アート）
 ex. 健康体操（保健×アート）

■ 展示のバリエーション

"S"

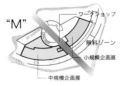
"M"

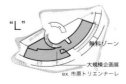
"L"

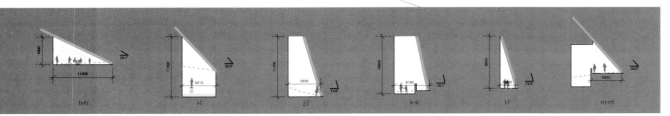

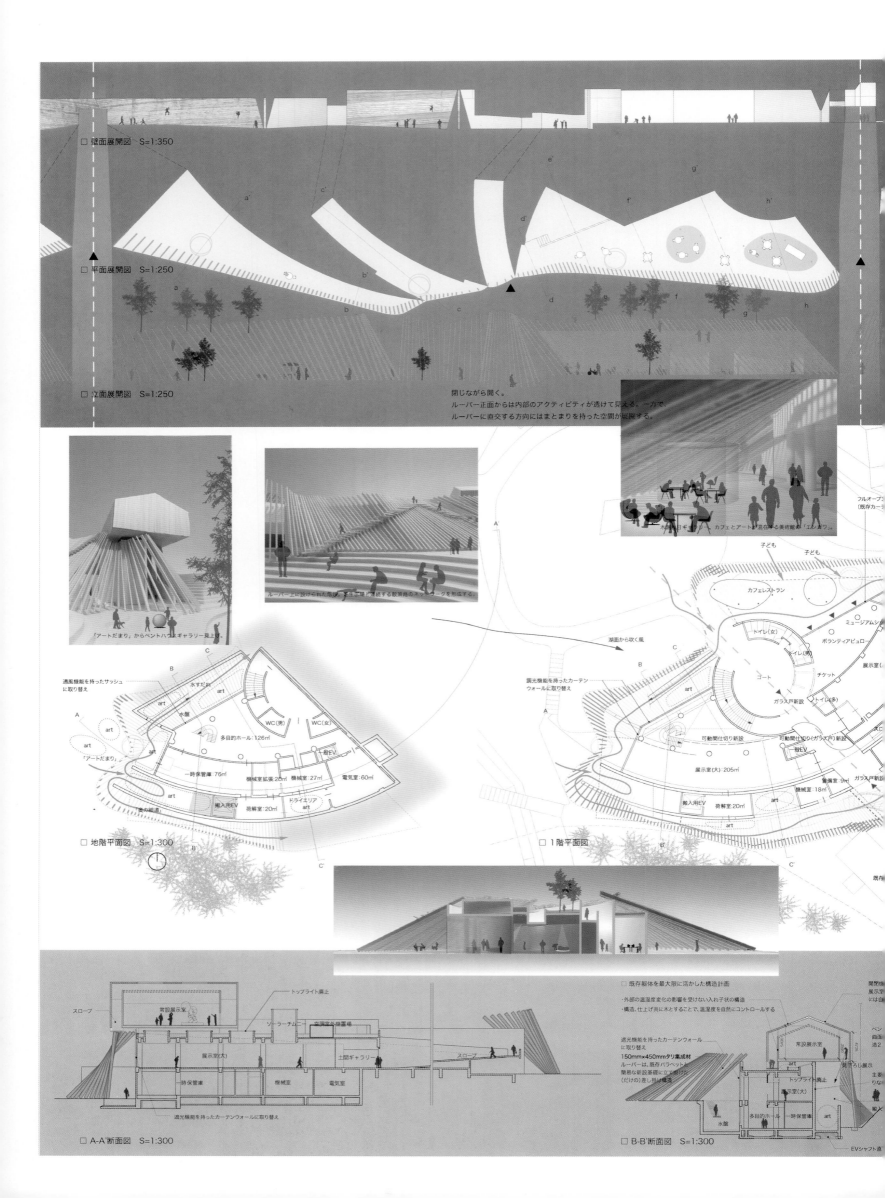

□ 壁面展開図　S=1:350

□ 平面展開図　S=1:250

□ 立面展開図　S=1:250

閉じながら開く。
ルーバー正面からは内部のアクティビティが透けて見える。一方で、
ルーバーに直交する方向にはまとまりを持った空間が展開する。

木造ルーバーギャラリー、カフェとアートが混在する美術館「エンガワ」。

「アートだまり」からペントハウス＆ギャラリー見上げ。

ルーバー上に設けられた斜路は、芝生広場と連続する散策路のネットワークを形成する。

湖面から吹く風

子ども　子ども

カフェレストラン

ミュージアムショップ

トイレ（女）

ボランティアビューロー

トイレ（男）

展示室

チケット

コート

ガラス戸新設

トイレ（多）

art

可動間仕切り新設

可動間仕切り（ガラス戸）新設

一般EV

調光機能を持ったカーテン
ウォールに取り替え

展示室（大）：205㎡

機械室：9㎡

搬入用EV

機械室：18㎡

荷解室 20㎡

art

通風機能を持ったサッシュ
に取り替え

水すだれ

art

水盤

art

art

WC（男）　WC（女）

多目的ホール：126㎡

一般EV

「アートだまり」

art

一時保管庫：76㎡

機械室拡張：20㎡　機械室：27㎡　電気室：60㎡

搬入用EV

荷解室：20㎡

ドライエリア
art

「姿の細道」

art

□ 地階平面図　S=1:300

□ 1階平面図

□ 既存躯体を最大限に活かした構造計画

・外部の温湿度変化の影響を受けない入れ子状の構造

・構造、仕上げ共に木とすることで、温湿度を自然にコントロールする

スロープ

トップライト廃止

常設展示室

ソーラーチムニー　全面芝生屋園場

展示室（大）

土間ギャラリー

スロープ

一時保管庫

機械室

電気室

遮光機能を持ったカーテンウォールに取り替え

□ A-A'断面図　S=1:300

遮光機能を持ったカーテンウォール
に取り替え

150mm×450mmタリ集成材

ルーバーは、既存パラペット・
簡易な新設基礎に立て掛け
（だけの）差し掛け構造

常設展示室

トップライト廃止

展示室（大）

art

多目的ホール

一時保管庫

art

水盤

EVシャフト

□ B-B'断面図　S=1:300

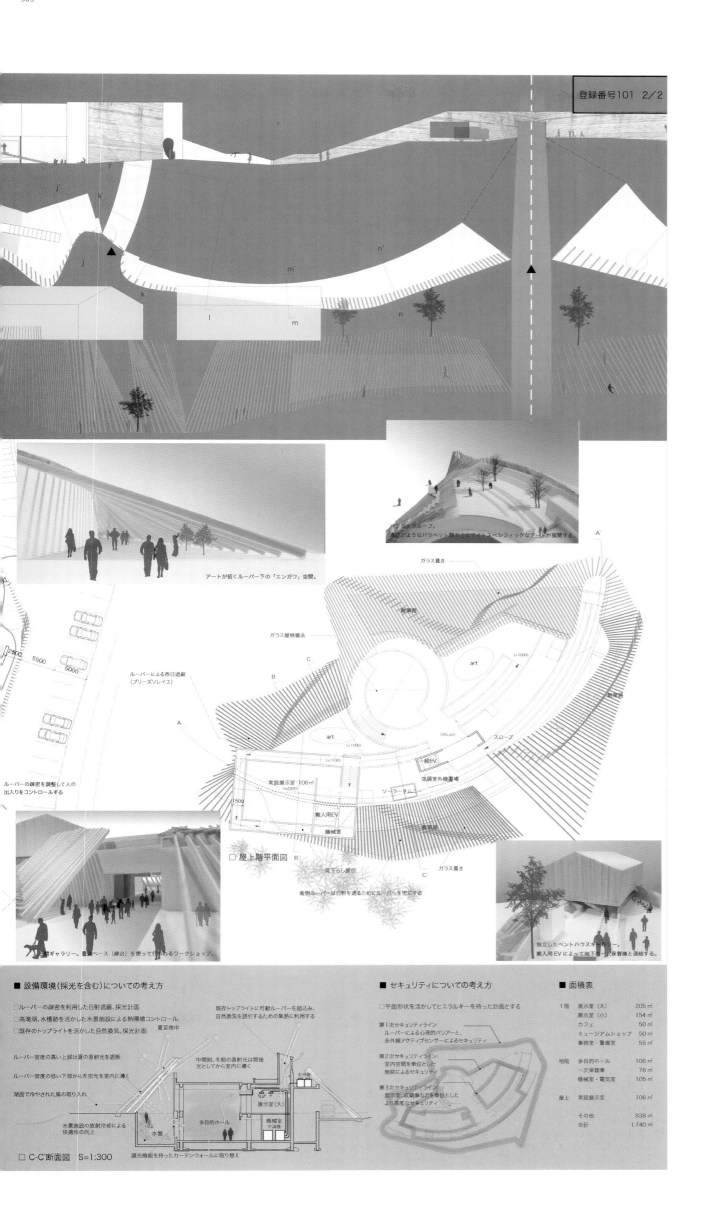

アートが招くルーバー下の「エンガワ」空間。

パブリックルーフ。
屏風のようなパラペット群の上にサイトスペシフィックなアートが展開する。

ガラス葺き

教室跡

art

ガラス屋根撤去

ルーバーによる西日遮蔽
（ブリーズソレイユ）

art

スロープ

空調室外機置場

歳EV

常設展示室　106㎡

ソーラーチムニー

搬入用EV

機械室

ルーバーの疎密を調整して人の
出入りをコントロールする

□屋上階平面図

見下ろし展示

ガラス葺き

南側ルーバーは日射を遮るためにルーバーを密にする

独立したペントハウスギャラリー。
搬入用EVによって地下1階、保管庫と直結する。

■設備環境（採光を含む）についての考え方

□ルーバーの疎密を利用した日射遮蔽、採光計画

□高滝湖、水槽跡を活かした水景施設による熱環境コントロール

□既存のトップライトを活かした自然換気、採光計画

既存トップライトに可動ルーバーを組込み、
自然換気を誘引するための集熱に利用する

夏至南中

ルーバー密度の濃い上部は夏の直射光を遮断

ルーバー密度の低い下部から天空光を室内に導く

中間期、冬期の直射光は間接
光としてから室内に導く

湖で冷やされた風の取り入れ

水景施設の放射冷却による
快適性の向上

水盤

調光機能を持ったカーテンウォールに取り替え

多目的ホール

展示室（大）

機械室
空調機

□C-C'断面図　S=1:300

■セキュリティについての考え方

□平面形状を活かしてヒエラルキーを持った計画とする

第1次セキュリティライン：
ルーバーによる心理的バリアーと、
赤外線アクティブセンサーによるセキュリティ

第2次セキュリティライン：
室内空間を単位とした
展認によるセキュリティ

第3次セキュリティライン：
展示室、収蔵庫などを単位とした
より高度なセキュリティ

■面積表

1階	展示室（大）	205㎡
	展示室（小）	154㎡
	カフェ	50㎡
	ミュージアムショップ	50㎡
	事務室・警備室	55㎡
地階	多目的ホール	106㎡
	一次保管庫	76㎡
	機械室・電気室	105㎡
屋上	常設展示室	106㎡
	その他	838㎡
	合計	1,740㎡

207

New Serlachius Museum | *XML Architecture Research Urbanism*

Architect : XML Architecture Research Urbanism
Program : Museum(expansion) - galleries, office, archive facilities, restaurant
Location : Mänttä, Finland
Area : 15000 m²

Client : Gösta Serlachius Fine Arts Foundation
Year : 2011 / Realization : Competition

Outside Inside -
Between Art and Nature

How to imagine a museum that liberates the experience of art from the dominance of the site's omnipresent landscape? Rather than organizing the museum's spaces in relation to the site's abundance of daunting nature, this proposal sets out to create a museum that mediates between two worlds: an external world of nature and an internal world of art.

The required programme has been distributed along a continuous route that connects different programmatic clusters such as galleries, storage, restaurant and office. By bending this route into a circle two conditions have been organized: on the inside of the circle a series of enclosed exhibition spaces allows visitors to focus on the experience of art, on the outside of the circle the continuous route that connects the programmatic clusters allows for alternating this intimate experiences with views on the surrounding nature.

The irregular residual space between the programmatic boxes is turned into a Gallery Garden, continuing the tradition of landscape architecture that is part of the museum's history. In contrast to the vastness of the surrounding landscape, this contained garden can be used to exhibit the sculpture collection of the museum but also as event space, accommodating lectures, interview-marathons or outside screenings and art-picnics. As a result, the floor area of the Museum is extended during summer, an idea that could reach as far as reconceptualizing the museum's identity into a twofold 'Wintermuseum' and 'Summermuseum' that host programs of different nature. As utopic garden at the heart of the museum, the Gallery Garden could become a plat-form to experiment with unexpected relations between art and nature.

Each of the requested gallery spaces is organized in separate rooms to create a maximum of curatorial freedom. The different galleries could be used together to host one exhibition, but also separated or in arrangements with the existing gallery space in Joenniemi Manor. The art hand-ling and storage facilities are combined in a programmatic cluster near the exhibition spaces for reasons of efficiency. However, this arrangement also allows curators to include the museum's archive into exhibitions offering the possibility to experiment with new curatorial models and modes of displaying art.

In the same way as the programmatic clusters at the ring's interior, the existing museum is con-nected at a single point to the continuous museum route. Like a diamond in a ring of gold, the Joenniemi Manor – as the only architectural volume on the outside of the ring – is re-contextua-lized as the jewel of the museum's expansion.

In reference to the Serlachius family-business, we propose to construct the extension of the mu-seum in wood. Wood not only refers to the industry that has created a great future for Männtä, but also adapts to the forest like surroundings of the museum. As an autonomous island of wood, the museum becomes the twin of Taavetinsaari island, anchoring the museum within the landscape.

Rather than provoking an opposition between nature and art - the continuous museum route is sequencing both conditions to exist in their own right. When strolling the museum, visitors will turn their bodies both to art and nature, depending on their location along the museum's routing. Whereas visitors leave the route to enter one of the enclosed museum spaces to engage with the museums' exhibitions, specific moments on the routing frame the surrounding landscape to contemplate the view on the beautiful nature. The continuous route is not only organising the museums' programme, but it also mediates between two worlds - the inner world of art and the external world of nature - that ultimately meet in the experience of the museum's visitor.

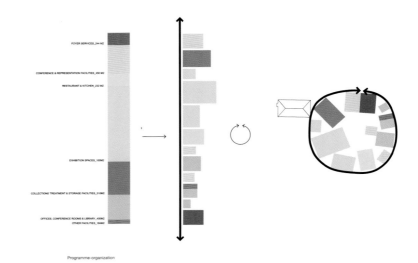

Programme-organization

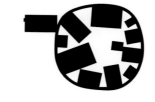

Winter-Museum

Summer Museum

Experiencing Art

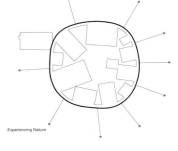

Experiencing Nature

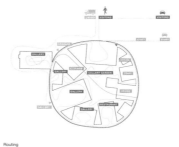

Routing

Routing: paid vs. unpaid

Joenniemi Manor as diamond in a ring of gold.

Gallery Garden

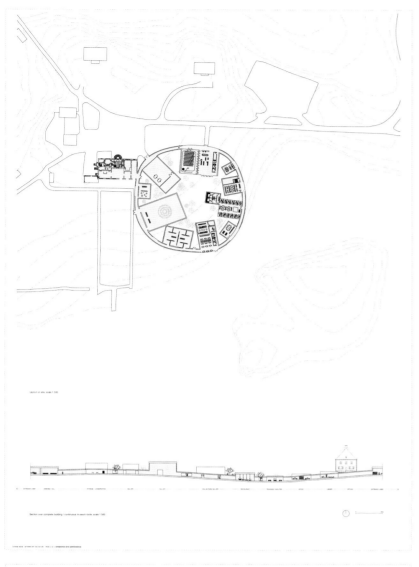

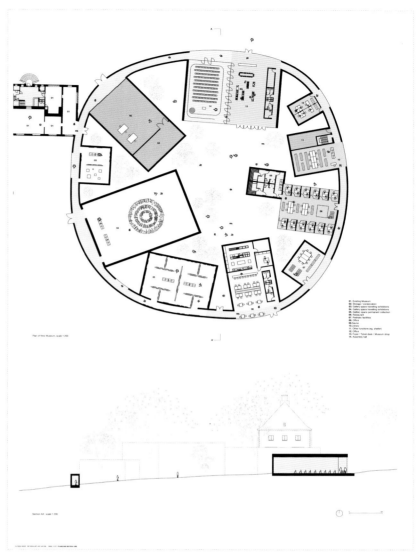

208

Lugar de la Memoria | *Lima Urban Lab*

Location : Lima, Peru
Project Team : Pablo Diaz,Diego Rodriguez, Johana Flores,Norly Endo, Jan Bludau,
Francis Rivera, Andrea Carranza, Angello Silva
Project area : 5000sqm

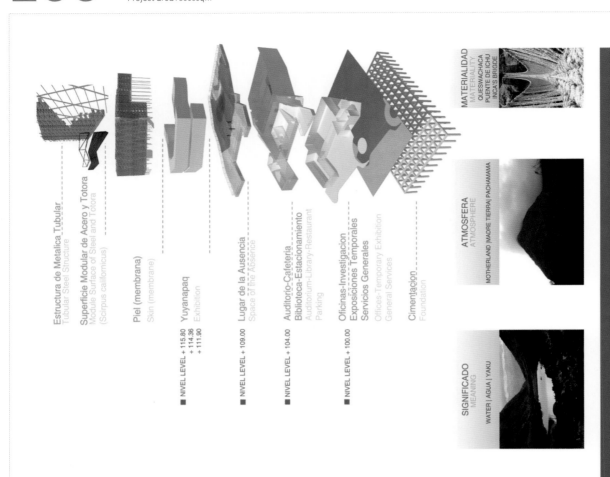

Estructura de Metalica_Tubular
Tubular Steel Structure

Superficie Modular de Acero y Totora
Module Surface of Steel and Totora
(Scirpus californicus)

Piel (membrana)
Skin (membrane)

■ NIVEL LEVEL + 115.80 Yuyanapaq
 + 114.36 Exhibition
 + 111.90

■ NIVEL LEVEL + 109.00 Lugar de la Ausencia
  Space of The Absence

■ NIVEL LEVEL + 104.00 Auditorio-Cafeteria
  Biblioteca-Estacionamiento
  Auditorium-Library-Restaurant
  Parking

■ NIVEL LEVEL + 100.00 Oficinas-Investigacion
  Exposiciones Temporales
  Servicios Generales
  Offices-Temporary Exhibition
  General Services

  Cimentacion
  Foundation

MATERIALIDAD
MATERIALITY
QUESWACHACA
PUENTE DE ICHU
INCA'S BRIDGE

ATMOSFERA
ATMOSPHERE
MOTHERLAND |MADRE TIERRA| PACHAMAMA

SIGNIFICADO
MEANING
WATER | AGUA | YAKU

DIAGRAMA DE LA EXPOSICION YUYANAPAQ
DIAGRAM OF THE YUYAPANAQ EXHIBITION

Lugar de la Memoria 01

Mapa de Memoria Colectiva

Red interconectada de Lugares.Un espacio de comunicación de la memoria colectiva y los derechos humanos. El modulo de la MEMORIA (Paradero o Objeto), es un interfaz que nos transmite información relacionada a los eventos de su emplazamiento y a su vez nos muestra los diversos sucesos vinculados a Yuyanapaq. Esta red de Modulos se convierte en una estrategia que permite al Lugar de la Memoria convertirse en un agente activo del paisaje urbano y rural.

A network of places. The space of the collective memory and the human rights information. The MEMORY module (Urban object or Busstop) is a interface that communicates information related to its location and to the events link to the Yuyanapaq.The network is a strategy so the Place of Memory will become an active agent of the urban and rural landscape.

interfaz paradero interface BUSTOP **interfaz objeto Urbano** interface Urban Object

Pantalla reflective screen **Interfaz Objeto Urbano** interface Urban Object

Place of the Absence Hace BAUU Disputation Accordion

Place of the Absence

interior yuyanapaq

air view

Lugar de la Memoria 02

Jossingfjord Competition P2-P6 | *David Garcia Studio*

Project : Mine Museum with Additional Facilities
Typology : Museum Building
Location : Jøssingfjord, Norway
Construction volume : 1,700m²

Client : NAL, National Norske Arkitekters Landsforbund –
National Association of Norwegian Architects
Participants : David A. Garcia (Architect MAA), Maria Tranebæk
Lindstrøm (Architect MAA),

Tom Doan (Intern), Sam Devanthery (Intern),
Rasmus Baes (Intern), Frederik Allan (Intern)
Year : 2011, 3rd prize

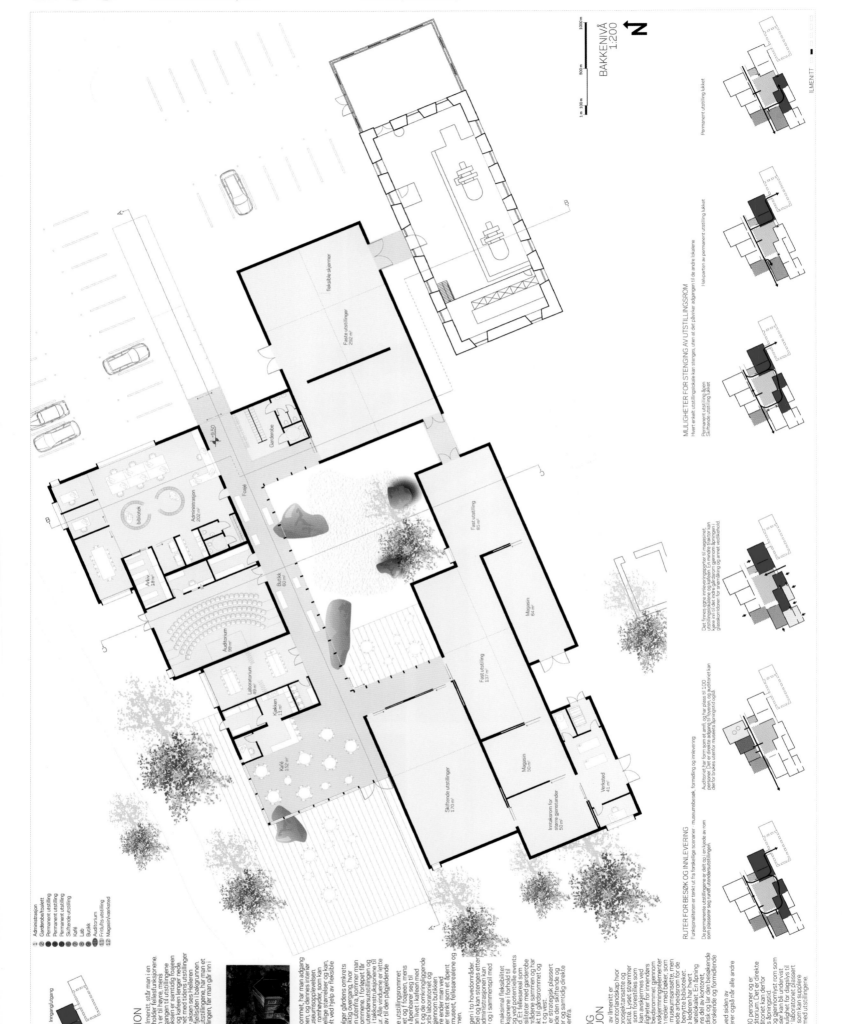

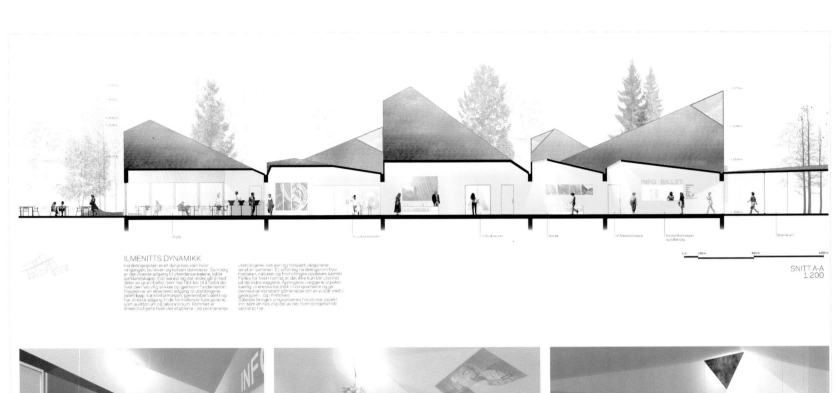

SNITT A-A
1:200

ILMENITTS DYNAMIKK

Fordelingsaksen er et dynamisk rom hvor inngangen, butikken og kaféen dominerer. Samtidig er det direkte adgang til utendørsarealene, både parklandskapet mot sørøst og den indre gård med delen av grunntrollet, som har fått lov til å forbli der hvor den naturlig stikker og gjennom fundamentet. Foajéen er en akse med adgang til utstillingene, billettskap, turistinformasjon, gjennombillettsalg og har direkte adgang til de formidlende funksjonene som auditorium og laboratorium. Rommet er ilmenitts hjerte hvor det etablerte - de permanente

utstillingene, naturen og forskerfunksjonene smelter sammen. Et offentlig fordelingsrom hvor historien, naturen og formidlingen oppleves samlet. Felles for hvert rom er at det ikke kun blir utstillet på de indre veggene. Åpningene i veggene utpeker særlig interessante blikk til omgivelsene og gir dermed en konstant gjenkjennelse om at vi står midt i geologien - og i historien. Således bringes omgivelsenes historiske aspekt inn, som en naturlig del av det formidlingsformål senteret har.

1. FOAJE

2. UTSTILLING

3. KAFÉ

VEST FASADE
1:200

SNITT B-B
1:200

LANDSKAP

På nordvestsiden er parkeringsplassen og inngangspartiet. Går man direkte gjennom senteret, forbi det indre gårdsrom, åpner det seg et parklandskap, hvor naturen er gjenninført uten å fjerne sporene fra den fortidige mineindustri.

Landskapet er bearbeidet med "stein-bjelker" som holder på landskapet og fører den besøkende gjennom delen, men blir brudd av Helleren-husene. Landskapsbearbeidelsen forholder seg til den historiske tradisjon ved å bruke naturlige og industrielle materialer som spor, som vil kunne ses fra klatreløypa og er en opplagt rasteplass.

Landskapet bearbeidet med "bjelker" som holder på landskapet, og dessuten fungerer som landskapsoppslepende matter.

ANKOMST

Man ankommer på Fv44 og svinger ned Titrania's vei gjennom sitet. Veien blir omlagt så Nedre Helleren kraftstasjon kan bli avstukket. Fra resten av Ilmenitt. Veien nedsenkes i forhold til bygningen for å forhindre støy fra fastbilene.

Som ansatt og som besøkende av senteret parkerer man utenfor inngangen.
Turbusser og klatrere som ankommer i bil, parkerer på den andre side av bekken. Bobilene parkerer langs fjellsiden i skogen.
Varer leveres fra sør til den pågjeldende side av bygningen.

Veien omlegges og føres til bygningens inngangsdom med parkering til gjester og ansatte på venstre side. På høyre side er det, plass til campingvogner, busser og ekstra personbiler.

Terrenget og bedjentrinene fungerer som støydempere for bygningen. Blot bakken skaper svall ornevaren på 3 m en naturlig skjerm, og trærne på skråfaten tar støy fra hovedveien.

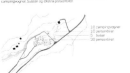 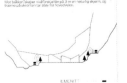

ØST FASADE
1:200

SNITT C-C
1:200

MATERIALEVALG

Bygningen er holdt i lokale, naturlige materialer, som understreker den sterke forbindelsen til fjellet, skogen og fjorden. På samme måte møte som titan utvinnes av malmen, bryter bygningen ut av grunnfjellet med sin titanstruktur og overflate. Materialevalget er viktig for å poengtere forholdet mellom naturen, teknologien og mennesket. Fasaden refererer til, og avspeiler den ytre kontteksten, mens de indre rommene er skapt til opphold og fordypelse. Vinduene i utstillingsrommene fokuserer på forholdet mellom det menneskelig bearbeidede interiør og rissiølfet utenfor, så det blir et intagent element av det utstilte. Den bærende konstruksjonen består av betongelementer bekledd med hvite gipsvegger på innsiden, som også brukes som romdelende vegger. Gulvene er belagt med lyse treplanker. Utendørsbelegningen er mørk stein, skifer eller lignende.

FASADE

Fasadematerialet titan markerer stedets natur og understreker forholdet mellom natur, teknologi og menneske. Med dets myke refleksjonsevne, vil omgivelsene og lyset spelle seg i bygningen. Fasadebekledningen av titanpaneler blir dermed er symbol på bearbeidelsen av landskapet - i en menneskelig håndterbar skala.
Som byggemateriale har titan mange fordeler. Det er et fleksibelt materiale, som kan motstå harde klimatiske forhold som en vestlandsk vintersrom. Det har en lang levetid med lav korrosjon, hvilket gjør det motstandsdyktig overfor vind og vann. Det er bærendyktig, da det er 100% resirkulerbart, og er energieffektivt med en høy isolasjonsverdi.
Titan er et lettvektsmateriale, så det oppnås kun minimal byrde på den bærende betongkonstruksjonen, som dermed kan dimensjoneres minimalt.

KONSTRUKSJON

Gulvene er belagt med lyse treplanker med en varm glød, lagt langs aksens horisontale retning, som understreke bygningens orientering mod fjorden. Taket holdes av en eksponert bjelkekonstruksjon, og henviser til tradisjonelle norske materialer og bygningskonstruksjon. Man kan skjule bjelkekonstruksjonen, så treverket framstår med hvite flater.
Vinduene bryter ut av titanfasaden i terrammer, som danner et fint samspill mellom den herde fasade utad og de myke materialer inni bygningen. På den måten sammenkobler vinduene bygningens konsept meget konkret og lett lesbart for den besøkende.
Rommene er bekledd med hvite gipsvegger som bakgrunn for utstillings- og oppholdsrom, og skillevegger er lette gipskonstruksjoner. Konstruksjonsprinsippet er enkel. Bygningen er konstruert av prefabrikkerte betongelementer.

POZ | *KLAIR Architecture*

Project description : Museum of History
City, country : Poznan, Poland
Designer / architect : KLAIR + Nenad Basic + IOSIS Polska
Date / expected year of completion / status of project : Competition Entry 2009

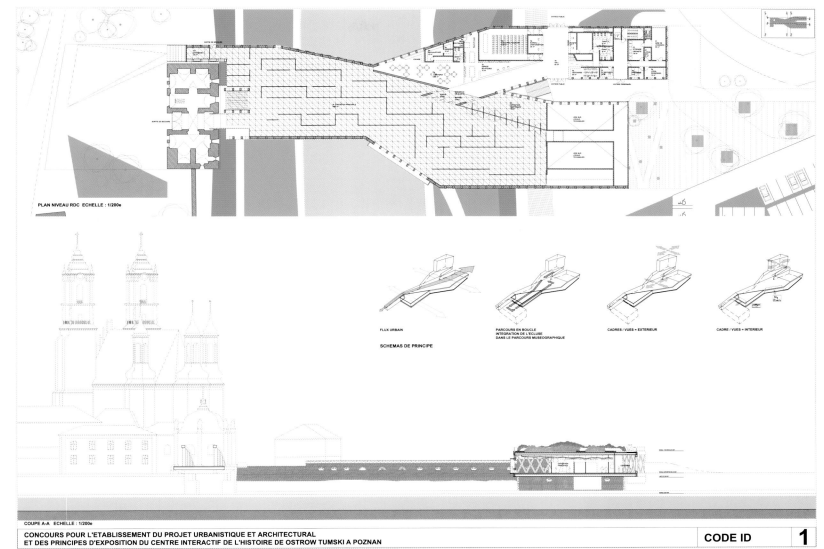

PLAN NIVEAU RDC ECHELLE : 1/200e

FLUX URBAIN

PARCOURS EN BOUCLE
INTEGRATION DE L'ECLUSE
DANS LE PARCOURS MUSEOGRAPHIQUE

CADRES / VUES = EXTERIEUR

CADRE / VUES = INTERIEUR

SCHEMAS DE PRINCIPE

COUPE A-A ECHELLE : 1/200e

CONCOURS POUR L'ETABLISSEMENT DU PROJET URBANISTIQUE ET ARCHITECTURAL
ET DES PRINCIPES D'EXPOSITION DU CENTRE INTERACTIF DE L'HISTOIRE DE OSTROW TUMSKI A POZNAN

CODE ID **1**

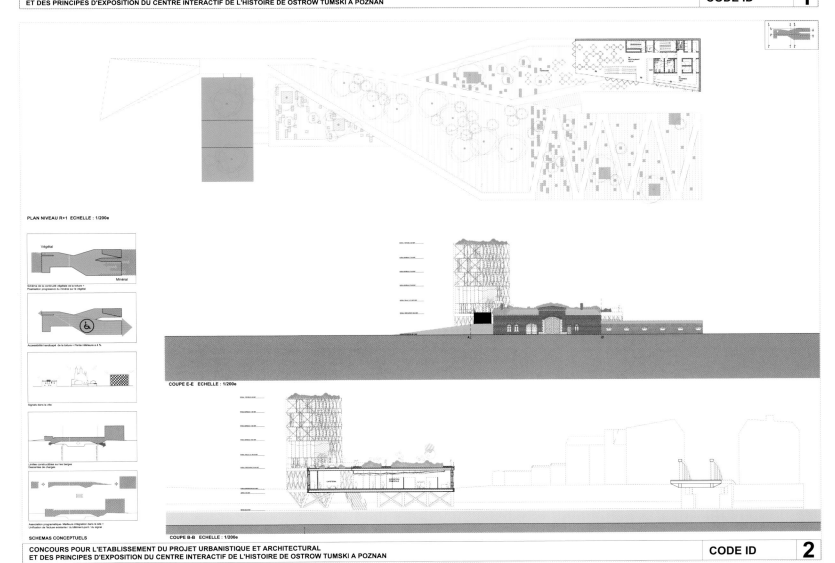

PLAN NIVEAU R+1 ECHELLE : 1/200e

Végétal

Minéral

Schéma de la continuité végétale de la toiture +
Pixelisation progressive du minéral sur le végétal

Accessibilité handicapé de la toiture + Pente inférieure à 4 %

Signals dans la ville

Limites constructibles sur les berges
Descentes de charges

Association programmatique. Meilleure intégration dans la ville +
Unification de l'écluse existante vs le bâtiment-pont / du signal

SCHEMAS CONCEPTUELS

COUPE E-E ECHELLE : 1/200e

COUPE B-B ECHELLE : 1/200e

CONCOURS POUR L'ETABLISSEMENT DU PROJET URBANISTIQUE ET ARCHITECTURAL
ET DES PRINCIPES D'EXPOSITION DU CENTRE INTERACTIF DE L'HISTOIRE DE OSTROW TUMSKI A POZNAN

CODE ID **2**

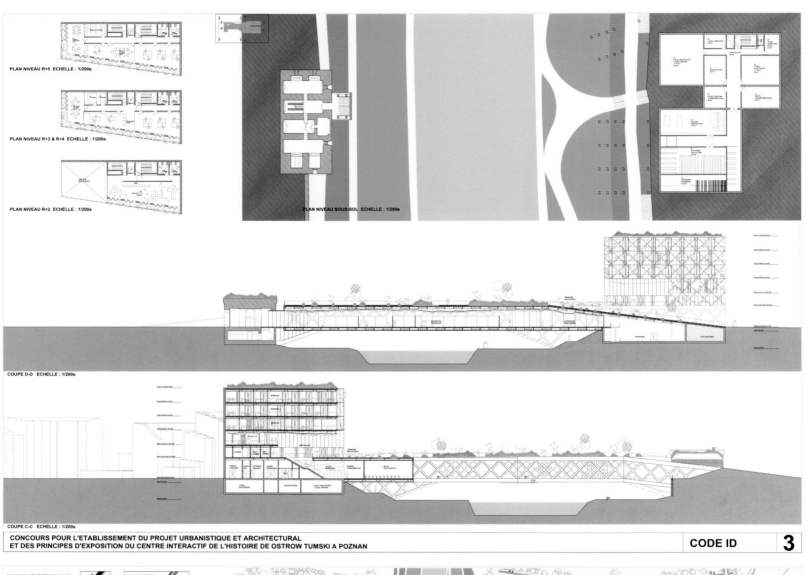

PLAN NIVEAU R+5 ECHELLE : 1/200e

PLAN NIVEAU R+3 & R+4 ECHELLE : 1/200e

PLAN NIVEAU R+2 ECHELLE : 1/200e

PLAN NIVEAU SOUS-SOL ECHELLE : 1/200e

COUPE D-D ECHELLE : 1/200e

COUPE C-C ECHELLE : 1/200e

CONCOURS POUR L'ETABLISSEMENT DU PROJET URBANISTIQUE ET ARCHITECTURAL
ET DES PRINCIPES D'EXPOSITION DU CENTRE INTERACTIF DE L'HISTOIRE DE OSTROW TUMSKI A POZNAN

CODE ID   3

SCHEMAS TRAITEMENTS PAYSAGERS

COUPE PAYSAGERE

PLAN MASSE ECHELLE : 1/1000e

VUE PERSPECTIVE 1 - DEPUIS LA PROMENADE SUD

CONCOURS POUR L'ETABLISSEMENT DU PROJET URBANISTIQUE ET ARCHITECTURAL
ET DES PRINCIPES D'EXPOSITION DU CENTRE INTERACTIF DE L'HISTOIRE DE OSTROW TUMSKI A POZNAN

CODE ID   4

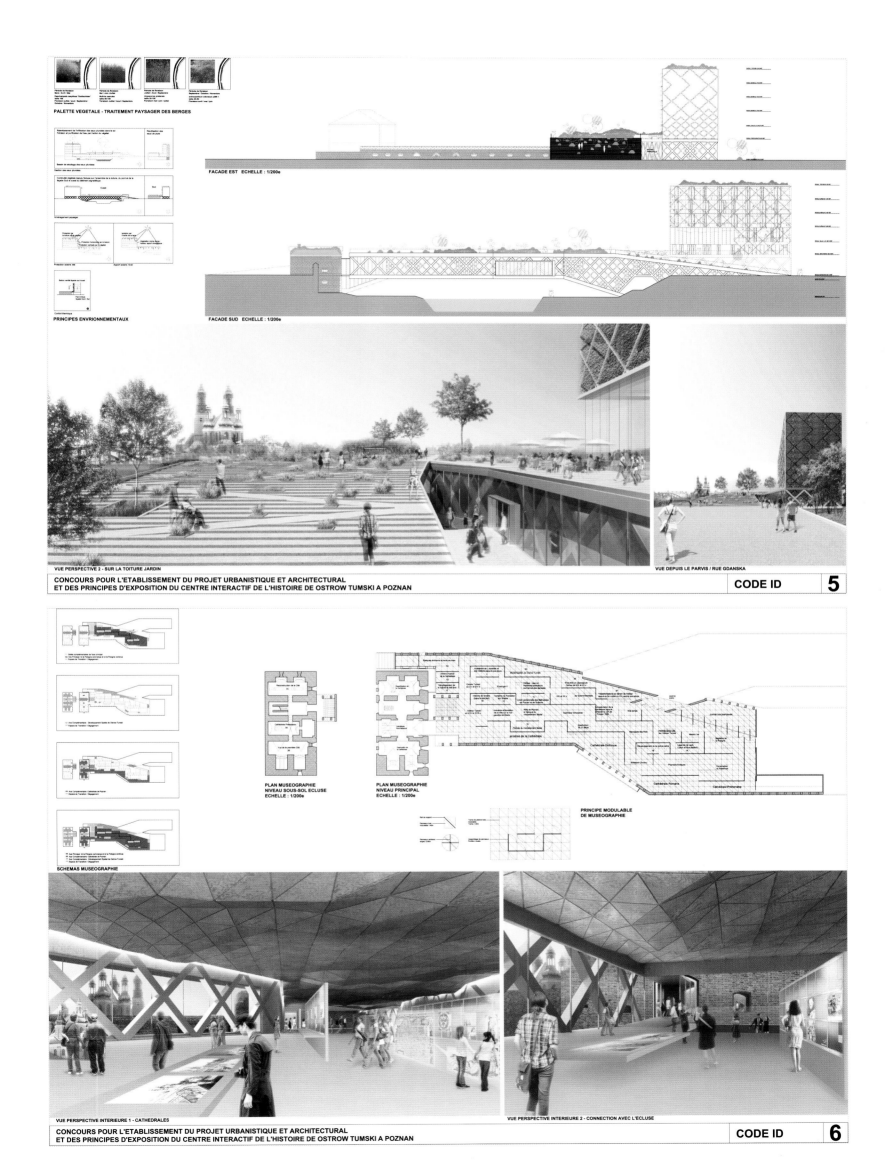

PALETTE VEGETALE - TRAITEMENT PAYSAGER DES BERGES

PRINCIPES ENVIRONNEMENTAUX

FACADE EST ECHELLE: 1/200e

FACADE SUD ECHELLE 1/200e

VUE PERSPECTIVE 2 - SUR LA TOITURE JARDIN

VUE DEPUIS LE PARVIS / RUE GDANSKA

CONCOURS POUR L'ETABLISSEMENT DU PROJET URBANISTIQUE ET ARCHITECTURAL
ET DES PRINCIPES D'EXPOSITION DU CENTRE INTERACTIF DE L'HISTOIRE DE OSTROW TUMSKI A POZNAN

CODE ID 5

SCHEMAS MUSEOGRAPHIE

PLAN MUSEOGRAPHIE
NIVEAU SOUS-SOL ECLUSE
ECHELLE : 1/200e

PLAN MUSEOGRAPHIE
NIVEAU PRINCIPAL
ECHELLE : 1/200e

PRINCIPE MODULABLE
DE MUSEOGRAPHIE

VUE PERSPECTIVE INTERIEURE 1 - CATHEDRALES

VUE PERSPECTIVE INTERIEURE 2 - CONNECTION AVEC L'ECLUSE

CONCOURS POUR L'ETABLISSEMENT DU PROJET URBANISTIQUE ET ARCHITECTURAL
ET DES PRINCIPES D'EXPOSITION DU CENTRE INTERACTIF DE L'HISTOIRE DE OSTROW TUMSKI A POZNAN

CODE ID 6

Participants : Cristina Goberna, Urtzi Grau, Akhsay Mehra
Project : Centre for Promotion of Science, Republic of Serbia
Typology : Science Museum
Location : Belgrade, Servia

Construction Volume : 10,000m²
Client : Goberment of Serbia

Centre for Promotion of Science, Republic of Serbia, a laboratory:

The fatal weakness of science museums is its dramatic inability to catch up with the speed of science. They are always running late. While the last one hundred years witnessed a tidal wave of new Copernican Revolutions – from relativity to string theory, from penicillin to genome, from steam engine to electric car, etc. – museums attempted to adapt to the continuous shift of paradigms renovating its collections, reorganizing master narratives and becoming a testing ground for innovative exhibition means; an endless documentation of the *state of the art*. Our proposal for the *Centre for Promotion of Science* brings to an end this perpetual chase of the latest scientific discoveries imagining the *Centre* as the actual site of innovation: a laboratory.

Precedents, Fragmentation:

Faced with new scientific paradigms historical museums – the *London Science Museum* (1857), the *Deutsches Museum* (1903), the *American Museum of Natural History* (1869), the *Chicago Museum of Science and Industry* (1933) – opted for a strategy of aggregation. Innovation equaled new space, and successive atomized extensions mimicked the structure of rooms of its original buildings in which Science is displayed as a fragmented aggregation of unrelated pieces.

Precedents, Box:

Following the revolution that the *Centre Pompidou* brought to the display of art, in 1986, the *Cite des Sciences* proposed that science should be display in a massive container, adapting to newness by reconfiguring its flexible interior. The *Cosmocaixa* (2004) in Barcelona, the *Phaeno Science* Center in Wolfsburg (2005) and the *California Academy of Sciences* (2008) opted for similar models, freeing their interiors of partitions and investing in new technologies rather than encyclopedic collections. Yet the *Centre for Promotion of Science* could not relay simply in the generic flexibility of a massive warehouse like the *Cosmocaixa*. Nor its laboratory-oriented flexibility could be constrained by formal eccentricities and rigid material configurations of the *Phaeno Science Center*. The new *Centre* needs to move beyond the heritage of the art museum and learn from spaces of experimentation.

Museum as a laboratory, Isolation and Flexibility:

Laboratories require a subtle equilibrium between isolation and connectivity. The controlled atmospheres where experiments are performed entail high levels of isolation, achieved by technical equipment relentlessly updated. Indeed, the last generation of science museums can be best described as a series of isolated environments that share its capacity to be actualized. They left the other side the scientific laboratory however out of the equation. Besides defining a flexible and secluded atmosphere the new *Centre for Promotion of Science* should display the porosity of any scientific pursuit.

Museum as a laboratory, Porosity:

Porosity refers to the intrinsic public value of scientific knowledge. Our proposal for the *Centre for Promotion of Science* contains the means to distribute that knowledge. The Exhibition Hall, the Science Club, the Science Park, the Conference Hall and the Inflatable Planetarium, isolated entities that define the new institution, can be combined into a single space to accommodate exhibitions and events that require bigger and more complex configurations. Scientific conferences, corporate presentations, experiments of grandiose dimensions can take advantage of a continuous single space 250 meter long and 50 meters wide, while the rest of the time the museum works as a series of isolated spaces. Nonetheless Science is always constructed using hybrids in which public representation and private research are seamlessly intertwined.

Museum as a laboratory, Intensification:

As a way of reinforcing its porosity, we imagine the new *Centre for Promotion of Science*, as the hub of the future research campus Blok 39. The regular hours of the museum are extended to meet the research institution requirements, and even further, to meet the researchers' needs for leisure. The Conference Hall and the Inflatable Planetarium, usually succinctly used in the Museum schedule, become a common facility for the campus directly connected to the future research facilities. And the means of connection, the Ring a 1.200 long racing track, expands the public façade of both the campus and the museum defining the identity of the new *Centre for Promotion of Science*.

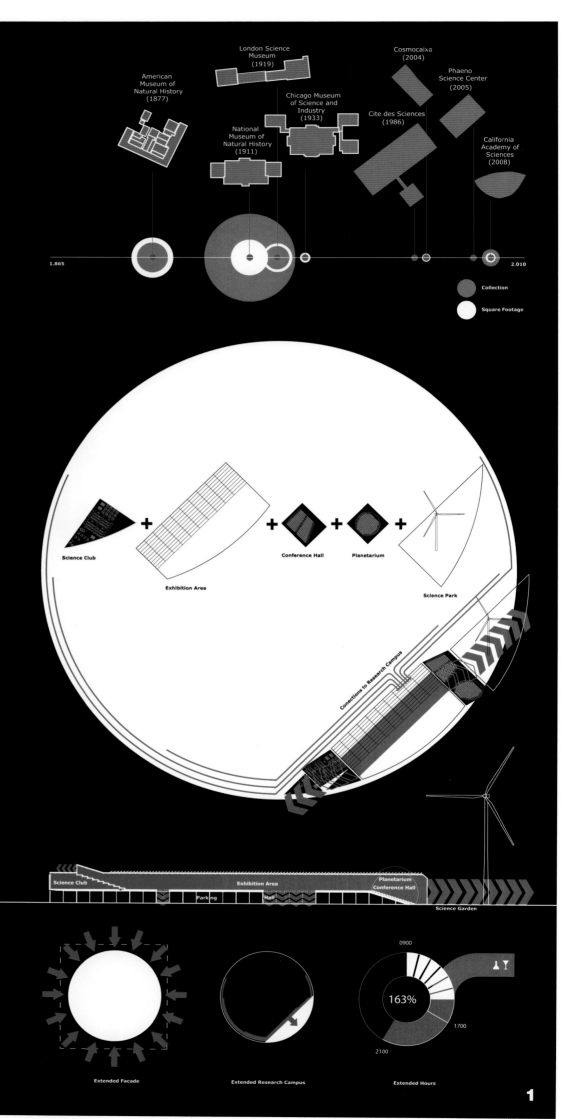

101126 OY

1

The Research Campus, an Urban Ring:

For decades the New Belgrade has been imagined as set of Cartesian pieces rigidly composed a priory to supposedly define "meaningful" urban spaces. In this composition many possibilities are sacrificed: The potential to organize large programs in informal arrangements; the potential to thematize the difference between then and know, the potential to inject into the New Belgrade a spectrum of complementary conditions. Our proposal for the Research Campus of the *Centre for Promotion of Science* injects a 350 meters diameter ring in Blok 39 that defines a large coliseum like virtual volume – a maximum envelope created through extrapolating zoning laws intended to protect a 80 meters diameter void in the center of the block From this envelope Buildings can be carved out, building an unforeseeable skyline connected by an external ring. It is both a closed block and a bundle of buildings, offering as alternative to the historical rigid frame of the New Belgrade a landscape of possibilities adaptable to the unstable future of scientific research.

The Ring: Running Track in the Sky

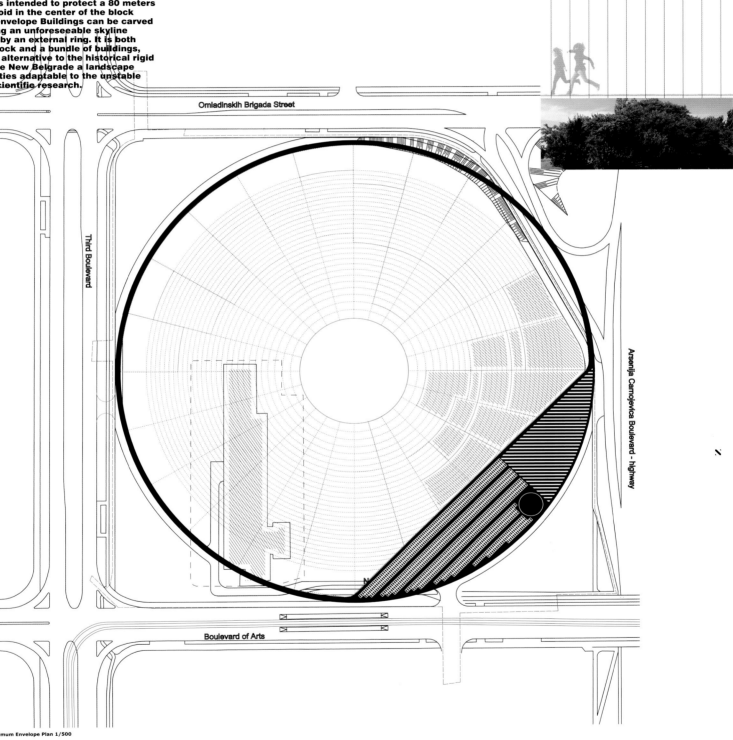

Omladinskih Brigada Street

Third Boulevard

Arsenija Carnojevica Boulevard - highway

Boulevard of Arts

Maximum Envelope Plan 1/500

Maximum Envelope Elevation 1/500

101126 OY

2

Ground Floor, Battlefield

A wind sweep oasis in the center of the New Belgrade, Blok 39, is the last (almost) untouched block. But what if we did not have to choose between preserving this open space and promoting science? What if we can have both the new center and the empty block? We propose a to insert 350 meter diameter elevated passage – the Ring, a 1200 meters long running track – that will eventually become the connection between the future research facilities of the *Centre for Promotion of Science*'s Campus. In the meantime however the projection of the Ring into the ground will define the divide between untouched land and urbanized space. Outside of the ring maximum artificiality will allow for an intense urban use of the land. Synthetic pavements and infrastructure in the underbelly of the ring will reinforce the façade quality on this virtual line. The interior will remain untouched, and the original nature of the region will take over.

Arriving to the *Centre for Promotion of Science*

If the Blok 39 is designed in two parts, the *Centre for Promotion of Science* occupies the spot of maximum dependency and interface between them. At the East corner of the site, the synthetic pavement accommodates the parking lot and the loading dock. The very same pavement guides the visitors through the porch towards the glass wall that connects with the main entrance. Through the crack that separates the Onference Hall and the Inflatable Planetarium, the Science Park and the escalators to access the upper level are visible. Beyond the wild interior of the blok39 continues.

Lobby

The Lobby is the central "nerve" of the *Centre*, where the building is accessed from the outside, and it is from where admission to all the functions of the *Centre* happens. A secondary level of services is placed in direct connection with the Lobby, as the shop and the Locker rooms, in order to serve all the areas of the complex. Dimensioned for the various visitor groups, the information and ticket counter, the booking office for events and guided tours are located in there.

After purchasing tickets at the centrally placed Info Desk, the visitors can take the escalators to access connection to the exhibitions hall, or directly enter Conference hall, the Inflatable Planetarium or and the Science Park. Seats and other rest areas are provided in the lobby; along with display panels and screens where information on the *Centre*. This information is both interactive and computer-based.

The store is visible and accessible without going into the exhibition area, i.e. without having to purchase an entry ticket and is designed to be flexible allowing easy reorganization of displayed items, including a small storage room.

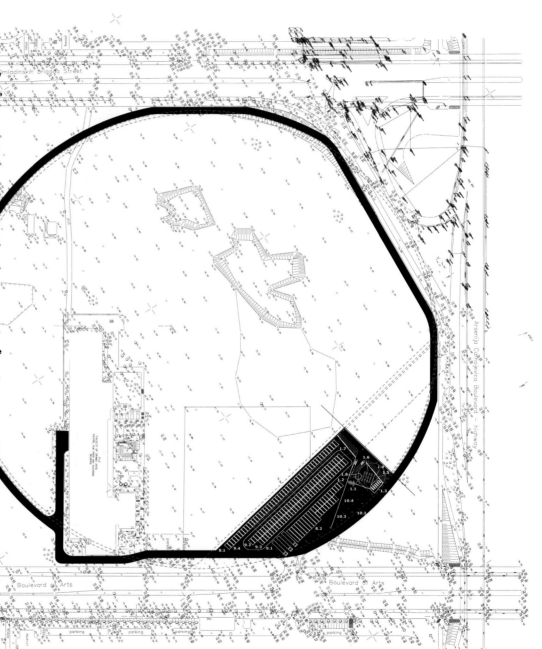

View of the Shop in Lobby from the Porch

GROUND FLOOR 1/500

1.0 LOBBY...502 m2
1.1 Entrance hall and main entrance...135 m2
1.2 Info desk...20 m2
1.3 Wardrobes and lockers...57 m2
1.4 Staff office with first aid...15 m2
1.5 Restrooms
1.6 Souvenir and book store
      with office and storage space...120 m2
1.7 Café and staff restroom...75 m2
1.8 Booking office...20 m2

8.0 GARAGE + PARKING...2750 m2
8.1 Cars (142 spaces)...2400 m2
8.2 Buses (10 spaces)...350 m2

9.0 LOADING/UNLOADING AREA...630 m2
9.1 Technical entrance with loading deck and
      service area...120 m2
9.2 Waste containers...100 m2
9.3 Security room/entrance control...10 m2
9.4 Storage space for exhibitions equipment...400 m2

10.0 OUTDOOR AREA...2,580 m2
10.1 Roads...1,000 m2
10.3 Bicycle...50 m2
10.4 Plato at the entrance...530 m2
10.5 Science garden...1,000 m2

101126 OY

Main Floor, the Great Hall:

Imagine a space 250 meters long and 50 meters wide, a massive laboratory where science happens. The space of the museum unfolds in three different levels connected by two inclined surfaces that house the Conference Hall –Inflatable Planetarium and the Science Club. The former connects the Science Park to the Exhibition Hall. The latter, gives access to the rooftop from the Exhibition Hall. Albeit each space works independently, the partitions can eventually vanish to unveil the magnificent space of the Great Hall.

Exhibition Hall

The *Centre for Promotion of Science* has two different exhibition areas – permanent and temporary exhibitions – both highly flexible with few load bearing columns and no permanent walls, but with a system of modular mobile walls.

The Permanent Exhibition area can be divided into four to five thematic areas, all areas easily accessible to the public, safeguard natural visitor flow, allowing for both quick review and in-depth study of exhibitions by individual visitors or larger groups. The temporary area is both separated and connected from the rest of the exhibition area, since is visually connected and has a separate entrance. 50% of floor the of the Exhibition hall is can be removed, increasing the celling high to 10 meters to accommodate exceptional exhibitions.

The space features total daylight control a light grid for various light/exhibition lighting/ projectors, electrical outlets in the technical floor, transport paths adapted for devices such as forklifts, pallet trucks or manual carts and an overhead crane to move heavy equipment easily.

Science Club

The Science club provides spaces for lectures, demonstrations, discussions and hands-on work with students and other visitors, mainly for Extracurricular and Co-curricular activities. It is organized along a ramp that grants views of the entire Great hall but is separate from the exhibition area and in close proximity to the maintenance and mechanical workshops. In includes four laboratories – 20 students per laboratory – featuring wet and dry facilities: Biology, Chemistry, Physics and Electronics, with the necessary equipment.

The Science club also includes teacher's preparation rooms for lab technicians, storage room for equipment a flexible classroom space, a science playground area, and visitors' restrooms

Conference Hall

The multifunctional hall, with a capacity of 250 seats, is enclosed by a textile wall that can vanish to allow for larger events. Its open lobby is directly connected to the ring that will communicate with the future research facilities. Its stage looks over the Science Park and can be open to enjoy a direct relation with the exterior. It is also possible to use it as a separate meeting and conference hall, stage for performance, gatherings, regular and 3D projections, etc. The independent access assures that the Conference Hall can be rented for commercial use not related to the *Centre*.

The Conference Hall also features a light grid for various light/exhibition lighting / projectors, an adjustable Conference Hall lighting and stage lighting, a retractable projection screen, electrical outlets in the stage floor, traction cable for control of light, sound and other equipment, necessary fixtures for cinema and equipment for simultaneous translation, room for speakers and storage, and its own restrooms.

Inflatable Planetarium

The Inflatable Dome Theatre, with a capacity of 100 seats and 12 meters diameter serves multipurpose functions in the *Centre*, through its variety of shows – skies & stars, educational/scientific films adapted for this format – through its shape and capacity for other types of potential activities – conferences, lectures, promotions, sponsored events, etc – Once deflated, it joins with the Conference Hall to increase its capacity to 350 seats. And even when it is functional all year round with multiple shows every day, it is design allows overlapping planetarium and non-planetarium use the very same day. Entrance is possible from the main lobby and the Exhibition Hall in case it requires separate ticket purchase.

The Planetarium will be equipped according to modern digital planetarium standards, combining both 2D and 3D projection capabilities.

The lighting of the dome should also be taken into consideration (controls, LED, fading ...). The Planetarium shall have good acoustic conditions and no daylight.

Restaurant and Canteen

The restaurant is accessible directly from the Lobby after the ticket checkpoint and in close connection with the conference hall the exhibition areas. Its siting area, (100 seats) is and open space with daylight and views to the outdoor areas. Necessary storage, refrigeration, and waste room are located by the kitchen and in the close proximity to the delivery areas.

Management and Administration

The management and administration offices facilities, located under the Science Club, are separated from the visitor areas with its own separate entrance.

FIRST FLOOR 1/300

2.0 EXHIBITION AREAS...3000 m2
2.1   Permanent exhibition area ...2500 m2
2.2   Temporary exhibition area...500 m2

3.0 SCIENCE CLUB...415 m2
3.1   Four laboratories (20 students per laboratory)...180 m2
3.2   Flexible classroom space...75 m2
3.3   2 preparation rooms for teachers...2x20 m2
3.4   Storage of equipment...20 m2
3.5   Science playground area...100 m2

4.0 SEMINARS/CONFERENCES...590 m2
4.1   Conference hall (250 seats)...500 m2
4.2   Conference hall lobby...75 m2
4.3   Room for speakers and storage, restroom...15 m2

5.0 PLANETARIUM...250 m2

6.0 RESTAURANT/CANTEEN...200 m2
6.1   Sitting area (80 seats)...100 m2
6.2   Delivery kitchen with counters and register...80 m2
6.3   Storage for chairs/supplies...20 m2

7.0 EMPLOYEES/STAFF...400 m2
  7.1 MANAGEMENT AND ADMINISTRATION...130 m2
    7.1.1 Director´s office and secretary...25 m2
    7.1.2 Manager, event project manager, business administration...62 m2
    7.1.3 Office space for volunteers...20 m2
    7.1.4 Copy room with storage...10 m2
    7.1.5 Meeting room (10 - 20 people)...30 m2
    7.1.6 reception area...10 m2
  7.2 MAINTENANCE ...170 m2
    7.2.1 Office space...20 m2
    7.2.2 Storage space...50 m2
    7.2.3 Repair and maintenance workshops...90 m2
  7.3 SECURITY...20 m2
    7.3.1 Security control room...20 m2
  7.4 SHARED STAFF AREAS...80 m2
    7.4.1 Changing room, restrooms with showers...40 m2
    7.4.2 Break room...40 m2

101126 OY

4

The Floor of the Exhibition Hall:

Two systems reinforce the flexibility of the Exhibition hall. The raised floor houses the mechanical and electrical services guarantying simple transformation of the space. And, in the Nord-West side of the hall, the area under the overhead crane, the slab can be completely removed, taking over sections of the parking lot underneath and increasing to 10 meters the celling high. That same area is used as loading dock, taking advantage of the two cranes and parking underneath.

Double Façade

The façade of Centre for Promotion of Science is a double layer of glass separated by a naturally ventilated corridor that increases dramatically the thermal insulation of the building. During the winter the external additional skin provides improved insulation by increasing the external heat transfer resistance. During the summer the warm air inside the cavity can be extracted when it is ventilated. It also lowers construction cost compared to solutions that can be provided by the use of electrochromic, thermochromic or photochromic panels, improving Energy savings and reducing environmental impacts. It multiplies the acoustic insulation, takes advantage of night time ventilation, while reducing wind pressure effects, allowing for spectacular levels of transparency without jeopardizing the shading protection.

Exhibition Hall

Cross Section 1/100

Cross Section 1/500

Longitudinal Section 1/500

Elevation 1/500

101126 OY

5

Construction. Big Box meets FastPark:

In order to optimize construction schedules and budget, two independent construction systems solve the entire building. The structure that supports the roof is solved with a generic and isotropic grid of columns, bays 15x15 meters cover with double system of unidirectional open web hoists, following the the standards of big box retail stores. The constructive solution for the roofing follows the same logic of light membranes adding a final layer of photovoltaic panels. This affordable solution – aprox. 500 €/ m² – guarantees a fast installation and long durability.

The main floor, ready to receive larger loads, is solved using a variation of the fastpark system, a 5.0m x 5.0m system of galvanized pillars and beams create the structural steel frame covered by a deck surface composed of 2.5m x 5.0m paving slabs in reinforced concrete. Its installation is even faster than the roofing, even if its cost is slightly higher – aprox. 700 €/ m² – but ensures the possible removal ofs part of the slabs to increase the ceiling high from 5 to 10 meters for exceptional exhibitions. This system, extensively deployed all along Europe, is also used in to solve the Ring.

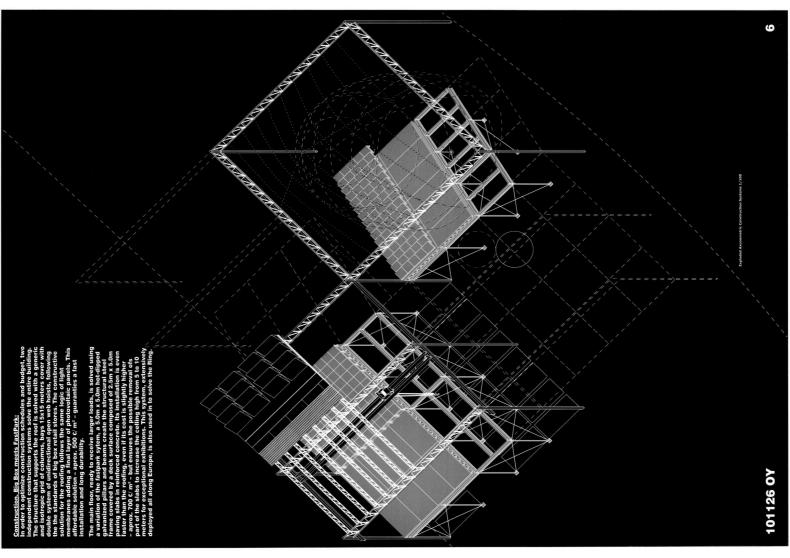

Exploded Axonometric Construction Systems 1/100

101126 OY

Whiteness Icon:

The facade a double layer of translucent materials – from glass to steal meshes, from fabric to Pet membranes — varies its materiality depending on the orientation, optimizing its energetic performance. Yet the 1:2 meter module remains constant, as well as is pristine whiteness.

Image P1

Image P2

Image P3

101126 OY

212

Museum of Contemporary | KWK PROMES

Client : Urząd Miejski Wrocławia
Authors : Robert Konieczny, Katarzyna Furgalinska, Michał Lisinski
Total Usable Area : 22,290m²
Location Wrocław, Poland

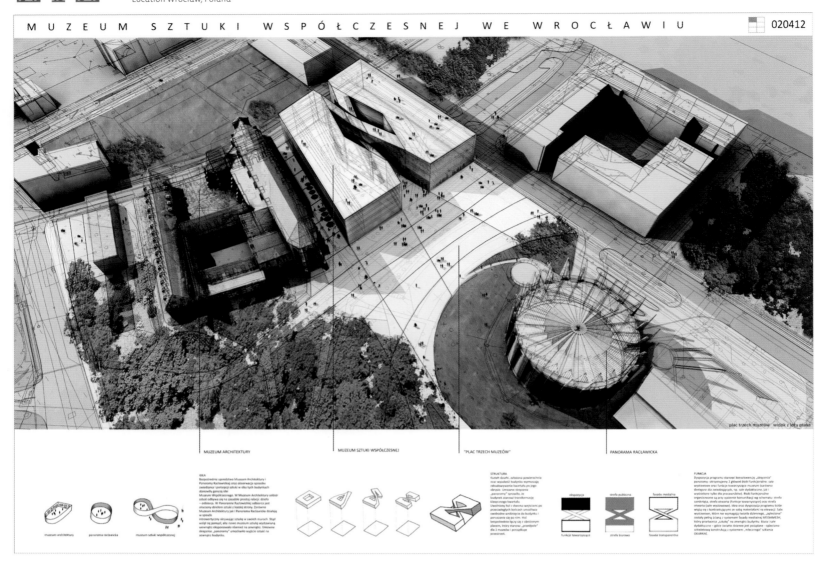

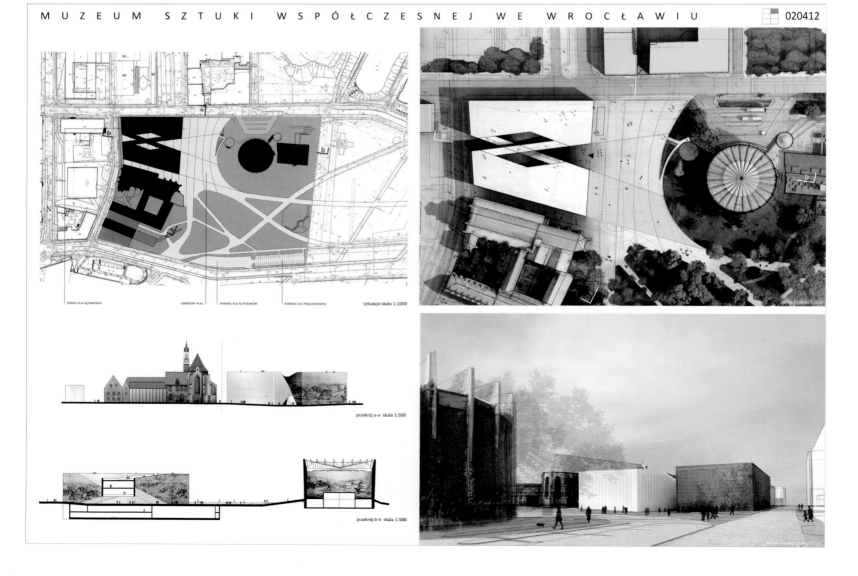

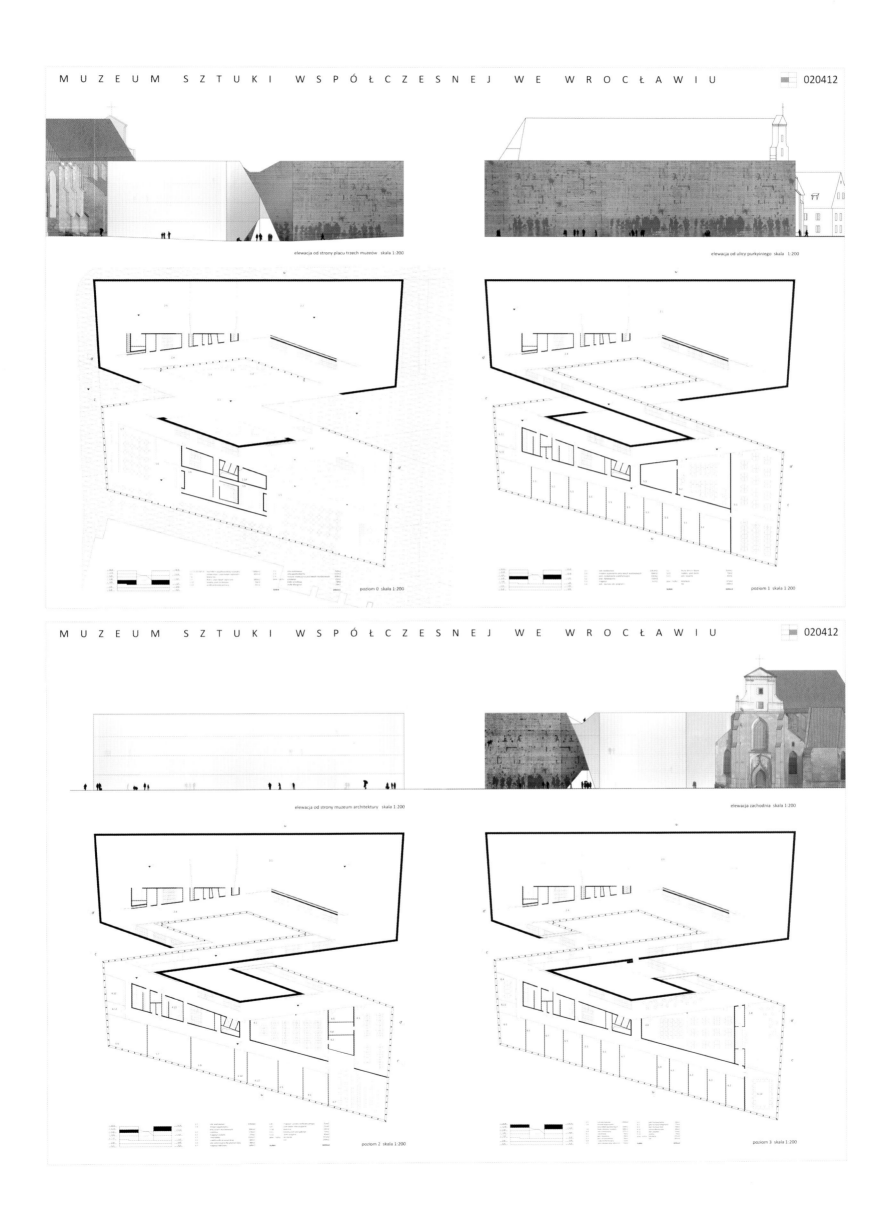

MUZEUM SZTUKI WSPÓŁCZESNEJ WE WROCŁAWIU   020412

elewacja od strony placu trzech muzeów skala 1:200

elewacja od ulicy purkyniego skala 1:200

poziom 0 skala 1:200

poziom 1 skala 1:200

MUZEUM SZTUKI WSPÓŁCZESNEJ WE WROCŁAWIU   020412

elewacja od strony muzeum architektury skala 1:200

elewacja zachodnia skala 1:200

poziom 2 skala 1:200

poziom 3 skala 1:200

M U Z E U M   S Z T U K I   W S P Ó Ł C Z E S N E J   W E   W R O C Ł A W I U

020412

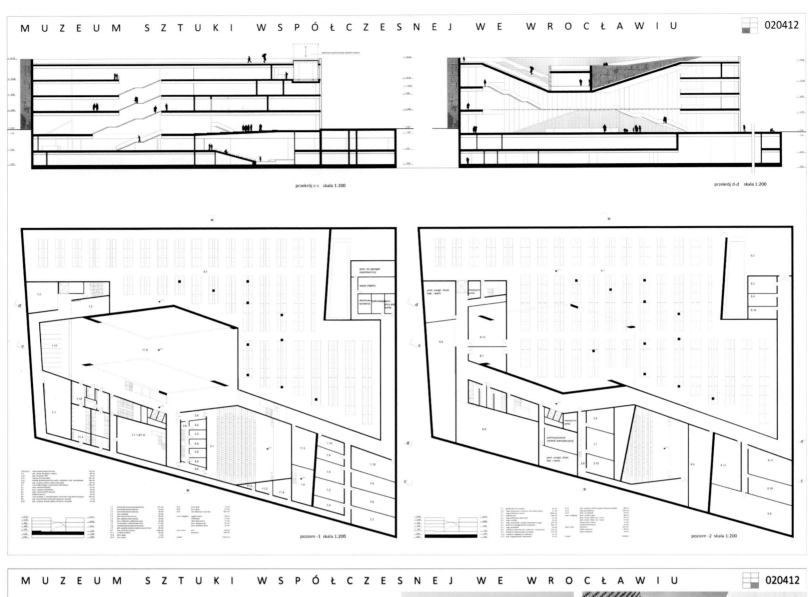

przekrój c-c skala 1:200

przekrój d-d skala 1:200

poziom -1 skala 1:200

poziom -2 skala 1:200

M U Z E U M   S Z T U K I   W S P Ó Ł C Z E S N E J   W E   W R O C Ł A W I U

020412

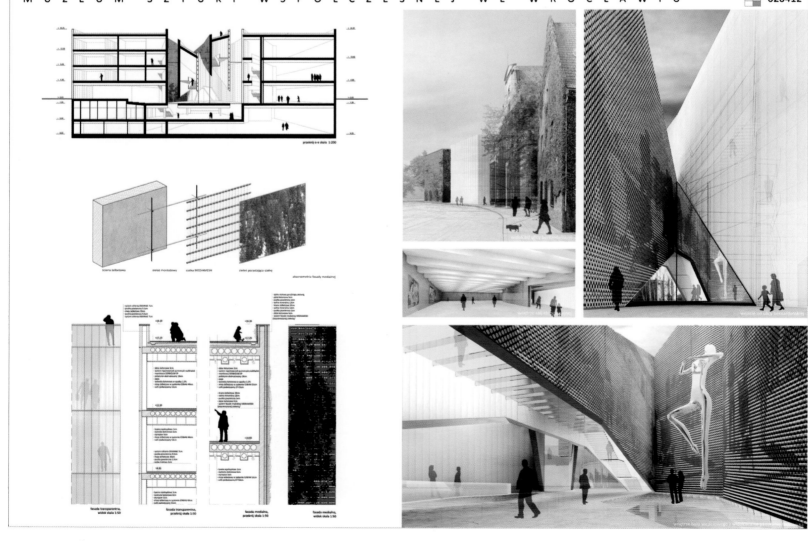

National Museum Przelomy | *KWK PROMES*

Cubic capacity : 15,845m²
Location : Szczecin, Poland

Client : National Museum in Szczecin
Authors : Robert Konieczny, Dorota Żurek, Katarzyna Furgalińska
Total usable area : 1,924m²

OBIEKT KOMUNIKACJI HISTORYCZNEJ **CENTRUM DIALOGU 'PRZEŁOMY'**

574003

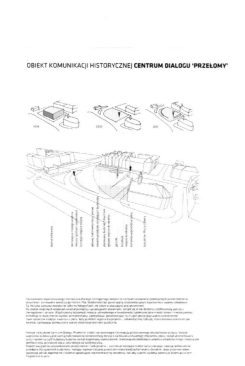

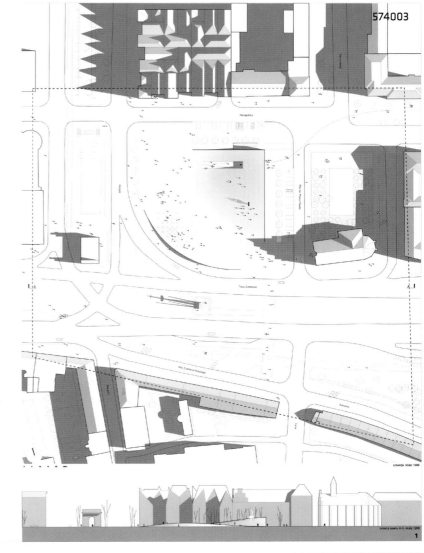

OBIEKT KOMUNIKACJI HISTORYCZNEJ **CENTRUM DIALOGU 'PRZEŁOMY'**

574003

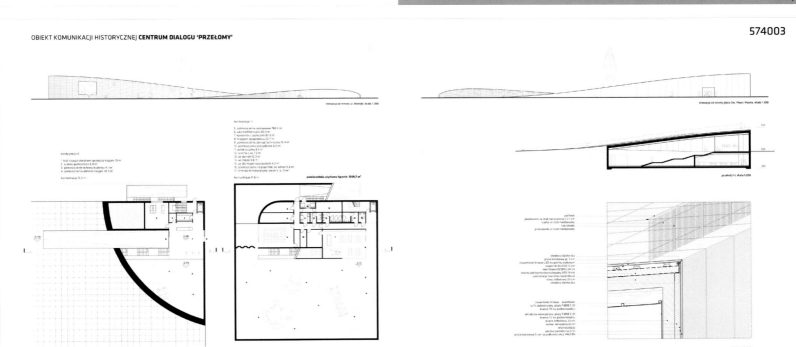

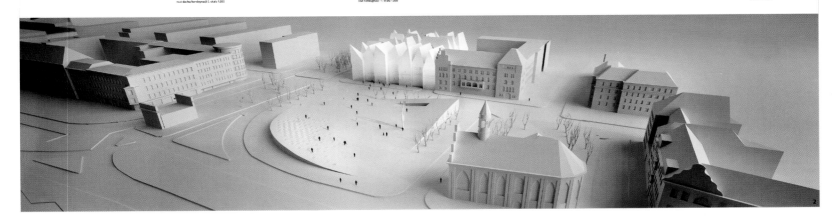

WONDERGROUND
THEATRE OF THE WORLD: STATENS NATHURHISTORISKE MUSEUM

"Al udvikling starter med forundring"
Socrates

Et Wunderkammer, eller på dansk: rarietetskabinet, var i renessancens europa betegnelsen på encyklopædiske samlinger af objekter hvis kategoriske grenser ikke endnu var definerede og kortlagte. I moderne terminologi kan man kategorisere objekterne som tilhørende den naturhistoriske verden (dog nogle gange forfalskede), etnografi, arkeologi, religiøse eller historiske relikvier, kunstværker og antikviteter. Wunderkammeret blev set på som værende et mikrokosmos eller et verdensteater og ikke mindst et hukommelsesteater. Det portrætterede symbolsk husets herres kontroll over verden gennem hans mikroskopiske reproduktiontil indendørs brug.

Et museum for de forunderlige skatte fra verdens naturhistorie, et Wunderkammer af objekter, lys og natur. Funderet nede i jorden, er det et fundet sted med masser af potentiale, der drømmende påkaller billeder fra arkeologihistorien, penetrerer jordoverfladen og inviterer os på eventyr ned i underverdenen. Det er et museum der legende inviterer den besøgende gennem poetiske lag af forskællige tider og skaler. Et dynamisk sted i konstant forandring i tagt med tidens, vejret og søsonernes rytmer. På magisk vis bliver vi ledet op mod overfladen, hvor man fra taget kan nyde de spektakulære omgivelser Botanisk Have tilbyder. Et museum der linker historierne fra de eksisterende museer, styrker minderne fra Københavns fortid og og byens kulturelle netværk. Et sted for samling og udveksling, for nysgærrighed og opdagelse. En scene for interaktionen mellem objekt, besøgende og rum. Et verdensteater.

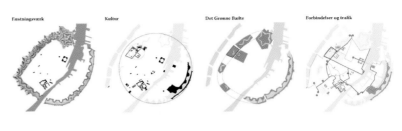

Fæstningsværk   Kultur   Det Grønne Bælte   Forbindelser og trafik

Stik fra Ferrante Imperato's Dell'Historia Naturale (Napoli 1599)

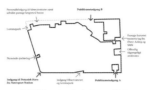

GRÆNSE - havens indhegning flyttes for at skabe kommer til offentlig brug.

ARKITEKTUR-

VÆKSTHUSE-

HISTORISK LANDSKAB-

FORBINDELSER-

MASTERPLAN

Samling

Overgang

Forbindelser

Udvikling

BYGNINGEN I LANDSKABET I BYEN

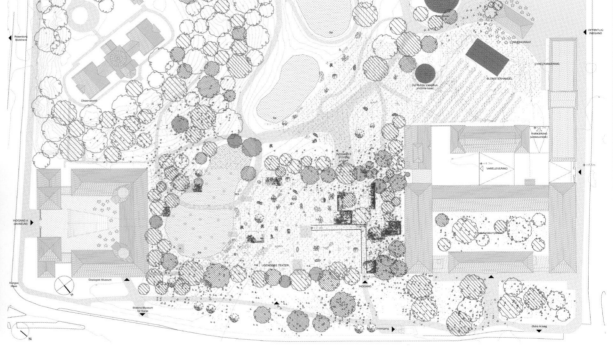

SITUATIONSPLAN 1:500

SNIT DER VISER FORHOLDET MELLEM BYGNINGENS TOPOGRAFI OG KONTEKST

KIG HENOVER MUSEETS HORISONTALE FACADE, DET GRØNNE TAG MED DEN NYE SØ OG GEOLOGISK MUSEUM I BAGGRUNDEN.

16214

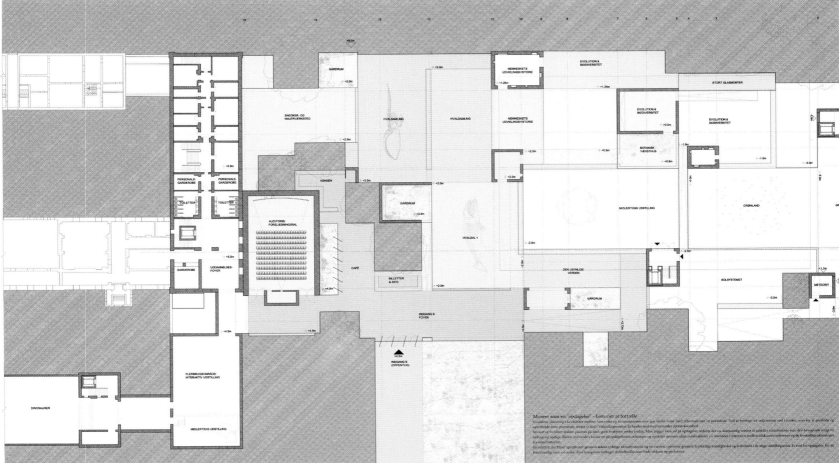

Museet som en "opdagelse" - historier at fortælle

PASSAGEN GENNEM MINERALSAMLINGENS GLASVITRINER DANNER EN FIN OVERGANG FRA DEN GEOLOGISKE AFDELING TIL DE NYE UDSTILLINGSRUM.

UDSYN FRA FOYEREN I INDGANG A.
HERFRA OVERSKUER MAN ISKÆRNERNE I GRØNLANDSUDSTILLINGEN OG STOREGENSTANDE I DEN MIDLERTIDIGE OG DE FASTE UDSTILLINGER

16 2 14

608

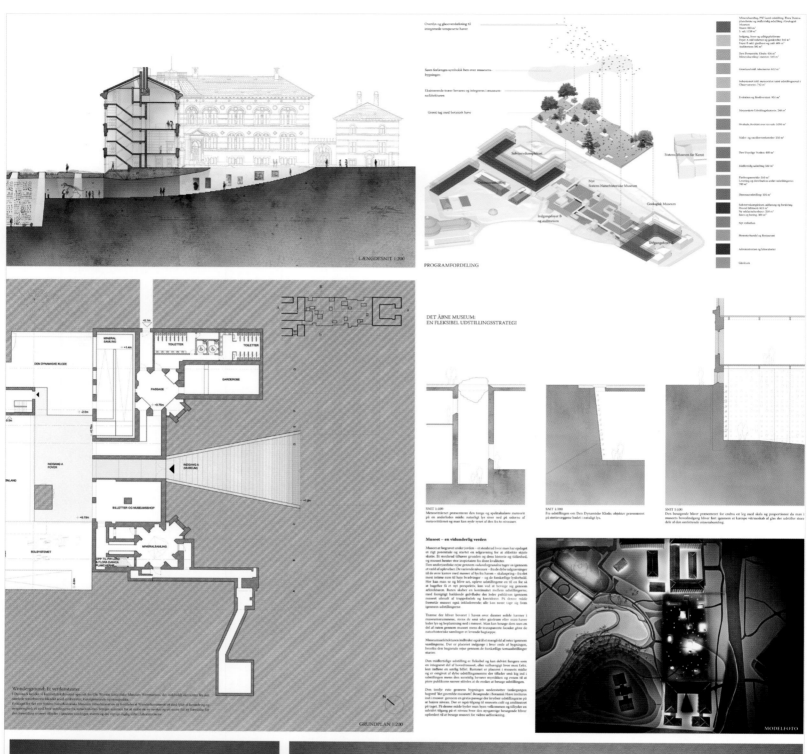

SAMLINGERNE PRÆSENTERES KATEGORISK OG GRUPPERET I TRÅD MED UDSTILLINGEN DEN DYNAMISKE KLODE, UDSTILLET PÅ STØTTEVÆGGENE OG SMUKT NATULIGT BELYST

KIG ETABLERES PÅ TVÆRS AF DE MANGE GÅRDRUM, OG DE FORSKÆLLIGE UDSTILLINGSOBJEKTER SUPERIMPOSERES PÅ ET LEVENDE BAGTÆPPE

16214

The House of Arts BEIRUT BEACON

A House of Arts. A House. A House echoing the form of traditional Lebanese Houses. A House sitting modestly between the glamorous highrises that mark the skyline of the City of Beirut. A Place of Art that starts by paying homage to the few remaining houses that are glimpsed by the visitor wondering around the streets of the city. Houses that bear the traces of the rich history of Beirut. A city that constantly revives itself after each outbreak of war or earthquake. Houses that beautifully surrender to the invasion of nature and to the decay of time.

This House of Arts simply starts by spatialising its own name to bear the spirit of these traditional Lebanese houses unique to the city. A house that wants to belong, through the spontaneity of its shape, to every citizen of Beirut and beyond. A shape or a line that every child could draw. A contextual House that speaks to the local and international Lebanese community, wherever they are around the world. Drawing them into its heart and becoming a Home. The House of Arts is an Open House that reflects the continuous under construction state of Beirut. It is an open structure. A Public space. A Place for continuous transformation. A place which expresses the passing of time through the seasonal changes of its hanging gardens. A House whose face evolves with the changing events in Beirut. Expressing information and events in the manner that the city displays its banners.

An Incubator for Activities and for the communication between the various arts it embraces around its public heart. A central open void. A space for the uncertain. A place for a varying public. An enticing void attracting differing fractions and origins. A heart embraced by the existing artistic networks of the city and inspiring new ones to grow. A space awaiting its visitors to fill it with their spontaneity. An intriguing space to discover. A place for reaching out into the city's events or just for laying back and enjoying an open projection.

A House that is a home for everyone - from Lebanon, the Arab world and Beyond.

Site Plan 1:1000

View to entrance from Existing Garden

View into Exhibition 1

1:500 Maquette (day view)

Floor Plans 1:500 and 1:250

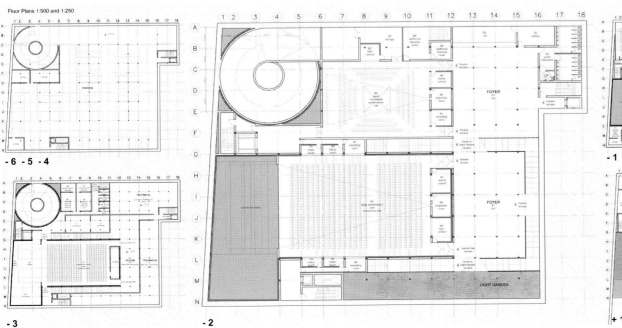

- 6 - 5 - 4

- 3 - 2

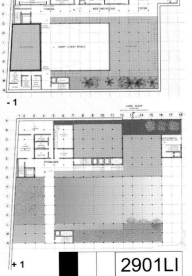

- 1

+ 1

2901LI

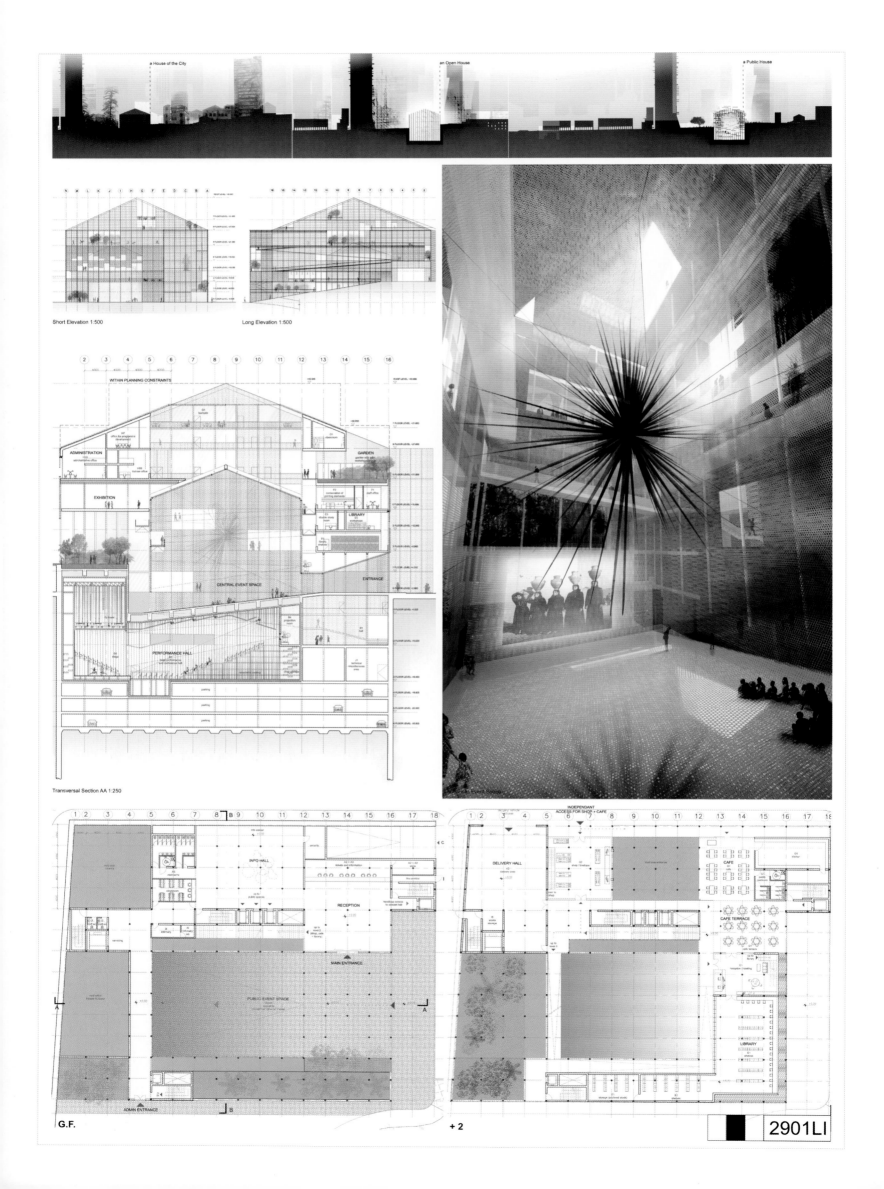

a House of the City   an Open House   a Public House

Short Elevation 1:500   Long Elevation 1:500

WITHIN PLANNING CONSTRAINTS

ADMINISTRATION

GARDEN

EXHIBITION

LIBRARY

CENTRAL EVENT SPACE

ENTRANCE

PERFORMANCE HALL

Transversal Section AA 1:250

INDEPENDANT
ACCESS FOR SHOP + CAFE

INFO HALL

RECEPTION

DELIVERY HALL

CAFE

CAFE TERRACE

PUBLIC EVENT SPACE

MAIN ENTRANCE

LIBRARY

ADMIN ENTRANCE

G.F.   + 2   2901LI

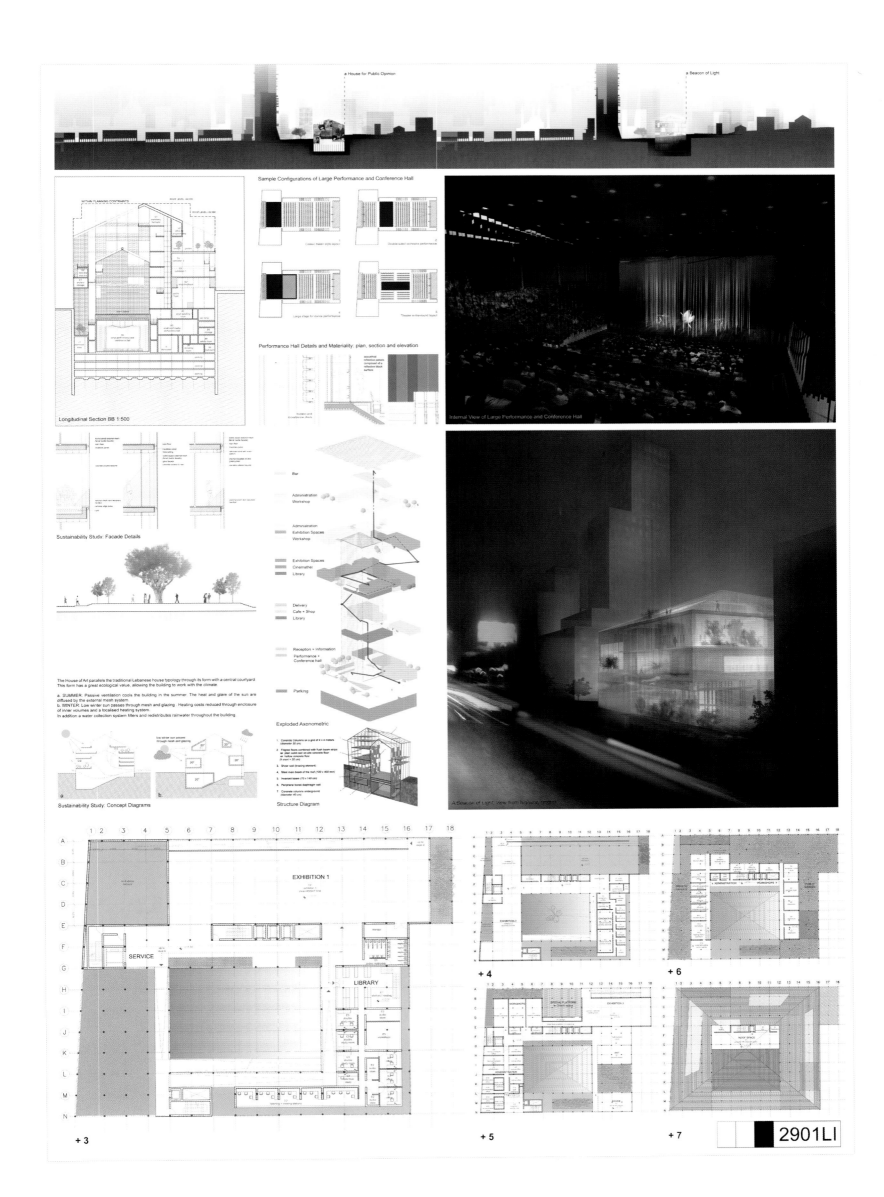

a House for Public Opinion

a Beacon of Light

Sample Configurations of Large Performance and Conference Hall

Performance Hall Details and Materiality: plan, section and elevation

Internal View of Large Performance and Conference Hall

Longitudinal Section BB 1:500

Sustainability Study: Facade Details

Bar

Administration
Workshop

Administration
Exhibition Spaces
Workshop

Exhibition Spaces
Cinematheque
Library

Delivery
Cafe + Shop
Library

Reception + Information

Performance +
Conference hall

Parking

Exploded Axonometric

The House of Art parallels the traditional Lebanese house typology through its form with a central courtyard. This form has a great ecological value, allowing the building to work with the climate.

a. SUMMER: Passive ventilation cools the building in the summer. The heat and glare of the sun are diffused by the external mesh system.
b. WINTER: Low winter sun passes through mesh and glazing. Heating costs reduced through enclosure of inner volumes and a focalised heating system.
In addition a water collection system filters and redistributes rainwater throughout the building.

Sustainability Study: Concept Diagrams

Structure Diagram

A Beacon of Light: View from Ivaivaba, project

EXHIBITION 1

SERVICE

LIBRARY

+ 3

+ 4

+ 6

+ 5

+ 7

2901LI

NTC Art museum | *B+U, llp*

Participants : [Principals] Herwig Baumgartner, Scott Uriu,
Team : Nema Ashjaee, Perla Aguayo, Steven Sun, Rebecca Gilbert
Partner : Schlaich, Bergermann and Partner (Structural engineer);
Transsolar (Energy consultant)

Project : Contemporary Art Museum
Client : New Taipei City Government, Department of Cultural Affairs
Typology : Museum
Location : New Taipei City, Taiwan

Construction Volume : 550,000 sq.ft.
Year : 2011

The proposed design for the New Taipei City Museum of Art (NTCArt) creates not only a visually stunning architectural landmark for the region and beyond, but also aims to redefine the museum typology, with a transformation from an exclusive territory for artist, patron and expert into a place that promotes art as a lifestyle and lifestyle as art: a "people's art museum."

The design embraces this concept by softening and removing traditional and spatial boundaries between the museum and the surrounding urban context. The creation of bright, relaxed exhibition spaces with plenty of daylight from above and large openings that frame stunning views of the surroundings—forming many visual connections between the city and the exhibition spaces—exemplifies this notion throughout the museum, establishing a visual dialogue that emphasizes art's ubiquity and centrality via the promotion of a seamless fusion of art and lifestyle.

On the ground floor, this connection is achieved by virtue of an open, outdoor lobby space—lined with shops, restaurants, art bookstores, and information centers—that is directly connected with the park. The museum is designed with multiple access points from the park, a large entrance plaza with drop-off areas for buses and cars, and a pedestrian bridge, which spans the creek and Huan-He Road, thereby connecting the museum to the city center. The landscape smoothly transitions upwards into the building while transforming into green roofs for the public service spaces below and creating continuous pathways from the park to the raised lobby space in the center of the building. From there, visitors are able to reach the top level of the museum through a center core that houses the museum archive, which becomes an active part of the museum. The core, expressed as an 85-meter-tall sculptural art vault that includes all main circulation elements, such as elevators and stairs, not only protects the art from exposure to sunlight and humidity, but also forms a central focal point as one moves through the galleries.

The exhibition spaces are organized in an upward spiral formation around the center core—a vertical staggering of the exhibition spaces that creates a large void above each gallery on the exterior and allows for natural daylight to enter through skylights above. The formation contributes to the dynamic and expressive morphology of the museum's envelope, which mimics this movement. The visitors are brought up to the top level with express elevators; after disembarking, they are able to wander back down in a spiral-like circulation through the different galleries.

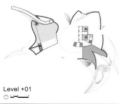
Level +01

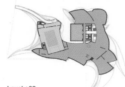
Level +02

Level +03

Level +04

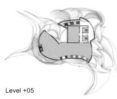
Level +05

Level +06

New Taipei City Art Museum, New Taipei City, Taiwan

B+U, LLP

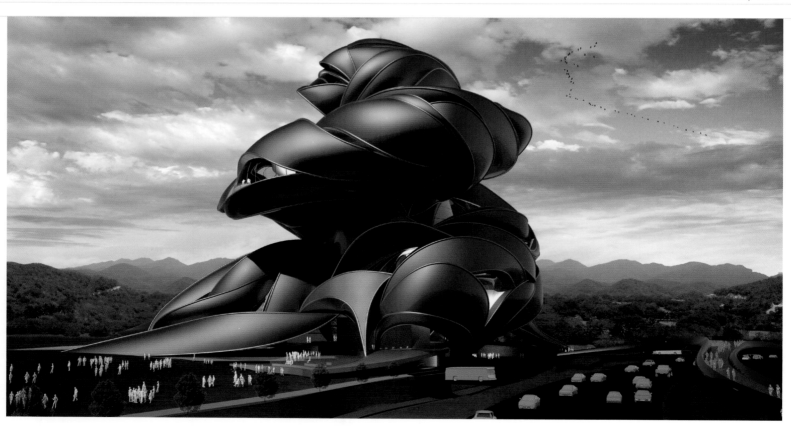

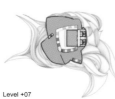
Level +07

Level +08

Level +09

Level +10

Level +11

Level +12

New Taipei City Art Museum, New Taipei City, Taiwan

B+U, LLP

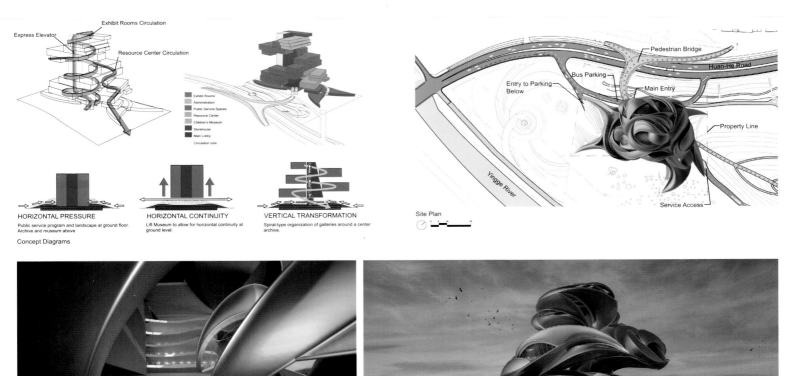

Concept Diagrams

HORIZONTAL PRESSURE
Public service program and landscape at ground floor.
Archive and museum above.

HORIZONTAL CONTINUITY
Lift Museum to allow for horizontal continuity at ground level.

VERTICAL TRANSFORMATION
Spiral-type organization of galleries around a center archive.

Express Elevator

Exhibit Rooms Circulation

Resource Center Circulation

Exhibit Rooms
Administration
Public Service Spaces
Resource Center
Children's Museum
Storehouse
Main Lobby
Circulation core

Site Plan

Pedestrian Bridge

Huan-He Road

Bus Parking

Entry to Parking Below

Main Entry

Property Line

Service Access

Yingge River

NEW TAIPEI CITY ART MUSEUM, NEW TAIPEI CITY, TAIWAN

B+U, LLP

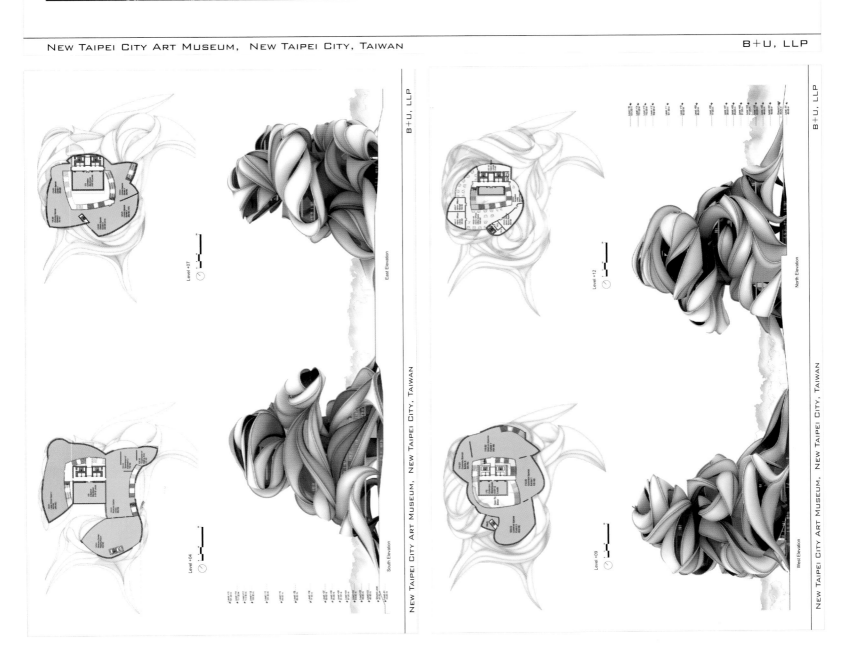

Level +07

Level +04

East Elevation

South Elevation

Level +12

Level +09

North Elevation

West Elevation

B+U, LLP

B+U, LLP

NEW TAIPEI CITY ART MUSEUM, NEW TAIPEI CITY, TAIWAN

NEW TAIPEI CITY ART MUSEUM, NEW TAIPEI CITY, TAIWAN

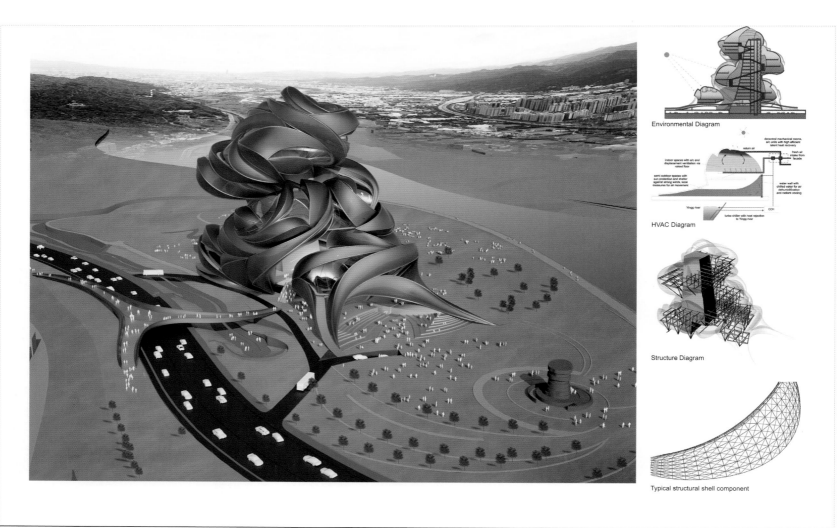

Environmental Diagram

HVAC Diagram

Structure Diagram

Typical structural shell component

NEW TAIPEI CITY ART MUSEUM, NEW TAIPEI CITY, TAIWAN

B+U, LLP

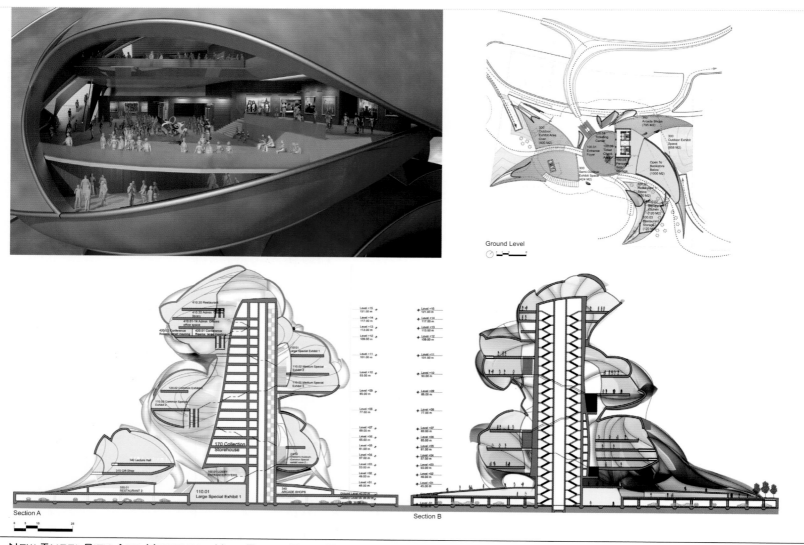

Ground Level

Section A

Section B

NEW TAIPEI CITY ART MUSEUM, NEW TAIPEI CITY, TAIWAN

B+U, LLP

wHY Architecture

9520 Jefferson Blvd.
Studio C
Culver City, CA 90232

Schéma de la Conception Architecturale, Connection Souterrain avec le Pavillon Charles Baillairgé, Illustration de l'Intégration du Nouveau Pavillon avec l'église, le SNBAQ et le Parc des Champs-de-Bataille, Analyse volumétrique des éléments du programme, Vue Globale du Musée et de son Intégration Urbaine

Participants : Sandra McKee, Hiroki Yoshihara, Carolina Buzzetti, Marcello Pacheco
Project : Supporting Facility for a Community Soccer Pitch with Stadium Seating, Community Room, Health Facilities
Typology : Sport Facility / Location : Buenos Aires, Argentina

Construction Volume : maximum Budget $50,000
Client : Architecture For Humanity, Nike Argentina

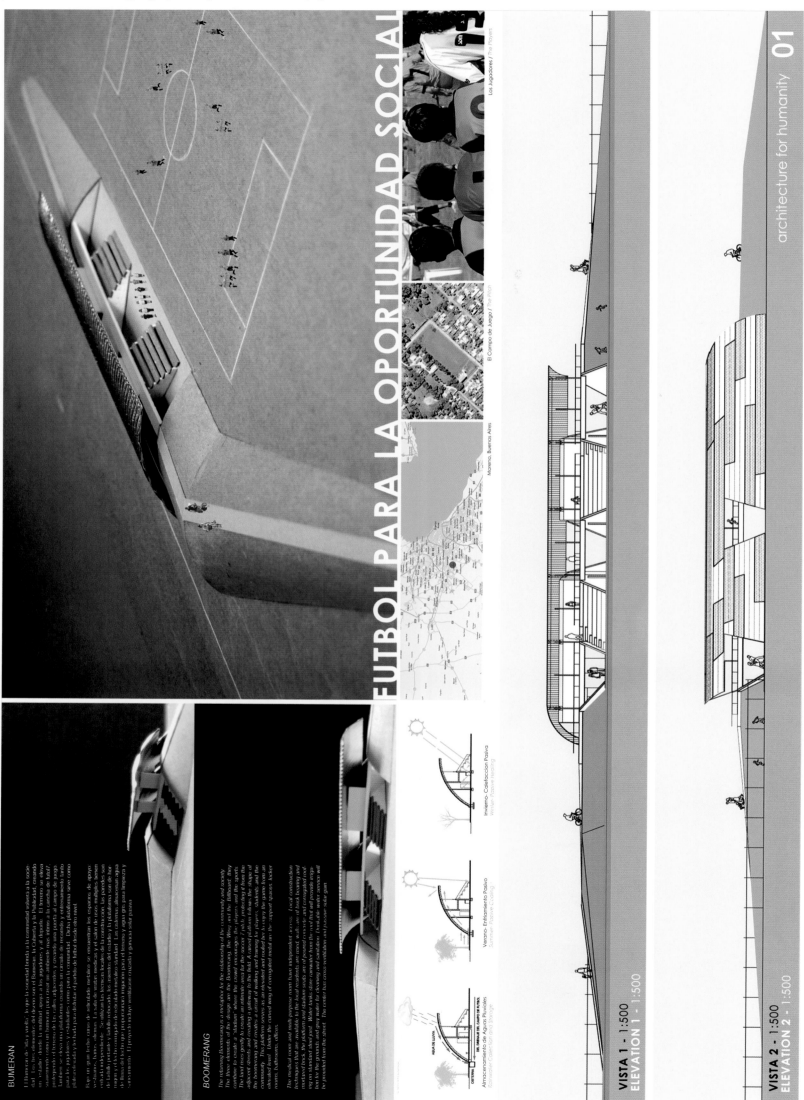

FÚTBOL PARA LA OPORTUNIDAD SOCIAL

Los Jugadores / The Players

El Campo de Juego / The Pitch

Moreno, Buenos Aires

Invierno - Calefacción Pasiva
Winter - Passive Heating

Verano - Enfriamiento Pasivo
Summer - Passive Cooling

Almacenamiento de Aguas Pluviales
Rainwater / Rainwater Storage

architecture for humanity 01

VISTA 1 - 1:500
ELEVATION 1 - 1:500

VISTA 2 - 1:500
ELEVATION 2 - 1:500

BUMERAN

El Bumeran de vida y vuelta, lo que la sociedad brinda a la comunidad vuelven a la sociedad. Los tres elementos del diseño son el Bumeran, la Cabecera y la Publicidad, creando un «estadio» donde la multitud apoya a los jugadores y el deporte. El terreno se eleva suavemente como un bumeran para crear un ambiente más íntimo a la cancha de fútol / protegiendo el terreno de las calles adyacentes y creando una puerta al campo de juego también se eleva una plataforma creando un círculo de encuentro y entretenimiento tanto para los jugadores, estudiantes, como para la comunidad. Dicha plataforma sirve como plataforma elevada y techada para disfrutar el partido. La forma del techo es un metal de hierro corrugado que proporciona espacios para el lobby, baños, oficinas.

Bajo un gran techo curvo de refractado metálicos se encuentran los espacios de apoyo que son comunes a los residentes locales y el salón de usos múltiples tienen técnicas de construcción locales de la concreto armado las partes tienen de la calla parante y ladrillo reforzado, los muentes, del esclato y la plataforma son de bar sangre y el techo son compuesto de techado metálico standard. Los cubierto, almacenan agua de lluvia del techo que proporcionara irrigación para el terreno y agua gris para limpieza y saneamiento. El proyecto incluye proporcionara irrigación cruzada y gana una solar piscina.

BOOMERANG

The returning Boomerang is a metaphor for the relationship of the community and society. The three elements of the design are the Boomerang, the Wing, and the Billboard, they combine to create a "stadium" where the crowd encourages the players, and the sports. The land rises gently to create an intimate area for the soccer / pitch, protecting it from the adjacent streets and creating a gateway to the field. A raised platform follows the shape of the boomerang and creates a circle of meeting and fronting to players, students, and the community. This platform provides an elevated and reached level to enjoy the game from an elevated level. Under the curved metal roof are the support spaces, locker rooms, bathrooms, offices.

The medical room and multi-purpose room have independent access. Local construction techniques that are available to the local residents are used, walls are of brick bearing and mortared brick, the platform and stadium seats are of poured concrete and corrugated roof on as standard sheet pool. Water tanks store rainwater from the roof that will provide irrigation for the grounds and grey water for cleaning and sanitation. Drinkable water services will be provided from the Street. The center has cross ventilation and passive solar gain.

617

BUENOS AIRES, ARGENTINA

architecture for humanity 02

LOS ELEMENTOS
THE ELEMENTS

LA CANCHA DE FÚTBOL
EL BUMERÁN
LA PLATAFORMA
LA PUBLICIDAD
EL TECHO

PLANTA - 1:100
PLAN - 1:100

1. VESTUARIO / LOCKER ROOM
2. BAÑO / RESTROOMS
3. BAÑO C/AN ACCESO A DISCAPACITADOS / HANDICAP RESTROOM
4. SALÓN DE USOS MÚLTIPLES / MULTIPURPOSE ROOM
5. COCINA / OFFICE
6. OFICINA / OFFICE
7. SALA DE VISITAS MÉDICAS / HEALTH VISITATION ROOM
8. ASIENTOS DEL ESTADIO / ROOM SEATING
9. CISTERNA / CISTERN

LADRILLO PORTANTE/
PARED DE REBOQUE/
PARED DE RETENCIÓN DE CEMENTO/
TECHO DE METAL CORRUGADO/
BASE PARA PARED DE RETENCIÓN/

PLANTA - 1:500
PLAN - 1:500

CALLE LEONARDO DI VINCI

CALLE S.M. DEL CARRIL

LOS MIEMBROS DEL EQUIPO DE ARQUITECTURA SON DE JAPÓN, ARGENTINA Y CANADÁ

1- CAMPO DE FÚTBOL /
2- CENTRO COMUNITARIO /
3- ASIENTOS DEL ESTADIO /
4- RAMPA /
5- PLATAFORMA /
6- BUMERÁN /
7- PLAZA PÚBLICA /

219

DGL Sportshall | *franz zt gmbh*

Function : Sports Hall
Location : Graz, Styria, Austria
Collaboration : Anna Gruber

618

wettbewerb dreifach-ballsporthalle graz liebenau

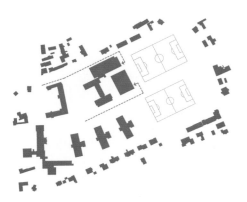

schwarzplan 1:2000

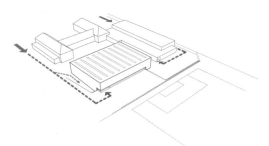

erschließung

der neubau steht als solitär losgelöst von den bestandsbauten und wird zum zentrum der umliegenden sportflächen. die besucher kommen über das natürlich ansteigende gelände. externe sportler kommen über die bestehende halle unterirdisch zu den garderoben.

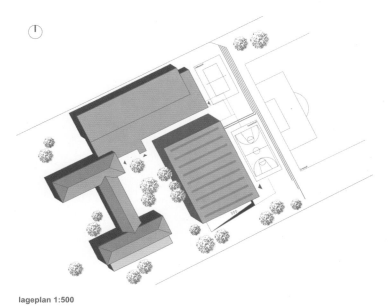

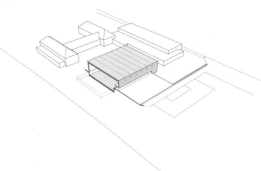

baukörper

die innentribüne geht über in die freiflächen und weiter in die aussentribüne. die über einem glasband schwebende hallenhülle ist als leichtbau konzipiert. die großflächig bedruckte fassade nach außen reduziert das subjektiv wahrgenommene volumen der halle.

lageplan 1:500

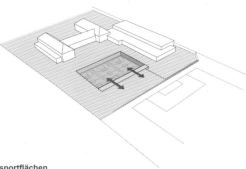

sportflächen

der bestehende fussballrasenplatz wird durch einen hartplatz für basketball und einen sandplatz für beachvolleyball ergänzt. die zentrale hallentribüne ist zu den freisportflächen verglast und ermöglicht witterungsgeschützte zuschauerbereiche.

freispiel

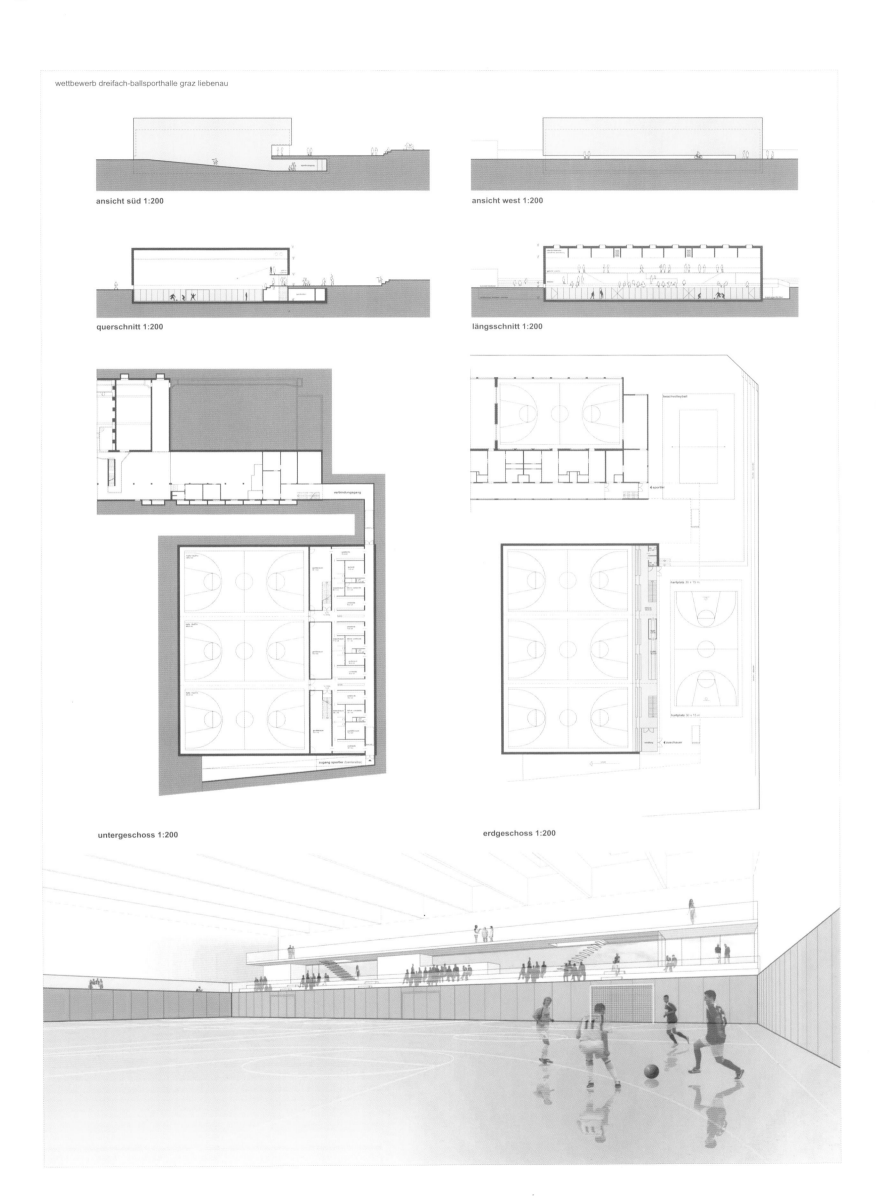

wettbewerb dreifach-ballsporthalle graz liebenau

ansicht süd 1:200

ansicht west 1:200

querschnitt 1:200

längsschnitt 1:200

untergeschoss 1:200

erdgeschoss 1:200

Site Plan
1:1000

Bird's Eye View

Top Aerial View

View From Akershus Fortress

Vestbanen Kulturatrium | National Museum of Art, Architecture and Design 9 0 0 2 6

4th Floor Plan
+15 M
1:500

security zone
private circulation
public circulation

6th Floor Plan
+25 M
1:500

security zone
private circulation
public circulation

open to below

2nd Floor Plan
+5 M
1:500

security zone
private circulation
public circulation
vehicular circulation
outdoor sculpture

5th Floor Plan
+20 M
1:500

security zone
private circulation
public circulation

3rd Floor Plan
+10 M
1:1000

security zone
public circulation
private circulation

1st Floor Plan
+0 M
1:1000

security zone
public circulation
private circulation

Tectonic and Material Strategy

The materiality of the building responds to the need of creating a stark contrast between the public open atrium and the rest of the project. Similarly as in the form and geometry of the building, the reflected and convoluted portions of the project are treated in a distinct manner. The exterior shell of the building will be finished in concrete and concrete cast panels. Fly ash will be utilized as a replacement for cement in all concrete portions of the project. This diminishes the environmental impact of the project.

Fly ash is a fine, glass-like powder recovered from gases created by coal-fired electric power generation. U.S. power plants produce millions of tons of fly ash annually, which is usually dumped in landfills. Fly ash is an inexpensive replacement for portland cement used in concrete, while it actually improves strength, segregation, and ease of pumping of the concrete. Fly ash is also used as an ingredient in brick, block, paving, and structural fills.

The roof/canopy as well as the manifold surfaces adjacent to the NMAAD main atrium are clad in custom made ceramic tiles. The color variation of these tiles follows five different tonalities to closely within neighboring regions and shifting from bluish grey, towards lavender purple. The gradation which responds to the interface points between the galleries and the movement systems adjacent to them so as to foreground the public areas and creating a quick sensation of dynamism when seen from outside.

Surfaces

Each shell is a compound surface that bridges six points in space, four of which are located within the circulation ramps connecting the galleries. The geometry utilized is that of minimal surfaces and complex manifold. The possibility of calculating this curvature counting with straight lines that conform the boundaries allow for a greater control and accuracy. The economy of means by which these surfaces are produced allow for the repetition of a same geometric family, where the issues, assembly, facets, and mechanism of detailing and assembly are the same, therefore allowing for a differential and yet serial logic of fabrication and assembly.

Visitors
Exhibition
Presentation, Library, Documentation and Art Depot
Workshops/ Studios
Vaults
Reception and Dispatch
Administration

Program Distribution

Courtyard / Core Access
Exterior Access
Interior Access
Interior Circulation Flow

Movement + Circulation

Vestbanen Kulturatrium I National Museum of Art, Architecture and Design 9 0 0 2 6

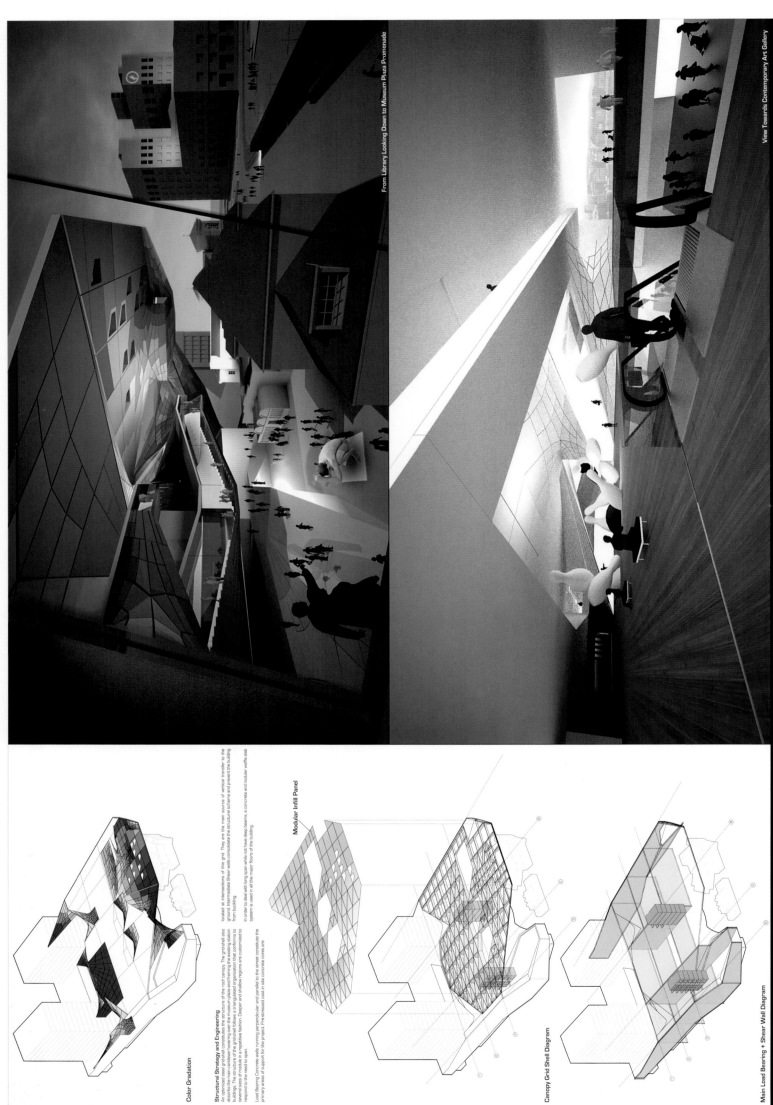

From Library Looking Down to Museum Plaza Promenade

View Towards Contemporary Art Gallery

Vestbanen Kulturatrium I National Museum of Art, Architecture and Design 9 0 0 2 6

Color Gradation

Structural Strategy and Engineering

An optimised steel grid-shell constitutes the structure of the roof canopy. The grid-shell also absorbs the main cantilever floating over the museum's plaza and framing the existing station buildings. The structure of the grid-shell follows a triangulated organisation that conforms to several sizes of module in a repetitive fashion. Deeper and shallow regions are customised to respond to the need to span.

Load Bearing Concrete walls running perpendicular and parallel to the street constitute the primary areas of support for the project. Pre-stressed cast-in-site concrete cores are

located at intersections of this grid. They are the main source of vertical transfer to the ground. Intermediate Shear walls consolidate the structural scheme and prevent the building from buckling.

In order to deal with long span while not have deep beams, a concrete and modular waffle slab system is used in all the major floors of the building.

Modular Infill Panel

Canopy Grid Shell Diagram

Main Load Bearing + Shear Wall Diagram

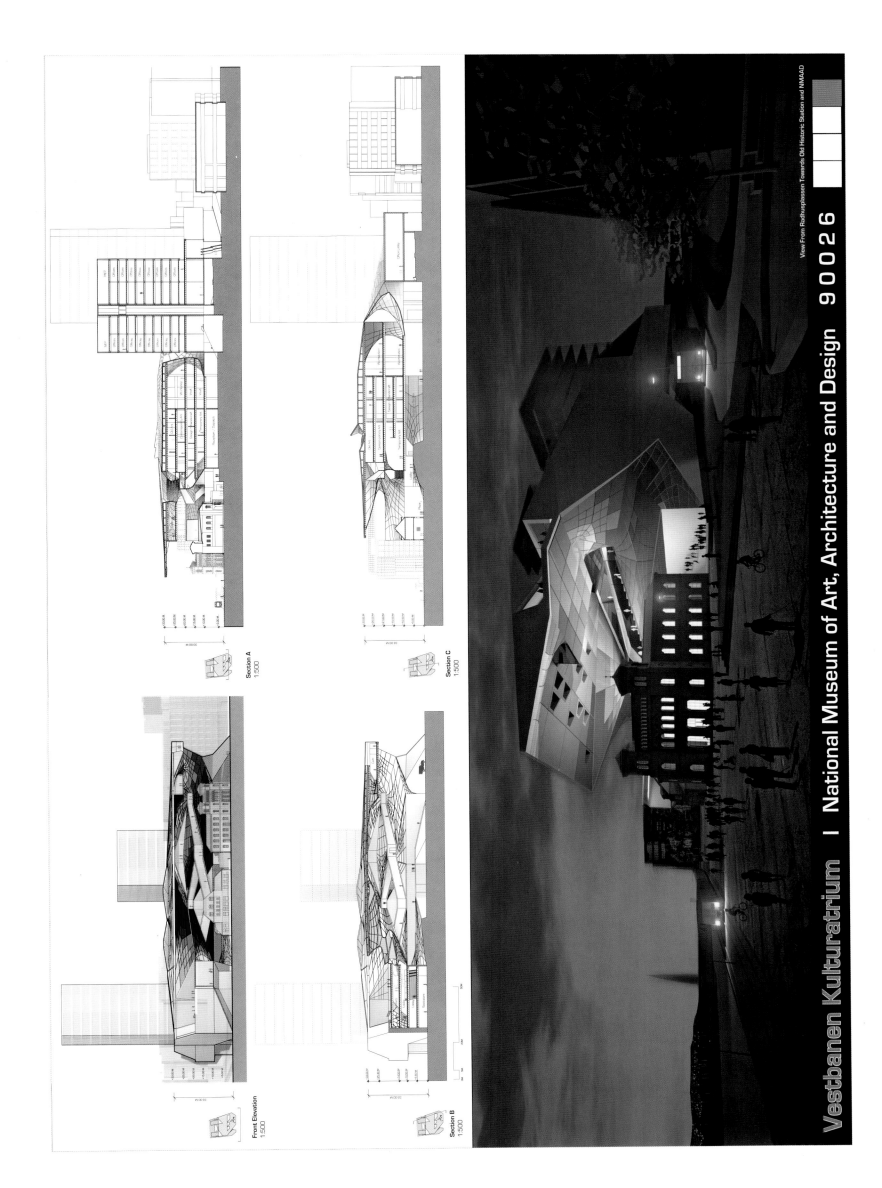

Front Elevation
1:500

Section A
1:500

Section B
1:500

Section C
1:500

View From Rødhusplassen Towards Old Historic Station and NMAAD

Vestbanen Kulturatrium I National Museum of Art, Architecture and Design 9 0 0 2 6

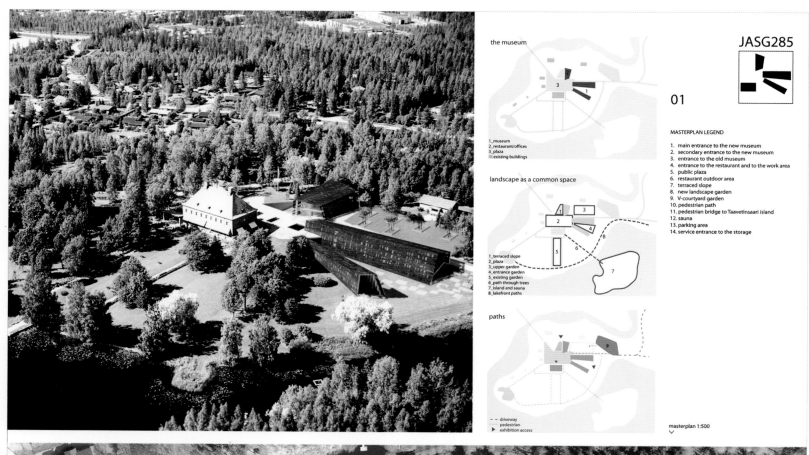

the museum

1_museum
2_restaurant/offices
3_plaza
▨ existing buildings

landscape as a common space

1_terraced slope
2_plaza
3_upper garden
4_entrance garden
5_existing garden
6_path through trees
7_island and sauna
8_lakefront paths

paths

‒ ‒ driveway
⋯⋯ pedestrian
▼ exhibition access

MASTERPLAN LEGEND

1. main entrance to the new museum
2. secondary entrance to the new museum
3. entrance to the old museum
4. entrance to the restaurant and to the work area
5. public plaza
6. restaurant outdoor area
7. terraced slope
8. new landscape garden
9. V-courtyard garden
10. pedestrian path
11. pedestrian bridge to Taavetinsaari island
12. sauna
13. parking area
14. service entrance to the storage

masterplan 1:500

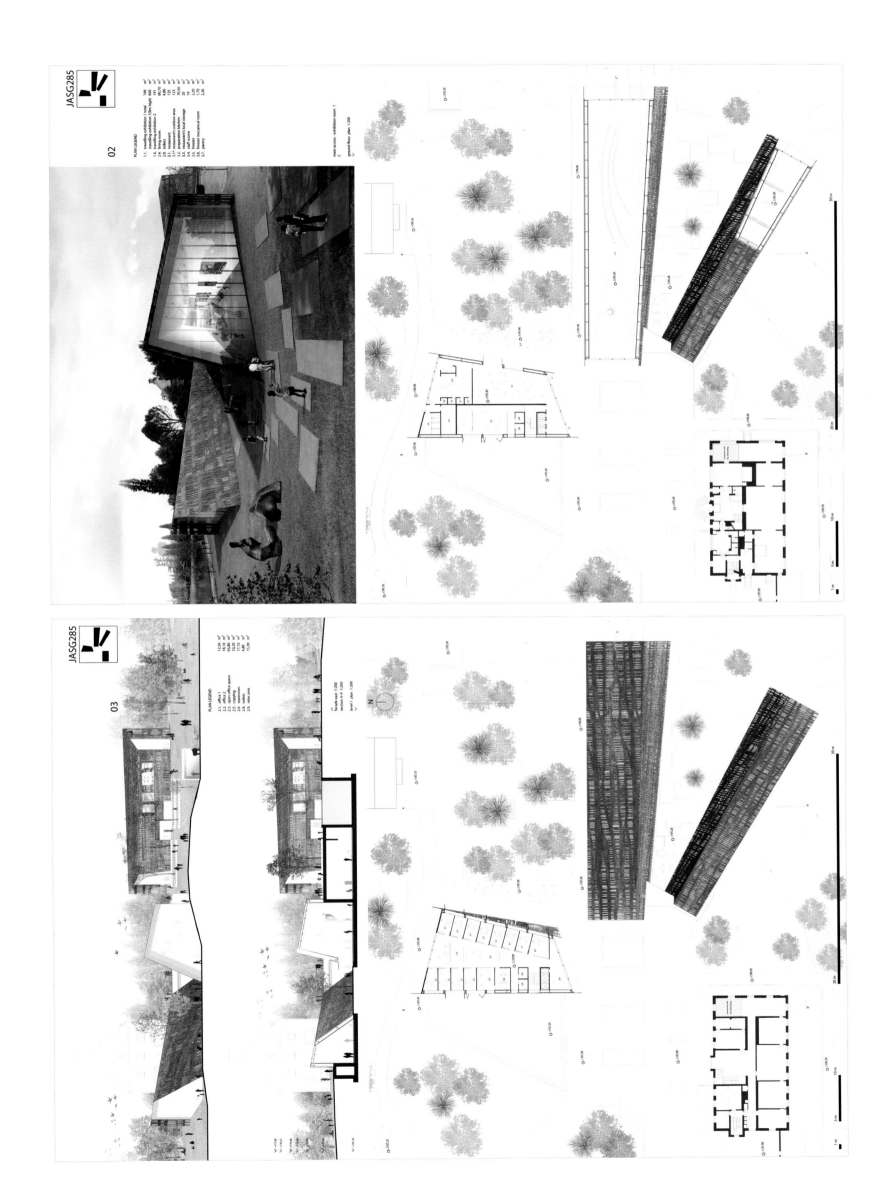

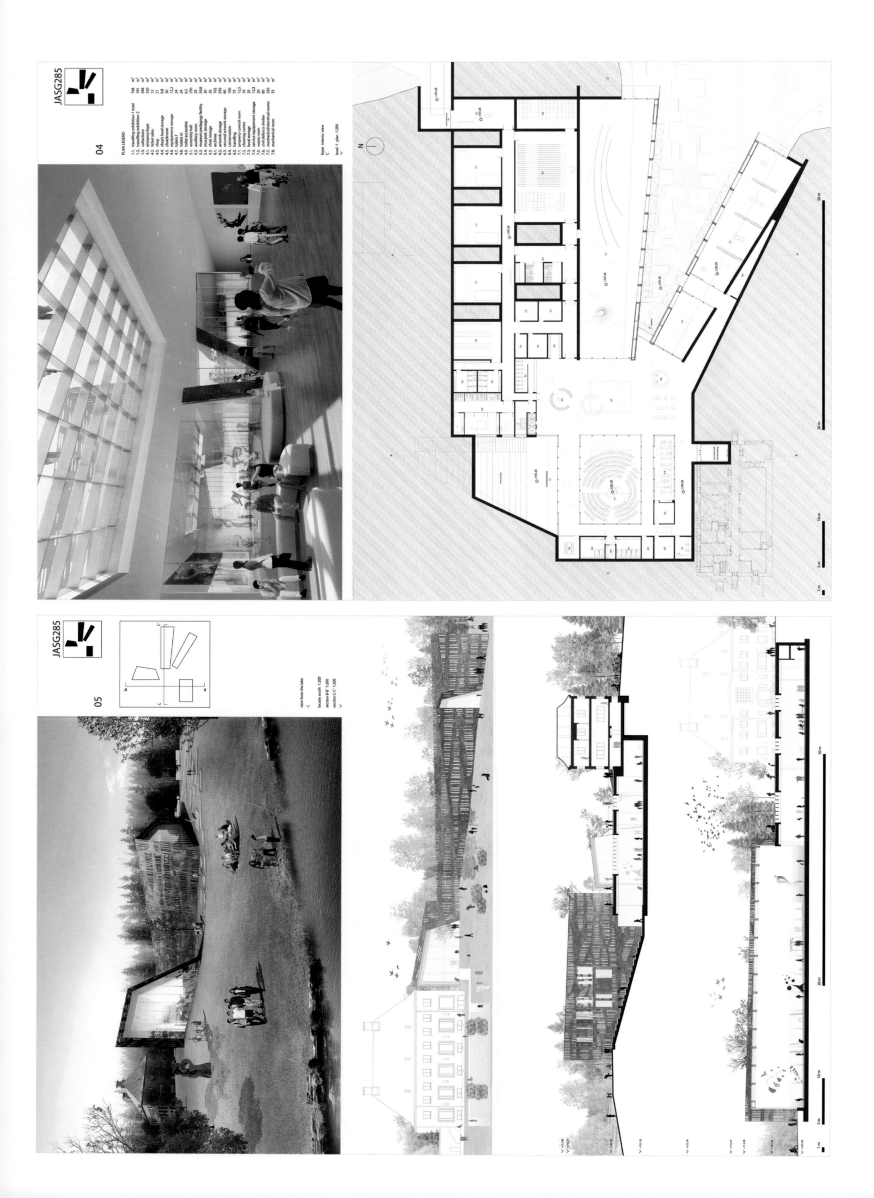

JASG285

04

PLAN LEGEND

1.1. travelling exhibition 1 total   748 m²
1.2. travelling exhibition 2   191 m²
1.3. collections   298 m²
4.1. entrance foyer   350 m²
4.2. ticket sales   12 m²
4.3. shop   21 m²
4.4. dough/food storage   30 m²
4.5. equipment storage   9.8 m²
4.6. cloakroom   12.3 m²
4.7. toilet m   24 m²
4.8. toilet accessible   6.5 m²
4.9. assembly room   250 m²
5.1. auxiliary room   20 m²
5.2. museum pedagogy facility   59.8 m²
5.3. workshop   20 m²
5.4. event storage   20 m²
5.5. chair storage   80 m²
6.1. archive   182 m²
6.2. secured artwork storage   250 m²
6.3. restoration   30 m²
6.4. handling   71 m²
6.5. food storage   12.3 m²
7.1. property control room   20 m²
7.2. building centre   20 m²
7.3. service equipment storage   12.3 m²
7.4. food storage   80 m²
7.5. civil defence shelter   250 m²
7.6. mechanical/electrical rooms   250 m²
7.8. mechanical room   35 m²

foyer interior view

level -1 plan 1:200

JASG285

05

view from the lake

façade south 1:200
section B-B' 1:200
section C-C' 1:200

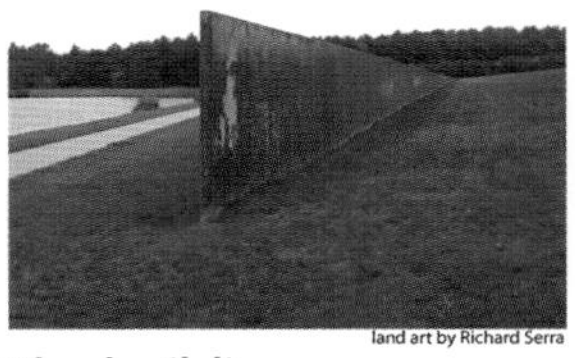
land art by Richard Serra

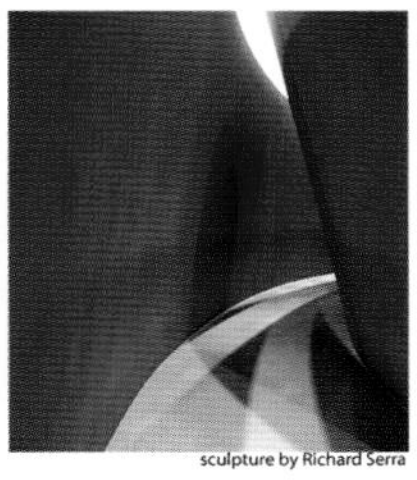
sculpture by Richard Serra

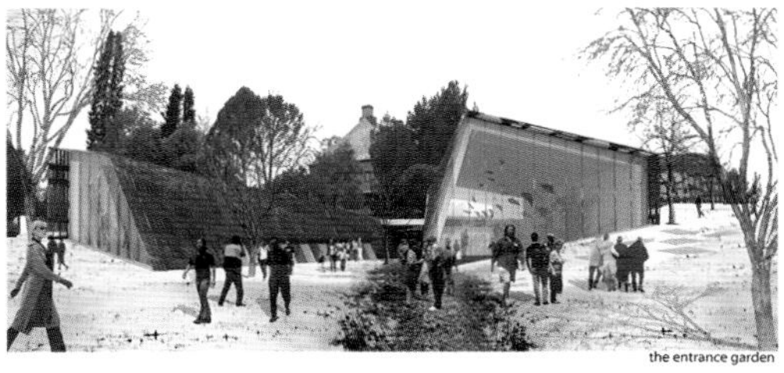
the entrance garden

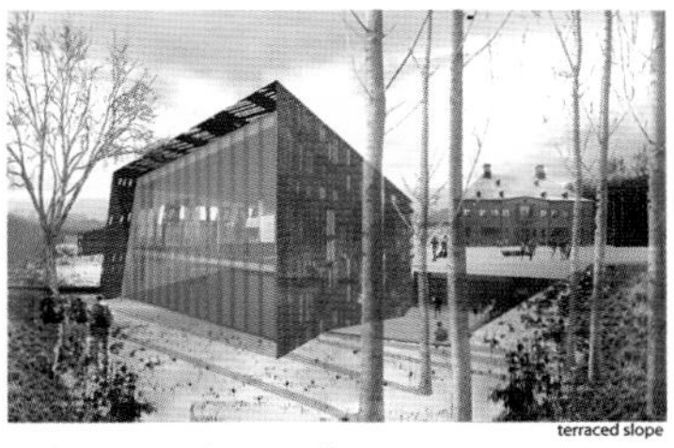
terraced slope

JASG285

The building:
a cut into the ground

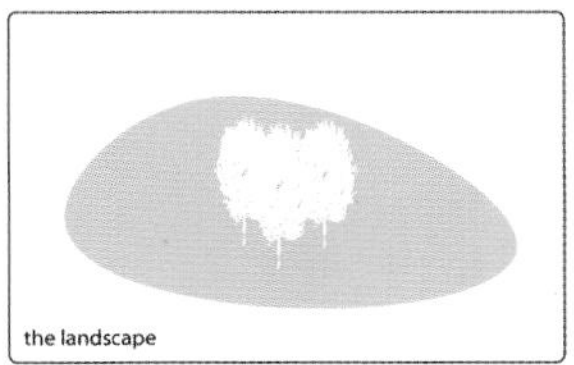
the landscape

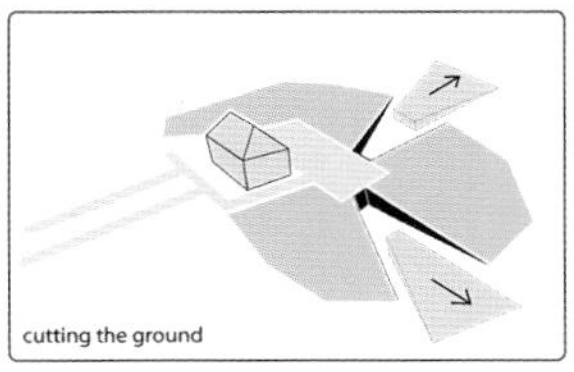
cutting the ground

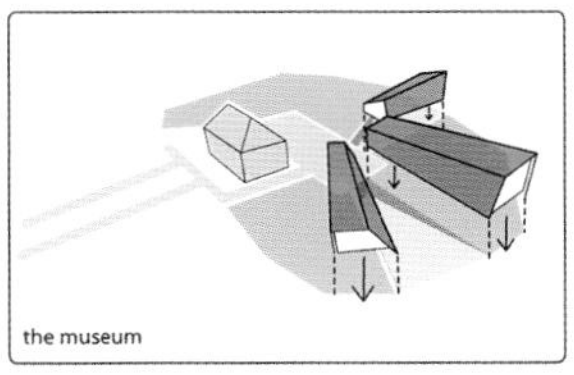
the museum

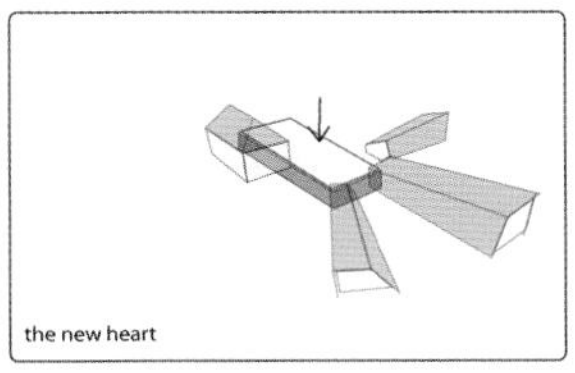
the new heart

The site suggested us the main idea to develop our design: since the beginning our clear intention has been not to propose just a building but a part of the nature, an open space system where **the building can re-activate the surrounding landscape.**

Architecture is intended as a natural extension of the landscape: **the project, inspired by land-art works**, creates an immersive experience among art, nature and architecture.

Walking through the landscape means exploring the museum, going through the museum means immerging into the landscape; the outdoor areas are in fact a natural extension of interiors. The building designs and structures a new natural landscape, which integrates the existing one.

The open spaces will perfectly integrate the new part with the old one; a system of ramps, walks and gardens are also "solving" the different heights of the slope (due to the ground topography).

The placement of the building within the site is dictated by the **desire to minimize the clear-cutting of the existing trees**. The pre-existing buildings, the villa, the restaurant and the pavilions constitute a widespread system, a series of fragments with different importance; **the new museum is composed of three Corten steel volumes** arranged in a way to consolidate this system, enhancing the relationship system among the various elements.

The offices and museum spaces have different orientations, they dialogue with the open space and constitute its ideal extension. The space that holds all the elements together, the very **heart of the project is the plaza** at the same level of the entrance to the villa, which stands above the foyer.

The new heart of the museum works on two superimposed levels:

- an open heart: the square which structures and holds together all the volumes, the Joenniemi manor, the new museum and the existing pavilions.
- a closed heart: the foyer, connecting all the old and new exhibition spaces, the offices, the restaurant and the storage areas.

The plaza: it is the access to the old building Joenniemi manor, it is the outdoor natural extension of the foyer; the restaurant looks out on it and from here all paths branch out, connecting to the park and to the lakefront area. From here, following the line of existing trees facing east, through a pedestrian bridge it is possible to reach the sauna located on the Taavetsinari island.

The square is punched by different dimension skylights, which guarantee the right illumination to the internal foyer space and, by night, they light the roofs on, turning them into public spaces, new marks into a shifting landscape.

The entrance garden: "trapped" between the two Corten steel facades, it leads visitors to the entrance of the new museum directly at foyer level, beneath the main square.

This garden works as a museum inner courtyard and it can become a real extension of the interior exhibition spaces.

On the entrance opposite side a **terraced slope** connects the foyer to the old restaurant and the pavilions. The stepped terrace will be used for outdoor performances and events, it constitutes an open-air extension of the conference room located in the foyer.

The **upper garden** facing the office wing is an area designed for relaxing and it lays right above the roof of the storage areas; trees will be planted in large pots placed between the warehouses.

The Taavetinsaari

The island as well will be part of the open spaces system, and it will be the **location of the sauna**, that comes back to its historical site. In this way the sauna acquires a special meaning because it refers to its original position, and it turns the island into a common discreet, space.

The lakefront, a place that now is not perceived as livable and pleasant because it lacks of attractive functions.

The pedestrian path along the waterside adds a strong quality to the fragmented building concept, allowing a high degree of permeability between the museum volumes, the lake and the wood. The different volumes of the complex will create new connections through activities and landscape.

The path through the trees becomes the junction axis between the square and the lakefront and, through a small pedestrian bridge, it extends on the island, where the sauna is placed.

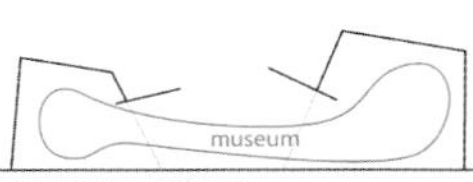

indoor / outdoor as a continuous exhibition space

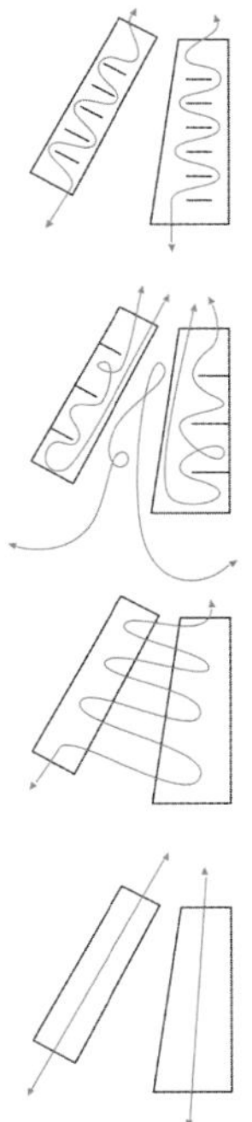
flexibility of spaces

The museum is organized into two 7x60 ml volumes, characterized by different heights, where a dimension predominates the other so to create a linear, continuous path. In both rooms it will be possible to use one of the long sides throughout all its length; the extremely flexible space can also be arranged through partitions perpendicular to the long side in order to establish a succession of variable size rooms, in case required by functional display needs.

urban and social sustainability

Our purpose is to design a sustainable Museum therefore it is very important for us to point out in the first place what is the meaning and the importance we give to sustainability. There are many acceptance of sustainability among which, of course, the ecological one. The sustainability we want to emphasize is the social sustainability. Since the beginning we conceived this project not simply as a new building but as a **system of open and closed spaces**.

Currently the museum has a small number of visitors, the new building through the use of open space will increase the accommodation in the area, taking advantage of the attractiveness of the park and outdoor exhibition spaces.

The new Museum wants to be the starting point for a life style, where the designed space is not simply the place to look at art but rather the **place of connections**, **relationships and cultural exchange**, an alive space where balances are different and changeable depending on users activities.

the building and energy saving system

Designing in a sustainable way is necessary to adjust the resource consumption as energy, water and waste; to review systems, processes and to reduce the impact of the structure on the environment, working on the thermal envelope as a main device for limiting energy consumption to the end of winter, while modifying the heat load in summer. For that is very important to design buildings with high standard energy efficiency.

Taking the advantage of today's construction techniques, the Museum uses an external corten steel plates skin, protecting an internal totally glazed facade. During the winter, the double skin creates an air buffer which increases the building thermal efficiency and also performs an optimal cold winds protection, reducing the convection on the glazed façade and roof. Since the openings of the corten plates holes are adjustable through movable louvers, they will close to generate a proper double façade during the cold long winter nights. On the other way round, the corten skin will be totally permeable in summer, allowing natural ventilation and sun shading, drastically reducing the air conditioning's energy consumption.

The heat loss from the mechanical air ventilation is the primary energy waste for a building. The high thermal capacity of the ground and the possibility of heat exchange with the existing water reserve of the lake, could provide heat recovery and a much better degree of energy saving efficiency for the air conditioning system.

Although the consumption of hot water for sanitary purposes are particularly low, it would be possible, during the summer, to produce no cost warm water through the recovery of heat extracted through the air conditioning circuits from the rooms, even with the possibility of transferring this hot water to neighboring existing structures.

The design choices of a transparent building envelope maximizes the gaining of natural light. The artificial lighting system will interact with it and with the needs of use of internal spaces in order to save energy. The whole building lighting could be coordinated by an advanced system of regulation and control of light level, activating artificial lamps only when its needed and in an appropriate quantity, according to the actual level of natural light. Presence controlled auto-off system will allow a general optimization of lighting sources, while a maintenance function will modulate the light intensity, depending from the lamps' efficiency due to the life cycle phase of every singular one.

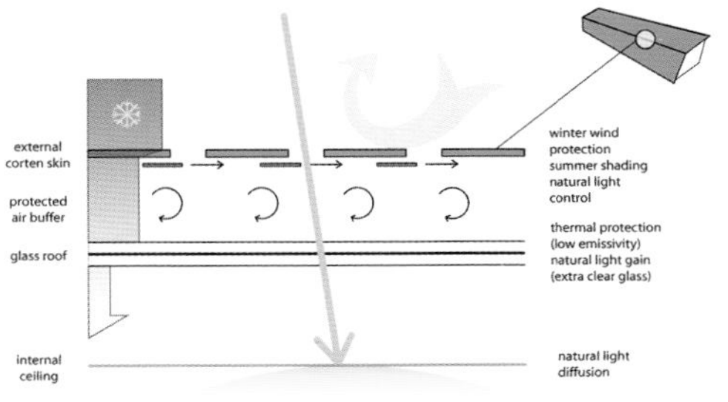

facade system

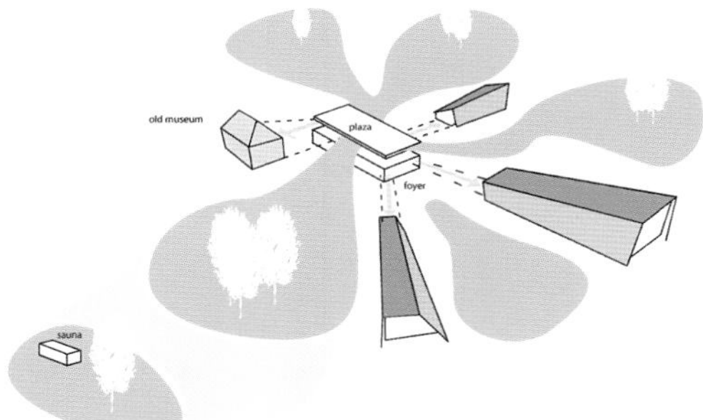

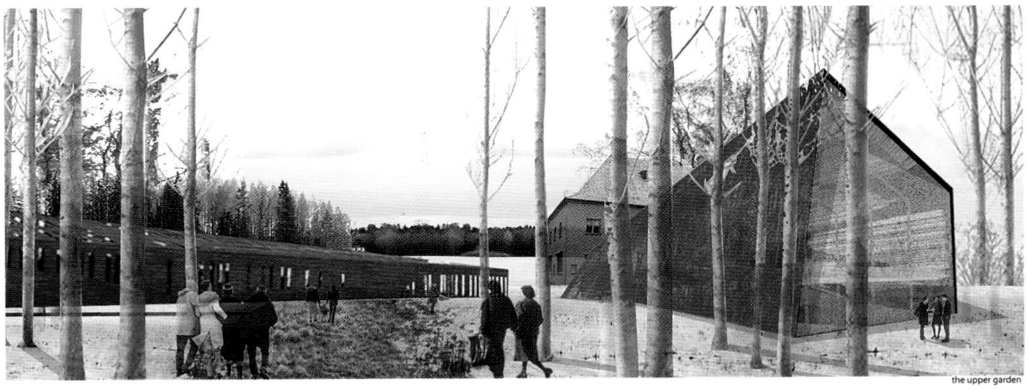
the upper garden

the landscape as a common space

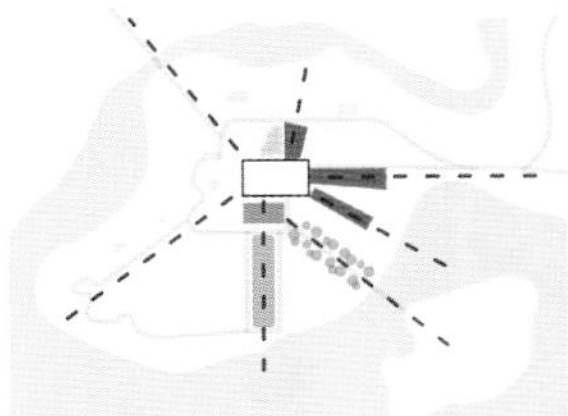
project guidelines

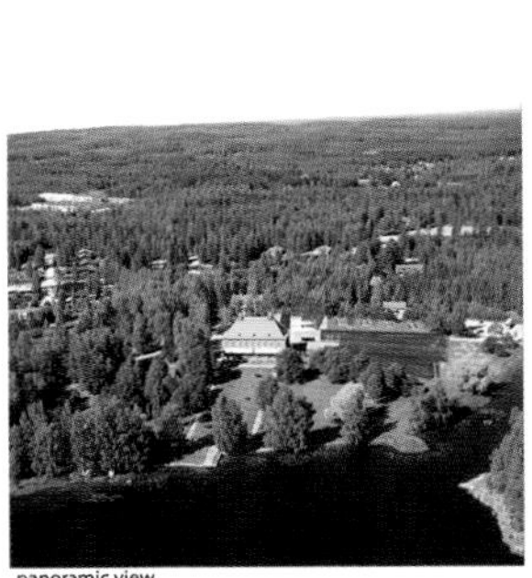
panoramic view

In our opinion, the existing landscape layout has certainly a big value, so that we decided to place the new building in a way to preserve the wooded areas and in particular the axis departing from the east side of the villa towards the island.

The design of the public space is characteristic of our approach to a project, especially when, as in this case, the building comes into dialogue with a fragmented fabric, full of natural suggestions. The common space (considered as the space surrounding the volumes) has a very important function in the project, since it's not conceived as void but rather as fulfillment of the indoor spaces and functions.

The building is not meant to be an iconography gesture that stands out into the nature but a **new part of the landscape** where public, semi-public and private spaces are mixed together and where outdoor and indoor spaces run after each other animating and every time renewing themselves by the users' experience.

The indoor exhibition spaces as well as the lounge area, find their own outdoor alter ego in the small squares, paths and ramps surrounding the volumes. The void builds up the structure of the project through indoor and outdoors connections. Each outdoor space have been designed and conceived to accommodate different functions and programs and, at the same time, to define an active connective tissue among the different volumes.

The access garden, the plaza, paths, the entrance steps to the foyer, the park, the existing garden: each open space has its own feature and quality related to a specific function of the museum.

functional+ design criteria

The fragmentation of the project into undifferentiated volumes responds to the "**reusable building**" concept. Each volume, accommodating a different function, is pretty much independent from the others, although they are connected to each other through the foyer, they can be arranged and organized in different ways. This means the complete fulfillment of each space potential in relation to the program and function it is suppose to accommodate.

The exhibition area is introduced inside the two volumes stuck into the ground arranged in a V-shape facing east; the entrance to the foyer of the museum is placed at the end, walking along the "V". From the foyer, where the ticket office, the conference room and the research area are placed, you can access to the exhibition areas in the house from one side, and from the other side to the restaurant, that overlooks the square. The first floor of the restaurant volume houses the offices.

From the foyer north side, through a large window, the visitors are taken to the stairs leading to the woods facing the main square, where the old restaurant, still operating, stands.

On the stepped terrace there is also the area dedicated to the restoration work, located adjacent to the warehouses bordering the main exhibition hall, 600 sqm with a constant height of 9 ml.

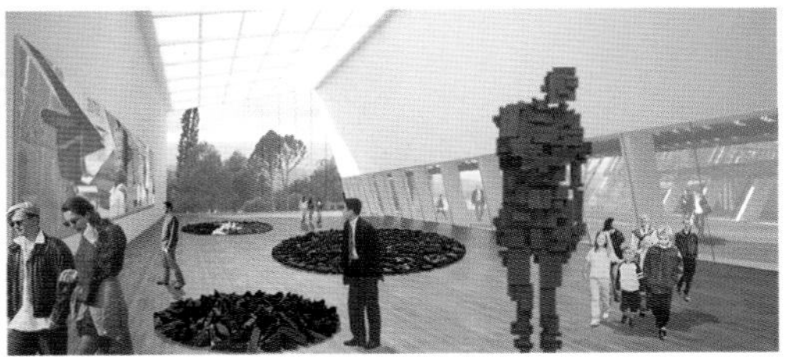

the natural lighting system

The fragmented design of the complex and the skylight will of course increase the natural light inside the volumes. We consider that a very good quality of the project especially because it will increase the flexibility of the art center and improve the quality of the rooms, particularly for the people working within the building. Natural light becomes a particular issue especially in the exhibition area, where a special darkening system has been conceived. Of course natural light has the optimal composition for people wellness inside built environment.

It is also an important issue the proper use of zenithal natural light for the inclined roof, avoiding direct light rays with a less glare, diffusing light device such as a special internal ceiling.

materials

The corten steel micro-perforated panels allow the natural light to filter inside the building, establishing a connection with the surrounding landscape, so that light marks the rhythm of daily time going by and the alternation of the seasons.

The glazed façades will be made by transparent and opaque glass. The transparent parts will be high performance glass which will need less maintenance thanks to the external skin protection.

By using recycled materials for construction (eg. recycled concrete, recycled plastic insulation) we intend to reduce even further the resource consumption giving an additional contribution to the sustainability of the new building.

The building techniques, based on structural frames composed by steel elements, will make the construction phase pretty fast and possible directly on site.

EXHIBITION SPACES: $1147 m^2$
OFFICES, CONFERENCE ROOM AND LIBRARY: $266{,}5 m^2$
RESTAURANT AND KITCHEN FACILITIES (SPACES FOR SERVICE FUNCTIONS): $241{,}1 m^2$
FOYER SERVICES (SPACES FOR SERVICE FUNCTIONS): $489{,}5 m^2$
CONFERENCE AND REPRESENTATION FACILITIES (SPACES FOR SERVICE FUNCTIONS): $369{,}8 m^2$
COLLECTIONS' TREATMENT AND STORAGE FACILITIES: $607{,}5 m^2$
OTHER FACILITIES: property management facilities: $414{,}6 m^2$
USABLE FLOOR AREA: $3360 m^2$
NET AREA: $4437{,}5 m^2$
GROSSFLOOR AREA: $4975 m^2$

" THE PANELS WILL BE SEEN WITH HUNDREDS OF OTHERS AND MUST STAND OUT. IT IS IMPORTANT TO HAVE A CLEAR AND EYE CATCHING IMAGES THAT BEST DESCRIBE THE IDEA OF YOUR PROJECT. "

222 Performing Arts Center | B+U, llp

Participants : [Principals] Herwig Baumgartner, Scott Uriu
Team : Nema Ashjaee, Perla Aguayo, Steven Sun, Rebecca Gilbert
Partner : Architektur Maurer (executive architect); Schlaich, Bergermann and Partner (Structural engineer); Transsolar (Energy consultant)

Project : Performing Arts Center
Typology : Multifunctional Hall
Location : Iserlohn, Germany
Construction Volume : 85,000 sq.ft.

Client : City of Iserlohn
Year : 2011

PERFORMING ARTS CENTER,   ISERLOHN, GERMANY   B+U, LLP

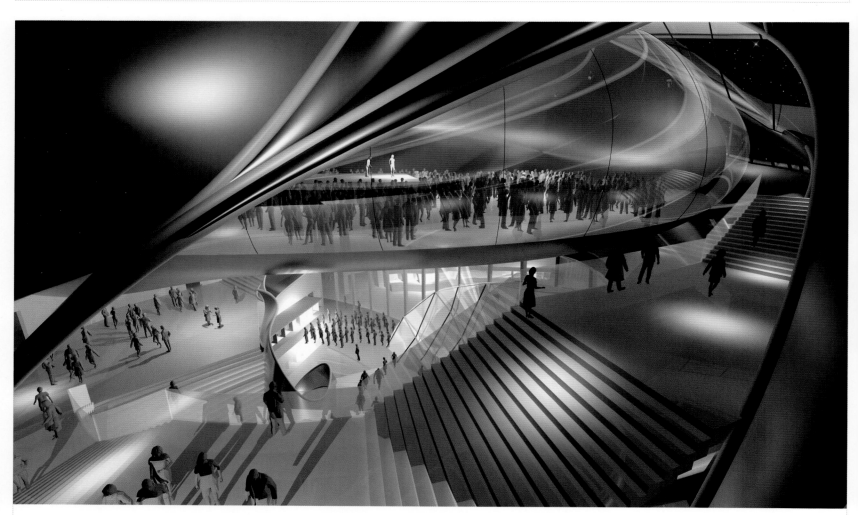

PERFORMING ARTS CENTER,   ISERLOHN, GERMANY   B+U, LLP

Lageplan

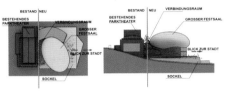

Entwurfs Konzept

The Performing Arts Center Alexanderhoehe in Iserlohn, Germany was an invitation-only competition that challenged entrants to redesign Alexanderhoehe, a large inner-city park, and add a multifunctional performance hall to the existing Parktheater, which is a classic proscenium-type performance space located on the park's north edge.

When situating the building on the site, it is important to redefine the urban relationship of Alexanderhoehe with the city center and to create a new gateway for the park. The proposal intends to position the structure as a landmark building for the city, particularly the region that is oriented towards its center, with the creation of a new pedestrian connection between the city center and the main train station. The design includes a large

public space that forms the plinth for the new hall and not only serves as the main entrance plaza for the theaters, but also becomes a destination and main access point to the park beyond.

The Performing Arts Center itself consists of three different types of venues: a large hall, adaptable to a wide variety of performances, for about 1,400 people; a small auditorium; and a multifunctional hall that can be rented out for balls, banquets, and other functions. The new Performing Arts Center forms a synergy between the existing Parktheater and the new multifunctional hall by virtue of a single, efficient, shared access point for visitors to both. In order to achieve this aim without blocking the existing views from the theater to the city center, we designed the

large hall to lift off of the ground, thereby creating a generous multilevel foyer space that connects all theaters with the entrance lobby.

This linkage space continues underneath the new large hall onto the plaza level and encompasses both the lobby and main entrances of both the old and new theaters. A central circulation element (a grand staircase) connects and provides access to the existing large hall on level five; to the existing Parktheater on level four; to the existing small theater and the small auditorium on level 2; and to the new multifunctional hall on the ground level, adjacent to the entrance lobby. The lobby space expands outside into a large plaza that is covered by the enclosure, floating above, of the large hall.

Süd Ansicht   Ost Ansicht   West Ansicht

PERFORMING ARTS CENTER,   ISERLOHN, GERMANY   B+U, LLP

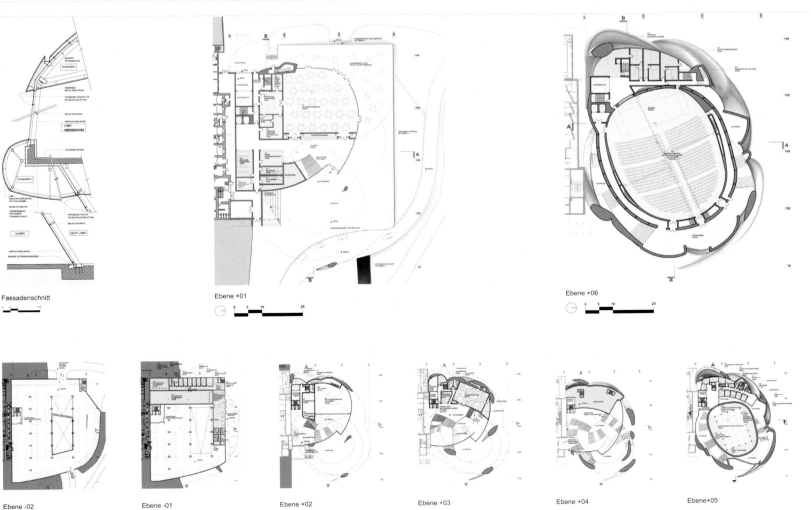

Fassadenschnitt   Ebene +01   Ebene +06

Ebene -02   Ebene -01   Ebene +02   Ebene +03   Ebene +04   Ebene+05

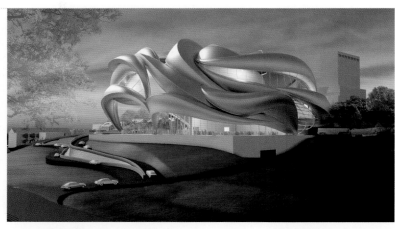

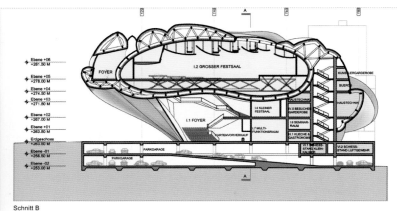

Schnitt B

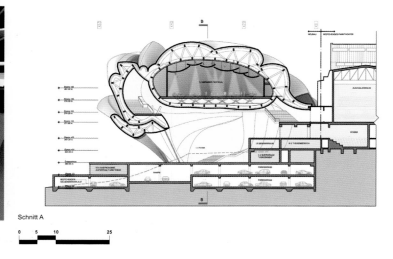

Schnitt A

PERFORMING ARTS CENTER,   ISERLOHN, GERMANY   B+U, LLP

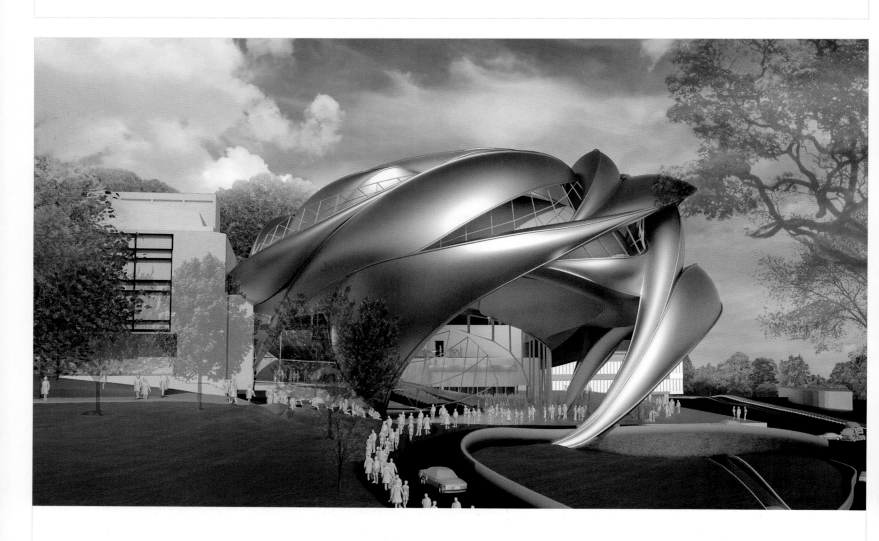

PERFORMING ARTS CENTER,   ISERLOHN, GERMANY   B+U, LLP

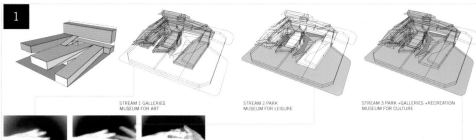

STREAM 1 GALLERIES
MUSEUM FOR ART

STREAM 2 PARK
MUSEUM FOR LEISURE

STREAM 3 PARK +GALLERIES +RECREATION
MUSEUM FOR CULTURE

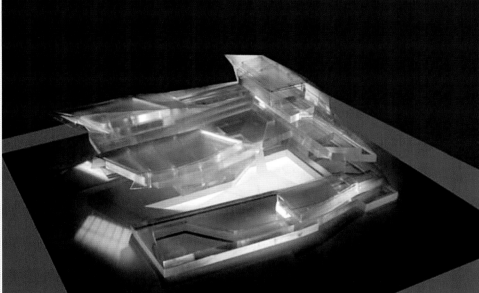

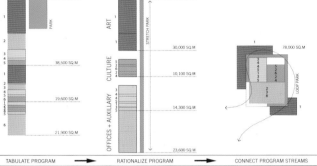

TABULATE PROGRAM → RATIONALIZE PROGRAM → CONNECT PROGRAM STREAMS

(1) EXHIBITION ZONE
A. GENERAL HALL
B. DESIGN HALL
C. EXPERIMENTAL HALL
D. SPECIAL DISPLAY AREA
(2) HOME COLLECTION STORAGE
(3) RESEARCH ZONE
(4) OFFICES AND ADMINISTRATIVE ZONE
(5) CULTURAL SERVICES ZONE

38,500 SQ.M

MOCA
MUSEUM OF CONTEMPORARY ART

(1) EXHIBITION ZONE
A. THE EXHIBITION OF URBAN DEVELOPMENT HISTORY
B. EXHIBITION OF THE URBAN CONSTRUCTION ACHIEVEMENTS
C. URBAN PLANNING EXHIBITION
D. PUBLIC INFORMATION AREA
(2) LIBRARY
(3) STORAGE ZONE FOR PE
(4) DEPARTMENT FOR URBAN PLANNING JOURNAL
(5) OFFICES AND ADMINISTRATIVE ZONE
(6) ZONE FOR PLANNING SERVICES

19,600 SQ.M

PE
PLANNING EXHIBITION

(1) FOYER
(2) MULTIPLE-PURPOSED HALLS AND AUDITORIUM
(3) CONFERENCE ROOM AND VIP RECEPTION
(4) AUXILIARY SERVICE ZONE
(5) UNDERGROUND GARAGE

21,900 SQ.M

COMMON AREA ALLOCATIONS
FOR MOCA + PE

CONNECTIVE TISSUE

Our design team, from the outset considered MOCAPE a synthesis of competing streams. The role of such a contemporary urban museum is seen as multi-layered:
1. External. As a social forum, an urban living room for Shenzhen.
2. Internal. As a place for disseminating contemporary art and as an academic, research institution.

Lao Tze, in the Tao Te Ching, expresses such a dilemma succinctly :

To experience without intention is to sense the world.
To experience with intention is to anticipate the world.
These two experiences are indistinguishable;
Their construction differ, but their effect is the same.

或曰 "欣赏艺术" 与 "认识城市规划" 的分别如老子的道德经所述：
故常無，欲以觀其妙；
常有，欲以觀其徼。
此兩者，同出而異名，同謂之玄。
玄之又玄，眾妙之門。

The precept becomes a powerful tool to resolve this seeming contradiction between a place of private reflection and one of public recreation. We envision MOCAPE therefore as an organism with interrelated parts, hands with fingers interlocked. The scheme unifies bands of gallery, public space and administration; each stream occasionally converging or diverging. The arrangement aims to ELIMINATE HIERARCHY within the Museum. Opportunities are forcibly created giving a typical user clear, distinct choice at each intersection. The streams fall primarily into two categories:

Circulation Stream 1. "SENSE" (without intention). A Museum as a civic event space. For people to visit, meet and experience through accident and recreation. As a continuous ring with a system of cafes and parks, it becomes a node for events, interaction, even recreation. Externalities.
Circulation Stream 2. "ANTICIPATE" (with intention). A Museum as a repository of knowledge. An interconnected system of galleries and academic areas. For users and supporters of an institution oriented toward education, display and research. Internalities.

The two experiences, as the premise goes, are indistinguishable. The streams reinforce each other and do not exist in opposition. At any point, a visitor can choose within or without, and connect the scroll in a unique yet legible way.

我们从设计的开始已认知，探测市当代艺术馆与城市规划展览馆的那种极端两种极端的概念，并提出能兼集因这两种概念用生的体验。从一方面，艺术本质的意识是投比例，投界版，投视性解释的。艺术可以是一座小雕像，一幅画像，一段影片，或瞬得一见的显示。所以，感受艺术是比较内向性，亲切的，个人的，又心灵相通的感受。相反，城市规划包含有计划的发展，俱有长线的远见，又结合别人的社会、文化、及经济的提高。艺术是和艺术相对这两种人物及团体的合作精神。我们自问，"这艺术展览馆的语言可有意或无意地感受及认识这两种概念？我们设计的空间能否被编制，或不受编制，以增长这两种接待但必需协调的体验为目的或同时？" 我们相信，在搜寻这些问题的答案过程中，我们将会为艺术展览馆找到最有逻辑，最有力，及最实际的提案。

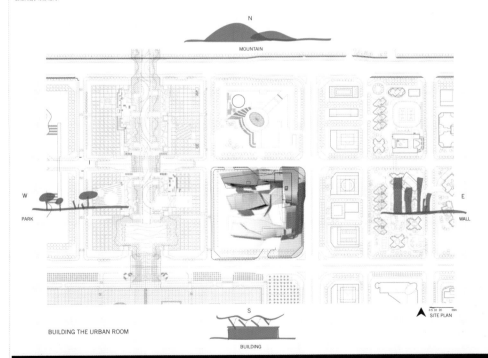

N

MOUNTAIN

W
PARK

E
WALL

S

SITE PLAN

BUILDING THE URBAN ROOM

BUILDING

ROOF — SUSTAINABLE SKIN

L07
L06
L05
L04
L03
— MOCA GALLERIES

L02
L01
— CAFE+SHOPS+THEATER +SUPPORT

L01 — PARK

B01 — PE GALLERIES

B02 — STORAGE+PARKING

PLANTING A TREE FOR SHENZHEN

PROGRAMMING

While consolidating the overall MOCAPE program, adjacencies within the Galleries were generated on the basis of a rigorous, intrinsic rationale. On the one hand, ART intrinsically constitutes no scale, no boundary, no pragmatic interpretations. Contemporary Art small sculptures, paintings, a video capture, or ephemeral once-in-a-life-time display. While art itself speaks to society, the experience and memory of art is primarily internal, intimate and personal, seizing a connection within. By contrast, PLANNING comprises primarily of large-scale social issues, development, long term vision, defined with a finite periphery. Such anticipation is more extroverted, explicit, communal, with collaboration among various individuals and groups. Could architectural space be organized, or disorganized, in such fashion to enhance these unique yet harmonized experiences? We proceeded to unify these two seamlessly so to visit MOCAPE would simultaneously experience and understand both noble ideals. With the two experiences "appreciating art" and "understanding planning" we intended for the two to be reversible or concurrent.

Our proposal for MOCAPE must be understood as a multi-layered project: as a network of urban space (to "anticipate") yet a public park for a communal use ("sense"); as an exploratory journey in search of an artistic identity yet a rational model for sustainable design. The overlay of values between Contemporary Art and Planning addresses a unique social interdependence.

Art, especially Contemporary Art required delving into social and cultural trends within present-day China. We focused exclusively on Chinese art, not only that produced in the liberation of thinking since Deng Xiaoping's open economic policy in the late 70s and the proliferation of mainland artists and works that followed, but also toward new methods of making and meaning within current works. We subsequently learnt that the development of contemporary Chinese art has not been too often from current social, cultural, and economic development. From the scale of Artist to Nation we the constant issue of confrontation; mediation between old and new, east and west, core values and external influences, patriotic pride and foreign admiration. Contemporary Chinese art, although experimentative in countless directions and in multidisciplinary media, was still forging an identity.

从艺术一端来看，我们先分析 "当代" 的意义，继而研究艺术纵横今中国社会及文化趋势下的动向。我们将焦点聚集思因为不，不只是因为在七十年代末期邓小平主席领导的经济改革下，人民思想开放，继而助长本地艺术家及艺术的生产量，还有是中国艺术的新意义，和更重要的，是新方法及媒介，从认识各艺术家中学到，当代中国艺术的发展，正如显微镜看，可反映国家的社会，文化，及经济发展。从一个艺术家到一个国家，两者都经营面对及卷辩的旧与新，东与西，自身评值与外来影响，爱国的骄傲与外国的仰慕之间。虽然当代中国艺术已试验各种不同的方向及媒介，仍然在寻找自我的风格和定向。

An analogy was drawn with an idea for an architectural space. We did not intend to design a gallery system with confusing paths drawing on lost causes or quick commodification. Our objective was to propose a curatorial flow path that would help museum visitors to synthesize an interpretation of contemporary Chinese art. As curators, we learnt from the work of artists who used or abused tradition in interesting ways by breaking apart, re-connecting and re-stitching in unique and new, yet characteristically Chinese ways. Such a body of work included ceramic robes made of broken china by Li Xiaofeng, and the detached-and-re-attached antique furniture of Shao Fan. We dare to predict, this could be a continuous and progressive system for designing MOCAPE, indeed for a nation defining a new identity for herself.

艺术风格其实与空间设计的概念开发相关，并不代表我们的艺术展览馆无日的地提供题乱的迷津。这不过是无意识的示范。我们提相那些拥我肢视的艺术品，为求一笑，不破幽地描述，沿用，及拖纽中国的传统典范成流传奇人物。相反，我们的方针，是要能引道这去找寻自我对艺术风格的观点，或自我对当代中国艺术的兴趣。

Planning required switching scales to configure MOCAPE as an urban project. Planning, as mentioned, constitutes long term social, cultural, and economical growth of a development, affecting the living conditions and standards of large group of people. Planners must have an exceptional and aspiring vision for the city at large, and the design problem is as much of a pragmatic urban nature as it is an artistic one. Planning issues have a pressing need to stay within the civic realm. This relevance is therefore crucial to configuring Planning Exhibition programming as a distinct portion of the museum, inextricably linked to the park, cafes and public circulation.

从城市规划一端来看，我们需要急急转思维以明白艺术城览馆是一个都市的项目。城市规划如上提及，包含长远的社会，文化，及经济增长与发展，对大众居民的生活状况及标准有莫大的影响。规划者身负重任，必须对整个城市由公类拔萃的远见，而设计问题是一个艺术本质与实际性并重的难题。

2

ART
CULTURE
ADMIN/OFFICE
PARKING/STORAGE

B01 PLAN -5m   L02 PLAN +5m   L03 PLAN +10m   L04 PLAN +15m   L05 PLAN +20m   L06 PLAN +25m   L07 PLAN +30m

PEDESTRIAN
CONNECTION

DROP-OFF

VISITOR
VEHICULAR PRIMARY
ACCESS

ART SHOP

MUSEUM SHOP

LOBBY

TICKETS

PE BOOKSHOP

LOBBY

PE GIFTSHOP

SERVICE
LOBBY

APPRAISAL
OFFICE

READING LOUNGE

THEATER LOBBY

BOOKSTORE

LIBRARY + READING ROOM

LIBRARY CAFE

LOBBY

LOBBY

A   A

PE ACADEMIC SALOON

RESTAURANT

LOBBY

PE GALLERY
CONNECTS L05 TO L03

PE JOURNAL OFFICE

VISITOR
VEHICULAR SECONDARY
ACCESS
PRIMARY SERVICE ACCESS

0 5 10   20   50m

SECTION A-A

+40M HEIGHT LIMIT

+5M

SOUTH ELEVATION

0 5 10   20   50m

+40M HEIGHT LIMIT

+5M

WEST ELEVATION

0 5 10   20   50m

+40M HEIGHT LIMIT

+5M

EAST ELEVATION

0 5 10   20   50m

+40M HEIGHT LIMIT

+5M

SOUTH ELEVATION

0 5 10   20   50m

3

As China is producing mega-cities in unprecedented rate that world has ever witnessed, an immediate and obvious subject matter came to our mind: the hot topic of Sustainable Design. Scientists used to predict China would surpass the U.S. as the leading carbon-emission country in the world in 2010, in a recent Time magazine article researchers corrected that it would happen by the end of this year. In respond to this phenomenon, government officials recognized the social challenge to create environmentally responsible projects of various scales. "Green Building", "Sustainable Architecture", "Renewable Resources" had almost replaced the former propaganda slogans in post-WWII China. Our challenge in the macro-scale was to create a true environmentally sensitive, or even environmentally productive project, both in the use and the making. At the same time when we were conceptualizing MOCAPE as an urban project, we must also carry a sense of social responsibility to enforce sustainable design for MOCAPE.

当中国以前所未见的速度生产了世界级的大都会城市，我司立刻联想到一个急切而明显的要点：近年最热门"资源循环再用设计"的议题。科学家曾经预算中国将会於2010年前超越美国成为碳化物放射率最高的国家。据近期时代杂志的报道，研究人员更正这状况将於本年年底前实现。回应这现象，各地政府官员已确认承担这议题，积极实施对环境负责的各大小项目。"绿化建筑物"，"资源循环再用设计"，"资源更新"等等大概已完全代替往日二次世界大战後的宣传口号。我司的有需要承担这挑战，不论在建造或启用的过程时，提出一项对环境负责，或甚至对环境改善的方案。当我们为艺术展览馆构思着MOCAPE这项目的概念时，必需承担这社会议责来实施资源循环再用设计。

As the research on sustainable design progressed, some of our green features not only proposed practical solution to reduction in energy and water consumption, also seamlessly integrated to the larger urban ideas for MOCAPE. For example, we were studying how traditional Chinese artists appreciated mountain and water scenary, and would capture the essence of such in the window of paintings. From a research visit to Yuzi Paradise in Guilin, we learnt how public art could blend in the natural environment, however, we began to ask ourselves, instead of bringing large scale public art to a park, how could architecture become part of the scenary, to become an extension of the urban fabric rather than a building on a site, further to bring the scale of landscape to the scale of art?

当我司在研究资源循环再用设计时，发现某中几项绿化特点不但能节省能源及用水，同时天衣无缝地与提案的都市概念。例如，中国传统画家对山水的热爱，缴而简情景收录进画面的関係内。从一次到桂林的愚自乐园的研究旅程中，我们体会到公共艺术品能无间地配合大然环境，我们自问，除了将大型的公共艺术品带入公园内，一座建筑物能否被引入成为园景的一部份，或伸延与都市组织的一部份，将大型的园景带进无比例的艺术世界？

The green roof idea naturally came to our mind, as it served dual purposes of a sustainable features as much as an urban solution for MOCAPE. We decided to create an "inviting" outdoor space for users to wander to MOCAPE without intention, to sense the transformation of the topography, to sense the museum, and to mediate through the more intimate exhibition spaces. Eventually, one would continue the journey, and through connecting pathways and bridges, re-connect with the urban surroundings.

绿化屋顶的概念很自然地萌芽，并提供双重效用。一来它是资源循环再用的设计，二来它是这提案的都市概念。意於提供一个点诱的户外空间，让访客能不自觉地被引进室内，感受地形的变化，再感受这艺术展馆及它较亲切的室内空间。不其然地，访客继继探求这探索的旅程，经过连接的走道及桥梁，再与世界的环境连上。

Our proposal for MOCAPE must be understood as a set of multi-layered social streams: As a museum for internal appreciation yet as a public park for community use, as bold artistic expression yet using a rational model for sustainable design. Dissimilar values we believe, need not be contradicting or exclusive, but co-existing and inter-dependent.

虽然我司的方案对"欣赏艺术"与"认识场市规划"的体验都以达到"同出出真名，同藏之玄"的效果。我司的方案是希望能达到两者互换及两者都全的体验。所以，我司的方案必需被理解为一个多层面的项目；一方面，是一所示切感受艺术的地方，另一方面是一个与众分享的公园；一方面，是探究艺术方计的旅程，另一方面是作为循环再用建筑设计的模范。从此可见，"艺术与城市规划"虽然意义不同，不一定是反对或互相排斥，反而可并存或有相辅相成的效果。

GALLERIES

VEHICULAR

PEDESTRIAN PARK

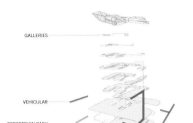

GALLERY AT L04   WAY-FINDING   SECURE SERVICE ACCESS

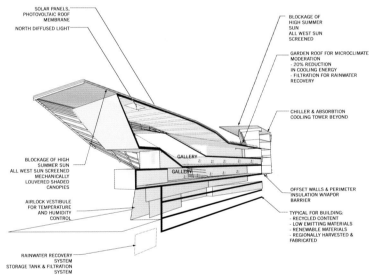

SOLAR PANELS, PHOTOVOLTAIC ROOF MEMBRANE

NORTH DIFFUSED LIGHT

BLOCKAGE OF HIGH SUMMER SUN ALL WEST SUN SCREENED

GARDEN ROOF FOR MICROCLIMATE MODERATION
- 20% REDUCTION IN COOLING ENERGY
- FILTRATION FOR RAINWATER RECOVERY

CHILLER & ABSORBTION COOLING TOWER BEYOND

BLOCKAGE OF HIGH SUMMER SUN ALL WEST SUN SCREENED MECHANICALLY LOUVERED SHADED CANOPIES

GALLERY
GALLERY

OFFSET WALLS & PERIMETER INSULATION W/VAPOR BARRIER

AIRLOCK VESTIBULE FOR TEMPERATURE AND HUMIDITY CONTROL

TYPICAL FOR BUILDING:
- RECYCLED CONTENT
- LOW EMITTING MATERIALS
- RENEWABLE MATERIALS
- REGIONALLY HARVESTED & FABRICATED

RAINWATER RECOVERY SYSTEM
STORAGE TANK & FILTRATION SYSTEM

CURATORIAL RATIONALE

MULTIPLE SCALE USES

▪ PHOTOGRAPHY, PAINTING (IN)

■ VIDEO, INSTALLATION (IN)

■ SCULPTURE, INSTALLATION (OUT)

SUSTAINABLE DEVELOPMENT IN SHENZHEN

Being established as the first Special Economic Zone (SEZ) of China in May 1980 and had shown exceptional urban development since. Shenzhen continues to re-invent herself as China's pioneering city by setting innovative and strategic goals for the city's economic and social development. In June 2000, Shenzhen won the Global 500 Roll of Honour Award given by the UN Environmental Programme for "its impressive achievement of marrying rapid and astonishing economic growth with environmental protection," as described in the South China Morning Post (June 5, 2002). In March 2006, the regional government of Shenzhen stressed a new five-year plan with specific measures to transform the city to a recycling society and to accelerate the development of four pillar industries (high-tech, finance, logistics, and cultural industry). Specifically on the building of an ecological city, besides putting emphasis on model enterprises including companies with less pollution, energy-saving and water-saving components, building ecological industrial and agriculture model parks, etc. great attention is given to integrate sustainable design to public projects. MOCAPE - being one of the major public projects to boost the cultural industry in the prominent area in Futian Central District - must set herself as a role model of sustainable design.

Just north of Hong Kong, Shenzhen shares a similar subtropical climate conditions with intense summer heat and lots of precipitations. Summers last for about six months out of a year and temperature can reach as high as 35°C. Winters in the city are more bearable with temperature rarely drops below 10°C. Raining last all year long, with most precipitations from May to September, and high humidity starting spring time.

With a wide array of "green" features and integrated engineering strategies, our MOCAPE proposal intends to save carbon dioxide emissions over conventional construction and to promote energy-saving and water-saving design. Some of major sustainable design strategies include:

ROOF
- Landscaped roof as an extension of the public park also serves the purpose for microclimate moderation. This results in reduction in cooling energy consumption for interior space as well as filtration system for rain water recovery.
- On top of billboard structure, we propose installation of roof solar panels for sanitary water heating. The design will specify a storage capacity of hot water at 55°C temperature.

EXTERIOR FACADE
- Optimal South and West fenestration and insulated glazing system to minimize heat gain during long summers, thus reducing cooling loads.
- Exterior walls to have vapor barrier on outside of insulation for humidity and moisture control.

WATER USE
- Sewer risers bring rainwater from roof to below grade recovery system with storage tank and filtration system for recycling uses, such as public toilets.
- Explore the use of underground water for cooling in the summer since temperature of underground water is relatively constant throughout the year at 15-18°C. A system of vertical underground pipes will collect water and bring to the heat pumps where energy will be exchanged between the underground water and water used for cooling.
- All sanitary-ware to have water dispense controls and automatic sensors. Consider dry urinals and environmental toilets.

MECHANICAL SYSTEM
- Displacement air system in museum lobby and main interior volume by using the difference in air densities to thermally separate hot dirty air and cool clean air. The idea of thermal stratification works when air comes through horizontal distribution below ground floor at extremely low velocity is cooler than the existing air, it's denser and stays near ground level. The warm, humid, and lighter air, which contains dirt, would be displaced to the ceiling.
- AHUs to run with 100% outside air at summer nights to pre-cool non-exhibition areas such as lobby, offices, restaurants, and shops using forced ventilation. The indoor temperature will then be lower during the early morning hours providing thermal comfort and improved air quality for the occupants.

DAYLIGHTING CONTROL
- Use of natural diffused light for non-exhibition, circulation, and lobby areas.
- Sun-shading devices to control direct sunlight as well as to protect art that are sensitive to harmful sunlight.
- Art lighting and other artificial lighting to be controlled by intelligent system to optimize energy efficiency, to be flexible for various art exhibitions, and to provide user comfort.

BUILDING MATERIALS
- Recycled, renewable, and low-emitting materials
- Regionally harvested and fabricated materials

RECYCLING PROGRAM
- Museum management team to promote and enforce recycling program to minimize waste production and to recycle materials.

深圳市的资源循环再用发展

自1980年5月作为中华人民共和国首度批准的第一个经济特区，深圳市在近况卓越的城市发展成果。深圳从多年来持续自我更新，以创新策略为城市的经济及社会发展方针，於2000年6月，深圳市获颁发由联合国环境署颁发的全球五百荣誉奖，以2002年6月5日南华早报所述"把人类相惊人的经济发展与环境保护结合"。於2006年3月，深圳市的区政府发表新一度的五年计划，包括详细的策略以创建成为一个资源循环再用的社会及加速发展四个主要行业（高科技，财经，运筹，文化）为目标。专注作为一个环保的城市，除了注重模范企业的发展外，包括了污染少的公司，节省能源和节省用水的设备公司，创建生态环保的工业及农业示范公园等，亦专注於公共项目设计内的整体资源再用设计。作为国际唯一个都市繁荣的文化区域及综合设施之一，深圳市当代艺术馆与城市规划展览馆定必成为一个模范资源循环再用的建筑设计。

位处香港之北，深圳市共有类同的亚热带气候，包括炎热的夏天及大量的降雨水。一年内夏天长达六个月，气温可高达摄氏35度。冬天比较温和，气温甚少低过摄氏10度。其四季全年多雨，在每年五月至九月期间的降雨量最多，同春天亦带着潮湿的季节。

我司透过设计的国际逐步采用各种绿化特点及城市规划整体策略以期达成节约的绿化项目及改善环境的工程效能，以减低区域碳排放量於二氧化物从传统建造业生产过程所产生的数量，同时为使用者节约能源，同时绿化建筑物以期减低水位过度利用。

屋顶
- 绿化屋顶及园景屋顶，亦为市园部分的城市环境提供一个微气候的环境调试分外亦减低冷房部份的用电量。
- 广告牌顶结构内，我们建议在安上太阳能设备以应付生水热的用电，设备包括一个可储藏热水於摄氏55度的贮藏室。

外墙
- 南方和西方合适的窗户，并采用隔热式的玻璃作隔热装置，以减少夏天长内的热量増加及分外降低冷房的用电压。
- 外墙内的绝缘设备外设有防气层障，以防止湿度和温度的入侵。

用水
- 污水管道从屋顶的雨水收集至下层的贮藏器及隔离处理装置，经过循环的雨水恢复。
- 由於城下水的比较恒常於摄氏15至18度。考虑使用地下水夏天冷却供用途，建议垂直地的水管组系统，导引地下水与冷却用水作能源的交换。
- 所有洁具设自动的水密控器及感应器，使用环保洁具或无用水的尿具。

机械系统
- 机械系统在美术馆内大厅用空气密度差别空间分隔概念及冷却密层隔间，以利用密度差别把热气分隔及导引，此概念的分隔原理是采用了隔气层的温差原理。新鲜的空气在下层低速导入的地板，因为空气的密度高又温度低会停留下层，热、湿、并含有尘的轻空气被导引到天花顶。
- 空气调节系统在夏天每晚全用百分百之百的室外气，以等提预冷非展览区，例如大厅、办公室、餐厅、及商场，藉以的空气内温度气先调降，为用者带来更佳的温适与空气质素。

日光控制
- 扩大自然散射的光源用于非展览之空间，流道，及复室的環境用灯。
- 遮阳器的设备是控制直射阳光及用以保护对光敏感的艺术品。
- 以所有智能的照明系统控制艺术灯光及照明设备，以节约能源及提供用途的灵活性，同时提供给予用者的舒适度。

建筑材料
- 采用循环再用，可重新，及生产时减少二氧化物放射的材料。
- 采用地方生成及制造的材料。

循环再用计划
- 馆管理部管理层推广及实施循环再用计划，以包括减少废物制及制度数

GALLERY AT L03

224

Buenosaires | *2:pm architectures*

Project : International Competition for a Vertical Zoo
Location : Buenos Aires, Argentina

Zoo as Network | *David Garcia Studio*

Typology : Zoo
Location : Urban Environment

Participants : David A. Garcia (Architect MAA)
Project : An Environmental Zoo Where Consideration Should be Given to
a Symbiotic Environment that Includes the Activities of Humans with Animals

225

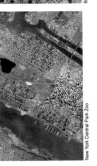

Berlin Zoo

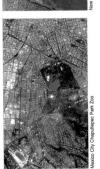

Paris Zoo

Tokyo Ueno Zoo

Barcelona Zoo

New York Central Park Zoo

Mexico City Chapultepec Park Zoo

San Diego Zoo

zoo as network

The aim of this proposal is to enrich both humans and animals by closer contact, while using the same environment.

If the contemporary aim of zoos is to understand how animals and humans can be enriched by each other, then the proximity between animals and people is essential.

This can be done by sharing simple rituals, like eating, resting or training. If these activities are done in the same architectural space, the natural environment becomes important to both, animals and humans.

Architecture is the perfect language to solve the physical challenges of such a proposal. This has to be understood as a serious undertaking and a way to enrich each

other's social necessities while creating new spaces.

Imagine your self, reading in a cloud of butterflies in the central library, swimming with dolphins in the public pool or eating close to grazing giraffes in a restaurant. These experiences will increase the responsibility in maintaining the environment, which both animals and humans use.

TRADITIONAL ZOO,
THE ISOLATED
STRUCTURE
ANIMALS AND
ENVIRONMENT
ARE ENCLOSED

URBAN LANDSCAPE

ISOLATED ZOO

ZOO AS NETWORK,
IN CONTACT WITH
CITY ACTIVITIES
BRINGS ANIMALS
AND ENVIRONMENT
CLOSER TO PEOPLE

ANTELOPE PARK AND TRACK AND FIELD
CENTRAL LIBRARY AND INSECTORIUM
VEGETARIAN RESTAURANT AND GIRAFFE PARK
PUBLIC POOL AND AQUARIUM

BEE FARM OFFICE BUILDING
PENGUIN HALL AND ICE RINK
CONCERT HALL AND BIRD AVIARY

ANIMAL SOCIAL GROUP SIZES

SOLITARY INDIVIDUALS
ROOM
SQUIRREL IN PRIVATE GARDEN
KOALA IN WORKSHOP

FAMILIES
HALL
LECTURE HALL AND GORILLA GARDEN
LIBRARY AND BUTTERFLY ROOM

GROUPS
PUBLIC SPACES
PUBLIC POOL AND DOLPHIN AQUARIUM
DANCING ROOM AND FLAMINGO PARK

HERDS
LARGE OUT DOOR SPACE
DEER FOREST AND STADIUM
ROWING CLUB AND TURTLE SANCTUARY

FLOCKS
LARGE ENCLOSED HALLS
CONCERT HALL AND BIRD AVIARY
MONKEY HOUSE AND GYMNASTICS HALL

SWARMS
PARKS
FOREST AND FIREFLY SANCTUARY
BEE FARM AND TRAINING PARK

CONCERT HALL AND BIRD AVIARY

VEGETARIAN RESTAURANT AND GIRAFFE PARK

PUBLIC POOL AND DOLPHIN AQUARIUM

CENTRAL LIBRARY AND INSECTORIUM

226

Reappropriation | *Arquipelago Studio*

Project Team : Gregory Marinic(Principal), Dario Badillo, Carlos Contreras,
Stephanie Garcia, Rodrigo Garza, Estefania Mendivil

638

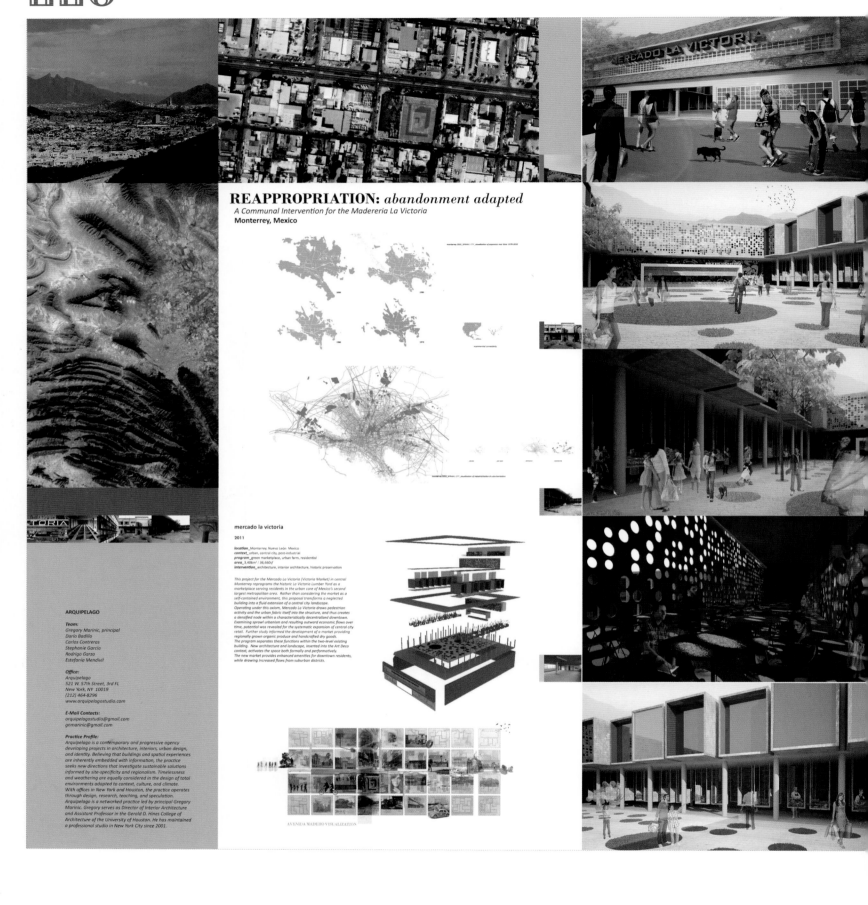

REAPPROPRIATION: *abandonment adapted*
A Communal Intervention for the Madereria La Victoria
Monterrey, Mexico

mercado la victoria

2011

*location*_Monterrey, Nuevo León Mexico
*context*_urban, central city, post-industrial
*program*_green marketplace, urban farm, residential
*area*_3,406m² / 36,660sf
*intervention*_architecture, interior architecture, historic preservation

This project for the Mercado La Victoria (Victoria Market) in central Monterrey reprograms the historic La Victoria Lumber Yard as a marketplace serving residents in the urban core of Mexico's second largest metropolitan area. Rather than considering the market as a self-contained environment, this proposal transforms a neglected building into a fluid extension of a central city landscape.
Operating under this axiom, Mercado La Victoria draws pedestrian activity and the urban fabric itself into the structure, and thus creates a densified node within a characteristically decentralized downtown.
Examining sprawl urbanism and resulting outward economic flows over time, potential was revealed for the systematic expansion of central city retail. Further study informed the development of a market providing regionally grown organic produce and handcrafted dry goods.
The program separates these functions within the two-level existing building. New architecture and landscape, inserted into the Art Deco context, activates the space both formally and performatively.
The new market provides enhanced amenities for downtown residents, while drawing increased flows from suburban districts.

AVENIDA MADERO VISUALIZATION

ARQUIPELAGO

Team:
Gregory Marinic, principal
Dario Badillo
Carlos Contreras
Stephanie Garcia
Rodrigo Garza
Estefania Mendivil

Office:
Arquipelago
521 W. 57th Street, 3rd FL
New York, NY 10019
(212) 464-8296
www.arquipelagostudio.com

E-Mail Contacts:
arquipelagostudio@gmail.com
gnmarinic@gmail.com

Practice Profile:
Arquipelago is a contemporary and progressive agency developing projects in architecture, interiors, urban design, and identity. Believing that buildings and spatial experiences are inherently embedded with information, the practice seeks new directions that investigate sustainable solutions informed by site-specificity and regionalism. Timelessness and weathering are equally considered in the design of total environments adapted to context, culture, and climate.
With offices in New York and Houston, the practice operates through design, research, teaching, and speculation.
Arquipelago is a networked practice led by principal Gregory Marinic. Gregory serves as Director of Interior Architecture and Assistant Professor in the Gerald D. Hines College of Architecture of the University of Houston. He has maintained a professional studio in New York City since 2001.

Jeongok Museum of Pre-History | *Paul Preissner*

Area : 6,500Sm
Cost : $24.5 Million

Location : Gyeonggi-Do, South Korea
Client : Gyeonggi-Do Prefecture
Program : Archeological Exhibtion, Preservation, Education, Banquets

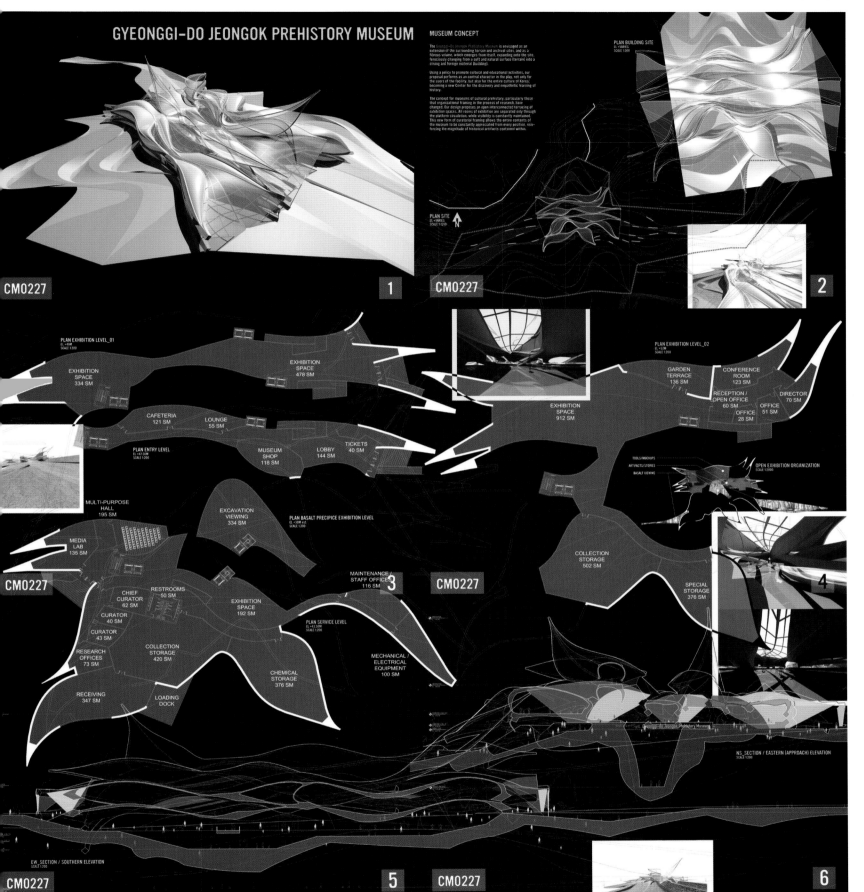

GYEONGGI-DO JEONGOK PREHISTORY MUSEUM

CM0227

MUSEUM CONCEPT

The Gyeonggi-Do Jeongok Prehistory Museum is envisaged as an extension of the surrounding terrain and archival sites, and as a fibrous volume, which emerges from itself, expanding onto the site, ferociously changing from a soft and natural surface (terrain) into a strong and foreign material (building).

Using a policy to promote cultural and educational activities, our proposal performs as an central character in the play, not only for the users of the facility, but also for the entire culture of Korea; becoming a new Center for the discovery and empathetic learning of history.

The concept for museums of cultural prehistory, particularly those that organizational framing in the process of research, have changed. Our design proposes an open interconnected terracing of exhibition spaces. All rooms of exhibition are separated only through the platform circulation, while visibility is constantly maintained. This new form of curatorial framing allows the entire contents of the museum to be constantly appreciated from every position, reinforcing the magnitude of historical artifacts contained within.

PLAN BUILDING SITE
EL +VARIES
SCALE 1:200

PLAN SITE
EL +VARIES
SCALE 1:200

CM0227

PLAN EXHIBITION LEVEL_01
EL +6M
SCALE 1:200

EXHIBITION SPACE 334 SM

EXHIBITION SPACE 478 SM

CAFETERIA 121 SM

LOUNGE 55 SM

PLAN ENTRY LEVEL
EL +2.50M
SCALE 1:200

MUSEUM SHOP 118 SM

LOBBY 144 SM

TICKETS 40 SM

PLAN EXHIBITION LEVEL_02
EL +5M
SCALE 1:200

GARDEN TERRACE 136 SM

CONFERENCE ROOM 123 SM

RECEPTION / OPEN OFFICE 60 SM

OFFICE 28 SM

OFFICE 51 SM

DIRECTOR 70 SM

EXHIBITION SPACE 912 SM

TOOLS/MOCKUPS
ARTIFACTS/STORES
BASALT VIEWING

OPEN EXHIBITION ORGANIZATION
SCALE 1:2000

MULTI-PURPOSE HALL 195 SM

EXCAVATION VIEWING 334 SM

PLAN BASALT PRECIPICE EXHIBITION LEVEL
EL +10M
SCALE 1:200

MEDIA LAB 135 SM

CHIEF CURATOR 62 SM

RESTROOMS 50 SM

MAINTENANCE / STAFF OFFICES 116 SM

CM0227

COLLECTION STORAGE 502 SM

SPECIAL STORAGE 376 SM

CURATOR 40 SM

EXHIBITION SPACE 192 SM

CURATOR 43 SM

RESEARCH OFFICES 73 SM

COLLECTION STORAGE 420 SM

PLAN SERVICE LEVEL
EL +3.50M
SCALE 1:200

MECHANICAL / ELECTRICAL EQUIPMENT 100 SM

RECEIVING 347 SM

LOADING DOCK

CHEMICAL STORAGE 376 SM

CM0227

NS_SECTION / EASTERN (APPROACH) ELEVATION
SCALE 1:200

EW_SECTION / SOUTHERN ELEVATION
SCALE 1:200

CM0227

CM0227

227

Hotel Liesma | *PRAUD*

Client : Hotel Liesma
Team : Dongwoo Yim, Rafael Luna, Emily Ko
Location : Jurmala, Latvia

Site Area : 15,000m²
Project Floor Area : 10,300m²

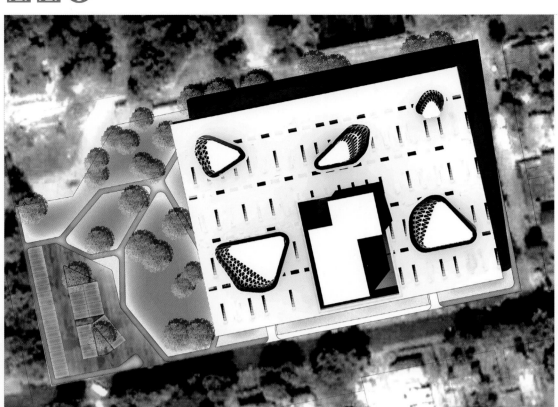

Site Plan (1:500)

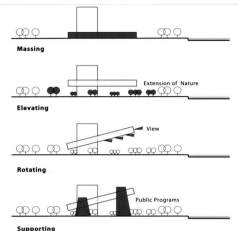

Massing

Elevating — Extension of Nature

Rotating — View

Supporting — Public Programs

Approach

There are two challenging questions we had when we first met the project. First, what type of architectural form can strengthen the concept of music hotel as well as this amazing landscape? Perhaps the architecture should not be an iconic building that tries to outstand itself amongs the environment, but a very gentle form that just sits on the site.

The next question was, is it able to bring in the nature into the site so that the whole site is conceived as park? To achieve this concept of music park, having a landscape field in the left over space in the site is not enough, perhaps we need more aggressive approach so that the music park we are trying to create is not something you can experience in other parts of the city.

Program Distribution

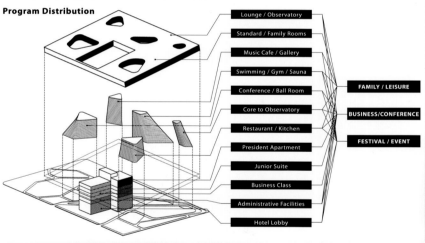

Lounge / Observatory
Standard / Family Rooms
Music Cafe / Gallery
Swimming / Gym / Sauna
Conference / Ball Room
Core to Observatory
Restaurant / Kitchen
President Apartment
Junior Suite
Business Class
Administrative Facilities
Hotel Lobby

FAMILY / LEISURE
BUSINESS/CONFERENCE
FESTIVAL / EVENT

ID:03346

Concept

The main concept of the project is to elevate the new hotel mass from the ground level. There are two major purposes of this approach; to have widely open public park on the ground level and to provide better view to the Baltic sea from hotel rooms.

Every single room in the new mass has direct view towards the sea and has access to the balcony on the roof. This new mat-type mass is held by multiple cones that contain public programs inside such as, music cafe, restaurants, conference hall, and swimming pool. By having private hotel rooms separated from the ground level and public programs sitting on the ground, the whole ground level, which we call it as music park, could be used as a dynamic and cultural park not only for the visitors to the hotel but also for all people who visits the city. Therefore, the music park becomes a new field for all those music concerts and festival of the city.

And by putting business class rooms and junior suites in the existing building, the hotel can be managed more efficiently. When it is in leisure season mostly for families, the hotel can only operate the new mat-type mass and couple of cones, while when it is for business conference, it can mainly operate the existing building, conference cone and restaurant cone. This efficient way of using the hotel facilities will let the hotel run viably through out the whole year.

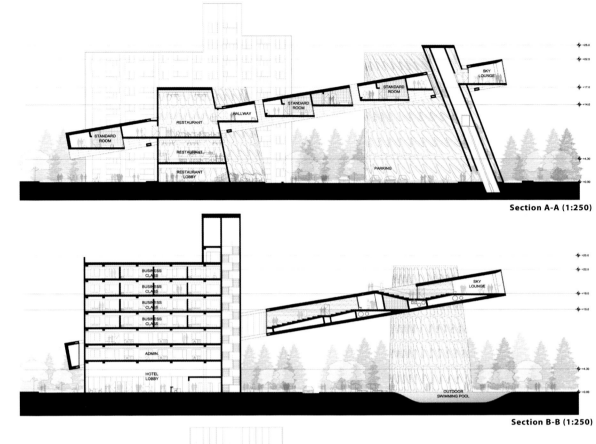

Section A-A (1:250)

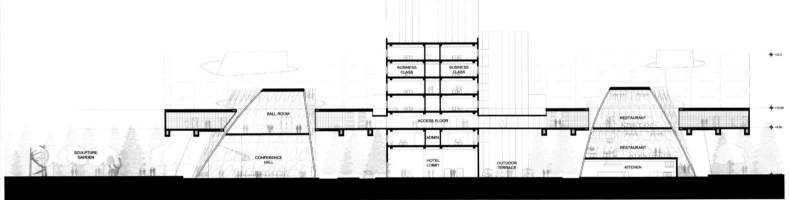

Section B-B (1:250)

Section C-C (1:250)

ID:03346

view from double room ▲

▼ view from single room

The biggest challenge of this mat-type building was to have a creative solution for structure. We introduced a structural system that basically resembles a tube system. A band of strip is composed with two layers of structure that is integrated with duct and shaft area, and the space in the middle is filled with programs such as hotel rooms and corridor.

This integrated system works as a whole structure, similar to truss or tube system, instead of space and structures being separated from each other. Therefore, we could create a sound system of structure that works well for long span floating mat-type building.

And this mat structure is supported by five major cones that cut through the mat. Each ring band around the whole transfers the force from the tube to each cone. Each cone also contains program inside just as the tube system at mat-type building above. Since the structural system in the cone is integrated at the periphery, each cone can have relatively free form. And as the loading force gets bigger on the ground, the shape of the cone and structural elements get bigger as well.

Structural Concept

Tube System

Cone

Truss Structure
Corridor
Light Well
Single Room
Double Room
Family Room
Truss Structure
Tube System

Hotel Floor Plan (1:250)

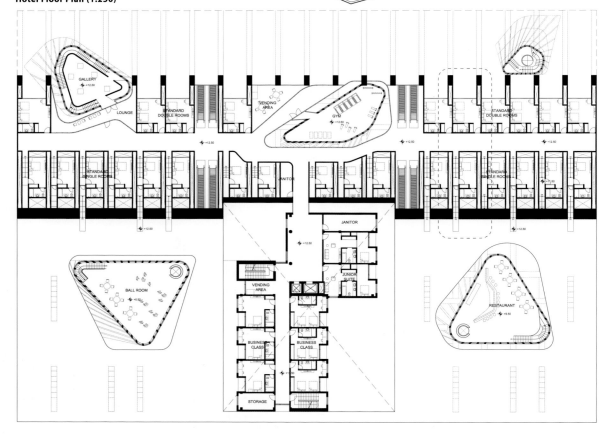

Unit Plan (1:150)

ID:03346

Ground Floor Plan (1:250)

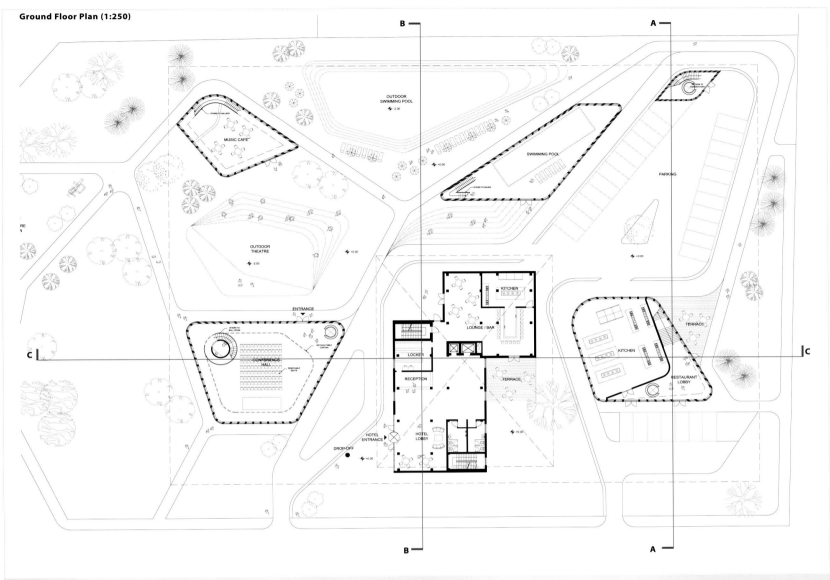

ID:03346

229

House of John Paul II "Do not Fear" | *Slot.*

Project Name : House of John Paul II "Do not Fear"
Location : Poland, Krakow
Program : Museum, Auditorium, Investigation Center, Chapel
Project Type : Open International Competition

Client : Board of the House of John Paul II Center Krakow
Construction Area : 13,168m²

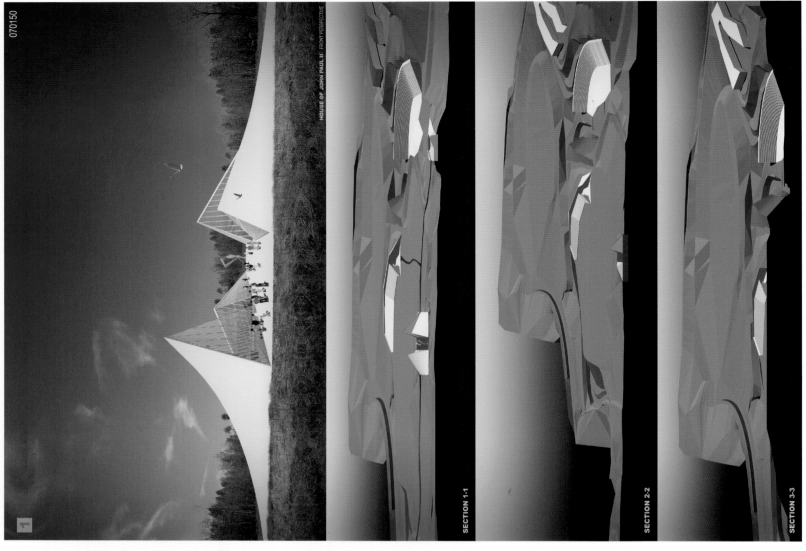

HOUSE OF JOHN PAUL II FROM PERSPECTIVE

SECTION 1-1

SECTION 2-2

SECTION 3-3

PUBLIC PLAZA NEAR THE SANCTUARY

WAY OF THE CROSS TOWARDS HOUSE OF JP II

PARKING FACILITIES NEAR HOUSE OF JP II

PROPOSAL FOR THE HOTEL FACILITIES

OPEN AIR THEATER USING THE EXISTING TOPOGRAPHY

LANDSCAPE AND RECREATIONAL PARK

LAND DEVELOPMENT

LAND DEVELOPMENT PLAN 1:2000

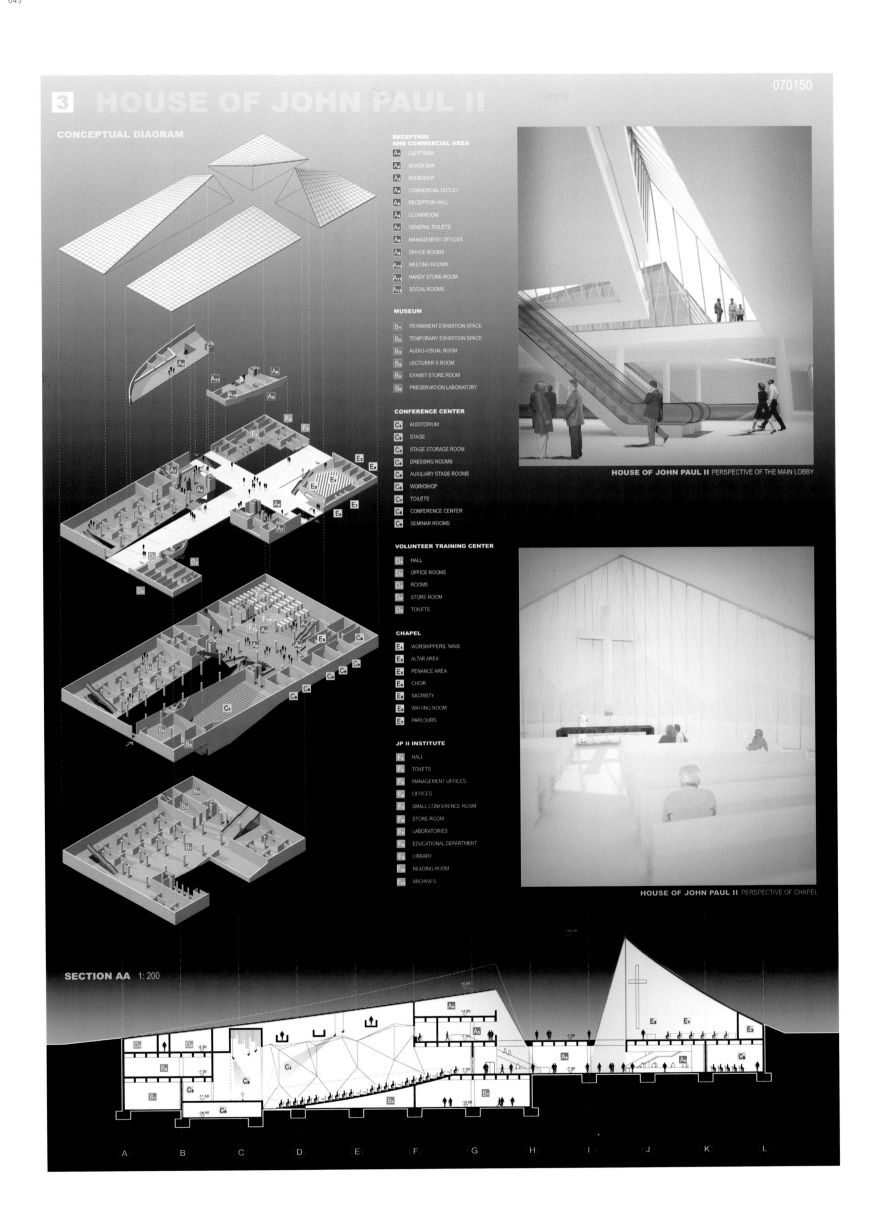

3 HOUSE OF JOHN PAUL II

070150

CONCEPTUAL DIAGRAM

RECEPTION AND COMMERCIAL AREA

A₁ CAFETERIA
A₂ SNACK BAR
A₃ BOOKSHOP
A₄ COMMERCIAL OUTLET
A₅ RECEPTION HALL
A₆ CLOAKROOM
A₇ GENERAL TOILETS
A₈ MANAGEMENT OFFICES
A₉ OFFICE ROOMS
A₁₀ MEETING ROOMS
A₁₁ HANDY STORE-ROOM
A₁₂ SOCIAL ROOMS

MUSEUM

B₁ PERMANENT EXHIBITION SPACE
B₂ TEMPORARY EXHIBITION SPACE
B₃ AUDIO-VISUAL ROOM
B₄ LECTURER'S ROOM
B₅ EXHIBIT STORE ROOM
B₆ PRESERVATION LABORATORY

CONFERENCE CENTER

C₁ AUDITORIUM
C₂ STAGE
C₃ STAGE STORAGE ROOM
C₄ DRESSING ROOMS
C₅ AUXILIARY STAGE ROOMS
C₆ WORKSHOP
C₇ TOILETS
C₈ CONFERENCE CENTER
C₉ SEMINAR ROOMS

VOLUNTEER TRAINING CENTER

D₁ HALL
D₂ OFFICE ROOMS
D₃ ROOMS
D₄ STORE-ROOM
D₅ TOILETS

CHAPEL

E₁ WORSHIPPERS NAVE
E₂ ALTAR AREA
E₃ PENANCE AREA
E₄ CHOIR
E₅ SACRISTY
E₆ WAITING ROOM
E₇ PARLOURS

JP II INSTITUTE

F₁ HALL
F₂ TOILETS
F₃ MANAGEMENT OFFICES
F₄ OFFICES
F₅ SMALL CONFERENCE ROOM
F₆ STORE ROOM
F₇ LABORATORIES
F₈ EDUCATIONAL DEPARTMENT
F₉ LIBRARY
F₁₀ READING ROOM
F₁₁ ARCHIVES

HOUSE OF JOHN PAUL II PERSPECTIVE OF THE MAIN LOBBY

HOUSE OF JOHN PAUL II PERSPECTIVE OF CHAPEL

SECTION AA 1:200

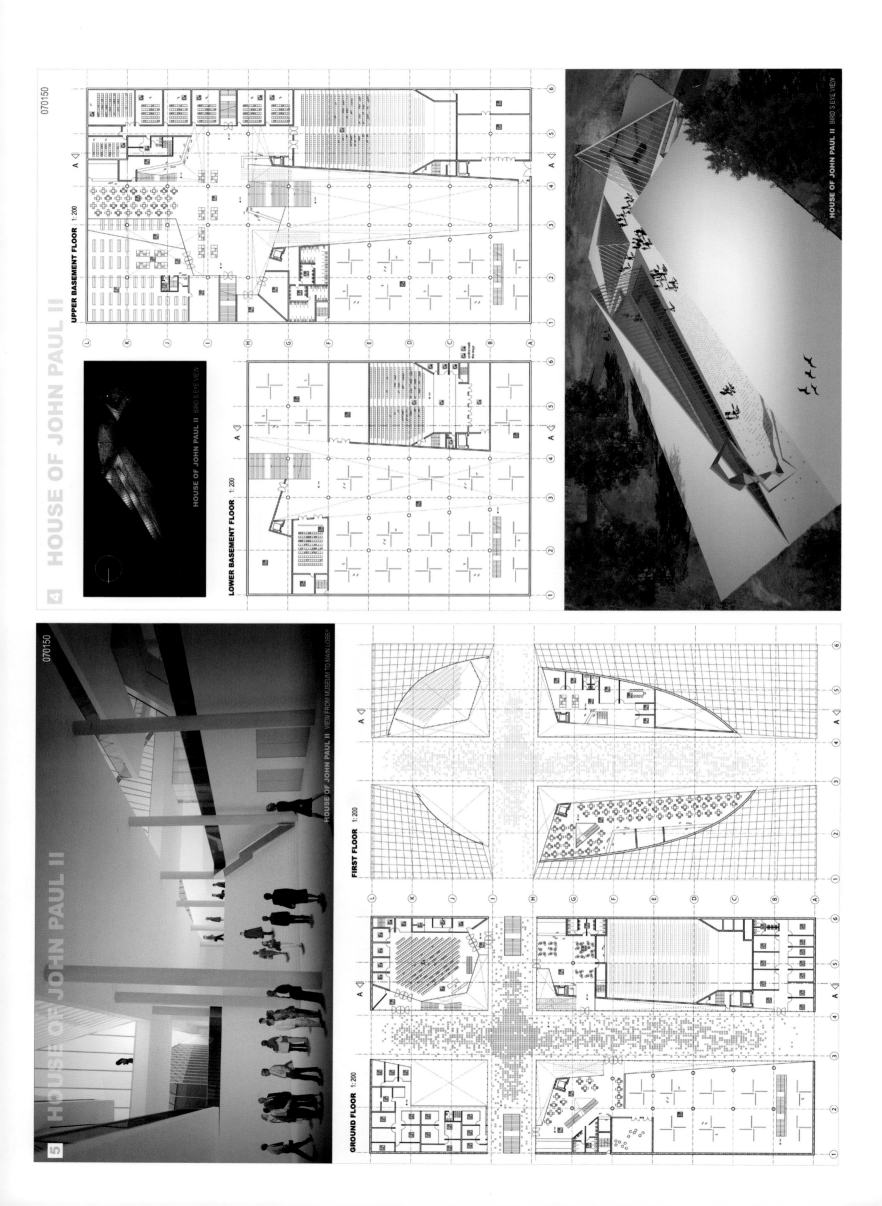

070150

4 HOUSE OF JOHN PAUL II

HOUSE OF JOHN PAUL II BIRD'S EYE VIEW

UPPER BASEMENT FLOOR 1:200

LOWER BASEMENT FLOOR 1:200

HOUSE OF JOHN PAUL II BIRD'S EYE VIEW

070150

5 HOUSE OF JOHN PAUL II

HOUSE OF JOHN PAUL II VIEW FROM MUSEUM TO MAIN LOBBY

FIRST FLOOR 1:200

GROUND FLOOR 1:200

RETREAT CENTER

VIEW INTO A DOUBLE BEDROOM OF THE RETREAT CENTER

1 reception hall	**6** group meeting rooms
2 chapel	**7** store room
3 administration	**8** single bedrooms
4 kitchen and dining-room	**9** double bedrooms
5 general toilets	**10** service flats

UPPER FLOOR 1: 200

LOWER FLOOR 1: 200

CONCEPTUAL DIAGRAM

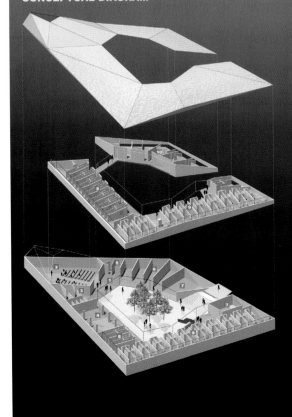

BIRDS EYE VIEW OF THE RETREAT CENTER

SECTION BB 1: 200

230

Mercedes Benz Business Center | *HTDSTUDIO DESIGNOFFICE™*

Client : Avangard Motors Co., Hotel InterContinental
Location : Yerevan, Armenia
Total Floor Area : 271,896ft2 / 25,260m2
Budget : Withheld / Status : Competition

Project Type : Mixed-Use Complex and Hotel
Renderings : ©HTDSTUDIO DESIGNOFFICE

648

Each Program Component is a Landmark.

Concept.

The Mercedes-Benz Business Center and Intercontinental Hotel stands alone as a singular business destination in the Northern Middle East region.

Situated atop a promontory overlooking the Old City via the axis of Terian Street, the Mercedes-Benz Business Center and Intercontinental Hotel will be a beacon of progress, sustainability and excellence that is customarily associated with both global brands.

The approach is to create a 'Living' program where each component maximizes the following:

• All exposures to city "walls" or old vs. new city
• Site access and traffic flow, both vehicular and pedestrian
• Dramatic Strategic views of the City of Yerevan & Mt. Ararat
• Discreet Separation vs. Consolidation of spaces
• Minimal site disturbance by main building
• Adaptive re-use of base of YYC into a museum, offices + storage
• Subgrade parking coupled with a green park and public gardens
• Re-use of at-grade wall-base of old Yerevan Youth Center as Museum

Inspiration.

The Mercedes-Benz Business Center and Intercontinental Hotel takes inspiration from the rich ancient and contemporary architectural history created by various civilizations over the centuries.

From Mother Armenia benevolently watching over the complex to the awe-inpsiring Cascades, to the power of Mount Ararat, MBBC is at once a structure futuristic and rational in its composition as well as reverent in its attempt to supplant the now demolished Yerevan Youth Center as a key landmark building standing sentry at the eastern Terminus of Terian Street.

Program Articulated.

Volume= + 25,260m2

Presidential Suite
Intercontinental Hotel
Serviced Apartments
Skypark + Theatre
Serviced Apartments
Fitness Center, Spa + Restaurant
Grand Ballroom
Core + Superstructure
Conference Rooms

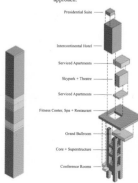

Program Volume   Program Components   Program Combined   Program Optimized

Exploded view of program components, structure and stacking. Minimal site disturbance approach.

Program components are arranged in literal to reflect user-flow in order to maintain a small overall building footprint; none of the building programmatics were concealed.

Hyper-rational program and massing accomodate consideration for future expansion.

Massing is achieved as a result of anticipated user-flow from public to private space.

Program components are pushed, pulled and arranged in order to address site views, massing, plan layouts and program stacking in order to maximize those features that make a world-class hotel desirable; dramatic views as well as public and private exposures that clients demand.

Various component volumes are pushed, pulled and arranged in order to address site views, massing, plan layouts and program stacking in order to maximize those features that make a world-class hotel desirable; dramatic views as well as public and private exposures that clients demand.

Building Systems.

Green Space   Geothermal Energy   Graywater Systems   Solar Array

In addition to the site, MBBC looks to take full advantage of its expansive roof areas with an abundance of green roofs, gardens, trees and other vegetation.

This technique has proven to assist with cooling in summer and heat insulation during winter.

This will also prove an asset as the site is at the center of a major vehicular route in and out of the capital city.

In an effort for Mercedes-Benz Business Center to achieve status as the standard in business destinations in the North Middle East, Geothermal energy systems are introduced for a clean efficient departure from fossil fuels utilized for heating and cooling.

This will help to insure that MBBC will exceed future energy expenditure treaties and requirements in the region.

With an extensive green space program set forth for the Mercedes-Benz Business Center, graywater systems are a logical solution to the heavy water use and upkeep requirements.

Waste water is filtered, treated, reintroduced into the system and diverted to sprinkler and other non-potable water delivery systems.

Strategic implementation of photovoltaic arrays can supplement low volume power for auxilliary systems. This system is maximized primarily by the high altitude climate of Yerevan where potential year-round sunlight is considered.

Superstructure.

The Superstructure was created for both enhanced integrity and seismic absorption. Constructed of steel (100% of which is now recycled) the four main pylons are tied together with trussed 'bridge' volumes at floor levels 2,3,8,9,16 and 17. A minimum of site area was disturbed to anchor the structure. Designed with subgrade pedestrian only access for enhanced building security.

Lower program volumes such as Fitness/Spa/Restaurant are suspended from main fitness/spa volume; they are meant to 'hang' from the building to anticipate and counteract seismic activity and oscillation.

Grand Ballroom and Conference halls are suspended from the larger building for clearly denoted typology as well as increased speed of construction. These volumes are constructed (and chemically isolated) of Aluminum construction for increased rigidity and weight savings of up to 30%.

Prefabrication.

The creation of a steel 'monocoque' was necessary as the basis for the tower portion of the complex to facilitate staggering of floor units while maintaining integrity. Each floor unit is composed of an inner box-truss system around the core opening and main suite walls are made up of a steel shear-wall truss system that extends from the center. The tower core super-structures penetrate floor plates at appropriate locations according to layout.

Reduced Footprint.

A smaller footprint adds value to a development project as there is reduced schedule in site prep. This approach is likened to how an oil rig would be constructed. Where the main pylon is built and key program components can be assembled and lifted into place. Construction scheduling may be enhanced as the building can be simultaneously assembled from above (jump crane) and below (assembly lift).

Floorplate Configurations.

With the Quad-Core Superstructure, the Client is free to design hotel floorplates as desired according to budget, anticipated occupancies, future expansion and so on. Each floorplate acts as a brace both vertically and horizontally throughout the building. Steel slab construction is also cross-braced to lock the structure in place.

Views, green space, suite configurations dictate staggered program elements.

Large Structure. Reduced Footprint.

Exploded Model of Complex Superstructure.

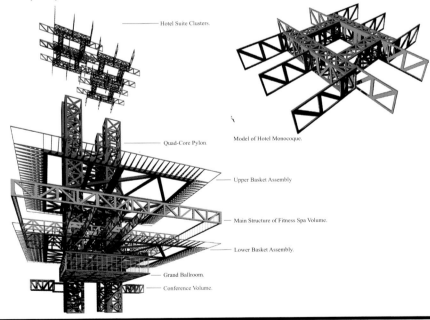

— Hotel Suite Clusters.

— Quad-Core Pylon.

Model of Hotel Monocoque.

— Upper Basket Assembly.

— Main Structure of Fitness Spa Volume.

— Lower Basket Assembly.

— Grand Ballroom.
— Conference Volume.

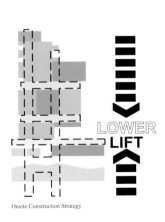

LOWER
LIFT

Onsite Construction Strategy

Floor Plate Variations.

Single-Core 10-room layout, views on all sides.

Dual-Core layout, 16-room plan, views with adjacent outdoor greenspace

Dual-Core layout, views with adjacent outdoor greenspace. Private garden(s).

Dual-Core layout, views with adjacent outdoor greenspace. Private garden(s)

Triple-Core layout, views with corner outdoor greenspace. Integrated structural bracing.

Quad-Core layout, Spa Center, hotel suites or serviced apartments or mechanical floor(s) Integrated superstructure.

Dual-Core layout, Senior suite(s) with private gardens

Mercedes-Benz Business Center Competition
Yerevan, Armenia

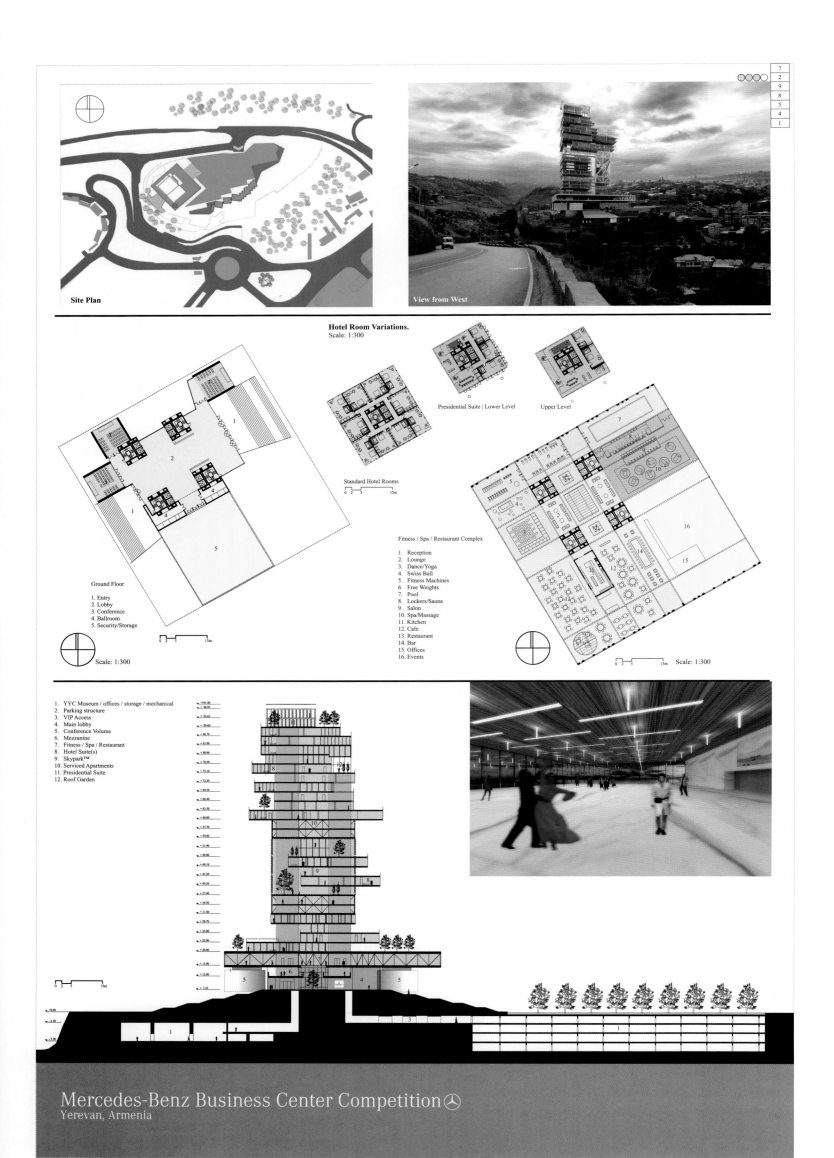

Site Plan

View from West

Hotel Room Variations.
Scale: 1:300

Presidential Suite | Lower Level   Upper Level

Standard Hotel Rooms

0 2 5   15m

Ground Floor

1. Entry
2. Lobby
3. Conference
4. Ballroom
5. Security/Storage

0 2 5   15m

Scale: 1:300

Fitness / Spa / Restaurant Complex

1. Reception
2. Lounge
3. Dance/Yoga
4. Swiss Ball
5. Fitness Machines
6. Free Weights
7. Pool
8. Lockers/Sauna
9. Salon
10. Spa/Massage
11. Kitchen
12. Cafe
13. Restaurant
14. Bar
15. Offices
16. Events

0 2 5   15m   Scale: 1:300

1. YYC Museum / offices / storage / mechanical
2. Parking structure
3. VIP Access
4. Main lobby
5. Conference Volume
6. Mezzanine
7. Fitness / Spa / Restaurant
8. Hotel Suite(s)
9. Skypark™
10. Serviced Apartments
11. Presidential Suite
12. Roof Garden

0 2 5   15m

Mercedes-Benz Business Center Competition
Yerevan, Armenia

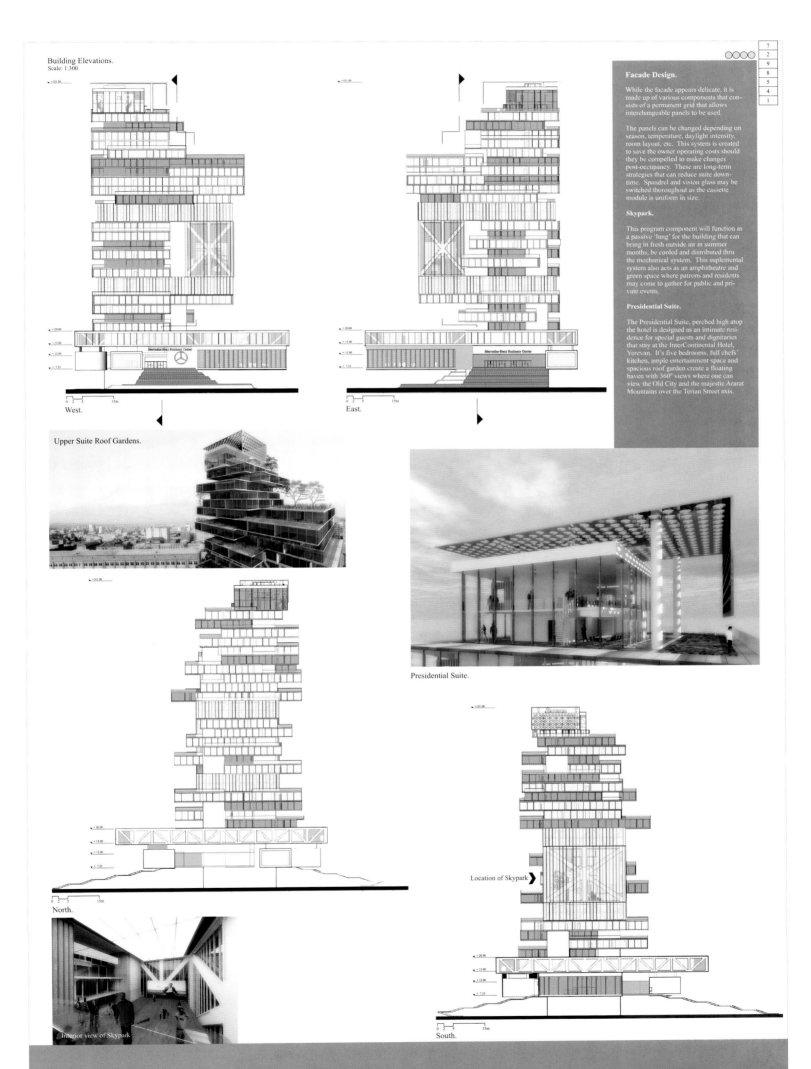

Building Elevations.
Scale: 1:300

West.

East.

Upper Suite Roof Gardens.

North.

Interior view of Skypark

Presidential Suite.

Location of Skypark

South.

Facade Design.

While the facade appears delicate, it is made up of various components that consists of a permanent grid that allows interchangeable panels to be used.

The panels can be changed depending on season, temperature, daylight intensity, room layout, etc. This system is created to save the owner operating costs should they be compelled to make changes post-occupancy. These are long-term strategies that can reduce suite down-time. Spandrel and vision glass may be switched thoroughout as the cassette module is uniform in size.

Skypark.

This program component will function as a passive 'lung' for the building that can bring in fresh outside air in summer months, be cooled and distributed thru the mechanical system. This suplemental system also acts as an amphitheatre and green space where patrons and residents may come to gather for public and private events.

Presidential Suite.

The Presidential Suite, perched high atop the hotel is designed as an intimate residence for special guests and dignitaries that stay at the InterContinental Hotel, Yerevan. It's five bedrooms, full chefs' kitchen, ample entertainment space and spacious roof garden create a floating haven with 360° views where one can view the Old City and the majestic Ararat Mountains over the Terian Street axis.

Mercedes-Benz Business Center Competition
Yerevan, Armenia

231
Small Hospitals Big Idea Competition | *HTDSTUDIO DESIGNOFFICE™*

652

Client : Kaiser-Permanente
Location : Los Angeles, California
Total Floor Area : 125,000 sq ft / 11,612.5m²

Budget : Withheld
Renderings : ©2011 HTDSTUDIO DESIGNOFFICE

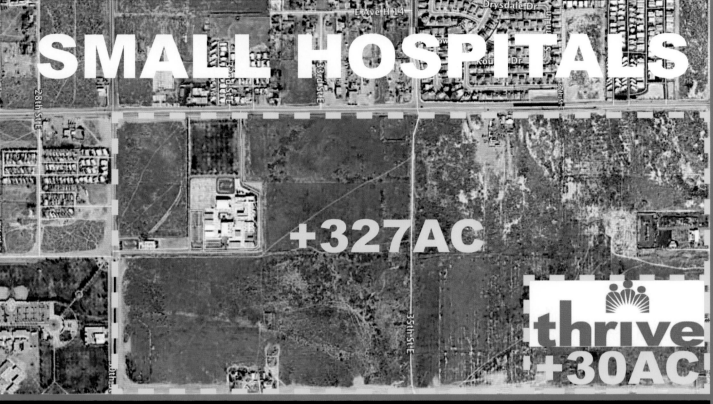

SMALL HOSPITALS BIG

+327AC

thrive
+30AC

40th St E & E Lancaster B

Case Study Site: Lancaster, California

This is a 30 Acre parcel of a sub-rural
327acre site in Southern California with a
close proximity to Alquist-Priolo Earthquake Fault Zones
to the west and south (<10 miles)

Targeted SB 1953 Compliance for 2030

This new facility will surpass 2013 deadlines and
meet the January, 2030 SB 1953 Senate Bill target for all
California Acute-Care Facilities to comply with both
Structural (SPC) and Non-Structural Performance (NPC)
Category requirements.

Excerpt from the 1975 Alquist-Priolo Earthquake Fault Zoning Act
2621.5. Purpose statement

*"...(a) It is the purpose of this chapter to provide for the adoption and administration
of zoning laws, ordinances, rules, and regulations by cities and counties in
implementation of the general plan that is in effect in any city or county.
The Legislature declares that this chapter is intended to provide policies and criteria
to assist cities, counties, and state agencies in the exercise of their responsibility
to prohibit the location of developments and structures for human occupancy across
the trace of active faults. Further, it is the intent of this chapter to provide the citizens
of the state with increased safety and to minimize the loss of life during and immediately
following earthquakes by facilitating seismic retrofitting to strengthen buildings,
including historical buildings, against ground shaking..."*

PROGRAM

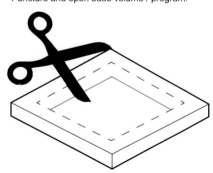

Circulation Ring
Pretreatment
Labs / Diagnostics
Radiology / Xray / MRI
Power / Storage
Entry / Reception
Waiting / Gifts / Cafeteria
Nursing / Clinics
Offices / Examination
Ambulance / Staff Entry
Service Ring
Main Entry
ER
ICU
General Care
Patient Suites (100 beds)

MASSING / AXIS / FLOW

Puncture and open base volume / program.

SERVICE RING

Prototype designed with all administration, consu
waiting, circulation, services, storage, power
facilities creating a perimeter ring.

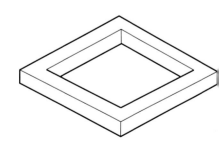

**SERVICES / ADMIN / SUPPORT
CONSULTATION / EXAM**

CIRCULATION

ER/ X-RAY / STERILIZATION

ICU

GENERAL SUITES / CARE / OUTPATIENTS

PROTOTYPE UNIT
A tranformable grid of suites, rooms and key units
as part of a larger network of medical departments.
Circulation spine bisects public and private spaces.

INSULAR CONFIGURATION
Ostensibly the ideal configuration, as suites,
ER, ICU and other sound-sensitive spaces are
located at the center of the facility.

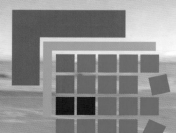

East Lancaster Boulevard

EA COMPETITION

Quake Zone Map

NSTANT ORIENTATION

hift with True North considered
re effective sunlight management.

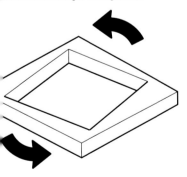

COMPLEX ENTRY

Patient and emergency vehicle entry points
bisect ring generating various zoned buildings
according to area of medical concentration.

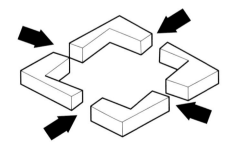

ARTICULATED COMPLEX

Typical hospital prototype with moveable
suites / ER / ICU units located at the
center of the complex.

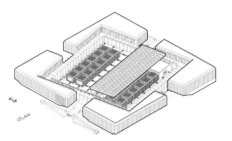

D CONFIGURATION

pated future expansion(s).
ates installation of additional suites
power systems redundancy

CATASTROPHIC CONFIGURATION

For high-alert emergency situations.
Redundant triage / surgery suites
Facilitates power systems redundancy

BUTTERFLY CONFIGURATION

Arranged to create large medical and academic campus
Accomodates installation of additional suites
Facilitates zoned power systems redundancy

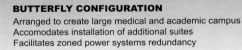
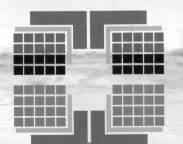

BASE PROTOTYPE

Multiple room units can be added or concentrated zonally withing the complex to meet the demands and scale of hospital.

Four base prototypes comprise of a 100-bed hospital. Hallway units are also reconfigurable, with all required systems and features built in.

Autonomous back-up power and connectivity to address catastrophic-level emergencies.

WELCOMING VISITOR'S ENTRANCE

The facility is celebrated in it's accessibility. Integrated ramps and stairs provide anticipation of entering the hospital.

The lightweight brise-soleil literally follows the daily sun position via hydraulically assisted sliding track.

Natural daylight is refracted into the perimeter building by way of reflective vertical fins; this system will supplement daylighting c

SUITE UNITS

Moveable, self-contained systems. Each suite contains 2 beds with all necessary equipment, services and connectivity. The suites can be subdivided for private configurations.

These units are arranged on an isolated grid of pylons where specific layouts can be created according to the hospital's specific programmatic requirements.

They are designed to provide controllable indirect natural light as well as enhanced air-filtering capabilites that mutually benefit patients, staff and the facility itself.

As expansion is required, pre-engineered units are delivered to the hospital site and 'launched' onto the network grid.

MOVEABLE ER

Multiple ER units can be added or concentrated zonally withing the complex to meet the demands and scale of an emergency.

Autonomous back-up power and connectivity to address catastrophe-level emergencies.

MOVEABLE SUITES

Capable of multitude of arrangements and configurations to meet changing hospital demands, expansions, future development, etc. All units self contained and equipped with required features.

PASSIVE VENTILATION

Warm surface air feeds under building and is drawn in and cooled through inner ring zone.

DYNAMIC SUN SH

Lightweight Brise Soleil follo throughout the day. Mirrore surface reflects ambient day interior spaces

MOBILE PV SYST

PV Cells are arrayed on bris to track sun phasing.

CHILLED BEAM S

Cooling in circulation areas the facility.

SEISMIC ISOLATION

Hospital Facility set on isolators for seismic stability

HEAT DISSIPATIO

Facility is cooled by way of g buried below grade.

COMPLETE 100-BED FACILITY

Although the hospital sits on a bed of isolators above-grade, the facility is fully accessible to the disabled, where the various entries welcome all those who visit.

A complete cluster creates an efficient, autonomous environment where local residents receive quality care, and where medical professionals and staff can work efficiently as never before.

The Kaiser-Permanente Thrive Center's configuration can be maximized literally 'on the fly', with its network of key moveable room units in order to meet the ever-changing and growing needs of the community.

DYNAMIC SUN SHADING

Lightweight Brise Soleil follows sun throughout the day. Mirrored under surface reflects ambient daylight into interior spaces.

CIRCULATION RING

The inner circulation ring provides access to the patient suites, emergency rooms, ICU and the other key room units that are designed to move and be reconfigured when the hospital's needs change.

INNER SANCTUARY

Wildflowers and local ground cover are planted in the central area inside the circulation ring; this helps to dissipate radiant heat and noise coming off the site's surface.

LOOMENERGY TECHNOLOGY

uilt with their patented solid oxide fuel cell technology, Bloom's Energy Server™ is a new class of distributed power generator, oducing clean, reliable, affordable electricity at the customer site. Fuel cells are devices that convert fuel into electricity through clean electro-chemical process rather than dirty combustion. They are like batteries except that they always run. Our particular be of fuel cell technology is different than legacy "hydrogen" fuel cells in four main ways:

ow cost materials – their cells use a common sand-like powder instead of precious metals like platinum or corrosive materials e acids.
gh electrical efficiency – they can convert fuel into electricity at nearly twice the rate of some legacy technologies
uel flexibility – their systems are capable of using either renewable or fossil fuels.
eversible – our technology is capable of both energy generation and storage.
ach Server provides 100kW of power, enough to meet the baseload needs of 100 average homes or a small office building...
iy and night, in roughly the footprint of a standard parking space.

ta and description courtesy Bloomenergy

ENERGY

Bloom Stacks / Servers
(50) Stacks for movable units (1 each @ 1 KW (for redundancy) = 50kW
(12) Stacks for 6 ER Units (for redundancy) =12 kW
(4) Stacks for 4 ICU's (for redundancy) =4 kW
(4) Bloom Servers (4x100kW=400kW / to serve 120,000 SF)

RMAL LOOP

SUBTOTAL 466kW @ +$8/ Watt = + $ 3,728,000.00

DYNAMIC SUN SHADING w/ INTEGRATED PV SYSTEM
Lightweight space-frame canopy with mirrored belly and integrated PV system feature. Industrial motorized and electronically timed gliding track conveyance.
SUBTOTAL +17,220 GSF x +$300 / SF = +$5,166,000.00

ARCHITECTURE

Infrastructure (masonry / steel / site dev / carpentry / MEP)
90,000 SF @+$150/PSF = $13,500,000.00
(Manufactured) Moveable Hospital Suites
20' x 20' = 400 SF x $600/PSF=$240,000 x 50 =$12,000,000.00
(Manufactured) Moveable ER's
20'x 40' = 800 SF x $1200/PSF= $960,000 x 6 = $4,140,000.00
(Manufactured) Moveable ICU
20'x 40' = 800 SF x $800/PSF= $640,000 x 6 = $3,840,000.00
Inner Ring (Circulation / Suite Access / MEP)
224 x 12' x 4= (10,572 SF) x $450 SF= $4,838,000.00
Service Ring (Perimeter Buildings)
90,000 SF x $500/SF = $45,000,000.00
TOTAL: +$83,318,000.00

ARCHITECTURE + INFRASTRUCTURE + ENERGY
TOTAL (+220,172 GSF)= +$92,212,200.00

232

Busan Opera House | *Alessandro Console Studio*

Competition : International Ideas Competition for Busan Opera House
Promoter : Busan Metropolitan City - BIACF
Location : Busan – Republic of Korea
Year : 2011

Project Team : Gina Oliva, Claudia Streuli, Giorgio Streuli

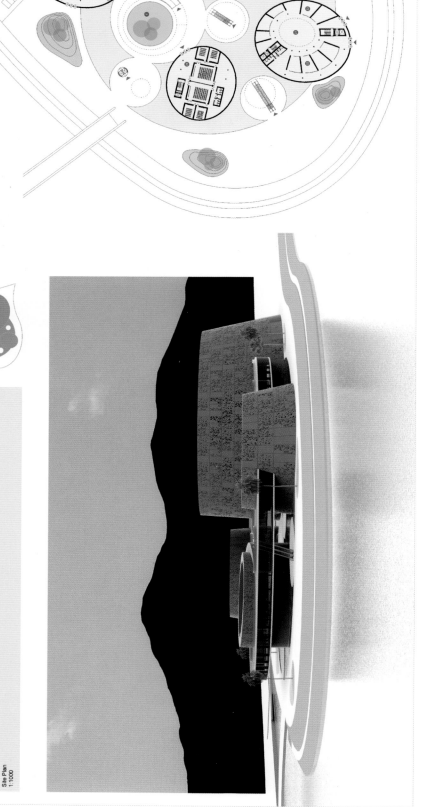

Plan Level 0
1:700

1. Exterior Space the Water Garden
2. Opera House Foyer
3. Event Room
4. Lounge Bar
5. Security Room
6. Cloakroom
7. VIP Lounge

8. Seats for Spectators
9. Orchestra Space

10. Technical Facilities

11. Space under the Main Stage
12. Space under the Stage Right
13. Area for Background Assembly

14. Staff Entrance
15. Dressing Rooms for Orchestra
16. Warehouse for Orchestra

17. Warehouse for Musical Instruments
18. Orchestra Library
19. Conductor Work Room
20. Conductor Room
21. Office for Orchestra Engineer
22. Marketing & Development Office
23. Company Office
24. Office for Presentation

25. Multi Purpose Theater Foyer
26. Seats for Spectators
27. Stage
28. Dressing Rooms
29. Make-up Rooms
30. Technical Facilities

31. Auxiliary Facilities Lobby
32. Specialized Shopping Center
33. Convention Room
34. Breakout Rooms

35. Staff Parking Area
36. Loading Dock

Public Entrances
Vertical Accesses to the Plate
VIP Entrance
Staff & Artists Entrances

BUSAN OPERA HOUSE

A opera house usually tends to be – just only due to its huge dimension and its peculiar features – a landmark, a "singular object" within a certain urban context. Thus, the sustainability of this kind of large and great intervention is based on the necessity of combining the outstanding character of the building itself with its environmental potentiality in generating and/or implementing urban quality of life within the city. The real goal then is to give the City an added value not only for economic and promotional purpose, but also for improving the quality and livability of its public and collective spaces.

Starting from these considerations, we conceive the Busan Opera House not merely as a "singular object", but rather as a "spatial system" able to match properly the programmatic and typological requirements scheduled by the competition, but also able to generate relations within the city, due to the creation of new public and collective space open and freely accessible to all people.

The Opera House complex is composed by four main elliptical blocks — with different heights and dimensions — located in the intervention area in a way to create an in-between open space.
The discontinuous and non-linear setting plan fosters the creation of a public space that is clearly defined and protected but, at the same time, opened towards the city and the sea, due to the presence of oriented crossings and selected visual connections through the area.
On a higher level (+7.00 meters), the unity of the "spatial system" is guaranteed by a circular floating plate that links each other the four main elliptical blocks.

The floating plate has a double role in the whole configuration of the project.
On one hand, to place the horizontal connecting element (the plate) among the other buildings (the blocks) on a higher level (+7.00 meters) allows to achieve more area in the lower one (0.00), that is the accessing level to the island along the coastline. This way, the lower level (0.00) becomes an open platform conceived as a further extension of the main waterfront scheduled in the general master plan of the North Port and located in the mainland side, in front of the Opera House area. Then, the complex becomes an integrated part of the wider maritime park, developed all around, with its own specific characterization.
On the other hand, the organization and the spatial relationship among the different parts of the complex allow to multiply and to increase the external greeneries and the public space available.
As a consequence, the public spaces developed vertically at various levels where it assumes different roles and features: at the lower level (0.00), underneath the floating plate, there is the **Water Garden**; at the intermediate level (+7.00 meters - within the plate), the **Public Hub**; at the higher level (+12.00 meters - the plate's roof), the **Floating Plaza**.
The connections among public spaces is assured by vertical access points (ramp, escalators, lifts). This way, public spaces works independently from use and times of the Opera House, so that it is open and freely accessible to all people.

01. FORMALIZING THE PROGRAM

02. ARRANGING THE PROGRAM IN THE AREA

03. IDENTIFYING THE COMMON AREA

04. LIFTING UP THE PUBLIC SPACE CONNECTING THE FOUR BLOCKS

OPERA HOUSE
MULTI PURPOSE THEATRE
FACILITIES
EXHIBITION SHOPPING CAFE
CONVENTION BANQUET RESTAURANT

01 02 03 04

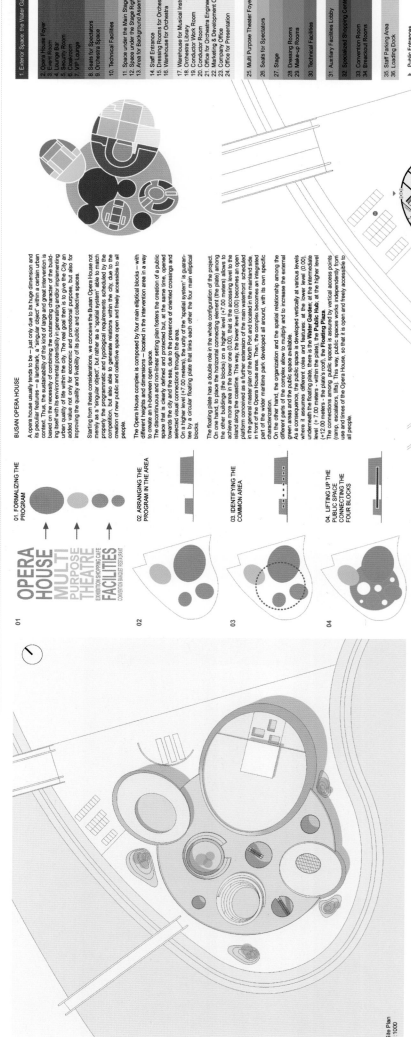

Site Plan
1:1000

View of the Floating Plaza

View of the Water Garden

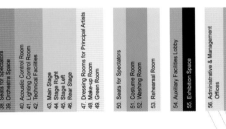

37. Ticket Office
38. Seats for Spectators
39. Orchestra Space
40. Acoustic Control Room
41. Lighting Control Room
42. Technical Facilities

43. Main Stage
44. Stage Right
45. Stage Left
46. Rear Stage

47. Dressing Rooms for Principal Artists
48. Make-up Room
49. Green Room

50. Seats for Spectators
51. Costume Room
52. Washing Room
53. Rehearsal Room

54. Auxiliary Facilities Lobby

55. Exhibition Space

56. Administrative & Management Offices
57. Cafe / Bar
58. Souvenir Store
59. Facilities for Childrens
60. Tourist Informations

Level 0
THE WATER GARDEN

Level 1
THE PUBLIC HUB

Level 2
THE FLOATING PLAZA

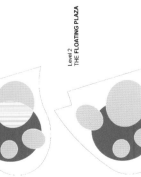

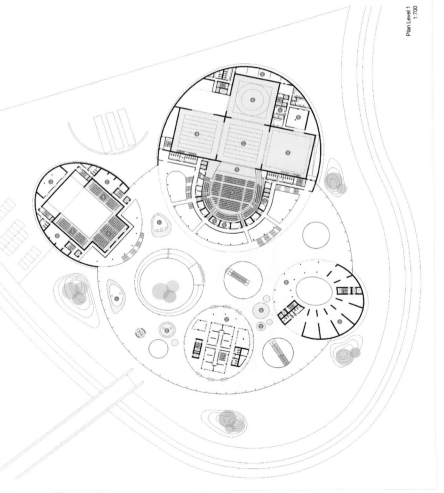

Plan Level 1
1:700

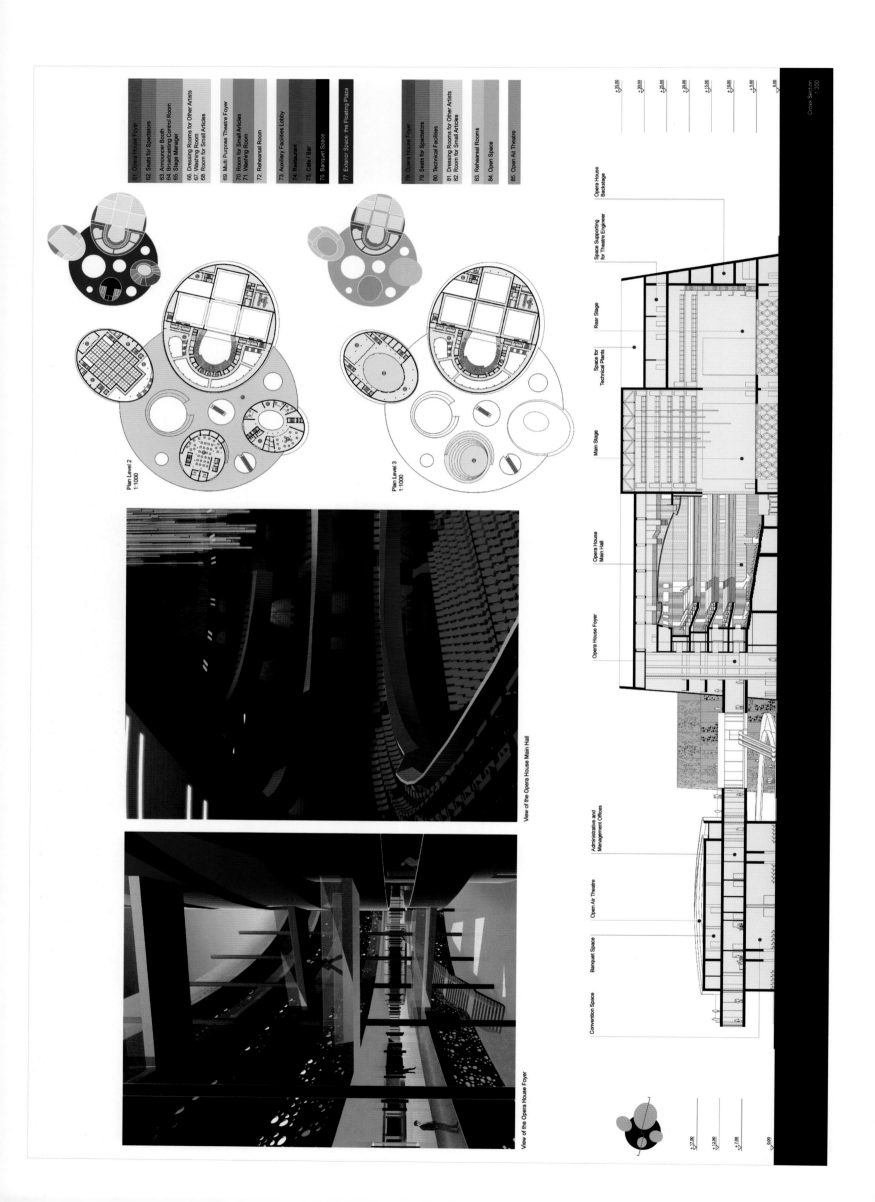

61. Opera House Foyer
62. Seats for Spectators
63. Announcer Booth
64. Broadcasting Control Room
65. Stage Manager
66. Dressing Rooms for Other Artists
67. Washing Room
68. Room for Small Articles

69. Multi Purpose Theatre Foyer
70. Room for Small Articles
71. Washing Room
72. Rehearsal Room

73. Auxiliary Facilities Lobby
74. Restaurant
75. Cafe / Bar
76. Banquet Space

77. Exterior Space the Floating Plaza

78. Opera House Foyer
79. Seats for Spectators
80. Technical Facilities
81. Dressing Rooms for Other Artists
82. Room for Small Articles

83. Rehearsal Rooms
84. Open Space
85. Open Air Theatre

Plan Level 2
1:1000

Plan Level 3
1:1000

View of the Opera House Main Hall

View of the Opera House Foyer

Convention Space

Banquet Space

Open Air Theatre

Administrative and Management Offices

Opera House Foyer

Opera House Main Hall

Main Stage

Space for Technical Plants

Rear Stage

Space Supporting for Theatre Engineer

Opera House Backstage

Cross Section
1:300

658

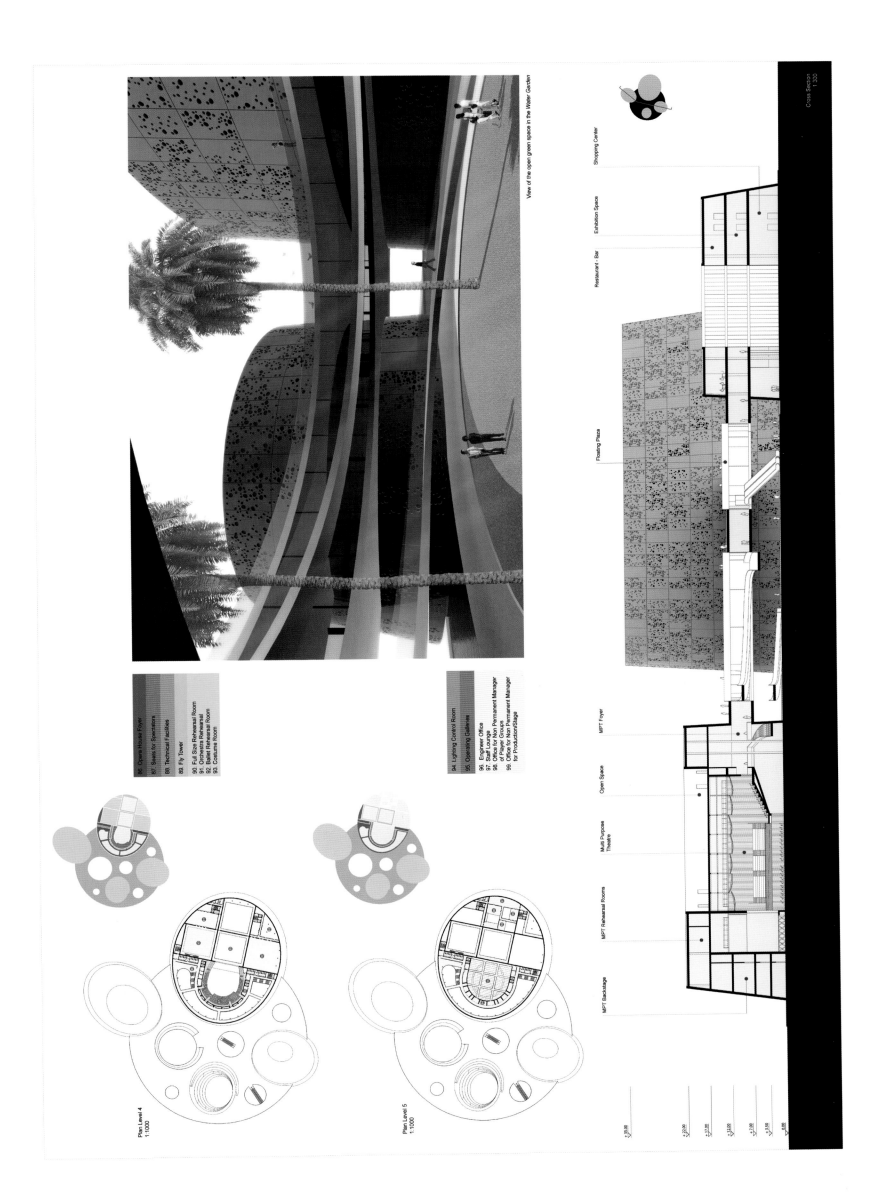

View of the open green space in the Water Garden

86. Opera House Foyer
87. Seats for Spectators
88. Technical Facilities
89. Fly Tower
90. Full Size Rehearsal Room
91. Orchestra Rehearsal
92. Ballet Rehearsal Room
93. Costume Room

94. Lighting Control Room
95. Operating Galleries
96. Engineer Office
97. Staff Lounge
98. Office for Non Permanent Manager of Player Groups
99. Office for Non Permanent Manager for Production/Stage

Plan Level 4
1:1000

Plan Level 5
1:1000

Cross Section
1:300

Shopping Center

Exhibition Space

Restaurant - Bar

Floating Plaza

MPT Foyer

Open Space

Multi Purpose Theatre

MPT Rehearsal Rooms

MPT Backstage

+35.00
+22.00
+17.00
+12.00
+7.00
+3.50
0.00

Busan Opera House | *Paul Preissner*

Location : Busan, South Korea
Client : Busan Metropolitan City
Program : Opera, Recital Hall, Public Plaza, Dining, Retail
Area : 34,938SM(Site) / 60,000SM(Building)

Cost : KRW130,000 million(US$140,500,000)
Status : Design 2011(Competition)

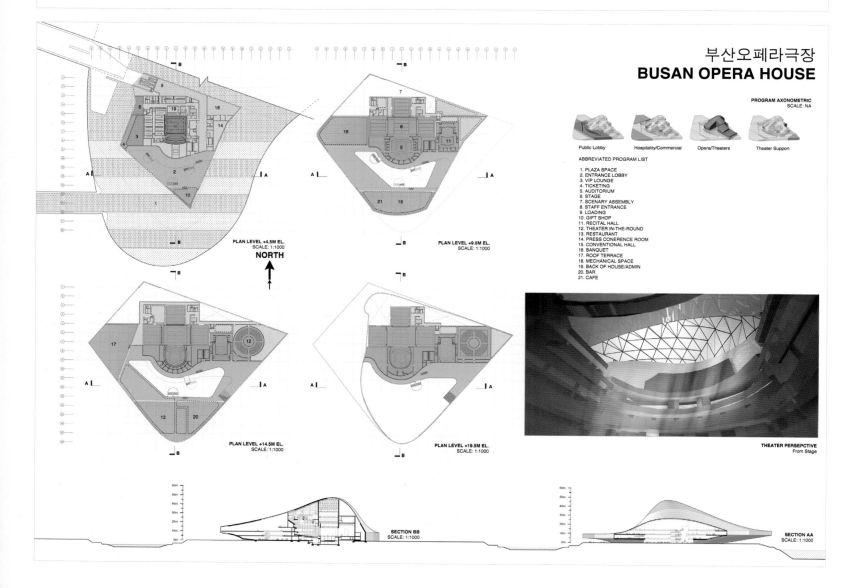

BUSAN OPERA HOUSE
LOCATION Busan, South Korea
CLIENT Busan Metropolitan City
PROGRAM Opera, Recital Hall, Public Plaza, Dining, Retail
AREA 34,938SM (Site) / 60,000SM (Building)
COST KRW130,000 million (US$140,500,000)
STATUS Design 2011 (Competition)

The design for the Busan Opera House relies on three main ideas:

To provide a strong urban statement in newly forming cultural district;
To develop a clear visual strategy for the identity of the Opera which is simultaneously familiar and never-before seen;
To create a unique building for the center of the cultural district with a contemporary architectural approach shaped to optimize active and passive energy use.

This project develops its personality by a combination of unique formal expression through the shape of the building, rational programmatic organization, and a curated graphic pattern (stripes) in order to produce a project that looks like nothing before it.

The project cantilevers its second level 5m above the entry level to allow for a very petit ground level footprint that enable the public to be welcomes by the building before even entering. This allows for a sequence from the pedestrian bridge that takes one over the creek, then onto the site, then within the buildings perimeter gallery sheltered from the elements by the cantilevered volume of the restaurant and convention spaces, to finally being within the major public lobby for the opera. The lobby is located within one of the glass stripes of the volume allowing for an impressive space and acts as the counterpart to the massive opaque volumes of the theaters.

//PAUL PREISSNER
/ ARCHITECTS //   CHICAGO ILL USA www.paulpreissner.com

부산오페라극장
BUSAN OPERA HOUSE

PROGRAM AXONOMETRIC
SCALE: NA

Public Lobby   Hospitality/Commercial   Opera/Theaters   Theater Support

ABBREVIATED PROGRAM LIST

1. PLAZA SPACE
2. ENTRANCE LOBBY
3. VIP LOUNGE
4. TICKETING
5. AUDITORIUM
6. STAGE
7. SCENARY ASSEMBLY
8. STAFF ENTRANCE
9. LOADING
10. GIFT SHOP
11. RECITAL HALL
12. THEATER IN-THE-ROUND
13. RESTAURANT
14. PRESS CONERENCE ROOM
15. CONVENTIONAL HALL
16. BANQUET
17. ROOF TERRACE
18. MECHANICAL SPACE
19. BACK OF HOUSE/ADMIN
20. BAR
21. CAFE

PLAN LEVEL +4.5M EL.
SCALE: 1:1000
NORTH

PLAN LEVEL +9.5M EL.
SCALE: 1:1000

PLAN LEVEL +14.5M EL.
SCALE: 1:1000

PLAN LEVEL +19.5M EL.
SCALE: 1:1000

THEATER PERSEPCTIVE
From Stage

SECTION BB
SCALE: 1:1000

SECTION AA
SCALE: 1:1000

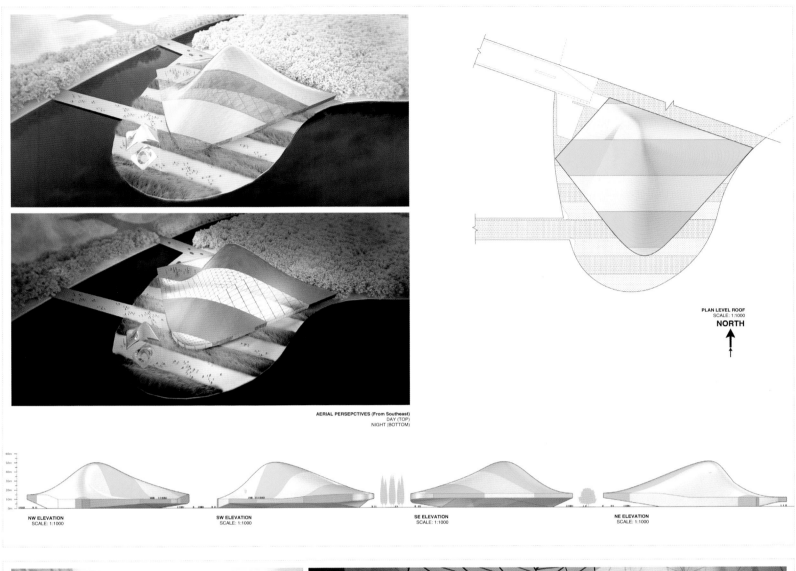

PLAN LEVEL ROOF
SCALE: 1:1000

NORTH

AERIAL PERSEPCTIVES (From Southeast)
DAY (TOP)
NIGHT (BOTTOM)

NW ELEVATION
SCALE: 1:1000

SW ELEVATION
SCALE: 1:1000

SE ELEVATION
SCALE: 1:1000

NE ELEVATION
SCALE: 1:1000

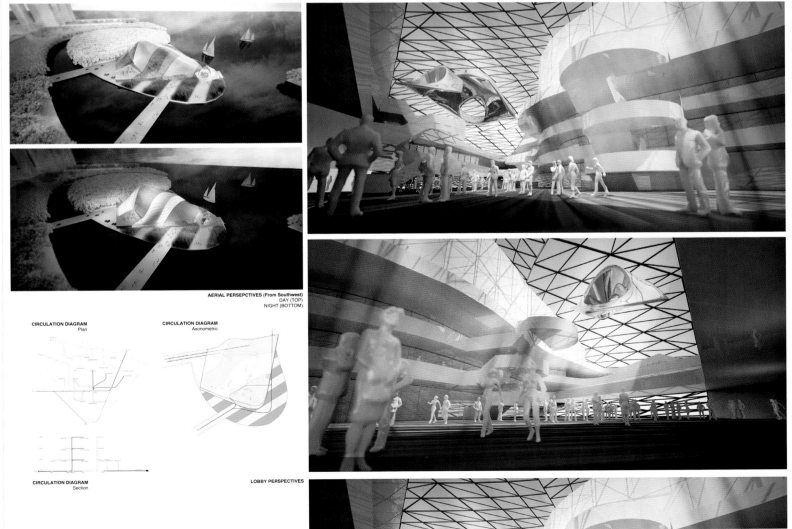

AERIAL PERSEPCTIVES (From Southwest)
DAY (TOP)
NIGHT (BOTTOM)

CIRCULATION DIAGRAM
Plan

CIRCULATION DIAGRAM
Axonometric

CIRCULATION DIAGRAM
Section

LOBBY PERSPECTIVES

234

Busan Opera House | *PRAUD*

Project : Competition Entry
Program : Opera House
Location : Busan, S.Korea

Program Area : 52,000m²
Team : Dongwoo Yim, Rafael Luna, Stacy Choi

CONCEPT

opera house + small theater + multi purpose theater + common area =

The concept starts from how multiple performance facilities can share common program. One way is to share public space such as foyers and the other is to share theatre function itself. We found out an interesting potential of theatre that when one performance facility share its theatre function with other facilities, various types of performance stages could be created by transformation of stage and chamber facilities. Unlike having a fixed performance stage and sharing common public space, it is a way of providing a variety of experience to the audience as well as using the opera house more efficient way.

To achieve this goal, we developed a transformable "cylinder" not only for stage/chamber function but also for structural stability. Multiple disks in the "cylinder" can move vertically depends on type and size of performance you need and numbers of performances at the same time. This vertical movement also creates void that provides visual connection between floors/masses so that a performance can be shown to audience in various ways. Also these disks can rotate so that performance can happen in multiple directions as well.

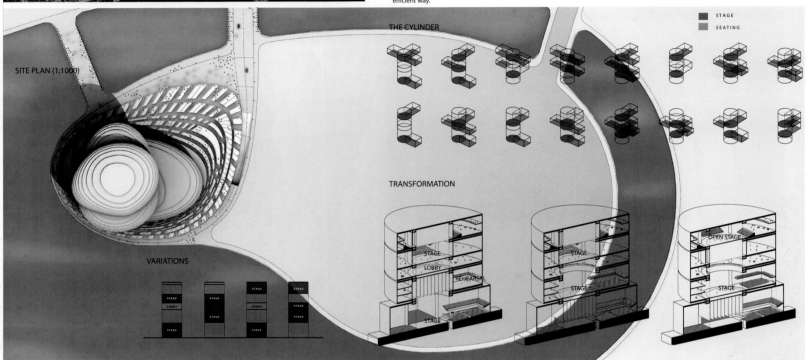

SITE PLAN (1:1000)

THE CYLINDER

STAGE
SEATING

VARIATIONS

TRANSFORMATION

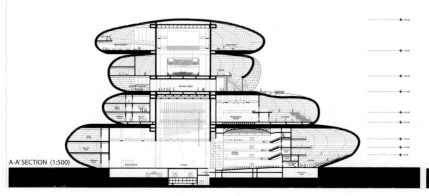

A-A' SECTION (1:500)

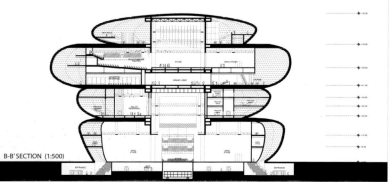

B-B' SECTION (1:500)

1st MASS PLAN (1:500)

2nd MASS PLAN (1:500)

3RD MASS PLAN (1:500)

4th MASS PLAN (1:500)

Participants : Miguel Mallaguerra, Susana Jesus, Bruno Martins, Hugo Aires, Lisa Borges
Project : Opera House
Typology : Public Building
Location : Busan , South Korea

Client : City of Busan
Year : 2011

Busan Opera House

International Ideas Competition
Arrival from the Sea

THE PLACE

Located on the southern Korean peninsula, Busan Port benefits from optimal conditions that make it an unique world-class port, such as the selter provided by surrounding mountains and its location adjacent to major arterial sea routes.
Being a part of the North Port development Plan, the site for the proposed project is in the heart of the Marine Culture District, in an artificial island that will allow the creation of an optimal water friendly environment.

THE PROJECT GUIDELINES

The construction of the Opera House will gather private and public spheres creating a dynamic flux of economy and culture. It will be an easily accessible cultural and leisure center that will benefit from stunning views over the city and the sea.
The scale of the future buildings included in the major Plan and the outlined silhouette of the mountains helps to define our project and the study of its proportions, imagining it in the context of tomorrow. All the accessibilities and means of transport were also thought for the future atmosphere and growing requests.
The Opera House will be surrounded by elegant skyscrapers and to delineate its special character it will be featured in a natural sculptural object that will seem to be emerging from the sea.

THE CONCEPT

The concept is supported by these realities, the surrounding mountains, the future tall buildings outlining the bay, an artificial island that now expands the territory towards the sea. This will set another scale to the city. To give the same dimensional scale to the Opera House, it was established a ratio between the height of the buildings and the length of the proposal. So the vertical became horizontal, and the land was shaped in order to highlight the building, establishing the same scale and respecting its identity as an unique object.

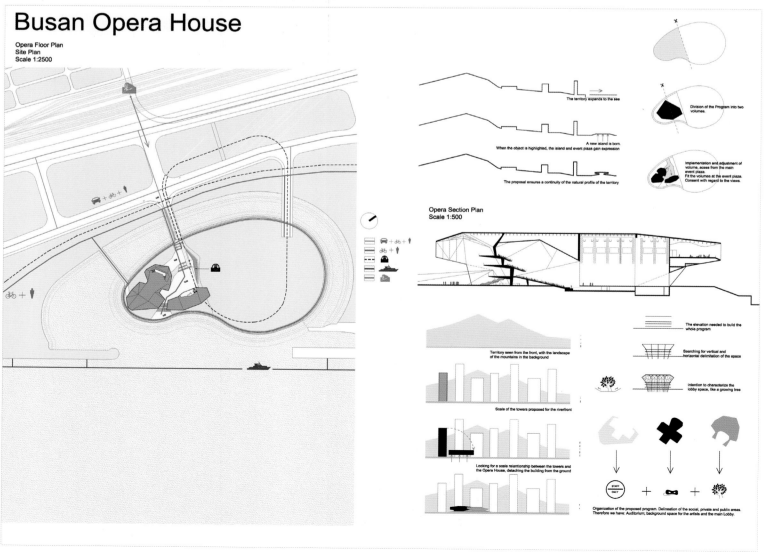

Busan Opera House

Opera Floor Plan
Site Plan
Scale 1:2500

Opera Section Plan
Scale 1:500

Busan Opera House

International Ideas Competition
Arrival from the City

THE OBJECT

Our proposal contemplates the distribution of the program in different levels according to its requirements. Morphologically the object appears as a result of plans connecting the edges that limit the interior space. The internal spaces adjustment defines the external shape, providing morphological movements and tensions.

The intention is to take this philosophy further, particularly in the interior, taking advantage of the structural elements, as it happens in the big auditorium main entrance.

As a result of the program, there is a multi-level division that is literally grabbed to the branching structure of pillars and beams, in a sculptural way, just like a tree. The light systems go along with this purpose, creating an impressive spectacle and giving dignity to the space. We can see the Opera from distant parts of the city

THE PROGRAM

The program allows the fraction of the proposal in two separate buildings. The result of this division and orientation of the two buildings is a creation of a large square, which is the arrival site. The square is drawn in order to take the best advantage of the views and also to enjoy interesting perspectives of these buildings sculptural forms and details.

The main building is organized in three distinct zones: social area, private area and public area, which corresponds to the lobby, the artist area and the auditorium. Its connections and functionality gave shape to this object.

Busan Opera House

Opera Floor Plan
Level 01 (+5.00)
Scale 1:750

Opera Floor Plan
Level 03 (+21.60)
Scale 1:750

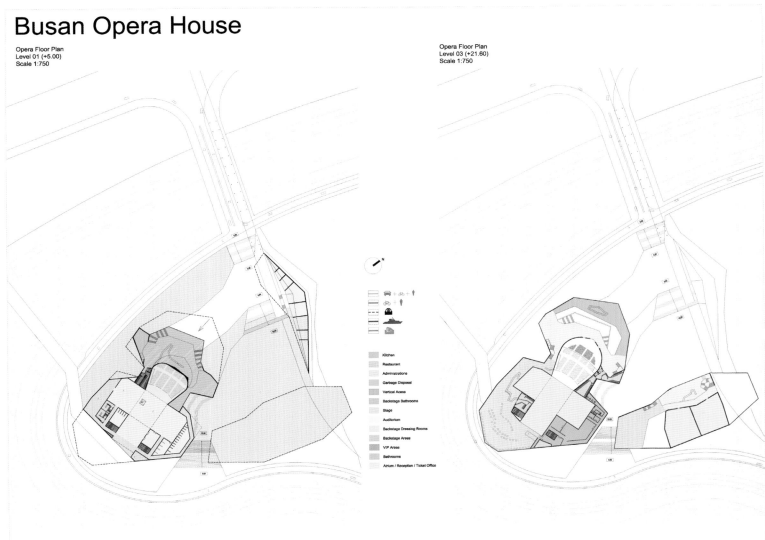

Kitchen
Restaurant
Administration
Garbage Disposal
Vertical Acess
Backstage Bathrooms
Stage
Auditorium
Backstage Dressing Rooms
Backstage Areas
VIP Areas
Bathrooms
Atrium / Reception / Ticket Office

International Ideas Competition for Opera House Busan, S.Korea. 2011
Client : Busan Metropolitan City, S. Korea
Project phase : International Idea Competition - Settled
Surface : 60.000m²

Collaborators : Agita Putnina, Furio Sordini, Alessandro Carabini, Lina Gronskyte, Dana Mazaarani, Daniel Ghutler, Liva Vilcina

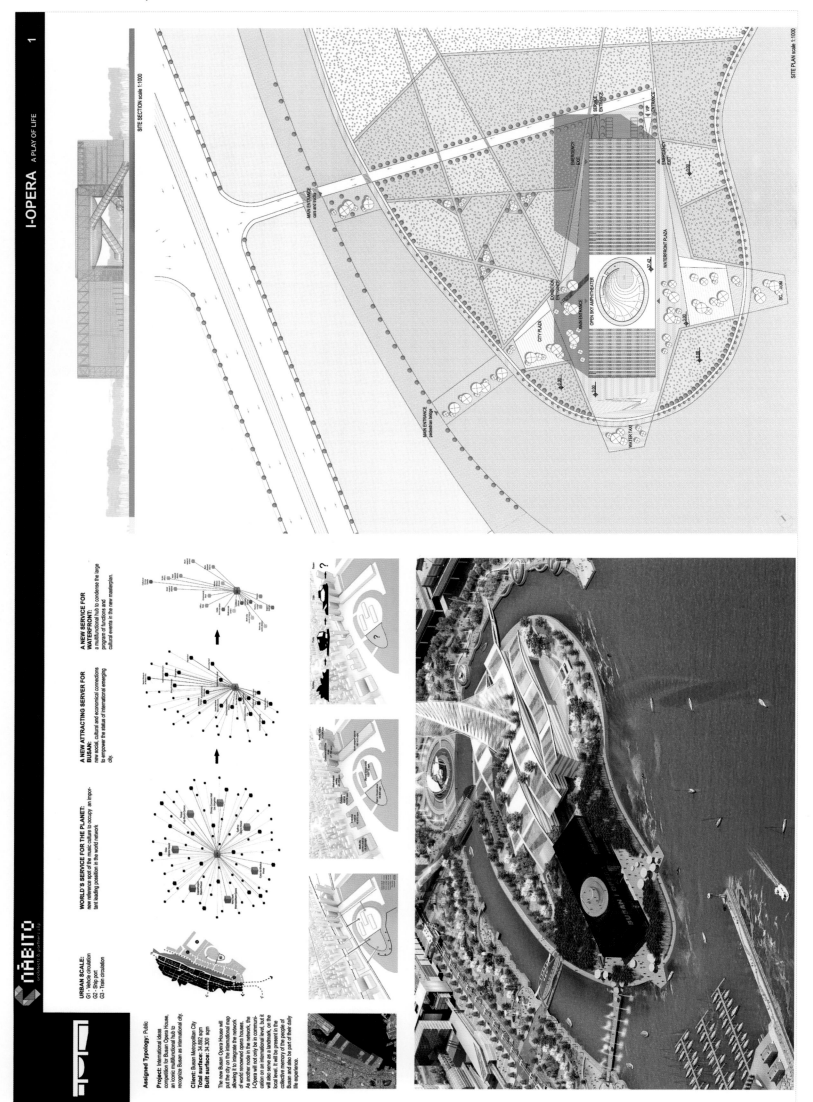

I-OPERA A PLAY OF LIFE

SITE SECTION scale 1:1000

SITE PLAN scale 1:1000

WORLD'S SERVICE FOR THE PLANET:
new reference spot of the music culture to occupy an important leading position in the world network

A NEW ATTRACTING SERVER FOR BUSAN:
new social, cultural and economical connections to empower the status of international emerging city.

A NEW SERVICE FOR WATERFRONT:
a multifunctional hub to condense the large program of functions and cultural events in the new masterplan.

URBAN SCALE:
01 - Vehicle circulation
02 - Ship port
03 - Train circulation

Assigned Typology: Public

Project: International ideas competition for Busan Opera House, an iconic multifunctional hub to recognize Busan as international city.

Client: Busan Metropolitan City
Total surface: 34.882 sqm
Built surface: 34.300 sqm

The new Busan Opera House will put the city on the international map allowing it to integrate the network of world renowned opera houses. As a central node in the network, the I-Opera will not only be in communication on an international level, but it will also serve as a landmark, on the local level. It will be present in the collective memory of the people of Busan and also be part of their daily life experience.

NABITO
architect & partners s.l.p.

URBAN CONCEPT

Public space between Busan and the sea

The podium expands into multiple platform

A green bamboo forest to generate social, economical and environmental sustainability

A multiscalar infrastructure

MULTIPLE CONFIGURATIONS AND INTERACTIONS

I-OPERA a play for life

In this Project for the Busan Opera House we reproduce and amplify this feeling over the entire concept. We interpret life as a play and the building is in itself a platform for various performances. We built an I-Opera, an integrated Building. We hung the program to the structure, mixing different functions and activities surrounded by various scenographies. We offer, manipulate and mix realities and allow users be a part of the performance. It is moreover a big infrastructure related to citizens and connected like a server to the world and to the city of Busan.

I-OPERA CONCEPT

Space   Space   Space

Identify three main spaces

Unify the all spaces and amplify

Multiply the connections

| Flexible Space | Public Space | Ritual Space |

A structure to transform the spaces into stages

| Flexible Stage | Public Stage | Ritual Stage |

Hanging the 'Spectacle of life'

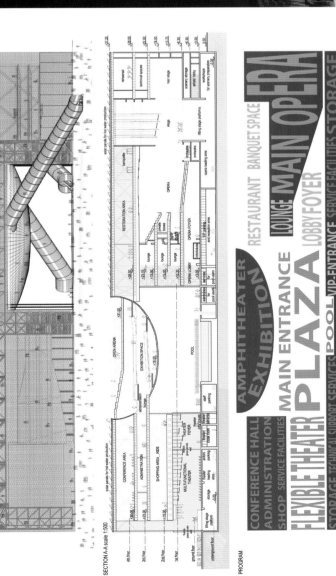

ELEVATION:

SECTION A-A scale 1:500

PROGRAM

CONFERENCE HALL

ADMINISTRATION

SHOP SERVICE FACILITIES

FLEXIBLE THEATER

STORAGE TECHNICAL SUPPORT SERVICES

AMPHITHEATER

EXHIBITION

MAIN ENTRANCE

PLAZA

POOL VIP-ENTRANCE SERVICE FACILITIES STORAGE

RESTAURANT BANQUET SPACE

LOUNGE MAIN OPERA

LOBBY FOYER

ERA

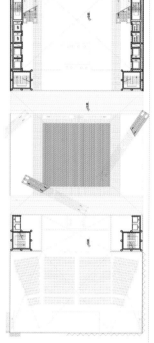

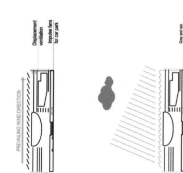

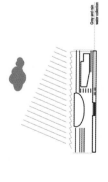

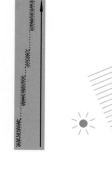

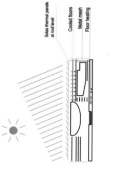

ñÃÈITO

GROUND FLOOR scale 1:500

1ˢᵗ FLOOR scale 1:500

2ⁿᵈ FLOOR scale 1:500

ENVIRONMENTAL STRATEGIES

Cooling will be provided by an innovative desiccant absorption and evaporative cooling system. Solar thermal hot water generated from roof mounted collectors will be used to regenerate the absorption in summer. In addition, an energy efficient surface cooling will be used to improve occupancy comfort. This is proposed to aid the control of heat gain generated by high occupancy densities.

VENTILATION STRATEGY:
It is envisaged that ventilation within the development will be provided through mechanical means for a considerable proportion of the year. The proposal is to deliver the ventilation air to all spaces in a displacement manner.

RECYCLED AND RECLAIMED WATER:
There are opportunities on the site the reclamation of water. A grey water and rain recovery system is proposed for the development. Stored water will be utilised for WC flushing and limited irrigation.

WATER EFFICIENCY
The principle of water efficiency is to reduce the quantity of water needed to satisfy any particular end use demand.

SOLAR THERMAL HOT WATER GENERATION
Solar thermal collectors will be used to generate hot water and harvesting solar energy. High solar radiation levels provide good opportunities for energy capture. An array of solar thermal collectors will be located in the roof of the building.

LED ECOFRIENDLY MEADIA WALL
The building works as a self-sufficient organic system, harvesting solar energy by day and using it to illuminate the screen on facade after dark, mirroring a day's climatic cycle.

Displacement ventilation

Impulse fans for car park

PREVAILING WIND DIRECTION

Grey and rain water collection

Solar thermal panels at roof level

Cooled floors

Metal mesh

Floor heating

Zero energy Meadia Wall

Day   Night

Solar Panels

LED Panels Coupled with Photovoltaic cells

CONFIGURATIONS OF MULTI-FUNCTIONAL THEATRE

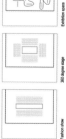

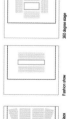
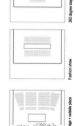
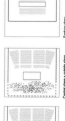
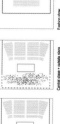

Banquet space

Exhibition space

360 degree stage

Fashion show

Central stage + outside plaza

Central stage

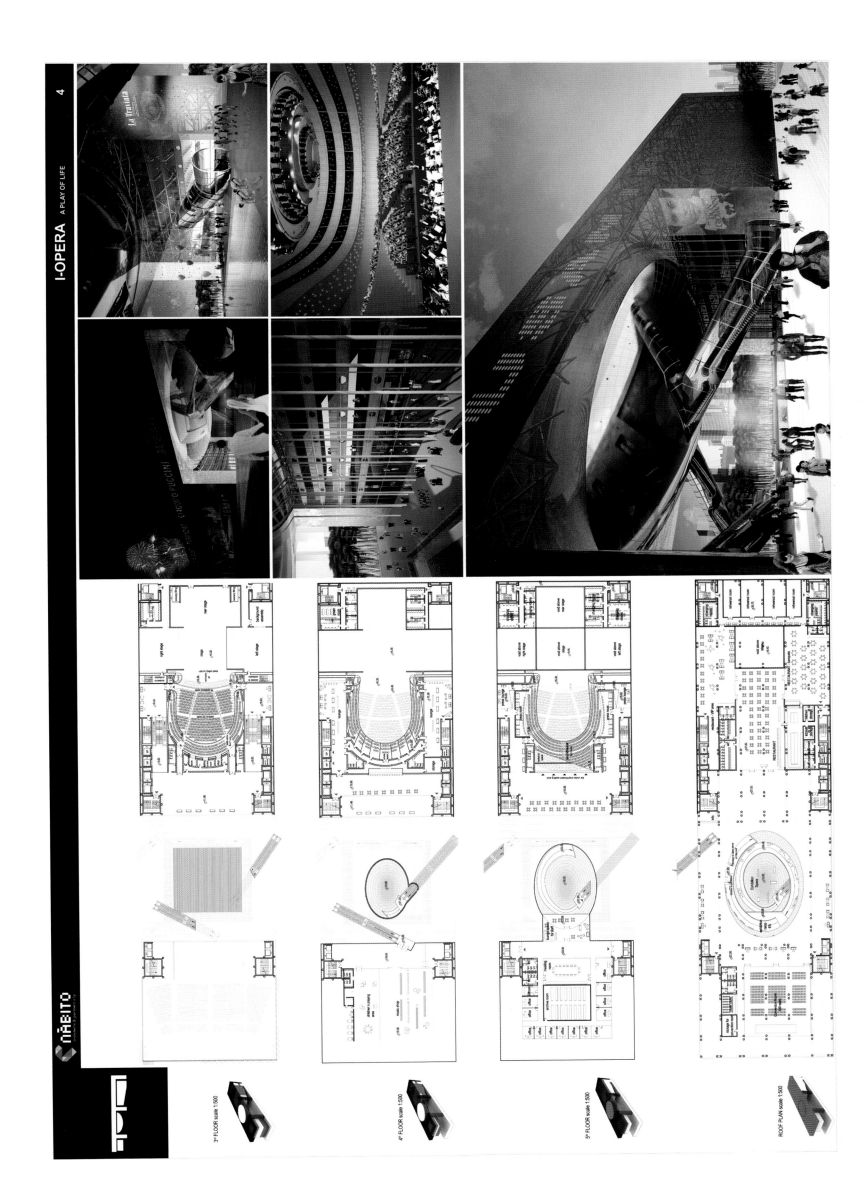

I-OPERA A PLAY OF LIFE

4

3rd FLOOR scale 1:500

4th FLOOR scale 1:500

5th FLOOR scale 1:500

ROOF PLAN scale 1:500

Stranded Shells.
Busan Opera House

Aerial View of Opera House

Stranded Shells I New Busan Opera House

Envelope Detail

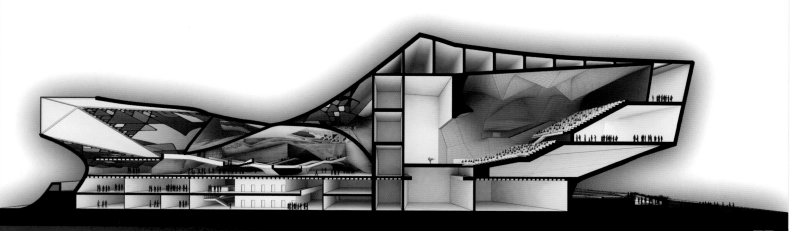

Stranded Shells I New Busan Opera House

Plinth

Interior of Atrium

Interior of Balcony

Stranded Shells I New Busan Opera House

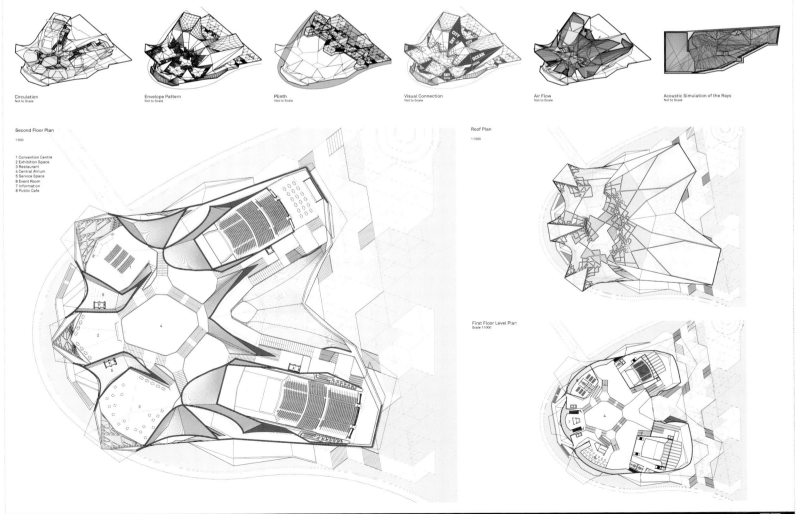

Circulation
Not to Scale

Envelope Pattern
Not to Scale

Plinth
Not to Scale

Visual Connection
Not to Scale

Air Flow
Not to Scale

Acoustic Simulation of the Rays
Not to Scale

Second Floor Plan
1:500

1 Convention Centre
2 Exhibition Space
3 Restaurant
4 Central Atrium
5 Service Space
6 Event Room
7 Information
8 Public Cafe

Roof Plan
1:1000

First Floor Level Plan
Scale 1:1000

Stranded Shells I New Busan Opera House

The Kaohsiung Maritime Cultural & Pop Music Center | *Leon11*

Team and working methodology : Made In architects, is a net_work horizontal
Studio that forms itselve from the union of various studios and spanish architects
working in distance positions
The main brains of this project were Manuel A-Monteserín and Beatriz Pachón.

Principal core : Manuel Álvarez-Monteserin (manu-facturas and Leon11), Beatriz
Pachón, Javier Simó, Lain Satrustegui (Zira02), Antonio Corona, Arsenio P. Amaral
(Corona, P. Amaral arquitectos), Guiomar Contreras (6+1), Sara Pérez,
Andrés Infantes, Jorge López (Leon11), Antonio Alejandro

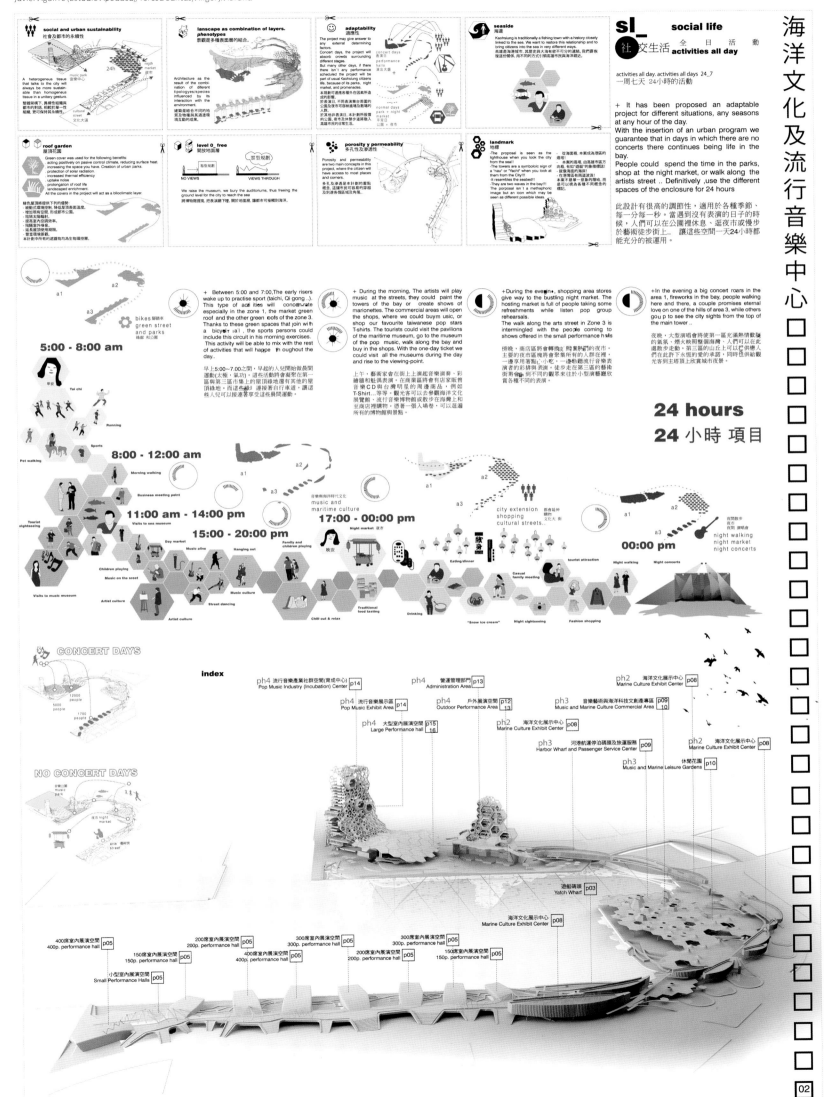

Second phases incorporations : Leon11 (Maria Mallo, Ignacio Álvarez-Monteserín, Jaime López, Javier Gutierrez, Beatriz Crespo, Laura Martín, Alicia Domingo Medrano, Ismael García Abad, Luis Marcos Nieto, Pablo Salvador), Javier Aguirre (Estudio Apodaca), Teresa Santás, Angel J. Abruña

social and urban sustainability
社會及都市的永續性

A heterogeneus tissue that talks to the city will always be more sustainable than homogeneus tissue in a unitary gesture.

整體裡面的不同組織，其具有異質性組織，相較於單一性組織，會可保持其永續性。

lanscape as combination of layers. phenotypes
景觀是多種表面層的結合。

Architecture as the result of the combination of different tipologies/species influenced by its interaction with the environment.

建築是結合不同的物種及各種典型組成，而這種典型是受到環境互動的影響。

adaptability
適應性

The project may give answer to any external determining factors.
Concert days, the project will absorb crowds surrounding different stages.
But many other days, if there isn´t any performance scheduled the project will be part of usual Kaohsiung citizens life, because of its parks, night market, and promenades.

seaside
海邊

Kaohsiung is traditionally a fishing town with a history closely linked to the sea. We want to restore this relationship and to bring citizens into the sea in very different ways.

高雄是傳統的漁村。其歷史與大海有著不可分的連結，我們要來復活從前的關係，用不同的方式引領高雄市民與海洋親近。

roof garden
屋頂花園

Green cover was used for the following benefits:
- acting positively on passive control climate, reducing surface heat.
- increasing the space you have. Creation of urban parks.
- protection of solar radiation.
- increased thermal efficiency.
- uptake noise
- prolongation of roof life
- landscaped enrichment.
All the covers in the project will act as a bioclimatic layer.

level 0_free
開放式面層

NO VIEWS   VIEWS THROUGH

We raise the museum, we bury the auditoriums, thus freeing the ground level for the city to reach the sea.

porosity y permeability
多孔及多滲透性

Porosity and permeability in the project mean concepts in this project, where the citizen will have access to most places and corners.

landmark
地標

- The proposal is seen as the lighthouse when you look the city from the sea!
- The towers are a symbolic sign of a "nau" or "yacht" when you look at them from the City!!!
- It resembles the seabed!!
- They are two waves in the bay!!!
- The proposal isn´t a methaphoric image but an icon which may be seen as different possible ideas.

activities all day. activities all days 24_7
一周七天 24小時的活動

+ It has been proposed an adaptable project for different situations, any seasons at any hour of the day.
With the insertion of an urban program we guarantee that in days in which there are no concerts there continues being life in the bay.
People could spend the time in the parks, shop at the night market, or walk along the artists street .. Definitely ,use the different spaces of the enclosure for 24 hours

此設計有很高的調節性，適用於各種季節、每一分每一秒。當遇到沒有表演的日子的時候，人們可以在公園裡休息、逛夜市或慢步於藝術徒步街上.. 讓這些空間一天24小時都能充分的被運用。

海洋文化及流行音樂中心

bikes
green street
and parks
腳踏車 松江路

5:00 - 8:00 am

+ Between 5:00 and 7:00,The early risers wake up to practise sport (taichi, Qi gong ..). This type of activities will concentrate especially in the zone 1, the market green roof and the other green roofs of the zone 3. Thanks to these green spaces that join with a bicycle trail , the sports persons could include this circuit in his morning exercises. This activity will be able to mix with the rest of activities that will happen throughout the day..

早上5:00~7.00之間，早起的人兒開始做晨間運動(太極、氣功)。這些活動將會凝聚在第一區與第三區市集上的屋頂綠地還有其他的屋頂綠地。而這些綠地 連接著自行車道，讓這些人兒可以接連享受這些晨間運動。

Tai chi
Running
Sports
Pet walking

8:00 - 12:00 am

+ During the morning, The artists will play music at the streets, they could paint the towers of the bay or create shows of marionettes. The commercial areas will open the shops, where we could buym usic, or shop our favourite taiwanese pop stars T-shirts. The tourists could visit the pavilions of the maritime museum, go to the museum of the pop music, walk along the bay and buy in the shops. With the one-day ticket we could visit all the museums during the day and rise to the viewing-point.

上午，藝術家會在街上上演起音樂演奏、彩繪塔樓和魁儡木偶表演。在商業區將會有店家販賣音樂CD與台灣明星的週邊商品，例如 T-Shirt....等等。觀光客可以去參觀海洋文化展覽館、流行音樂博物館或散步在海灣上和至商店裡購物，憑著一張入場卷，可以逛遍所有的博物館與景點。

Morning walking
Business meeting point

music and maritime culture
音樂與海洋時代文化

11:00 am - 14:00 pm
15:00 - 20:00 pm

Visits to sea museum
Day market
Music alive
Hanging out
Children playing
Music on the street
Visits to music museum
Artist culture
Street dancing
Artist culture
Tourist sightseeing

17:00 - 00:00 pm

+During the evening, shopping area stores give way to the bustling night market. The hosting market is full of people taking some refreshments while listen pop group rehearsals.
The walk along the arts street in Zone 3 is intermingled with the people coming to shows offered in the small performance halls.

傍晚，商店區將會轉換成熱鬧非凡的夜市。主要的夜市區瀰漫會聚集所有的人群在裡頭，一邊享用著點心小吃，一邊聆聽流行音樂表演者的彩排與表演。徒步走在第三區的藝術街將會連接到不同的觀眾來往於小型演藝欣賞各種不同的表演。

Night market
Family and children playing
Eating/dinner
Casual family meeting
Traditional food tasting
Chill out & relax
Drinking
"Snow ice cream"
Night sightseeing
Fashion shopping

city extension shopping cultural streets..
都會延伸 逛街 文化大街

00:00 pm

+In the evening a big concert roars in the area 1, fireworks in the bay, people walking here and there, a couple promises eternal love on one of the hills of area 3, while others goup to see the city sights from the top of the main tower ..

夜晚，大型演唱會將使第一區充滿熱情載歌的氣氛、煙火映照整個海灣、人們可以在此處散步走動。第三區的山丘上可以見到供情人們立在此許下不悔的愛的承諾，同時也供給觀光客到主塔頂上欣賞城市夜景。

night walking
night market
night concerts

夜間散步 逛街 夜間 演唱會

night walking
night concerts

24 hours
24 小時 項目

CONCERT DAYS
12000 people
5000 people
1700 people

NO CONCERT DAYS
music park
night market
arts street

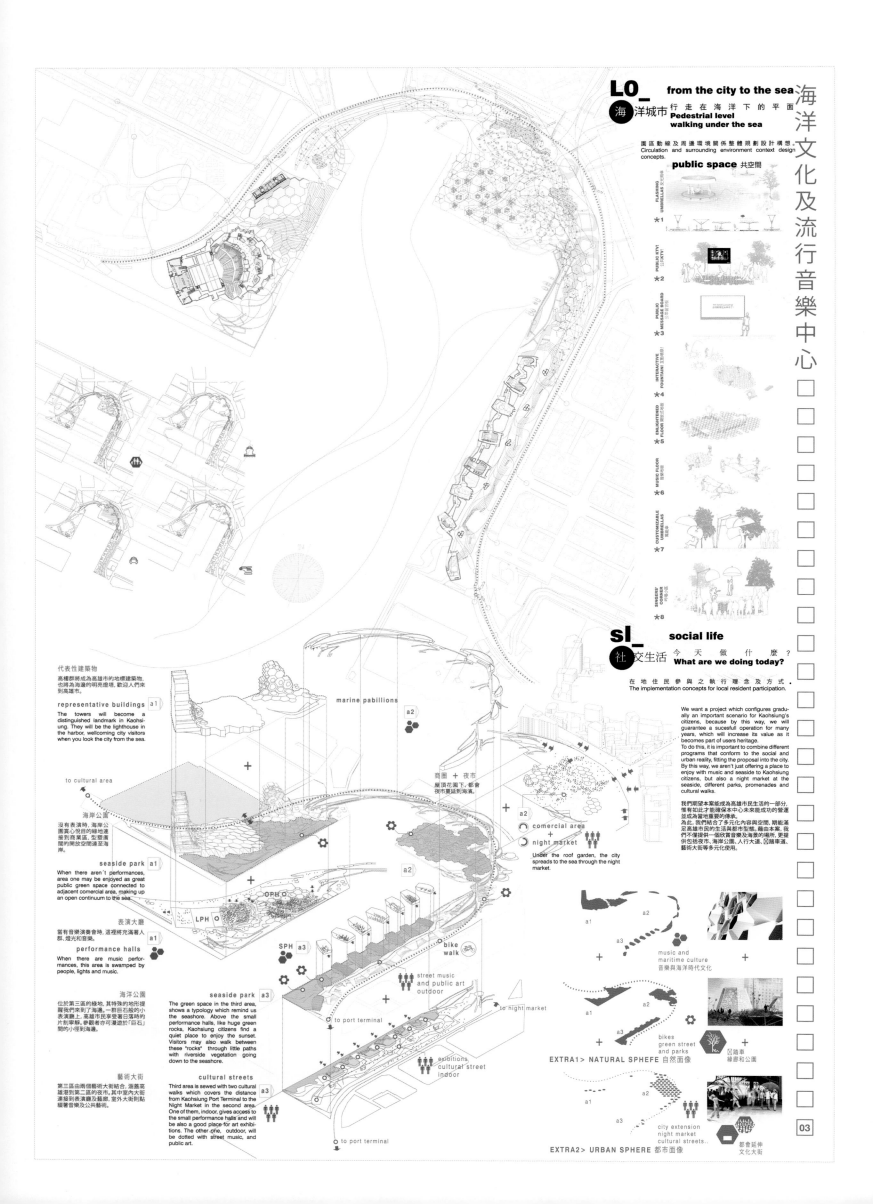

LO_
海洋城市

from the city to the sea
行走在海洋下的平面
Pedestrial level
walking under the sea

園區動線及周邊環境關係整體規劃設計構想。
Circulation and surrounding environment context design concepts.

public space 共空間

*1 FLASHING UMBRELLAS 反光傘群
*2 PUBLIC KTV 公共KTV
*3 PUBLIC MESSAGE BOARD 公共留言板
*4 INTERACTIVE FOUNTAIN 互動噴泉
*5 ENLIGHTENED 5 FLOOR 發光式地板
*6 MUSIC FLOOR 音樂地板
*7 CUSTOMIZABLE UMBRELLAS 客製傘
*8 SINGERS' CORNER 歌唱角落

sl_
社交生活

social life
今天做什麼？
What are we doing today?

在地住民參與之執行理念及方式.
The implementation concepts for local resident participation.

We want a project which configures gradually an important scenario for Kaohsiung's citizens, because by this way, we will guarantee a sucesfull operation for many years, which will increase its value as it becomes part of users heritage.
To do this, it is important to combine different programs that conform to the social and urban reality, fitting the proposal into the city. By this way, we aren't just offering a place to enjoy with music and seaside to Kaohsiung citizens, but also a night market at the seaside, different parks, promenades and cultural walks.

我們期望本案能成為高雄市民生活的一部分，惟有如此才能確保本中心未來能成功的管運並成為當地重要的得承。
為此，我們結合了多元化內容與空間，期能滿足高雄市民的生活與都市型態。藉由本案，我們不僅提供一個欣賞音樂與海濱的場所，更提供包括夜市、海洋公園、人行大道、腳踏車道、藝術大街等多元化使用。

海洋文化及流行音樂中心□□□□□

代表性建築物
高樓群將成為高雄市的地標建築物，也將為海邊的明亮燈塔，歡迎人們來到高雄市。

representative buildings a1
The towers will become a distinguished landmark in Kaohsiung. They will be the lighthouse in the harbor, wellcoming city visitors when you look the city from the sea.

marine pabillions a2

to cultural area

海洋公園
沒有表演時，海岸公園賞心悅目的綠地連接到商業區，型塑廣闊的開放空間連到海岸。

seaside park a1
When there aren't performances, area one may be enjoyed as great public green space connected to adjacent comercial area, making up an open continuum to the sea.

表演大廳
當有音樂演奏會時，這裡將充滿著人群、燈光和音樂。

performance halls a1
When there are music performances, this area is swamped by people, lights and music.

海洋公園
位於第三區的綠地，其特殊的地形提醒我們來到了海邊。一群巨石般的小表演廳，讓您享受著日落時的片刻寧靜。參觀者亦可漫遊於「巨石」間的小徑到海邊。

藝術大街
第三區由兩個藝術大街結合，涵蓋高雄港到第二區的夜市。其中室內大街連接到表演廳及藝廊，室外大街則點綴著音樂及公共藝術。

seaside park a3
The green space in the third area, shows a typology which remind us the seashore. Above the small performance halls, like huge green rocks, Kaohsiung citizens find a quiet place to enjoy the sunset. Visitors may also walk between these "rocks" through little paths with riverside vegetation going down to the seashore.

cultural streets a3
Third area is sewed with two cultural walks which covers the distance from Kaohsiung Port Terminal to the Night Market in the second area. One of them, indoor, gives access to the small performance halls and will be also a good place for art exhibitions. The other one, outdoor, will be dotted with street music, and public art.

商圈＋夜市
屋頂花園下，都會夜市蔓延到海濱。

comercial area
＋
night market
Under the roof garden, the city spreads to the sea through the night market.

OPH
LPH
SPH a3
bike walk
street music and public art outdoor
to port terminal
exhibitions cultural street indoor
to port terminal
to night market

a1 a2 a3
music and maritime culture
音樂與海洋時代文化

a1 a3
bikes green street and parks
EXTRA1> **NATURAL SPHEFE** 自然面像
腳踏車 綠廊和公園

a1 a3
city extension night market cultural streets..
EXTRA2> **URBAN SPHERE** 都市面像
都會延伸 文化大街

03

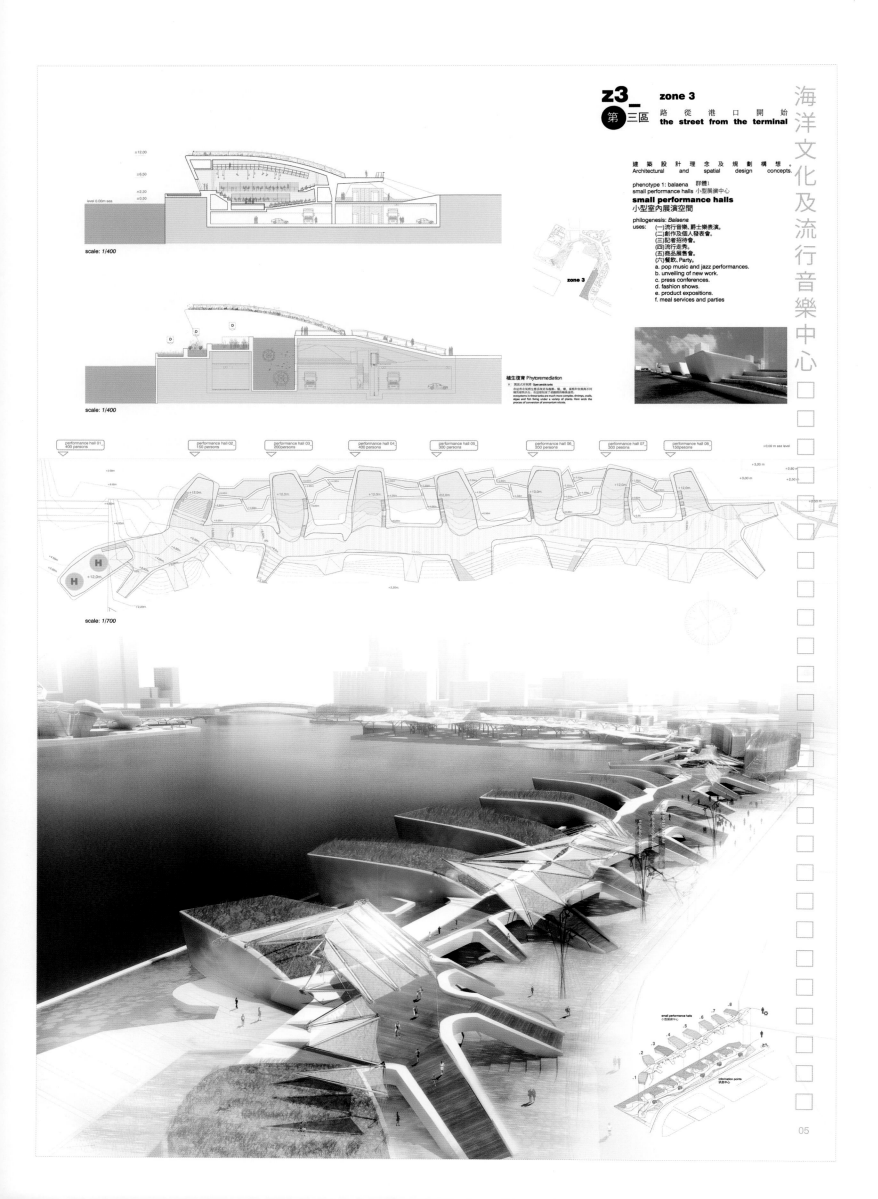

第三區 路 從 港 口 開 始
the street from the terminal

海洋文化及流行音樂中心

建 築 設 計 理 念 及 規 劃 構 想。
Architectural and spatial design concepts.

phenotype 1: balaena   群體1
small performance halls 小型展演中心
small performance halls
小型室內展演空間

philogenesis: *Balaena*
uses: (一)流行音樂、爵士樂表演。
         (二)創作及個人發表會。
         (三)記者招待會。
         (四)流行走秀。
         (五)商品展售會。
         (六)餐飲、Party。
         a. pop music and jazz performances.
         b. unveiling of new work.
         c. press conferences.
         d. fashion shows.
         e. product expositions.
         f. meal services and parties

level 0.00m ses

scale: 1/400

scale: 1/400

植生復育 Phytoremediation

scale: 1/700

05

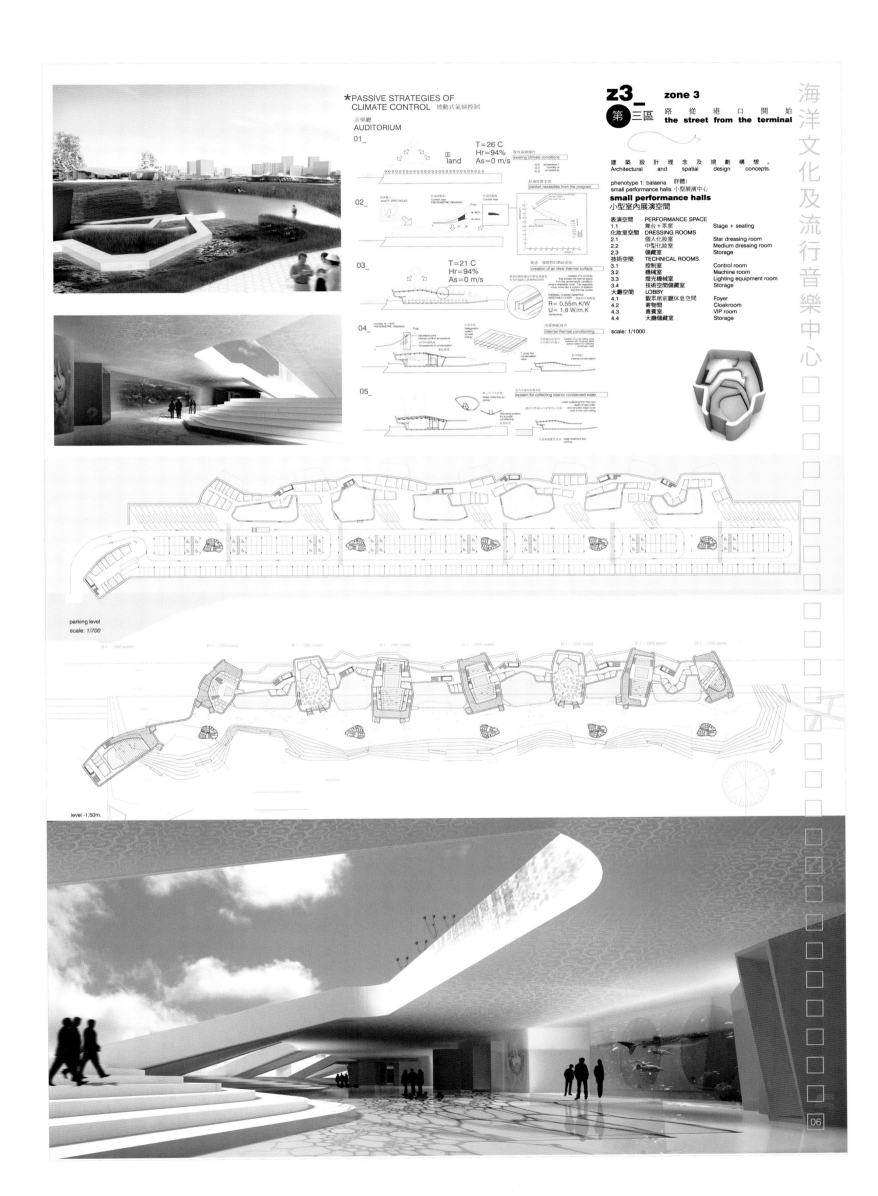

*PASSIVE STRATEGIES OF CLIMATE CONTROL 被動式氣候控制

音樂廳
AUDITORIUM

01_ land
T=26 C
Hr=94%
As=0 m/s

02_

03_
T=21 C
Hr=94%
As=0 m/s

creation of an ideal thermal surface

R= 0,55m.K/W
U= 1,8 W/m.K

04_ internal thermal conditioning

05_ system for collecting interior condensed water

z3_ **zone 3**
第三區 路從港口開始 the street from the terminal

建築設計理念及規劃構想。
Architectural and spatial design concepts.

phenotype 1: balaena 群體1
small performance halls 小型展演中心
small performance halls
小型室內展演空間

表演空間	PERFORMANCE SPACE	
1.1	舞台＋眾席	Stage + seating
化妝室空間	DRESSING ROOMS	
2.1	個人化妝室	Star dressing room
2.2	中型化妝室	Medium dressing room
2.3	儲藏室	Storage
技術空間	TECHNICAL ROOMS.	
3.1	控制室	Control room
3.2	機械室	Machine room
3.3	燈光機械室	Lighting equipment room
3.4	技術空間儲藏室	Storage
大廳空間	LOBBY	
4.1	觀眾席前廳休息空間	Foyer
4.2	寄物間	Cloakroom
4.3	貴賓室	VIP room
4.4	大廳儲藏室	Storage

scale: 1/1000

parking level
scale: 1/700

level -1,50m.

海洋文化及流行音樂中心

06

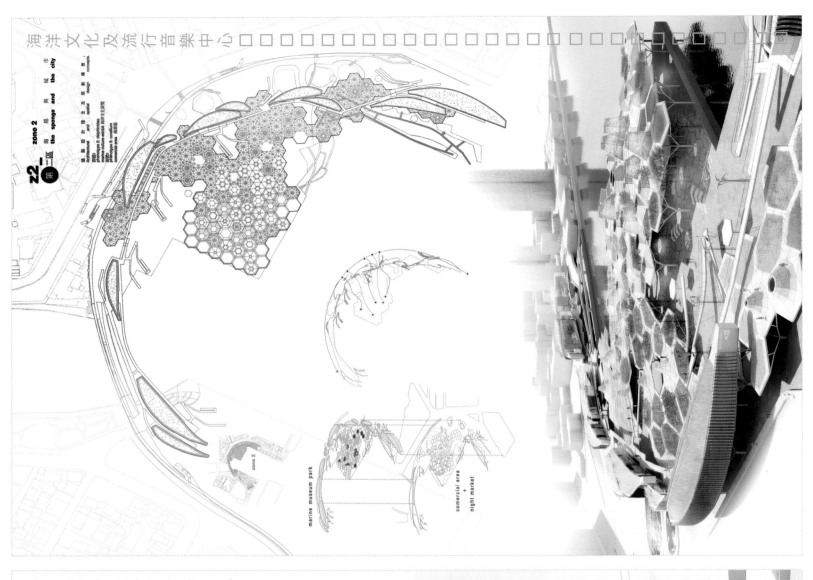

海洋文化及流行音樂中心

z2_ zone 2 第二區 the sponge and the city

marine museum park

comercial area + night market

zone 2

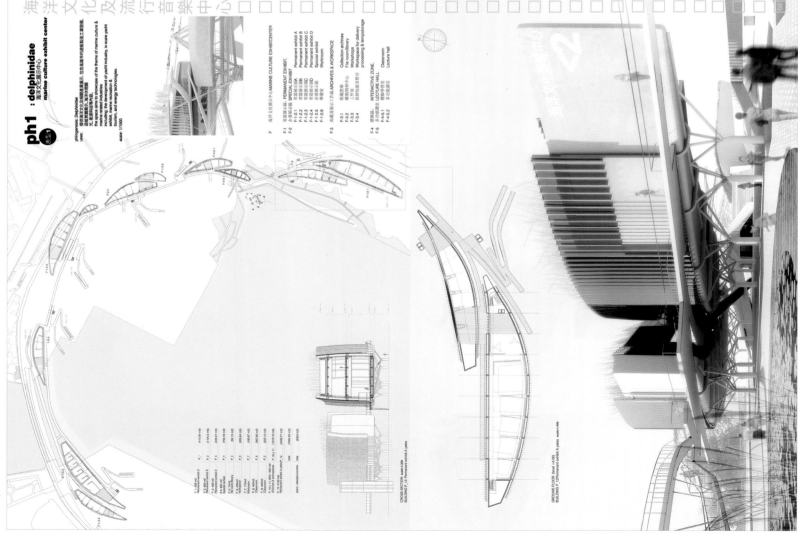

海洋文化及流行音樂中心

ph1 : delphinidae
海洋文化園所中心
marine culture exhibit center

use: the space aims to showcase the theme of marine culture & marine related industries, including the development of yacht industry, in-scale yacht exhibit, marine recreation & tourism, and energy technologies.

scale: 1/1500

F 海洋文化館小中心／MARINE CULTURE EXHIBIT CENTER.

F-1 常設展示區 PERMANENT EXHIBIT.
F-2 特設展示區 SPECIAL EXHIBIT.
   F-1/2.1 常設展示館A Permanent exhibit A
   F-1/2.2 常設展示館B Permanent exhibit B
   F-1/2.3 常設展示館C Permanent exhibit C
   F-1/2.4 常設展示館D Permanent exhibit D
   F-1/2.5 企劃展示館 Special exhibit
   F-1/2.6 工作坊 Workroom

F-3 典藏及館務工作區 ARCHIVES & WORKSPACE
   F-3.1 典藏空間 Collection archives
   F-3.2 檔案室／圖書室 File room/library
   F-3.3 工作坊 Workshops
   F-3.4 貨物收送及整理室 Workspace for delivery processing & temp.storage

F-4 體驗區 INTERACTIVE ZONE.
F-5 多功能演講廳
   F-4/5.1 教學教室 Classroom
   F-4/5.2 多功能演講廳 Lecture hall

CROSS SECTION scale:1/300
BUILDING P_1/2 Permanent exhibit A yates

GROUND FLOOR (level +6.00)
BUILDING P_1/Permanent exhibit A yates scale:1/500

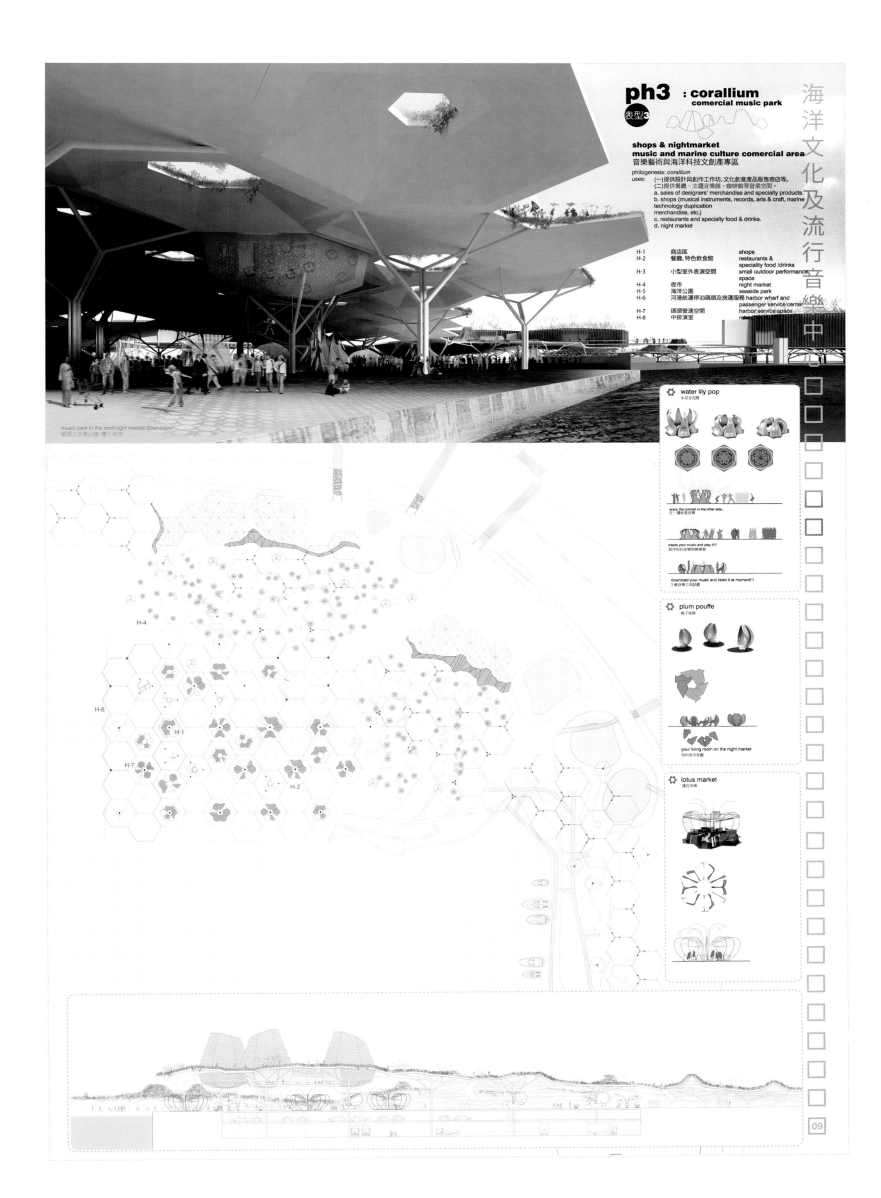

ph3 : corallium
comercial music park

表型3

shops & nightmarket
music and marine culture comercial area
音樂藝術與海洋科技文創產業專區

philogenesis: *corallium*
uses: （一）提供設計與創作工作坊、文化創意產品販售商店等。
（二）提供餐廳、主題音樂館、咖啡館等營業空間。
a. sales of designers' merchandise and specialty products.
b. shops (musical instruments, records, arts & craft, marine technology duplication merchandise, etc.)
c. restaurants and specialty food & drinks.
d. night market

H-1	商店區	shops
H-2	餐廳、特色飲食館	restaurants & speciality food /drinks
H-3	小型室外表演空間	small outdoor performance space
H-4	夜市	night market
H-5	海洋公園	seaside park
H-6	河港航運停泊碼頭及旅運服務	harbor wharf and passenger service center
H-7	碼頭營運空間	harbor service space
H-8	中排演室	rehearse

music park in the roof/night market downstaire
屋頂上音樂公園/樓下夜市

海洋文化及流行音樂中心

water lily pop
水百合花開

enjoy the concert in the other side...
在一邊欣賞音樂

create your music and play !!!!
創作你的音樂即興演奏會

download your music and listen it at moment!!!
下載音樂立刻試聽

plum pouffe
梅子坐椅

your living room on the night market
你的夜市客廳

lotus market
蓮花市攤

H-4
H-6
H-1
H-7
H-2

09

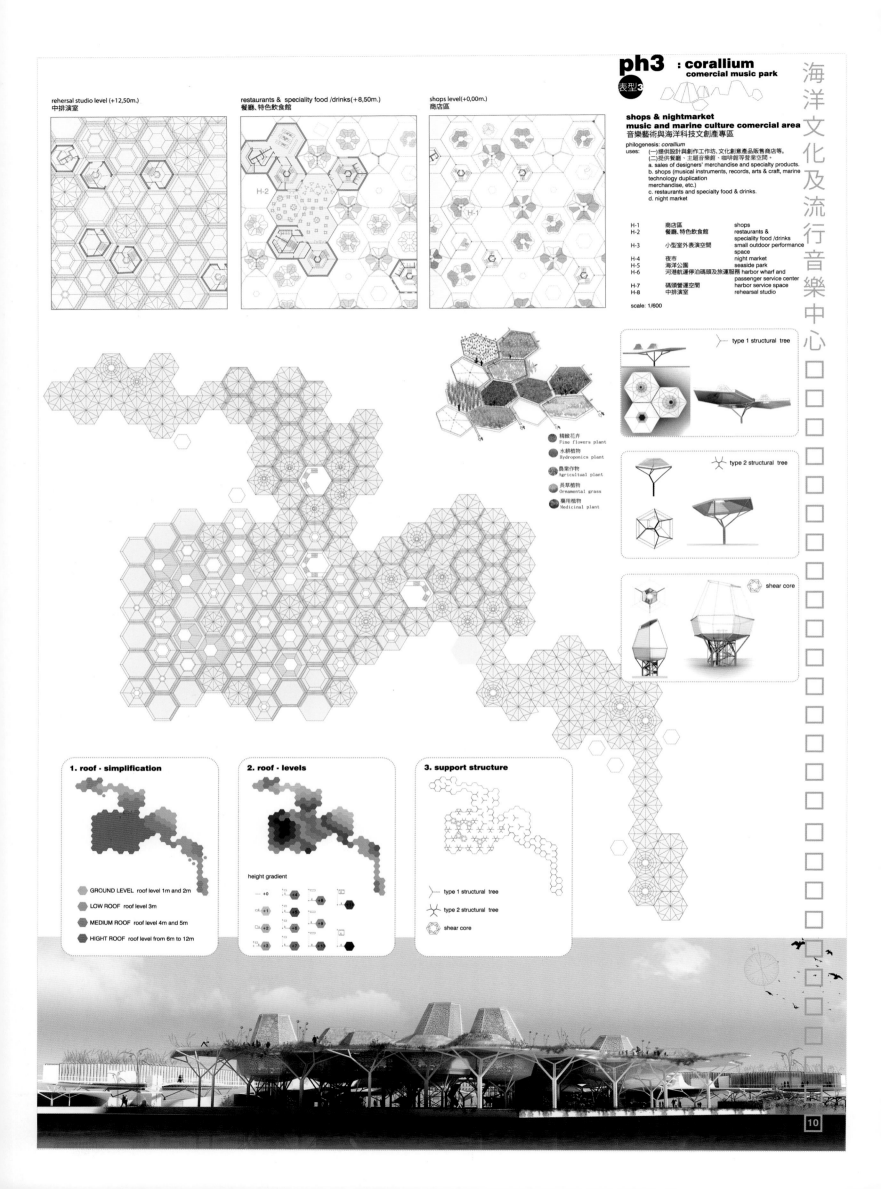

shops & nightmarket
music and marine culture comercial area
音樂藝術與海洋科技文創產專區

philogenesis: *corallium*
uses: (一)提供設計與創作工作坊、文化創意產品版售商店等。
(二)提供餐廳、主題音樂館、咖啡館等營業空間。
a. sales of designers' merchandise and specialty products.
b. shops (musical instruments, records, arts & craft, marine technology duplication merchandise, etc.)
c. restaurants and specialty food & drinks.
d. night market

H-1	商店區	shops
H-2	餐廳、特色飲食館	restaurants & speciality food /drinks
H-3	小型室外表演空間	small outdoor performance space
H-4	夜市	night market
H-5	海洋公園	seaside park
H-6	河港航運停泊碼頭及旅運服務	harbor wharf and passenger service center
H-7	碼頭營運空間	harbor service space
H-8	中排演室	rehearsal studio

scale: 1/600

rehersal studio level (+12,50m.)
中排演室

restaurants & speciality food /drinks(+8,50m.)
餐廳、特色飲食館

shops level(+0,00m.)
商店區

H-2

H-1

精緻花卉
Fine flowers plant

水耕植物
Hydroponics plant

農業作物
Agricultural plant

長草植物
Ornamental grass

藥用植物
Medicinal plant

type 1 structural tree

type 2 structural tree

shear core

1. roof - simplification

GROUND LEVEL roof level 1m and 2m
LOW ROOF roof level 3m
MEDIUM ROOF roof level 4m and 5m
HIGHT ROOF roof level from 6m to 12m

2. roof - levels

height gradient

3. support structure

type 1 structural tree
type 2 structural tree
shear core

681

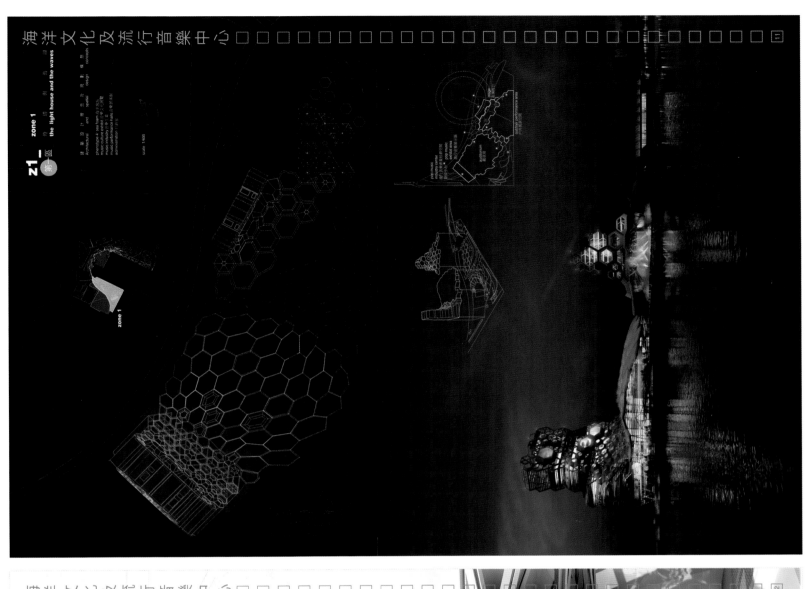

海洋文化及流行音樂中心

z1 第一區

zone 1
the light house and the waves

Architectural and spatial design

prototype a: wave form v / 5 %
music culture exhibit / 少 / 文化
music industry / 少 / 少
music performance halls / 少演 /少少展
astronomation / 天文
scale: 1:500

zone 1

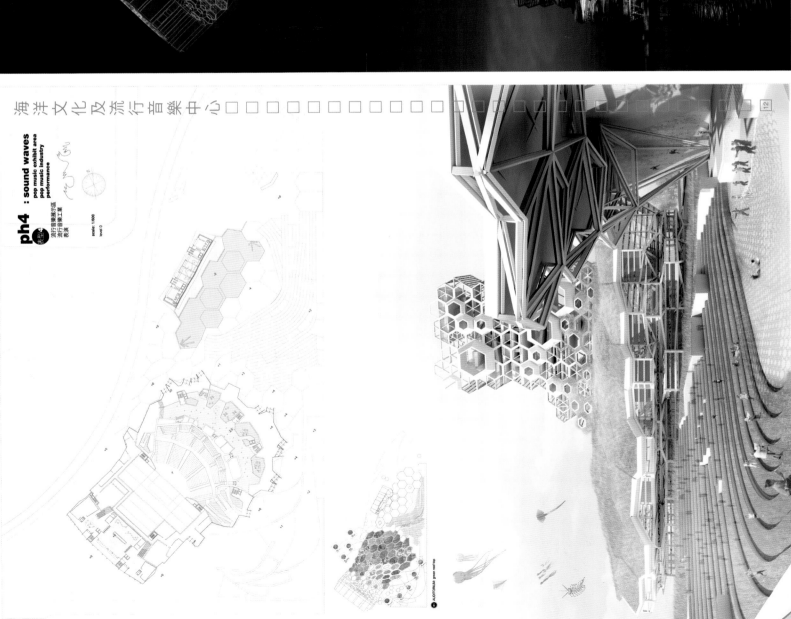

海洋文化及流行音樂中心

ph4 長洲 : sound waves

流行音樂展示區 pop music exhibit area
流行音樂工業 pop music industry
表演 performance

scale: 1:500
level 0

AUDITORIUM: green reef top

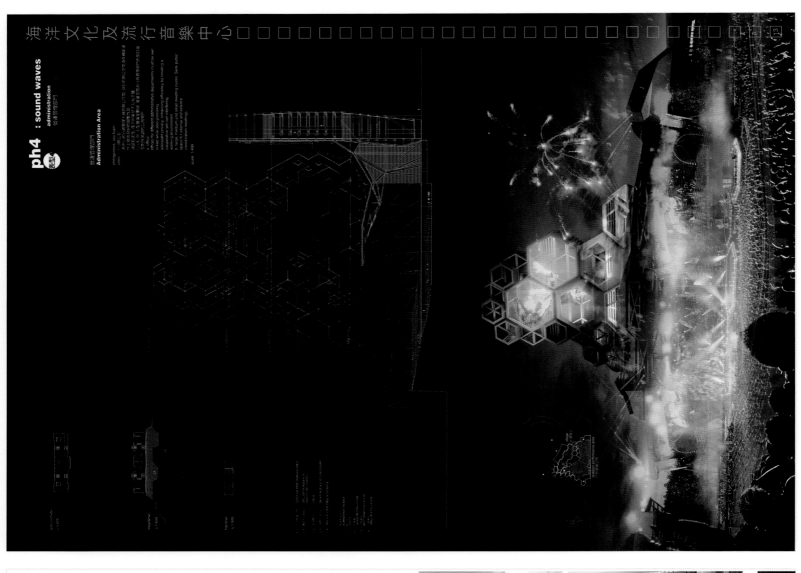

海洋文化及流行音樂中心

ph4 : sound waves

administration
公事管部門

Administration Area

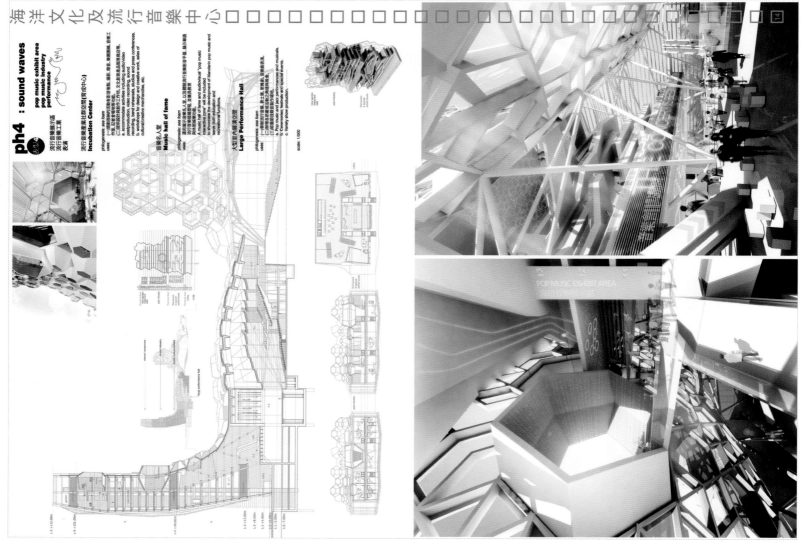

海洋文化及流行音樂中心

ph4 : sound waves

pop music exhibit area
流行音樂展示區
pop music industry
流行音樂工業
performance
表演

流行音樂孵化器空間(育成中心)
Incubation Center

phagenesis: sea foam

大型室內展演空間
Large Performance Hall

phagenesis: sea foam

音樂名人堂
Music hall of fame

phagenesis: sea foam

scale: 1:900

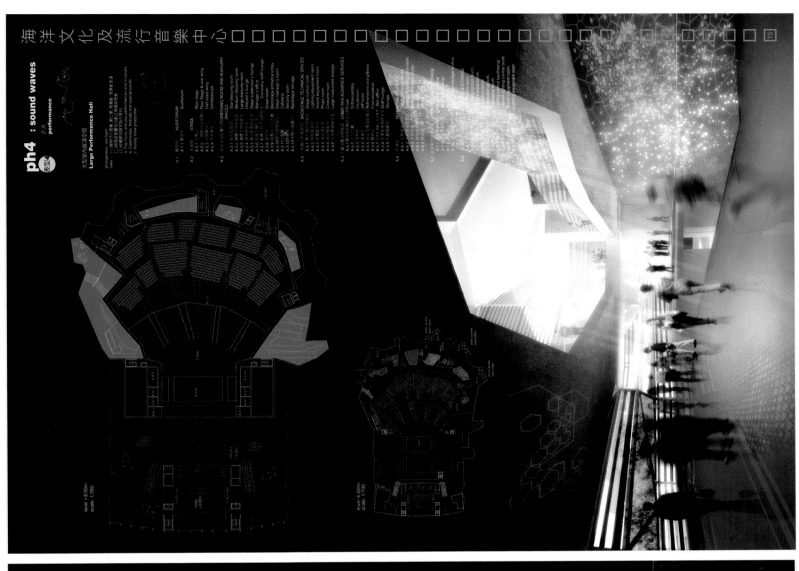

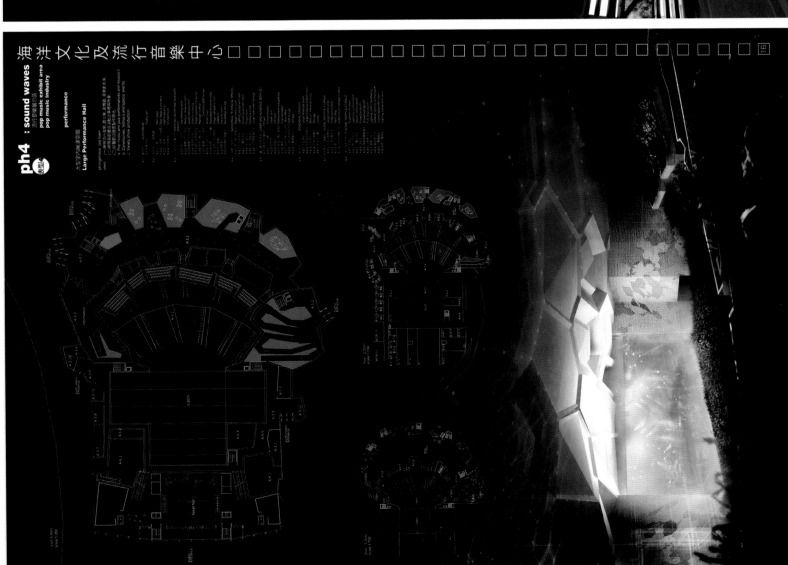

239

Hotel Music Skin | *NABITO ARCHITECTS & PARTNERS*

684

International Competition "Hotelliesma" for a 4Star Hotel. Jurmala, Latvia, 2011
Project Phase : International Competition, Settled
Date : 2011
Surface : 4750m²

Collaborators : Agita Putnina, Madara Villere, Leonards Kalnins, Lina Gronskyte, Mona Shaar

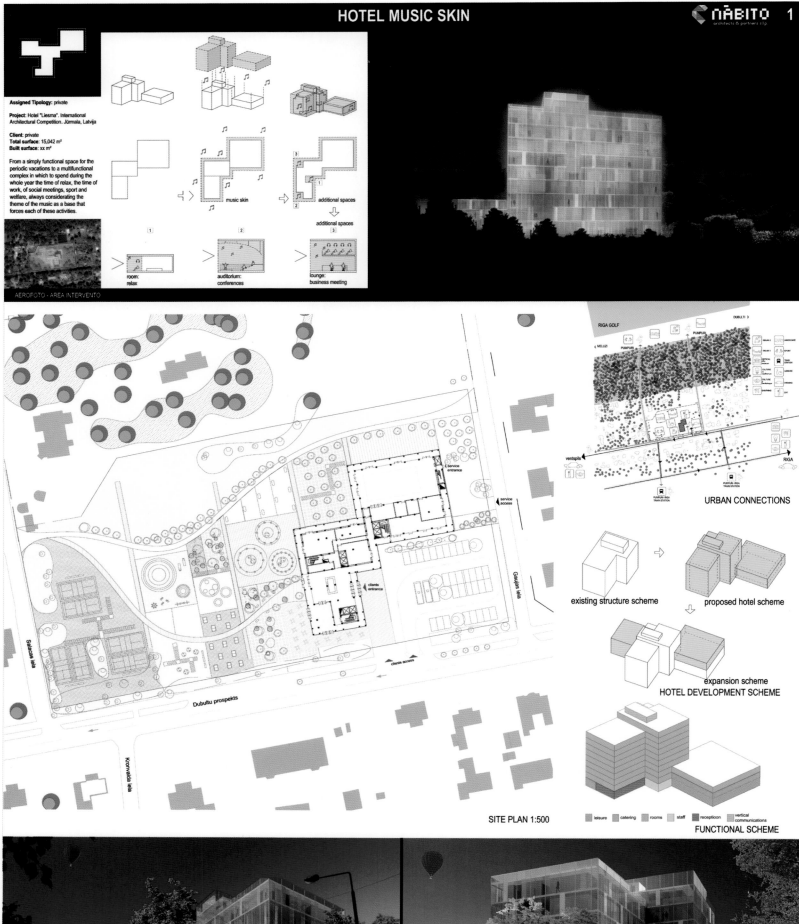

MUSIC SKIN HOTEL

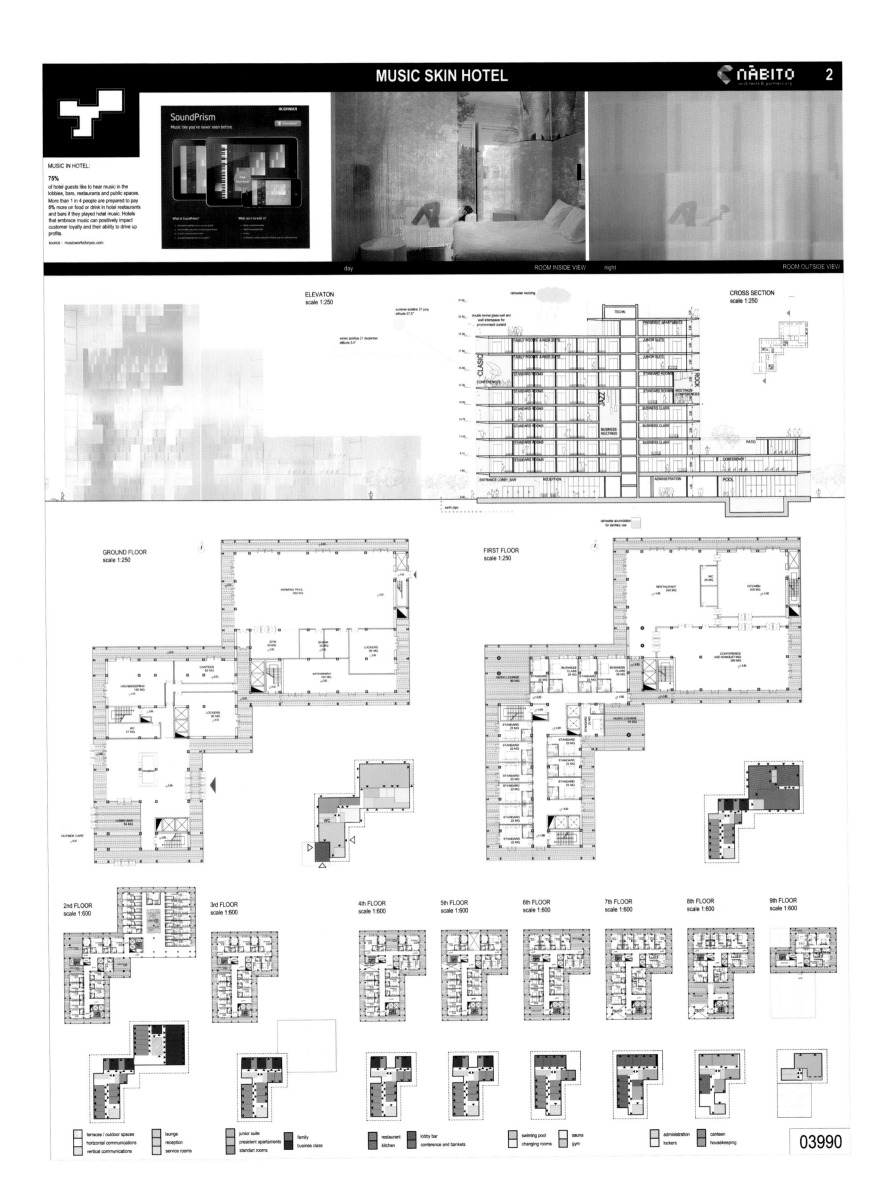

MUSIC IN HOTEL:

75%
of hotel guests like to hear music in the lobbies, bars, restaurants and public spaces. More than 1 in 4 people are prepared to pay **5%** more on food or drink in hotel restaurants and bars if they played hotel music. Hotels that embrace music can positively impact customer loyalty and their ability to drive up profits.

source : musicworksforyou.com

SoundPrism
Music like you've never seen before

day   ROOM INSIDE VIEW   night   ROOM OUTSIDE VIEW

ELEVATON
scale 1:250

CROSS SECTION
scale 1:250

GROUND FLOOR
scale 1:250

FIRST FLOOR
scale 1:250

2nd FLOOR
scale 1:600

3rd FLOOR
scale 1:600

4th FLOOR
scale 1:600

5th FLOOR
scale 1:600

6th FLOOR
scale 1:600

7th FLOOR
scale 1:600

8th FLOOR
scale 1:600

9th FLOOR
scale 1:600

terraces / outdoor spaces
horizontal communications
vertical communications
launge
reception
service rooms
junior suite
president apartaments
standart rooms
family
busines class
restaurant
kitchen
lobby bar
conference and bankets
swiming pool
changing rooms
sauna
gym
administration
lockers
canteen
housekeeping

03990

Auditorium Poliedro | *NABITO ARCHITECTS & PARTNERS*

International competition for Auditorium. Acilia – Dragona (Rome), Italy, 2011
Client : Municipality of Rome
Project phase : International Competition / Final Stage
Estimate : € 4.242.300,00

Date : 2011
Surface : 2786m²
Collaborators : Valentina Esposito, Andrea Rojas, Agita Putnina

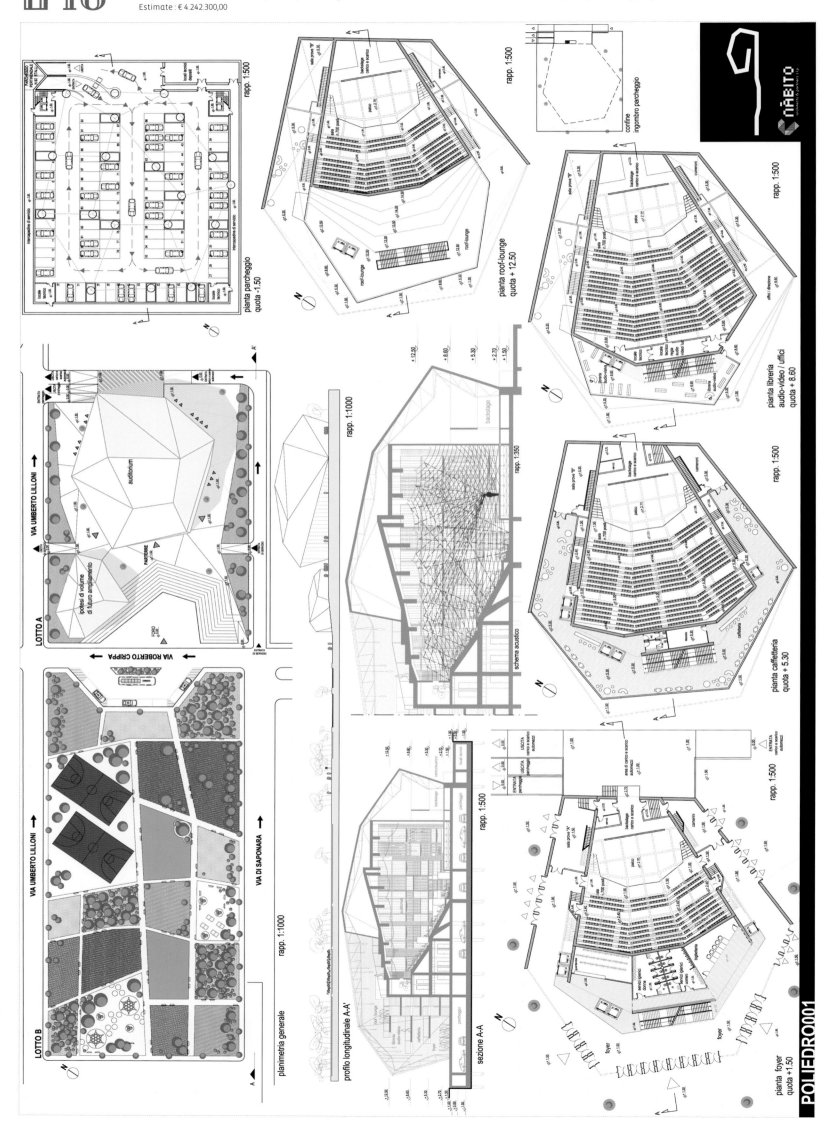

POLIEDRO001

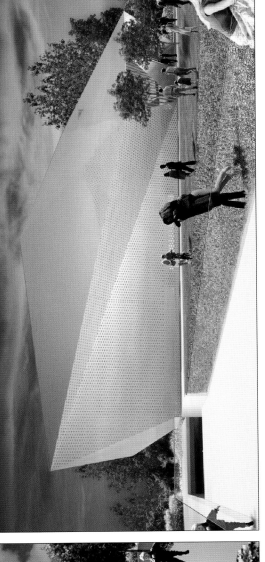
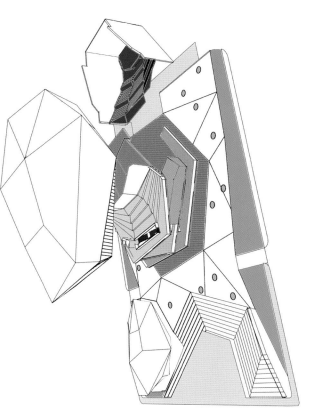

sala

locali tecnici

foro

+ 8.60 _ libreria audio-visiva

uffici/direzione

+ 12.50 _ roof garden

verde

foyer

+ 5.30 _ caffetteria

nabito
architetti & partner s.l.p

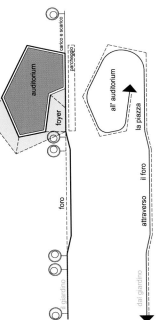
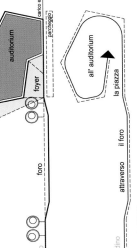

auditorium

foyer

carico e scarico

parcheggio

all'auditorium

la piazza

attraverso   il foro

dal giardino

il giardino   foro

LA PASSEGGIATA POLIEDRICA

La decisione di denominare il nuovo auditorium di Acilia "POLIEDRO" e' nata dall'esigenza di generare uno spazio estremamente flessibile e molteplice che riesca ad accogliere il quartiere durante tutte le ore della giornata e ad essere un forte polo di attrazione ad una scala piu' amplia. Uno Spazio Poliedrico dal molteplice carattere da un'identità ben chiara.

Dal "Giardino", nel lotto B, l'hortus, (una reinterpretazione che prende spunto dal tessuto agricolo dell'agro romano) si attraversa il foro, la piazza, il foyer multifunzionale verticale, entrando nell'Auditorium, un poliedro in un poliedro di relazioni.

Il percorso progettuale, le tipologie strutturali e le tecnologie costruttive scelte, perseguono i seguenti obbiettivi:

- Inserimento urbano-ambientale e possibilità che il nuovo intervento costituisca un "elemento poliedrico" capace di riqualificare la morfologia e le caratteristiche dello spazio su cui insiste e diverga, al tempo stesso, nucleo di condensazione di attività qualificate per un processo piu' amplio di riqualificazione urbana, in linea con Il PRU, il nuovo polo intermodale e la prevista stazione ferroviaria Acilia - Dragona.

- Caratterizzazione e riconoscibilità dell'intervento attraverso un linguaggio architettonico contemporaneo ed in grado di sottolineare la valenza pubblica del complesso, amplificando le relazioni con l'immediato intorno urbano e tra l'interno dell'edificio e gli spazi esterni.

- Innovazione tecnologica ed utilizzazione di materiali dalle elevate caratteristiche prestazionali, dai costi compatibili con il budget.

Punti chiave del progetto sono stati la versatilità dello spazio di rappresentazione, la flessibilità dell'intero complesso, la funzionalità della "macchina armonica", il comfort dello spettatore, fisico, acustico e visivo, attraverso:

- elevazione della platea e del palcoscenico dalla quota stradale creando un'ottima "cassa armonica".

- assetto della sala per un miglior rapporto visibilità-acustica.

- scelta del legno come materiale per i rivestimenti ed i pavimenti, ottimo veicolo per la propagazione delle vibrazioni sonore.

- versatilità dell'involucro interno per adeguare il comportamento acustico della sala alle differenti manifestazioni: attraverso il movimento dei pannelli acustici in legno di rivestimento il suono viene indirizzato in modo omogeneo in tutti i posti della sala; la loro rotazione e la traslazione controlla la diffusione delle onde acustiche e assicura la modifica del volume acustico in funzione dei diversi tipi di manifestazione

POLIEDRO001

Tabella 1	Concorso di progettazione per l'Auditorium di Acilia - Dragona				
ambienti	funzioni	superfici mq	costo parametrico unitario (€/mq)	Importo Totale (€)	incidenze percentuali dei componenti funzionali
1.00	SPAZI PER LO SPETTACOLO	mq	600,00	1.140.000,00	
1.01	SALA	mq	1.900,00	1.140.000,00	
1.02	PALCO E RETROPALCO	mq	200,00	140.000,00	
1.03	SALA PROVE (A e B)	mq	150,00	165.000,00	
	TOTALE 1	mq	950,00	1.445.000,00	49,49%
2.00	SPAZI PER IL PUBBLICO				
2.01	ATRIO FOYER E DISTRIBUZIONE	mq	600,00	540.000,00	
2.02	BIGLIETTERIA	mq	40,00	28.000,00	
2.03	GUARDAROBA	mq	55,00	38.500,00	
2.04	CAFFETTERIA E RELATIVI SERVIZI	mq	540,00	486.000,00	
2.05	LIBRERIA	mq	120,00	108.000,00	
2.06	SERVIZI IGIENICI PER IL PUBBLICO	mq	100,00	60.000,00	
	TOTALE 2	mq	1.455,00	1.260.500,00	43,18%
3.00	SPAZI PER GLI INTERPRETI				
3.01	REGIA E CABINA TRADUZIONE	mq	57,00	45.600,00	
3.02	CAMERINI	mq	50,00	30.000,00	
3.03	CAMERONI	mq	50,00	30.000,00	
	TOTALE 3	mq	157,00	105.600,00	3,62%
4.00	SPAZI PER GLI ADDETTI				
4.01	UFFICI E AMBIENTI DI SERVIZIO	mq	100,00	65.000,00	
	TOTALE 4	mq	100,00	65.000,00	2,23%
5.00	SPAZI ACCESSORI				
5.01	DEPOSITI	mq	24,00	8.400,00	
5.02	LOCALI TECNICI	mq	100,00	35.000,00	
	TOTALE 5	mq	124,00	43.400,00	1,49%
	TOTALE A		2.786,00	2.919.500,00	
6.00	AREE ACCESSORIE				
6.01	PARCHEGGIO INTERRATO	mq	2.500,00	875.000,00	
6.02	AREA CARICO E SCARICO	mq	25,00	2.500,00	
6.03	SISTEMAZIONI ESTERNE	mq	73,00	445.300,00	
	TOTALE B: AREE ACCESSORIE		6.100,00	1.322.800,00	
	TOTALE LAVORI			4.242.300,00	

Client : Toulon Provence Méditerranée and City of Six Fours les Plages
Location : Six-Fours-les-Plages, France
Program : Music and Dance School, 1350-Capacity Performance Hall
Surface area : 6,700m² + 6,000m² parking

Cost : 13,890,000€
Design Period : 2010
Architect : Brisac Gonzalez Architects - Cécile Brisac, Eleftherios Ambatzis, Antoine Pascal, Miguel Gonçalves, João Baptista

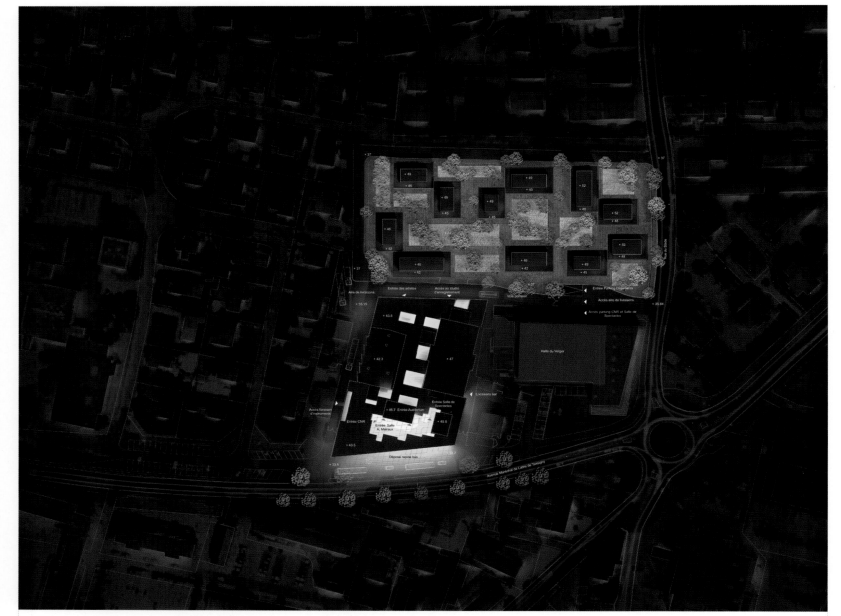

Plan de situation - 1/500°

+ 47
+ 43.5
+ 33.7

Façade Avenue Maréchal de Lattre de Tassigny - 1/200°

Un véritable pôle

Le long de l'Avenue de Lattre de Tassigny, le Pôle Musical devient réellement un nouveau 'pôle'.

III Parti fonctionnel, technique et économique

Un bâtiment compact et aussi un bâtiment plus économique.

Intérieur de l'auditorium

Halls en enfilade

Configuration debout 1350 personnes

Scène centrale 594 personnes

Configuration en croix 486 personnes

Défilé

POLE MUSICAL CNR DE SIX-FOURS-LES-PLAGES

1

Design team : VP&Green (Structural Engineer, Nicholas Green),
Ducks Scéno (Theatre Consultant, Pierre Jaubert de Beaujeu), LTA (cost consultant),
INEX + Terao (Services, Environmental), Point d'Orgue (Acoustics, Damien Dupouy),
MIR (Visualisations)

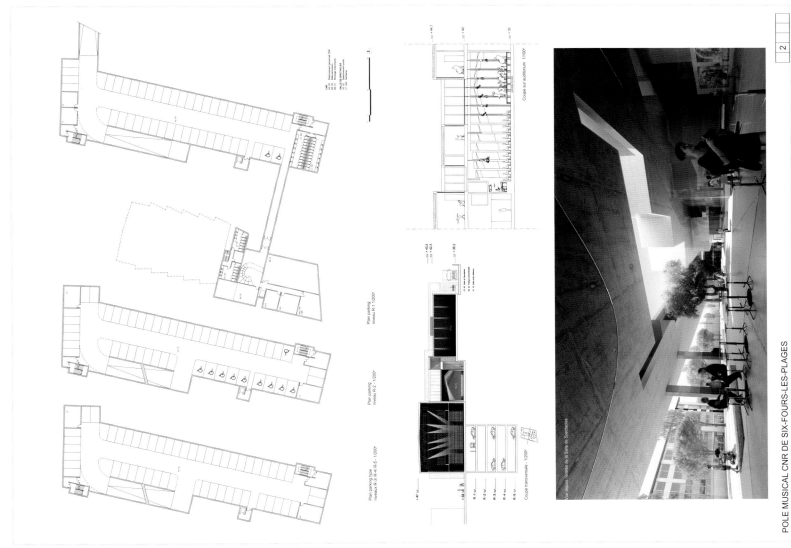

POLE MUSICAL CNR DE SIX-FOURS-LES-PLAGES

2

POLE MUSICAL CNR DE SIX-FOURS-LES-PLAGES

3

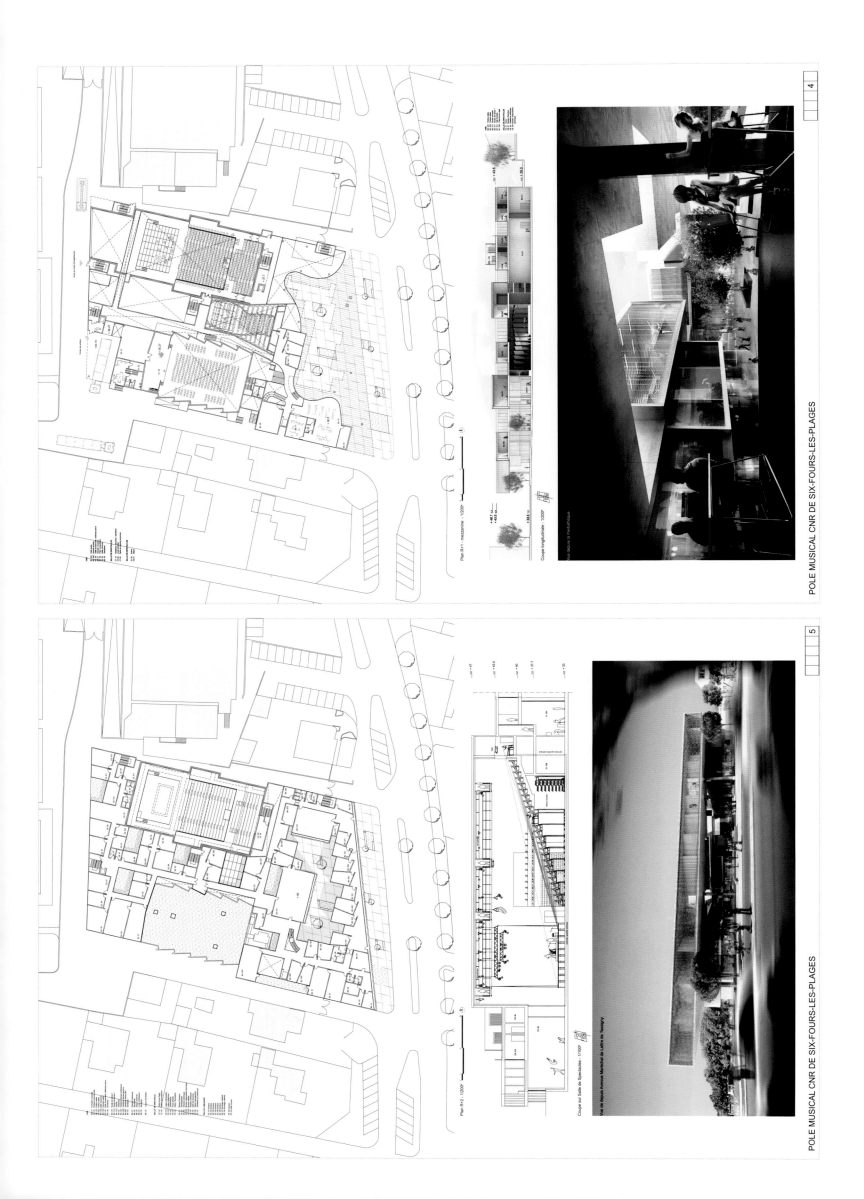

POLE MUSICAL CNR DE SIX-FOURS-LES-PLAGES

POLE MUSICAL CNR DE SIX-FOURS-LES-PLAGES

Ballet Center, Restaurant, Library, School, Conference Hall, Cultural Facilities And Youth Center
Architect : Brisac Gonzalez Architects (Edgar Gonzalez, Cécile Brisac, João Baptista, Eleftherios Ambatzis,Husain Jaorawala, Miguel Goncalves, Gordon Swapp,

Client : Kristiansund Kommune
Location : Kristiansund, Norway
Surface Area : 15,000m²
Program : New Opera and Culture House, Comprising a 650 Seat Auditorium, Symphony,

TRE STERKE IDENTITETER FORENT

OUVERTURE

I kombinasjonen Opera, Bibliotek, Skole, frivillig kulturarbeidsfasiliteter og Ungdomshus, ligger det optimisme, ambisjon og stort potensial. De samme egenskapene som i sin tid utnyttet den lokale klippfisksuksessen til et nasjonalt operaløft : i Kristiansund.

Det nye Opera- og Kulturhuset i Kristiansund (OKK) vil representere kultur i sin mest inkluderende og nyskapende form. Samtidig kan sammenstillingen av de ulike funksjoner ønsket, behov og muligheter risikere en læringsorientert nøytralitet og ende opp med en generisk tilnærming, spesifikk verken for stedet eller for det visjonære. A skape rom for det uventede, det kollektive og det individuelle, for forandring, inspirasjon, eksperimentering, nyskaping, ulikhet og frihet – er å frigjøre kultur.

Den nye OKK må åpne for den samme dynamikk og frihet som sjudt produksjonen av Orfeus – totalt sosialt engasjement. Folkeopera i ordets rette forstand. Kulturhus er altfor ofte et konglomerat av ulike programmer koplet sammen i et opplag og forenklet urban grep. De offentlige rom er ofte en serie av tilfeldige soner innenfor en labyrintisk organisasjon.

Vår strategi er enkel. Hvordan artikulere en stor masse og samtidig tydeliggjøre de ulike programmatiske elementene og utnytte deres nye naboskap? OKK vil fremstå som et samlet anlegg : og som en serie med mindre, men håndterlige bygninger.

OKK krystalliserer ambisjonene om flere sterke identiteter i en kollektiv kulturinstitusjon. Sammensetningen åpner for synergieffekter som vil optimalisere potensialene for hver komponent. Vår strategi går videre ved å utvikle nye synergier som fremdyrker og utnytt.

DEN RØDE LØPEREN

Den røde løperen markerer en kontinuerlig bevegelse fra inngang og lobby til restauranten på toppen, og avtegner samtidig et dynamisk interiør og utsikt over Kristiansund. Dette øynerøre tredimensjonale publikumsareal kobler sammen alle tilgjengelige områder, som filter og buffersone – men også som rom for improviserte forestillinger, resepsjon, kafé og informasjonssenter. Visjonen om uavhengighet og gjensidig avhengighet er lett i den horisontale lagdelingen av funksjoner : operaen, der undergruppen får sin egen plass i bygningen; en etasje for frivillig kulturliv, ballett- og dansehaller, øvingslokale for symfonien, administrasjonsbasen, og toppetasjen med kantine, restaurant og utsiktsterasse. Den røde løper er publikumsarealet som åpner for omtolkning og flerfoldig bruk. Vårt forslag ønsker å skape nye relasjoner og synergier mellom utøvere og besøkende og legger til rette for et åpent miljø med nærhet mellom de ulike brukere. Bevegelsen fra lobby til restauranten på toppen blir en egen akt : en spektakulær forestilling : byen som huset sett kan by på. En montasje av to miljøer – et nikt interaktivg byens dynamiske liv.

SALEN

Vår målsetting er enkel. Flest mulig tilskuere skal være nærmest mulig scenen, med perfekte siktlinjer. Fra scenen, skal utøveren se et hav av mennesker : fra vegg til vegg : og oppnå nær kontakt med dem. Den tradisjonelle flerbuksskalen – som prioriterer behovet for fleksibilitet, ble ofte et offer for mistettingen mellom det praktiske og det vakre, det store og det lille, det uynlige og det eksponerte. Vår design for hovedsalen er et karakteristisk og klart definert interiør skapt av balgende brecanmer som gir konstruktet i rommet, og fleksibiliteti akustisk definisjon. Salen er fleksibel, men aldri generisk. Et rom med en sterk arkitektonisk identitet som kan justeres til flere tilstander og bruk uten å miste en karakter og sine egenskaper.

Symfoniorkesterets rom kan åpnes til restauranten som igjen åpner til tak-terrassen. Den østlige delen av scenen kan åpnes for et publikum på utsiden. Den vestlige fasaden fungerer som skjerm for projeksjon med sitteplasser i parken. Mulighetene er uendelige.

SMUGTITT

Møtet mellom virkelighet og fantasi motiverer vår design, og eksponerer nye ønsker og nye synergier. Stablingen av servicerealene : OKK frigjør de offentlige delene av operaen, og sikrer en unik åpenhet mellom tilskuere og forestilling. Konstruksjonen : den nye bygningen er en metafor for den overordnede strategien. Vertikalkjernene bærer hovedsalen som igjen bærer aktivitetsrommene rundt i bygget. Denne enestående konstruksjonen gir den første operaen i Norge et anneT unikt pioner

...

projekt : det svevende snorloft : der publikum får et glimt inn i den verden hvor fantasien er konstruert – et backstagepass for alle, et kort øyeblikk. Disse smugtittene blir øyeblikk der husets maskineri og tilskuereri : mates. Denne ambisjonen er en refleksjon av den ideologien som allerede er unik og åpenbar i Kristiansund : fullbyrdelsen av the spectator og spectacle (Operafestoken).

ET ROM MED UTSIKT

På byens tak har vi samlet soner for mat og fritid : restaurant og kantine, sammen med orkesterets øvingsrom. I kombinasjon vil disse tre individuelle funksjoner skape en stor festsal for musikken.

KUNNSKAP

Biblioteket er en av de siste åpne og ukommersielle offentlige rom i byen, dermed også en av de mest sårbare. Det moderne biblioteket et åpent forum for utvikling av informasjon : musikk, film, mikrofilm, magasiner, aviser, kart, web-innhold. Like viktig er den rollen det moderne biblioteket har som en katalysator for den sosiale dynamikken i byen – voksenopplæring, utdannelse, utstillinger, ungdomstjenester, diskusjonsgrupper, og folkemøter.I dette perspektivet representerer skolen et perfekt union med det fremtidige biblioteket. Folkets Hus er i dag en skygge av sitt opprinnelig selv. Slitt og brukt – og aventende. Vår strategi er tredelt: en full renovering av bygningens fasade :en historisk tilbakeføring), med en kunstnerisk utsmykking som en skjerm inspirert av klippfisk, en oppgradering av konstruksjonen (forbedrede til fremtiden), og en gjennopbygging og utvidelse av øverste etasje (utvide potensialet). Kaféen har en inviterende front mot Kongensplass, med en urban hage. Veggene blir fulle av bøker – hyller som kan roteres og åpnes mot plassen : en inspirerende og fargerik tettet av tilgjengelig informasjon. Første etasje er tenkt som en felles "bystue", med plass til musikk, magasiner og aviser, for studie, informasjon og spill. Bevegen mot seg gjennom denne plassen møter en et utendørsteater fra Pedersens plan. En sjenerøs trapp forbinder "stua" både opp og ned :opp mot øvingsflor skole, bibliotek, og utstillingsbroen, og ned som tribune til "black box" for film- og videovisninger.

ANSIKT UTAD

Fasaden er en refleksjon av det som skjer innenfor. Utenfra vil den assosieres med scenetepe eller en myk kjole dekket i små reflekterende pajetter, glitrende, flytende.

...

heltaftener med servering og underholdning med en spektakulær utsikt over byen. Restauranten vil uten tvil bli enestående og antagelig et renomeret – en destinasjon i seg selv. Med luksusen av en fantastisk utsikt, stor terrasse, og med mulighet for synergi med orkesteralfen midt i kulturkvartalet der alt kan og vil skje vil dette bli et unikt Room with a View.

SERVICE

Servicedelen av huset henvender seg til de forskjellige behov i bygningen ved å plassere hver servicefunksjon med optimal tilknytning til de områder de skal tjene. På bakkenivå, er den en bred og klar servicekorridor mellom vareleveríng, work shops, back stage og lobby. Miljøvennlige løsninger er enkelt og effektivt løst; det kompakte bygningsprinsippet gir automatisk energibesparelse. Felles energianlegg for komplekset gir fleksibilitet i gjenvinning og for funksjoners skiftende krav, og sikrer effektivitet. Valgene som er gjort for prosjektet er forankret i det oppnåelig mål Leeds Platinum Sertifisering.

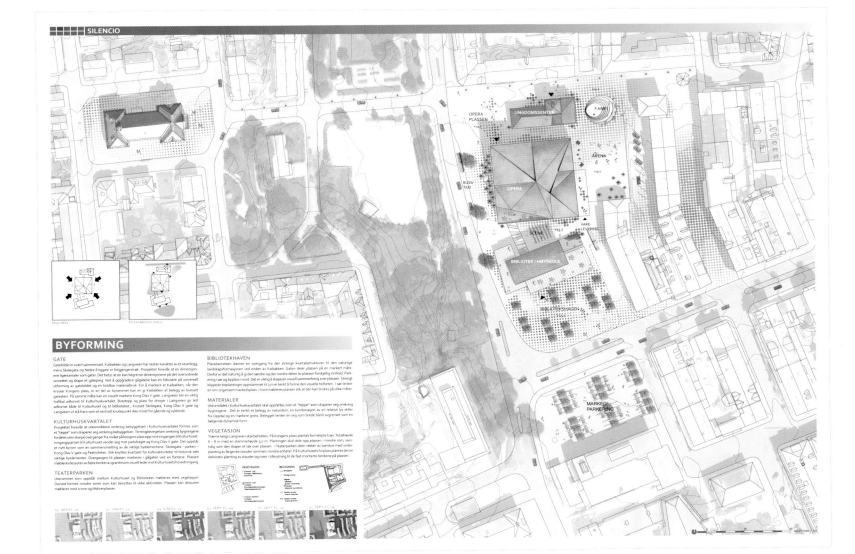

BYFORMING

GATE

Gatebildet er svært sammensatt. Kaibakken og Langveien har nesten karakter av et veianlegg, mens Skolegata og Nedre Enggate er fotgjengerstrøk. Prosjektet foreslår at en dimensjonerer kjørearealer som gater. Det betyr at en kan begrense dimensjonene på det overordnede veinettet og skape et gaterpreg. Ved å oppgradere gågatene kan en fokusere på universell utforming av gatebildet og en holdbar materialstruk. For å markere at Kaibakken, når den krysser Kongens plass, er en del av byrommet kan en gi Kaibakken et belegg av bussatt gatesten. På samme måte kan en visuelt markere Kong Olav V gate. Langveien blir en viktig trafikal adkomst til Kulturhuskvartalet. Busstopp og plass for dropsgert i Langveien gir lett adkomst både til Kulturhuset og til biblioteket, krysset Skolegata, Kong Olav V gate og Langveien vil stå fram som et sentralt knutepunkt ikke minst for gående og syklende.

KULTURHUSKVARTALET

Prosjektet foreslår at uterommene omkring bebyggelsen i Kulturhuskvartalet formes som et "teppe" som draperer seg omkring bebyggelsen. Teronggebevegelsen omkring bygningene fordeles den skaper overgangene fra et gateløp på nye Kongens plass opp mot inngangen til Kulturhuset. Inngangspartiet til Kulturhuset vender seg mot parkdraget og Kong Olav V gate. Det oppstår et nytt byrom som en sammensmelting av de viktige byelementene. Skolegata - parken – Kong Olav V gate og Festiviteten. Slik knyttes kvartalet for Kulturaktiviteter til historisk sett viktige byelementer. Overgangen til plassen markeres i gågaten ved en fontene. Plassen møbleres dessuten av faste benker av granitt som visuelt leder mot Kulturhusets hovedinngang.

TEATERPARKEN

Uterommet som oppstår mellom Kulturhuset og Biblioteket møbleres med vegetasjon. Derved formes mindre soner som kan benyttes til ulike aktiviteter. Plassen kan dessuten møbleres med scene og tilskuerplasser.

BIBLIOTEKHAVEN

Plassdannelsen danner en overgang fra den strenge kvartalsstrukturen til den naturlige landskapsformasjonen ved enden av Kaibakken. Gaten deler plassen på en markert måte. Derfor er det naturlig å gi den søndre og den nordre delen av plassen forskjellig innhold. Parkering i sør og byplass i nord. Det er viktig å skape en visuell sammenheng over plassen. Strengt klippede trepiantinger oppstammet til 3 m er tenkt å forme den visuelle helheten. I sør tenker en om organisert markedsplass. I nord møbleres plassen slik at den kan brukes på ulike måter.

MATERIALER

Uteområdet i kulturhuskvartalet skal oppfattes som et "teppe" som draperer seg omkring bygningene. Det er tenkt et belegg av naturstein, en kombinasjon av en rolige hovedstruktur hvor et fargerike skygge som markere gjens. Belegget tenker en seg som brede bånd avgrenset som en belgende dynamisk form.

VEGETASJON

Trærne langs Langveien skal beholdes. På Kongens plass plantes formklipte trær. Totalhøyde 6 – 8 m med en stammehøyde 3,0 m. Plantingen skal dele opp plassen i mindre rom, samtidig som den skaper et tak over plassen. I teaterparken deles rekke av trær, men under planting av fargerike stauder former i mindre enheter. På kulturhusets forplass plantes det en dekorativ planting av stauder og roser i bånd. Bygningstil de fast monterte benkene på plassen.

Franck Lebouc-Mazé), Space Group (Gary Bates, Gro Bonesmo, Adam Kurdahl, Wenche Andreassen, Gesine Gummi, Ingjerd Sandven Kleivan, Naofumi Namba, Jens Noach, Erich Gerlach, Sassi Heiskanen, Tudor Vlasceanu, Jens Niehues, Rebekah Schaberg) Design team : Adams Kara Taylor (Structural Engineer / Albert Taylor, Paul Scott, Rob Partridge,

Clemens Neugart), Atelier 10 (Services, Environmenta / Rudolf Duncan-Bosu), Norconsult as / Akustikon (Acoustics / Enno Swets, Jan-Inge Gustafsson), Ducks Sceno (Theatre Consultant : Michel Cova, Frans Swarte, Alina Delgadillo, Analyse Duperrier), Sundt ⊕ Thomassen AS (Landscape / Trygve Sundt, Marianne Thomassen, Knut Andreas Øyvang), Atkins (Logistics), Luxigon (Visualisations : Eric de Broche des Combes, Laurent Ménabe)

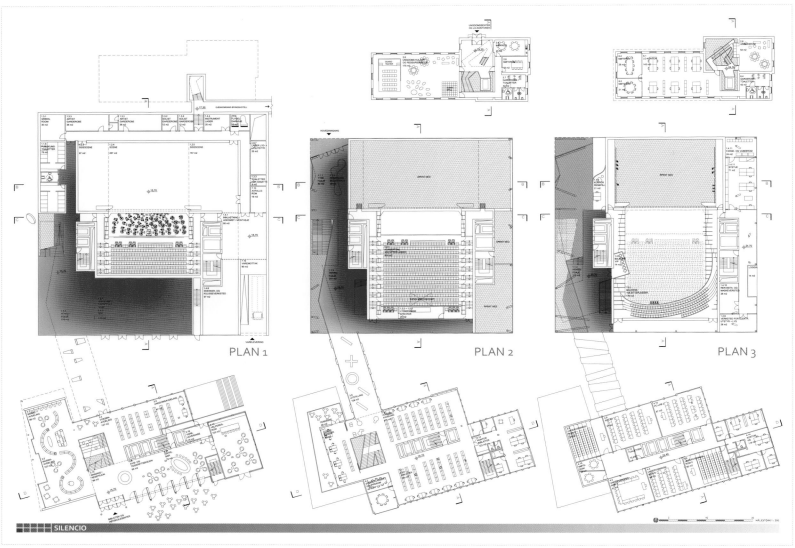

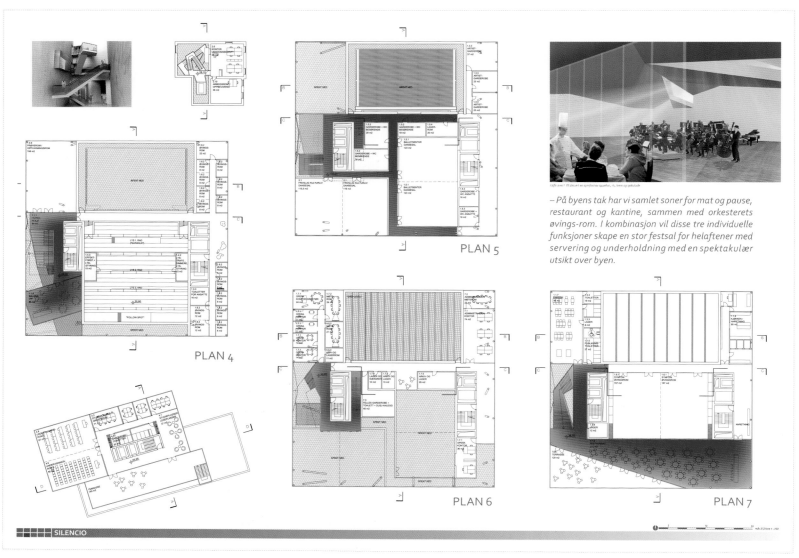

— På byens tak har vi samlet soner for mat og pause, restaurant og kantine, sammen med orkesterets øvings-rom. I kombinasjon vil disse tre individuelle funksjoner skape en stor festsal for helaftener med servering og underholdning med en spektakulær utsikt over byen.

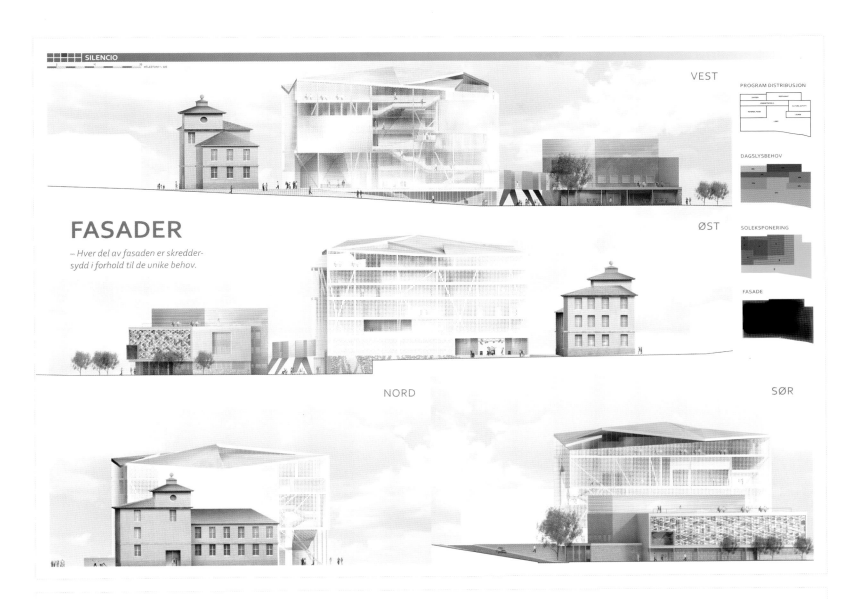

SILENCIO

VEST

PROGRAM DISTRIBUSJON

DAGSLYSBEHOV

ØST

SOLEKSPONERING

FASADE

FASADER

– Hver del av fasaden er skredder-sydd i forhold til de unike behov.

NORD

SØR

SILENCIO

OPERAEN

Vår målsetting er enkel: Flest mulig tilskuere skal være nærmest mulig scenen, med perfekte siktlinjer. Fra scenen, skal utøveren se i hav av mennesker - fra vegg til vegg – og oppnå nær kontakt med dem. Et rom med en sterk arkitektonisk identitet som kan justeres til flere tilstander og bruk uten å miste sin karakter og sine egenskaper.

DYNAMISK AKUSTIKK

SCENEVARIASJONER

Scenen kan ved enkle grep tilpasses ulike typer forestillinger.

OPERA, OPERETTE, DANS: ORKESTERGRAV

KONSERT, ENSEMBLE: ORKESTERSKALL

MODERNE TEATER, DANS: ÅPEN SCENE

UTFORMING

TEATERROM OG SCENETEKNIKK

SCENETEKNIKK

Proscenium

Lysplassering

Kontrollrposisjoner

Inn- og utlasting

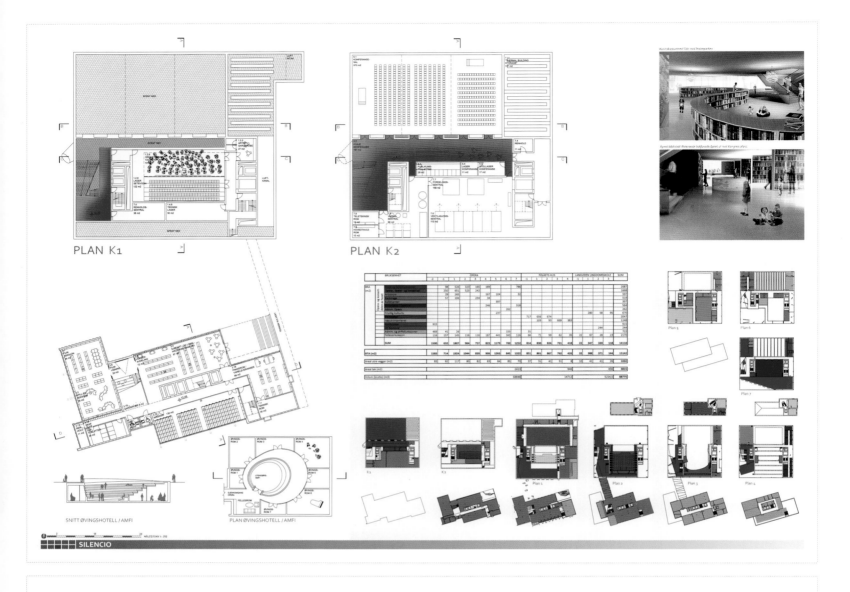

PLAN K1

PLAN K2

SNITT ØVINGSHOTELL / AMFI

PLAN ØVINGSHOTELL / AMFI

SILENCIO

SNITT

Ambisjonen er å skape nye relasjoner og synergier mellom utøvere og besøkende og legger til rette for et åpent miljø med nærhet mellom alle brukere.

SNITT BB

SNITT CC

SNITT DD

VARME, VENTILASJON OG KLIMA

VENTILASJONSSTRATEGI

Generelt

Naturlig ventilasjon

Fortrengningsventilasjon

VARME OG KJØLING

Termisk labyrint

Grunnvanns-varmepumpe

Oppvarming og kjøling

VANN

ENERGIKOSTNADER

SERTIFISERINGER OG BÆREKRAFTIGE MATERIALER

NØKKELTILTAK SOM VIL INTEGRERES I PROSJEKTET FOR Å REDUSERE ENERGIFORBRUK ER:

MATERIALER

MILJØ & ENERGI

— Det kompakte bygningsvolumet gir automatisk energibesparelser. Felles energianlegg for komplekset gir fleksibilitet i gjenvinning og for funksjoners skiftende krav, og sikrer effektivitet. Valgene som er gjort for prosjektet er forankret i et oppnåelig mål: Leeds Platinum Sertifisering.

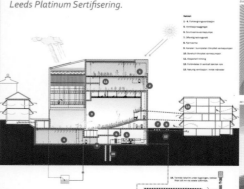

SILENCIO

███ SILENCIO

KONSTRUKSJON
BYGGETEKNISKE ASPEKTER

INNLEDNING

Denne rapporten er en beskrivelse av det bærestrukturelle konseptet og byggetekniske aspekter for det nye opera- og kulturhuset i Kristiansund. Informasjonen som kreves er underlagt utviklingsgrad er i henhold til nedinforstående designstadier. Videre arbeid vil omfatte alternativavurderinger og forundersøkelser for å etablere optimale løsninger for alle bærekonstruksjoner i form av kostnader, konstruksjon, designintegrering og klientkrav.

Prosjektet omfatter en ny kulturbygning bestående av en stor konsertsal for ulike kulturelle aktiviteter som opera og ballett. Videre inneholder det en restaurant på taknivå, et stort konferanserom i understasjon og flere mindre rom for kulturelle aktiviteter og avslasformål. Det nye operahuset vil bli plassert mellom to eksisterende bygninger. Deler av disse vil bli revet for å gi plass til det nye bygget, og gjenværende arealer vil bli bygget om. Ettersom bygningene er fra ulike epoker, er målet å integrere den nye strukturen og å slå sammen de ulike arkitektoniske visjoner til én. En kobling mellom den nye og de eksisterende bygningene vil bestå av en stålbro.

SEISMIKK

På en global seismisk skala er verdiene i Norge lave til middels, selv om de er de høyeste i Nordvest-Europa. Tilgjengelige historiske data viser at et jordskjelv med større (magnitude på Richters skala) Ms eller større inntreffer i gjennomsnitt hvert 30 år og en M6 eller større hvert 100. år.

Ifølge det seismiske farekartet som vises på denne siden, er det et lavt potensial for seismisk aktivitet i området nær stedet. PGA (Peak Ground Acceleration) tyder på svært lav seismisk aktivitet. Derfor ser ikke dette ut til å bli et problem. Faren uttrykker at PGA har en forventet 10 % sannsynlighet for overskridelse i løpet av 50 år. PGA-verdiene for Kristiansund og regionen er i området 0.2-0.8/1.6g.

BYGGSTEDS-BEGRENSNINGER

De nye operaen begrenses av de to eksisterende bygningene på nord- og sørsiden og ved "Langveien" i vest. Det er også en mindre adkomstvei og et torgområde, så vel som et underjordisk anlegg i området øst på tomta.

Terrengnivået på tomten skråner fra nord til sør med den eksisterende skolebygningen i nord fundamentert ca. 5 m høyere enn kontorbygget i sør.

EKSISTERENDE BYGNINGER

Langveien skole ble bygd på 1920-tallet, og opptar det meste av den nordlige halvdelen av tomten. Forslaget er å rive større deler av bygningen for å få plass til det nye operahuset. Den eksisterende bærestrukturen antas å være bærende betongvegger på grunne fundamenter med betongdekker. Deler som skal beholdes er nordfløyen, en to etasjes bygning som huser gymsalen og et fire etasjes høyt tårn. Det er antatt at bygningen har vært ubebodd i flere år og ville kreve betydelige reparasjoner og rehabilitering. Forslaget er å konvertere gjenværende arealene til et ungdomssenter og kontorer.

Folkets Hus er et kontorbygg som ligger på den sørlige delen av området. Det ble bygget på 1960-tallet. Bygningen består av en armert betongramme trolig fundamentert på peler til fjell. Noen av de bærende betongelementene er eksponert utvendig og vil kunne kreve mindre reparasjoner, men det har blitt rapportert at selve bygningen er i relativt god stand. Målet er å bygge om bygningen til et bibliotek og senturm for læring og å rehabilitere den ved å endre strukturen samt å bygge på en ekstra etasje på toppen. Endret bruk av den eksisterende bygningen til bibliotek vil føre til en økning i belastning på gulvet med uunngåelige forsterkningstiltak av bærekonstruksjonen. Dessuten vil den ekstra etasjen øke belastningen på de vertikale elementene og fundamentet. Der for anbefales det at påbygget etableres med et lettvekts bæresystem av stål eller tre. På et senere tidspunkt vil lastkapasitet av den eksisterende bærestrukturen bli vurdert nærmere for å undersøke om forsterkning av søyler og fundamenter er påkrevet.

OPERAHUSET

Overbygning

Bæresystemet kan grovt deles inn i to deler. Den første er hoveddelen i betong, som rommer auditoriet og tårnet, begge støttet av to betongsjakter. Betongkassen i auditoriet støtter de forskjellige etasjene og er rundt hallen og krager ut fra sjaktene i den ekstra søylen under og skaper dermed inntrykk av at bærestrukturen henger i luften. Sideveggene på tårnet er forankret til bakken i endene via søyler og fungerer som en endefelt som gir nødvendige motvekt til utkragningen. Ideen er å eksponere de viktigste betongtverveggene og å justere veggtykkelsen i henhold til det belastningen. Å forme veggen på denne måten vil resultere i en glidende overflate som tilfredsstiller både de arkitektoniske og bærende visjoner.

Den andre bærestrukturen er rammen over og rundt den sentrale hallen, som består av vertikale og diagonale stålsøyler og bjelker, som i sin tur understøtter gulvdekkene og ytterkledningen. Diagonalene tar opp lastene fra gulvdekker og kledning på kanten av dekkene og overfører dem gjennom strekk eller trykk til hovedbæresystemet i betong. Dekkene fungerer dermed avstivende og som en forbindelse som lukker lasttrekanten.

Disse to bæresystemene danner kjernen i det interne og eksterne arkitektoniske språk og søker å uttrykke kraften i integrasjonen mellom byggeteknikk og arkitektur.

GRUNNKONSTRUKSJONER

Det nye operahuset skal bygges inn i skråningen med en to etasjes kjeller, ca. 7 til 12 m dyp. Det antas at løsmassformasjonene er relativt grunne, og at deler av kjelleren vil ligge nedsprengt i fjell. Dype utgravninger i løsmasser vil være utfordrende, og det vil være påkrevet å undersøke fjellnivå og fjellets beskaffenhet som del av den videre utviklingen av prosjektet. Bærekonstruksjon og type kjellervegger vil være avhengig av grunnforhold og avstand til eksisterende bebyggelse. Potensiell undergraving av eksisterende fundamenter og setninger i grunnen må også tas i betraktning. Hvis kjelleren i hovedsak bygges inn i fjell, antas det at jordtrykket vil være minimalt. I så fall kan en åpen utgraving og kjellervegger i armert betong benyttes.

Naturen og plasseringen av området tatt i betraktning, er det lite sannsynlig med mulige forkytninger der store konsentrerte laster kommer ned. Mulige oppdriftskrefter på grunn av den store utkragningen av overbygningen skal vurderes og fundasjonen utformes deretter.

BYGG

Bestemmelse av rekkefølgen av konstruksjonene må vurderes nøye, spesielt hva angår utkragningen og de fremgående etasjedekkene. Det bør merkes at dimensjoneringen av bærestrukturen mht. byggeperioden er like viktig som for den endelige tilstanden. En forstått rekkefølge av arbeidene er vist på de tilstående bildene.

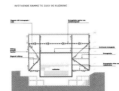

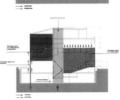

Huset som svever!

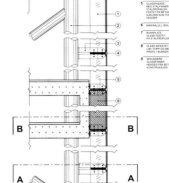

B — B

A — A

PRINSIPP SNITT   M 1:20

Snitt A-A   M 1:20

Snitt B-B   M 1:20

1. GLASSFASADE MED GLASSFINNER OG STÅLPROFILER FESTET PÅ STÅLKONSTRUKSJON
2. STÅLKONSTRUKSJON HENGT FRA BETONG
3. STÅLPLATER SVEISET TIL STÅLKONSTRUKSJON
4. SILIKON FUGE
5. GLASSFASADE MED STÅLFINNER OG STÅLPROFILER FESTET PÅ BETONG VEGGER
6. MINERALULL ISOLASJON
7. BUNNPLATE GLASS FESTET PÅ STÅLPROFILER
8. GLASS INFESTET MED STÅLFINNER MED LIM I TOPP OG MED PROFIL I BUNNEN
9. SEKUNDÆR GLASSFINNER HENGES FRA BETONG KONSTRUKSJON

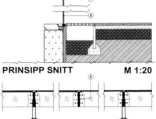

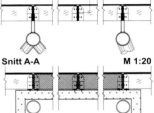

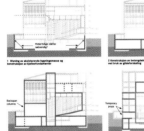

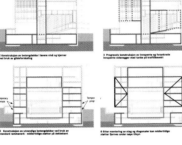

SNITT AA

En "rød løper" binder huset sammen

BALLETT

VIP LOUNGE

BLACK BOX   FOAJE

KANTINE

UTSTILLING

FOAJE   FOAJE

— Publikum får et glimt inn i den verden hvor fantasien er konstruert — et backstagepass for alle, et kort øyeblikk

███ SILENCIO

243

Moulin Rouge | *Horhizon consortium*

Type : Civic and Art
Design : Justin C. K Lau, Tobias Klein

perspective section

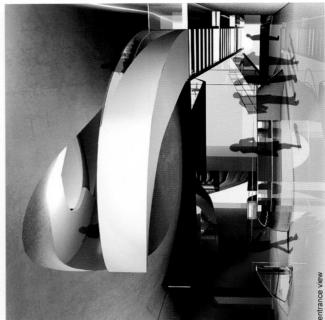

entrance view

front view

Choreographed circulation and curvelinear design is best described y the design of the main walkway that floats over the auditorium 1, allowing it to be used as part of the stage set. Further along, the ramp dramatically leads the public through the ceiling, allowing a full 3d spatial experience with glimpses to the dancers and overview of the entire double hight ground floor. The choreographed infrastructure allows interaction between space, dance, public and building

Moulin Rouge
curve-linear choreography

The main concept for our design of the new Rouge is to transform and utilize the iconic windmill silhouette while creating a fluid choreographed space that allow the encounter between visitor and dancer, displays the narrative history of the place and 3 dimensionally explores it. Two main points are very important in our design.

The choreographed circulation is a gentle meandering path that climbs through the building and ending in an impressive suspended walkway that becomes even part of the auditorium. This core pathway is centered around a void space that penetrates the entire building, and acts as a view corridor but at the same time naturally ventilates the the building. The height of this dynamic vertical form creates a stack effect to allow air travels from ground to the roof level. It encourages stale air to rise out of the ground and pulling through cooler external air

The constant interaction between visitor and dancer (public and private) is crucial and key to the organisation and the design; we expressed this relationship by multitude of view glimpses and a dramatic insertion within the fluid ceiling form ove the ground-floor. The public program has been considerately choreographed into a breathtaking spatial and historical experience which reflects the exciting history of the Moulin Rouge

Both design concepts together form a narrative infrastructure/journey that inform the organization and expression of the building in every detail ation and spatial experience.

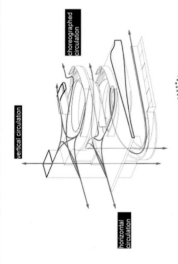

vertical circulation

choreographed circulation

horizontal circulation

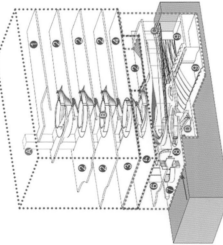

1. office
2. dance studio
3. gym
4. changing room
5. cafe
6. bookstore / exhibition archive
7. souvenir shop
8. entrance
9. auditorium

A. lift
B. *helix staircase*
C. performance ramp
D. grand foyer stair

········· private
········· puplic
■■■■■■ public/private

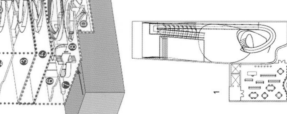

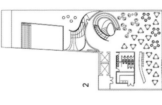

2

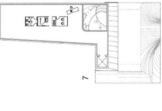

7

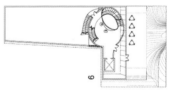

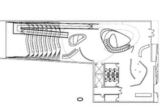

1

6

0

4-5

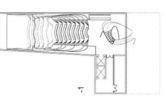

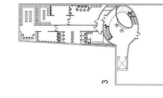

-1

3

Built Area (GFA) : 17028 sqm
Client : Ministry of Culture, Republic of Lebanon

Project : Multi-Functional Cultural Center in Beirut
Typology : Cultural Building
Location : Beirut, Lebanon

Participants : Luis Aguirre Manso, Sergio Blanco Fernández,
James Tendayi Matsuku, Noelia Cervero Sánchez,
Victoria González Gómez, Yitzhak B. Samun
Collaborators : Max Gerthel, Qin Yuxi, Dinah Zhang, He Wei

open arte-fact

o1

CONNECTIONS
MANIFESTATION
MANAGEMENT

CLASSIFICATION
SERVICES

DEBATE

CREATION
INTERACTION
EXCHANGE

The core idea of the scheme hinges upon the building being a framework, a series of slipping planes, within which independent pods are inserted. This framework provides interstitial spaces and behaves like a test tube rack. Each pod encloses a distinct function, offering enclosure and seclusion amongst the backdrop of the framework. These pods extend vertically, linking different levels of the building together and provoking the exchange of ideas between the different disciplines.

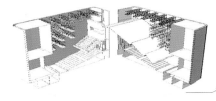

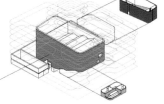

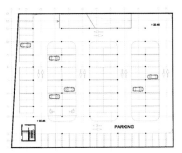

PARKING

10m level -2

PARKING

DELIVERY AREA

10m level -1

MULTIMEDIA HALL

PARKING ACCESS

FOYER

CHALGHOUL STREET

MAIN
ENTRANCE

10m site plan level 0

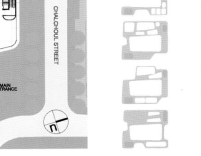

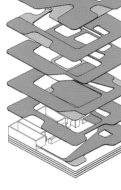

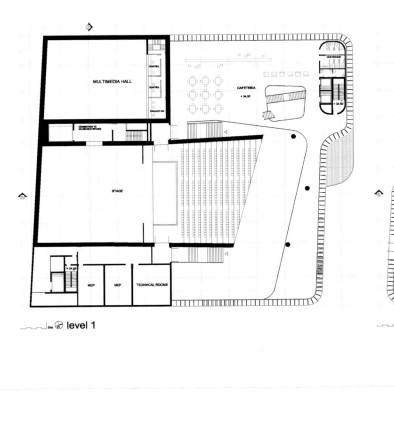

MULTIMEDIA HALL

CAFETERIA

STAGE

MEP   MEP   TECHNICAL ROOM

5m level 1

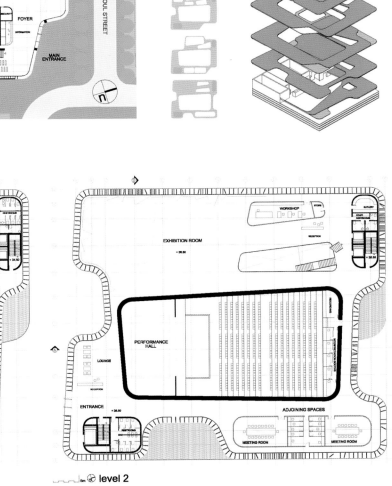

WORKSHOP   STORE

EXHIBITION ROOM

RECEPTION

PERFORMANCE
HALL

LOUNGE

ENTRANCE

ADJOINING SPACES

MEETING ROOM   MEETING ROOM

5m level 2

exterior view, north elevation

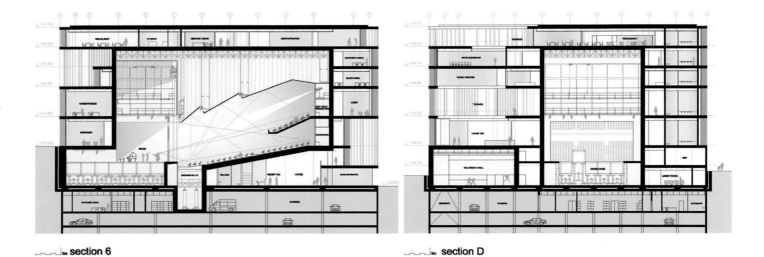

section 6

section D

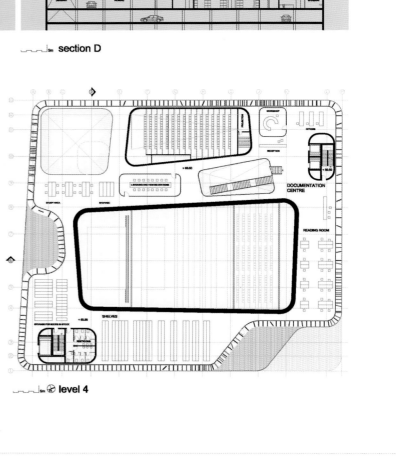

level 3

level 4

o2

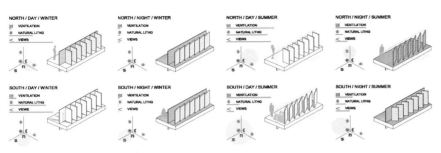

Facade

Permeability/porosity on the perimeter creates and intriguing and appealing elevation, an osmotic layer, which encourages users to explore the inside.

Adjustable glass louvers cover the building skin allows maximum heat control, where heat will be trapped in winter and ventilation during summer. In addition, they control the light and the permeability of the skin, offering shade during the day and illumination at night time. Control systems monitor outside temperature and when it is low it enough at night, windows are opened to allow night purge to cool the internal spaces.

The perimeter facade louvers extends from floor slab to ceiling, and enclosing a central axel which also acts as columns, supporting the building vertically.

west elevation

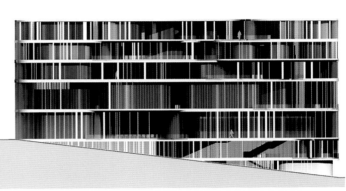

east elevation

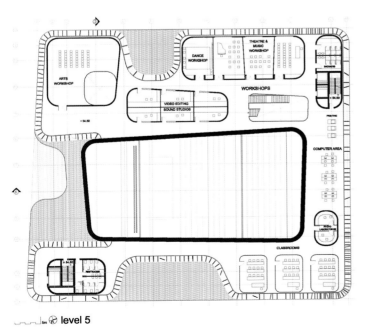

level 5

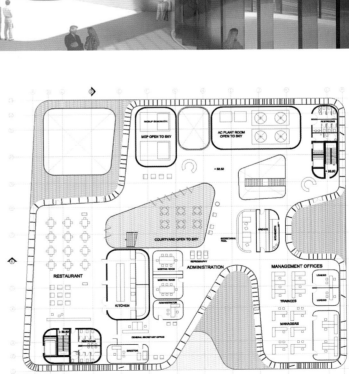

level 6

245

Atienza Music Hall | *AQSO arquitectos office*

Participants : Luis Aguirre Manso
Project : Chapel restoration and outdoor concert hall
Typology : Cultural building
Location : Huete, Cuenca, Spain

Built area (GFA) : 200 sqm / Site area : 948 sqm
Client : Huete future Foundation (Spain)

01

En las partes del edificio que se conservan la intervención pasa principalmente por la consolidación de las estructuras y realce de los acabados, sin grandes operaciones. En la necesaria ampliación se ha buscado la puesta en valor del edificio histórico contraponiéndolo a una volumetría simple que, por su mera disposición, de escala y acerca la percepción de los restos históricos según sus características originales.

La intervención se materializa en un gesto sencillo que a través de una sola pieza cubre los restos existentes, crea un espacio que permite observar el ábside desde la perspectiva original de la nave central y, solucionando cotas de acceso y desnivel, se convierte en espacio apto para el nuevo uso.

Formalmente el edificio es una piel que, doblada como un material continuo, delimita el espacio original de la nave central con dos muros paralelos, forma una cubierta plana y se extiende en voladizo para cubrir el ábside. Su actitud protectora es tan extrema que ni tan siquiera toca el monumento, resguardándolo tan sólo como si de una uña que protege una obra de arte se tratase.

El resultado es una pieza austera que se recorta en función de la geometría y las visuales, un refugio para la mirada. Una ventana rasgada recorta la piel buscando el horizonte, de manera que el público pueda disfrutar, además de la imagen del ábside, de la vista del valle.

SECCIÓN LONGITUDINAL

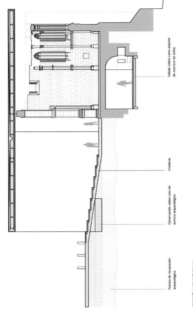
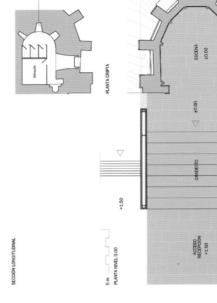

PLANTA CRIPTA

PLANTA NIVEL 0.00

ACCESO RECEPCIÓN +1.50

GRADERÍO

ESCENA ±0.00

ACCESO CRIPTA

MIRADOR

5 m

La diferencia de cota y superposición de la vía pública con la planta original del templo se soluciona con un tratamiento del pavimento y un escalonamiento gradual hacia el ábside. Esto facilita por un lado la lectura del monumento, al dibujarse sobre el suelo su impronta, mientras el tratamiento del desnivel crea una situación de graderío óptima para la sala de conciertos en la que se convierte el espacio.

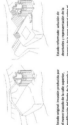

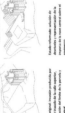

opt969

REHABILITACIÓN DEL ÁBSIDE DE SANTA MARÍA DE ATIENZA
un refugio para la mirada

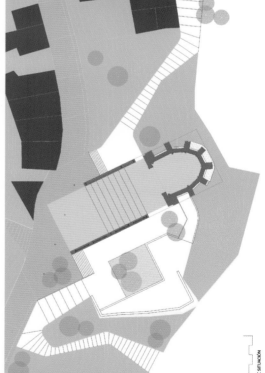

10 m

PLANTA DE SITUACIÓN

o2

opt 969

REHABILITACIÓN DEL ÁBSIDE DE SANTA MARÍA DE ATIENZA
un refugio para la mirada

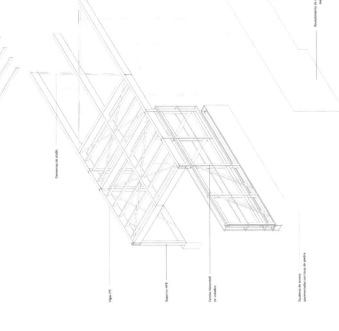

Viguetas IPE

Elementos de atado

Vigas IPE

Soportes HEB

Cordón transversal en voladizo

Escaleras de acceso pavimentadas con losas de piedra

Revestimiento de chapa metálica

La simplicidad del nuevo edificio se materializa con un sistema constructivo avanzado que permite su aspecto ingrávido y respetuoso con el ábside. Una estructura de acero formada por perfilería atornillada crea el armazón necesario para soportar el elemento metálico que lo cubre de forma continua.

El acabado tanto exterior como interior del edificio se plantea de chapa de cobre cuya oxidación y tonalidad esté controlada.

Dado que la pieza se concibe como un solo elemento, el tratamiento de las piezas será tal que la junta se minimice y su lectura sea la de un material continuo, similar a una pieza entera de fundición.

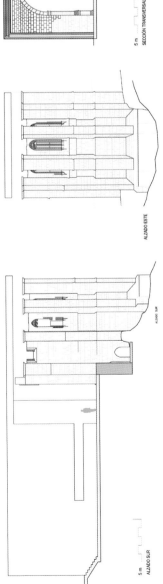

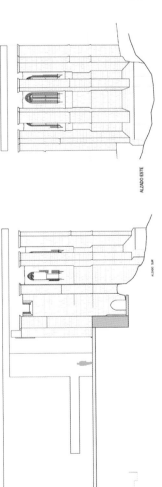

5 m — ALZADO NORTE

ALZADO ESTE

5 m — ALZADO SUR

ALZADO ESTE

5 m — SECCIÓN TRANSVERSAL

246

Music of Rock Music | *Brisac Gonzalez Architects*

Client : Danmarks Rockmuseum
Location : Roskilde, Denmark
Program : Building Complex Comprising a Museum,
High School, Dormitories and Administrative Building

Surface Area : 11,000m²
Cost : 25,500,000 € / Design Period : 2011
Architect : Brisac Gonzalez Architects(Edgar Gonzalez, João Baptista, Antoine Pascal, Fidy Radaody, Theodosia Evdori
Panangiotopoulou, Karl Karam, Kristine Jacobsen)

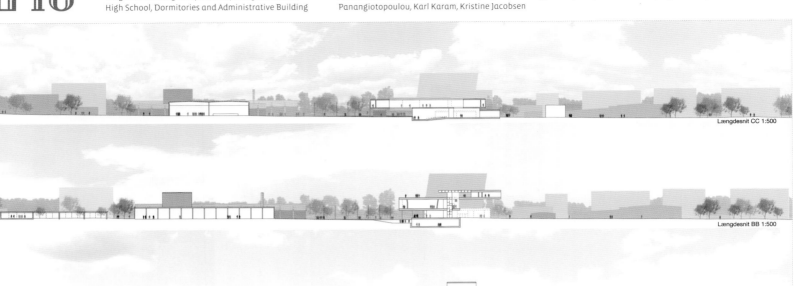

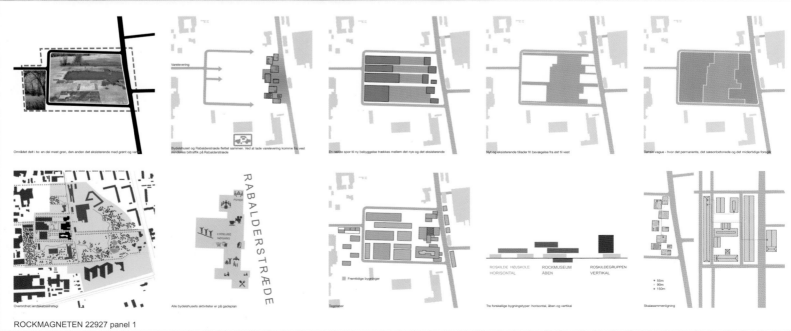

ROCKMAGNETEN 22927 panel 1

Design Team : Ai-gruppen (Local Architect / Tomas Snog, Bjørn Mogensen, Lau Markussen Raffnsøe, Jørgen Peter Nielsen), Thornton Tomasetti (Structural Engineer / Les Postawa), Algren & Bruun Landskabsarkitekter ApS (Landscape Architect / Svend Algren, Adam Bang, Jens Linnet), Ducks Scéno (Theatre Consultant / Michel Cova, Frans Swarte), Davis Langdon (cost consultant / Simon Downing, Daniel Pomfrett), Max Fordham (Services, Environmental / Henry Luker), Jordan Akustik (Acoustics / Neils Jordan), Speirs+Majors (Light designer / Jonathan Speirs, Keith Bradshaw, Carrie Donahue Bremner), VIA Trafik (Traffic consultant / Martin Kristian Kallesen), MIR (Visualisations / Mats Andersen, Jan-Erik Sletten)

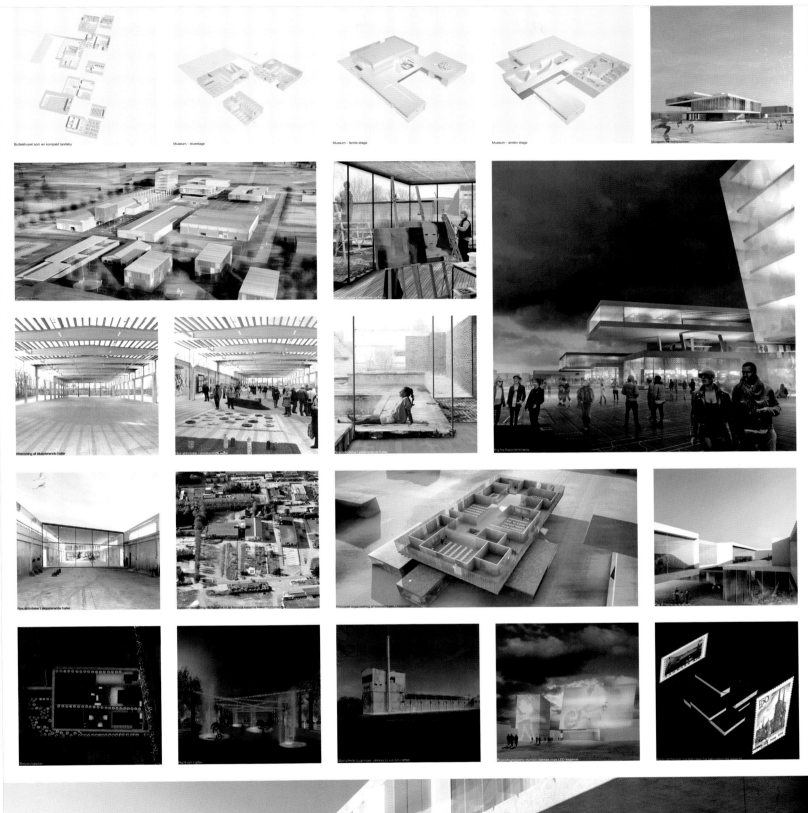

ROCKMAGNETEN 22927 panel 2

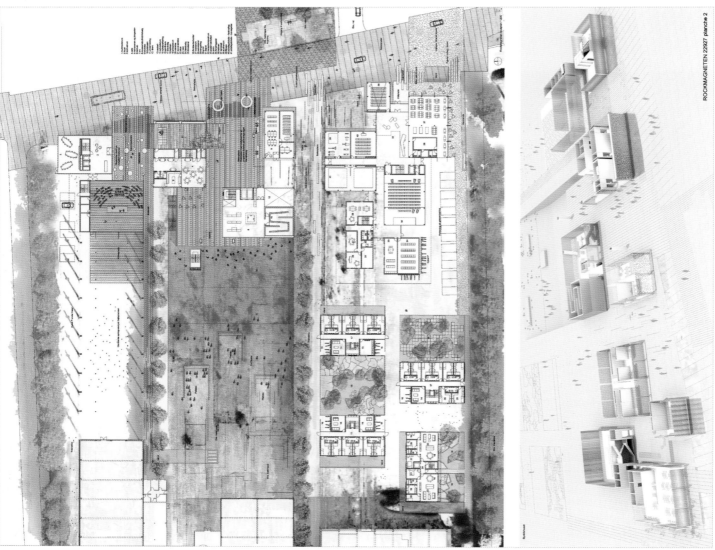

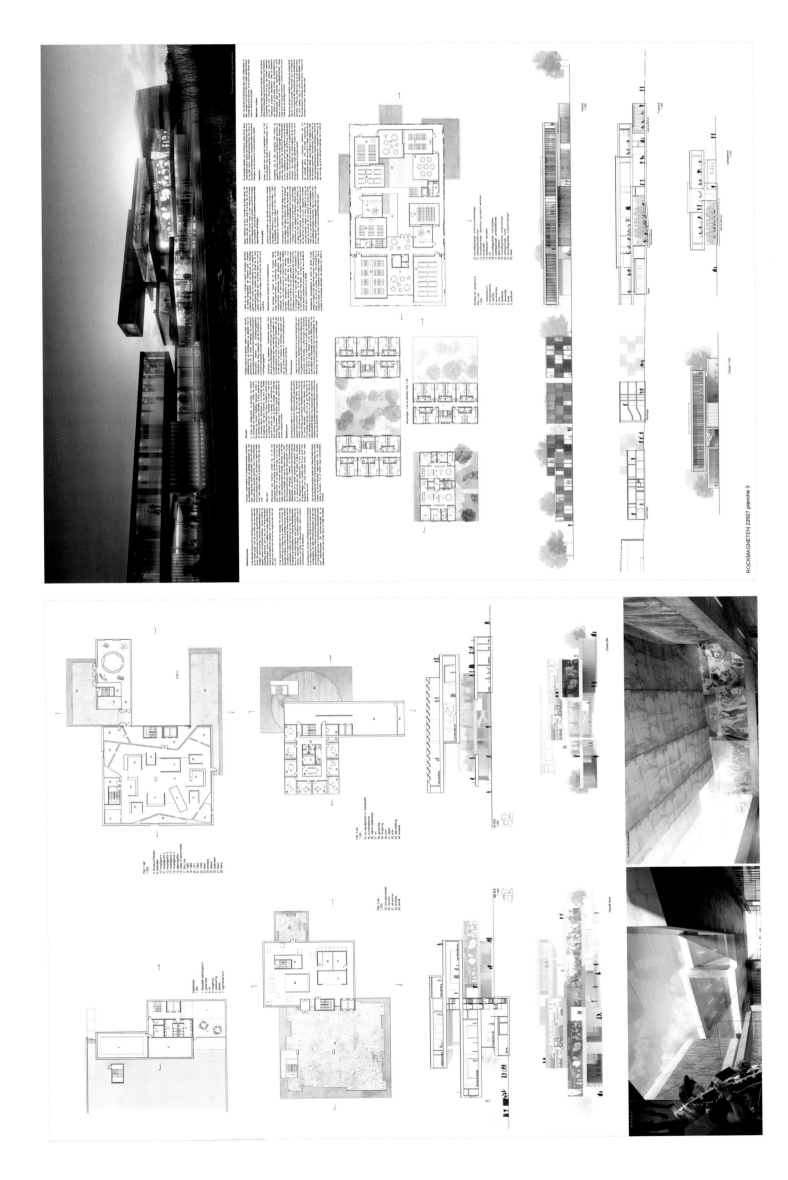

ROCKMAGNETEN 22927 planche 3

247

Sekretu Bat Orion | *LUIS ARREDONDO_ARCHITECT*

Project : Cultural equipment in Orio
Participants : Luis Arredondo, Ekain Olaizola, Amaia Artaetxebarria
Typology : Cultural
Location : Orio, Pais Vasco, Spain

Client : Orio Goberment
Year : 2011

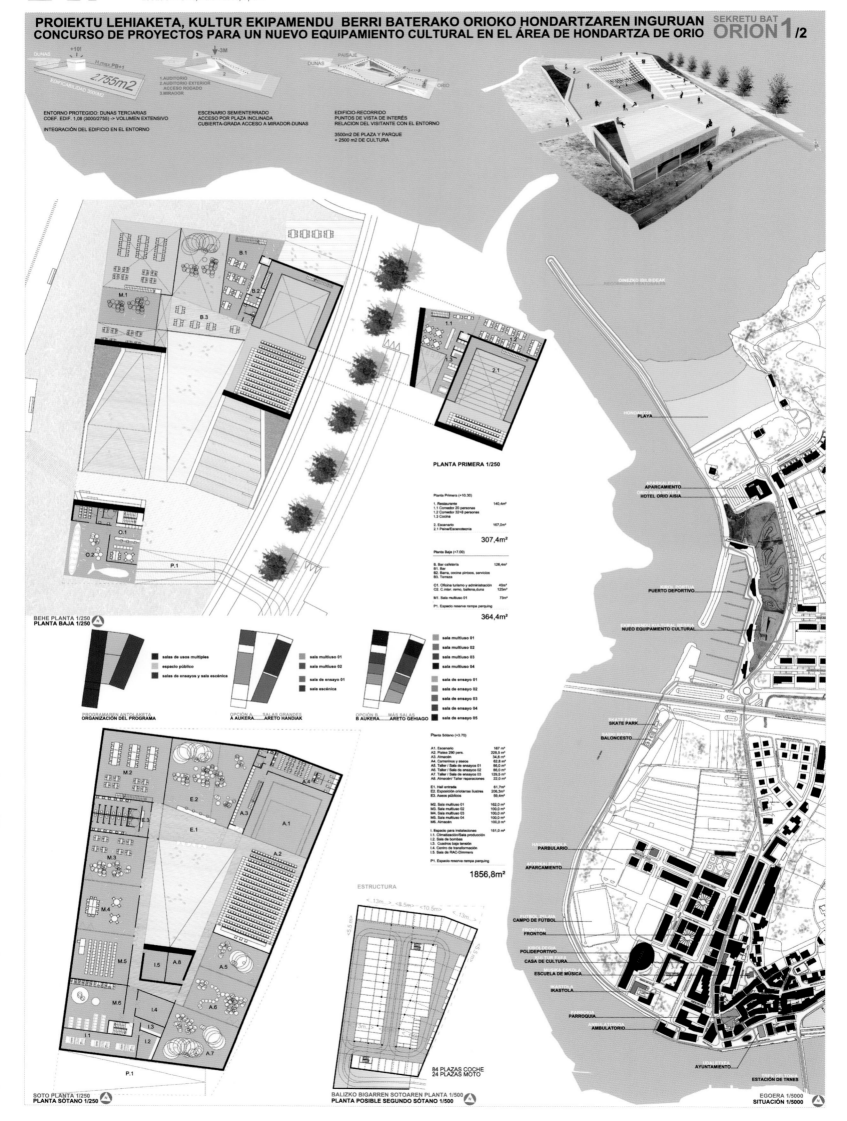

PROIEKTU LEHIAKETA, KULTUR EKIPAMENDU BERRI BATERAKO ORIOKO HONDARTZAREN INGURUAN
CONCURSO DE PROYECTOS PARA UN NUEVO EQUIPAMIENTO CULTURAL EN EL ÁREA DE HONDARTZA DE ORIO

SEKRETU BAT
ORION 1/2

ENTORNO PROTEGIDO: DUNAS TERCIARIAS
COEF. EDIF. 1,08 (3000/2755) -> VOLUMEN EXTENSIVO

INTEGRACIÓN DEL EDIFICIO EN EL ENTORNO

ESCENARIO SEMIENTERRADO
ACCESO POR PLAZA INCLINADA
CUBIERTA-GRADA ACCESO A MIRADOR-DUNAS

EDIFICIO-RECORRIDO
PUNTOS DE VISTA DE INTERÉS
RELACIÓN DEL VISITANTE CON EL ENTORNO

3500m2 DE PLAZA Y PARQUE
+ 2500 m2 DE CULTURA

1.AUDITORIO
2.AUDITORIO EXTERIOR
  ACCESO RODADO
3.MIRADOR

PLANTA PRIMERA 1/250

Planta Primera (+10.30)

1. Restaurante 140,4m²
1.1 Comedor 20 personas
1.2 Comedor 32+8 personas
1.3 Cocina

2. Escenario 167,0m²
2.1 Peine/Escenotecnia

307,4m²

Planta Baja (+7.00)

B. Bar cafetería 126,4m²
B1. Bar
B2. Barra, cocina pintxos, servicios
B3. Terraza

O1. Oficina turismo y administración 40m²
O2. C.inter. ismo, ballena,duna 125m²

M1. Sala multiuso 01 .... 73m²

P1. Espacio reserva rampa parquing

364,4m²

BEHE PLANTA 1/250
PLANTA BAJA 1/250

■ salas de usos multiples
□ espacio público
■ salas de ensayos y sala escénica

□ sala multiuso 01
■ sala multiuso 02
■ sala de ensayo 01
■ sala escénica

□ sala multiuso 01
□ sala multiuso 02
□ sala multiuso 03
■ sala multiuso 04
□ sala de ensayo 01
■ sala de ensayo 02
■ sala de ensayo 03
■ sala de ensayo 04
■ sala de ensayo 05

PROGRAMAREN ANTOLAKETA
ORGANIZACIÓN DEL PROGRAMA

OPCIÓN A..........SALAS GRANDES
À AUKERA...........ARETO HANDIAK

OPCIÓN B..........MÁS SALAS
B AUKERA..........ARETO GEHIAGO

Planta Sótano (+3.70)

A1. Escenario .... 167 m²
A2. Platea 290 pers. .... 228,5 m²
A3. Almacén .... 34,6 m²
A4. Camerinos y aseos .... 62,8 m²
A5. Taller / Sala de ensayos 01 ...... 86,0 m²
A6. Taller / Sala de ensayos 02 ...... 96,0 m²
A7. Taller / Sala de ensayos 03 ...... 129,5 m²
A8. Almacén/ Taller reparaciones ...... 22,0 m²

E1. Hall entrada 61,7m²
E2. Exposición criotarras ilustres ... 206,3m²
E3. Aseos públicos 59,4m²

M2. Sala multiuso 01 .... 162,0 m²
M3. Sala multiuso 02 .... 100,0 m²
M4. Sala multiuso 03 .... 100,0 m²
M5. Sala multiuso 04 .... 100,0 m²
M6. Almacén .... 100,0 m²

I. Espacio para instalaciones ...... 151,0 m²
I.1. Climatización/Sala producción
I.2. Sala de bombas
I.3. Cuadros baja tensión
I.4. Centro de transformación
I.5. Sala de RAC-Dimmers

P1. Espacio reserva rampa parquing

1856,8m²

ESTRUCTURA

BEHE PLANTA 1/250
PLANTA SÓTANO 1/250

84 PLAZAS COCHE
24 PLAZAS MOTO

BALIZKO BIGARREN SOTOAREN PLANTA 1/500
PLANTA POSIBLE SEGUNDO SÓTANO 1/500

OINEZKO IBILBIDEAK
RECORRIDOS PEATONALES

HONDARTZA
PLAYA

APARKALEKUA
APARCAMIENTO
HOTEL ORIO AISIA

KIROL PORTUA
PUERTO DEPORTIVO

EKIPAMENDU KULTURAL BERRIA
NUEO EQUIPAMIENTO CULTURAL

SKATE PARK
SASKI BALOIA
BALONCESTO

HAUR ...
PARBULARIO

APARKALEKUA
APARCAMIENTO

FUTBOL ZELAIA
CAMPO DE FÚTBOL

FRONTOIA
FRONTON

KIROLDEGIA
POLIDEPORTIVO

CASA DE CULTURA

MUSIKA ESKOLA
ESCUELA DE MÚSICA

IKASTOLA
IKASTOLA

PARROKIA
PARROQUIA

ANBULATORIOA
AMBULATORIO

UDALETXEA
AYUNTAMIENTO

ESTACIÓN DE TRNES

EGOERA 1/5000
SITUACIÓN 1/5000

PROIEKTU LEHIAKETA, KULTUR EKIPAMENDU BERRI BATERAKO ORIOKO HONDARTZAREN INGURUAN
CONCURSO DE PROYECTOS PARA UN NUEVO EQUIPAMIENTO CULTURAL EN EL ÁREA DE HONDARTZA DE ORIO

SEKRETU BAT
ORION2/2

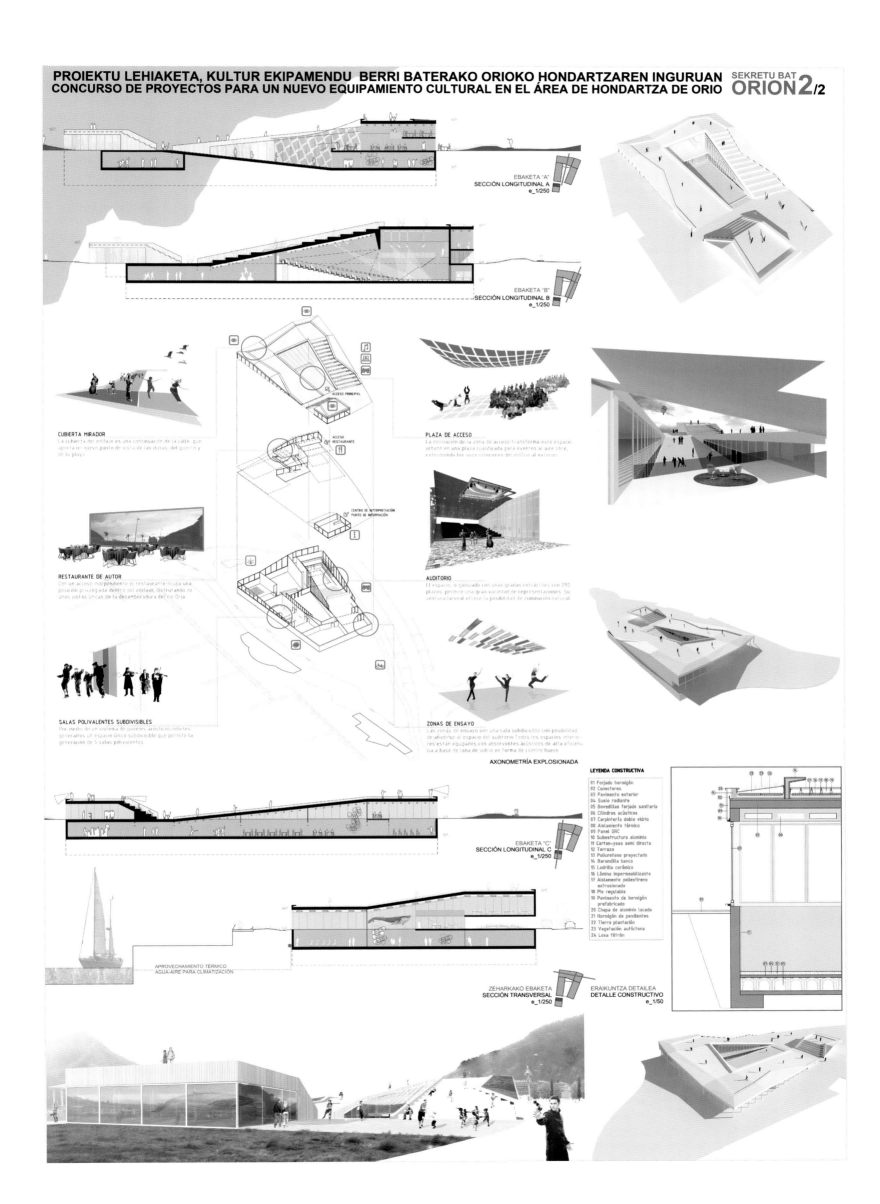

248

Lamina | *Arquipelago Studio*

Submitted to the d3 Natural Systems Competition 2011
Department of Art, Architecture, and Design Universidad de Monterrey
Team : Jaime Garcia, Ivan Aguirre
Faculty Advisors : Prof. Ziad Qureshi, Prof. Gregory Marinic

HEART
HEPPENSTALL ART CENTER

existing museums.

brownfields

Heppenstall belo
due to the decl
become zones
security, and a
abandoned fact
industrial buildin

river front

site

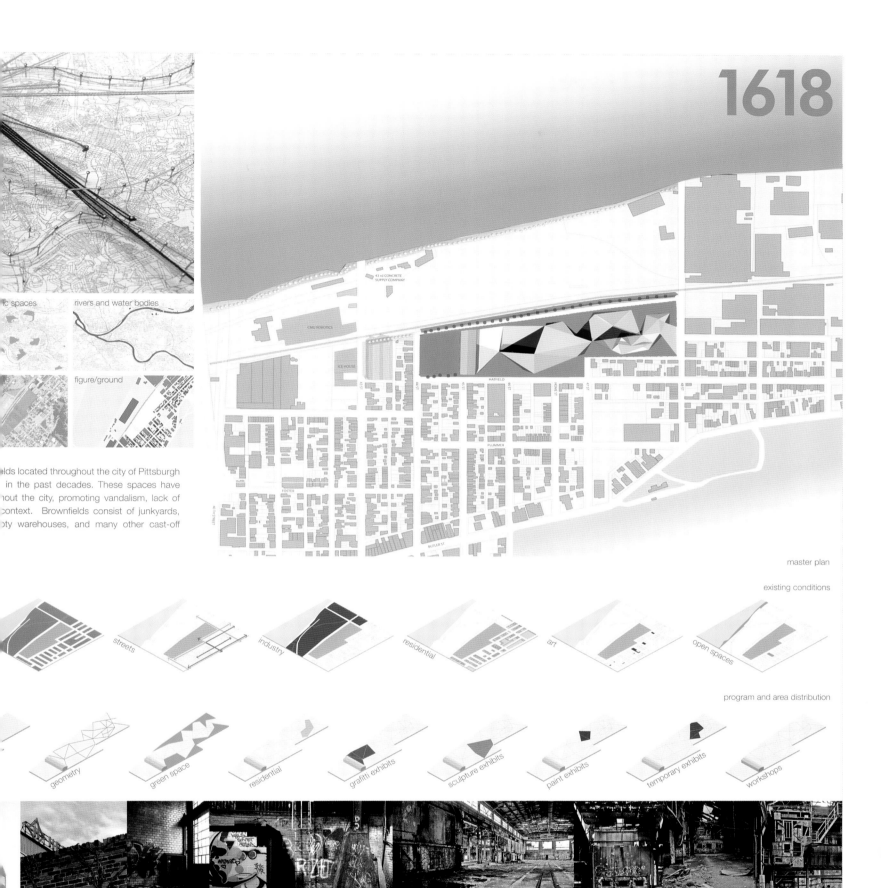

1618

...ic spaces

rivers and water bodies

...figure/ground

...lds located throughout the city of Pittsburgh
... in the past decades. These spaces have
...hout the city, promoting vandalism, lack of
...context. Brownfields consist of junkyards,
...pty warehouses, and many other cast-off

43 rd CONCRETE
SUPPLY COMPANY

CMU ROBOTICS

ICE HOUSE

HARFIELD

PLUMMER

FOSTER

BUTLER ST

master plan

existing conditions

streets   industry   residential   art   open spaces

program and area distribution

geometry   green space   residential   grafitti exhibits   sculpture exhibits   paint exhibits   temporary exhibits   workshops

HEART
HEPPENSTALL ART CENTER

The proposal consists in creating a big open space to contrast with the high residential density that surrounds Heppenstall. It will be a home for the local arts and their creators, by providing working space, living space, and art galleries with permanent and temporal exhibits.

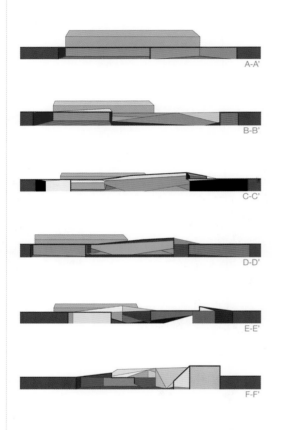

A-A'
B-B'
C-C'
D-D'
E-E'
F-F'

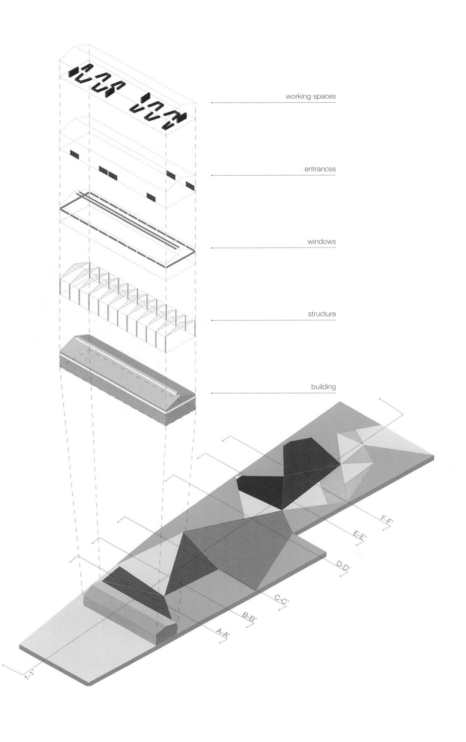

working spaces

entrances

windows

structure

building

Jumbo Jet Theater | *OCDC*

Project Team : Andy Ku, Kam Ku
Location : BOS-LAX
Typology : Theater
Size : 400 Seat / Flexible

713

Creating a Digital Culture | *Lima Urban Lab*

Location : Taiwan, China
Project Team : Pablo Diaz, Diego Rodriguez, Gonzalo Rodriguez, Christian Abugattas, Martin Cruz

250

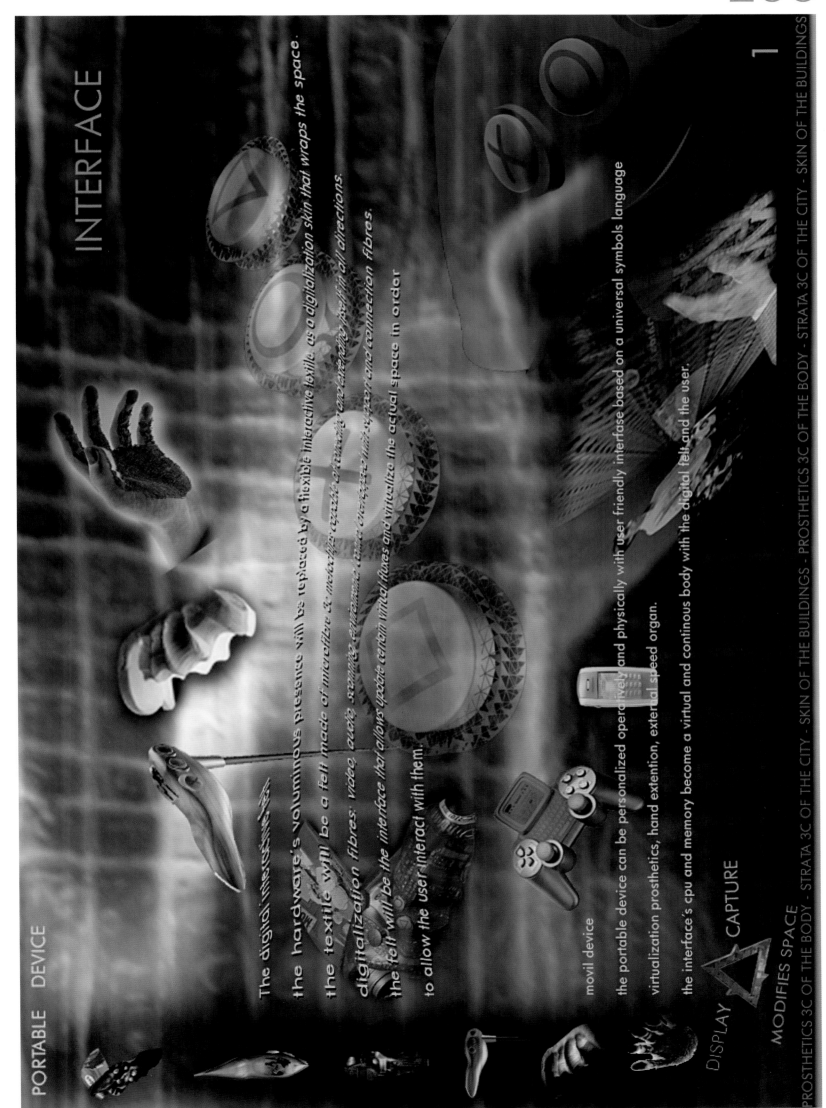

INTERFACE

PORTABLE DEVICE

The digital interface as

the hardware's voluminous presence will be replaced by a flexible interactive textile, as a digitalization skin that wraps the space.

the textile will be a felt made of microfibre to match the exact amount of current operating systems built in all directions.

digitalization fibres: video, audio, scanning, cellphones, data, emotions with a touch and connection fibres.

the felt will be the interface that allows update certain virtual fluxes and virtualize the actual space in order

to allow the user interact with them.

movil device

the portable device can be personalized operatively and physically with user friendly interfase based on a universal symbols language

virtualization prosthetics, hand extention, external speed organ.

the interface's cpu and memory become a virtual and continous body with the digital felt and the user.

DISPLAY CAPTURE

MODIFIES SPACE

1

ON THE GROUND - HORIZONTAL SPACE

FIT WITH TWO TYPES OF INTERACTION, ONE BY USING THE PORTABLE DEVICE (SENDING A CODE) AND THE
OTHER BY DIRECT TOUCH. THE FELT IS THE NEW SPATIAL STRATA OF VIRTUAL DIGITALIZATION

URBAN SPACE
DIFERENT FOLD INTERACTION SCALES
A - ADVERTISING,SIGNAGE,PUBLIC PHONES
B - BUS STATIONS,RAIL STATIONS
C - PUBLIC SIDEWALKS

SPATIAL MODULE

FLEXIBILITY

A VIRTUAL INTERFACE SPACE IN THE CITY , A SPACE WRAPPED WITH A DIGITAL FELT WITH SCREEN, COMUNI-
CATION AND DATA ACCESS FUNCTIONS AND MULTIPLE CONECTIONS WITH THE INFORMATION NETWORK.

PROSTHETICS 3C OF THE BODY - STRATA 3C OF THE CITY - SKIN OF THE BUILDINGS - PROSTHETICS 3C OF THE BODY - STRATA 3C OF THE CITY - SKIN OF THE BUILDINGS

ON THE WALL VERTICAL SPACE

VIRTUAL

SYMBIOSIS

SHOPPING

THE VERTICAL SPACE IS A MEMBRANE MADE OF AN INTERACTIVE AND SENSITIVE FELT, A SKIN THAT WRAPS SECTIONS OF A COMMERCIAL BUILDING FACADE. THE STRATEGY IS TO USE THE POTENTIAL FORCE AND FLUXES OF TODAY'S COMMERCIAL SPACE IN ORDER TO ATTRACT COSTUMERS.

THE MEMBRANE'S PURPOSE IS TO ALLOW PEOPLE INTERACT WITH THIS NEW TECHNOLOGY, TO EXPLORE ITS POSSIBILITIES. A SPATIAL EXPERIENCE LABORATORY.
THE VIRTUAL SPACE IS ANOTHER STRATA OF THE CITY'S ARTIFICIAL LANDSCAPE. THE INFORMATION MESH-WORK. A PLACE WHERE IS POSSIBLE TO BRING TOGETHER AN INTENSE INTERACTION BETWEEN PEOPLE AND THE 3C TECH. A SPACE OF MULTIPLE CONECTIONS AND RELATIONS BETWEEN THE USER AND THE NET.

THE NEW PUBLIC SPACE WHERE THE INTERACTION HAPPENS IN THE NET AND THE CITY. THE FELT THAT WRAPS THE FACADE AND WRAPS US WITH THE VIRTUAL CODIFICATION. WE'LL BE SUBMERGED IN AN INTENSE INTERACTION EXPERIENCE.

3

PROSTHETICS 3C OF THE BODY - STRATA 3C OF THE CITY - SKIN OF THE BUILDINGS - PROSTHETICS 3C OF THE BODY - STRATA 3C OF THE CITY - SKIN OF THE BUILDINGS

251

Geneve | *Marchi_Architectes*

Team : Architecture project(Adelaïde et Nicola Marchi[Marchi_Architectes]),
Aassociate architect(Federico Kraus), 3D images(Federico Kraus)

716

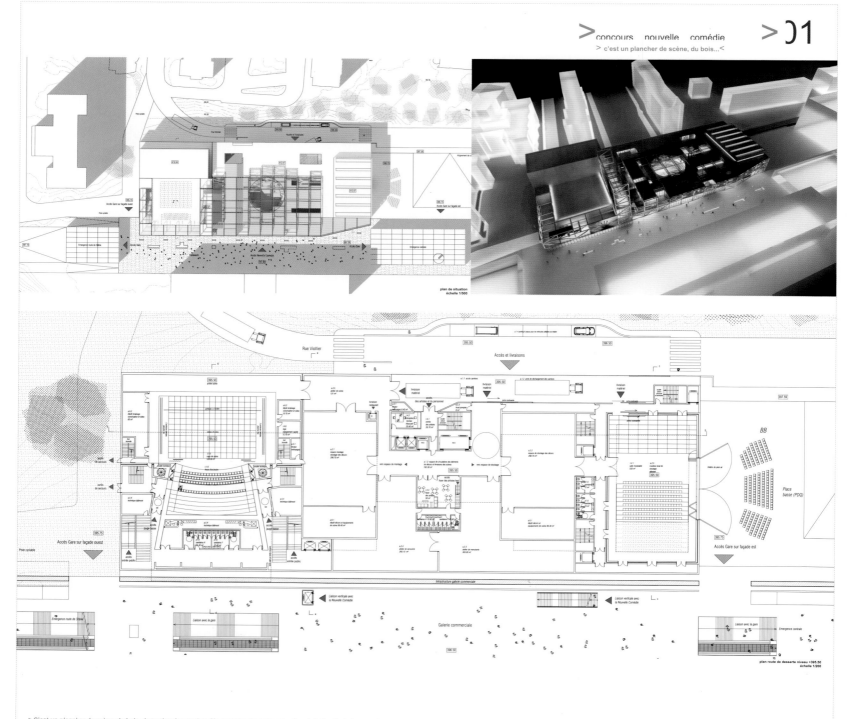

> concours nouvelle comédie   > 01
> c'est un plancher de scène, du bois...<

> C'est un plancher de scène, du bois, du papier, des cordes. C'est un plan avec des planches de bois, placé dans une longue perspective ou structuré dans
d'autres compositions. C'est en tout cas du vieux bois avec des clous et des trappes qui s'ouvrent sur le mystère. <
                                                                                                                    Giorgio Strehler, 1972

Machu Picchu Rain Forest Resort | *Lima Urban Lab*

Location : Machu Picchu,Cusco, Peru
Project Team : Pablo Diaz,Diego Rodriguez,Gonzalo Rodriguez,
Sandra Almenara, Rebeca San Roman, Christian Abugattas
Project area : 500 sqm

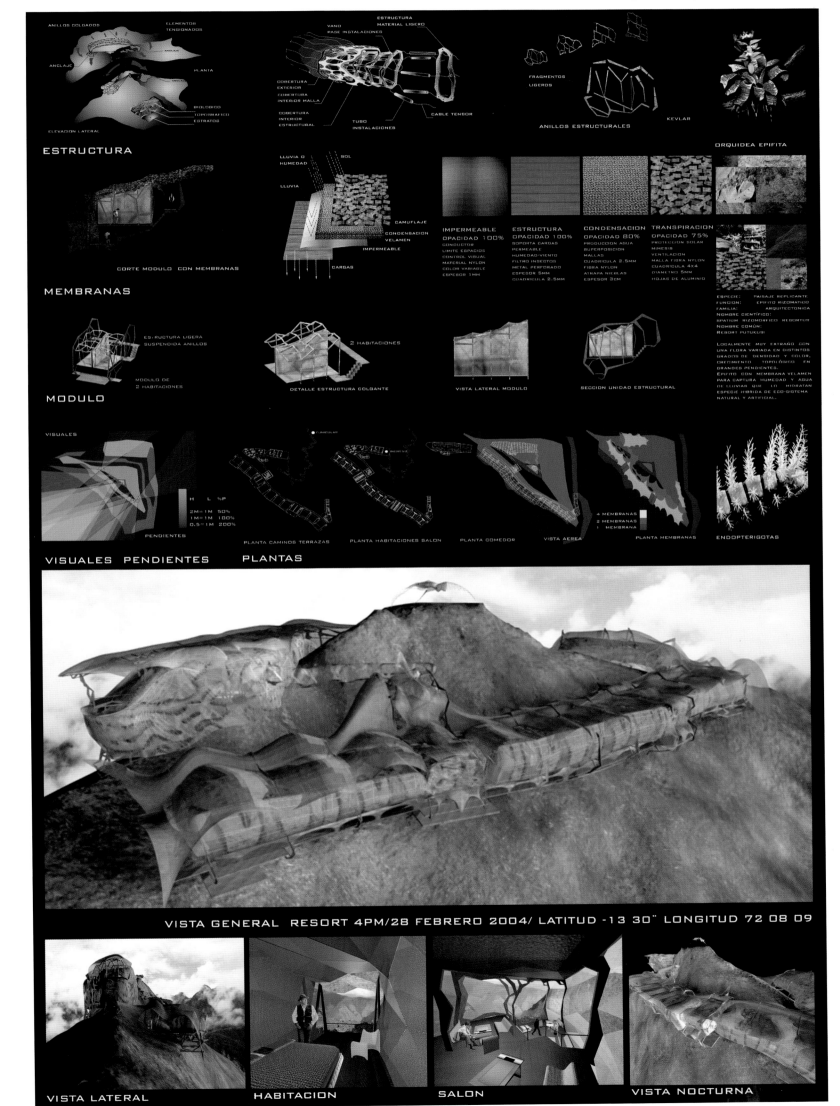

253 Big Leaves Dream Carriers | *MOTOElastico*

International Design Idea Competition for the Big-O of Expo 2012 Yeosu Korea-
Project by : Simone Carena | Marco Bruno + Jooyeon Kim + The One
Design Team : Minji Kim, Vivien Serveau, Davide Barreri
Location : Yeosu, South Korea

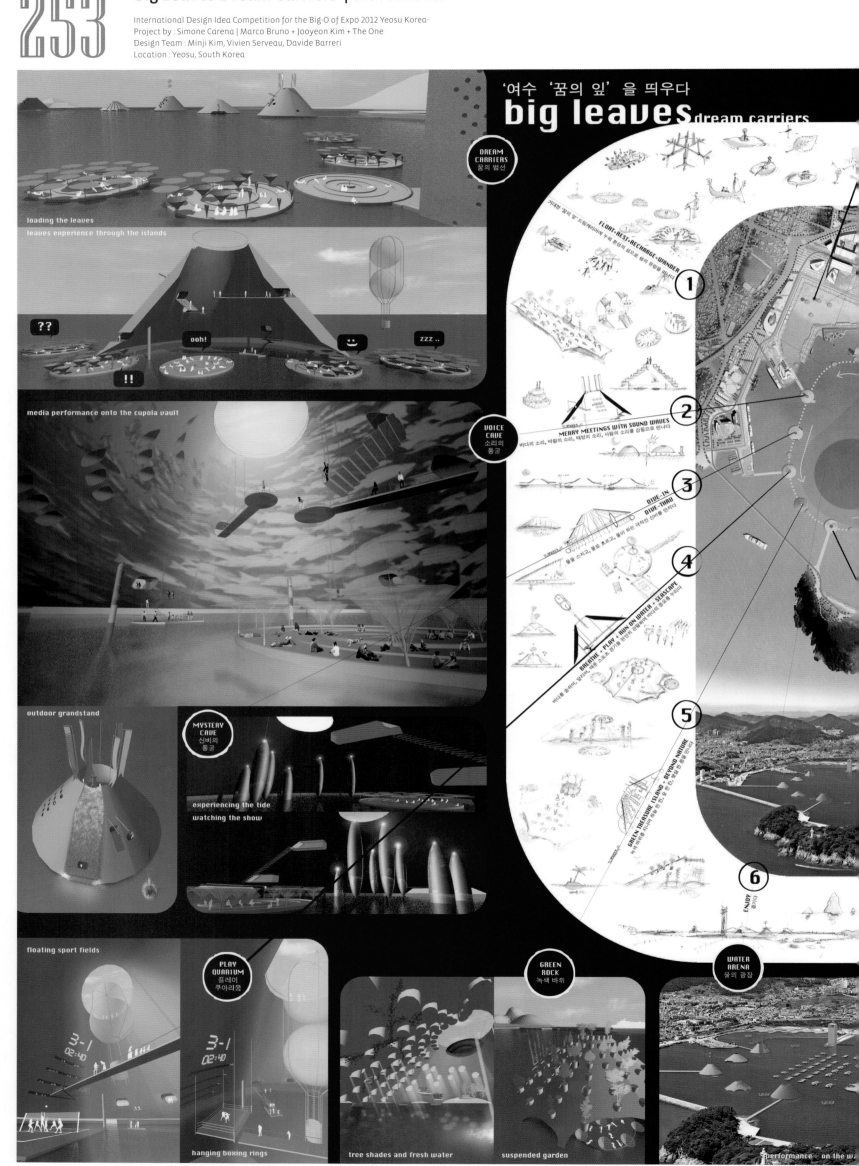

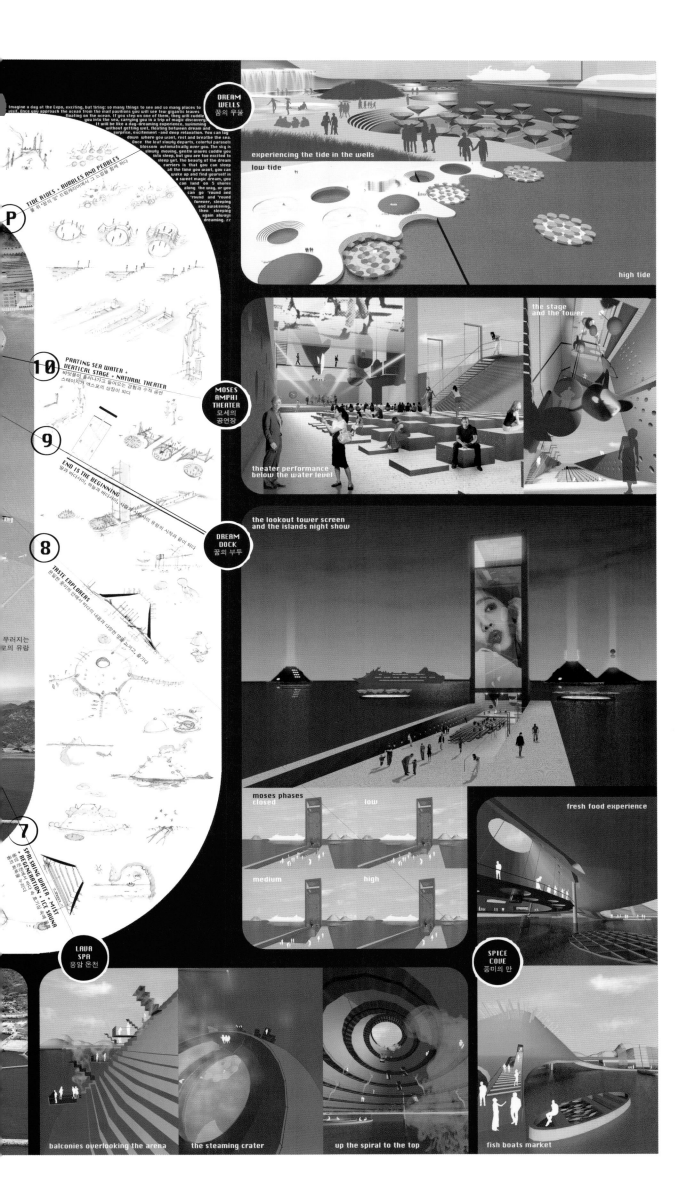

Imagine a day at the Expo, exciting, but tiring: so many things to see and so many places to visit. Once you approach the ocean from the mail pavilions you will see few gigantic leaves floating on the ocean. If you step on one of them, they will cuddle you into the sea, carrying you in a trip of magic discovery. It will be like a day-dreaming experience, swimming without getting wet, floating between dream and surprise, excitement - and deep relaxation. You can lay down where you want, rest and breathe the sea. Once the leaf slowly departs, colorful parasols blossom automatically over you. The sky is slowly moving, gentle waves cuddle you into sleep, but you are too excited to sleep yet. The beauty of the dream carriers is that you can sleep all the time you want, you can wake up and find yourself in a sweet magic dream, you can land on 5 shores along the way, or you can go 'round and 'round and 'round forever, sleeping and awakening, then sleeping again always dreaming. zz

TIDE RIDES + BUBBLES AND PEBBLES
풀 밑 '웅덩' 앞 '드워'라인'에서 그 느낌을 함께 하다

P

10 PARTING SEA WATER + VERTICAL STAGE + NATURAL THEATER
바닷물이 흘러나가고 들어오는 경험과 수직 공연
스테이지가 엑스포의 상징이 되다

9 END IS THE BEGINNING
앞의 바다이야, 뒤쪽의 바다이야, 시작과 끝이 유랑의 시작계 끝이 되다

DREAM WELLS
꿈의 우물

experiencing the tide in the wells
low tide

high tide

MOSES AMPHI THEATER
모세의 공연장

the stage and the tower

theater performance below the water level

DREAM DOCK
꿈의 부두

the lookout tower screen and the islands night show

8 TASTE EXPLORERS
관능적 풍미의 맛깔스런 바다의 내용의 다양함 맛을 느끼고, 즐기다

우러지는
쿨의 유랑

7 SPLASHING WATER + MIST + ICE SAUNA
REGENERATION
코물과 물장구와 안개의 분사 그리고 얼음의 유쾌한 엑스포의 회복을 찾다

moses phases
closed   low
medium   high

fresh food experience

LAVA SPA
용암 온천

SPICE COVE
풍미의 만

balconies overlooking the arena   the steaming crater   up the spiral to the top   fish boats market

254

Yeosu Pavilion Competition | *Thurlow Small Architecture*

Location : Yeosu, Korea
Design Team : Andrew Thurlow, Maia Small, Carlos Endriga
Competition Sponsor : Organizing Committee of the Expo 2012 Yeosu

720

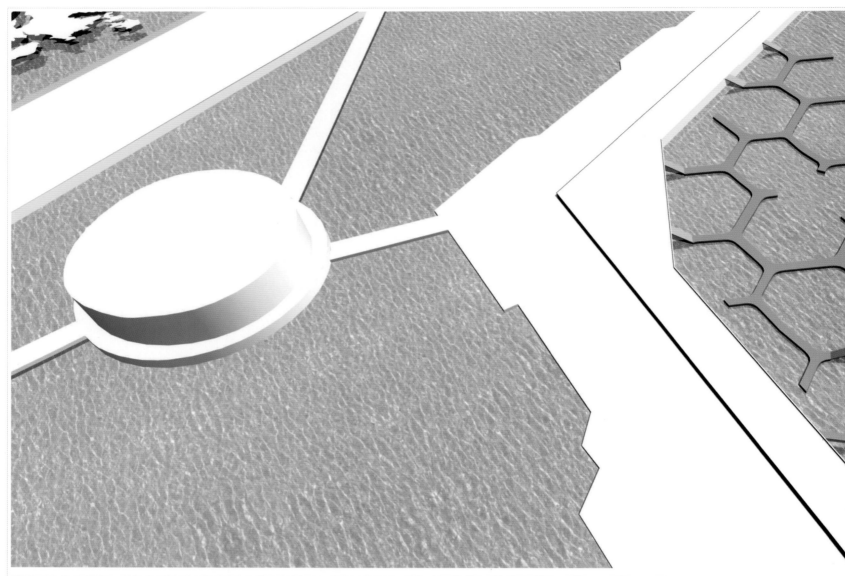

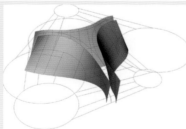
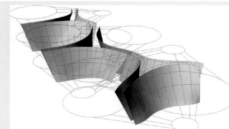

POOLS ARE A SPATIAL NET.

The geometry of the pools comes from a set of
spatial relationships derived from the program brief.
We first began by describing a network of open
centers between the two main galleries and support
spaces, then we experimented with proximities
and adjacencies to test out the potential effects.
We sought the best option to highlight porosity,
overflow potential, and density to contrast the
narrow walls with the openness of the pools.

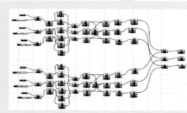

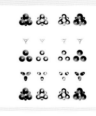
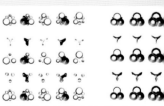

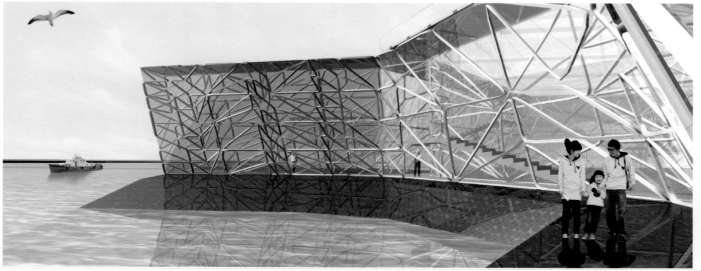
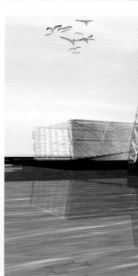

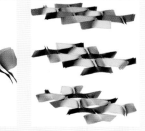

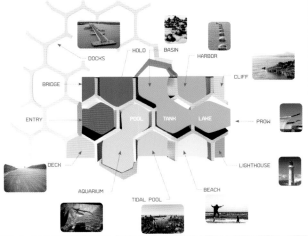

...OPLE MOVE LIKE WATER.

...avilion is a place to learn about and inhabit ...perience of all of the forms of water as life, ..., value and meaning through a set of interior ...xterior pools. Some pools are literal and some ...ural; pools contain water, wildlife, people, ex-...ce, and texture. Each one is named as shown ...o express the variety of types, uses, percep-...and interactions between water, land, people ...e earth. While the wall geometry is complex, ...aces are simple to allow for the exhibits.

DOCKS HOLD BASIN HARBOR

BRIDGE CLIFF

ENTRY POOL TANK LAKE PROW

DECK LIGHTHOUSE

AQUARIUM BEACH

TIDAL POOL

POOL
GALLERIES

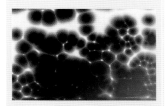

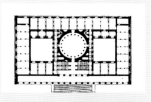

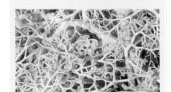

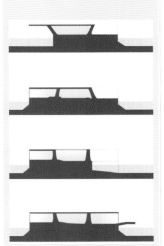

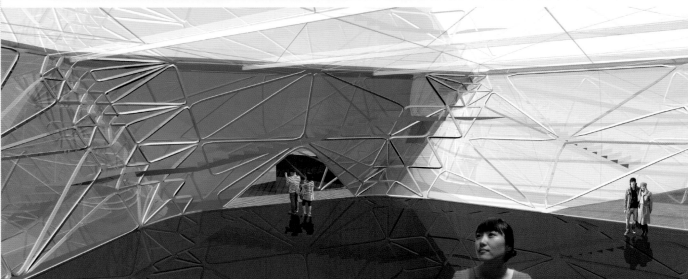

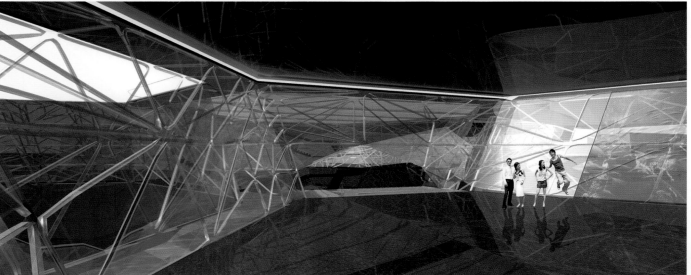

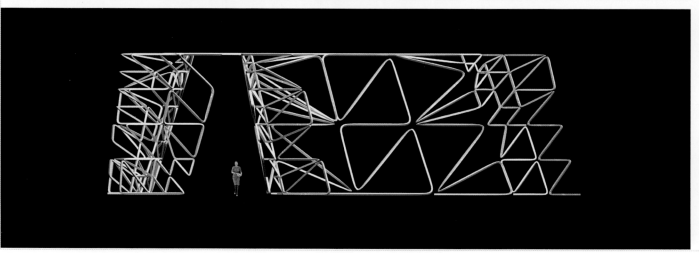

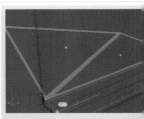

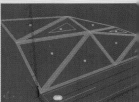

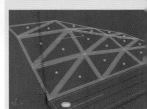

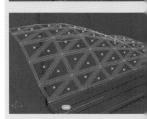

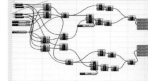

RESPONSIVE WALL SYSTEM.

Parametric modeling (RhinoScript / Grasshopper) was used to both create and control a system of structure and panelization for the networked wall system, dubbed "butterfly clip." The integrative workflow model incorporates design criteria, programmatic & site analysis (both internal and external constraints), as well as fabrication requirements as generative devices for the creation of the self-similar wall system as architectural prototype.

WATER AFFECT.

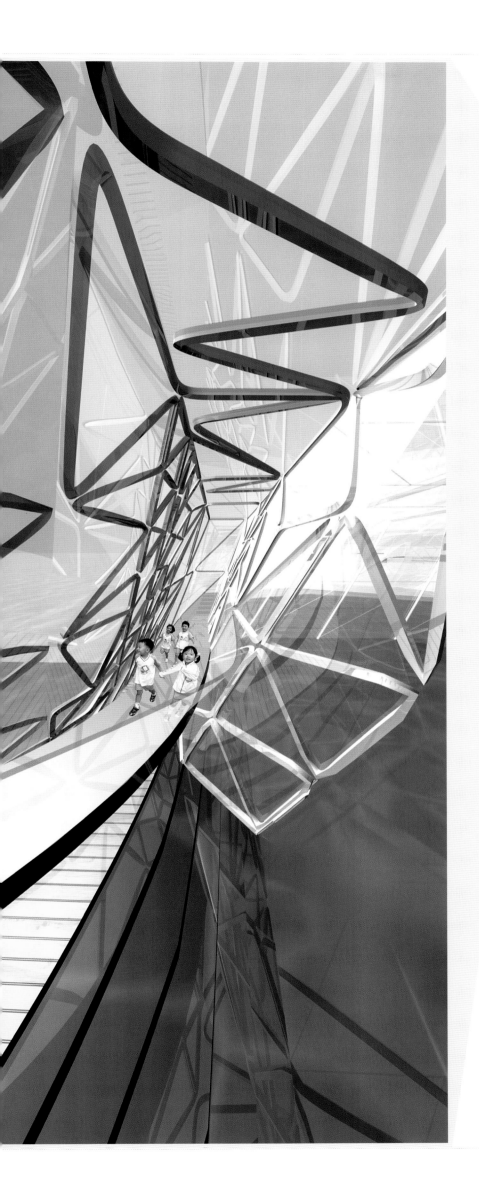

WATERFALL WALLS

WALLS LIKE WATER.

Moving through pools of program is more than going between rooms. The walls themselves are delicate structures of bent aluminum, a cage of circulation that varies in density and porosity. Thus one falls from one pool to the next, swirling through the basins, from interior to exterior. The paperclip walls are translucent and open slightly differently for everyone such that movement is unpredictable and dynamic. The waterfall walls, on the inside, would have a variety of panel enclosures to allow for or restrict movement and, on the outside, to create a solid barrier as necessary for the roof and exterior edges.

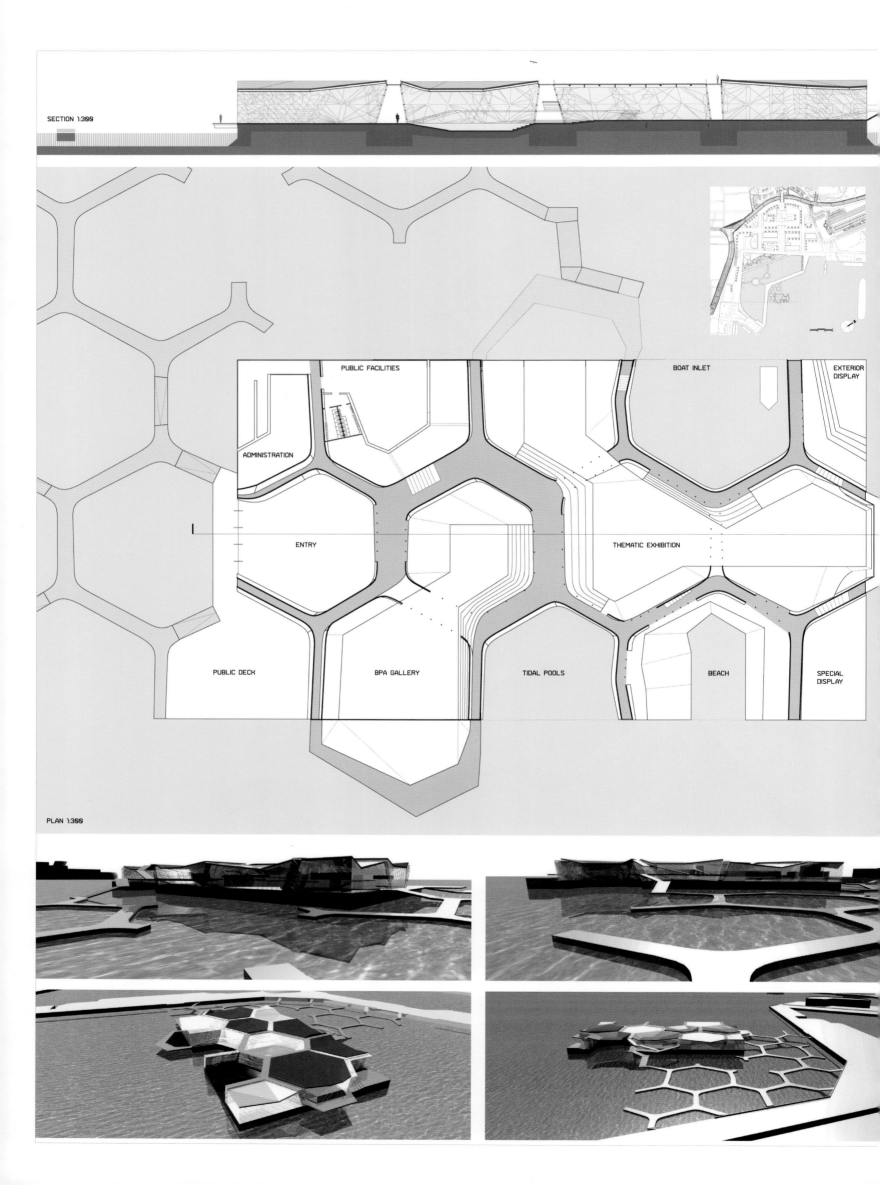

SECTION 1:300

PLAN 1:300

PUBLIC FACILITIES

BOAT INLET

EXTERIOR
DISPLAY

ADMINISTRATION

ENTRY

THEMATIC EXHIBITION

PUBLIC DECK

BPA GALLERY

TIDAL POOLS

BEACH

SPECIAL
DISPLAY

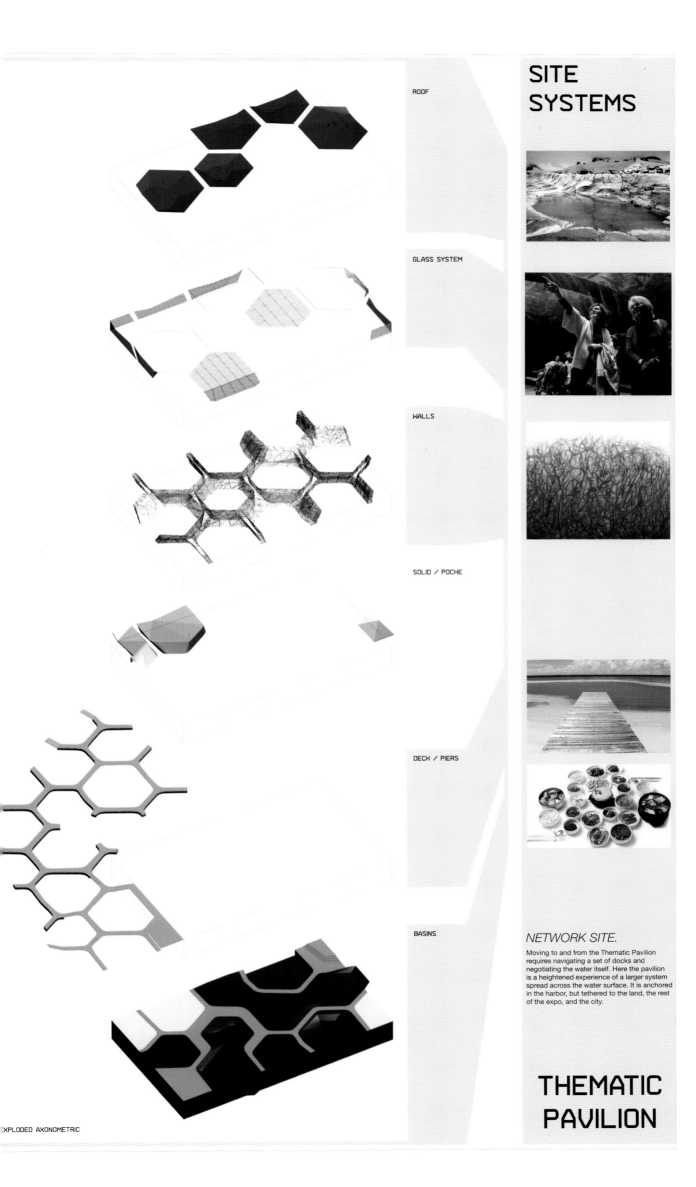

ROOF

GLASS SYSTEM

WALLS

SOLID / POCHE

DECK / PIERS

BASINS

EXPLODED AXONOMETRIC

SITE SYSTEMS

NETWORK SITE.

Moving to and from the Thematic Pavilion requires navigating a set of docks and negotiating the water itself. Here the pavilion is a heightened experience of a larger system spread across the water surface. It is anchored in the harbor, but tethered to the land, the rest of the expo, and the city.

THEMATIC PAVILION

255

Expo Yeosu 2012 Korea | *Slot.*

Location : Korea, Yeosu, Expo Area in the Open Sea
Program : Thematic Pavilion with Outdoor/ Indoor Exhibition Area, Access Pier with Lobby & Restaurant
Project Type : Open International Competition

Client : Organizing Committee for Expo 2012 Yeosu Korea
Construction Area : 6,236m²

THE MOST SUCCESSFUL WORLD EXPO EVER WILL BE SYMBOLIZED BY THE MOST ICONIC BUILDING

NEW VISION
IT SUGGESTS A NEW OCEAN VISION FOR THAT THE GLOBAL SOCIETY SHOULD LEARN

NEW EXPERIENCE
THE MOST INSIGHTFUL AND DRAMATIC EXPERIENCE PROVIDING THE STRONGEST IMPRESSIONS FOR THE VISITOR

AN INNOVATION
WITH THE MOST ADVANCED TECHNOLOGIES AVAILABLE IN KOREA AND THE WORLD

INTEGRATION
EVERY DETAIL DELIVERS THE MESSAGE OF THE EXPO THEME, NOT JUST THE EXHIBITION BUT ALSO THE BUILDING ITSELF

AN ICON
WITH A UNIQUE DESIGN WHICH LEAVES THE MOST VIVID IMPRESSION TO VISITORS

A LANDMARK
AS A BUILDING, AS AN EXHIBITION, AND AS THE NEW CENTER FOR THE BLUE ECO-PARK

AN INVESTMENT
CREATING VALUE TODAY AND WEALTH TOMORROW

A FUTURE
BEING AN EDUCATIONAL FACILITY THAT WILL SHAPE FUTURE GENERATIONS

PERSPECTIVE AT ROOF TOP LEVEL

INTEGRATION IN THE MASTERPLAN

The building is located in the open sea off the breakwaters with an approximate distance of 35 meters. It is however well connected with the Expo site.

Similar to an umbilical cord, a wooden pier connects the building to land and allows **good accessibility** from the pedestrian loop of the breakwaters. The pier is in one line with the Ocean Tower and forms an axis, so **the Big "O" and other major Expo facilities are well considered** in our planning.

In conjunction with its location, the **simple but meaningful form** and façade of the Thematic Pavilion makes the building a **core attraction of the Expo Yeosu 2012**.

AN IDEA OF THE WORLD

A PLATFORM

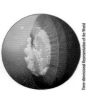

The Edge of the World

Three-dimensional Representation of the World

ANCIENT MODEL OF THE EARTH AS FLAT DISK

Through out all civilizations, the Earth has been seen as a flat disk. First three-dimensional representations have subsequently been flat and showed the Earth with a defined edge.

A VOLUME

Three-dimensional Model of the World

Section through the Square Model

MODERN MODEL OF THE EARTH AS GLOBE

For first time in history, in the 6th century B.C. the Earth was considered by Indian and Greek cultures to be a globe. This was finally proven centuries later by flat pictures taken from the Earth from outer space.

AN INTERIOR VISION

Representation of the South Pole

Representation of the North Pole

UNDERSTANDING THE EARTH FROM ITS INTERIOR

The Earth is the only planet in our solar system from which we definitely know that it is holding a liquid surface. 72% of the Earth's surface is covered by water and sweet water holds a share of merely 3%.

THE MESSAGE

The "Floating World" Conceptual Image of the Project

AN IDEA ABOUT THE WORLD

Thinking about the Ocean (and water) means thinking in a global trend. Our proposal intends to be a signal in a big scale and represents the important aspects of water from its origins of perceiving the world as a flat disk up to its own evolution, taking water to its extreme; the synthesized metaphor of the idea of the **plain** and the **global World**.

BIRD'S EYE VIEW OF THE THEMATIC PAVILION

MASTERPLAN 1/2000

THE BUILDING CONCEPT

The project emerges from a simple idea: **water**. Our proposal introduces **a new way of building in the water and with the water**, developing a new prototype of Ocean Architecture.

Covered all over in water, its facades reflect the theme "Oceans and Costs" and illustrate a powerful message about the theme by **integrating exterior space, interior space, architecture and the exhibition.**

The architectural expression is potentially the most striking aspect of the project. The formal expression of the pavilion is as simple as possible, a large bowl which grows from the surface of the water, hardly touching it. This is where the project stands out.

THE EXHIBITION CONCEPT

As the architecture itself is already showcase for the living exhibition and education and giving strong indications about the Pavilion's theme, visitors are in any case stimulated once entering the exhibition.

Implicative and dramatic exhibition methods are giving strong impressions and present images full of hidden meanings to people by associating with simple but symbolic ideas.

Visitors are lead through the particular exhibition spaces, while **different spatial experiences** are provoked, **giving the most impressive memory to visitors.** All experiences have to do with water and the transition between land and water.

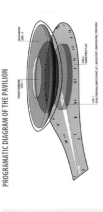

ENTRANCE AND PUBLIC PLAZA

In order to reduce resource and costs, foundations are accommodating considerable space of the building program such as the **access, the lobby, waiting areas, the administration and restrooms.**

A public plaza at open-air with different coffee shops and restaurants is accommodated right above, taking advantage of existing roof surfaces. **The plaza is shaded and cooled** by the building volume above and the breeze of the falling waters is cooling down the air temperature considerably.

CIRCULATION AND FLOW DIAGRAM

After moving down the **access ramp**, visitors gather in the **lobby** below the water surface, waiting to be lifted up by an elevator and arrive at the **Roof Top**. Their first impression is an endlessly seeming water surface against the horizon.

From there, visitors descent into the building and circulate along a horizontal donut to visit the **BPA Exhibition.** Later on, visitors continue their way entering the globe and once inside, **gradually move down along a ramp.** The Globe symbolizes the earth's interior and hosts the **Thematic Exhibition.**

PROGRAMATIC DIAGRAM OF THE PAVILION

Walking along the pedestrian loop of the breakwaters, a wooden pier appears which **connects the building with the breakwaters.** This pier is divided in a ramp disappearing in the ocean, which defines the **entrance to the exhibition** and a loop enlacing the building and forming a public plaza with bars and restaurants being completely independent from the exhibition.

The exhibition's additional program such as lobby, administration and public bathrooms is accommodated in the basement and the bowl houses the different exhibition areas.

MOVEMENT OF WATER - SUSTAINABILITY

Water is omnipresent in the building concept. **The whole building is covered in water, from the ground, the roof and its facades.** By this, the building acts as an exemplary for sustainable architecture and is a representative for an **environmentally friendly architecture.**

The water surface on the roof protects the building against heat in the summer months. Falling water from the edge of the roof causes evaporation of water and helps to **cool down the air temperature** considerably.

THEMATIC PAVILION IN FORM OF A BOWL

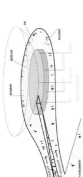

This bowl with a **diameter of 82 meters and a height of nearly 18 meters** accommodates **all exhibition spaces** of the Thematic Pavilion. It is composed of 16 steel trusses in radial formation and covered by a reflective titanium surface.

A skeleton of steel serves as structural element in the center and accommodates an elevator and an emergency stairway. It also transports water from the sea to the roof of the building.

USE OF ROOF TOP

After stepping out of the elevator, the visitor arrives at an **open platform, with no visual limitation at all.** His first impression is an endlessly seeming water surface against the horizon, with reflections of the sky.

The water surface actually is only some centimeters thick and allows visitors to move freely on it, which evokes the impression of **"walking on the water".** This is the first of three steps to evoke sensibility with the subject water.

EXHIBITION IN DONUT - BPA

Visitors descent into the building and **circulate along a horizontal donut to see the BPA Exhibition,** showing the most innovative articles and materials of marine technology from Korea and the world.

This exhibition considers the need for a rather traditional exhibition concept with sufficient area for the **exposition of marine articles and materials.** The exhibition is accommodated between the steel trusses of the structure.

EXHIBITION IN THE EARTH'S INTERIOR

Core attraction of the exhibition **is to be inside our planet and feel surrounded by the oceans.** This emphasizes the idea of the **ocean as origin of life** and breeding ground of all living organisms of the Earth.

Gradually moving down along a ramp, visitors experience the **Thematic Exhibition,** which delivers insight into the past, highlights problems of the present and seeks for answers in the future. **The most advanced exhibition technologies** available in Korea and the world will be applied.

PERSPECTIVE OF THE THEMATIC EXHIBITION

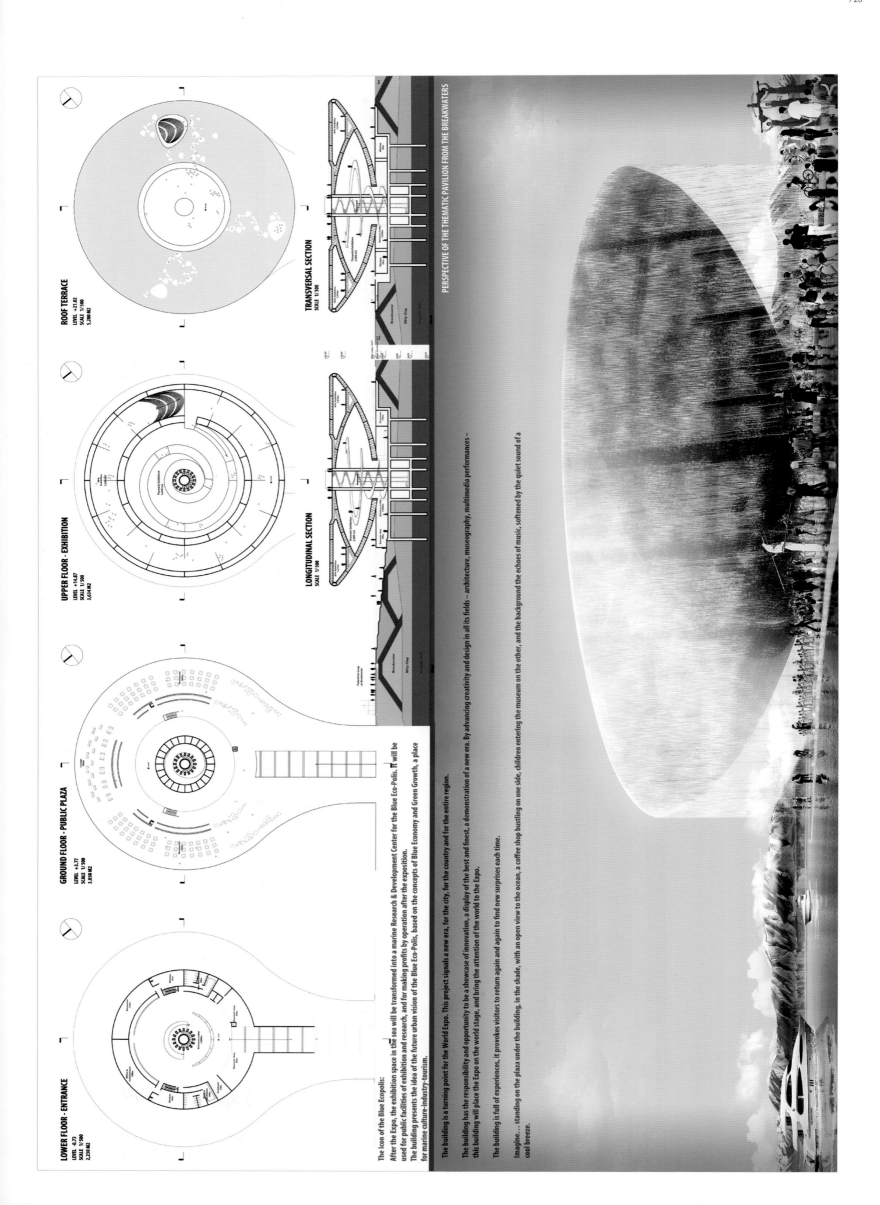

LOWER FLOOR - ENTRANCE
LEVEL -4.73
SCALE 1/500
2,230 M2

GROUND FLOOR - PUBLIC PLAZA
LEVEL +4.77
SCALE 1/500
3,050 M2

UPPER FLOOR - EXHIBITION
LEVEL +14.47
SCALE 1/500
3,634 M2

ROOF TERRACE
LEVEL +21.02
SCALE 1/500
5,200 M2

LONGITUDINAL SECTION
SCALE 1/500

TRANSVERSAL SECTION
SCALE 1/500

PERSPECTIVE OF THE THEMATIC PAVILION FROM THE BREAKWATERS

The Icon of the Blue Ecopolis:
After the Expo, the exhibition space in the sea will be transformed into a marine Research & Development Center for the Blue Eco-Polis. It will be used for public facilities of exhibition and research, and for making profits by operation after the exposition.
The building presents the idea of the future urban vision of the Blue Eco-Polis, based on the concepts of Blue Economy and Green Growth, a place for marine culture-industry-tourism.

The building is a turning point for the World Expo. This project signals a new era, for the city, for the country and for the entire region.

The building has the responsibility and opportunity to be a showcase of innovation, a display of the best and finest, a demonstration of a new era. By advancing creativity and design in all its fields – architecture, museography, multimedia performances – this building will place the Expo on the world stage, and bring the attention of the world to the Expo.

The building is full of experiences, it provokes visitors to return again and again to find new surprises each time.

Imagine… standing on the plaza under the building, in the shade, with an open view to the ocean, a coffee shop bustling on one side, children entering the museum on the other, and the background the echoes of music, softened by the quiet sound of a cool breeze.

Expo 2012 'Ocean Partner' | *REC ARQUITECTURA*

Competition : EXPO 2012 "Ocean Partner"; COREA (2011)
Team : REC ARQUITECTURA(Aika Yamakita, Hugo Candanedo, Ulises Rodriguez,
Mariano Arias, Gerardo Recoder)

257

Thematic Pavilion Expo 2012 Yeosu | *WWAA*

Authors : Natalia Paszkowska, Marcin Mostafa
Collaboration : BURO HAPPOLD(arch. Iwona Borkowska, arch. Maciej Burdalski, arch. Mikołaj Molenda, arch. Artur Gosk)

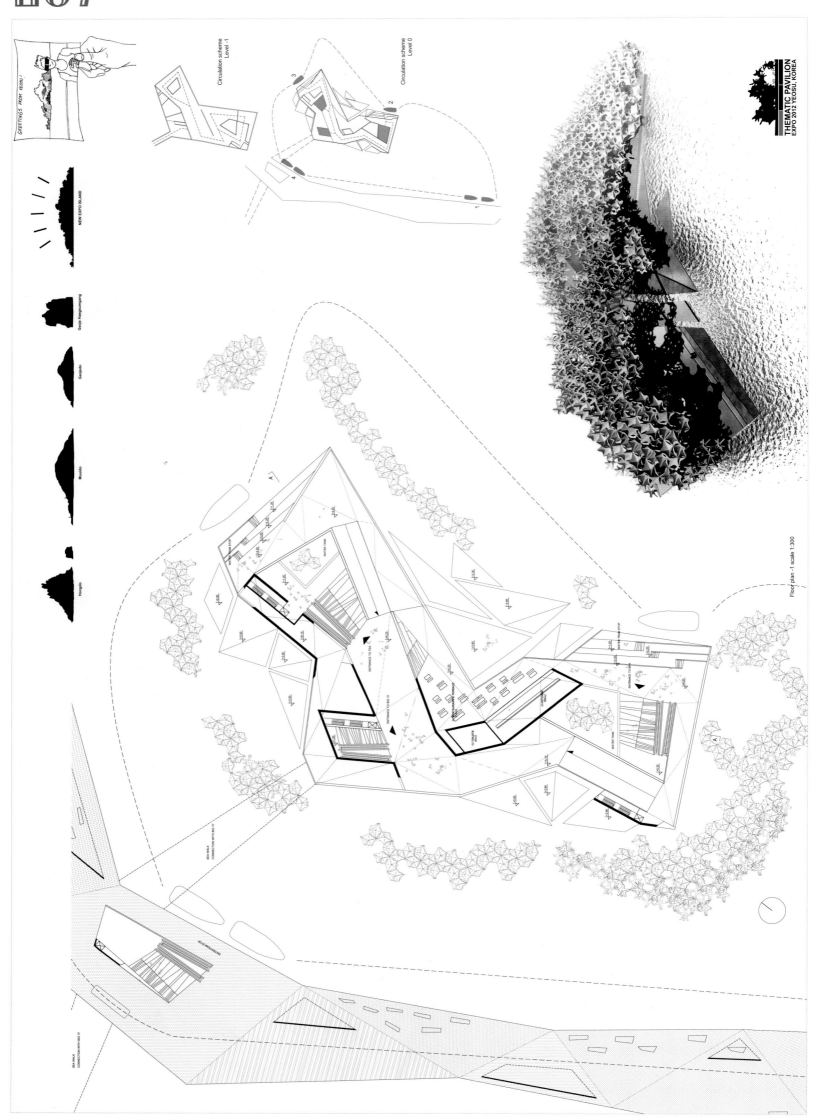

THEMATIC PAVILION
EXPO 2012 YEOSU KOREA

Space filling geometry

Variety of the moduls

Harvest of tidal energy

Algae plantation

Module fabrication

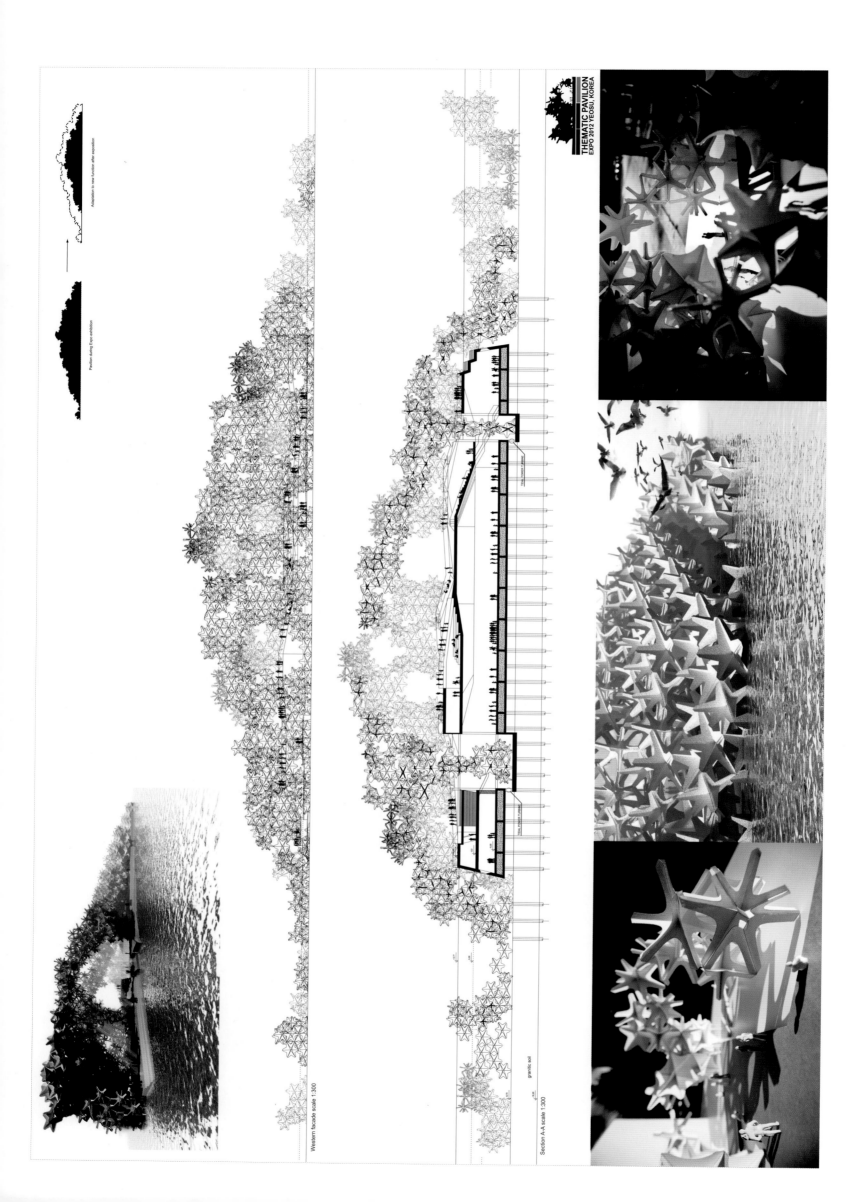

Pavilion during Expo exhibition

Adaptation to new function after exposition

Western facade scale 1:300

Section A-A scale 1:300

granitic soil

THEMATIC PAVILION
EXPO 2012 YEOSU, KOREA

Built Area (GFA) : 6128sqm
Client : Organizing Committee of the Expo 2012 Yeosu

Wavescape | *AQSO arquitectos office*

Participants : Luis Aguirre Manso, James Tendayi Matsuku, Howard Jiho Kim, Tony Yam
Project : Thematic pavilion for the Yeosu Expo 2012
Typology : Cultural Building
Location : Yeosu, South Korea

258

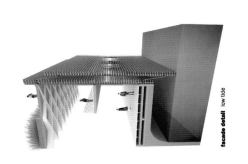

facade detail low tide

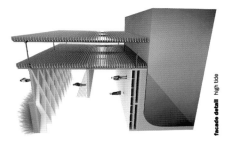

facade detail high tide

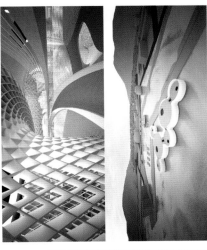

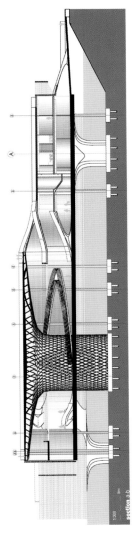

section a-b

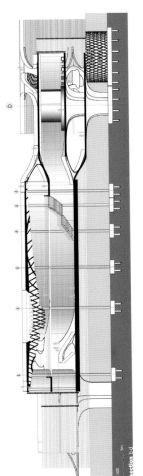

section b-d

water molecule
THE WAVE-SCAPE

The thematic pavilion of the international exhibition aspires to be an iconic element located on the Yeosu port. It will be iconic not only because it is going to be the main pavilion of the exposition, but also because it will represent the major theme and the aim of this event: the oceans. The site has been purposely proposed to be situated at an axis that symbolizes a transition between the mountain, the city, the coast and the water, all of which serves to condition the character of the building. Therefore the thematic pavilion has a focus for the people to experience and understand this liquid element through the specific place in which it is located: the ocean.

In order to represent water through architecture, the dynamic and translucent qualities of the fluid are translated into details of the pavilion. The pavilion is not bound to a solid state. It is always in action materializing both dynamicity and the varying layers of transparency. The visitor will be guided directly into a zone of coexisting space of ocean and architecture.

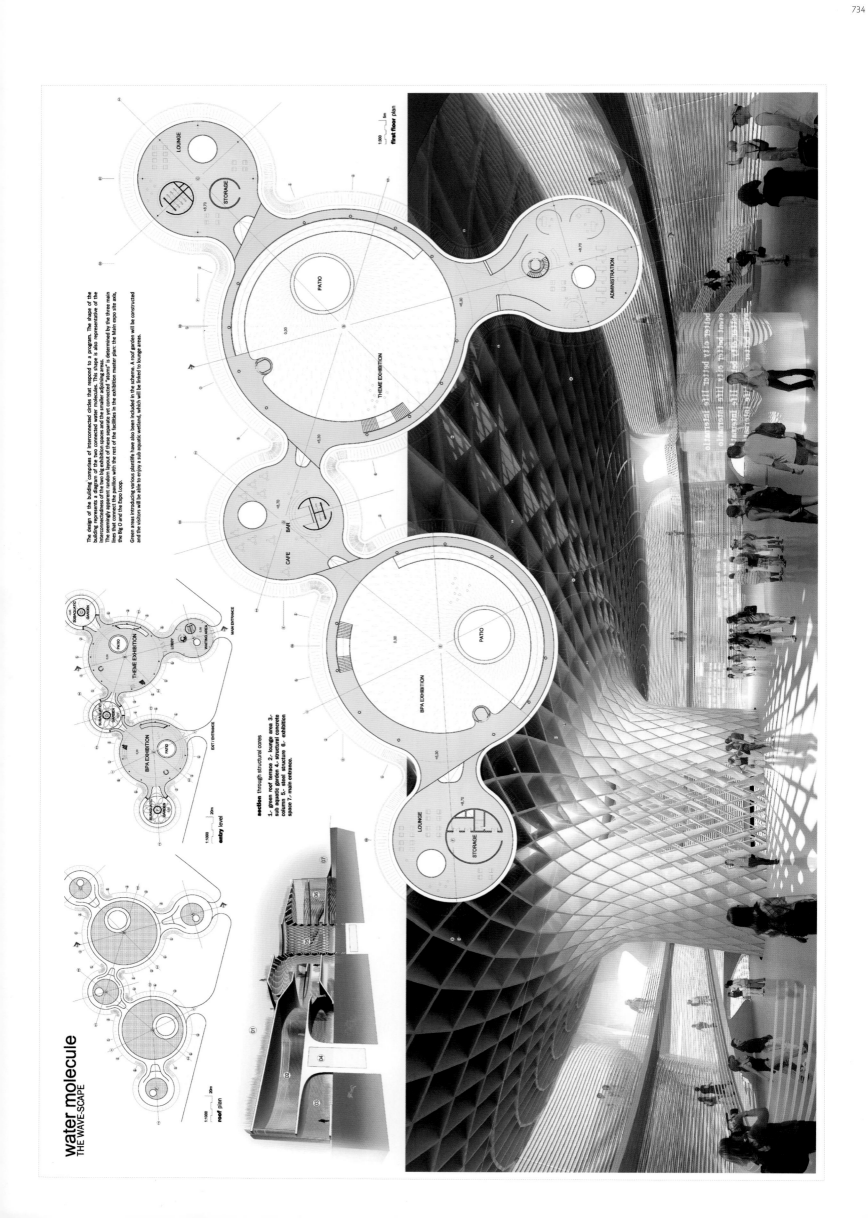

water molecule
THE WAVE-SCAPE

The design of the building comprises of interconnected circles that respond to a program. The shape of the building represents a diagram of the two connected water molecules. This shape is also representative of the interconnectedness of the two big exhibition spaces and the smaller adjoining areas.

The seemingly apparent random layout of these separate yet connected "atoms" is determined by the three main lines that connect the pavilion with the rest of the facilities in the exhibition master plan: the Main expo site axis, the Big O and the Expo Loop.

Green areas introducing various plantlife have also been included in the scheme. A roof garden will be constructed and the visitors will be able to enjoy a sub aquatic wetland, which will be linked to lounge areas.

section through structural cores

1.- green roof terrace 2.- lounge area 3.- sub aquatic garden 4.- structural concrete column 5.- steel structure 6.- exhibition space 7.- main entrance.

1:1000   20m   **entry level**

1:1000   20m   **roof plan**

1:300   6m   **first floor plan**

water molecule
THE WAVE-SCAPE

1:100 ___ 2m **façade detail**

1.- green roof 2.- double glazing 3.- steel structure 4.- raised floor 5.- aluminum louvers 6.- pivoting steel linkage 7.- floating galvanize steel case 8.- flat roof 9.- concrete slab 10.- reinforced concrete column.

1:300 ___ 10m
elevation low tide

elevation high tide

The skin is made by two layers with a series of horizontal louvers that give a varying transparent quality to the building. The outer skin translates the energy of the ocean to move itself vertically up and down. It creates a dynamic atmosphere that is always in motion as the waves and tides.

The moving louvers create a fuzzy image on the outside and also create interesting lighting effects inside through the moiré effect. The inner louvers are fixed on to the glass of the pavilion, whereas the outer louvers are floating on water, becoming a unique element that moves and changes with no energy consumption.

The superposition of these two osmotic layers give an intriguing image of the breathing building, making the water nature alive for the public to experience.

0 divisions
no vertical deformation / -0m / no wave

2 divisions
fixed vertical deformation / 2m / weak constant wave

8 divisions
fixed vertical deformation / 6m / strong constant wave

8 divisions
fixed vertical deformation / 3m / medium constant wave

2 divisions
fixed vertical deformation / 6m / strong constant wave

4 divisions
fixed vertical deformation / 6m / strong constant wave

8 divisions
random vertical deformation / -2 to 2m / weak natural wave

8 divisions
random vertical deformation / -4 to 4m / strong natural wave

259

Polish Pavilion Expo 2010 Shanghai | *WWAA*

Design : WWAA(Marcin Mostafa , Natalia Paszkowska, Maciej Burdalski,
Mikołaj Molenda, Zofia Pichelska, Maciej Siczek, Maciej Walczyna)
with Wojciech Kakowski(BURO HAPPOLD)
Client : Polish Information and Foreign Investment Agency(PAIiIZ),

Polish Agency for Enterprise Development(PARP)
Area : 2400 sqm

KONCEPCJA PAWILONU POLSKIEGO SEKCJI POLSKIEJ PODCZAS EXPO 2010 W SZANGHAJU

275221

RZUT PARTERU 1:200

RZUT SALI KONCERTOWEJ 1:200

ELEWACJA ZACHODNIA 1:200

ELEWACJA PÓŁNOCNA 1:200

ENTRANCE TICKET POLISH PAVILLION EXPO 2010

ELEWACJA WSCHODNIA 1:200

RZUT ANTRESOLI 1:200

KONCEPCJA PAWILONU POLSKIEGO SEKCJI POLSKIEJ PODCZAS EXPO 2010 W SZANGHAJU

275221

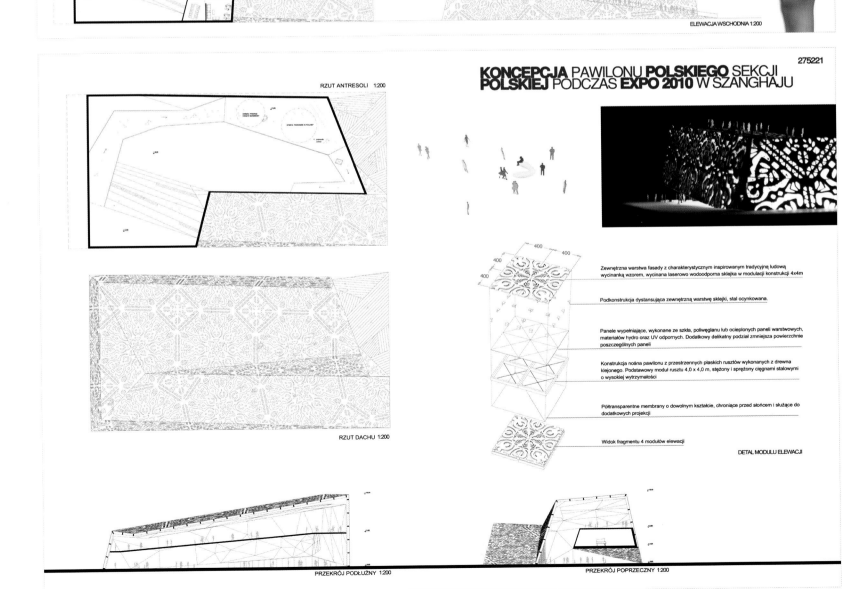

Zewnętrzna warstwa fasady z charakterystycznym inspirowanym tradycyjną ludową wycinanką wzorem, wycinana laserowo wodoodporna sklejka w modulacji konstrukcji 4x4m

Podkonstrukcja dystansująca zewnętrzną warstwę sklejki, stal ocynkowana.

Panele wypełniające, wykonane ze szkła, poliwęglanu lub ocieplonych paneli warstwowych, materiałów hydro oraz UV odpornych. Dodatkowy delikatny podział zmniejsza powierzchnie poszczególnych paneli

Konstrukcja nośna pawilonu z przestrzennych płaskich rusztów wykonanych z drewna klejonego. Podstawowy moduł rusztu 4,0 x 4,0 m, stężony i sprężony cięgnami stalowymi o wysokiej wytrzymałości

Półtransparentne membrany o dowolnym kształcie, chroniące przed słońcem i służące do dodatkowych projekcji

Widok fragmentu 4 modułów elewacji

DETAL MODUŁU ELEWACJI

RZUT DACHU 1:200

PRZEKRÓJ PODŁUŻNY 1:200

PRZEKRÓJ POPRZECZNY 1:200

Kujira | *REC ARQUITECTURA*

Competition : Nissinkogyo, Japan
Team : Aika Yamakita, Gerardo Recoder

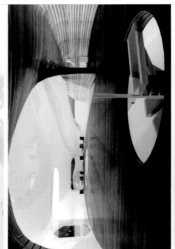

N10593

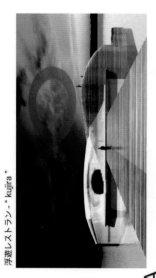

浮遊レストラン-"kujira"

Floating Restaurant and Water Treatment Plant....K U J I R A

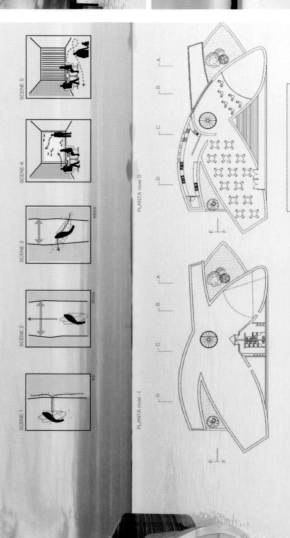

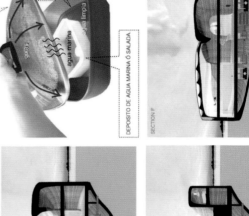

AGUA DESALINIZADA

ESCURRIMIENTO DE AGUA EVAPORADA SIN SAL

DEPOSITO DE AGUA MARINA Ó SALADA

agua marina

agua limpia

SECTION F

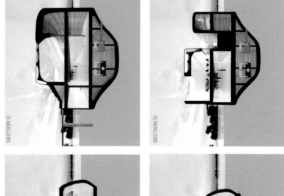

SECTION C

SECTION D

SECTION A

SECTION B

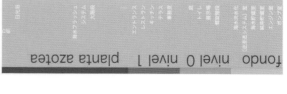

fondo nivel 0 nivel 1 planta azotea

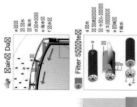

Tourist Facilities | *Donner Sorcinelli Architecture*

International Competition Cyprus
Built Surface : 160 sq.m. each Building
Client : Ministry of Culture and Education

261

MAX001

photovoltaic totem

steel brise soleil

steel structure

movable platform and stairs

scale 1/175

SEA STAR

new structure for leisure

sun deck

belvedere

LEVEL 2

cocktail house

relax area

LEVEL 1

tanks and systems entrance

LEVEL 0

What happens?

There is a Sea Star on the water.

Really?

Yes.

What is its function?

What they say is a new structure for leisure.

But it is not on the beach.

No, it's on water. Inside and on the upper deck there are cocktail house, small kiosks, areas for relaxation, for playing, sun deck, but also belvedere to admire the landscape, school areas for diving, windsurfing, water skiing and much more.

Beautiful! But how can we go there?

By a shuttle service, pedal boats, jet-ski or inflatable floating piers.

Great! I immediately go there to know how you can see the beach and the ruins on the hill from there. So, what you think to go together and drink something while taking the sun?

Come on. Let's go!

Kube Kong | *b4architects*

Location : Hong Kong, China
Year : 2011
Type : Competition
Object : Hong Kong Alternative Car Park Tower

Client : AC-CA
Area : 30000sqm
Programme : Car Park, Café, Restaurant, Multifunctional Space, Art Exhibitions, Fashion Shows, Open Spaces

Project Team : Gianluca Evels & Stefania Papitto - b4architects
with Sebastiano Maccarrone, Alessia Tonnetti

entrance

event square garden

interactive metropolitan scenery

function

reception hall
car parking
moto parking
bike parking
café/lounge bar
clear space
backstage area
storage space
loading area
plant room
administration
offices/space for rent
public restroom
roof garden
glasshouse garden
helicopter platform

1st STEP
car's cube/
primitive form definition
n. 1500

2nd STEP
raise the cube

3rd STEP
remodelling the form

4th STEP
Kube Kong

concept process

urban self sufficient microcosmos

1. steel structure
2. cor-ten screen
3. aluminum screen
4. reinforced concrete slabs
5. reinforced concrete columns
6. prefab composite slabs of concrete on corrugated sheeting
7. glass walls

+135.00
+127.50 observation deck
+114.75 roof garden/café lounge bar
+79.00 helicopter platform
+49.70 offices/space for rent
+33.40 offices/administration
+17.20 podium/event square/roof garden
±0.00 m

flow

technical flow
pedestrian flow
vehicular flow

section

highrise urbanity

structure

city hall

city hall

exit

city hall

Book your Place everywhere

use your card

kube kong Skyscraper CAR Park
停车场
文化活动
Personal Code

N   0mt   entrance   50mt   ground floor

floors: from 1st to 5th

025782

KUBE
KONG
SKYSCRAPER
CAR PARK

KUBE KONG
SKYSCRAPER
CAR
PARKING

WATCHING
HONG KONG

complex experience
of perception

6th floor   7th floor   floors: from 21st to 29th

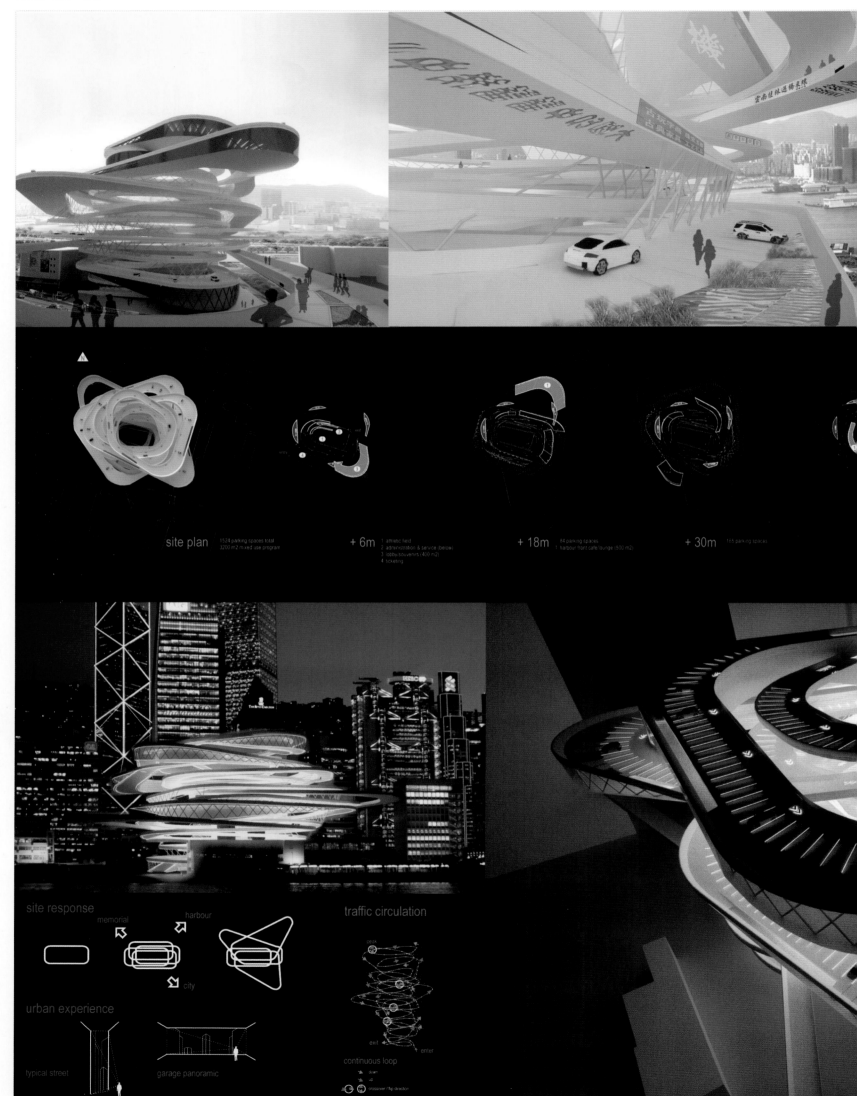

site plan   1524 parking spaces total
3200 m2 mixed use program

+ 6m   1 athletic field
2 administration & service (below)
3 lobby-souvenirs (400 m2)
4 ticketing

+ 18m   64 parking spaces
1 harbour front cafe/lounge (500 m2)

+ 30m   165 parking spaces

site response
memorial   harbour
city

urban experience

typical street   garage panoramic

traffic circulation

continuous loop

crossover / flip director

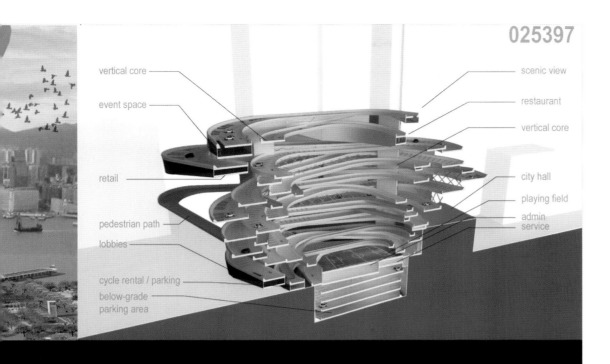

025397

vertical core
event space
retail
pedestrian path
lobbies
cycle rental / parking
below-grade parking area

scenic view
restaurant
vertical core
city hall
playing field
admin service

CAR PARK

Hong Kong's relationship to the car is defined by a small ratio of people to automobiles. In a city of over 7 million, only 461,000 cars are registered to local drivers. This massively dense city contains only 566,618 parking spaces.

We see this as an opportunity. While so many cities are forced to "store" a massive volume of automobiles in ways that don't negatively impact the street, Hong Kong can be different. Hong Kong likes to wear its infrastructure on its sleeve. From the Old Airport, to richly layered pedestrian walkways, to outdoor escalators, to floating water-borne neighborhoods – the city pulses with circulation, both horizontal and vertical. Despite new development which continues to emulate western approaches to hiding cars, our proposal looks to capture new potentials for Hong Kong's infrastructural personality.

The Car Park is just that. It romanticizes the car as an active urban object while also adding a new storm water management strategy that creates landscape retreats in the sky and irrigates the athletic field at the ground plane. The park is a civic, mixed-use armature of landscape, shopping, food, sports, views, and parking spaces tangled up in a kinetic rotation of animated circulation.

programs

structure

parking

car ramp

pedestrian ramp

Location : Hong Kong + China
Design Team : CJ Lim/Studio 8 Architects with Alex Gazetas, Lik San Chan
Consultants : Techniker (structural engineers)

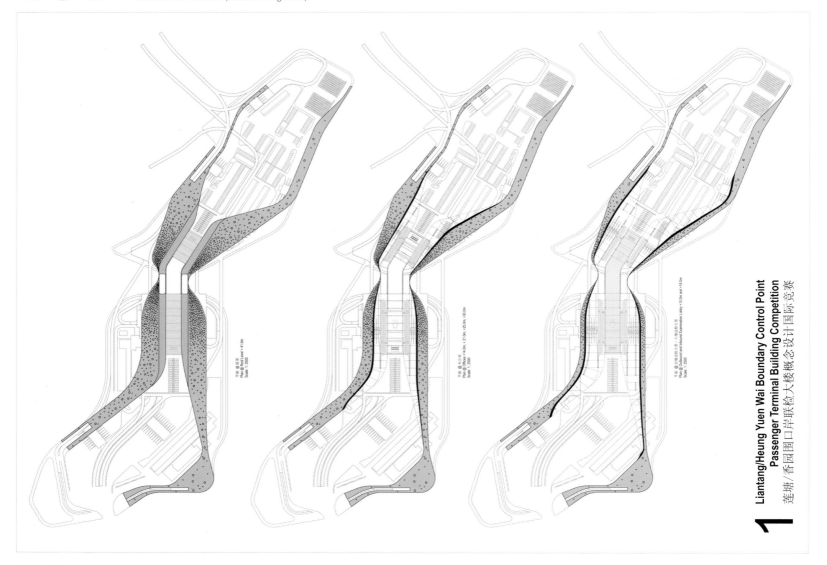

1 Liantang/Heung Yuen Wai Boundary Control Point
Passenger Terminal Building Competition
蓮塘/香園圍口岸聯檢大樓概念設計國際競賽

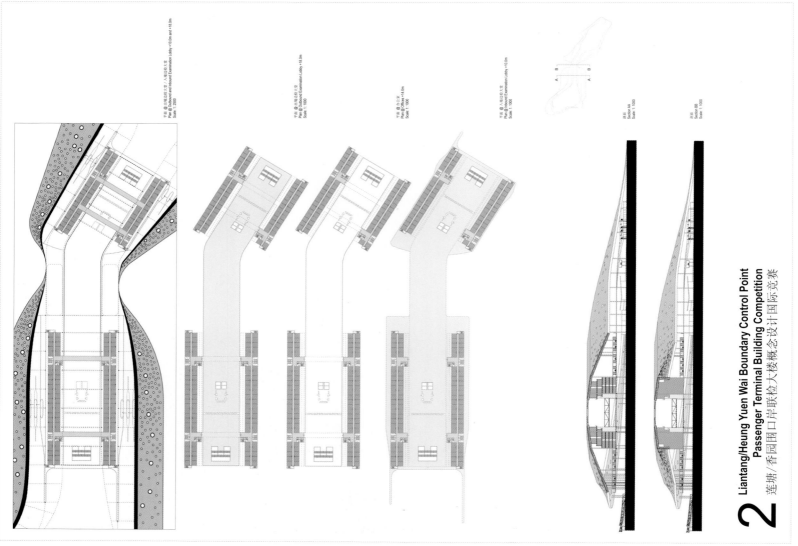

2 Liantang/Heung Yuen Wai Boundary Control Point
Passenger Terminal Building Competition
蓮塘/香園圍口岸聯檢大樓概念設計國際競賽

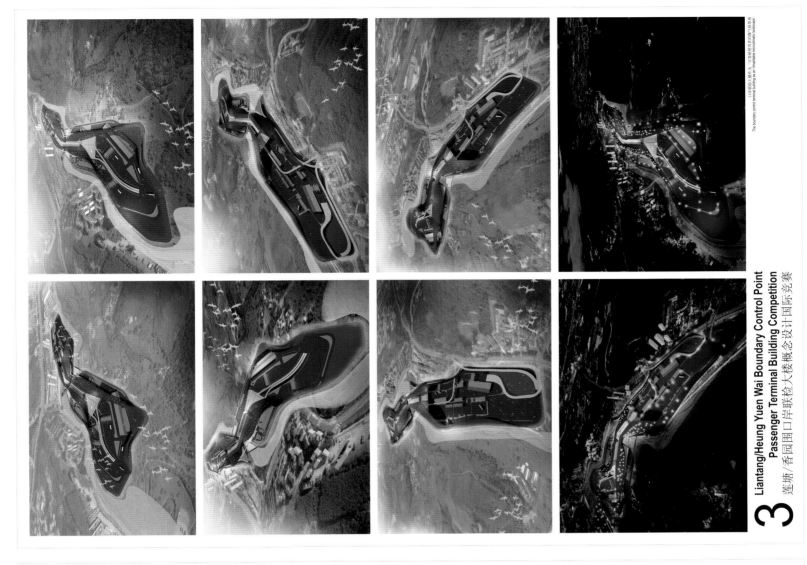

The boundary control terminal building as an immutable microthematic landscape
山的景观从大楼形态为一可持续性微观气候景观

3 Liantang/Heung Yuen Wai Boundary Control Point
Passenger Terminal Building Competition
莲塘/香园围口岸联检大楼概念设计国际竞赛

Instead of enforcing the notion of borders and barriers, the proposal creates maximum territorial and visual connections, mobility, environmental water and architectural continuity
我们建议一个最小的空间界定，且没有一种界定并以最大性建筑的空间界定连续性建筑与水

4 Liantang/Heung Yuen Wai Boundary Control Point
Passenger Terminal Building Competition
莲塘/香园围口岸联检大楼概念设计国际竞赛

景天绿色屋顶帮助降低建筑对热能的吸收
Sedum Roof help reducing Heat Gain

建筑通过天井采光
Sun light enter the building through Light Wells

景天绿色屋顶蒸发式降温
Evaporative cooling from Sedum Roof

自然对流式通风
Natural Cross Ventilation

烟囱效应通风系统
Ventilation by Stack effect

屋顶收集雨水
Roof as Rain Water Harvester

视觉透明
Visual Connections

Glazed Roof

■ Enclosures 围合式空间
■ Open Spaces 开放式空间

Immigration Hall
出入境大堂

Outbound Examination Lobby
Inbound Examination Lobby

■ Arrival / Departures 到达/出发
■ Offices 行政管理部门的建筑体块

Lightweight Steel / Concrete Composite Decks on Steel Framing — Toughened Glass Canopy — In-situ Reinforced Concrete Main Deck

施工分析图
Construction Diagram 2

Precast Destressed Concrete Roof Deck — Steel Truss Supporting Lightweight Steel / Concrete Composite Deck — Pre-stressed Concrete Vehicular Bridge

行人穿越 Pedestrian Crossing

机动车穿越 Vehicles Crossing

Construction Diagram 1

红景天种植
Roof Top Sedum

屋顶结构网络
Roof Structural Grid

Movement Provisions across
Main Trusses

结构柱网
Structural Column Grid

Steel Frame
Super Structures

Construction Strips
Cast in Masoed/Situ Slab

红景天种植
Roof top Sedum
太阳能电池板
Solar Voltaic cells
玻璃
Glass

太阳能电池板，取材于中国国旗和香港区旗的图案
Photovoltaic cells harvest sun-energy and is inspired by the flags' motifs of Hong Kong and China.

莲塘/香园围口岸联检大楼概念设计国际竞赛

口岸联检大楼被设计成一个连续的'可容纳使用者的微气候景观'，用来庆贺香港与中国大陆的关系。移民部门与海关部门的布局方式向类似功能的建筑形态提出挑战。相比较于强调边境的概念，本设计最大限度地在地域以及视觉上创造了联系性、移动性、环境庇护以及建筑的连续性。

'微气候景观'屋顶分成两个部分，由五座桥梁（四座机动车桥梁和一座行人桥梁）汇聚而成。同时，在中间部分设置有玻璃构造的行政办公块块。红景天植物屋顶为当地居民提供了一个公共空间，重新定义了横穿建筑的边境的角色。基础设施由预制预应力混凝土板支撑，这些混凝土板又通过顶部的现浇钢筋混凝土连接在一起。主要柱体上架有钢制桁架结构，实心楼板由桁架支撑。屋顶形成了连续起伏的表面，覆盖建筑的两个部分。同时，在横跨河流的较窄处设置有变形缝。屋顶灯光被预先安装在防水的主甲板上。热位移通过主要中央柱体以及两侧滑动轴承的屈曲获得抵消。

两座行政办公楼从两侧掩映中间的行人流线，自然光线透射而下。简洁的平面布局提供了灵活可控的工作空间，并且由垂直电梯和楼梯连接。轻钢混凝土楼板由钢框架结构支撑，提供了灵活高效的楼板空间。建筑的边缘采用轻钢支撑结构的大玻璃屏风，同时建筑中部的玻璃空间采用强化玻璃、玻璃梁、以及管状钢桁架结构。玻璃的行政办公空间在视觉上和寓意上代表了透明的政治边界。

景观策略促进了人与活动的集中与空间流动。遍布建筑的植物红景天创造了建筑与视觉的连续性。地面层包括一个连续的人行道、停车场和机动车道；上方的主楼采用大跨度预应力混凝土楼板，圆形的支撑柱子随下方的流线形态分布。四座机动车桥梁采用预应力混凝土结构横跨河流。跨越边境的行人桥梁采用大型钢结构楼板，并且连接两座行政办公楼。大跨度的钢结构复合楼板由桁架支撑。

被动式环境设计策略非常适宜本地区，防止热量获得以及通过建筑表皮消散多余热量可以减少制冷需求。'微气候景观'的植物屋顶为巨大的开放场地提供了最大限度的遮阳，促进自然烟囱效应和水平通风。狭窄的行政办公块块促进了自然通风和过滤自然光。　在景天植物屋顶上的太阳能电池板可以为建筑提供能源。太阳能电池板的布局类似于所种植的红色植物，取材于中国国旗和香港区旗。

Liantang/Heung Yuen Wai Boundary Control Point Passenger Terminal Building Competition

The boundary control terminal building is developed as a continuous 'inhabitable microclimaticlandscape' to celebrate the relationship between Hong Kong and China. The arrangement of immigration and customs operation also challenges the architectural typology of similar function. Instead of enforcing the notion of borders and barriers, the proposal creates maximum territorial and visual connections, mobility, environmental shelter and architectural continuity.

The 'inhabitable microclimatic landscape' roof forms the two halves of the new building, joined by five bridges (four vehicle and a central pedestrian bridges) with a glazed centre section containing the administration blocks. The red 'sedum' planted roof is also a new public space for local inhabitants, redefining the role of a border crossing building. The infrastructure is supported on a pre-cast pre-stressed concrete panel deck, which is locked together with an in-situ cast reinforced concrete topping. The solid slab is carried on steel truss elements spanning between the main columns. The roof forms continuous folded plates over each half of the building with movement joints in the narrower section spanning the river. Roof-lights are pre-assembled and carefully waterproofed onto the main deck. Thermal movements are accommodated by flexure in the main central columns and sliding bearings at the perimeters.

The two administration blocks flank the central pedestrian circulation, washed with natural daylight. The simple floor plans allows flexible and controlled workspaces, and are vertically serviced by lifts and stairs. Steel and lightweight concrete composite decks are supported on steel frames to provide flexible, high capacity floor plates. The edges of the buildings are sealed with large glass screens on lightweight steel framing and the glazed centre section of the building is formed of toughened glass on structural glass beams and lightweight tubular steel truss elements. The glazed administration spaces presents transparency literally and metaphorically of the political boarders.

The landscape strategies facilitate easy spatial flow and concentration between activities and people. The use of red 'sedum' planting through the building allows architectural and visual continuity.The ground floor comprises a continuous plane of pavement, parking and roadways; and the principal deck above is a wide-span reinforced concrete plate on simple circular columns evenly distributed to suit the circulation patterns below. Vehicles cross this level onto four bridges of pre-stressed concrete spanning the river. The main pedestrian walkway across the border is a large steel-framed deck linking the two administration blocks. Deep truss elements support a wide-span steel and composite floor.

The passive environmental design strategies are applicable for this region, resisting heat gain and allowing excess heat dissipation through the building fabric to reduce the cooling demand. The 'inhabitable microclimatic landscape' sedum roof provides maximum shade to the vast opensite, and encourage natural stack and cross ventilation. The narrow plan of the administration blocks allows natural ventilation with maximum use of filtered daylight.The constellations of photovoltaic cells in the sedum roof harvest sun-energy and contribute to the energy management of the building. The arrangement of the cells, similar to application of the red planting, is inspired by the flags of Hong Kong and China.

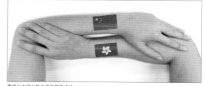

香港与中国大陆关系的概念表达
Conceptual representation of the relationship between Hong Kong and China

5 Liantang/Heung Yuen Wai Boundary Control Point
Passenger Terminal Building Competition
莲塘/香园围口岸联检大楼概念设计国际竞赛

遍布建筑的植物红景天创造了建筑与视觉的连续性。
The use of red 'sedum' planting through the building allows architectural and visual continuity.

6 **Liantang/Heung Yuen Wai Boundary Control Point**
Passenger Terminal Building Competition
莲塘/香园围口岸联检大楼概念设计国际竞赛

265

Metro Station 20 | *MSB ARQUITECTOS*

Participants : Miguel Mallaguerra, Susana Jesus,
Bruno Martins, Hugo Aires, Lisa Borges, Ivan Jorge
Typology : Public Building

Location : Sofia, Bulgaria
Client : City os Sofia / Year : 2011

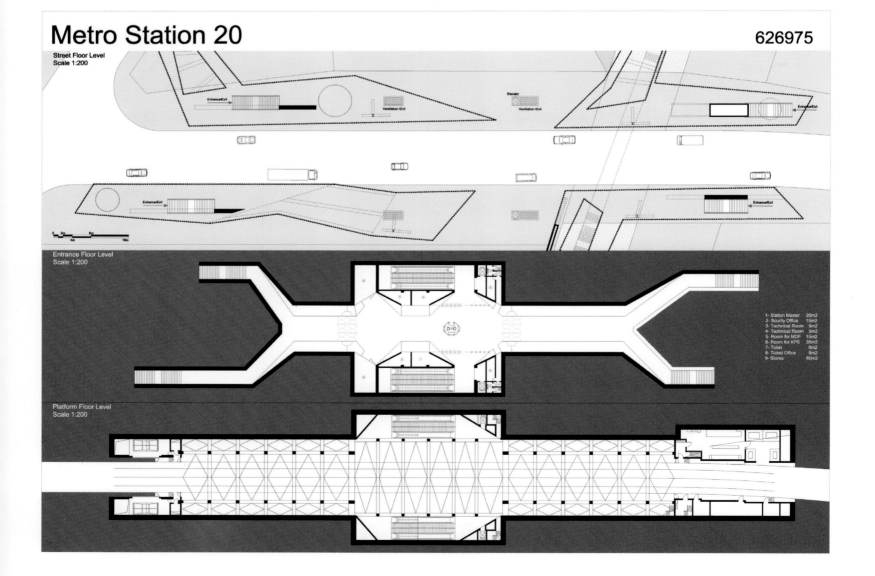

Metro Station 20 626975

Situation Plan
Scale 1:500

Street Level Image

Street Level Image 02

Metro Station 20 626975

Street Floor Level
Scale 1:200

Entrance/Exit

Ventilation Grid

Elevator

Ventilation Grid

Entrance/Exit

Entrance/Exit

Entrance/Exit

Entrance Floor Level
Scale 1:200

1- Station Master   20m2
2- Scurity Office   15m2
3- Technical Room   9m2
4- Technical Room   9m2
5- Room for MDF   15m2
6- Room for KPS   35m2
7- Toilet   8m2
8- Ticket Office   8m2
9- Stores   60m2

Platform Floor Level
Scale 1:200

Metro Station 20

Territory - The site of is located in a non-urbanized area, between two parts of high-density residential area of Druzhba. It is a peripheral zone of the city center which is near the airport.

The proposal aims to create passing spaces, with the creation and delineation of structures and trees that provide the amenities for this occupation.

The intervention area is between future buildings, between highways outlined in the existing urban design and is characterized by a pronounced change in their occupation, where a rapid development is estimated, and a great mobilization of people to this site. The plan that was delivered in the tender documents has been respected, and the intervention was adapted to the existing plan

Pre-Existence - Despite being a non-urbanized area, there is a prior plan of development and expansion, where the blocks are defined, the access road and footpaths, the implementation and specification of the number of floors of buildings, and explicitly, the deployment of the future metro station and constraints to further action. The gas pipes running through the area, and how they would be integrated into the project, were taken into consideration in our proposal.

Objective - The proposed idea for the implementation of the Metro station 20, and organization of the territory around it, according to the assumptions of competition

Assuming that the city will grow to this area, this project developments that may be structured in this new area of the city through the creation of common spaces - above and below ground - with a philosophy of unity at a visual and functional language .

Platform Level Image

Section AA
Scale 1:200

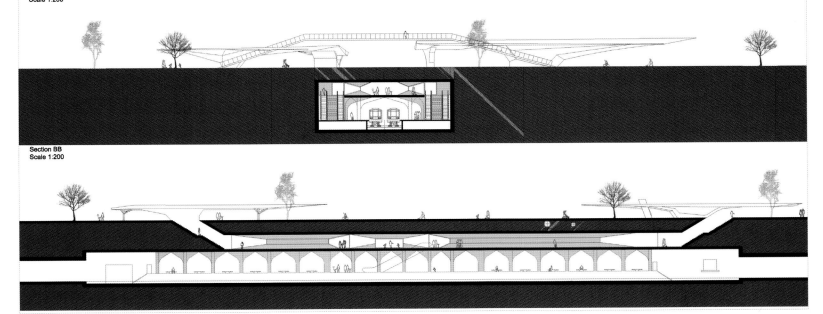

Section BB
Scale 1:200

Metro Station 20

626975

Entrance Hall Image

Proposal - The way in which we live this space, and walk through was a determining factor in the collection of possible solutions, both at the Street level zone, as in the entrance hall, and finally to the platform zone. The sense of unity and communication between levels, in order to establish a dialogue, is an important message to retain.

According to the characteristics of the surrounding paths and assumed level of the road, we propose four entrance / exit, to settle in areas that allow more and better movement of pedestrians and ensure the necessary comfort to this intervention. These entries are embedded within the framework of the urban network, assuming a sculptural character which extends horizontally and which is reflected in its implementation. Thus, there is a strong marking of the entrance / exits of the metro, and an approach which ensures that the new intervention is assumed not only inside but also at the street level.

With this strategy, we seek a very clear definition of access points to the subway, but in the intermediate level we have a moment of meeting and passing. In the transition there are two references very clear: the first to absorb other people and release them. Here, the slopes that climb the walls in the coverage, create a tunnel that leads to a great comfort and provide a security nature.

The lower level is characterized by a strong network of pillars. Rather than eliminate them, our proposal sought to take advantage of these elements, while objects that define this space. Instead of fighting against the pillars, they became a driving force in the environment of the project. Our approach is to unite the pillars that glide through hoops to each other, creating a space of multiple domes that share platforms in waiting areas and entrance to the underground, creating a wealth of great comfort and formal richness.

The implementation suggested in the tender documents, the coordinates where the levels are developed, the program and location of access, and even the provided pillars were fully respected in our proposal. The gas pipelines that cross this block are buried between the entrance hall and the street level zone.

Night Bird's eye view of Crossing
Not to Scale
夜嫌鋤錫亮蚨

751

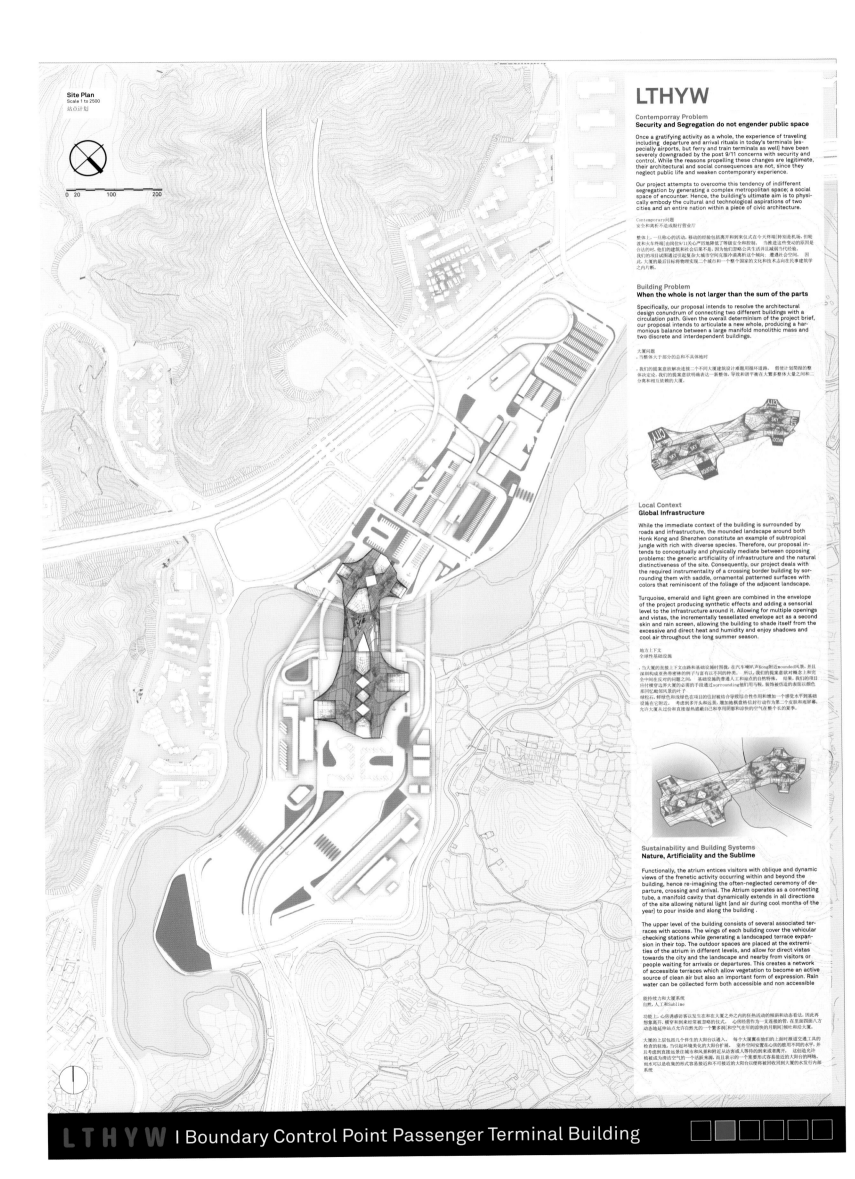

Site Plan
Scale 1 to 2500
站点计划

0 20   100   200

LTHYW

Contemporray Problem
Security and Segregation do not engender public space

Once a gratifying activity as a whole, the experience of traveling including departure and arrival rituals in today's terminals (especially airports, but ferry and train terminals as well) have been severely downgraded by the post 9/11 concerns with security and control. While the reasons propelling these changes are legitimate, their architectural and social consequences are not, since they neglect public life and weaken contemporary experience.

Our project attempts to overcome this tendency of indifferent segregation by generating a complex metropolitan space; a social space of encounter. Hence, the building's ultimate aim is to physically embody the cultural and technological aspirations of two cities and an entire nation within a piece of civic architecture.

Contemporary问题
安全和离析不成成眼行营业厅

整体上，一只称心的活动，移动的经验包括离开和到来仪式在今天终端(特别是机场，但轮渡和火车终端)由岗位9/11关心严格降低了等级安全和控制。当推这些变动的原因是合法的，他们的建筑和社会后果不是，因为他们忽略公共生活并且城弱当代经验。我们的项目试图通过引起复杂大城市空间立服冷漠离析这个倾向。遭遇社会空间。因此，大厦的最后目标将要将物理实现二个城市和一个国家的文化和技术志向在民事建筑学之内片断。

Building Problem
When the whole is not larger than the sum of the parts

Specifically, our proposal intends to resolve the architectural design conundrum of connecting two different buildings with a circulation path. Given the overall determinism of the project brief, our proposal intends to articulate a new whole, producing a harmonious balance between a large manifold monolithic mass and two discrete and interdependent buildings.

大厦问题
当整体大于部分的总和不具体地时

我们的提案意欲解决连接二个不同大厦建筑设计难题用循环道路。假使计划简报的整体决定论，我们的提案意欲明确表达一新整体，导致的谐平衡在大厦多整体大量之间和二分离和相互依赖的大厦。

Local Context
Global Infrastructure

While the immediate context of the building is surrounded by roads and infrastructure, the mounded landscape around both Honk Kong and Shenzhen constitute an example of subtropical jungle with rich with diverse species. Therefore, our proposal intends to conceptually and physically mediate between opposing problems: the generic artificiality of infrastructure and the natural distinctiveness of the site. Consequently, our project deals with the required instrumentality of a crossing border building by surrounding them with saddle, ornamental patterned surfaces with colors that reminiscent of the foliage of the adjacent landscape.

Turquoise, emerald and light green are combined in the envelope of the project producing synthetic effects and adding a sensorial level to the infrastructure around it. Allowing for multiple openings and vistas, the incrementally tessellated envelope act as a second skin and rain screen, allowing the building to shade itself from the excessive and direct heat and humidity and enjoy shadows and cool air throughout the long summer season.

地方上下文
全球性基础设施

当大厦的直接上下文由路和基础设施时围接，在汽车喇叭声Honk Kong附近mounded风景，并且深圳构成亚热带密林的例子与富有以不同的种类。所以，我们的提案意欲对概念上和完全中间在反对的问题之间，基础设施的普通人工和站点的自然特殊。结果，我们的项目应付横穿边界大厦的必要了手段通过围接们用马鞍，装饰性图纹的表面以颜色那同忆起邻近风景的叶子。

绿松石，鲜绿色和浅绿色在项目的信封结合导致综合性作用和增加一个感觉水平到基础设施备点它它围接。考虑到多开头和远景，增加地模齿格包封行动作为第二个皮肤和雨屏蔽，允许大厦从过份和直接湿热遮蔽自己和享用阴影和凉快的空气在整个长的夏季。

Sustainability and Building Systems
Nature, Artificiality and the Sublime

Functionally, the atrium entices visitors with oblique and dynamic views of the frenetic activity occurring within and beyond the building, hence re-imagining the often-neglected ceremony of departure, crossing and arrival. The Atrium operates as a connecting tube, a manifold cavity that dynamically extends in all directions of the site allowing natural light [and air during cool months of the year] to pour inside and along the building.

The upper level of the building consists of several associated terraces with access. The wings of each building cover the vehicular checking stations while generating a landscaped terrace expansion in their top. The outdoor spaces are placed at the extremities of the atrium in different levels, and allow for direct vistas towards the city and the landscape and nearby from visitors or people waiting for arrivals or departures. This creates a network of accessible terraces which allow vegetation to become an active source of clean air but also an important form of expression. Rain water can be collected form both accessible and non accessible

能持续力力和大厦系统
自然，人工和Sublime

功能上，心房诱使访客以发生在和在大厦之外之内的狂热活动的倾斜和动态看法，因此再想象离开，横穿和到来经常被忽略的仪式。心房经营作为一文连接的管，在里面西面八方动态地延伸站点允许自然光的一个繁多例和空气在年的凉快的月期间(倒注inside和沿大厦)

大厦的上层包括几个伴生的大阳台以通入。每个大厦翼在他们的上面时报道交通工具的绿的的的站地。当引起环境美化的大阳台开展，室外空间安置在心房的使用不同的水平，并且考虑到直接远景在城市和风景和附近从访客来源，人等待的到来或离开。这创造成为清洁空气的一个活跃来源，而且表示的一个重要形式容易接近的大阳台的网络，雨水可以收集的形式容易接近和不可接近的大阳台以便将被回收回到大厦的水发打内部系统

L T H Y W | Boundary Control Point Passenger Terminal Building

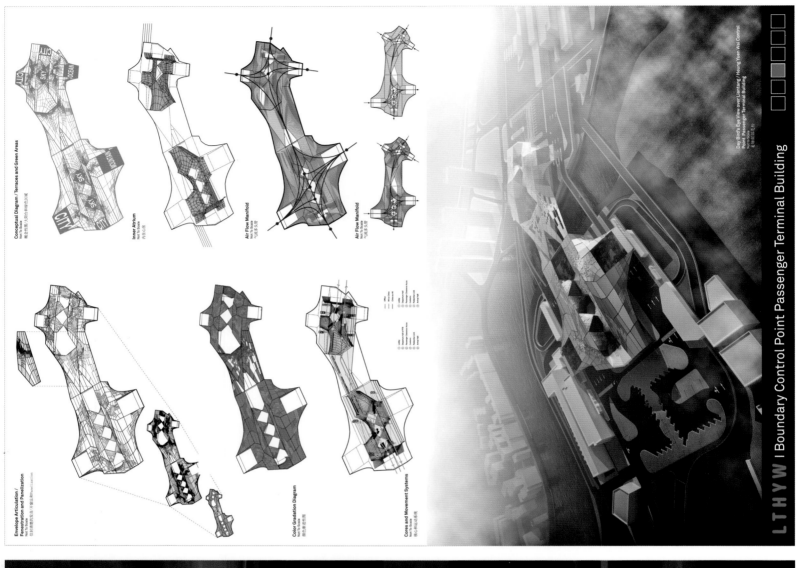

Conceptual Diagram / Terraces and Green Areas
Not To Scale

Inner Atrium
Not To Scale

Air Flow Manifold
Not To Scale

Air Flow Manifold
Not To Scale

Envelope Articulation /
Fenestration and Panelization
Not To Scale

Color Gradation Diagram
Not To Scale

Cores and Movement Systems
Not To Scale

Day: Bird's Eye View over Lisntang / Heung Yuen Wai Control
Point Passenger Terminal Building
Not To Scale

LTHYW I Boundary Control Point Passenger Terminal Building

Evening View towards crossing bridge from Liangtang Side
Not To Scale

Pedestrian View Looking up towards Pedestrian Bridge
Not To Scale

LTHYW I Boundary Control Point Passenger Terminal Building

753

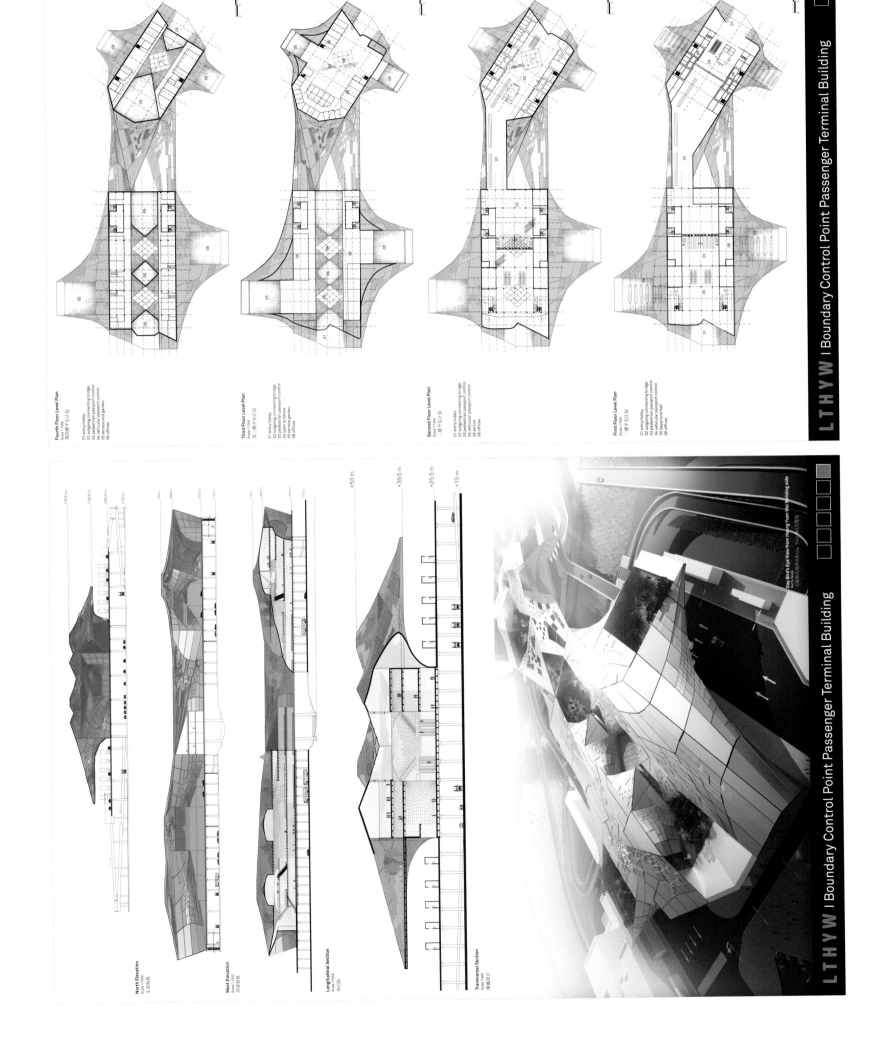

Fourth Floor Level Plan
Scale 1:1000
四层楼平面计划

01 entry/lobby
02 outgoing connecting bridge
03 pedestrian passport control
04 vehicular passport control
05 terrace and garden
06 offices

Third Floor Level Plan
Scale 1:1000
三、楼平面计划

01 entry/lobby
02 outgoing passport control
03 pedestrian passport control
04 vehicular passport control
05 terrace garden
06 offices

Second Floor Level Plan
Scale 1:1000
二楼平面计划

01 entry/lobby
02 outgoing connecting bridge
03 pedestrian passport control
04 vehicular passport control
05 open to below
06 offices

First Floor Level Plan
Scale 1:1000
楼平面计划

01 entry/lobby
02 outgoing connecting bridge
03 pedestrian passport control
04 vehicular passport control
05 departure hall
06 offices

North Elevation
Scale 1:1000
北部海视

West Elevation
Scale 1:1000
西方位视

Longitudinal Section
Scale 1:1000
纵切面

Transversal Section
Scale 1:1000
横截部分

+53 m
+39.5 m
+25.5 m
+15 m

Day Bird's Eye View from Heung Yuen Wai Building side
Not to Scale
天海视向近顺苑华大楼侧视图

LTHYW I Boundary Control Point Passenger Terminal Building

267

Airbaltic Terminal | *MSB ARQUITECTOS*

Participants : Miguel Mallaguerra, Susana Jesus, Bruno Martins, Hugo Aires, Claudia Alves, Wojciech Hydzik
Partners : MSB Architects + AHAD Architects
Project : AirBaltic Terminal
Typology : Public Building

Location : Riga, Latvia
Client : AirBaltic / Year : 2010

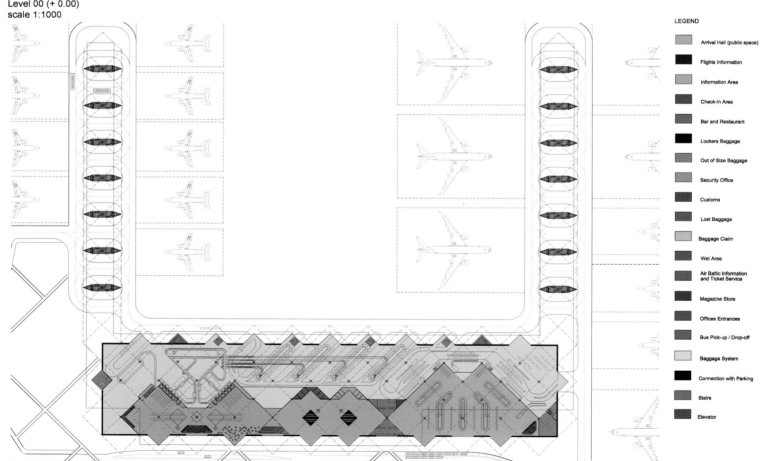

airBaltic Passenger Terminal

nr 206 // 01

Project description //

Our proposal embodies the essence of Latvia's cultural heritage and symbolises national historical values. The result is a building comprised of a diamond grid where the diagonals manage the spatial organization, strongly related to local traditions.

Latvia has a very ancient, rich and multi-faceted culture. The traditional forms found in artwork have played and still play an important symbolic role in the preservation of national values and cultural heritage. They also create a feeling of unity amongst the people, affirming a link with the past.

It is possible that the patterns are a form of writing, a way of communicating a concept or a wish. Latvians passion for dance and music coupled with their love of nature has formed a naturally balanced ambiance found in our proposal.

Architectural Concept //

The proposed design is intended to be read as one object, one entity where both piers play an inner complicity. This reflects airBaltic's aspirations, reinforcing the idea of linking earth and sky, Eastern and Western Europe.

The diamond like configuration and the diagonal grid are fundamental for the development of the terminal. The main façade with the angular entrances has a dramatic effect, whether arriving or departing. It adopts a dynamic image, which reflects the true dynamism of flying. It also enhances the terminal's presence, giving a more theatrical transition between the interior and exterior, welcoming and embracing the passengers in an engaging experience.

Our aim was to deliver an airport terminal that reflects the community's values, and exceeds customer expectations. We believe that our design successfully combines airline aspirations, national charisma and its development, passenger flows and technical / operational requirements.

We have proposed the new terminal to reflect airBaltic's progress, to be attractive and dignified. The terminal acts as a statement of airBaltic's achievements, success, image and promising future, it encompasses a look of permanence and solidity.

Site Plan
scale 1:3500

Terminal Floor Plan
Level 00 (+ 0.00)
scale 1:1000

LEGEND

- Arrival Hall (public space)
- Flights Information
- Information Area
- Check-in Area
- Bar and Restaurant
- Lockers Baggage
- Out of Size Baggage
- Security Office
- Customs
- Lost Baggage
- Baggage Claim
- Wet Area
- Air Baltic Information and Ticket Service
- Magazine Store
- Offices Entrances
- Bus Pick-up / Drop-off
- Baggage System
- Connection with Parking
- Stairs
- Elevator

Front Elevation

airBaltic Passenger Terminal

Terminal Floor Plan
Level 01 (+ 5.50)
scale 1:1000

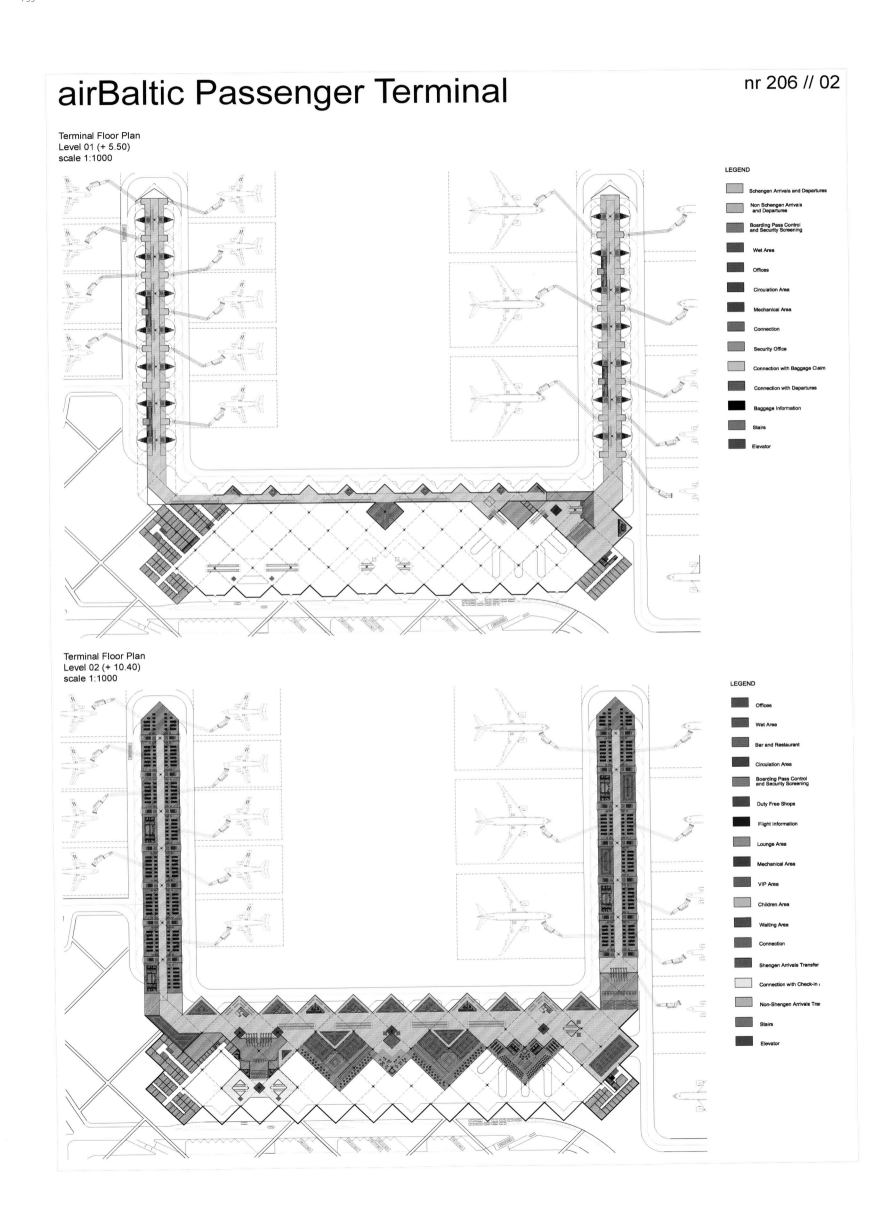

LEGEND

- Schengen Arrivals and Departures
- Non Schengen Arrivals and Departures
- Boarding Pass Control and Security Screening
- Wet Area
- Offices
- Circulation Area
- Mechanical Area
- Connection
- Security Office
- Connection with Baggage Claim
- Connection with Departures
- Baggage Information
- Stairs
- Elevator

Terminal Floor Plan
Level 02 (+ 10.40)
scale 1:1000

LEGEND

- Offices
- Wet Area
- Bar and Restaurant
- Circulation Area
- Boarding Pass Control and Security Screening
- Duty Free Shops
- Flight Information
- Lounge Area
- Mechanical Area
- VIP Area
- Children Area
- Waiting Area
- Connection
- Shengen Arrivals Transfer
- Connection with Check-in /
- Non-Shengen Arrivals Tra
- Stairs
- Elevator

airBaltic Passenger Terminal

airBaltic Passenger Terminal

Passenger Flow Diagram
Level 00

Passenger Flow Diagram
Level 01

Passenger Flow Diagram
Level 02

CM_Lamina | *LUIS ARREDONDO_ARCHITECT*

Location : Santany, Mallorca, Spain
Client : Blai Bonet Foundation

Project : Blai Bonet Museum
Participants : Luis Arredondo
Typology : Cultural

268

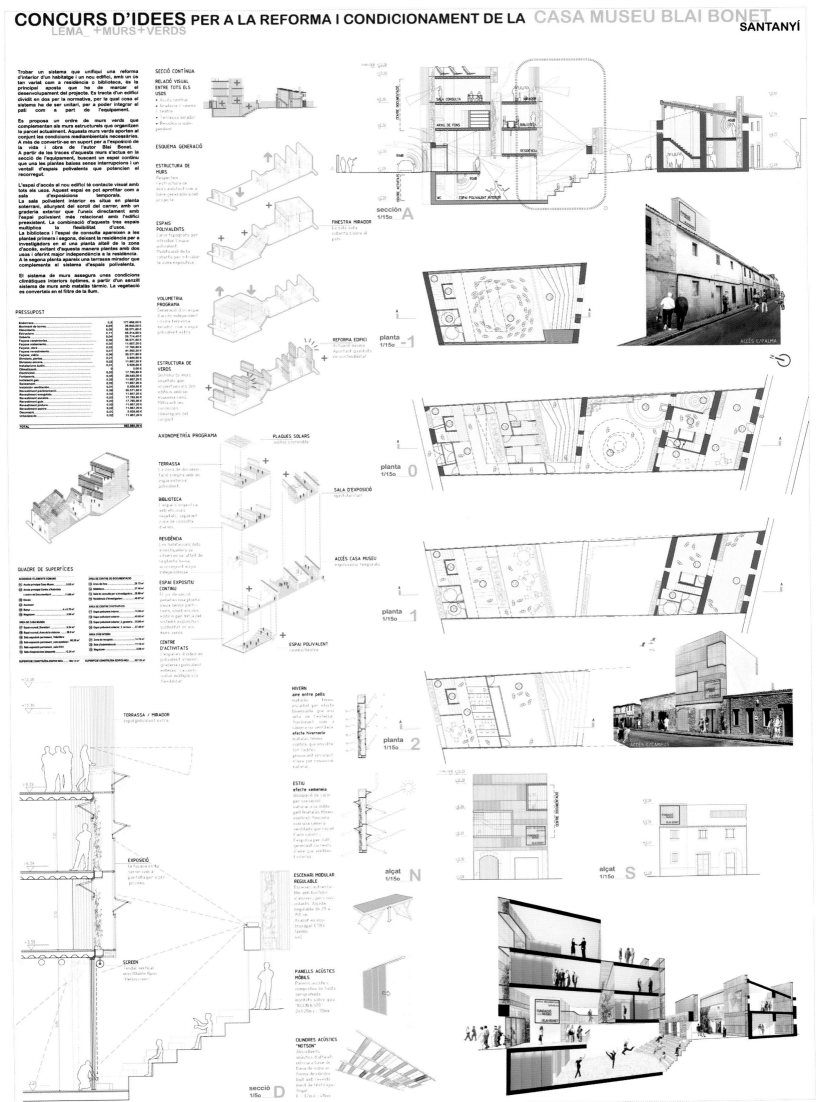

269

El Cementerio de la Cornisa | *XML Architecture Research Urbanism*

Program : Cemetery
Location : Madrid, Spain
Area : 10 HA

Client : City of Madrid / Europan Spain
Realization : Competition, Honorable Mention

SR 045
MADRID 1/3

MADRID
EL CEMENTERIO DE LA CORNISA

In the history of Madrid's urban development, the area now known as the Manzanares Cornice has been an ambiguous void ever since some buildings were constructed there in the 13th century. As an area that was peripheral to the city but also contained an influential religious center, the Cornice played a double role in Madrid's social and cultural fabric. During the following centuries, the San Francisco el Grande area prospered and gradually merged with the city, but to this day and age the heart of the Cornice is like an abyss that cuts through Madrid's urban structure.

This project seeks to maximize the true potential of a void within the city. Our proposal is based on the precept that, for a site to be absorbed within the public space of a city, meaning is more important than program. Therefore, instead of reacting with the typical neo-liberal reflex bent on allocating a program to each and every available location within a city, this proposal aims to attribute meaning to the intrinsic qualities of the site's emptiness.

The project centers on the hypothesis that emptiness is an essential part of urban life. As in most European cities, Madrid's population is waning. Urban growth has come to a standstill, exacerbated by the current recession, and the median age of urban populations has risen considerably. A strong city should have the capacity to give place and meaning to the crucial forces of its day. Hence, cities with a graying population need to address the crucial issue of how rituals of death and mourning are to be incorporated into urbanity. Instead of viewing death as a taboo and displacing burial rituals to its periphery, the city should accommodate the reality of death and mourning within its center.

The Cornice offers a unique opportunity for the city of Madrid to realize conditions that relate to today's changed urban demographics. This project proposes that the Cornice's emptiness is preserved by pursuing a program characterized by emptiness: death. The proposal transforms the site into a grid of cemeteries on various plateaus, modestly following the morphology of the landscape. The Cementerio de la Cornisa contains a variety of burial sites such as a Zen garden, a children's graveyard, bamboo gardens and a columbarium for cinerary urns. With each burial ritual, the Madrileños incorporate part of their personal histories into the site, which becomes an invisible but indelible element of the city's mental map over the years. Each grave establishes new, unexpected links with the population in other parts of the city. The routes through this grid weave into the surrounding urban areas. In this way, the Cementerio de la Cornisa project revives the aura of the convent established here centuries ago, thus strengthening the identity of the San Francisco el Grande area within the city. The Cornice is transformed into a tranquil, serene park within Madrid's highly developed urban landscape, a unique and fundamental part of the city's public space. Death becomes an integral part of urban life.

This proposal pushes the intrinsic quality of the Cornice site to its extreme and, instead of solely offering programmatic filling, attributes meaning to the site's emptiness. The new cemetery weaves past and future together to create a new urban space within the city of Madrid, a space that will be a container for the rituals and events of its inhabitants and become a historic and cultural showcase for all time.

Site: Urban Growth (1656, 1910, 2008)

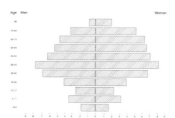

Population Pyramid Madrid

Madrid Cemeteries

Lamina | *scandurrastudio*

Location : Mexico City, Mexico
Team : Alessandro Scandurra, Davide Sala, Marina Malavasi, Cristian Del Giudice

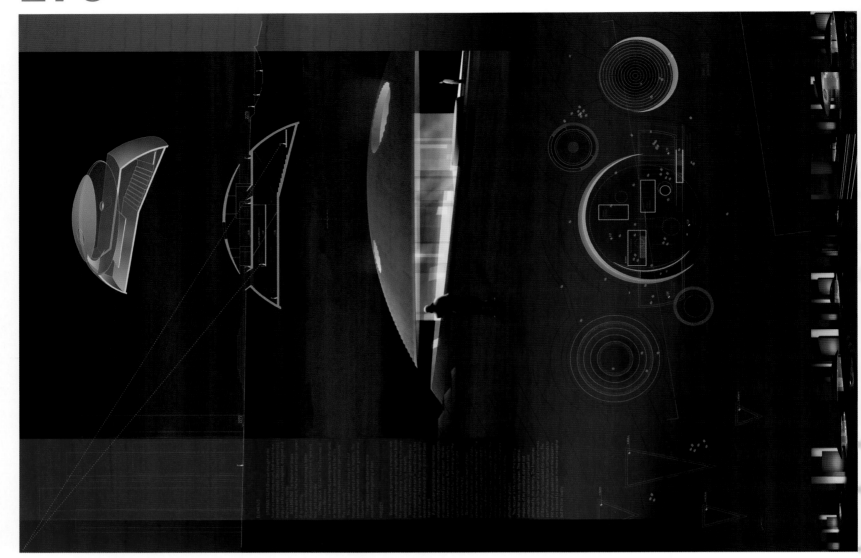

761

New Apostolic Church | *BKK-3*

Location : Vienna, Austria
Design competition for realisation of a church 2011
Team : Franz Sumnitsch, Norman Jargstorff, Tina Krischmann, Renate Rodel, Cora Vollnagel

271

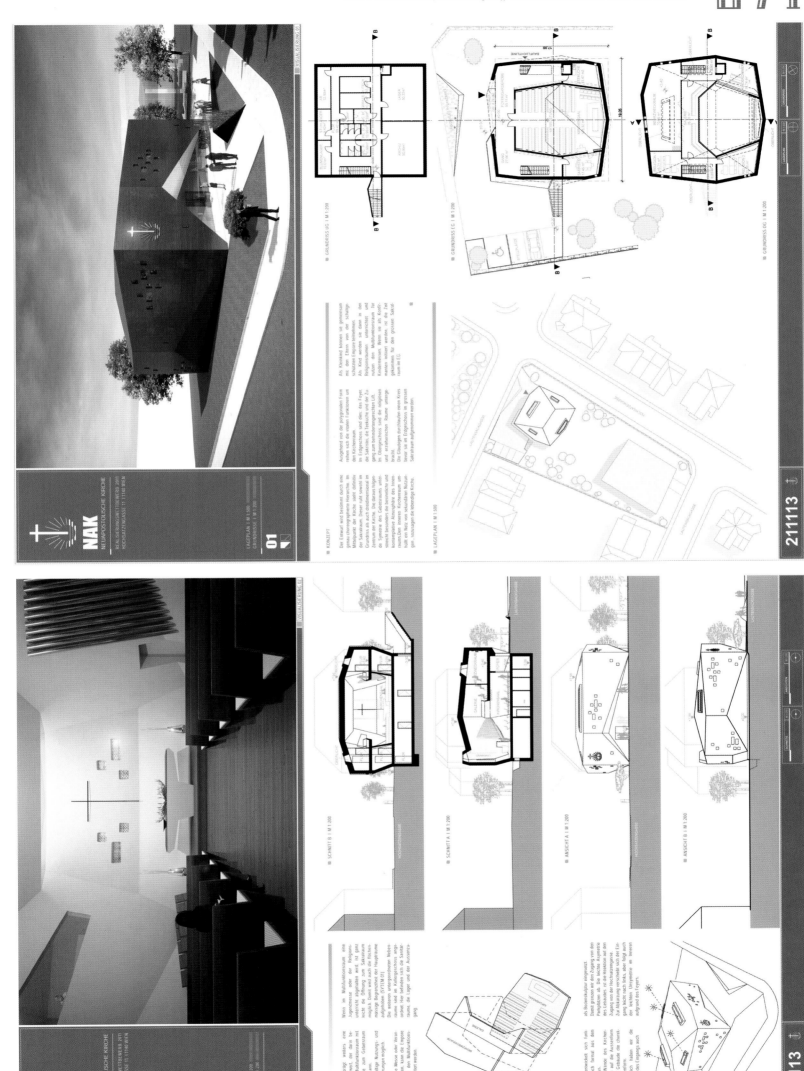

272

Piazza Dante | *ZO_loft*

Architect : Filomena Acquaviva, Andrea Cingoli, Francesca Fontana,
Michele Manigrasso, Luigi Di Paolo, Roberto Potenza
Collaborators : Immacolata Palma, Nicoletta Daniele

Client : Comune di Teramo (TE)
Location : Teramo (TE) Italy

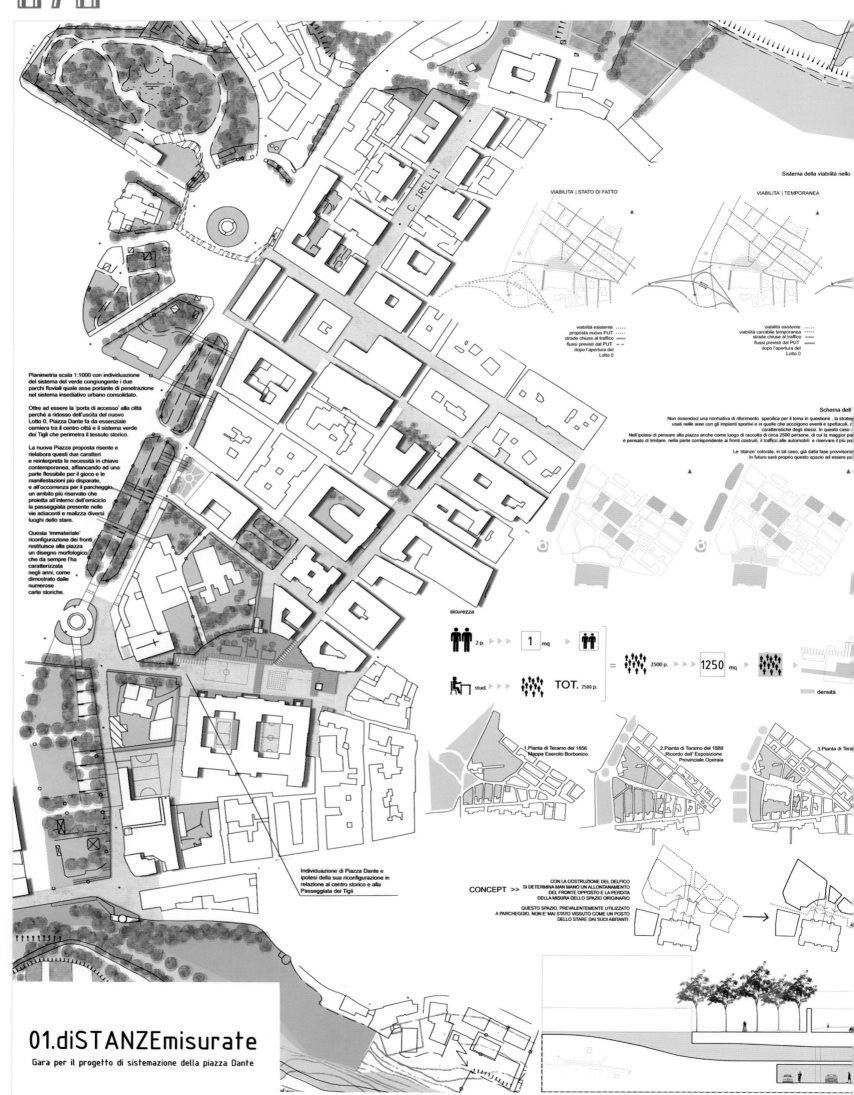

Planimetria scala 1:1000 con individuazione
del sistema del verde congiungente i due
parchi fluviali quale asse portante di penetrazione
nel sistema insediativo urbano consolidato.

Oltre ad essere la 'porta di accesso' alla città
perché a ridosso dell'uscita del nuovo
Lotto 0, Piazza Dante fa da essenziale
cerniera tra il centro città e il sistema verde
dei Tigli che perimetra il tessuto storico.

La nuova Piazza proposta risente e
rielabora questi due caratteri
e reinterpreta le necessità in chiave
contemporanea, affiancando ad una
parte flessibile per il gioco e le
manifestazioni più disparate,
e all'occorrenza per il parcheggio,
un ambito più riservato che
proietta all'interno dell'emiciclo
la passeggiata presente nelle
vie adiacenti e realizza diversi
luoghi dello stare.

Questa 'immateriale'
riconfigurazione dei fronti
restituisce alla piazza
un disegno morfologico
che da sempre l'ha
caratterizzata
negli anni, come
dimostrato dalle
numerose
carte storiche.

Individuazione di Piazza Dante e
ipotesi della sua riconfigurazione in
relazione al centro storico e alla
Passeggiata dei Tigli

Sistema della viabilità nello

VIABILITA' | STATO DI FATTO

VIABILITA' | TEMPORANEA

viabilità esistente .....
proposta nuovo PUT .....
strade chiuse al traffico ───
flussi previsti dal PUT ──
dopo l'apertura del
Lotto 0

viabilità esistente .....
viabilità carrabile temporanea
strade chiuse al traffico ───
flussi previsti dal PUT ──
dopo l'apertura del
Lotto 0

Schema dell

Non essendoci una normativa di riferimento specifica per il tema in questione, la strateg
usati nelle aree con gli impianti sportivi e in quelle che accolgono eventi e spettacoli, c
caratteristiche degli stessi. In questo caso i

Nell'ipotesi di pensare alla piazza anche come luogo di raccolta di circa 2500 persone, di cui la maggior par
è pensato di limitare, nella parte corrispondente ai fronti costruiti, il traffico alle automobili e riservare il più po

Le 'stanze' colorate, in tal caso, già dalla fase provvisori
In futuro sarà proprio questo spazio ad essere pa

sicurezza

2 p. ▸▸▸ 1 mq

stud. ▸▸▸ TOT. 2500 p.

= 2500 p. ▸▸▸ 1250 mq

densità

1.Pianta di Teramo del 1856
Mappa Esercito Borbonico

2.Pianta di Teramo del 1888
Ricordo dell' Esposizione
Provinciale Operaia

3.Pianta di Tera

CONCEPT >> CON LA COSTRUZIONE DEL DELFICO
SI DETERMINA MAN MANO UN ALLONTANAMENTO
DEL FRONTE OPPOSTO E LA PERDITA
DELLA MISURA DELLO SPAZIO ORIGINARIO

QUESTO SPAZIO, PREVALENTEMENTE UTILIZZATO
A PARCHEGGIO, NON E' MAI STATO VISSUTO COME UN POSTO
DELLO STARE DAI SUOI ABITANTI.

01.diSTANZEmisurate

Gara per il progetto di sistemazione della piazza Dante

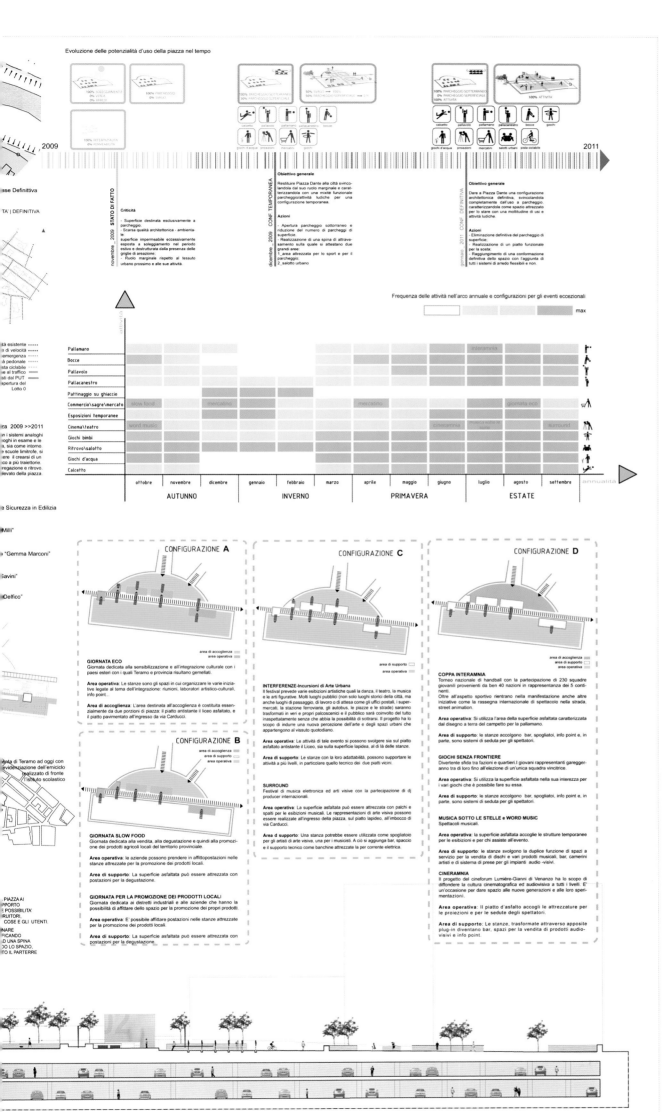

Evoluzione delle potenzialità d'uso della piazza nel tempo

2009 ... 2011

Frequenza delle attività nell'arco annuale e configurazioni per gli eventi eccezionali

max

	ottobre	novembre	dicembre	gennaio	febbraio	marzo	aprile	maggio	giugno	luglio	agosto	settembre	annualità
Pallamano										interamnia			
Bocce													
Pallavolo													
Pallacanestro													
Pattinaggio su ghiaccio													
Commercio\sagre\mercato	slow food	mercatino					mercatino				giornata eco		
Esposizioni temporanee													
Cinema\teatro	word music							cineramnia		surround			
Giochi bimbi													
Ritrovo\salotto													
Giochi d'acqua													
Calcetto													

AUTUNNO — INVERNO — PRIMAVERA — ESTATE

CONFIGURAZIONE A

area di accoglienza
area operativa

GIORNATA ECO
Giornata dedicata alla sensibilizzazione e all'integrazione culturale con i paesi esteri con i quali Teramo e provincia risultano gemellati.

Area operativa: Le stanze sono gli spazi in cui organizzare le varie iniziative legate al tema dell'integrazione: riunioni, laboratori artistico-culturali, info point..

Area di accoglienza: L'area destinata all'accoglienza è costituita essenzialmente da due porzioni di piazza: il piatto antistante il liceo asfaltato, e il piatto pavimentato all'ingresso di via Carducci.

CONFIGURAZIONE B

area di accoglienza
area di supporto
area operativa

GIORNATA SLOW FOOD
Giornata dedicata alla vendita, alla degustazione e quindi alla promozione dei prodotti agricoli locali del territorio provinciale.

Area operativa: le aziende possono prendere in affittopostazioni nelle stanze attrezzate per la promozione dei prodotti locali.

Area di supporto: La superficie asfaltata può essere attrezzata con postazioni per la degustazione.

GIORNATA PER LA PROMOZIONE DEI PRODOTTI LOCALI
Giornata dedicata ai distretti industriali e alle aziende che hanno la possibilità di affittare dello spazio per la promozione dei propri prodotti.

Area operativa: E' possibile affittare postazioni nelle stanze attrezzate per la promozione dei prodotti locali.

Area di supporto: La superficie asfaltata può essere attrezzata con postazioni per la degustazione.

CONFIGURAZIONE C

area di supporto
area operativa

INTERFERENZE-Incursioni di Arte Urbana
Il festival prevede varie esibizioni artistiche quali la danza, il teatro, la musica e le arti figurative. Molti luoghi pubblici (non solo luoghi storici della città, ma anche luoghi di passaggio, di lavoro o di attesa come gli uffici postali, i supermercati, la stazione ferroviaria, gli autobus, le piazze e le strade) saranno trasformati in veri e propri palcoscenici e il pubblico sarà coinvolto del tutto inaspettatamente senza che abbia la possibilità di sottrarsi. Il progetto ha lo scopo di indurre una nuova percezione dell'arte e degli spazi urbani che appartengono al vissuto quotidiano.

Area operativa: Le attività di tale evento si possono svolgere sia sul piatto asfaltato antistante il Liceo, sia sulla superficie lapidea, al di là delle stanze.

Area di supporto: Le stanze con la loro adattabilità, possono supportare le attività a più livelli, in particolare quello tecnico dei due piatti vicini.

SURROUND
Festival di musica elettronica ed arti visive con la partecipazione di dj producer internazionali.

Area operativa: La superficie asfaltata può essere attrezzata con palchi e spalti per le esibizioni musicali. Le rappresentazioni di arte visiva possono essere realizzate all'ingresso della piazza, sul piatto lapideo, all'imbocco di via Carducci.

Area d supporto: Una stanza potrebbe essere utilizzata come spogliatoio per gli artisti di arte visiva, una per i musicisti. A ciò si aggiunga bar, spaccio e il supporto tecnico come banchine attrezzate la per corrente elettrica.

CONFIGURAZIONE D

area di accoglienza
area di supporto
area operativa

COPPA INTERAMNIA
Torneo nazionale di handball con la partecipazione di 230 squadre giovanili provenienti da ben 40 nazioni in rappresentanza dei 5 continenti.
Oltre all'aspetto sportivo rientrano nella manifestazione anche altre iniziative come la rassegna internazionale di spettacolo nella strada, street animation.

Area operativa: Si utilizza l'area della superficie asfaltata caratterizzata dal disegno a terra del campetto per la pallamano.

Area di supporto: le stanze accolgono bar, spogliatoi, info point e, in parte, sono sistemi di seduta per gli spettatori.

GIOCHI SENZA FRONTIERE
Divertente sfida tra fazioni e quartieri.I giovani rappresentanti gareggeranno tra di loro fino all'elezione di un'unica squadra vincitrice.

Area operativa: Si utilizza la superficie asfaltata nella sua interezza per i vari giochi che è possibile fare su essa.

Area di supporto: le stanze accolgono bar, spogliatoi, info point e, in parte, sono sistemi di seduta per gli spettatori.

MUSICA SOTTO LE STELLE e WORD MUSIC
Spettacoli musicali.

Area operativa: la superficie asfaltata accoglie le strutture temporanee per le esibizioni e per chi assiste all'evento.

Area di supporto: le stanze svolgono la duplice funzione di spazi a servizio per la vendita di dischi e vari prodotti musicali, bar, camerini artisti e di sistema di prese per gli impianti audio-visivi.

CINERAMNIA
Il progetto del cineforum Lumière-Gianni di Venanzo ha lo scopo di diffondere la cultura cinematografica ed audiovisiva a tutti i livelli. E' un'occasione per dare spazio alle nuove generazioni e alle loro sperimentazioni.

Area operativa: Il piatto d'asfalto accoglie le attrezzature per le proiezioni e per le sedute degli spettatori.

Area di supporto: Le stanze, trasformate attraverso apposite plug-in diventano bar, spazi per la vendita di prodotti audio-visivi e info point.

Sezione longitudinale significativa scala 1:200

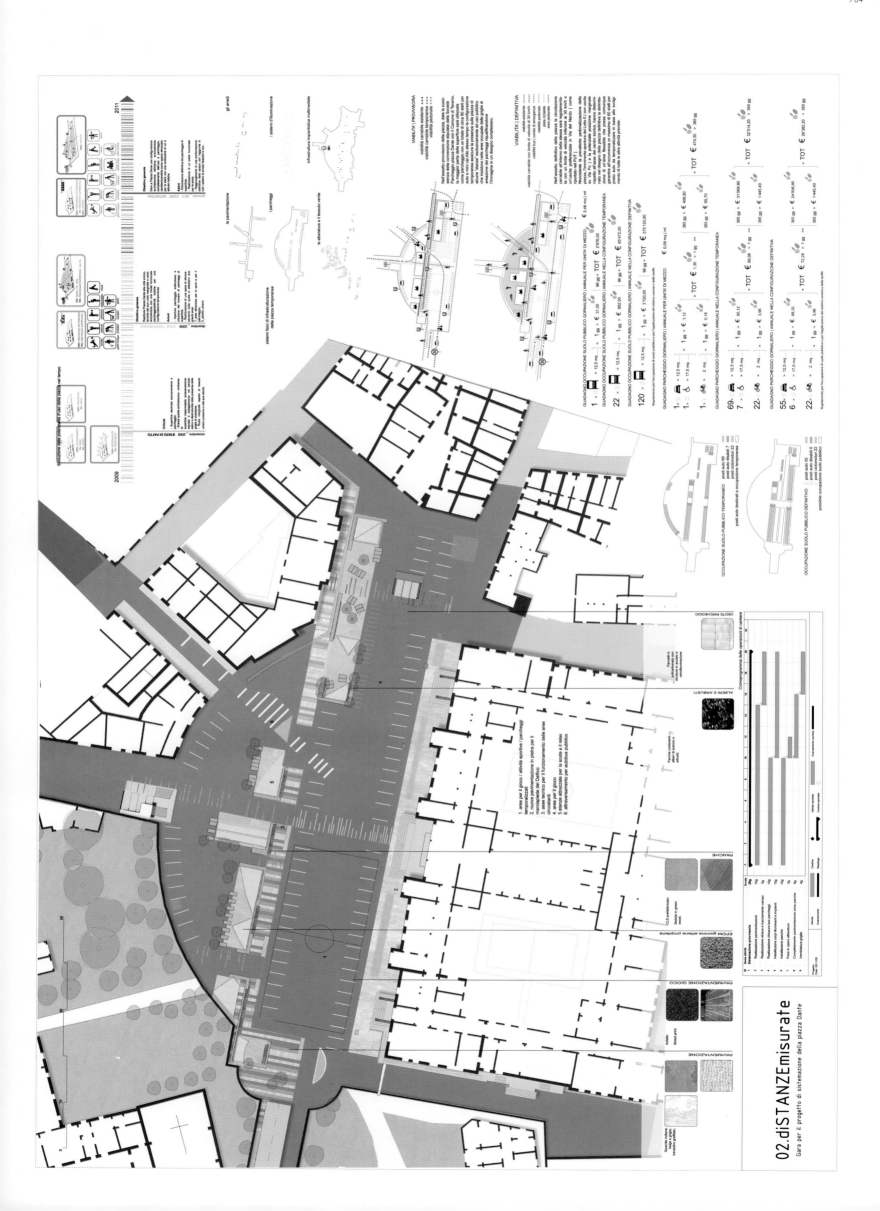

02.diSTANZEmisurate

Gara per il progetto di sistemazione della piazza Dante

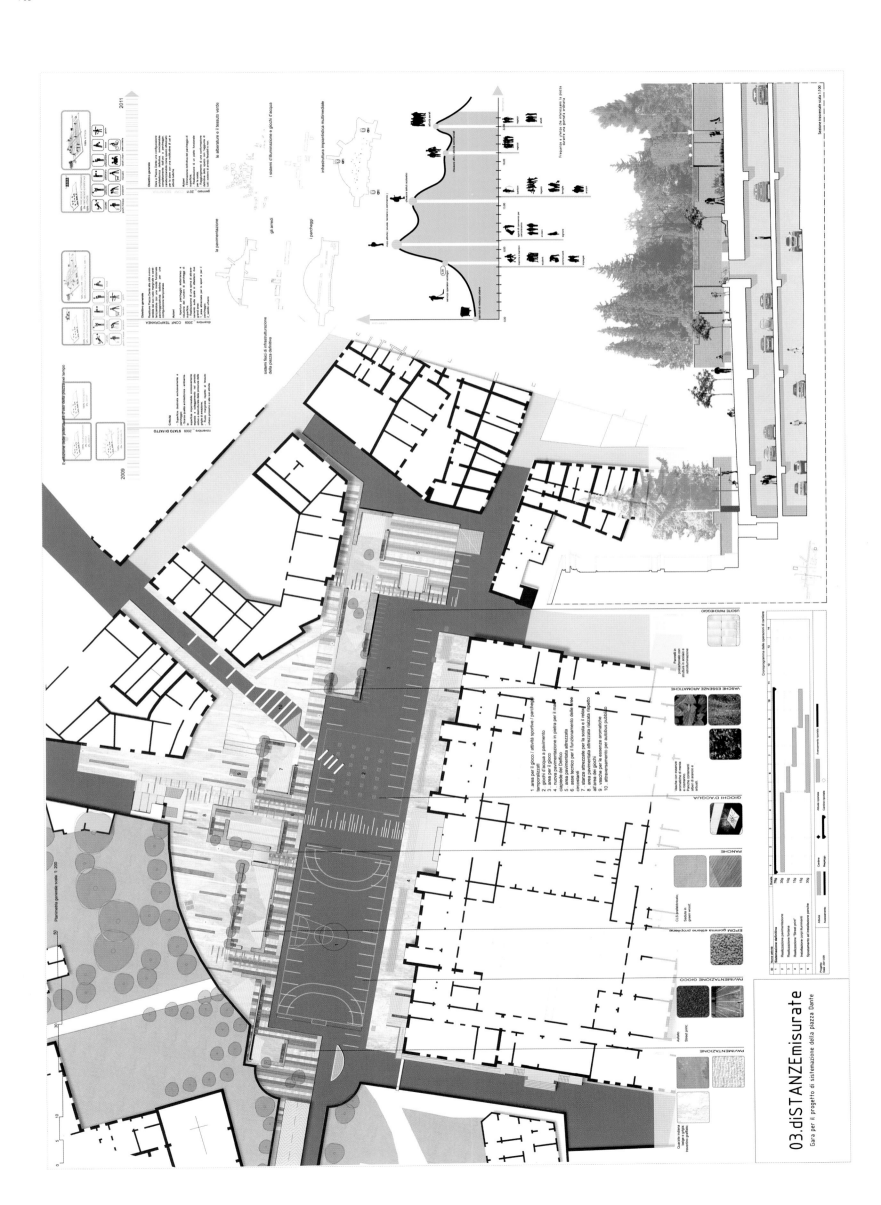

03.diSTANZEmisurate

Gara per il progetto di sistemazione della piazza Dante

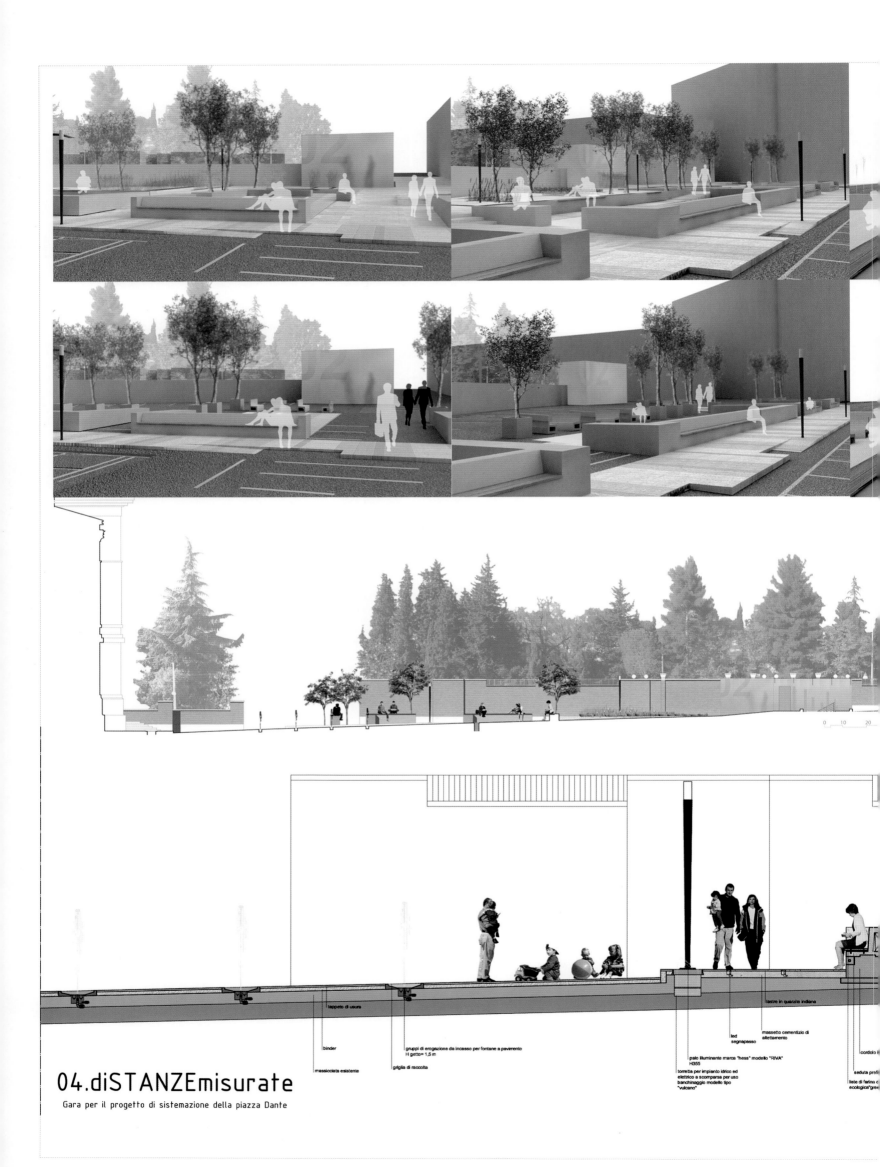

04.diSTANZEmisurate

Gara per il progetto di sistemazione della piazza Dante

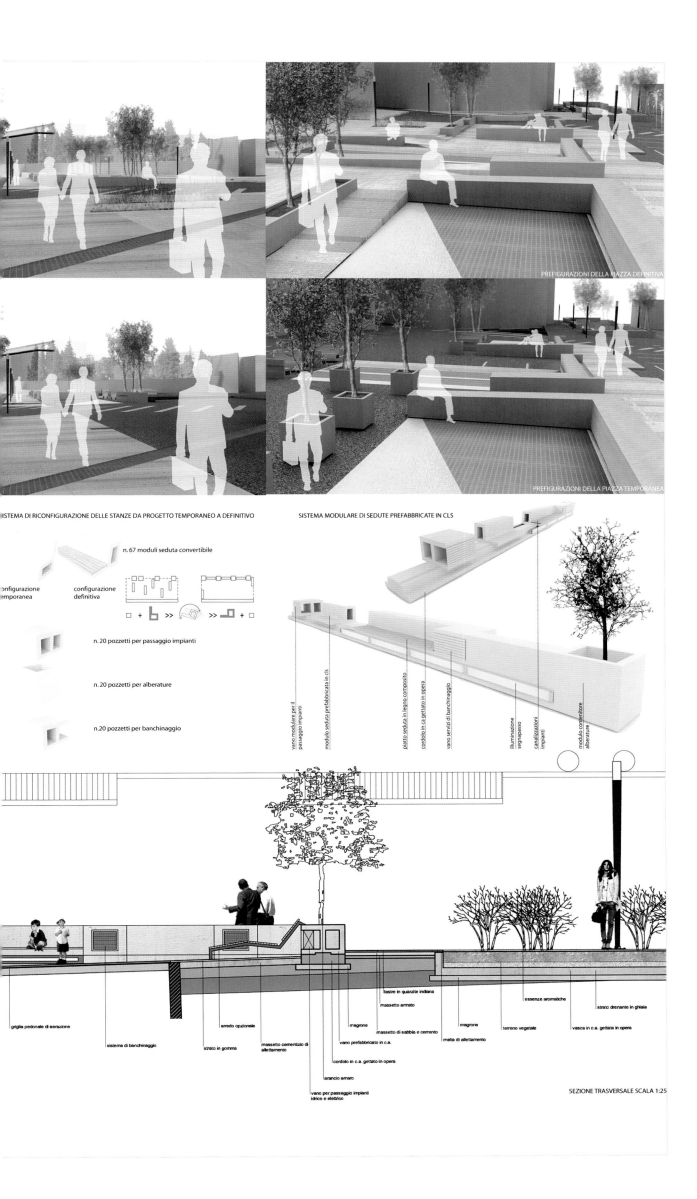

PREFIGURAZIONI DELLA PIAZZA DEFINITIVA

PREFIGURAZIONI DELLA PIAZZA TEMPORANEA

SISTEMA DI RICONFIGURAZIONE DELLE STANZE DA PROGETTO TEMPORANEO A DEFINITIVO

SISTEMA MODULARE DI SEDUTE PREFABBRICATE IN CLS

n. 67 moduli seduta convertibile

configurazione temporanea

configurazione definitiva

n. 20 pozzetti per passaggio impianti

n. 20 pozzetti per alberature

n. 20 pozzetti per banchinaggio

vano modulare per il passaggio impianti

modulo seduta prefabbricata in cls

piatto seduta in legno composito

cordolo in ca gettato in opera

vano servizi di banchinaggio

illuminazione segnapasso

canalizzazioni impianti

modulo contenitore alberature

griglia pedonale di aerazione

sistema di banchinaggio

strato in gomma

amredo opzionale

massetto cementizio di allettamento

cordolo in c.a. gettato in opera

arancio amaro

vano per passaggio impianti idrico e elettrico

vano prefabbricato in c.a.

magrone

massetto di sabbia e cemento

massetto armato

lastre in quarzite indiana

magrone

malta di allettamento

terreno vegetale

essenze aromatiche

vasca in c.a. gettata in opera

strato drenante in ghiaia

SEZIONE TRASVERSALE SCALA 1:25

273

Piazza Duomo | *ZO_loft*

Architect : Filomena Acquaviva, Andrea Cingoli, Francesca Fontana,
Michele Manigrasso, Roberto Potenza
Client : Comune di Cerignola (FG)
Location : Cerignola (FG) Italy

768

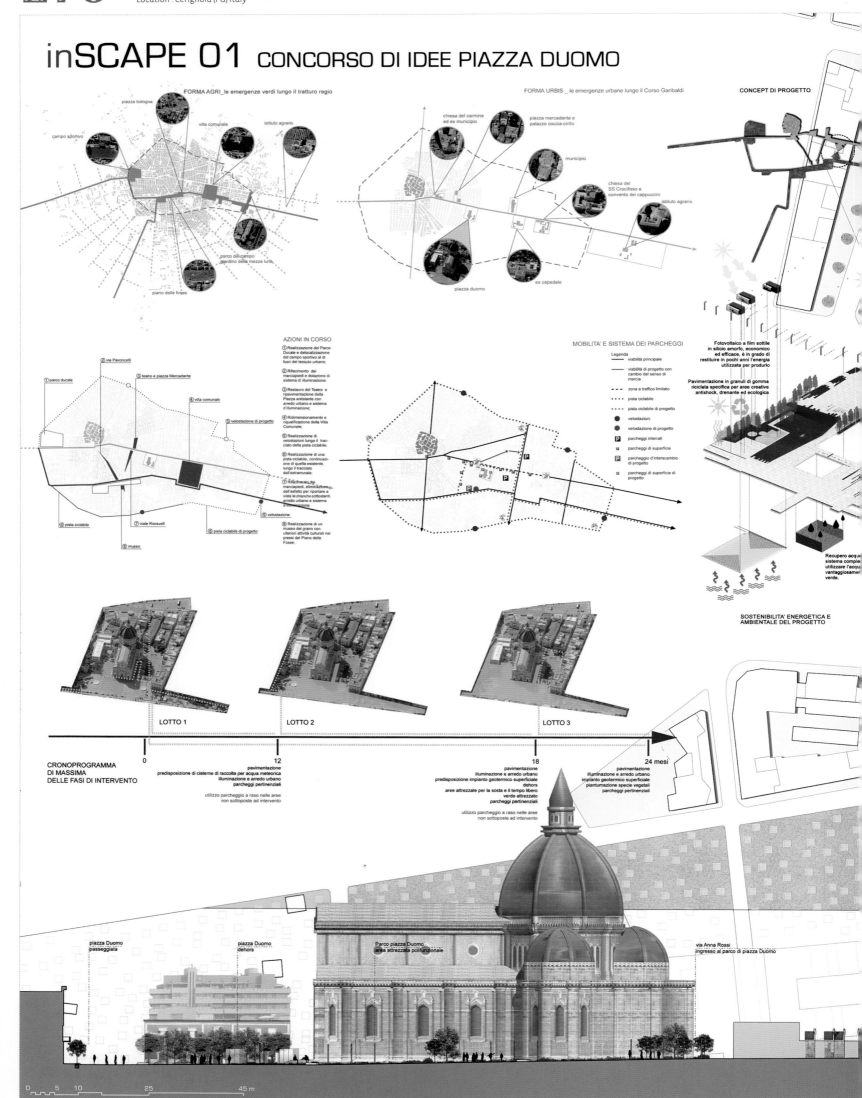

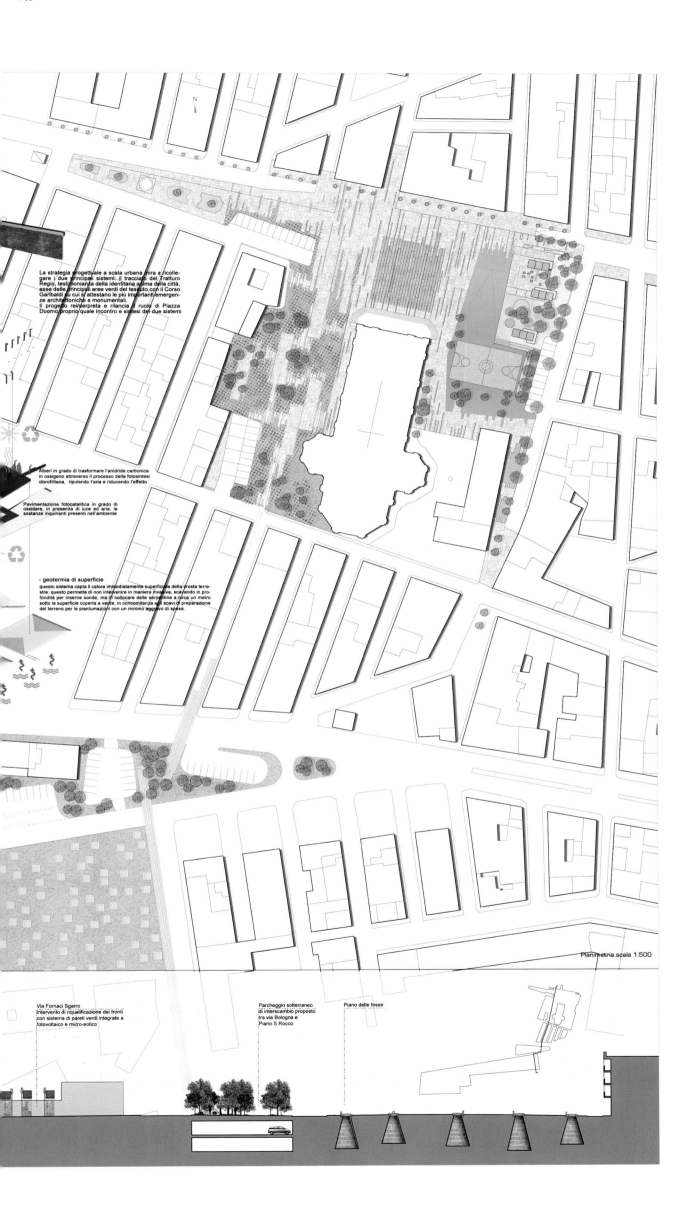

La strategia progettuale a scala urbana mira a ricollegare i due principali sistemi: il tracciato del Tratturo Regio, testimonianza della identitaria anima della città, asse delle principali aree verdi del tessuto, con il Corso Garibaldi su cui si attestano le più importanti emergenze architettoniche e monumentali.
Il progetto reinterpreta e rilancia il ruolo di Piazza Duomo proprio quale incontro e sintesi dei due sistemi

Alberi in grado di trasformare l'anidride carbonica in ossigeno attraverso il processo della fotosintesi clorofilliana, ripulendo l'aria e riducendo l'effetto

Pavimentazione fotocatalitica in grado di ossidare, in presenza di luce ed aria, le sostanze inquinanti presenti nell'ambiente

- geotermia di superficie

questo sistema capta il calore immediatamente superficiale della crosta terrestre: questo permette di non intervenire in maniera invasiva, scavando in profondità per inserire sonde, ma di collocare delle serpentine a circa un metro sotto la superficie coperta a verde, in concomitanza agli scavi di preparazione del terreno per le piantumazioni con un minimo aggravio di spesa

Planimetria scala 1:500

Via Fornaci Sgarro
intervento di riqualificazione dei fronti con sistema di pareti verdi integrate a fotovoltaico e micro-eolico

Parcheggio sotterraneo di interscambio proposto tra via Bologna e Piano S.Rocco

Piano delle fosse

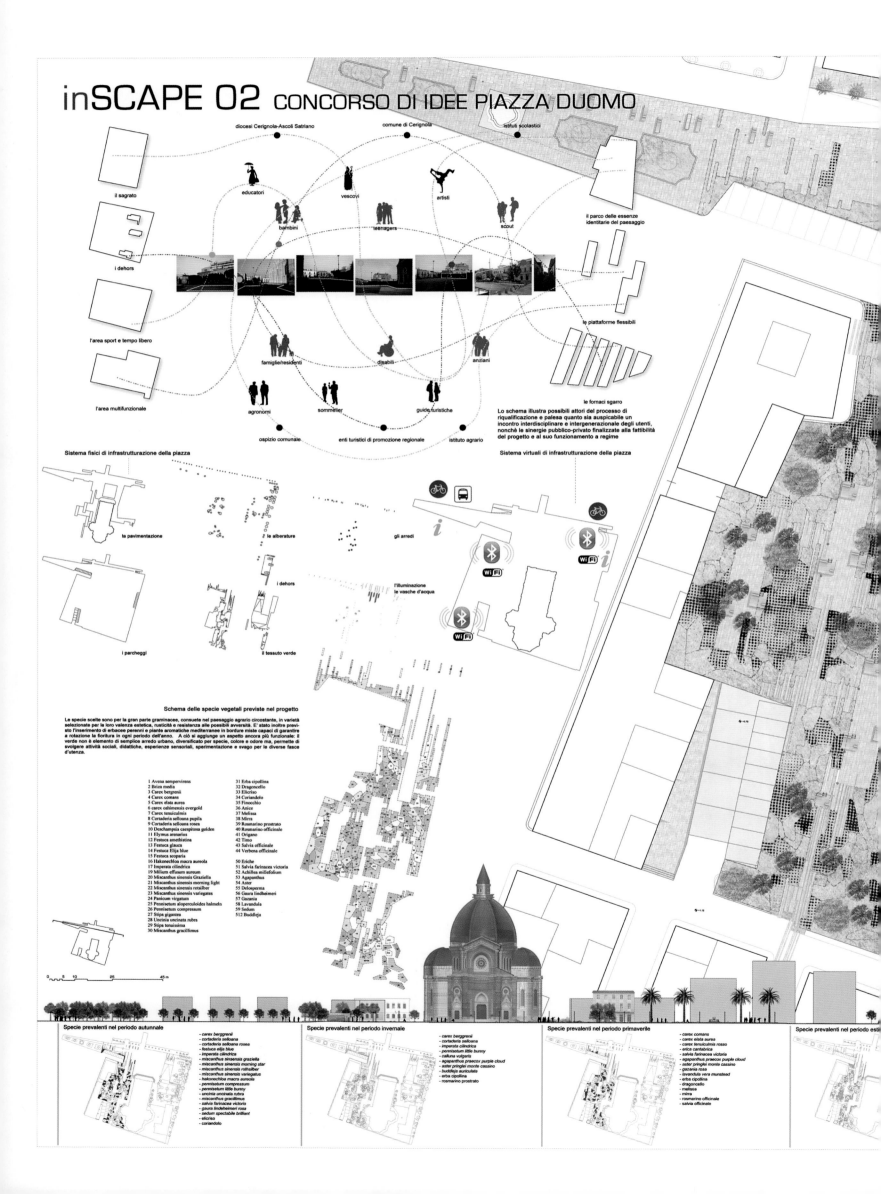

771

planivolumetria scala 1:200

N

Legenda degli elementi costituenti il progetto
1 area polifunzionale sport/tempo libero
2 area gioco per bimbi
3 internet café
4 urban center
5 ludoteca/ritrovo per anziani
6 sagrato
7 giochi d'acqua
8 parco delle specie vegetali autoctone
9 aree attrezzate
10 spazi flessibili per eventi
11 parcheggi

ABACO DELLE SUPERFICI

SISTEMA DEL VERDE

alberi

erbe

erbe_officinali

fiori

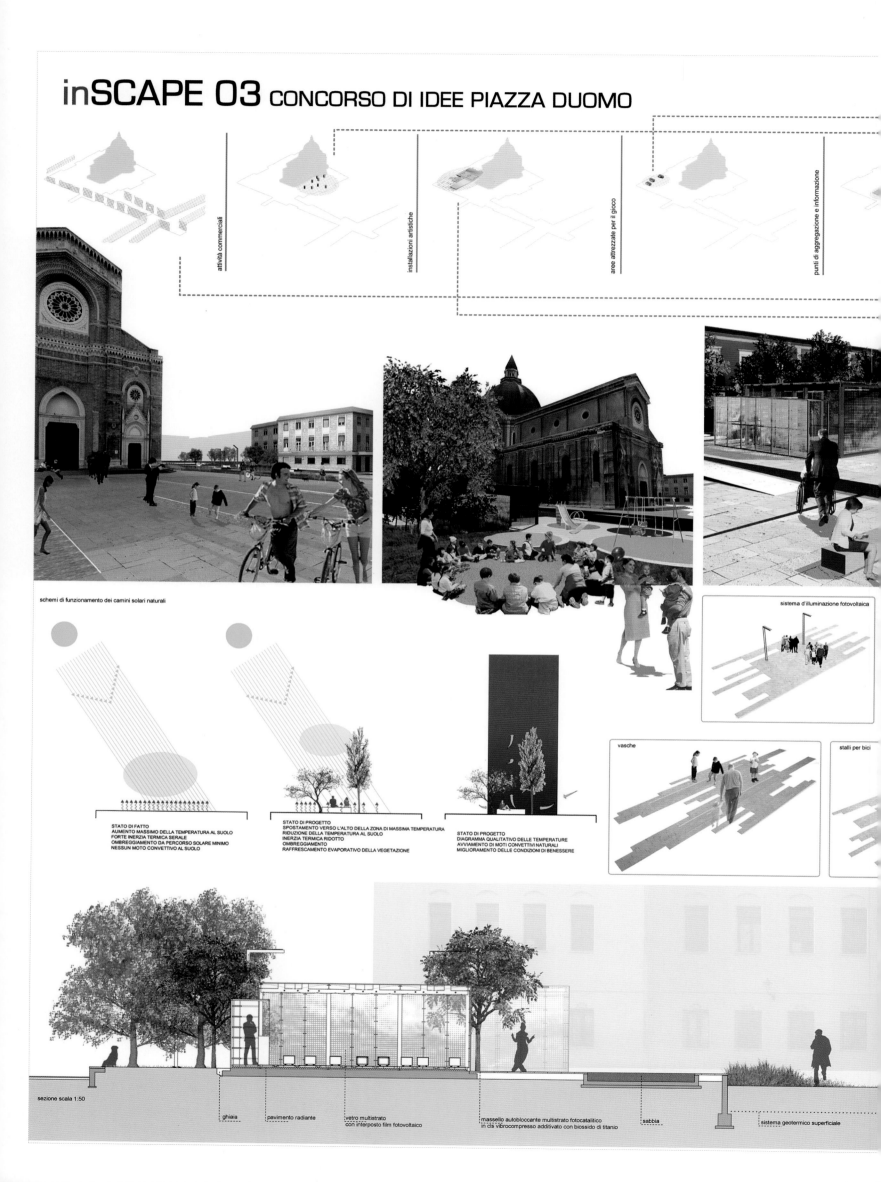

inSCAPE 03 CONCORSO DI IDEE PIAZZA DUOMO

attività commerciali

installazioni artistiche

aree attrezzate per il gioco

punti di aggregazione e informazione

schemi di funzionamento dei camini solari naturali

sistema d'illuminazione fotovoltaica

vasche

stalli per bici

STATO DI FATTO
AUMENTO MASSIMO DELLA TEMPERATURA AL SUOLO
FORTE INERZIA TERMICA SERALE
OMBREGGIAMENTO DA PERCORSO SOLARE MINIMO
NESSUN MOTO CONVETTIVO AL SUOLO

STATO DI PROGETTO
SPOSTAMENTO VERSO L'ALTO DELLA ZONA DI MASSIMA TEMPERATURA
RIDUZIONE DELLA TEMPERATURA AL SUOLO
INERZIA TERMICA RIDOTTO
OMBREGGIAMENTO
RAFFRESCAMENTO EVAPORATIVO DELLA VEGETAZIONE

STATO DI PROGETTO
DIAGRAMMA QUALITATIVO DELLE TEMPERATURE
AVVIAMENTO DI MOTI CONVETTIVI NATURALI
MIGLIORAMENTO DELLE CONDIZIONI DI BENESSERE

sezione scala 1:50

ghiaia   pavimento radiante   vetro multistrato con interposto film fotovoltaico   massello autobloccante multistrato fotocatalitico in cls vibrocompresso additivato con biossido di titanio   sabbia   sistema geotermico superficiale

modalità d'uso degli ambiti della piazza predisposta a continue riconfigurazioni

attività liturgiche

commercio ambulante

aree attrezzate per il tempo libero e il relax

spazi dedicati a spettacoli e grandi eventi

dehor autosufficienti

sistema integrato di captazione

turbina microeolica
pannello fotovoltaico

sistema di panche-gavone modulari

totem informativo-pubblicitario

modulo base

moduli aggregati

giardino tematico

graminacee
aromatiche
erbacee perenni da fiore

postazione di biomonitoraggio ambientale

hipericum
dacylis
plantago
verbascum
picris
daucus
chicorium

pavimentazioni eco-compatibili

pavimentazione antitrauma in gomma riciclata
massello autobloccante fotocatalitico

prato rustico calpestabile a base di *festuca sp.*

panca gavone prefabbricata

lampione fotovoltaico

lastre in pietra di Apricena

led fotovoltaico

vasca d'acqua a sfioro

274

Piazza Gregis | *ZO_loft*

Architect : Paolo Emilio Bellisario, Andrea Cingoli, Giorgio Giurdanella, Hyung Seon Kwak
Collaborators : Giuseppe Bandieramonte, Ivea Butkute, Francesca Fontana, Gabriele Martinelli,
Roberto Potenza, Emanuela Spiotta

Client : Comune di Gorlago (BG)
Location : Gorlago (BG) Italy

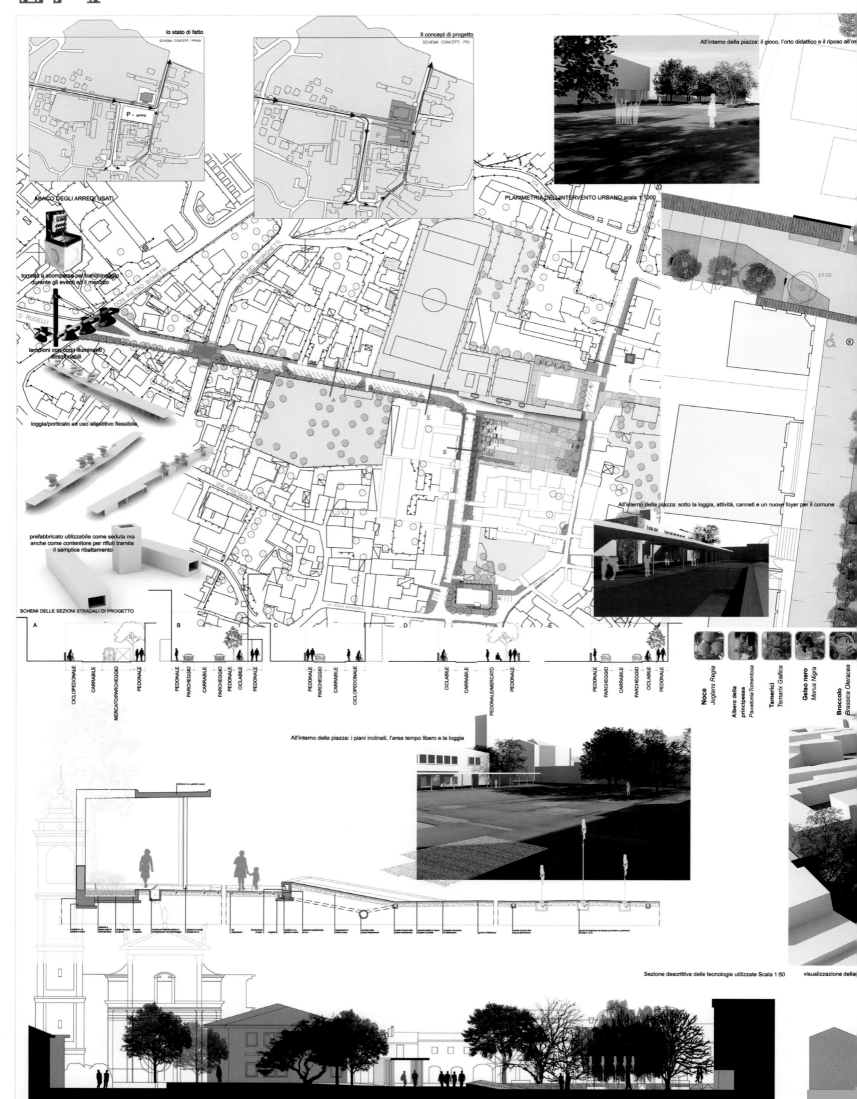

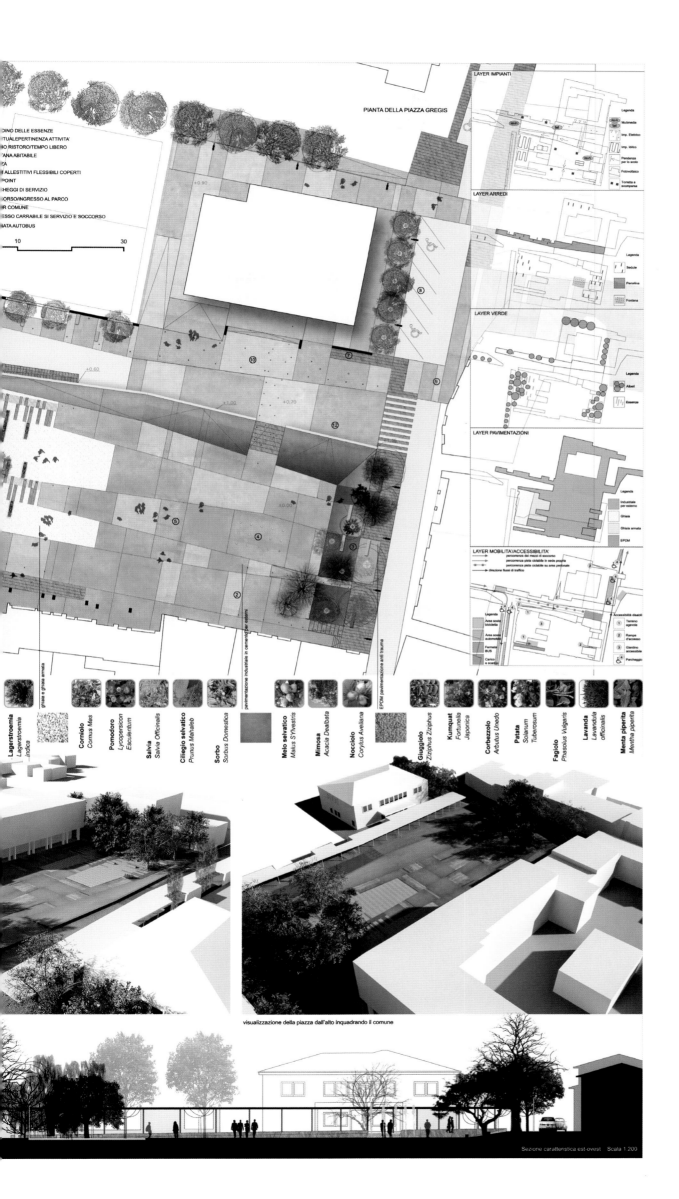

PIANTA DELLA PIAZZA GREGIS

LAYER IMPIANTI

LAYER ARREDI

LAYER VERDE

LAYER PAVIMENTAZIONI

LAYER MOBILITA'/ACCESSIBILITA'

RDINO DELLE ESSENZE
ITUALEPERTINENZA ATTIVITA'
IO RISTORO/TEMPO LIBERO
'ANA ABITABILE
'A'
II ALLESTITIVI FLESSIBILI COPERTI
POINT
HEGGI DI SERVIZIO
ORSO/INGRESSO AL PARCO
R COMUNE
ESSO CARRABILE SI SERVIZIO E SOCCORSO
IATA AUTOBUS

10   30

Lagerstroemia *Lagerstroemia indica*

ghiaia e ghiaia armata

Corniolo *Cornus Mas*

Pomodoro *Lycopersicon Esculentum*

Salvia *Salvia Officinalis*

Ciliegio selvatico *Prunus Mahaleb*

Sorbo *Sorbus Domestica*

pavimentazione industriale in cemento/per esterni

Melo selvatico *Malus S'Yivestris*

Mimosa *Acacia Dealbata*

Nocciolo *Corylus Avellana*

EPDM pavimentazione anti trauma

Giuggiolo *Ziziphus Ziziphus*

Kumquat *Fortunella Japonica*

Corbezzolo *Arbutus Unedo*

Patata *Solanum Tuberosum*

Fagiolo *Phasolus Vulgaris*

Lavanda *Lavandula officinalis*

Menta piperita *Mentha piperita*

visualizzazione della piazza dall'alto inquadrando il comune

Sezione caratteristica est-ovest Scala 1:200

Project : International Competition for Requalification of Capital Garden Block
Location : Abu Dhabi(UAE)
Design Team : 2:pm architectures + G. Benais(arch)
Competition Results : Special Mention

//panel:01//

capitalDIAGONAL garDen

How to develop the site of "capital garden" as a central powerfull place in the urban, economic and social context of Abu Dhabi city?

We answer with a strategy based on the tourism development. Using the analysis of the population of the city wich is very specific, we transform the tourists as real protagonists of Abu Dhabi's population. We define appropriate program elements wich answer to each kind of population (locals/foreigners(expatriates)/tourists) needs.

To merge all the functions of the building, we decide the leisure become the main central and common part of our project (2 big swimming-pools/body-centers/spa/sport spaces/cultural center/art gallery/library/convention center..). Leisure is the central zone whereas hotels/business/housing and shopping are satellites.

There are 3 main elements constituent in our architecture. firstly, there is a tower typology wich answer to the urban density of the site. Secondly, we keep the idea of a big park relative to capital garden like a "big ground floor slab", wich is the link Between city and nature. Thirdly, we organize an underground complex network to enjoy the coolness of the soil with a big main street to offer a "diagonalisation" of our site block (this part is called "underground medina).
We consider the existing mosque as a social link and an important landmark/point of reference in the neighbourhood.Thus, we keep it.

We really want to propose a self-sufficient project using wind-proppelers, desalted water and photovoltaic-cells panels on the top of the towers.

Methods ; temporalizing + territorializing data
It is vital element for us to adapt our ways of thinking with the context of our architectural production. We want to conceive new methods of analysis and new instruments of urban planning that will introduce a dynamic and open dimension into our procedure. every urban elements or function is reduced to its digital existence and is quantified before it is given its shape in the town. That is why we illustrate all our intentions by means of diagrams, explaining different kind of complexity in the processing.

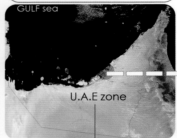

GULF sea

U.A.E zone

ABU DHABI ZONE

GEOGRAPHY

ABU DHABI CITY

site

city blocks urban grid

diagrams colors ID

[---] 212.247.199
[-] 186.239.165
[.] 148.244.110
[+] 94.243.35
[++] 71.180.28
[+++] 46.117.18

U.A.E:population
38% foreigners men
15% foreigners women
10% nationals men
nationals women

documentation sources :
all numeric datas from 2004 or 2005 updates
"dictionary of advanced architecture" actar
"wikipedia" "tourism" U.A.E and "abu dhabi" research
"gulf analysis" "geography" "tourism" urbanism..
"gulf rem koolhaas.AMO las muller publishers

the most spendthrift countries in term of tourism in the world

between 5 and 10   Billions of USD
between 10 and 15 Billions of USD
between 15 and 20 Billions of USD
between 20 and 30 Billions of USD
between 30 and 50 Billions of USD
more than 50 Billions of USD

the region origin of worldwide tourists

Africa : 17.7 millions of travellers
Americas : 115.3 millions of travellers
Asia : 155.4 millions of travellers
Europe : 408.5 millions of travellers

worldwide travellers : 690.9 millions
worldwide travellers in the same region : 561.8 millions
worldwide travellers in different regions : 117.7 millions

Gulf analysis
The coastal development is a new regional and global order. The ancient nomad site's 50 years ago are now making a big production of urban substance. The initial development due to the oil-natural reserves and production is now the base for an hyper-growing of the Gulf region in different categories of analysis: economy, culture, Tourism, urbanism...
The Gulf is in construction now. This construction is based on the repertoire of current urban prototypes: community (expats+local) + hotel (themed) + shopping center (largest), cemented together by public space. To resume, we can say that the population is the Gulf alternative energy source, as the ultimate configuration of the urban substance.

Why tour...
Demogr...
question...
Dhabi is...
Dhabi's...
developed...

Tourism i...
Since ab...
people)...
a relative...
The deve...
new kind...
that the...
emergen...
with the e...
(hot and...
desert ze...
ties.

Accordin...
rism is the...
slowing...
rism has...
become...
way to i...
text. Yet,...
to prope...
Dhabi is...
New tou...
tourism is...
and urb...

for u...
iden...
gon...
dha...

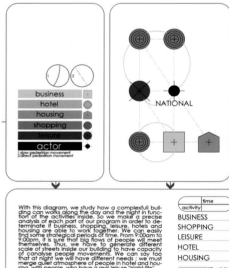

business
hotel
housing
shopping
leisure
actor
1:slow pedestrian movement
2:direct pedestrian movement

NATIONAL

With this diagram, we study how a complexfull building can works along the day and the night in function of the activities inside. So we make a precise analysis of each part of our program in order to determinate if business, shopping, leisure, hotels and housing are able to work together. We can easily find some strategical periods of time. From 9:00am to 9:00pm, it is sure that big flows of people will meet themselves. Thus, we have to generate different scale of streets inside our building to have capacity of canalyse people movements. We can say too that at night we will have different needs ; we must merge quiet atmosphere of people in hotel and housing. with people who have a real leisure "night-life".

activity	time
BUSINESS	
SHOPPING	
LEISURE	
HOTEL	
HOUSING	

0% activities
1-25% activities
25-50% activities
50-75% activities
75-100% activities

N

empty diagonals relative to full interaction spaces

to merge the street defined inside the building with the regular grid (5x5m in alignment with the diagonale)

...as, we start ...ults and mix ...We decide ...ur modular ...give more ...masterplan. ...grid is a ...n essential ...us the real ...e a project

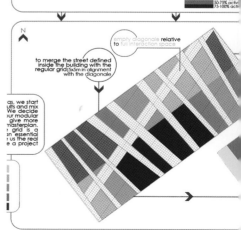

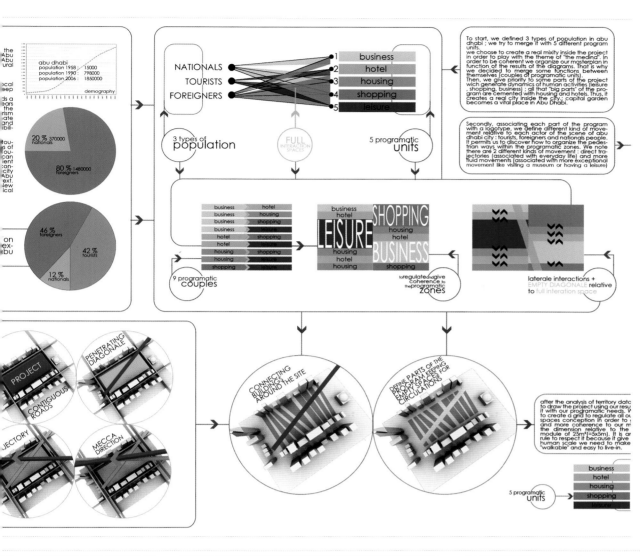

abu dhabi
population 1958 : 15000
population 1990 : 798000
population 2006 : 1850000

demography

3 types of
population

FULL
INTERACTION
SPACES

5 programatic
units

NATIONALS
TOURISTS
FOREIGNERS

1 business
2 hotel
3 housing
4 shopping
5 leisure

20 % 370000 nationals

80 % 1480000 foreigners

46 % foreigners

42 % tourists

12 % nationals

To start, we defined 3 types of population in abu dhabi ; we try to merge it with 5 different program units.
we choose to create a real mixity inside the project in order to play with the theme of "the medina". In order to be coherent we organize our masterplan in function of the results of the diagrams. That is why we decided to merge some functions between themselves (couples of programatic units).
Then, we give priority to some parts of the project wich generate dynamics of human activities (leisure , shopping, business) ; all that "big parts" of the program are cemented with housing and hotels. Thus, it creates a real city inside the city ; capital garden becomes a vital place in Abu Dhabi.

Secondly, associating each part of the program with a logotype, we define different kind of movement relative to each actor of the scene of abu dhabi city : tourists, foreigners and nationals people. It permits us to discover how to organize the pedestrian ways within the programatic zones. We note there are 2 different kinds of movement : direct trajectories (associated with everyday life) and more fluid movements (associated with more exceptional movement like visiting a museum or having a leisure).

business hotel
business housing
business shopping
business leisure
hotel shopping
hotel leisure
housing shopping
housing leisure
shopping leisure

9 programatic couples

LEISURE SHOPPING
business hotel housing housing
hotel hotel
housing housing
shopping business

to regulate and give coherence to the programatic zones

laterale interactions + EMPTY DIAGONALE relative to full interaction space

PROJECT
PENETRATING DIAGONALE
CONTIGUOUS ROADS
JECTORY
MECCA DIRECTION

CONNECTING BUILDINGS AROUND THE SITE

DEFINE PARTS OF THE PROGRAM KEEPING EMPTY SPACE FOR CIRCULATIONS

after the analysis of territory data to draw the project using our resu it with our programatic needs. to create a grid to regulate all ou spaces conception in order to and more coherence to our m the dimension relative to the module of 25m²(=5x5m). It is ar rule to respect it because if give human scale we need to make "walkable" and easy to live-in.

business
hotel
housing
shopping
leisure

5 programatic units

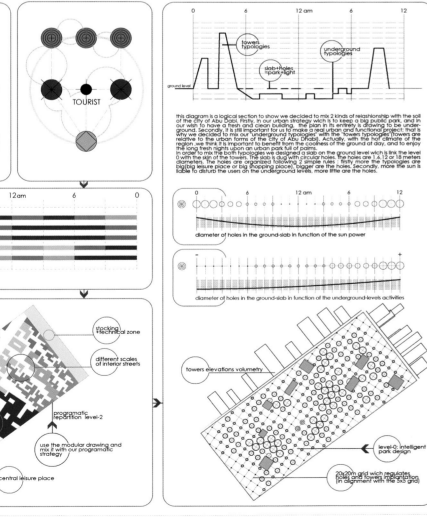

TOURIST

12am 6 0

stocking +Technical zone

different scales of interior streets

programatic repartition level-2

use the modular drawing and mix it with our programatic strategy

central leisure place

towers typologies

underground typologies

slab++holes +park+light

ground level

this diagram is a logical section to show we decided to mix 2 kinds of relashionship with the soil of the city of Abu Dabi. Firstly, in our urban strategy wich is to keep a big public park, and in our wish to have a fresh and clean building, the plan in its entirety is drawing to be underground. Secondly, it is still important for us to make a real urban and functional project; that is why we decided to mix our "underground typologies" with the "towers typologies" (towers are relative to the urban forms of the city of Abu Dhabi). Actually, with the hot climate of the region ,we think it is important to benefit from the coolness of the ground at day, and to enjoy the long fresh nights upon an urban park full of palms.
In order to mix the both typologies we designed a slab on the ground level wich is link the level 0 with the skin of the towers. The slab is dug with circular holes. The holes are 1.6, 12 or 18 meters diameters. The holes are organized following 2 simple rules : firstly more the typologies are big(big leisure place or big shopping place), bigger are the holes. Secondly, more the sun is liable to disturb the users on the underground levels, more little are the holes.

0 6 12 am 6 12

diameter of holes in the ground-slab in function of the sun power

diameter of holes in the ground-slab in function of the underground-levels activities

towers elevations volumetry

level-0: intelligent park design

20x20m grid wich regulates holes and towers implantion (in alignment with the 5x5 grid)

wind proppelers to keep benefits from sea wind corridor wind pomp connected with a self sufficient energy network

level-0-slab planted with natural palms +"intelligent-artificial-palms"

holes in the slab : it permits an urban park on level-0 + light in the underground levels

level -1 : level -2 : 2 levels of "underground-medina"

desalted water tank +technical network

level -3 : parking zone

the soil of the park is dug in order to enjoy the coolness for the underground levels

horizontal network : it transports water from sea to the building to be desalted

Environmental strategy
The concept is to reinvent a landscape based on the analysis of spatial and temporal processes of the accumulations and energies that ceaselessly deconstruct and reconstruct territory. As we see it, ecology is the priority for the development of contemporary cities. Ecology is not only environmental but also social. The disappearance of architecture is due to "the domestication of nature" and to "the naturalization of the domestic".

Our wish to be respectful of the environment gives us a real quality requirement in the building functionnent's elaboration. U.A.E are the third water consumers (after USA and Canada). U.A.E represents 20% of total worldwide palms. There are only 43mm of rainwater per year in Abu Dhabi, so the city has 130 millions of trees alimented by desalted water from the sea.

We choose to respect this cycle between the trees growing and the sea water. We decide to make a real network of wind propellers in order to use sea wind to generate a very-clean energy for the building alimentation. moreover we create on the "level:0-slab" a palm forest added to an "intelligent-artificial-palm" forest (see the text below). the soil inside the slab gives inertia for the building insulation.
We want minimize the conditionned-air making an underground building which keeps the benefits of the coolness of the soil.The holes in the "level0-slab" permit a natural ventilation of the building. With the windpomp, we can use the desalted sea-water for the trees of the park and for the 2 big swimming-pools in

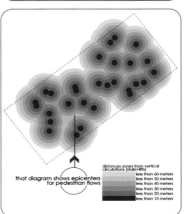

distances zones from vertical circulations (stairs-lifts)
less than 60 meters
less than 50 meters
less than 40 meters
less than 30 meters
less than 20 meters
less than 10 meters

that diagram shows epicenters for pedestrian flows

Flexible amorphous silicon photo-voltaic cells mounted on a silicon tree leaf (thickness: 2mm)

Flexible aluminium framework holding out a LED network

Our artificial Tree is an alternative urban object to answer to the soil-need for a tree, and the compulsory shadow need. Virtual tree is made of two kind of leaf: upper layer is photo-voltaic cells to capture sun light, and underneath a LED network for a night public lighting. Energy is stocked in batteries hidden in the trunk.

//panel:02//

1: master plan scale : 1/3000
2: plan level:-1 scale : 1/2000
3: section aa' scale : 1/2000
4: "underground-medina" typologies
development with 5x5m modular units grid
5: towers typologies
implantation/sections/plan levels
6: project axonometry

business
hotel
housing
shopping
leisure

1

2x25=50m²   4x25=100m²   5x25=125m²

3x25=75m²

little office big office meeting room   open space workshop

main leisure typologie
= swimming pool complex

retail shop   middle size shop   supermarket/mall
                   big shop

2

The masterplan shows a big park on the site's entirety. All
the holes on the "level:0 slab" are entries for light or people
inside the undergound-medina levels:-1and-2.

the level:-1 plan shows a high diversity of typologies inside
the streets of our underground medina. The diversity is
very present too in term of mixity of uses. All needs of users
are connected between themselves.The level:-1 drawing
is based on the level:-2 drawing. We cans say : "level:-2
less "level:-1" equal "a lot of terraces for the level:-1".

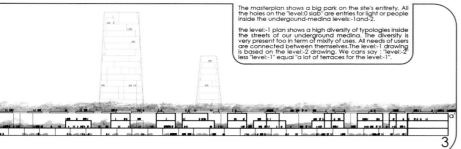

3

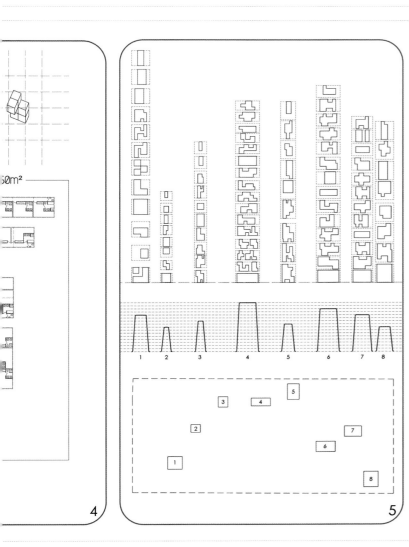

4

5

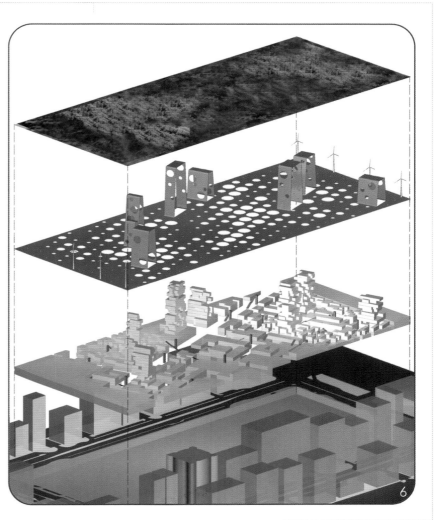

6

aerial view 1

aerial view 2

ound-medina view

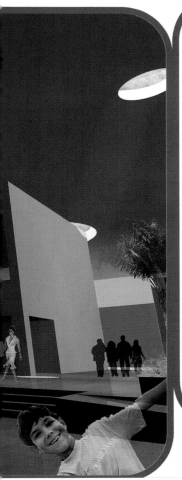

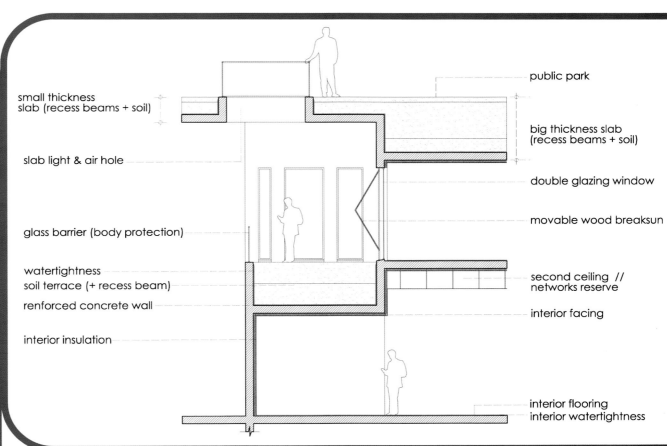

small thickness
slab (recess beams + soil)

slab light & air hole

glass barrier (body protection)

watertightness
soil terrace (+ recess beam)

renforced concrete wall

interior insulation

public park

big thickness slab
(recess beams + soil)

double glazing window

movable wood breaksun

second ceiling //
networks reserve

interior facing

interior flooring
interior watertightness

detail section : 1/50

OO-000 tampere - alice in wonderwall

01

POROSITY

CONTINUITY WITH
THE ENVIRONMENT

URBAN FRONT
3 storeys
buildings
in continuity
with the avenue
front

NATURAL
ENVIRONMENT
dispersed
2 storeys dwellings
enacting a deser onto

CONTEXTUAL
APPROACH

VUOREKSEN
PUISTOKATU FRONT

VUOREKSEN PUISTOKATU

SITE PLAN - 1/2000

0   20   100   200

I dreamt
I was hiding
within the walls,

FACADE ON VUOREKSEN PUISTOKATU - 1/300

OO-000 tampere - alice in wonderwall

1. PROGRAMMATIC SURFACE
2. DIVIDING INTO A REGULAR GRID
3. INSERTING ACTIVITIES BLOCKS
4. REACHING A NEW BALANCE
5. DOUBLE SKIN AS A BUFFER INT/EXT ZONE

INTERSTITIAL COLLECTIVE SPACE
DOMESTIC EXTERIOUR AREAS
IN-SKIN COLLECTIVE MIN. EXHIBITION SPACES
IN-SKIN COLLECTIVE MULTIPURPOSE SPACES
FOUR SIDES ORIENTATION

02

2nd FLOOR PLAN - 1/500

0 · · · 10 · · · 20 · · · · · 50

walking through
the gardens,
running up
the stairs,

1ST FLOOR PLAN - 1/500

0 · · 10 · · 20 · · · · 50

SITE PLAN - 1/200

0 · 2 · · · 10 · · · · 20

LONGITUDINAL SECTION - 1/200

0 · 2 · · · 10 · · · · 20

OO-000 tampere - alice in wonderwall

There is a constant interaction between the domestic space, the urban space and nature, elements which interfere one with the other through every aspect of the project.

Nature infiltrates the inner space through the winter gardens, while the outdoor squares get a domestic scale and the walls of the houses give urban value to the network of collective spaces.

"LA PEAU EST CE QU'IL Y A DE PLUS PROFOND"
("What is most deep is the skin", P. Valéry)

All the buildings are of high energetic efficiency while no special technology is added. The typologies themselves are rethought to reach a minimal thermal dispersion (passive houses) and to optimize the temperature in relation to the needs of the single spaces.

The peripheral walls of every house become conceptual and physical double skins, integrating two different levels of insulation: an inner skin (the house structural core), constituted by opaque Poroton® hollow bricks, providing a first level of thermal insulation through Perlite® infills; and an outer skin of translucent Polycarbonate containing Nanogel®, in order to get a complete insulation.

The distance between the inner and outer surfaces is large enough to host inhabitable areas. This space acts as a buffer zone: it thermally insulates the rooms inside from the cold and at the same time it creates unusual domestic ambiances within the house. Here one can find the elements of the house which require a lower level of warmth, like storage rooms and closets, staircases, corridors, or even a winter garden, an atelier, a mini gym or a space with no specific function (or whose function has to be invented by the inhabitants).

Here the double skin loses its original technical purpose to become a real tool for defining, adapting or generating space.

WINTER GARDEN -
STAYING OUTSIDE WHILE IN THE HOUSE

DOUBLE SKIN
UNUSUAL DOMESTIC AMBIENCES

until I was
no longer
inside
nor outside.

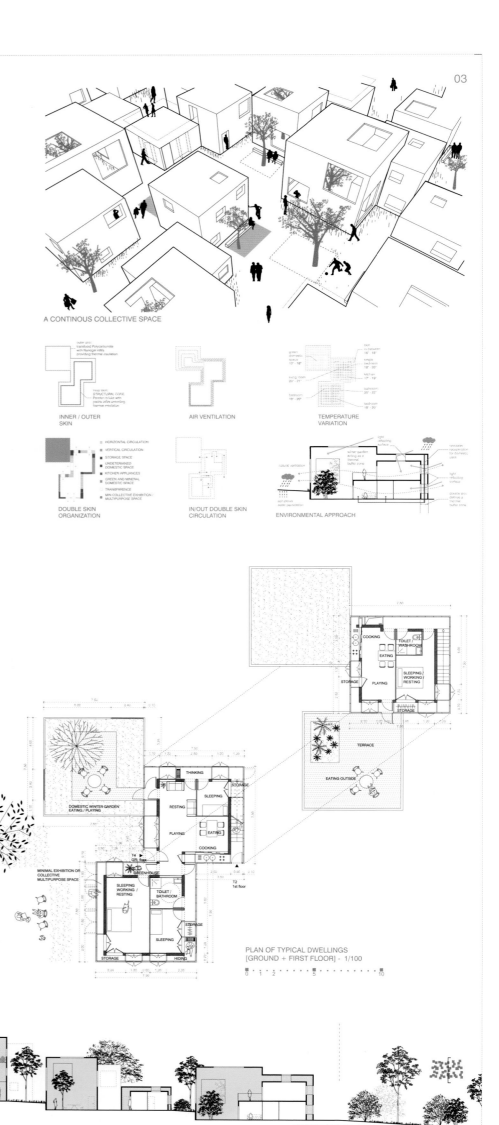

A CONTINOUS COLLECTIVE SPACE

INNER / OUTER SKIN

AIR VENTILATION

TEMPERATURE VARIATION

DOUBLE SKIN ORGANIZATION

IN/OUT DOUBLE SKIN CIRCULATION

ENVIRONMENTAL APPROACH

PLAN OF TYPICAL DWELLINGS
[GROUND + FIRST FLOOR] - 1/100

CROSS SECTION - 1/200

Ploughed Fields | *Alessandro Console Studio*

Typology : Masterplan
Project Team : Alessandro Console, Gina Oliva, Claudia Streuli, Giorgio Streuli

Competition : Europan 10
Promoter : Europan Europe – Local Municipality
Location : Jarvenpaa, Finland

XY 004
JÄRVENPÄÄ - FINLAND

T0

T1: structuring

T2: adding

T3: linking

system #1: HOUSING

system #2: COMMON SPACES & SERVICES

system #3: LARGE GREEN AREAS

system #4: CULTIVATIONS

system #5: PRIVATE GARDENS

system #5: EQUIPPED GREEN AREAS

PLOUGHED FIELDS

1

PLOUGHED FIELDS is made by two main categories: the Landstripes and the Public Services Band.

LANSTRIPES
The Landstripes are the leading infrastructure of the new urban system and they play a dual role in defining and managing the configuration and organization of the whole area:

1. The Landstripes allows to link and to connect all the elements existing in the area (residential, cultural, agricultural elements) by creating a widespread network within the study site.
As a matter of fact, all the existing elements in the area currently seems to be isolated, so that they need to be integrated within a structured and well-oriented system.
Like the staff for the musical notes and like the sea for the achipelago's islands, the Landstripes are the backbone of the system that reaches out from the west shoreline of Lake Tuusula, to the railway line, eastward. The Landstripes define the main links within the area and the city centre and manage the traffic flows and the streets network.

2. The Landstripes allow to steer the development of new residential areas within the project site by playing a programmatic role and undertaking different characterizations.
Within the project site, indeed, there are three different kind of Landstripes characterized by a different percentage of anthropic and natural elements settled within them. The variation of these elements creates the specific feature of each Landstripes.

The 3 main Landstripes are:
- RESIDENTIAL LANDSTRIPES where there is a higher percentage of anthropic elements.
Each RL is characterized and structured by various morfphological combinations of residential typologies.
- GREEN LANDSTRIPES where natural elements are predominant. There are 2 green landstrips: the first one (northwards) is an open green area that creates an ecological corridor between the railway and the lake; the other is a green infilling area that continues and implements the existing wood.
- AGRICULTURAL LANDSTRIPES that host togheter residential areas and cultivations.

PUBLIC SERVICES BAND
The Public Services Band crosses the area linking in North-South direction all the leading Landstripes.
The Band hosts three main categories of public services:
A. Sport Facilities: sport fields - areas for physical and training activities indoor and outdoor;
B. Social, Cultural and Educational Services: day-care centre, school, elderly centre etc..
C. Areas and Plants for Energy Production: small-scale wind farms, photovoltaic panels, solar collectors etc..

This band represents and defines the main direction for connecting the residential areas in the south (Terioja and Ristinummi) and the north (Lepola and Kyrola) to the city center. The Band also becomes the main axis able to link all the public service facilities existing in the area and to orient their future location and development within the site.

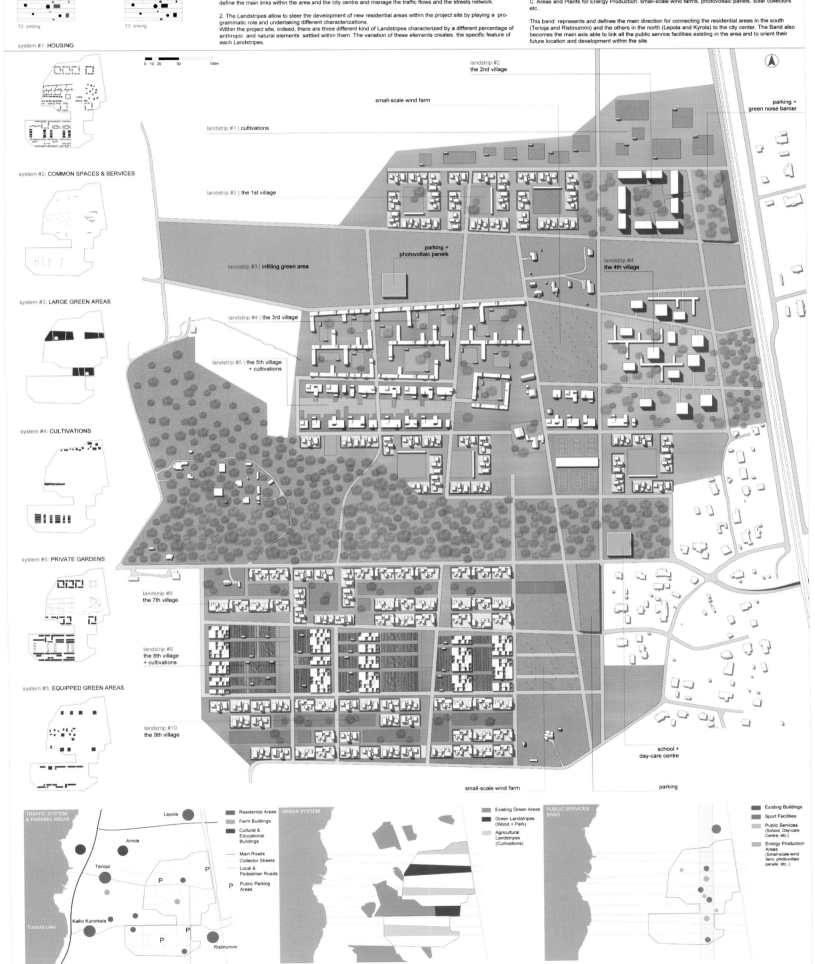

landstrip #2
the 2nd village

small-scale wind farm

parking +
green noise barrier

landstrip #1 | cultivations

landstrip #2 | the 1st village

parking +
photovoltaic panels

landstrip #4
the 4th village

landstrip #3 | infilling green area

landstrip #4 | the 3rd village

landstrip #5 | the 5th village
+ cultivations

landstrip #8
the 7th village

landstrip #9
the 8th village
+ cultivations

landstrip #10
the 9th village

school +
day-care centre

small-scale wind farm

parking

TRAFFIC SYSTEM
& PARKING AREAS

Lepola

Ainola

Terioja

Kallio Kuninkala

Tuusula Lake

Ristinummi

Residential Areas
Farm Buildings
Cultural & Educational Buildings
Main Roads
Collector Streets
Local & Pedestrian Roads
P Public Parking Areas

GREEN SYSTEM

Existing Green Areas
Green Landstripes (Wood + Park)
Agricultural Landstripes (Cultivations)

PUBLIC SERVICES BAND

Existing Buildings
Sport Facilities
Public Services (School, Day-care Centre, etc.)
Energy Production Areas (Small-scale wind farm, photovoltaic panels etc.)

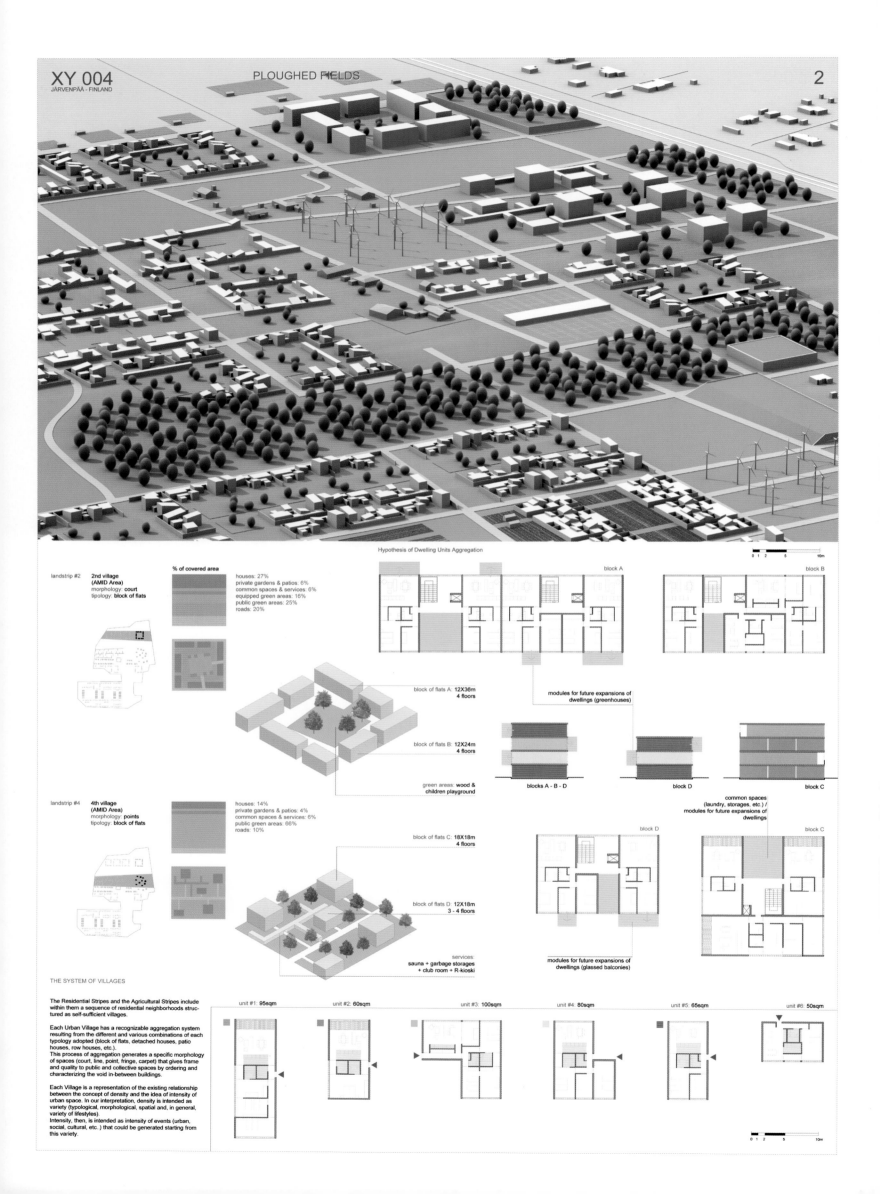

Hypothesis of Dwelling Units Aggregation

0 1 2 5 10m

landstrip #2   **2nd village
(AMID Area)**
morphology: **court**
tipology: **block of flats**

% of covered area

houses: 27%
private gardens & patios: 6%
common spaces & services: 6%
equipped green areas: 16%
public green areas: 25%
roads: 20%

block A

block B

block of flats A: **12X36m**
4 floors

modules for future expansions of
dwellings (greenhouses)

block of flats B: **12X24m**
4 floors

green areas: **wood &
children playground**

blocks A - B - D   block D   block C

landstrip #4   **4th village
(AMID Area)**
morphology: **points**
tipology: **block of flats**

houses: 14%
private gardens & patios: 4%
common spaces & services: 6%
public green areas: 66%
roads: 10%

common spaces
(laundry, storages, etc.) /
modules for future expansions of
dwellings

block D

block C

block of flats C: **18X18m**
4 floors

block of flats D: **12X18m**
3 - 4 floors

services:
**sauna + garbage storages
+ club room + R-kioski**

modules for future expansions of
dwellings (glassed balconies)

THE SYSTEM OF VILLAGES

The Residential Stripes and the Agricultural Stripes include
within them a sequence of residential neighborhoods structured as self-sufficient villages.

Each Urban Village has a recognizable aggregation system
resulting from the different and various combinations of each
typology adopted (block of flats, detached houses, patio
houses, row houses, etc.).
This process of aggregation generates a specific morphology
of spaces (court, line, point, fringe, carpet) that gives frame
and quality to public and collective spaces by ordering and
characterizing the void in-between buildings.

Each Village is a representation of the existing relationship
between the concept of density and the idea of intensity of
urban space. In our interpretation, density is intended as
variety (typological, morphological, spatial and, in general,
variety of lifestyles).
Intensity, then, is intended as intensity of events (urban,
social, cultural, etc.) that could be generated starting from
this variety.

unit #1: **95sqm**   unit #2: **60sqm**   unit #3: **100sqm**   unit #4: **80sqm**   unit #5: **65sqm**   unit #6: **50sqm**

0 1 2 5 10m

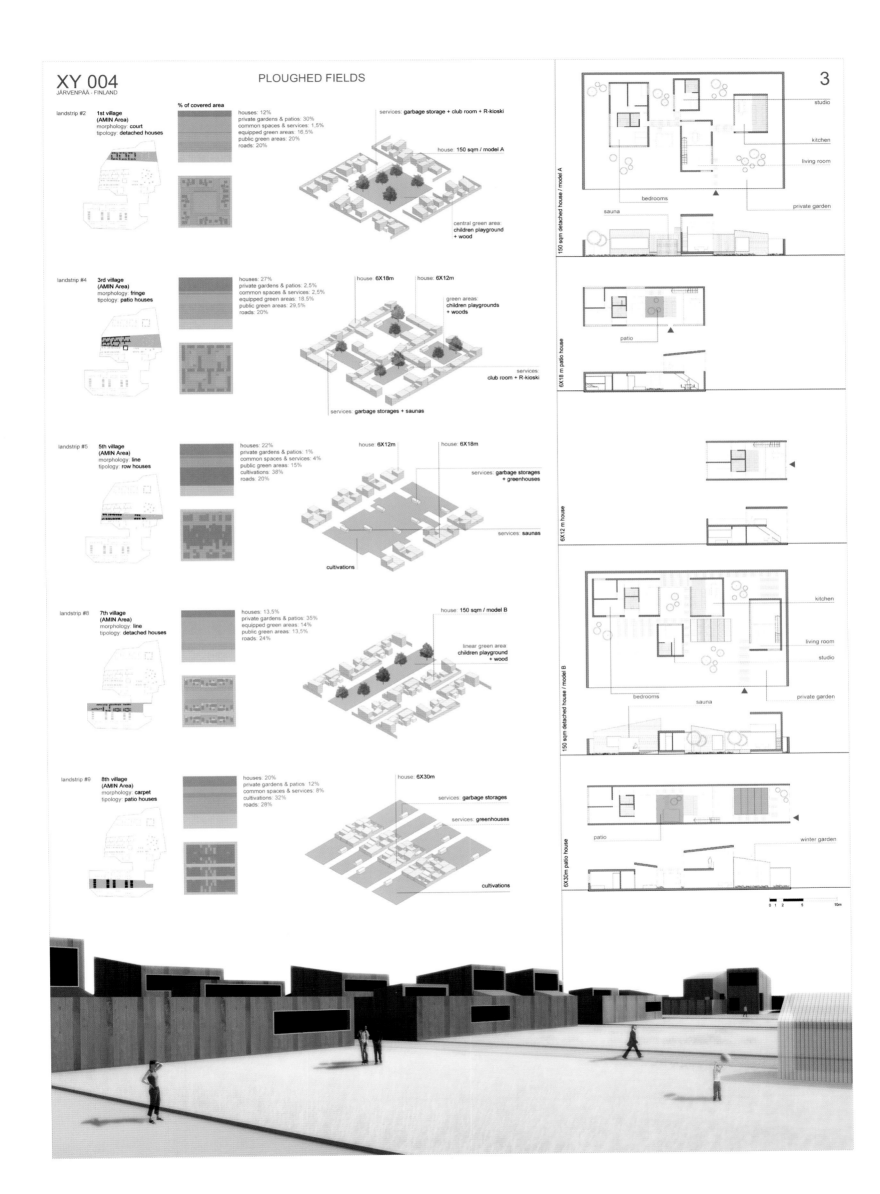

XY 004
JÄRVENPÄÄ - FINLAND

PLOUGHED FIELDS

3

landstrip #2 | **1st village**
(AMIN Area)
morphology: **court**
tipology: **detached houses**

% of covered area

houses: 12%
private gardens & patios: 30%
common spaces & services: 1,5%
equipped green areas: 16,5%
public green areas: 20%
roads: 20%

services: **garbage storage + club room + R-kioski**

house: **150 sqm / model A**

central green area:
**children playground
+ wood**

landstrip #4 | **3rd village**
(AMIN Area)
morphology: **fringe**
tipology: **patio houses**

houses: 27%
private gardens & patios: 2,5%
common spaces & services: 2,5%
equipped green areas: 18,5%
public green areas: 29,5%
roads: 20%

house: **6X18m**   house: **6X12m**

green areas:
**children playgrounds
+ woods**

services:
club room + R-kioski

services: **garbage storages + saunas**

landstrip #5 | **5th village**
(AMIN Area)
morphology: **line**
tipology: **row houses**

houses: 22%
private gardens & patios: 1%
common spaces & services: 4%
public green areas: 15%
cultivations: 38%
roads: 20%

house: **6X12m**   house: **6X18m**

services: **garbage storages
+ greenhouses**

services: **saunas**

cultivations

landstrip #8 | **7th village**
(AMIN Area)
morphology: **line**
tipology: **detached houses**

houses: 13,5%
private gardens & patios: 35%
equipped green areas: 14%
public green areas: 13,5%
roads: 24%

house: **150 sqm / model B**

linear green area:
**children playground
+ wood**

landstrip #9 | **8th village**
(AMIN Area)
morphology: **carpet**
tipology: **patio houses**

houses: 20%
private gardens & patios 12%
common spaces & services: 8%
cultivations: 32%
roads: 28%

house: **6X30m**

services: **garbage storages**

services: **greenhouses**

cultivations

studio
kitchen
living room
bedrooms
sauna
private garden

150 sqm detached house / model A

patio

6X18 m patio house

6X12 m house

kitchen
living room
studio
bedrooms
sauna
private garden

150 sqm detached house / model B

patio
winter garden

6X30m patio house

0 1 2   5   10m

278

Art Wood | *2A+P/A*

Type : Design Competition "EPK - Drava River 2010"
Program : Museum
Team : 2A+P/A, Andrea Branzi
Location : Maribor, Slovenia / Year : 2010

Model : Marco Galofaro/Modelab
Photo : Sebastiano Costanzo

1 ARCHITECTURAL COMPETITION
EPK DRAVA 2012

91660 / 3

SITE PLAN - SCALE 1:1000

1 Gallery Shops
2 Apartments
3 Information Centre
4 Bar
5 Restaurant
6 Club
7 Catering Terrace

Ecological Roof

Pine-wood Art Museum

Greenhouses

Public Functions

Public Square

Underground Art Museum

GROUND FLOOR PLAN (PUBLIC SPACE) - SCALE 1:400

AXONOMETRIC VIEW

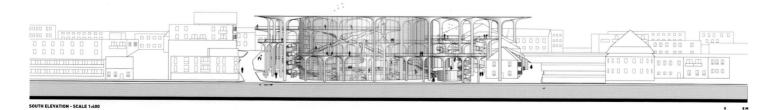

SOUTH ELEVATION - SCALE 1:400

2 ARCHITECTURAL COMPETITION
EPK DRAVA 2012

91660 / 3

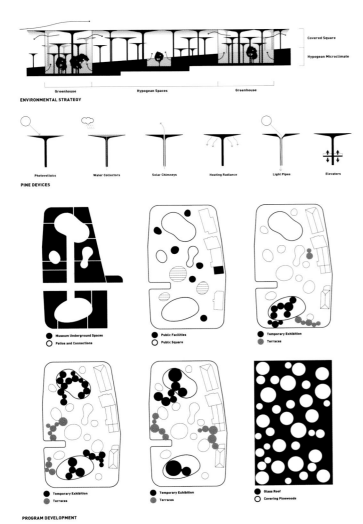

Covered Square

Hypogean Microclimate

Greenhouse   Hypogean Spaces   Greenhouse

ENVIRONMENTAL STRATEGY

Photovoltaics   Water Collectors   Solar Chimneys   Heating Radiance   Light Pipes   Elevators

PINE DEVICES

● Museum Underground Spaces   ● Public Facilities   ● Temporary Exhibition
○ Patios and Connections   ○ Public Square   ● Terraces

● Temporary Exhibition   ● Temporary Exhibition   ● Glass Roof
● Terraces   ● Terraces   ○ Covering Pinewoods

PROGRAM DEVELOPMENT

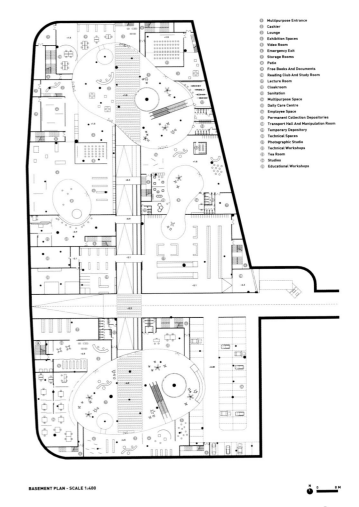

1. Multipurpose Entrance
2. Cashier
3. Lounge
4. Exhibition Spaces
5. Video Room
6. Emergency Exit
7. Storage Rooms
8. Patio
9. Free Books And Documents
10. Reading Club And Study Room
11. Lecture Room
12. Cloakroom
13. Sanitation
14. Multipurpose Space
15. Daily Care Centre
16. Employee Space
17. Permanent Collection Depositories
18. Transport Hall And Manipulation Room
19. Temporary Depository
20. Technical Spaces
21. Photographic Studio
22. Technical Workshops
23. Tea Room
24. Studies
25. Educational Workshops

BASEMENT PLAN - SCALE 1:400

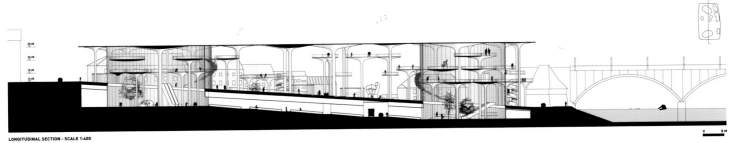

LONGITUDINAL SECTION - SCALE 1:400

3 **ARCHITECTURAL COMPETITION**
EPK DRAVA 2012

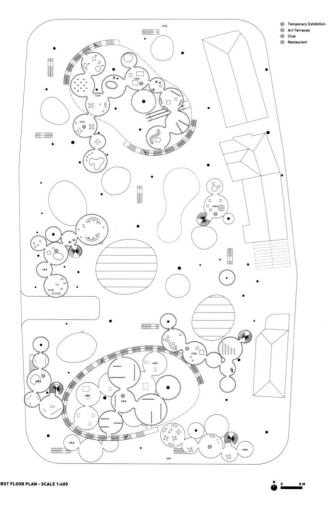

① Temporary Exhibition
② Art Terraces
③ Club
④ Restaurant

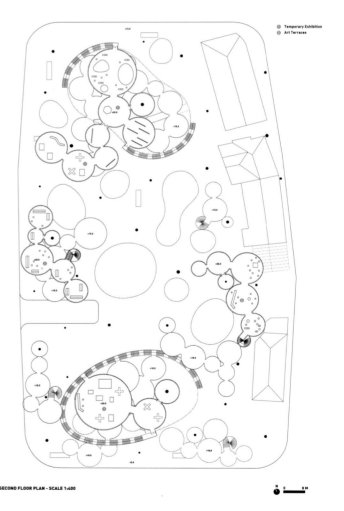

① Temporary Exhibition
② Art Terraces

FIRST FLOOR PLAN - SCALE 1:400

SECOND FLOOR PLAN - SCALE 1:400

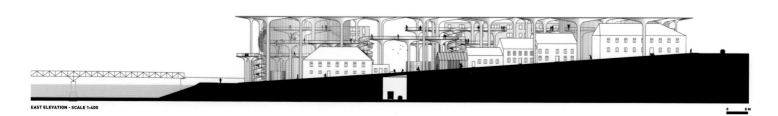

EAST ELEVATION - SCALE 1:400

CROSS SECTION - SCALE 1:200

0   4 M

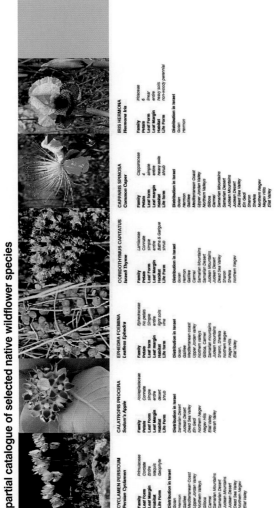

partial catalogue of selected native wildflower species

partial catalogue of selected migratory bird species

fields of dreams
A performative metamorphosis of BatYam

What about air quality?

A series of small-scale adaptive urban gardens embedding nature into the heart of the city...

As an adaptive system, **airfield BatYam** offers an opportunity to embed performative small- and large-scale landscapes throughout the city over time. Native plant life and migrant wildlife from throughout the Levant will be reintroduced into the heart of the Tel Aviv metropolitan area. As a flexible network, **airfield BatYam** establishes a platform for Bat Yam's residents to engage themselves in the re-naturalization of their own neighborhoods. Beyond serving the medicinal needs of residents, **airfield BatYam** will offer sanctuaries for birds and butterflies. The construct shown above, provides a found nesting habitat for urban birds, as well as a sculptural architectural folly for the visual curiosity and enjoyment of residents and visitors. Small steps toward improving citywide air quality...

airfield BatYam
pocket parks

fields of dreams
A performative metamorphosis of BatYam

What about nature?

An adaptive cellular system that can be deployed citywide

A wildflower promenade serving residents and visitors alike...

Let's take back the streets for pedestrians and bike riders! Flowering medicinal plants and wildflowers form the basis of the **flowerfield BatYam** performative landscape. These plants, native to the Middle East, propagate throughout the region and are commonly found in all nations of the Levant. Transcending time and national borders, such medicinals offer Bat Yam's residents and visitors an opportunity to directly connect with a shared natural resource. Medicinal plants for **flowerfield BatYam** were selected for their curative and performative, as well as visual qualities.

flowerfield BatYam
international peace park

fields of dreams
A performative metamorphosis of BatYam

What about food?

Before   After

"By partnering in with the city's Fields of Dreams programme, I was able to transform my sidelot from a plot of grass and weeds into a communal food production space. A vertical herb garden, pear tree, and perennial meadow generate curative and cooking herbs for my own family and my neighbors. Instead of using a petrol-fueled lawn mower, we now harvest our own food that supplements our needs year-round."

Vertical Gardens
deployable, modular, soil-based

A supportive system allowing citizens to participate in the re-greening of their city...

By reappropriating lost territories within their own districts, the system offers a chance to activate underperforming public, as well as private, landscapes. This ground-up strategy combines top-down and bottom-up interventions allowing the system to determine a balance between the built and natural environments. By merging both realms, **commonfield BatYam** works to engage all citizens in the greening and improved performance of their city.

commonfield BatYam
home-based food production

fields of dreams

Team : Enrique Badillo, Roberto Cantu, Myles Chumchal, Mohammed Gowayed, Amanda Kroll, Rigoberto Moreno, Mirna Ovalle, Marc Whitmore

Won an Honorable Mention from the Association of Collegiate Schools of Architecture(ACSA)
Institution : University of Houston Gerald D. Hines College of Architecture
Faculty : Prof. Gregory Marinic

DIASPORIC LANDSCAPES

Greater Houston is the fourth largest metropolitan area in the United States. Over the last 30 years, the region has witnessed an unprecedented expansion. Dramatic growth and demographic shifts have transformed the city into a thoroughly international place. With over 90 languages are spoken, Houston is undeniably a multicultural region and home to an estimated 1.1 million foreign-born residents. Two international airports and a major seaport make the city a natural base for the nation's third-largest concentration of consular offices. Houston's unzoned land use policy promotes inherently fluid occupancies. Cultural shifts correspondingly register considerably faster in Houston than in cities governed by more conventional regulation. With demographic diversity and free market commercialism as a filter, it may be argued that a singularly Western perspective has become increasingly irrelevant.

If architecture and landscape reflect culture, how can contemporary architects engage influences that more accurately convey recent flows and influences on the region?
How might we engage the cultural, territorial, and temporal memory of the 'new' Houstonians?
How might we appropriate aspects of their experience into the built and natural landscapes of the city?

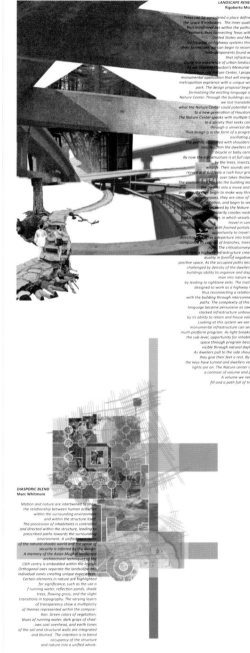

LANDSCAPE RENEWAL
Rigoberto Moreno

DIASPORIC BLEND
Marc Whitmore

PERSIAN PATHS
MIRNA OVALLE

Through an analysis of Persian gardens and Houston's Memorial Park Arboretum & Nature Center site, my collage conveys an interaction between nature and building. Given the task of designing a public and private space on Memorial Park, my design will combine Houston and Iranian landscape. By taking the ancient Persian concept of having a series of thresholds that bring together the elements of light, space, and courtyards, my building will itself become the transition from the urban city to a natural landscape.

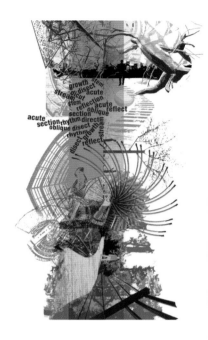

CULTURAL LAYERS
Roberto Cantu

Studying the culture of Persian miniature painting, I identified a specific technique of creating a sense of space through paintings. Since Persian miniature painting started and peaked at a very early point in time, their painting technique may be considered somewhat primitive.

TEMPORAL LIGHT
Amanda Kroll

NATURAL TRANSFORMATION
Myles Chumchal

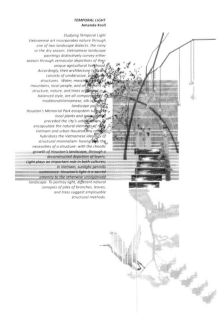

CHALLENGING SYMMETRY
Mohammed Gowayed

In this collage I convey the symmetry and balance in Moghul gardens and landscapes. Moghuls use a Charbagh system that was influenced by the Persians. The top photo is the Tomb of Humayun, an example of the symmetry employed in Moghul gardens.

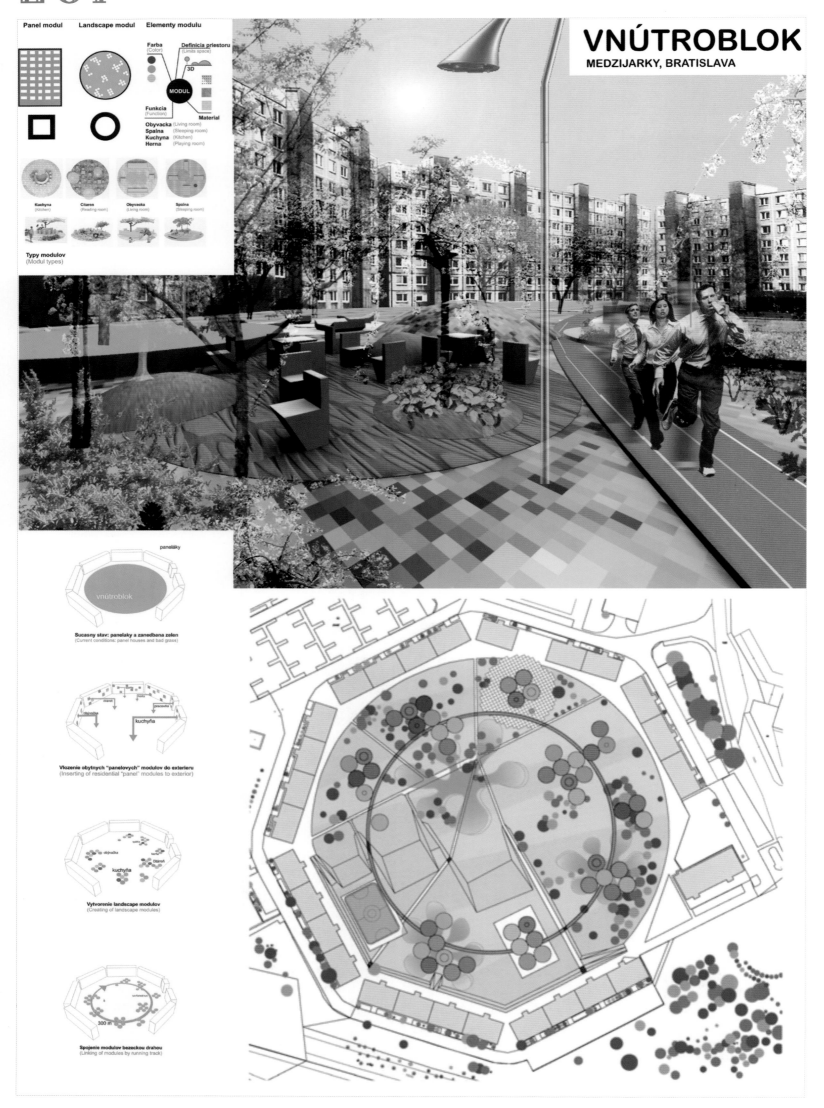

Panel modul **Landscape modul** **Elementy modulu**

Farba (Color)
Definícia priestoru (Limits space)
3D
MODUL
Funkcia (Function)
Material

Obyvacka (Living room)
Spalna (Sleeping room)
Kuchyna (Kitchen)
Herna (Playing room)

Kuchyna (Kitchen)
Citaren (Reading room)
Obyvacka (Living room)
Spalna (Sleeping room)

Typy modulov (Modul types)

VNÚTROBLOK
MEDZIJARKY, BRATISLAVA

paneláky

vnútroblok

Sucasny stav: panelaky a zanedbana zelen
(Current conditions: panel houses and bad grass)

Vlozenie obytnych "panelovych" modulov do exterieru
(Inserting of residential "panel" modules to exterior)

Vytvorenie landscape modulov
(Creating of landscape modules)

300 m

Spojenie modulov bezeckou drahou
(Linking of modules by running track)

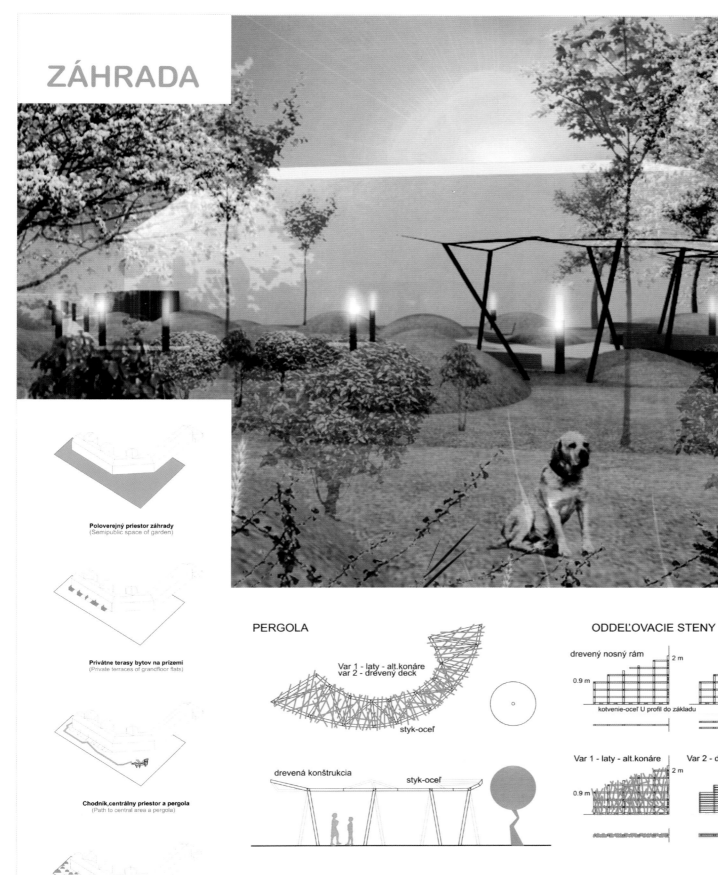

ZÁHRADA

Poloverejný priestor záhrady
(Semipublic space of garden)

Privátne terasy bytov na prízemí
(Private terraces of grandfloor flats)

Chodník, centrálny priestor a pergola
(Path to central area a pergola)

Kopcový landscape
(Landscape of hills)

Vloženie privátnych záhradiek a ovocných stromov
(Inserting of private gardens and fruit trees)

PERGOLA

Var 1 - laty - alt. konáre
var 2 - dreveny deck

styk-oceľ

drevená konštrukcia

styk-oceľ

ODDEĽOVACIE STENY

drevený nosný rám   2 m

0.9 m

kotvenie-oceľ U profil do základu

okolo steny

Var 1 - laty - alt. konáre   Var 2 - drevený deck   2 m

0.9 m

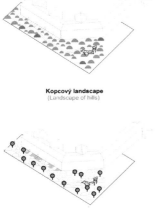

283

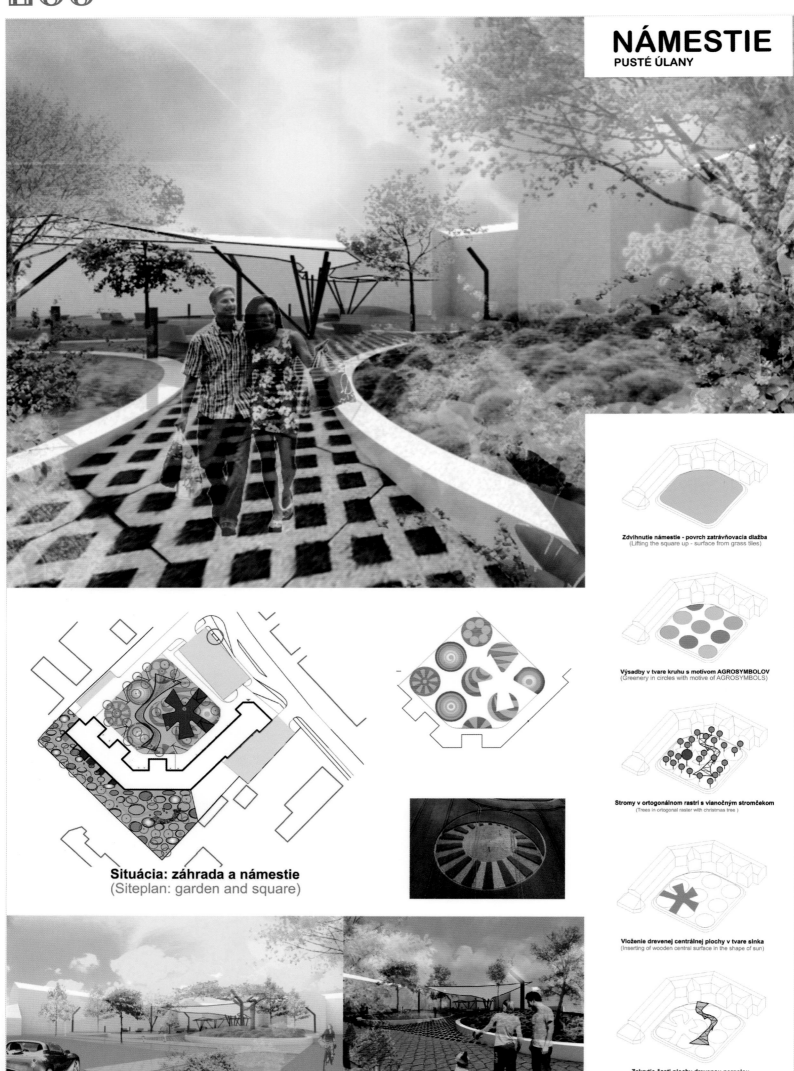

NÁMESTIE
PUSTÉ ÚLANY

Zdvihnutie námestie - povrch zatrávňovacia dlažba
(Lifting the square up - surface from grass tiles)

Výsadby v tvare kruhu s motívom AGROSYMBOLOV
(Greenery in circles with motive of AGROSYMBOLS)

Stromy v ortogonálnom rastri s vianočným stromčekom
(Trees in ortogonal raster with christmas tree)

Vloženie drevenej centrálnej plochy v tvare slnka
(Inserting of wooden central surface in the shape of sun)

Zakrytie časti plochy drevenou pergolou
(Roofing part of the square with wooden pergola)

Situácia: záhrada a námestie
(Siteplan: garden and square)

Cityscape 1 | *Horhizon consortium*

Team : Eva Sommeregger
Build the City Around Yourself
Type : Film

Antananarivo Barcelona Berlin Brasilia Damascus Hong Kong Johannesburg Lahore London Muscat New York Paris Rome Sao Paolo Tokyo Vienna

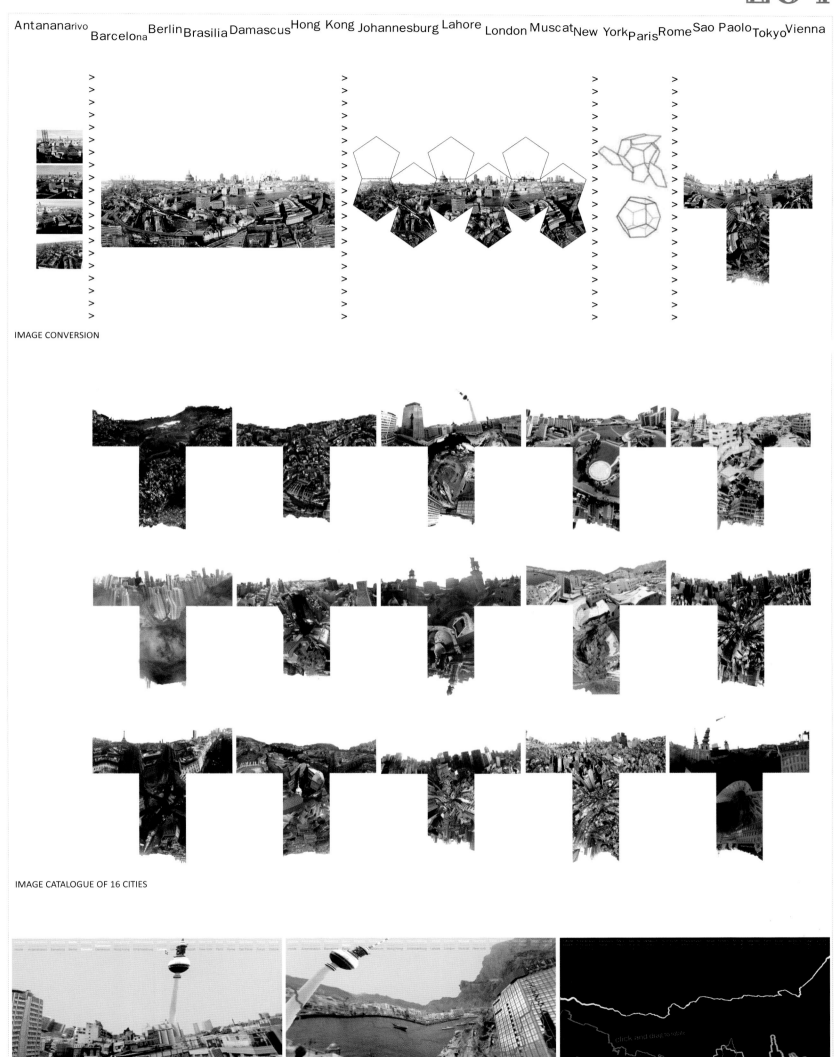

IMAGE CONVERSION

IMAGE CATALOGUE OF 16 CITIES

CITYSCAPE.AT 360°ONLINE APPLICATION

285

Las | *scandurrastudio*

Location : New York, USA
Design : Gregory Marinic, Principal

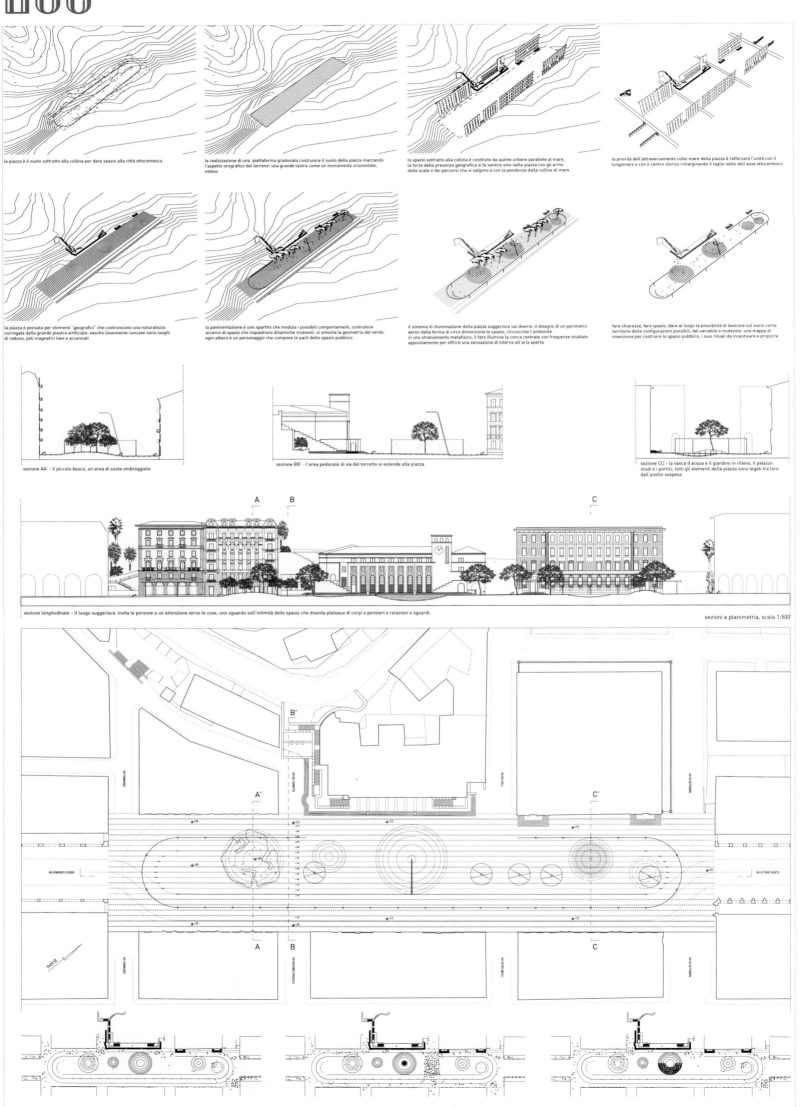

la piazza è il vuoto sottratto alla collina per dare spazio alla città ottocentesca

la realizzazione di una piattaforma gradonata costruisce il suolo della piazza marcando l'aspetto orografico del terreno: una grande lastra come un monumento orizzontale, esteso

lo spazio sottratto alla collina è costituito da quinte urbane parallele al mare, la forza della presenza geografica si fa sentire sino nella piazza con gli arrivi delle scale e dei percorsi che vi salgono e con la pendenza dalla collina al mare

la priorità dell'attraversamento colle-mare della piazza è rafforzare l'unità con il lungomare e con il centro storico rimarginando il taglio netto dell'asse ottocentesco

la piazza è pensata per elementi "geografici" che costruiscono una naturalezza surrogata della grande piastra artificiale: vasche lievemente concave sono luoghi di raduno, poli magnetici lievi e accennati

la pavimentazione è uno spartito che modula i possibili comportamenti, costruisce accenni di spazio che inquadrano dinamiche mutevoli. si smonta la geometria del verde, ogni albero è un personaggio che compone le parti dello spazio pubblico

il sistema di illuminazione della piazza suggerisce usi diversi: il disegno di un perimetro aereo dalla forma di circo dimensiona lo spazio, circoscrive l'ambiente in uno straniamento metafisico, il faro illumina la conca centrale con frequenze studiate appositamente per offrire una sensazione di interno all'aria aperta

fare chiarezza, fare spazio, dare al luogo la possibilità di lavorare sul vuoto come territorio delle configurazioni possibili, del variabile e mutevole: una mappa di invenzione per costruire lo spazio pubblico, i suoi rituali da incentivare e proporre

sezione AA' – il piccolo bosco, un'area di sosta ombreggiata

sezione BB' – l'area pedonale di via del torretto si estende alla piazza

sezione CC' – la vasca d'acqua e il giardino in rilievo, il palazzo studi e i portici, tutti gli elementi della piazza sono legati tra loro dall'anello sospeso

sezione longitudinale – Il luogo suggerisce, invita le persone a un'attenzione verso le cose, uno sguardo sull'intimità dello spazio che diventa plateaux di corpi e pensieri e relazioni e sguardi.

sezioni e planimetria, scala 1:500

nord

gli elementi geografici della piazza si rivelano un palcoscenico di comportamenti possibili, di relazioni tra persone e parti di città, cerniera tra mare e colla: concerti, eventi e ogni tipo di manifestazione di carattere pubblico.

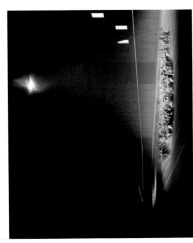

286

Bastion Lattice | *Thurlow Small Architecture*

800

Hadspen Parabola Garden Competition Proposal
Location : Somerset, England
Design Team : Andrew Thurlow, Snehal Intwala
Competition Sponsor : Hadspen House and Garden

bastion lattice

In the shadow of the Hadspen wall, this project conflates the social and spatial traditions of the bastion and the parterre into a contemporary landscape experience. The bastion system, like Lucca Italy's now pedestriated ramparts, are more than a physical edifice, they sponsor a social event-structure, the passeggiata, a viewing promenade in an elevated garden. As an archipelago, the bastions are a series of episodic, yet interconnected, terraces for viewing the subdivided ornamental arrangement of flowerbeds and the surrounding walls. Each bastion organizes a series of landscape systems: the first, the bastion edges, are socles that replicate the lenticular pattern of the whole garden as a smaller-scale, textural, stone lattice. The pattern modulates down its length and forms diamond shaped planters as well as a system for vertical garden walls. The second are ramps that allow access on top of the bastions that literally and figuratively elevate the pedestrian to a performer in the promenade. The

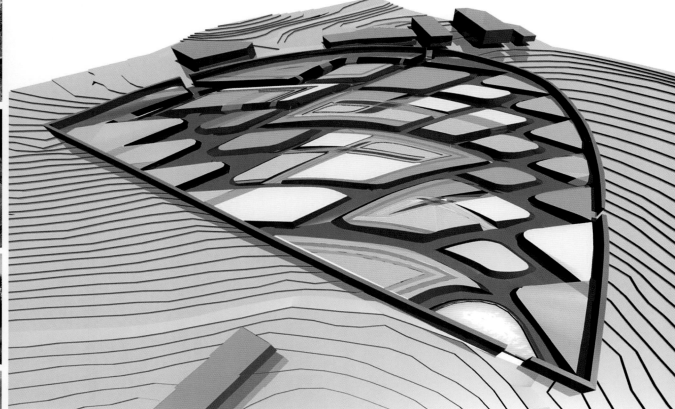

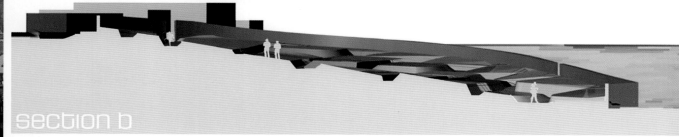

section b

section c

flower types

Name:
Common Foxglove
Species:
purpurea

Name:
Windflower
Species:
anemone

Name:
Fusilier Carnation
Species:
Dianthus

that create the parterres, a highly controlled, floral field space composed of
The hedges are a series of permeable vegetative boundaries that organize the
allow for visual continuity. And finally, the fourth are parterre beds that proj-
nd texture horizontally as a quilt of mini-fields. A series of registrations from
ulled across and expanded in section define the geometry of the garden. While
ied to the space of each bastion, the geometry links across, tying the lenticular
a larger system that allows the viewer to reference and rereference the tex-
e garden as a whole. Here, the passage of the passegiata involves an infinitely
ce of moving through the primary and secondary systems of the FOA paths
ew paralleling tertiary and quaternary systems of rising and falling, moving and
nd being viewed across a series of berms and hedges, through fields of horizon-
vertical stones.

beaulieu

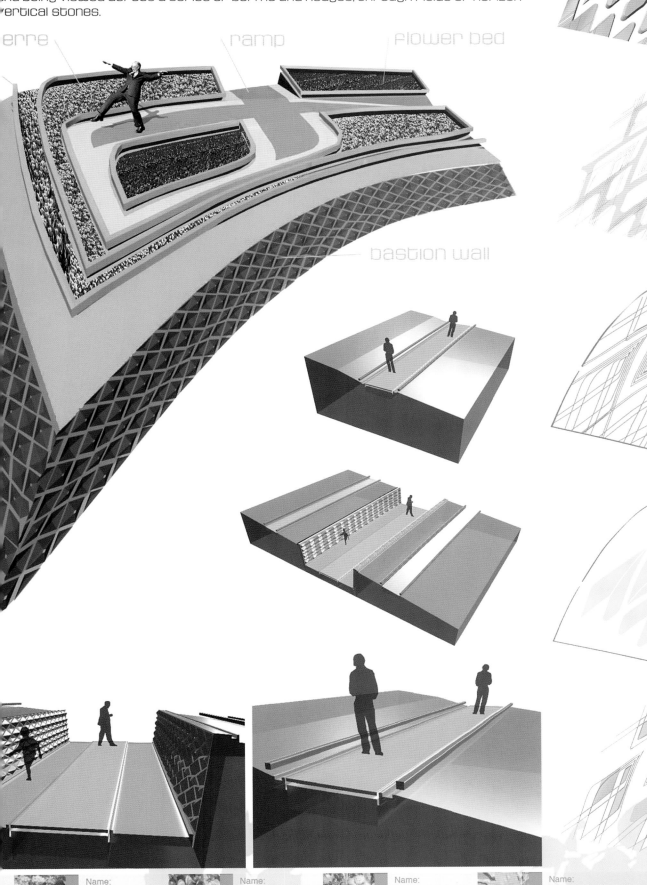

erre   ramp   flower bed

bastion wall

Name:
Golden Garlic
Species:
moly

Name:
Aubretia
Species:
x cultorum

Name:
Mexican Sunflower
Species:
rotundifolia

Name:
Marvel of Peru
Species:
jalapa

287

Cracow Triennial of Architecture | ZALEWSKI ARCHITECTURE GROUP

Participants : Krzysztof Zalewski, Adam Gil, Paweł Zalewski
Project : The Third Dimension of Architecture – 50 high-rise buildings for a historical city – Cracow
Typology : Ideas Competition

802

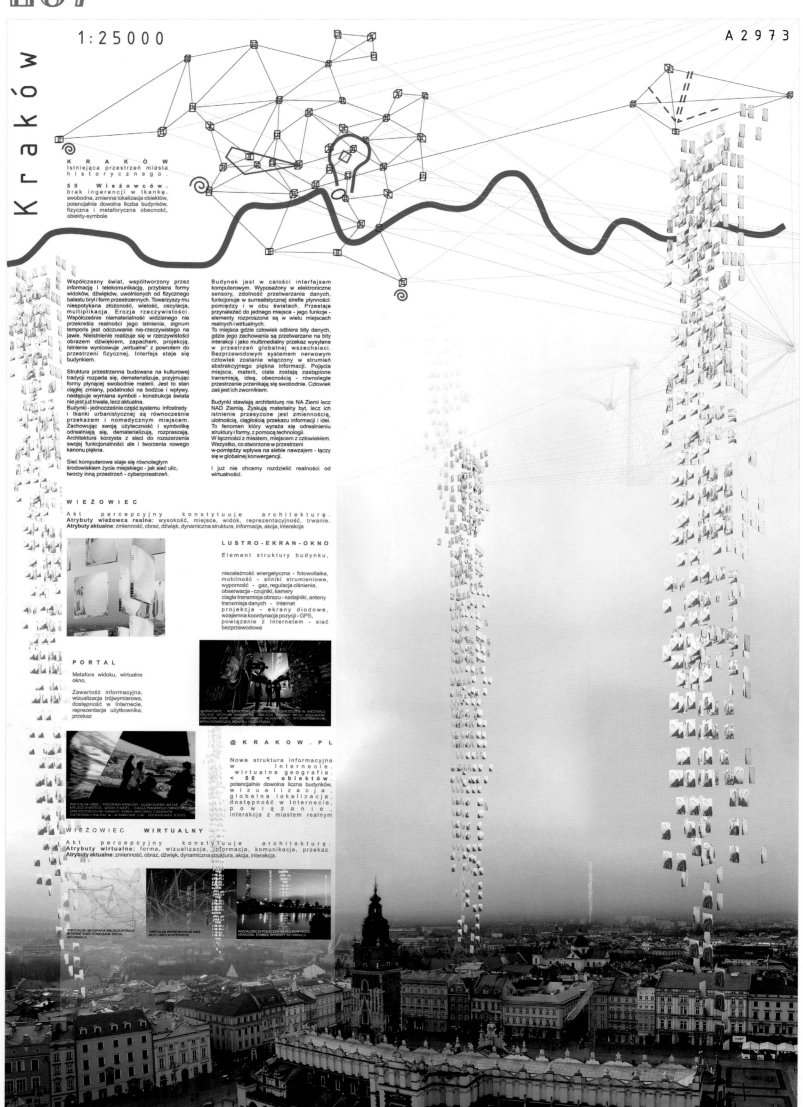

A 2 9 7 3

@krakow

Highline Proposal
Location : New York, NY
Design Team : Maia Small, Andrew Thurlow

Competition Sponsor : Friends of the Highline
Awards : Selected for Exhibition at Grand Central Terminal

GREENHOUSE / WAREHOUSE

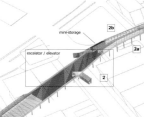

mini-storage 2b

escalator / elevator 2a

2

3

mini-storage

escalator / elevator 1

2

GREENHOUSE / WAREHOUSE

FARMER'S / FLOWER MARKET

SPLIT STREET CONNECTIONS

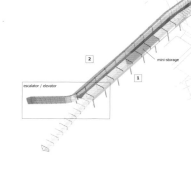

THE GREEN RAY

The Green Ray: a rare kind of green flash, in which an actual beam of green light is seen shooting up from the horizon where the Sun has just set or from the Sun itself.

Le Rayon Vert, Jules Verne 1882.   A young girl refuses to marry the man her uncles have selected for her until she sees the "Green Ray." Legend has it that this is an indication of true love.

Le Rayon Vert, Eric Rohmer 1986. Delphine bolts, heading back to Paris. As she waits at the Biarritz train station, a young man catches her eye; perhaps a sunset and the sun's green ray await.

"I need my space." Manhattan Mini-storage Logo, 2001

Over the past two hundred years, New Yorkers have simultaneously reveled in dense urbanity and fought for breathing space. In times of abundance, cultivated natural environments have been places of luxury, leisure time and reflection; in times of hardship, open green space has been a salvation, an escape from the melifluous miasma of industrialization and poverty to spiritual, cultural and physical purity. This false dichotomy between paradise and rehabilitation has denied the unique opportunities of blending environments— the opportunities of allowing the urban condition to in fact heighten the experience of cultivated vegetative landscape. In the 21st century, in a 19th century structure, we propose a new pleasure ground: an interior and exterior, public and communally owned, elevated greenhouse landscape that folds together the presumed antagonists of urban and natural life. It is not a natural environment as escape from city life, but rather exalts it by drawing it through the blocks themselves in one of the most unique conditions of the city. The main feature of the system is a network of greenhouses that follow the continuous surface of the elevated plane; they are ephemeral atmospheres of mist, luscious hothouses, translucent night beacons, community saturnalia, that foster private indulgence and wicked collective cultivation. They offer Babylon in the 21st century— real foliage in the concrete jungle: the decadent urges of the boom city

have come to rest in the space above the street. This Babylon is not a decadence of simple carnal desires for the pleasures of the 21st century city are indulgences in time and space: the time for the slow speed of plant cultivation, the time to meander, the time to literally stop and smell the roses-- the space for non-profitable life, the space for collective behavior, the space of personal territory. Social butterflies mix with real ones.

Rather than transgress the existing structure, we treated it as a linear container that could hold insertions that would foster both attachments to the city and allow for vegetation to drip and permeate into the city. Different profiles respond to various programs communally owned greenhouse gardens, personal storage units as either cabanas or mini-storage, farmer's / open markets for produce and flowers grown on the green ray, and escalator/elevator units to connect to the street. The space under the highline would be organized in support of these activities--special parking/loading zones for material for storage and goods for market, extensions of the circulation system to experience the vertical transition through milky glass escalator tubes.

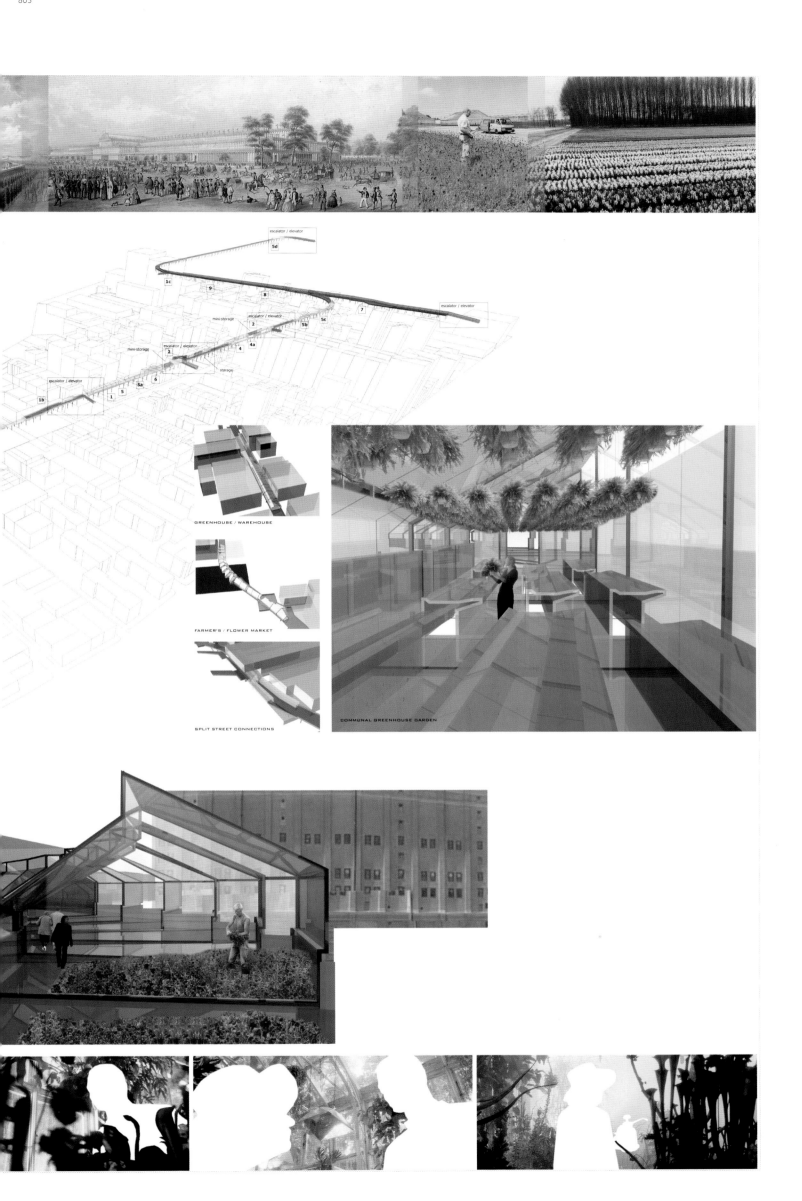

GREENHOUSE / WAREHOUSE

FARMER'S / FLOWER MARKET

SPLIT STREET CONNECTIONS

COMMUNAL GREENHOUSE GARDEN

289

Square in the Sky | *Leon11*

Date : Juny 2011
Project director : Ignacio Alvarez-Monteserín
Architects : Ignacio Alvarez-Monteserín, Beatriz Crespo and Maria Mallo

COVERED GARDEN

LIGHTHOUSE IN THE HORIZON

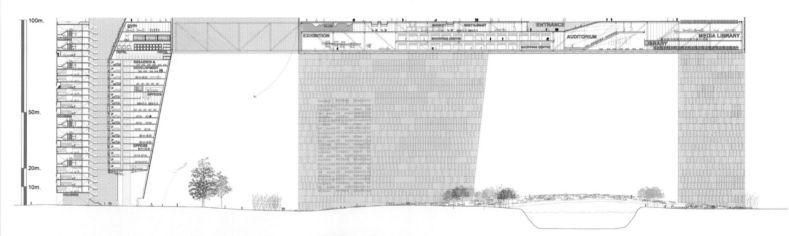

CONCEPT BRIEF

- We raise the public space till get "the height of the clouds". With this action we get a maximum quality of public space, gaining a position that used to be reserved to offices of executives of large companies.
- We provide two new icons to Parramatta city: the building itself, and the Sydney skyline.
- We create a powerful attractor to bring tourism and business visitors to the neighbourhood.
- We improve and expand existing endowments and services.
- We offer a variety of dwellings in an unbeatable location.
- We offer business Incubators that will attract human capital.

GENERATION SCHEMES

Current activities are lifted in order to release the ground floor. Below, the natural garden connects the city.
Big towers appear to support the platform with complementary activities inside.

SQUARE IN THE SKY

VIEWPOINTS COMPARATIVE

Parramatta Square Building. Australia
Hight = 100 m
Viewpoint Surface = 13.300 m2
Visitors = ?.000.000 each year

Eiffel Tower. France
Hight = 300 m
Viewpoint Surface = 225m2
Visitors = 6.000.000 each year

The most important icons of cities are used in many cases as viewpoints in small surfaces.
Why not make an icon intended as a viewpoint with a big surface that works to raise the influx of visitors?

PROGRAM / BIOCLIMATIC SCHEMES

The Golden Lane | *Leon11*

Date : Juny2011
Architects : Ana Peñalba Estebanez, Jaime López,
Javier Gutierrez, Laura Dominguez, Alicia Domingo
Illustrator : Quique de la Rubia

290

The aim of the proposal is to regenerate the Parramatta Riverside with two core elements developing three precise actions:

01. the Golden Lane:
a plot perimetre shaped street in the sky configurates linear public spaces that qualify the existing programs.

02. the Wild Nature:
Parramalta Riverside becomes a small wild park in the middle of the city. Hugged by the Golden Lane in the wildness we can find cultural and sport facilities with nature-like characteristics.

+Versus Décolletage the Backless Dress strategy: to enphasize mistery and surprise is a must in this plot. All adjacent buildings show their back to the riverbank, in order to transform this condition into a capital gain we propose the Riverside to become a new meeting point.

+Versus Communication Breakdown the Vueling Strategy: The golden lane gives unity to the existing area, connecting both sides of the river.

+Versus Alienation the Grow and Sow strategy: Every program has the opportunity of having an added value, by extending their activities to the wild park or connecting to the new programs in the lane.

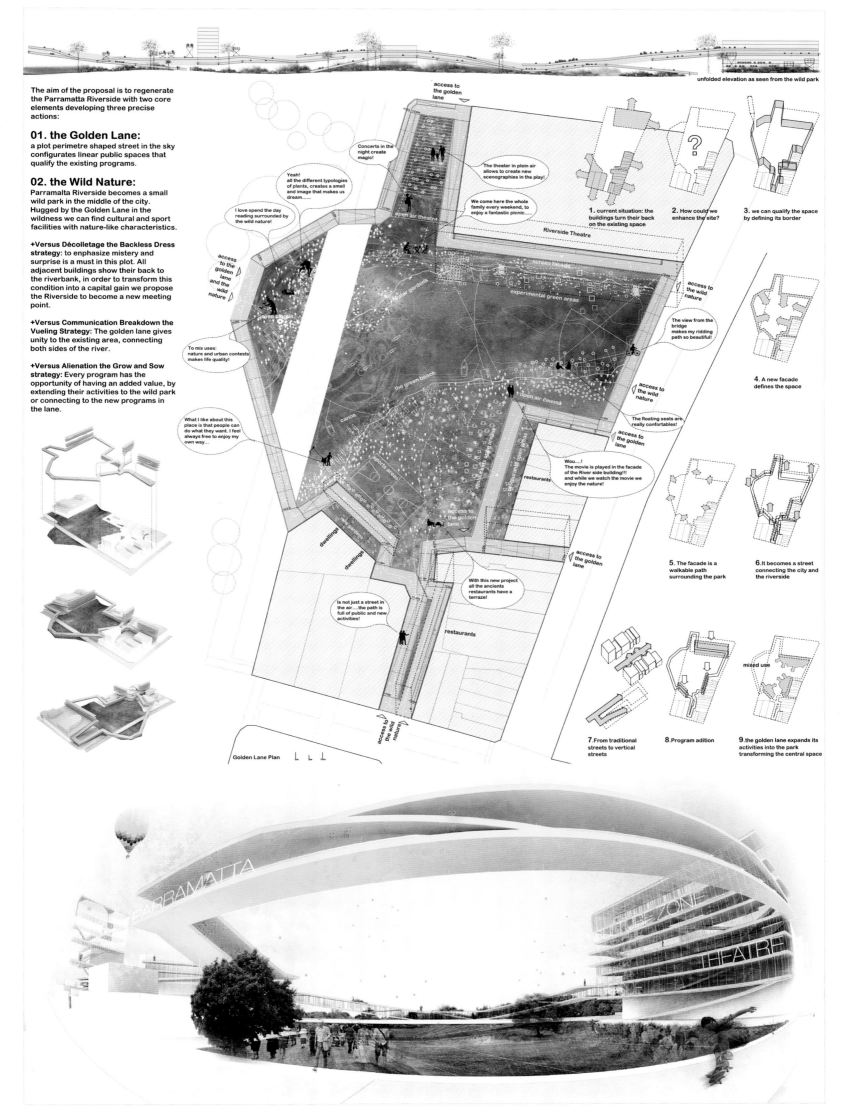

unfolded elevation as seen from the wild park

1. current situation: the buildings turn their back on the existing space

2. How could we enhance the site?

3. we can qualify the space by defining its border

4. A new facade defines the space

5. The facade is a walkable path surrounding the park

6. It becomes a street connecting the city and the riverside

7. From traditional streets to vertical streets

8. Program adition

9. the golden lane expands its activities into the park transforming the central space

Golden Lane Plan

291

Hong Kong Boundary Crossing | *Slot.*

Location : Hong Kong-Zhuhai-Macao
Program : Bridge, Boundary Crossing Facilities
Project Type : Open International Competition

Client : Government of the Hong Kong Special Administrative Region (HKSARG)
Construction Area : 479,563m²

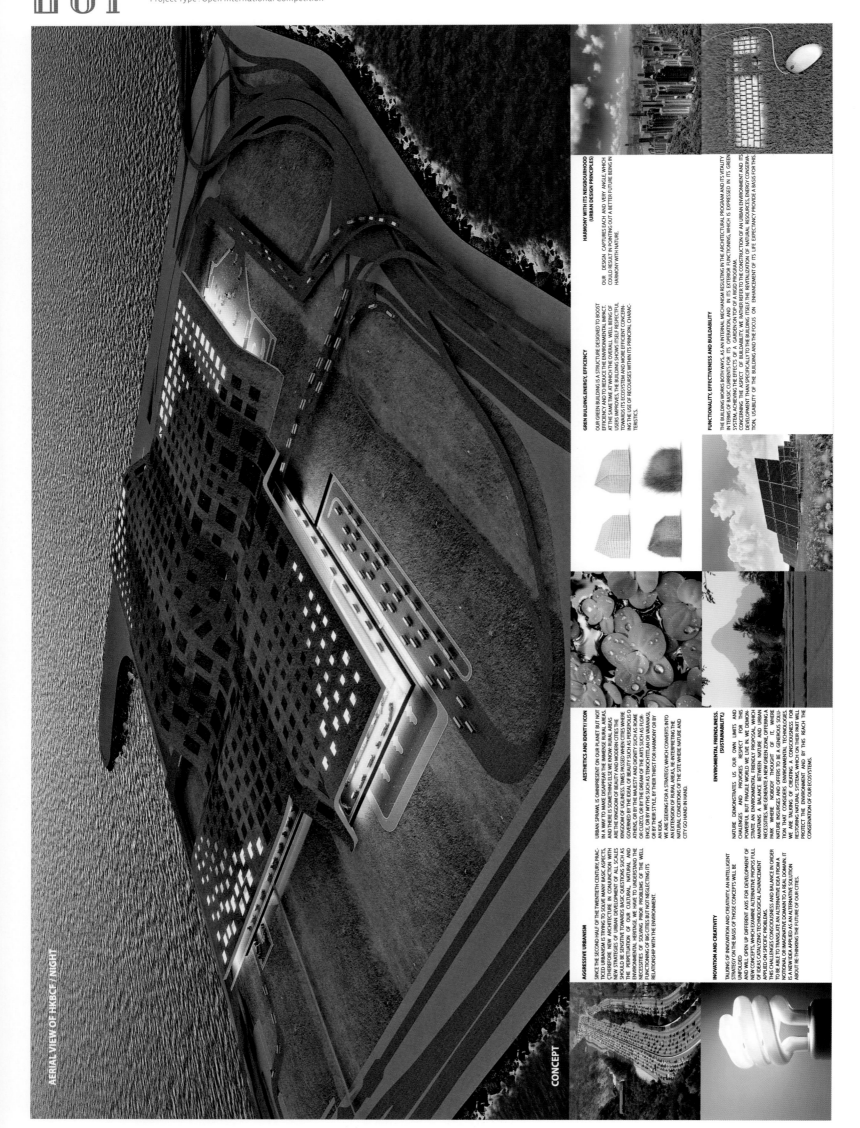

AERIAL VIEW OF HKBCF / NIGHT

CONCEPT

AGGRESSIVE URBANISM

SINCE THE SECOND HALF OF THE TWENTIETH CENTURY, PRACTICED URBANISM IS TRYING TO SOLVE MANY BASIC ASPECTS, OTHERWISE NEW ARCHITECTURE IN CONJUNCTION WITH NEW STRATEGIES OF URBAN DEVELOPMENT OF ALL SCALES SHOULD BE SENSITIVE TOWARDS BASIC QUESTIONS SUCH AS THE PERPETUATION OF OUR CULTURAL, NATURAL AND ENVIRONMENTAL HERITAGE. WE HAVE TO UNDERSTAND THE WELL FUNCTIONING OF BIG CITIES BUT NOT NEGLECTING ITS RELATIONSHIP WITH THE ENVIRONMENT.

INNOVATION AND CREATIVITY

TALKING OF INNOVATION AND CREATIVITY, AN INTELLIGENT STRATEGY ON THE BASIS OF THOSE CONCEPTS WILL BE UNFOLDED AND WILL OPEN UP DIFFERENT AXIS FOR DEVELOPMENT OF NEW CONCEPTS, WHICH EXAMINE ALTERNATIVE PROPOS FULL OF IDEAS CATALYZING TECHNOLOGICAL ADVANCEMENT APPLIED ON SPECIFIC PROBLEMS. THIS CHALLENGES CONSCIOUSNESS AND BALANCE IN ORDER TO BE ABLE TO TRANSLATE AN ALTERNATIVE IDEA FROM A NOTIONAL AND IMAGINATIVE DOMAIN TO A REAL DOMAIN. IT IS A NEW IDEA APPLIED AS AN ALTERNATIVE SOLUTION ABOUT RE-THINKING THE FUTURE OF OUR CITIES.

AESTHETICS AND IDENTITY/ICON

URBAN SPRAWL IS OMNIPRESENT ON OUR PLANET BUT NOT IN A WAY TO MAKE DISAPPEAR THE IMMENSE RURAL AREAS, AND THERE IS SOMETHING ELSE WE KNOW, RURAL AREAS ARE THE KINGDOM OF BEAUTY AND MODERN CITIES THE KINGDOM OF UGLINESS. TIMES PASSED WHEN CITIES WHERE GOVERNED BY THE IDEAL OF BEAUTY SUCH AS PERSEPOLIS O ATHENS, OR BY THE MAJESTY AND DIGNITY SUCH AS ROME OR COLOSSEUM OR BY THE DRAMA OF THE ARTS SUCH AS FLORENCE, OR BY MYTHS SUCH AS TENOCHTITLAN OR VARANASI, OR BY THEIR STYLE, BY THEIR THIRST FOR HARMONY OR BY AN IDEA. WE ARE SEEKING FOR A STRATEGY, WHICH CONVERTS INTO AN EXTERIOR OF RURAL AREAS, RE-INTERPRETING THE NATURAL CONDITIONS OF THE SITE WHERE NATURE AND CITY GO HAND IN HAND.

ENVIROMENTAL FRIENDLINESS. (SUSTAINABILITY.)

NATURE DEMONSTRATES US OUR OWN LIMITS AND CHALLENGES AND PROVOKES RESPECT. FOR THIS POWERFUL BUT FRAGILE WORLD WE LIVE IN. WE DEMONSTRATE AN ENVIRONMENTAL FRIENDLY PROPOSAL, WHICH MAINTAINS A BALANCE BETWEEN NATURE AND URBAN NECESSITIES. WE GENERATE A NEW GREEN ZONE, OFFERING A PARK WHERE NOBODY THOUGHT OF IT, WHERE NATURE BUILDS AND OFFERS TO BE A GARDEROUS SOLUTION THAT CONSIDERS ENVIRONMENTAL TECHNOLOGIES. WE ARE TALKING OF CREATING A CONSCIOUSNESS FOR RESTORING NATURAL SYSTEMS, WHICH ON THEIR PART WILL PROTECT THE ENVIRONMENT AND BY THIS REACH THE CONSERVATION OF OUR ECOSYSTEMS.

GREEN BUILDING.ENERGY. EFFICIENCY

OUR GREEN BUILDING IS A STRUCTURE DESIGNED TO BOOST EFFICIENCY AND TO REDUCE THE ENVIRONMENTAL IMPACT. AT THE SAME TIME AT WHICH THE OVERALL WELL BEING OF USERS IMPROVES, THE BUILDING SHOWS ITSELF RESPECTFUL TOWARDS ITS ECOSYSTEM AND MORE EFFICIENT CONCERNING THE USE OF RECOURSES WITHIN ITS PRINCIPAL CHARACTERISTICS.

HARMONY WITH ITS NEIGBOURHOOD (URBAN DESIGN PRINCIPLES)

OUR DESIGN CAPTURES EACH AND VERY ANGLE WHICH COULD RESULT IN POINTING OUT A BETTER FUTURE BEING IN HARMONY WITH NATURE.

FUNCTIONALITY, EFFECTIVENESS AND BUILDABILITY

THE BUILDING WORKS BOTH WAYS, AS AN INTERNAL MECHANISM RESULTING IN THE ARCHITECTURAL PROGRAM AND ITS VITALITY IN TERMS OF BASIC CURRENTS FOR ITS OPERATION AND IN ITS EXTERIOR FUNCTIONING, WHICH IS EXPRESSED IN ITS GREEN SYSTEM, ACHIEVING THE EFFECTS OF A GARDEN ON TOP OF A RIGID PROGRAM. CONCERNING THE ASPECT OF BUILDABILITY, WE RATHER REFER TO THE CONSTRUCTION OF AN URBAN ENVIRONMENT AND ITS DEVELOPMENT IN A SPECIAL WORLD WE LIVE IN. THE REVITALIZATION OF NATURAL RESOURCES, ENERGY CONSERVATION, USABILITY OF THE BUILDING AND THE FOCUS ON ENHANCEMENT OF ITS LIFE EXPECTANCY PROVIDE A BASIS FOR THIS.

MASTER LAYOUT PLAN ESC.1:200
HKBCF

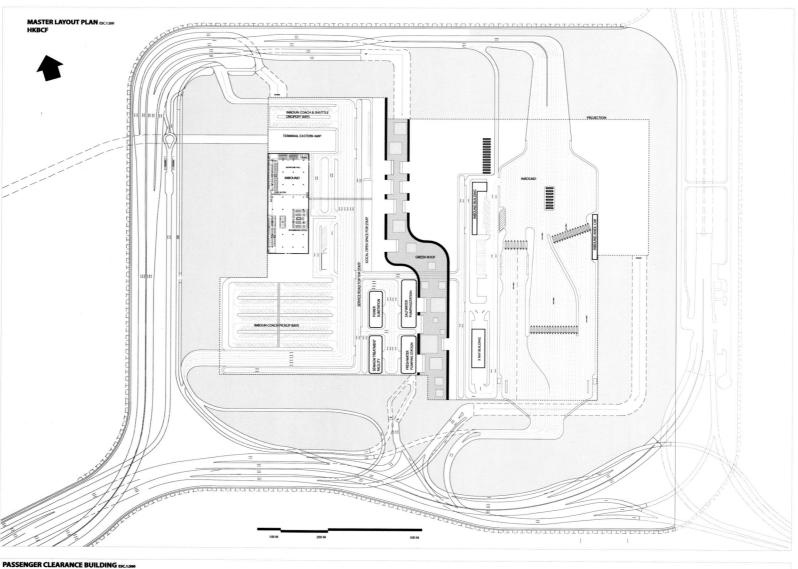

PASSENGER CLEARANCE BUILDING ESC.1:500
HKBCF

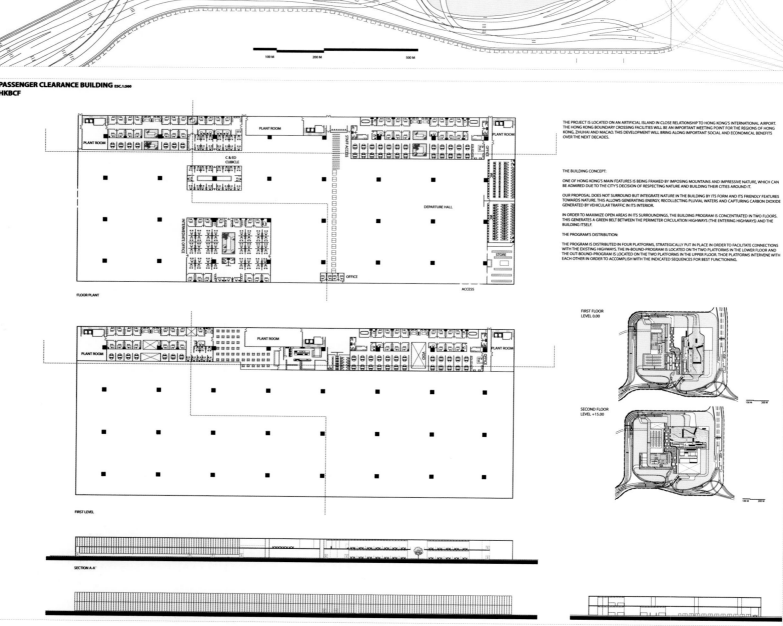

THE PROJECT IS LOCATED ON AN ARTIFICIAL ISLAND IN CLOSE RELATIONSHIP TO HONG KONG'S INTERNATIONAL AIRPORT. THE HONG KONG BOUNDARY CROSSING FACILITIES WILL BE AN IMPORTANT MEETING POINT FOR THE REGIONS OF HONG KONG, ZHUHAI AND MACAO. THIS DEVELOPMENT WILL BRING ALONG IMPORTANT SOCIAL AND ECONOMICAL BENEFITS OVER THE NEXT DECADES.

THE BUILDING CONCEPT:

ONE OF HONG KONG'S MAIN FEATURES IS BEING FRAMED BY IMPOSING MOUNTAINS AND IMPRESSIVE NATURE, WHICH CAN BE ADMIRED DUE TO THE CITY'S DECISION OF RESPECTING NATURE AND BUILDING THEIR CITIES AROUND IT.

OUR PROPOSAL DOES NOT SURROUND BUT INTEGRATE NATURE IN THE BUILDING BY ITS FORM AND ITS FRIENDLY FEATURES TOWARDS NATURE. THIS ALLOWS GENERATING ENERGY, RECOLLECTING PLUVIAL WATERS AND CAPTURING CARBON DIOXIDE GENERATED BY VEHICULAR TRAFFIC IN ITS INTERIOR.

IN ORDER TO MAXIMIZE OPEN AREAS IN ITS SURROUNDINGS, THE BUILDING PROGRAM IS CONCENTRATED IN TWO FLOORS. THIS GENERATES A GREEN BELT BETWEEN THE PERIMETER CIRCULATION HIGHWAYS (THE ENTERING HIGHWAYS) AND THE BUILDING ITSELF.

THE PROGRAM'S DISTRIBUTION:

THE PROGRAM IS DISTRIBUTED IN FOUR PLATFORMS, STRATEGICALLY PUT IN PLACE IN ORDER TO FACILITATE CONNECTIONS WITH THE EXISTING HIGHWAYS. THE IN-BOUND-PROGRAM IS LOCATED ON THE TWO PLATFORMS IN THE LOWER FLOOR AND THE OUT-BOUND-PROGRAM IS LOCATED ON THE TWO PLATFORMS IN THE UPPER FLOOR. THOSE PLATFORMS INTERVENE WITH EACH OTHER IN ORDER TO ACCOMPLISH WITH THE INDICATED SEQUENCES FOR BEST FUNCTIONING.

OF THE VEHICLE CLEARANCE KIOSK
HKBCF

FLOOR PLAN

STRUCTURALLY, THE KIOSKS WILL WORK AS COLUMNS SUPPORTING THE WEIGHT
AND CLEARANCE OF THE ROOF STRUCTURE.

C&ED EQUIPMENT ROOM

CRASH BARRIER

TRAFFIC DIRECTION LINE BAR

SECTION A-A

FACADE 1

FACADE 2

FACADE 3

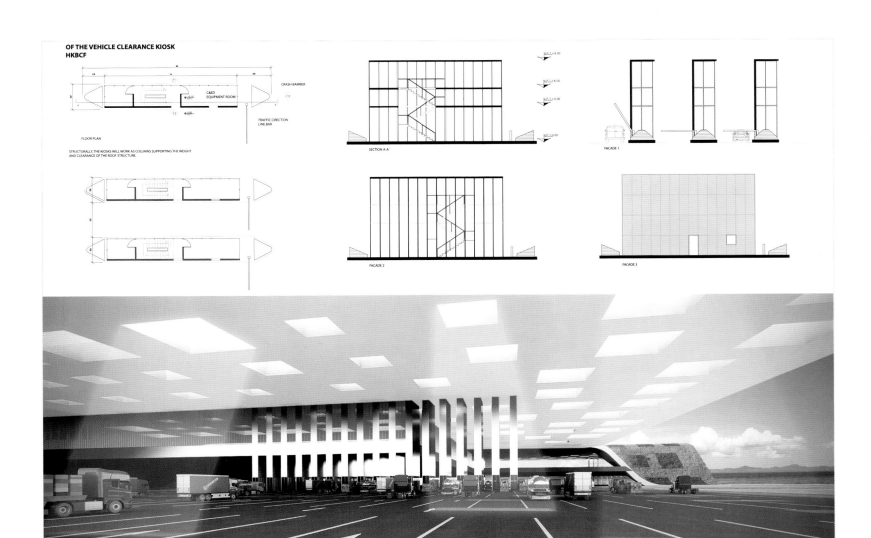

PASSENGER CLEARANCE BUILDING ESC. 1:500
HKBCF

THE SUSTAINABLE COVER:

THE FOUR PLATFORMS CONCENTRATED IN THE CENTER OF THE ISLAND ARE ALL CANOPIED BY ONE SINGLE COVER, WHICH WORKS FOR BOTH, THE ACCOMMODATION OF THE PROGRAM AND THE APPEARANCE OF THE LANDSCAPE AS AN ELEMENT INTEGRATING BEST WITH NATURE WHILE HIDING VEHICULAR TRAFFIC. AIR CAN MOVE FREELY UNDERNEATH THE COVER, WHICH INDEED IS TO BE UNDERSTOOD AS A PERFORATED ROOF SURFACE WITH NO FACADES IN ITS PERIMETER.

AN INTERESTING VISUAL RELATION IS ESTABLISHED BETWEEN THE PERFORATED COVER AND THE SPACES UNDERNEATH IT, ALLOWING DAYLIGHT AND NATURAL VENTILATION COMING IN AND ARTIFICIAL LIGHT COMING OUT AT NIGHT, WHICH CONVERTS THE HONG KONG BOUNDARY CROSSING FACILITIES INTO A LANDMARK.
THE ROOF SURFACE WILL SATISFY DIFFERENT SUSTAINABLE NEEDS SUCH AS THE GENERATION OF ENERGY BY SOLAR PANELS AND THE CATCHMENT OF PLUVIAL WATERS BY THE INCLINED ANGLE OF THE SURFACE ITSELF.
CARBON CAPTURING TECHNOLOGIES WILL BE USED AS MATERIAL OF THE CEILING. CO2 GASSES, GENERATED BY VEHICULAR TRAFFIC UNDERNEATH, WILL BE TRAPPED RESULTING IN HIGHLY EFFICIENT CAPTURE OF CARBON.

PHOTOVOLTAIC ROOF GENERATES ELECTRICITY TO MEET ENERGY NECESSITIES OF THE BUILDING

GREEN ROOF AVOIDS OVERHEATING OF THE BUILDING AND HELPS TO SAVE ENERGY

DAYLIGHT ENTERS DEEP INTO THE BUILDING

CARBON CAPTURING TECHNOLOGIES WILL BE USED AS MATERIAL OF THE CEILING

OPEN FACADES ALLOW WIND TO BLOW THROUGH THE BUILDING AND HELP TO COOL IT DOWN

CARBON CAPTURING TECHNOLOGIES WILL BE USED AS MATERIAL OF THE CEILING

OPEN FACADES ALLOW WIND TO BLOW THROUGH THE BUILDING AND HELP TO COOL IT DOWN

RAINWATER FROM THE ROOF SURFACE IS COLLECTED AND STORED IN AN UNDERGROUND TANK

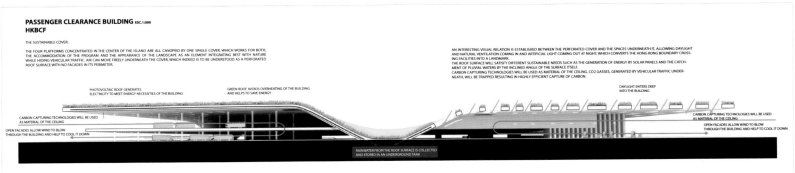

AERIAL VIEW OF HKBCF / DAY

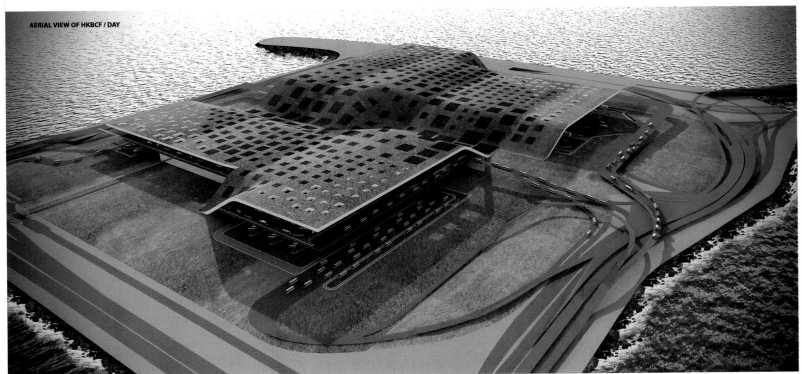

292

Prancing Zebra | *MOTOElastico*

Gwangju Design Biennale 2011 Urban Folly Competition
Project by : Simone Carena, Marco Bruno
Design Team : Minji Kim, Jihyun Hong
Location : Gwangju, South Korea

812

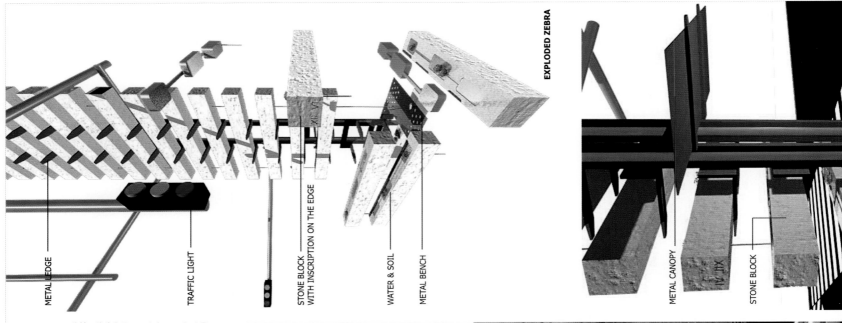

EXPLODED ZEBRA

METAL LEDGE

TRAFFIC LIGHT

STONE BLOCK
WITH INSCRIPTION ON THE EDGE

WATER & SOIL

METAL BENCH

METAL CANOPY

STONE BLOCK

PRANCING ZEBRA

Walls used to be the no-trespass limits of ancient cities. You needed a gate or a ladder to go through. In a contemporary metropolis, streets with busy traffic are the new no-trespass limits. They often delimitate areas more effectively then ancient walls. To cross these limits we use urban devices such as traffic lights and zebras. Our site is at the corner of the ancient Gwangju walls but now the real border to cross is the heavy traffic of the street at the front.

Our Prancing Zebra Urban Folly proposes a giant leap in space and time: a conceptual rotation that will shift your sense of gravity. It is a zebra crossing that turns 90 degree and reaches towards the sky. It crosses the street and then climbs up trying to surpass a wall that used to be there but now it is not visible any longer. It is the memory of the past that stretches its path towards an uncertain future. To lift the zebra we used a metal structure similar to a multiple forklift: metal ledges hold the blocks of stones up in the sky allowing the wind to go through and the water to wash the surface of each block. Each block's topside is carved to host soils and seeds and allow natural essences to freely grow. The edges of the prancing zebra will bloom into flying gardens that will naturally adapt to the height and to the seasons. Visitors will peacefully rest on the covered bench at the feet of this ramping urban beast!

옛 도시에서 성벽이란 무단침입금지를 나타내는 경계였다. 때문에 밖을 넘기 위해서 사람들은 사다리나 문을 이용해야만 했다. 현대 도시에서 무단침입금지의 경계를 형성하는 것은 바로 붐비는 교통 량이다. 때로는 이 차들이 고대의 벽들보다 효과적으로 구역의 한계를 지정해준다. 이 경계를 넘을 때 우리는 신호등과 횡단보도와 같은 도시장치들을 이용한다. 대지는 옛 광주성의 성벽이 있었던 자 리이고 있다. 예전엔 벽이 있었지만 지금은 자리에 있어 앞을 바로 보여 붐비는 교통량이 진정한 우선의 도로의 횡단이 건너야 할 실제 경계로 존재한다.

Prancing Zebra Urban Folly(발랄한 얼룩말 도발란 도시의 빌딩)는 당신의 중력감각의 변화를 가져올 것이다. 이는 90도 회전을 하여 하늘을 향해 뻗어나가는 zebra crossing (횡단보도) 돌들로 이뤄져 있다. 도로를 가로지른 후 예전엔 존재했지만 지금은 보이지 않는 어떤 벽을 타고 올라간다. 우리가 지안하는 돌리가 지안하는 90도 회전을 하여 하늘을 향해 뻗어나가는 것이다. Zebra(얼룩말)를 들어올리기 위해서 우리는 다중 지게차와 같은 금속구조물을 사용하였다. 금속 지지대들은 석재를 들어올려줌으로써 바람이 그 틈 사이로 불고, 물도 돌에서 석재 표면을 각각 씻겨줄 수 있도록 해준다. 각각의 석재들은 윗부분이 움푹 파여 흙과 씨앗을 담을 수 있다. 발랄한 자연의 정수가 자유롭게 자랄 수 있는 환경이 만들어진다. prancing zebra 의 모서리는 공중정원으로 꽃을 피워 자연스럽게 높이와 계절에 적용하게 될 것이다. 관람객들은 이 헛발로 서 있는 도시 짐승의 발치에 놓인 벤치에 놓인 편화롭게 휴식할 것이다.

Prancing Zebra.
Folli

BENCH VIEW

SIDEWALK EXTENSION

EXPLODED ZEBRA

METAL LEDGE

TRAFFIC LIGHT

STONE BLOCK

WATER DRIP

METAL BENCH

PRANCING ZEBRAS/ 날뛰는 얼룩말

293

Venice | *REC ARQUITECTURA*

Competition : Museum -Bridge; Venice/Italy
Team : Ignacio Salas Sánchez, Jonathan Tapia Bernal, Juan Manuel Vargas, Gerardo Recoder Déciga

"...finally the fish cross through the bridge"

1 ACCESS 64.38 m2
2 RAMPS 119.88 m2
3 BATHROOMS 58.00 m2
4 ROOM STORM 71.20 m2
5 ROOM STORM 94.45 m2
6 COFFE 98.06
7 PERMANENT ROOM 132.09 m2
8 FISHBOWL 58.05 m2
9 VIEWER 75.33 m2

TOTAL 776 M2

Sharing volumes and basic **proportions** of the surroundings and understanding the opened thing of its seats, a traditional bridge comes near giving access to **old and new boats**, an architecture organized by bodies of easy reading with lines of vision and shared circulations, in where two regular **towers** make the transition of vertical buildings to horizontal volumes, with a **classic silhouette of an old bridge and plates** that arrives and large themselves giving sense that the fish cross from an end **fishbowl** to the other, being a marked and sharp volume. The museum recover **nostalgia**, in where the oxidized steel belts of old boats are placed to give a contemporary skin. Another plate covers the cafeteria-viewpoint and it is proposal with the same **black of Venetian gondolas**, the glass as a display cabinet material is made by the great craftsmen of venecia, mixed artistic with the fish of colors that in certain places interpose between the pedestrian and the city.

Swiss Pavillion Expo 2015 | *Donner Sorcinelli Architecture*

Built surface : 4,400 sq.m.
Budget : € 9,861,000 / Client : DFAE

Location : Milan, Italy
International Competition
Year : 2011
Area : 4,420 sq.m.

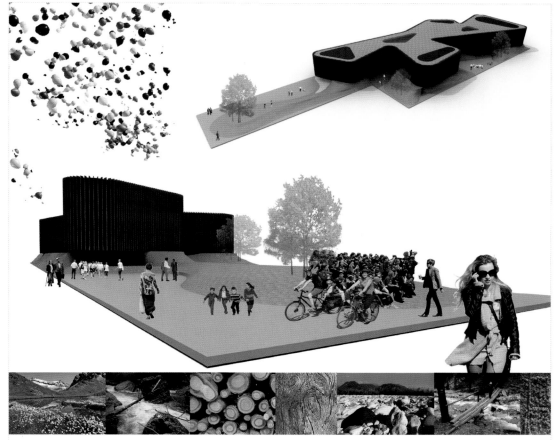

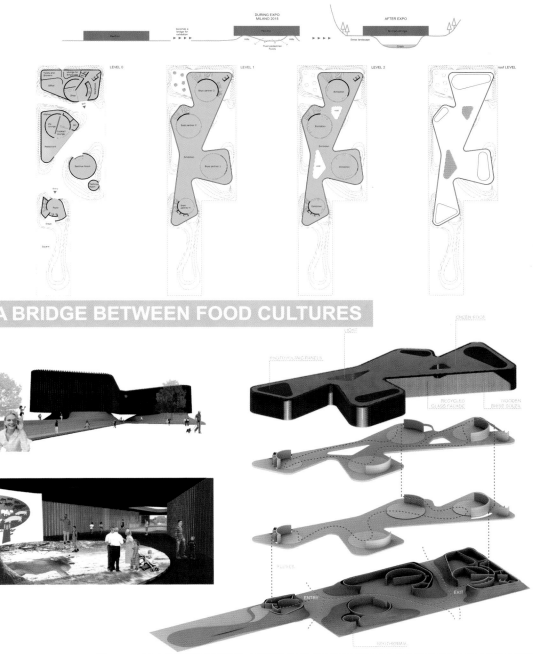

A BRIDGE BETWEEN FOOD CULTURES

295

Urban Sky Link Poster | *David Garcia Studio*

816

Participants : David A. Garcia (Architect MAA)
Project : Skyscraper as a High FAR Structure in the Urban Fabric
Typology : Bridge

Location : New York, NY, United States of America
Construction Volume : 35,000m²

URBAN SKY LINK

CONCEPT

The history of the skyscraper is inherently linked to that of the elevator. It is interesting to note that although structurally speaking the skyscraper has evolved enormously, it is still a vertical structure, dictated by the elevator, which in its effort to go up, it only meets a dead end. The lack for alternative methods of moving through floors (the elevator's refusal to bend) has determined the typology of the skyscraper for the last hundred years or so.

This proposal wishes to expand the understanding of high-rises, beyond a high FAR structure, or an extrusion of a plan. The proposal's main concept is simple: that the idea of moving up in a building can also mean moving to somewhere else in the urban fabric, taking the pedestrians' relationship to the city as decisive design factor.

The concept converts the traditional structure into a double-ended skyscraper, making it rise and fall again, linking two sites and transforming the structure into a wormhole in the city. As thus, the building also becomes a public transport system, and accessible landscape. The skyscraper could link unconnected sites, or salvage topographic barriers such as rivers, or link different levels with in a city.

SITE

The sites chosen for this proposal are by the East river edge, close to the UN building in Manhattan, and the opposite shore, at Hunters Point in Queens. This is a relevant test scenario, partly because of the existing density and skyscraper tradition in Manhattan, and mainly because of the strong geographical barrier that is the East river. Mainly an industrial site now in full development, Hunters Point is far from a lively city area. Nonetheless, it is the site of a vital railroad link and station, with breathtaking sights of the Manhattan, and a water edge full of potential.

Although bridges exist across the East river, and a main traffic artery tunnel is next to the site, they are primarily non-pedestrian territories, existing only as moments between here and there. On the other hand, the double-ended skyscraper becomes in itself a topography, an artificial landscape, linking these two areas in the city, where the individual can dwell, live and work, or simply ride from one end to the other. The building would become an extension of Hunters Point reaching downtown Manhattan, or a continuation of East 39th street into Queens.

SKYSCRAPER

Spanning just over a kilome... on the Manhattan riverside... curve towards the East rive... non-existent, only the stru... skyscrapers is possible by ...

Immediately above, the flo... around a central core or a ... top of the structure, given it... and shopping areas. On the ... aviary. A series of empty fl... rotating air turbines and g... offering leisure, office spac...

The total built up area is 34...

ally, amongst other high-rises
for the first 50 floors, only to
level, the footprint is almost
park, where access to the

and apartments distributed
ed by an atrium garden. The
ulated by restaurants, cafés
separated by a park and an
o go through the structure,
tions as a street extension,
loor areas and energy parks.

450 m

268 m

TRANSPORT

To solve the challenge of transportation in a curved high-rise, we looked at existing technologies related to large spans. Gondola lifts, used in ski resorts, travel at 6m/s, span kilometres, and shift angle constantly. They can seat up to 51 persons per gondola, have several gondolas per line and move over 2000 persons per hour. This system would be used to travel to designated stop/stations along the skyscraper. Angled elevators, and escalators would do the job of distributing the user to the individual floors. Almost like riding a cabin through the Alps, the user/commuter, would travel through the building, experiencing the various spaces and typologies within the latticed structure.

RESTAURANTS AND HIGH ED FLATS

HOTEL   OFFICE

APARTMENTS

OFFICE   OFFICE

OFFICE   APARTMENTS

ELEVATOR GROUPING

GONDOLA LIFT STOPS

STRUCTURE

The arched form provides an efficient structural solution for a double-ended skyscraper. The primary vertical loads distribute through the floors to the node points on the tube inducing axial compression in the arch form. As with a conventional skyscraper there is only limited bending forces induced under gravitational loads. Horizontal wind loads are resisted at the apex by bending induced in the tube. As these forces are distributed to the ground, the bending turns to torsion within the arch. The torsionally rigid tube provides an ideal form to resist these loads. Vertical loads to the foundations are resisted by a conventional basement and pile solution. The lateral thrust from the arch would b resisted by a deep basement with additional ground anchors to reduce movement. The superstructure would be constructed using large-scale steelwork erection and fabrication methods as used in the bridge and offshore oil industry.

01 SPIRAL NODES

02 LATTICE NODES

03 SPIRAL AND RING NODES

04 SPIRAL AND DECK NODES

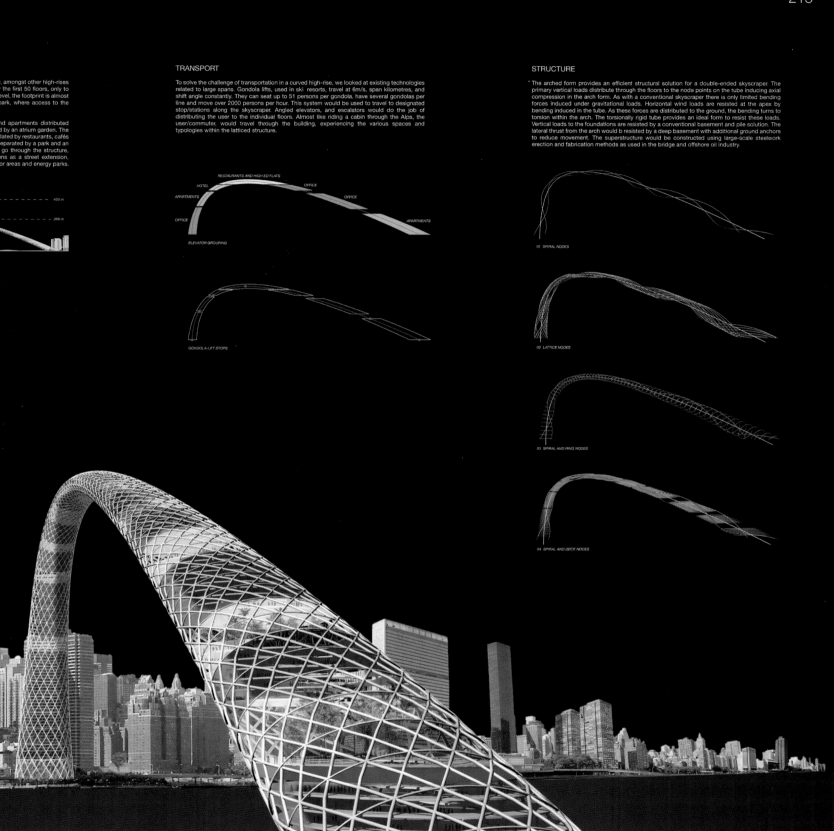

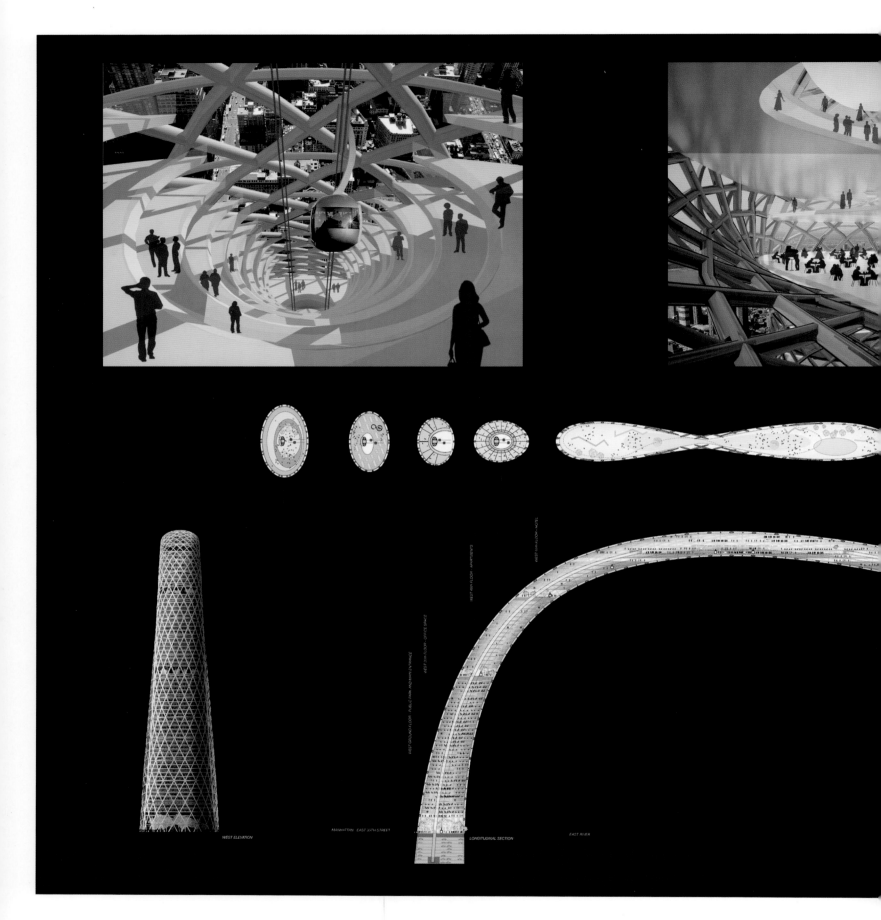

WEST ELEVATION   MANHATTAN: EAST 35TH STREET   LONGITUDINAL SECTION   EAST RIVER

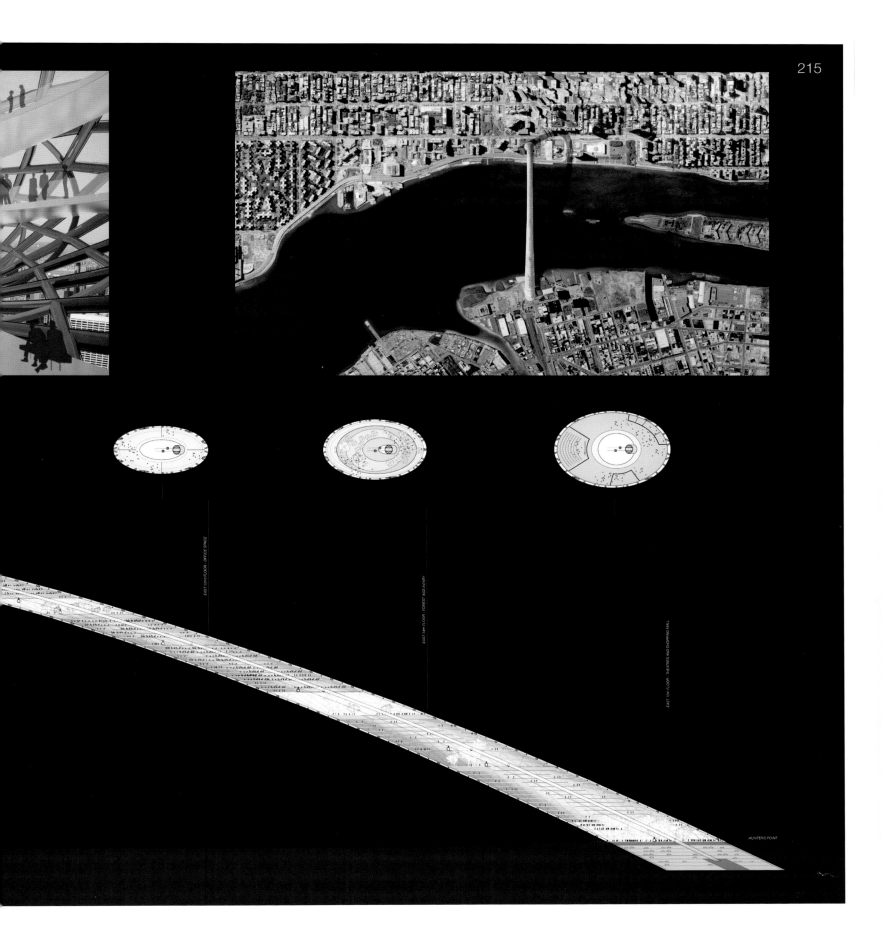

EAST 12TH FLOOR: OFFICE SPACE

EAST 34TH FLOOR: FOREST AND AVIARY

EAST 13TH FLOOR: THEATRES AND SHOPPING MALL

HUNTERS POINT

296

Reflections Poster | *David Garcia Studio*

820

Participants : David A. Garcia (Architect MAA)
Project : Link Between Bronx and Manhattan to Re-establish the Significance
of the Derelict High Bridge as a Historic and Cultural Point/landmark
Typology : Bridge, Rehabilitation / Client : City of Brooklyn

Location : New York, NY, United States of America
Construction Volume : 15,000m²

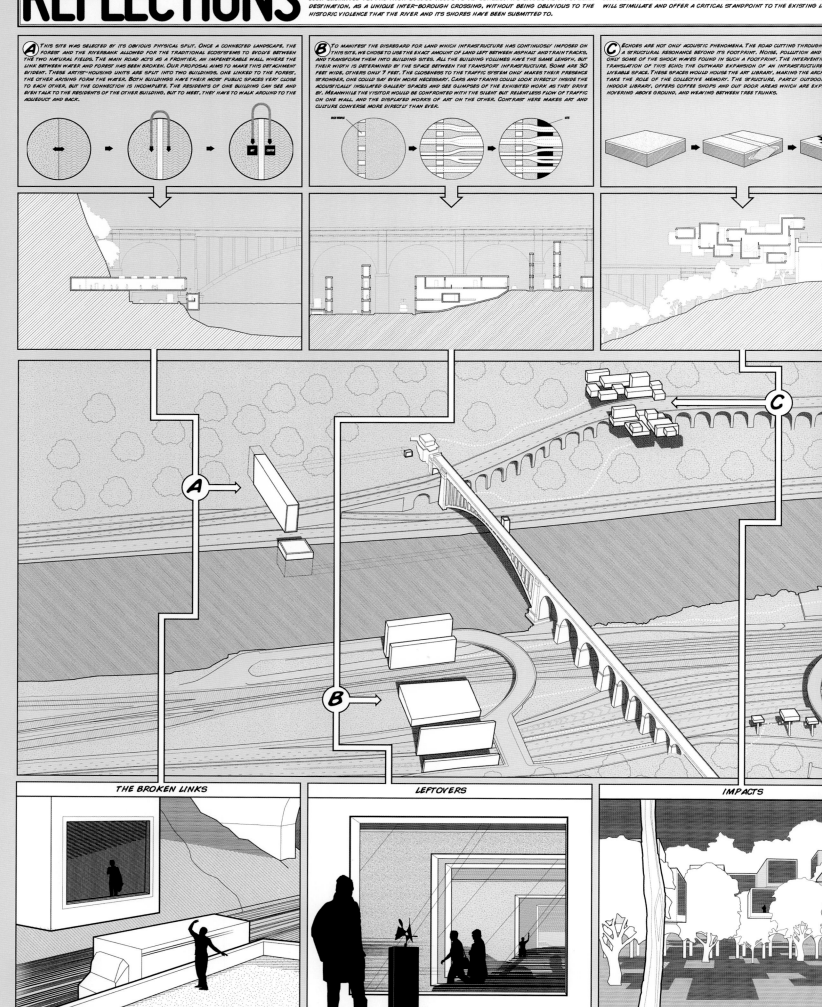

(A, B, C, D AND E) HAVE BEEN CHOSEN TO DESCRIBE A VOCABULARY OF DISRUPTED
NTIONS THAT HAVE TAKEN PLACE IN THE PAST. ALL LINKED TO THE HIGH BRIDGE
ARTERY AND ACCESS POINT, THESE SITES ARE USED TO RESOLVE CULTURAL SPACES
THEIR IMMEDIATE STATUS. AVOIDING THE ROMANTIC OR UTOPIAN, WE CHOSE A
PROACH AS A DESIGN GUIDELINE, MAKING EACH INTERVENTION A REFLECTION ON
AL LOST BY PAST ACTIONS.

*T*HE CHOSEN SITES HAVE BEEN THE RESULT OF PAST ISOLATION, NEGLECT, DISPLACEMENT
AND DISREGARD FOR NATURE AND SOCIAL NEEDS. WE HAVE CHOSEN TO TURN THESE
RESULTS INTO POSITIVE ACTIONS. INSTEAD OF TURNING OUR BACK TO THE REALITY THAT
SURROUNDS THESE SITES, THE INTERVENTIONS USE THIS CONTEXT TO GENERATE SPACES WITH
CONSCIOUSNESS, AN ARCHITECTURE WHICH IS THE PHYSICAL EXPRESSION OF A HISTORY OF
NEGLECT.

A BIOGRAPHY OF COUNTLESS DISPLACEMENTS, THIS SIDE OF THE SHORE HAS BEEN SUBMITTED
ONSTANT RE-SHIFTING. ROADS, TRAIN TRACKS AND NOW A DISPOSAL SITE, THE SHORE HAS
TRIPLET OF IMPOSSIBILITIES. WE HAVE DESIGNED ARTIST WORKSHOPS AND GALLERIES AS A
, A FINAL LAYER TO LOOK BACK ON TO THE SHORE, AND UNDER THE WATER LEVEL. HALF SUNK
ER, THEY ARE A MIRRORING OF THE TREATMENT THAT THE RIVER HAS RECEIVED IN ITS RECENT
WORKSHOPS RECEIVE NATURAL LIGHT FROM ABOVE, WHILE STRATEGIC WINDOWS SHOW
D CHARACTER OF THE RIVER BED. THESE SPACES AIM TO EMPHASIZE THE ENVIRONMENTAL
ORGETFULNESS, ALLOWING THE ARTIST AND VISITORS TO REFLECT ON THE SURROUNDING

E A CRISSCROSS OF INFRASTRUCTURE HIGH BRIDGES HAS ISOLATED THIS FOREST LANDSCAPE,
RENDERING IT INACCESSIBLE AND TRAPPED BY CONCRETE AND STEEL. IT IS AN ISLAND OF
TEMPTATION AND CONSTANT FRUSTRATION. WE PROPOSE TREE LIKE, THIN AND ELEVATED STRUCTURES,
WHICH REFLECT ON THIS ISOLATION. ABLE ONLY TO GAZE AT THE TREES AS WELL AS AT THE CONSTANT
TRAFFIC, IT BECOMES ALMOST IMPOSSIBLE TO REACH THE GROUND. THESE SPACES HOUSE MULTIMEDIA
WORKSHOPS AND EXHIBITION SPACES, ALLOWING FOR THE 3D SPACE THAT SURROUNDS EACH CUBICLE
TO BE EXPLORED THROUGH THE DIGITAL MEDIUM. FILMS AND DIGITAL MEDIA CAN BE PROJECTED ON TO
THE UNREACHABLE FOREST FLOOR, LEAVES OF TREES, OR THE UNDERBELLIES OF THE INFRASTRUCTURE
HIGHWAYS. THIS VIRTUAL MEDIUM (YOU CAN SEE DIGITAL PROJECTIONS WITHOUT TOUCHING THEM) IS A
WAY OF EXPLORING THE SURROUNDING REALITY THROUGH ART.

ART CENTER

D

E

HISTORY OF DISPLACMENT

ISOLATED RESIDUES

297

STM Foot Bridge Margaretengürtel | *franz zt gmbh*

Function : Urban Bridge for Cyclists And Pedestrians
Collaboration : Christian Petz (Structural Engineering), Henning Grahn, Joe Suntinger, Anna Gruber

blatt 1   wettbewerb fuss- und radwegsteg magaretengürtel

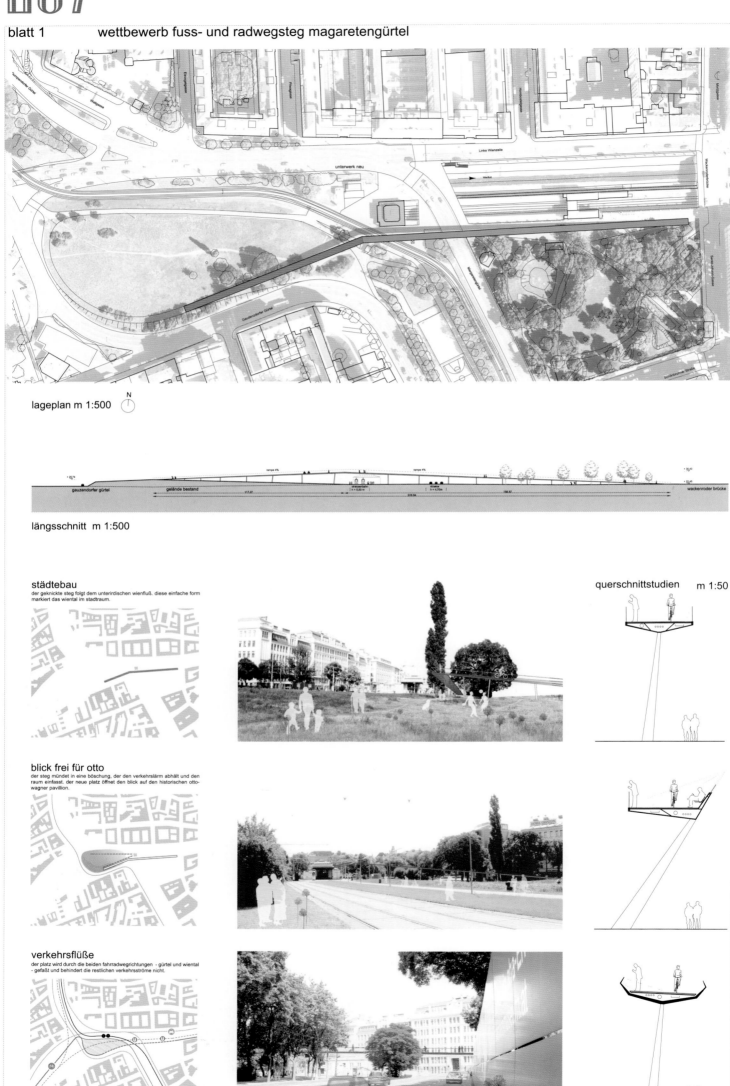

lageplan m 1:500   N

längsschnitt m 1:500

städtebau
der geknickte steg folgt dem unterirdischen wienfluß. diese einfache form
markiert das wiental im stadtraum.

blick frei für otto
der steg mündet in eine böschung, der den verkehrslärm abhält und den
raum einfasst. der neue platz öffnet den blick auf den historischen otto-
wagner pavillion.

verkehrsflüße
der platz wird durch die beiden fahrradwegrichtungen - gürtel und wiental
- gefaßt und behindert die restlichen verkehrsströme nicht.

querschnittstudien   m 1:50

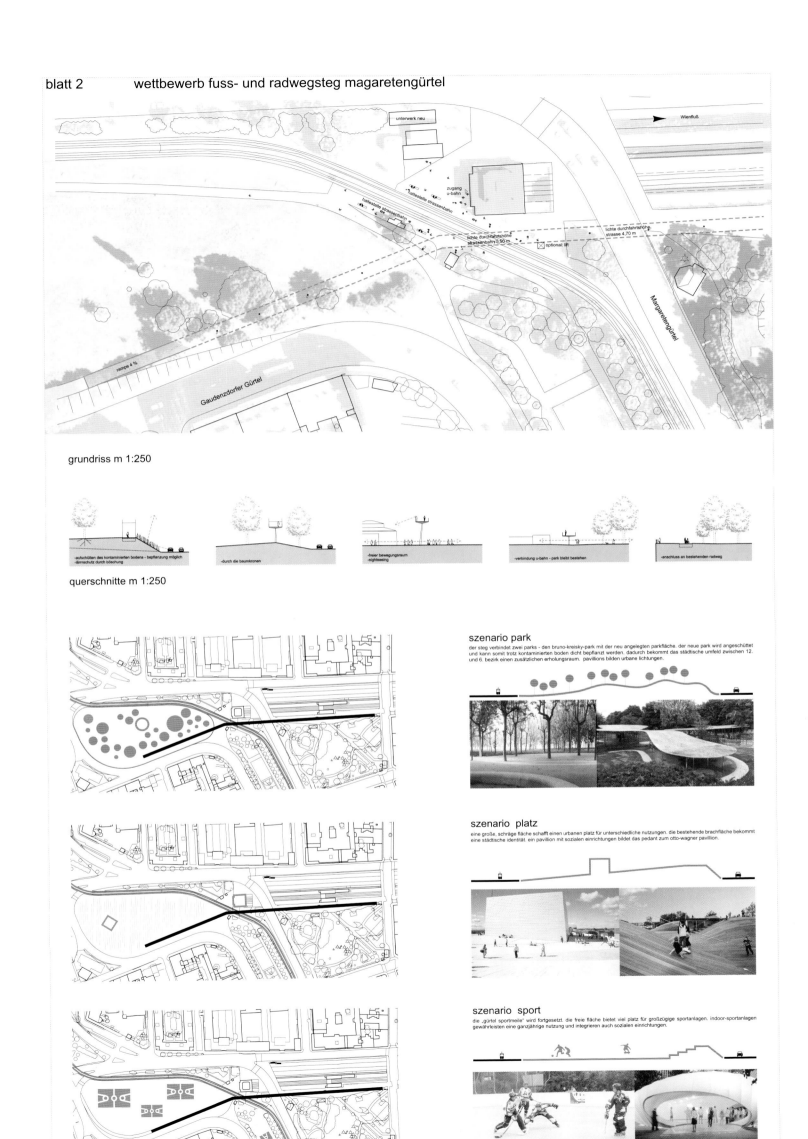

Living Bridge | *Marchi_Architectes*

Team : Architecture Project(Adelaïde et Nicola Marchi[Marchi_Architectes]),
Project Manager(Chen Xi), Art director(Emiko Boun Xun), 3D images(Federico Kraus)

>0.316

international competition
vertical density
skyscraper
> the living bridge <

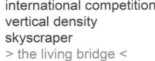

Michel Etienne Turgot, Borough President of the City of Paris in 1734, commissioned to the drafter Louis Bretez the most beautiful and accurate representation of Paris in the "Ancien Régime".
Based on this representation, it is evident that most bridges in the City at that time are living quarters and perform as actual buildings, fully integrated to the bridge itself. The same typology is found in the historic "Ponte Vecchio" in Florence that survives unaltered to this date, with its direct relationship between "bridge architecture" and the river.

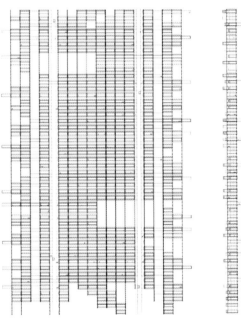

The center of Paris is deeply characterized by the extraordinary presence of the Seine River, touching the historic monuments such as the Louvre, the Eiffel Tower and the Grande Palais. These are all landmarks that provide orientation in the city, as authentic milestones. The historic city can still develop and grow its density vertically, respecting and highlighting the existing context.

The grand open spaces of Paris, and particularly the Place de la Concorde, have the potential of integrating the new 400-meter high building, made of two narrow (12 meter) and long (216 meter) volumes, separated by 30 meter space. The building is integrated by the Seine, becoming a new landmark and offering to the historic center the development of the most varied programmatic elements, from landscape to culture, museum and performance spaces. The new bridge for the city is a living one.

>0.316

international competition
vertical density
skyscraper
> the living bridge <

Use : Exhibition Space
Theme : Better City, Better Life
Project Type : Open Competition, First Prize, Built Project
Site : Shanghai, China. Expo Fair, American pavilions area, zone C, number 8

Total Area : 4000m²
Built area : 3500m²
Dimensions : 80m long X 50m wide

Client : Promexico
Completed : May 2010

Pabellón de México en la Exposición Universal Shanghai 2010

1353893676

Exposición Universal Shanghai 2010
"Better City, Better Life"

En 2010 la comunidad internacional hace presente el deseo de mejorar la calidad de vida en las urbanizaciones del futuro. La Exposición Universal de Shanghai expondrá el **potencial de la vida urbana en el siglo XXI**, y será un escaparate para exponer estrategias e ideas vanguardistas de urbanización y desarrollo sustentable.

Foto aerea del recinto ferial

Pabellón de México
"Vivir Mejor"

El pabellón de México se presenta con el tema "Vivir Mejor", mostrando la **originalidad de nuestra vida cotidiana y una proyección clara sobre como definimos el proceso de la planeación urbana** y el fomento de la sustentabilidad en el 2010 con la finalidad de que los mexicanos vivamos mejor.

Tendrá como reto mostrar las grandes riquezas del país a nivel cultural, de recursos naturales e historia, además de saberse sus deficiencias en las grandes urbes para mostrar los proyectos de mejora y por consecuencia aumentar la calidad de vida en un país que cuenta con una de las ciudades más grandes del mundo.

La ubicación del pabellon se encuentra en la zona de los Pabellones de América en la zona C numero 8, tipo de pabellon 1 construído por participantes.

Plano de ubicación

Proceso de Urbanización en México
Retos

Las ciudades en México crecen a partir de la sobreposición de la ciudad colonial sobre la prehispánica, heredando una retícula concéntrica a una plaza como influencia de los españoles, sin embargo el crecimiento acelerado y la sobrepoblación hicieron que la espontaneidad rigiera la traza urbana.

Hoy en día México cuenta con la segunda ciudad más grande del mundo después de Tokio, y con una población total que rebasa los **106.7 millones de habitantes.** Como consecuencia, la ciudad se enfrenta actualmente a retos importantes que permitan generar mejores condiciones de vida.

Generadores	Consecuencias
Sobrepoblación	Problemas ambientales
Urbanización espontanea	**Falta de areas verdes**
Concentración económica	Desempleo

1900   1950   1970

1980   1990   2005

Diagrama area verde vs. mancha urbana s. XX

El proceso de urbanización generó el uso y la explotación desmedidos; las manchas urbanas desbordaron los límites de sus emplazamientos, provocando su deterioro y el desequilibrio físico y ambiental del medio.

Áreas verdes por habitante

De acuerdo con la Organización de la Naciones Unidas (ONU), **es recomendable tener un mínimo de 12 m de área verde por habitante** para poseer un ambiente aceptablemente sano, tanto física como mentalmente. En la Ciudad de México, se calcula una superficie de 3 metros cuadrados de área verde por habitante, con lo cual el déficit es muy notable.

1m   1m

Ciudad de México   Recomendación de la ONU

Diagrama m² x habitante

Actualidad
Espacios públicos

En la Ciudad de México, Chapultepec es el pulmón verde por excelencia en medio del asfalto, a el se arrastran los problemas comunes de las áreas verdes cuando son visitadas por miles de personas. En la actualidad los espacios existentes no son suficientes para cubrir las necesidades de los millones de personas que habitan esta gran urbe.

Con la perdida de la gran mayoría de las áreas verdes, los ciudadanos se ven obligados a apropiarse de espacios públicos urbanos para realizar diversas actividades, a los que se les adjudica un uso informal diferente al establecido, generando nuevos problemas.

Un ejemplo claro de este fenomeno es el tianguis, la utilización de las calles y avenidas con puestos desmontables y una cubierta con lonas, en distintas zonas de la ciudad, crean un espacio y una atmosfera que delimita el área de venta de productos, esto forma parte de la cotidianeidad de la ciudad.

Foto tianguis Ciudad de México

Con la espontaneidad y frecuencia con la que surgen estos espacios informales en las grandes metropolis y restando cada vez mas áreas verdes, **los niños y las nuevas generaciones crecen dentro de este contexto** carente de áreas de esparcimiento, utilizan la vía pública como zonas de juego o centros de reunión, que limitan su bienestar y buen desarrollo.

La vegetación y la naturaleza refuerzan nuestro equilibrio físico y mental, permiten que nuestro sistema sensorial se relaje y libera del estrés.

Foto Zócalo Ciudad de México

Futuro de mariposas
"Visión a futuro"

La propuesta es mirar el futuro con espacios destinados, pensados y planeados esp[...] camente al esparcimiento, la recuperación de parques y áreas verdes donde ni[...] generaciones puedan reconocerse dentro de una ciudad donde se puede "vivir me[...]

Foto Papalote

Papalote: nombre regional mexicano
del náhuatl papálotl, "mariposa"

Es un artefacto volador, más pesado que el aire, que vuela gracias a la fuerza del vie[...] a uno o varios hilos que la mantienen desde tierra en su postura correcta de vuelo[...] **origen en China.** Se sabe que alrededor del año 1200 a. C. se utilizaban como disp[...] de señalización militar.

Los movimientos y los diferentes colores de las cometas constituían mensaje[...] se comunicaban en la distancia. Actualmente es un juego infantil tradicional.

Como propuesta utilizamos el papalote como **elemento que une a la cultura Ch[...] México**, proponiendo a este como un símbolo de progreso, **llegar alto mirand[...] futuro**, imaginando una ciudad con espacios donde los niños jueguen entre un bo[...] de papalotes.

Foto niña volando papalote

829

1353893676

Secuencia del México que queremos

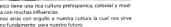

Despegar

México del futuro

Presente

México del pasado

Saliendo del presente, se nos ofrecen varios caminos de interpretar y presentar nuestro país.

México del Pasado

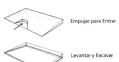

Zona Arqueológica de Mitla

México tiene una rica cultura prehispanica, colonial y moderna con muchas influencias.
Vemos atrás con orgullo a nuestra cultura la cual nos sirve como fundamento para nuestro futuro.

México del Futuro

Bosque de Chapultepec, México DF

México será más verde en el futuro, devolviendo áreas verdes a sus ciudades. Después del caos que se generó en las grandes urbes de nuestro país, queremos buscar soluciones sustentables para nuestras ciudades.

México que queremos

Papalotes

México quiere moverse adelante y presentarse como un país atractivo.
Queremos que el mundo nos reconosca como un país abierto para recibir a turistas e inversiones extranjeras.

Contexto Urbano dentro de la Expo

La propuesta para el pabellón aprovecha su ubicación céntrica adentro del conjunto de los pabellones americanos en el terreno de la Expo Shanghai 2010. El desplante del pabellón aprovecha del terreno completo y el proyecto se desarrolla en un solo nivel.

Talud + Excavación

Empujar para Entrar

Levantar y Excavar

Terreno Disponible

El proyecto se concibe formalmente como un gran talud que se convierte en una plaza accesible desde el nivel de las plazas y circulaciones de la Expo. Al mismo tiempo se crea una apertura generosa en el talud que crea la entrada del pabellón.

El visitante tiene dos opciones de acceder al pabellón: subir a la plaza elevada, que simboliza el México del futuro (el México que queremos), y bajar a las áreas programáticas que contienen entre otras la exhibición y el restaurante. Esta última parte simboliza el México del pasado/ presente (el México que tenemos).

Accesos a las 2 Partes del Pabellón

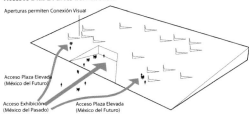

Aperturas permiten Conexión Visual

Acceso Plaza Elevada (México del Futuro)

Acceso Exhibición (México del Pasado)

Acceso Plaza Elevada (México del Futuro)

Distribución del Programa debajo del Talud

Lectura Horizontal

Altura promedio de 6 metros
Altura promedio de 4 metros
Talud relleno con tierra

Lectura Vertical

Servicios
Áreas públicas
Servicios

El programa abajo del talud comprende todas las áreas del programa arquitectónico necesario para su funcionamiento.

Funcionalmente, el vestíbulo de entrada actúa como distribuidor para las diversas atracciones que ofrece el pabellón mexicano. De un lado se ubica el restaurante y del otro lado promoción turística. En frente la sala de exposición permanente.

El recorrido típico de un visitante empieza en el vestíbulo de entrada del cual procede la exhibición y continúa con la exposición temporal. Esta última le invita a atravesar la tienda para salir del pabellón.

Programa Desglosado

Área de Exposición
Bodegas y Maquinas
Bodegas y Maquinas
Restaurante
Vestíbulo
Tienda
Oficinas y Business Center
Promoción Turística
Expo Temporal

El Talud como Plaza Pública

La Plaza como Tribuna de un Espectáculo

La Plaza como Plataforma para una Feria Empresarial

La superficie del talud se convierte en una plaza que sube con una pendiente ligera desde el nivel de acceso hasta una altura de 6 metros.

Las posibilidades de uso de esta plaza son casi inagotables: un lugar similar a un bosque que con sus hojas proporciona sombra, invita a todos los visitantes de la Expo para descansar y reunirse. También podría servir como tribuna de espectáculos en una escala mucho muy grande. Un lugar que con sus cualidades agradables da una visión hacia el futuro verde y sustentable de México.

Techo Formado por Papalotes

Zoom rampa escalonada Pendiente de la Plaza 8 %

Plaza Pública para Usos Múltiples

Los Papalotes y su Significado

Los papalotes abstractos tienen sus raíces en el talud que cubre nuestra historia, estos papalotes simbolizan nuestras ambiciones de despegar sin olvidarnos de nuestro pasado.

Se pueden de igual manera también entender como una ofrenda del pueblo mexicano al pueblo chino, honorando los papalotes como unas de las invenciones chinas que se dispersaron en todo el mundo hace siglos y ayudaron a formar el presente que hoy tenemos. Por eso proponemos la reutilización de dichos elementos como mobiliario urbano en la República China una vez que terminó la Expo.

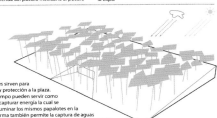

Los papalotes sirven para dar sombra y protección a la plaza.
Al mismo tiempo pueden servir como fuente para capturar energía la cual se usará para iluminar los mismos papalotes en la noche. Su forma también permite la captura de aguas pluviales y convierte los papalotes en elementos sustentables.

Construcción + Estructura

Estructura del Techo

Cajón de Cimentación e Indicación de Claros

La construcción del gran talud está basada en un sistema de ejes tanto perpendiculares como diagonales. Los ejes diagonales generan una malla de aperturas en el techo, expresándose en triángulos que suben en tres puntos.

De igual manera los ejes permiten una modulación del techo en elementos prefabricados los cuales en conjunto funcionan como una trilidosa. Los elementos prefabricados del techo están hechos de acero y cubiertos con una losa de concreto in situ. Los muros perimetrales y el muro interno por el eje longitudinal son estructurales y están hechos de concreto.

Ejes Constructivos + Estructurales

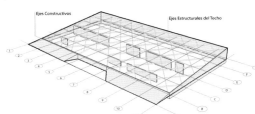

Ejes Constructivos
Ejes Estructurales del Techo

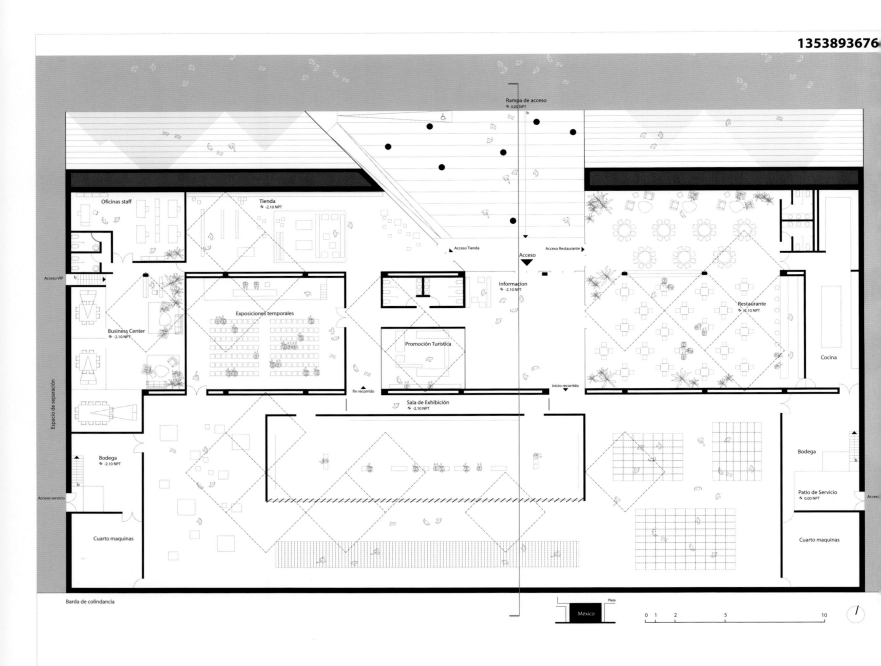

Opciones de museografía exposición permanente
Flexibilidad del espacio, diferentes escenarios y recorridos

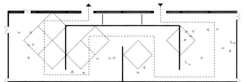

Exposición en salas conectadas

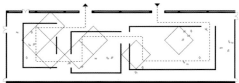

Exposición en salas independientes

Opciones de museografía exposición temporal
Diferentes escenarios y actividades

Exposición varias salas

Función: exposición de piezas en diferentes ambientes

Exposición de piezas de arte

Función: exposición de una o varias piezas de gran tamaño

Video proyección

Función: proyecciones en un solo espacio

Escenario conciertos

Función: escenario pa realizar conciertos, ma performance, etc.

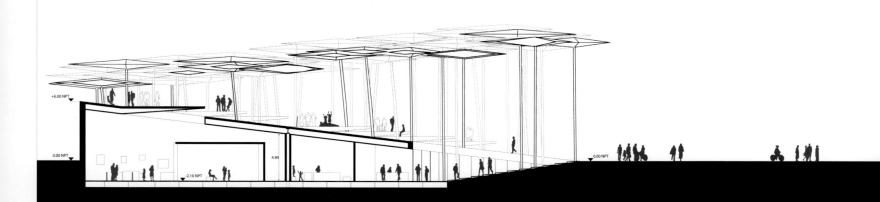

useografía en espacio de Exposición Permanente
opuesta para el desarrollo de contenidos

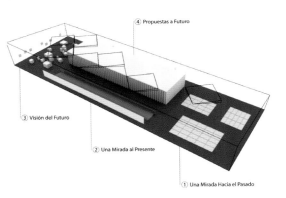

④ Propuestas a Futuro

③ Visión del Futuro

② Una Mirada al Presente

① Una Mirada Hacia el Pasado

espacio central del pabellon de México es el area de exposiciones
manentes, en ella se pretende mostrar un recorrido sobre la
olucion y desarrollo de las ciudades de México, contemplando la
apa historica, el presente, los planes a futuro y las nuevas propues-
para "Vivir Mejor".

① Una Mirada Hacia el Pasado
Tres pantallas en el piso con imagenes de ciudades prehispanicas,
ciudades de la colonia y ciudades del siglo XIX, que cambian
constantemente. Transladarse, caminar y recorrer antiguos espacios
permite al visitante sentirse dentro de nuestra historia.

② Una Mirada Al Presente
Sobre una banda electrica se observa a un lado un muro de leds
proyectando imagenes de la actualidad en las ciudades de México y
otra pantalla paralela muestra escenarios urbanos cotidianos, donde
el visitante experimenta el presente en constante movimiento.

Una vez adentrado en el espacio, el visitante puede ver entre las
bandas verticales rotadas de leds, pedazos de escenas del México en
el que queremos vivir, haciendo analogia a ventanas en el presente
que periten vislumbrar el futuro.

3. Vision del Futuro
Varias mesas interactivas al alcance de todos los visitantes, sirven de
escaparate de informacion para comunicar los planes de desarrollo a
futuro asi como programas de sustentabilidad ambiental que
permitiran crear un México mejor.

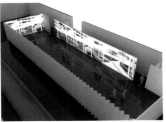

4. Propuesta a Futuro
Dentro del espacio confinado por tres pantallas, el visitante se
encuentra frente a imagenes en tiempo real de la plaza de papalotes
ubicada en la cubierta del pabellón, mostrando que esa plaza
representa el México que queremos.

Estas pantallas muestran las actividades que se realizan en la plaza
para invitar al visitante a subir a este bosque de papalotes y que sea
parte de la experiencia.

Pasto Sintético "TIGERTURF" Modular
Recubrimiento Exterior Lamina Plana Cempanel Smooth 1.22 x 2.44 M
Recubrimiento Interior Lamina Plana Cempanel Smooth 1.22 x 2.44 M
Sección Cuadrada, PTR Estructural
Estructura Principal Vigas PPR, 353 x 415 - 34 KB
Estructura Secundaria Sección Cuadrada PTR Largeros
Cama de Elemento Organico para Filtración de Agua
Piezas Modulares de Prefabricado de Concreto
Impermeabilizante Asfaltico
Firme de Concreto Armado
Falso Piso para Paso de Instalaciones
Plafon de Tablaroca
Paraboloides Prefabricados de Concreto

Corte Detallado en 3D

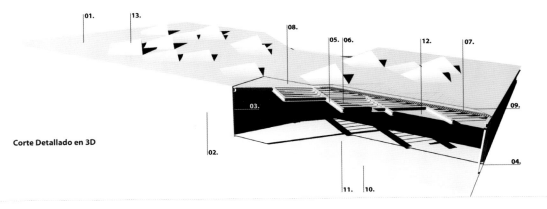

300

Mersey Observatory | *CJ Lim / Studio 8 Architects*

Location : Liverpool, UK
Design Team : CJ Lim/Studio 8 Architects with Barry Cho
Consultants : Techniker(structural engineers), Fulcrum Consulting(environmental engineers), KMCS(quantity Surveyors)

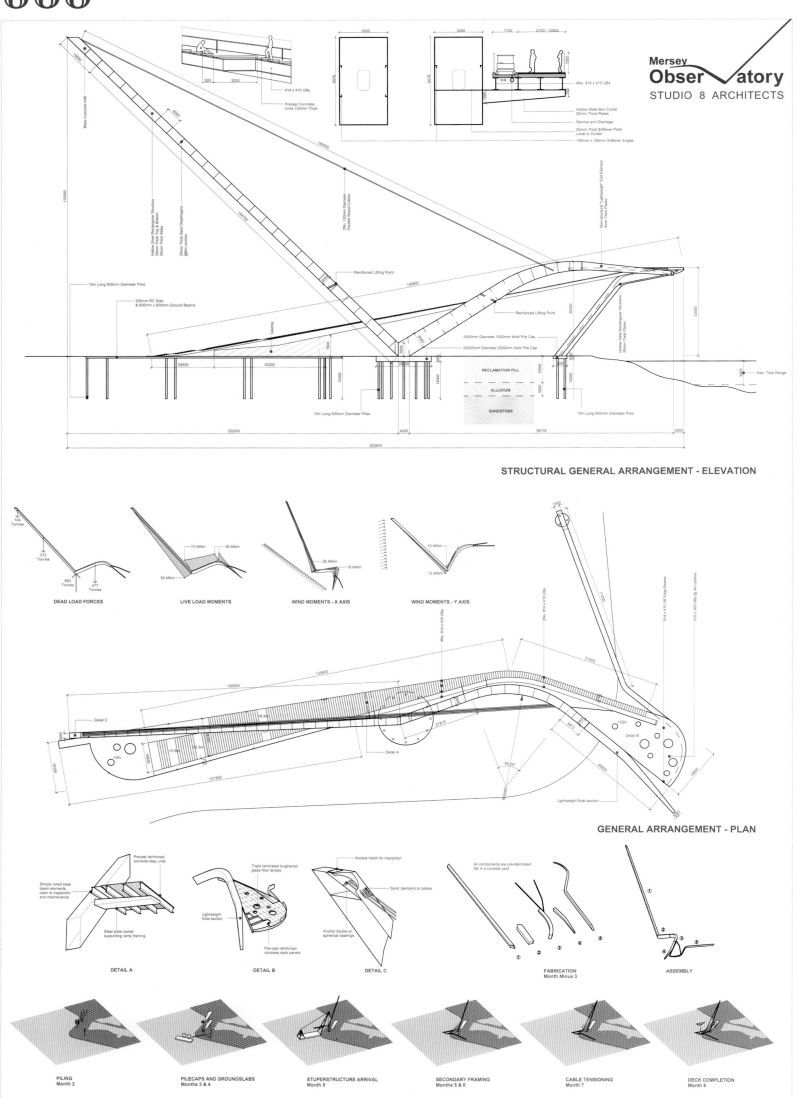

Mersey Observatory
STUDIO 8 ARCHITECTS

STRUCTURAL GENERAL ARRANGEMENT - ELEVATION

DEAD LOAD FORCES

LIVE LOAD MOMENTS

WIND MOMENTS - X AXIS

WIND MOMENTS - Y AXIS

GENERAL ARRANGEMENT - PLAN

DETAIL A

DETAIL B

DETAIL C

FABRICATION
Month Minus 3

ASSEMBLY

PILING
Month 2

PILECAPS AND GROUNDSLABS
Months 3 & 4

STUPERSTRUCTURE ARRIVAL
Month 5

SECONDARY FRAMING
Months 5 & 6

CABLE TENSIONING
Month 7

DECK COMPLETION
Month 8

Mersey
Obser**V**atory
STUDIO 8 ARCHITECTS

The new Mersey Observatory presents a unique 21st Century icon for Liverpool reflecting the city's strong sense of identity, a sculptural structure rather than a building, something which people will want to come and see from all over the world. The elegant V-shaped structure gracefully inscribes the Mersey-Liverpool skyline and can be seen from land, sea and sky - miles away, day and night.

The observatory elegantly negotiates land and water with a dynamic structure to present maximum views of the Mersey and its surrounding attractions. It comprises a visitors pavilion on the ground and an observation deck supported on a cantilevered arm, which is braced and counter-balanced by a stay and pylon support. An additional strut provides lateral support.

Refer to the report for more information.

Images: (Clockwise from top-left): Day View from Crosby Beach; Dusk View from Crosby Beach; View from Crosby Dunes; Site Plan; Suspended Observatory Deck from Ground Level; Scenic Compass on Observatory Deck; Stepped Ramp to Observatory Deck; View from Cafe in Pavilion; Night View from Existing Path

Visitors Pavilion
Scale 1:500

Key:
1 - Main Entrance
2 - Tickets / Information
3 - Door towards External Deck
4 - Multi-functional Room
5 - Cafe
6 - Shop
7 - Staff Office
8 - WCs (including disabled)
9 - Furniture Store
10 - Plant Room / Bin Store
11 - Performance Space
12 - External Terrace

Mersey Observatory: 120m   Liverpool Cathedral: 101m   Metropolitan Cathedral: 89m   Gateshead Bridge: 50m   Angel of the North: 20m

301 Panoramic Tower and Congress Building | *Donner Sorcinelli Architecture*

International Competition
Location : Dubai, UAE
Area : 21.000 sq.m.
Height : 165 mt

Built Surface : 1.200 sq.m.
Client : ThyssenKrupp / Dubai Municipality

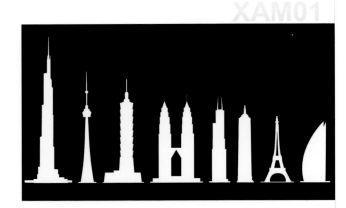

the "hourglass"
a new iconic landmark

XAM01

1_gatehouse 6
2_restaurant
3_square
4_arch
5_oasis
6_underground parking
7_parking entrance
8_pedestrian path
9_garden
10_services
11_lake

N

1

master plan   1_1000

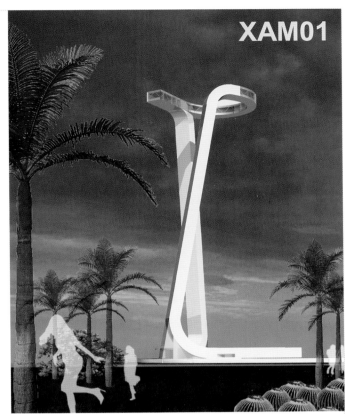

XAM01

south view

THE "HOURGLASS"

Dynamism, flexibility, innovation and striving for the future, are the keys of Dubai, both in economic and urban strategies, as at cultural level.

Such attitude should also be reflected in its iconographic symbols.

The Arch, with its formal intrinsic tension, seemed suited to represent this specific internal dynamism.

Cause of its cultural specificity and atypicality in the globalized world, Dubai needs an unique interpretation of its recognizable landmarks.

The figurative element from which the project evolved, should have contain within itself, not just symbolism associated with the current international vision of Dubai, but also a deep relationship with the cultural identity of this land.

Infact, the sudden change of this city, transformed in a few decades from fishing village to the city of business and leisure, is clearly linked to the concept of time.

From the birth of the universe, time marks our lives and it is determined by changes in space and materials.

Therefore it is the factor that unites peoples, different cultures and traditions.

In the final analysis, it's the only global element combining all mankind from the beginning.

The Arch represents the different souls of Dubai: its history, the present and the great vision of the future that awaits.

The idea came out from the transposition and formal abstraction of a "hourglass".

This instrument, among the oldest, is a universal symbol in the figurative representation of the concept of time.

The particular shape of the hourglass, sinuous and smooth, has led to the development of a strong sculptural form, as main figure, created by the distortion and twist of a single stretched element with a rectangular section.

The result was an asymmetrical and atypical Arch, with a strong iconographic impact and universal symbolism.

The sculptural final mass is characterized by a dominant figurative continuity, where the plasticity, the essentiality and the dynamism of forms, mark both the appearance that the functional composition, in keeping with the nature of the surrounding park.

The asymmetrical shape, will permit, with the passing of seasons and according to the points of view, to perceive the building in a different and unique way, making this vision a unique experience at sensory level.

aerial view
west side

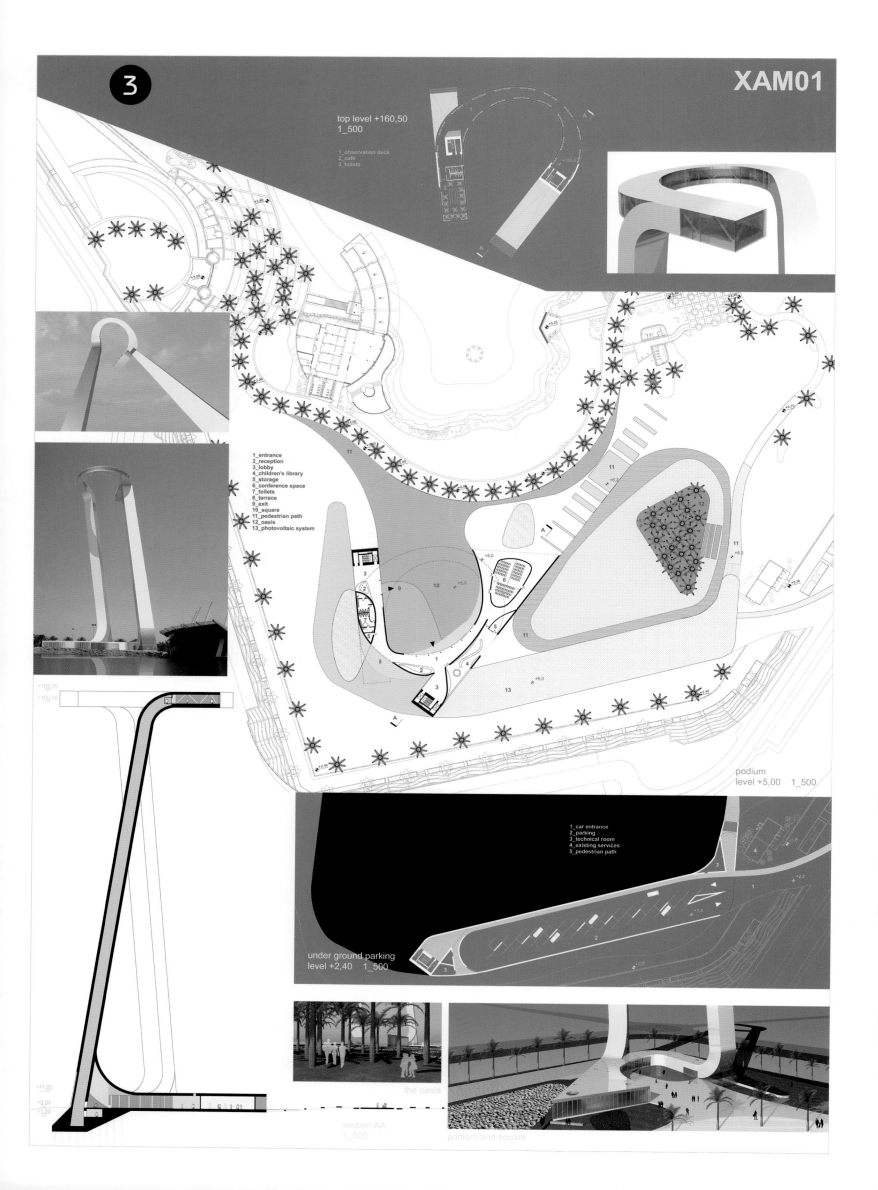

3

XAM01

top level +160,50
1_500

1_observation deck
2_café
3_toilets

1_entrance
2_reception
3_lobby
4_children's library
5_storage
6_conference space
7_toilets
8_terrace
9_exit
10_square
11_pedestrian path
12_oasis
13_photovoltaic system

podium
level +5,00   1_500

1_car entrance
2_parking
3_technical room
4_existing services
5_pedestrian path

under ground parking
level +2,40   1_500

the oasis

section AA
1_500

podium and square

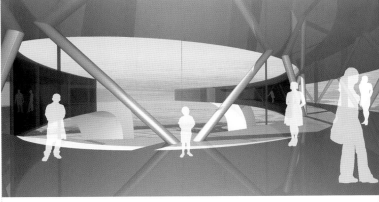

XAM01

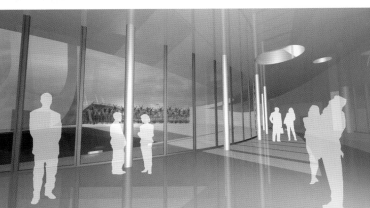

flows

stairs and lifts

down   up

no interferences

sustainability

structure

steel structure

concrete cores

concrete basement

concrete podium

The structural system adopted, has two components integrated with each other.

The first, for the podium and the two vertical cores, consists of self compacting concrete, cast in place, allowing an easy workability and ductility.

These parts, permit to maintain a stiff structure in relation to the specific shape of the arch.

The top is provided with a reticular structure made of steel, in order not to burden excessive structural loads, including in relation to seismic loads and those of the wind.

Furthermore, the particular shape of the structure allows you to favour wind flows in a progressive manner, just like a modern sail lets the wind pass, reducing the pressure on the top of the mainmast in a progressive way.

From a safety and circulation point of view, the two cores with rectangular section are provided of two fire resistant stairs and three lifts.

Structural cores are also provided of compartments and facilities for the conduct of pre-natural cooling (using conceptually similar facilities to ancient Qanat system).

The cladding will be in white concrete panels, reinforced with fibre C, mounted on a metal substructure applied to main structure.

The curtain walls, with ventilated double glazed and active technology, complete the cladding. Their use will ensure a high thermal and acoustic comfort, such as a high grade of transparency will reduce the consumption of artificial light.

The formal and structural separation in two vertical cores, connected to the top, lays the groundwork for a possible separation and management of ascent and descent in the various activities in the tower. There is therefore a real possibility to reduce interference and optimize the flows according to the daily and seasonal visitors and users of the structure. Three elevators and two stairwells to safety, ensure the daily movement and security in the event of evacuation from the building.

aerial view north side

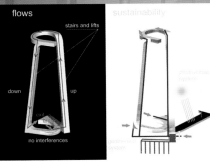

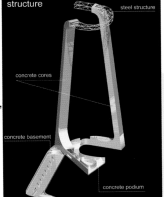

Sustainability is a fundamental aspect of the project.

Photovoltaic systems, geothermal energy and natural ventilation plant, integrated each other for the needs of the building, are planned with the intention of making the building self-sufficient in energy by reducing the consumption and emissions of CO2.

The roof of the car park has been provided with integrated photovoltaic cells, to produce electricity, sufficient to cover the consumption of internal and external activities.

The air-conditioning system is structured on a system with heat pumps associated with a geothermal vertical plant.

The natural ventilation is used in conjunction with the installation of air conditioning, using the planimetric configuration of the tower.

Exploiting the specific planimetric configuration of the building, the breezes coming from all quadrants can be collected, pre-cooled (under ground) and directed into suitably arranged ducts. In this way the wind will be used to reduce energy consumption.

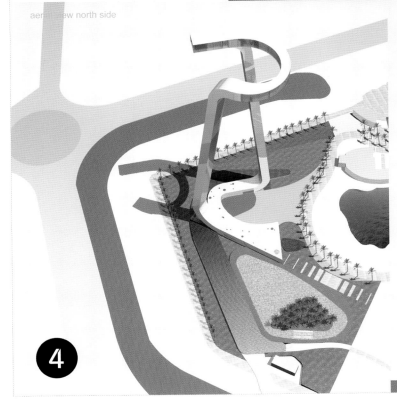

4

south- west facade
1_500

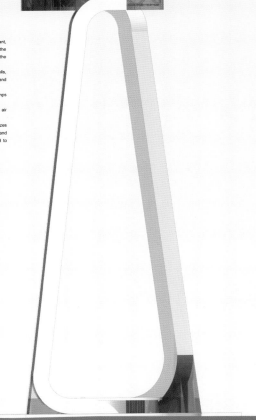

302

Tea House | *Thurlow Small Architecture*

Peepshow Competition Proposal
Location : Calgary, Canada
Design Team : Andrew Thurlow, Maia Small, Nate Del Vecchio, Brandon Massey

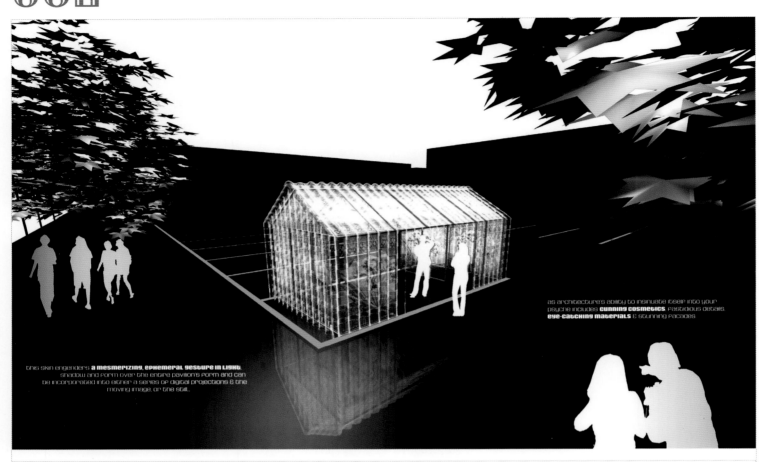

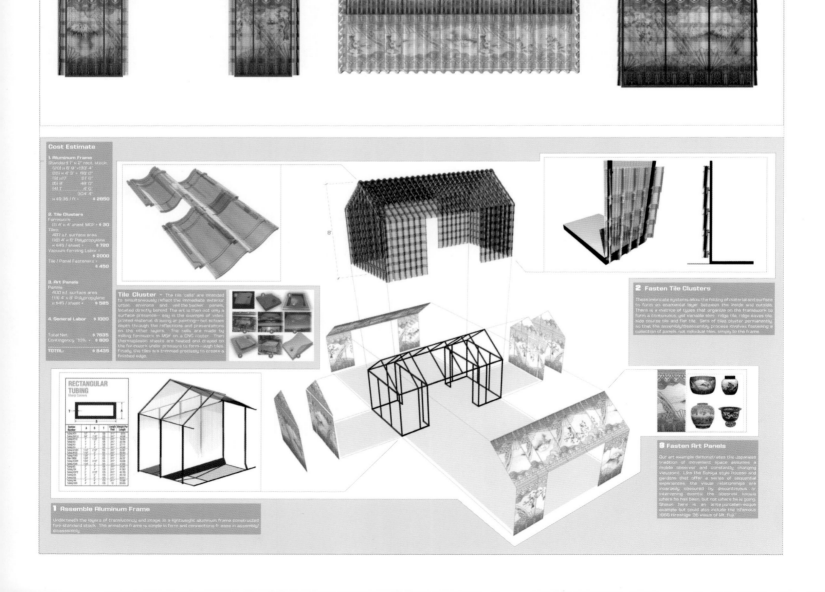

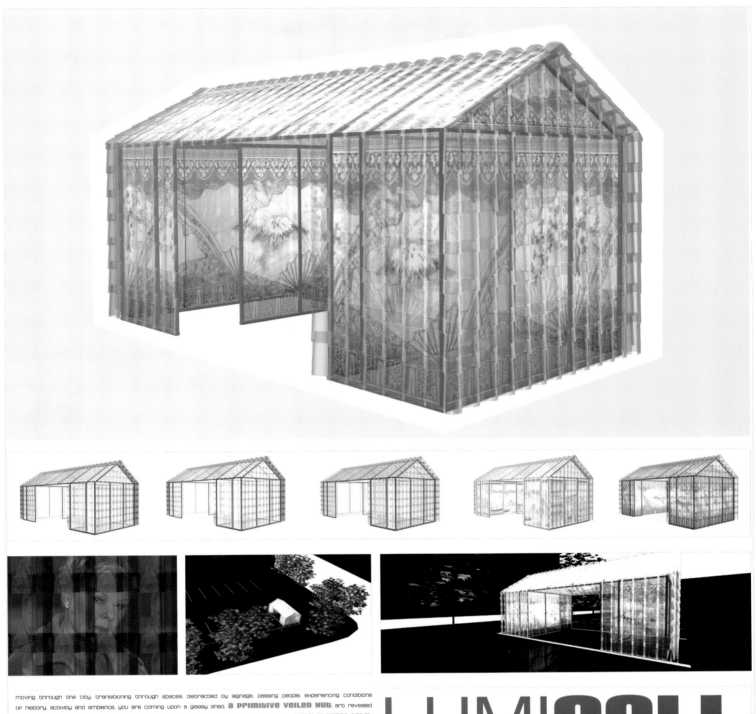

moving through the city, transitioning through spaces, distracted by signage, passing people, experiencing conditions of history, activity and ambience, you are coming upon a glassy shed. **a primitive veiled hut,** and revealed through interior and exterior views. The form is simple and the formation easy, but the **affect intriguing. the intarsia complex.** it is **a surface landscape of luminescence** formed into a distinct object, embedded within an urban logic. it orchestrates **a private atmosphere** temporarily captured for each viewer, it projects **an aura for each of us,** a precise moment of presence in daily life, where the meaning of art and thus our meaning, is realized.

LUMI**CELL**

the irreconcilability of the **intoxicating, almost erotic allure** of the compoundly curved, **luxurious** acrylic roof-like tiles as both architectural ornament & enclosure...

creating in monolithic uniformity with the functional rationalization of the overall system, or **primeval form,** resulting in a combinatorial set of powerful **effects**

303

Glowworm | *REC ARQUITECTURA*

Competition : STEEDMAN; NY/E.U.A
Team : Gerardo Recoder Déciga

Glowworm Pavilion

Taking the NYC subway system and its train cars as reference point while inserting a rigorous grid on it, the pavilion is generated with proportion; able to be inserted in a variety of locations, but now in a single location we have different pavilion variants, conceived with three main elements: floor, ceiling and axis; easy to built and assemble; floor and ceiling are movable, they slide independently from the main structure while generating new points of reference, this three simple elements are susceptible bodies to get dressed for different expression skins: glass, marble, concrete, copper, stainless steel, fiberglass. Etc.

An Axis-Pavilion which concentrates on the individual instead of the surroundings; having the senses as main tool, perceiving, associating and playing with the overlapping of virtual and real, supported in the virtual technology of hologram, they will put on in juxtaposition oneself object, in the day virtual inside the boxcar and real in the exterior, and at night, vice versa, understanding that the boxcar will be able to have different positions, moreover, this configuration generates more opportunities to engage dialogue with nature: light and shadow, inside and outside, cover and exposed, rain, speed, wind and reflections are some of the elements that change depending on the different configuration the pavilion may adopt.

The senses help the observer to interact with the human and non-human, while allowing different forms of expression. Freing it self from a single form of reference.

The architecture moves now, stopping to be sedentary for now returning to be nomadic.

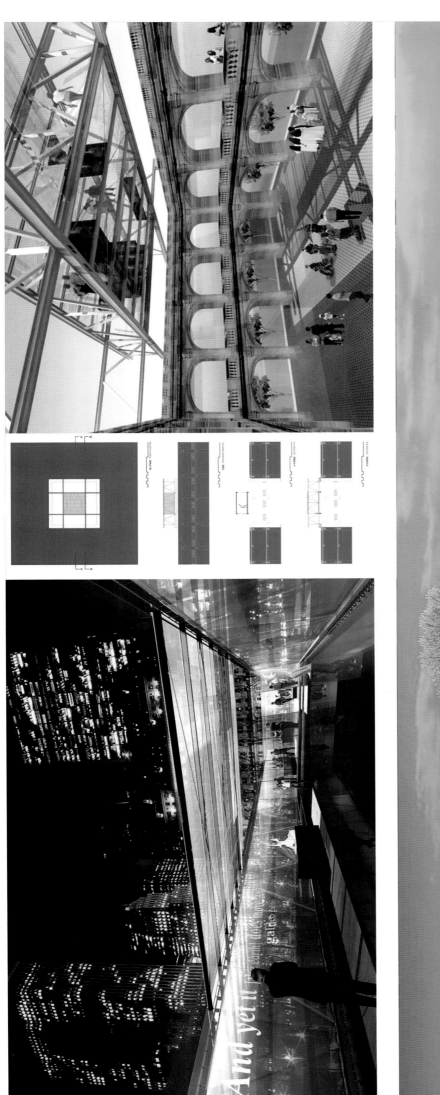

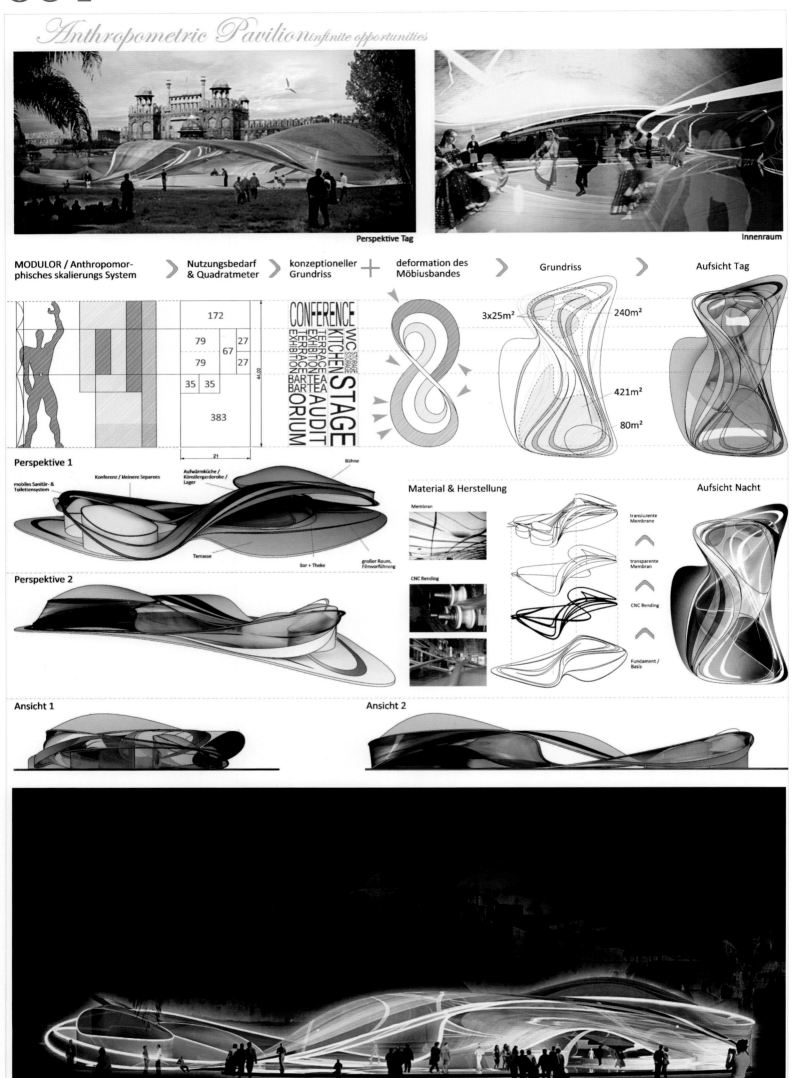

Anthropometric Pavilion *infinite opportunities*

Perspektive Tag

Innenraum

MODULOR / Anthropomor-
phisches skalierungs System

Nutzungsbedarf
& Quadratmeter

konzeptioneller
Grundriss

deformation des
Möbiusbandes

Grundriss

Aufsicht Tag

172

79   27
        67
79   27

35   35

383

44.00

21

3x25m²   240m²

421m²

80m²

CONFERENCE
KITCHEN STAGE
WC STORAGE
STORAGE
TERRACE
EXHIBITION
EXHIBITION
TERRACE
TERRACE
BARTEA
BARTEA
ORIUM
AUDIT

Perspektive 1

mobiles Sanitär- &
Toilettensystem

Konferenz / kleinere Separees

Aufwärmküche /
Künstlergarderobe /
Lager

Bühne

Terrasse

Bar + Theke

großer Raum,
Filmvorführung

Material & Herstellung

Aufsicht Nacht

Membran

transluzente
Membrane

transparente
Membran

CNC Bending

CNC Bending

Fundament /
Basis

Perspektive 2

Ansicht 1

Ansicht 2

Perspektive Nacht / Projektion

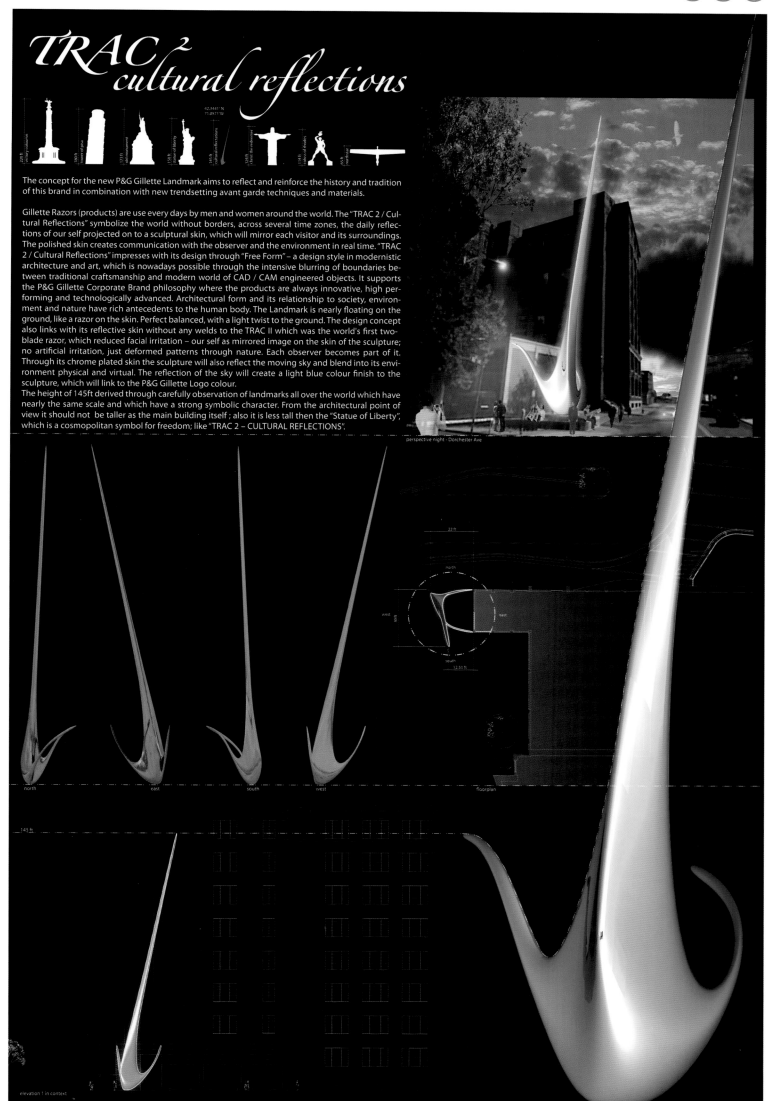

TRAC² cultural reflections

The concept for the new P&G Gillette Landmark aims to reflect and reinforce the history and tradition of this brand in combination with new trendsetting avant garde techniques and materials.

Gillette Razors (products) are use every days by men and women around the world. The "TRAC 2 / Cultural Reflections" symbolize the world without borders, across several time zones, the daily reflections of our self projected on to a sculptural skin, which will mirror each visitor and its surroundings. The polished skin creates communication with the observer and the environment in real time. "TRAC 2 / Cultural Reflections" impresses with its design through "Free Form" – a design style in modernistic architecture and art, which is nowadays possible through the intensive blurring of boundaries between traditional craftsmanship and modern world of CAD / CAM engineered objects. It supports the P&G Gillette Corporate Brand philosophy where the products are always innovative, high performing and technologically advanced. Architectural form and its relationship to society, environment and nature have rich antecedents to the human body. The Landmark is nearly floating on the ground, like a razor on the skin. Perfect balanced, with a light twist to the ground. The design concept also links with its reflective skin without any welds to the TRAC II which was the world's first two-blade razor, which reduced facial irritation – our self as mirrored image on the skin of the sculpture; no artificial irritation, just deformed patterns through nature. Each observer becomes part of it. Through its chrome plated skin the sculpture will also reflect the moving sky and blend into its environment physical and virtual. The reflection of the sky will create a light blue colour finish to the sculpture, which will link to the P&G Gillette Logo colour.

The height of 145ft derived through carefully observation of landmarks all over the world which have nearly the same scale and which have a strong symbolic character. From the architectural point of view it should not be taller as the main building itself ; also it is less tall then the "Statue of Liberty", which is a cosmopolitan symbol for freedom; like "TRAC 2 – CULTURAL REFLECTIONS".

perspective night - Dorchester Ave

north   east   south   west   floorplan

145 ft

elevation 1 in context

Pa LASTE UND ELASTE

Lageplan

Dietmar Koering   02/08/2007

Leicht und formschön aus der Retorte

Perspektive 1

Front

Side L

Back

Side R

Es war einmal ein Kind welches sich ‚Palast der Republik' nannte; aufgewachsen im schoße seiner Mutter, doch die Bewohner konnten nicht von der so grossen Mutter lassen. Erst gesprengt nun wieder kodiert und zu neuem Leben erwacht. Um die Mutter mit hilfe der Magie in die physika-lische Welt zu holen muss das Kind jedoch weichen. Warum haben die Bewohner angst vor neuem, warum Tote wieder-beleben?

Den glanz vergangener Epochen erstre-ben mit dem wiederaufbau eines längst verlorenen Gebäudes. Die alleinige diskussion eine Farce - die Erschaffung eines Zombies – aus Plaste-Elaste, dem was bleibt in unserer polymeren Welt.

Das Schloss der zukunft – virtuell real, physisch eine Wolke, eine Idee – optisch ein Krebsgeschwür im herzen der Stadt.

Recycling -Eine struktur aus den resten der Republik, Baustoff der Zukunft zugleich, symbolisierend wie ein alter Knochen... das Fleisch was einst so leben-dig war, gegessen von der Nachtigall... geblieben die verwurzelung zur Erde, was wir Heimat nennen. Groß und thronend im urbanen Kontext, punk in der Geste, keine rücksicht auf vorhandene Bauschät-ze, erstrahlendes weiss, ein schatten über dem Rathaus... ein schatten über alles, denn das ist was immer bleiben wird: der Palast der Republik, ein schatten in unserem Geist. Auch wenn in trümmern, er wird immer da-sein. Geschichte lässt sich verändern, biegen oder manipulie-ren, jedoch nie auslöschen.

Perspektive 1

Schnitt urbaner Kontext

Freude im Haushalt

Welche Hausfrau hat die Vorzüge dieses praktischen Materials noch nicht erkannt? Es ist geruch- und geschmackfrei, hygienisch, leicht und bruchfest, form-schön und farbenfreudig. Plaste ist für Ihren Haushalt kein Ersatz, sondern ein unentbehrlicher vollwertiger Rohstoff.

Capitoné | *gutiérrez-delafuente arquitectos*

Client : City of Madrid
Team : Natalia Gutiérrez & Julio de la Fuente

Project : National Competition Book Fair Pavilion in Madrid
Program : Temporary Book Fair Pavilion
Location : Madrid, Spain

307

CAPITONÉ

CONCURSO PABELLÓN AYUNTAMIENTO
FERIA DEL LIBRO DE MADRID 2008

CONTEXTO

-LA IDENTIDAD TIPOLÓGICA DE LA FERIA DEL LIBRO DE MADRID REALIZADA EN EL PASEO DE COCHES DEL RETIRO ES LA LINEALIDAD, SU DESARROLLO LONGITUDINAL Y EL FLUJO QUE ESTE PROVOCA EN DOS SENTIDOS.

-EL OBJETIVO DEL PABELLÓN DEL AYUNTAMIENTO, ADEMÁS DEL PROGRAMÁTICO DEBE SER EL DE SERVIR DE REFERENCIA, DE PUERTA VIRTUAL DE LA FERIA. CONVERTIRSE EN UN HITO RECONOCIBLE. EL AYUNTAMIENTO COMO MARCA.

-LA HERRAMIENTA UTILIZADA PARA ARTICULAR ESTAS DOS VARIABLES SERÁ UN OPERACIÓN DE LAND-ART.
UN MURO. AZUL.

PROGRAMA

-UN MURO. CONTÍNUO QUE CONDUCE AL VISITANTE. LA ENTRADA Y LA SALIDA SE PRODUCEN EN EL SENTIDO NATURAL DE LA MARCHA. EL LONGITUDINAL.

-UNA GRIETA. UN ESPACIO INTERSTICIAL ABOCINADO EN FUNCIÓN DEL FLUJO DE VISITANTES Y DE LA AGLOMERACIÓN EN TORNO A LA ENTRADA Y LA TIENDA. ESTE ESPACIO ES UN PASEO ABIERTO EN EL QUE CASITE CUELAS SIN QUERER Y EN EL QUE SE DESCUBREN LAS PROYECCIONES REALIZADAS SOBRE EL FALSO TECHO EN DIENTE DE SIERRA. EN EL ACCESO Y EN LA SALIDA DOS PUERTAS PIVOTANTES PERMITEN UN CORRECTO CIERRE NOCTURNO.

-UN VOLUMEN. CON EL PROGRAMA ESTRICTO DEL PABELLÓN: TIENDA, ALMACÉN, INSTALACIONES Y SALA POLIVALENTE, QUE SE PLANTEA COMO UN ESPACIO INDEPENDIENTE, NO DE PASO.

MATERIALIDAD

-EL MURO SE REALIZA EN **CAPITONÉ AZUL**. EL CAPITONÉ ES UNA REFERENCIA AL ESPACIO DOMÉSTICO, ENTENDIENDO ESTE COMO UN ESPACIO DE LECTURA, DE REPOSO...DE LOS LIBROS.

SE REALIZARÁ EN LONA ABOTONADA Y ACOLCHADA CON UN MÓDULO DE 30CM.

-LAS PUERTAS DE ACCESO Y SALIDA SON DOS FRAGMENTOS DE UNA BIBLIOTECA QUE PIVOTAN.LA ENTRADA Y LA SALIDA SE REALIZA A TRAVÉS DE LOS **LIBROS**. SE CONSTRUYE CON ELLOS.

-LA GRIETA DE PASO TIENE UN FALSO TECHO EN DIENTE DE SIERRA FORMADO POR **LONA BLANCA** DE PVC SOBRE LA QUE SE PROYECTAN IMÁGENES DESDE EL INTERIOR.LAS IMÁGENES SOLO SE VAN DESCUBRIENDO AL ANDAR, MISTERIO... CURIOSIDAD....

-EL VOLUMEN QUE CONTIENE EL PROGRAMA SE PLANTEA COMO UN ESPACIO NEUTRO, BLANCO Y NEGRO. EL CERRAMIENTO EXTERIOR ESTÁ FORMADO POR PLANCHAS DE **ACERO INOX PLEGADO** PARA CONFUNDIR LOS LÍMITES REALES DEL PABELLÓN CON REFLEJOS DEL RETIRO Y LOS VISITANTES.

CAPITONÉ

CONCURSO PABELLÓN AYUNTAMIENTO
FERIA DEL LIBRO DE MADRID 2008

ALZADO MURO DE CAPITONÉ AZUL 1/150
IMAGEN EXTERIOR FERIA DEL LIBRO

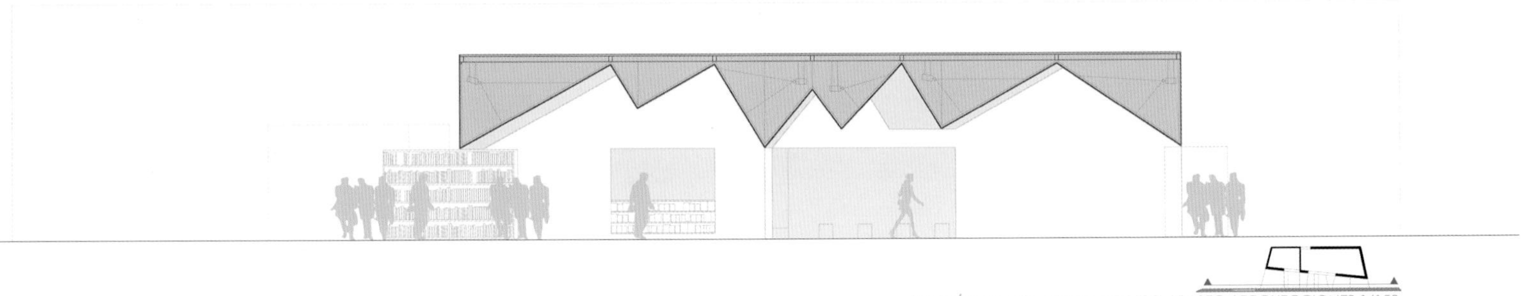

SECCIÓN AA POR GRIETA ACCESO / PASEO / PROYECCIONES 1/150
IMAGEN INTERIOR GRIETA ACCESO / PASEO / PROYECCIONES

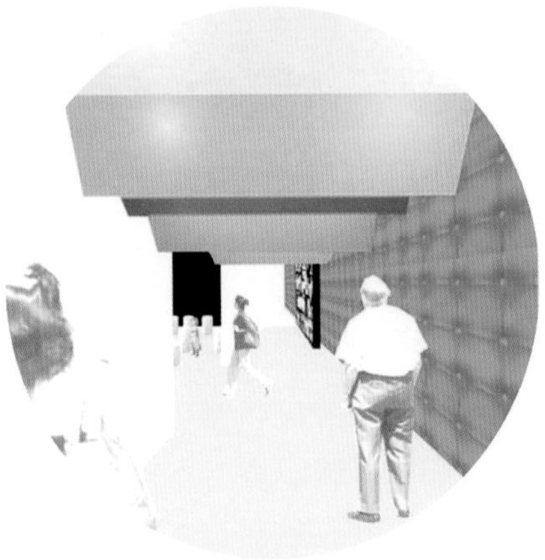

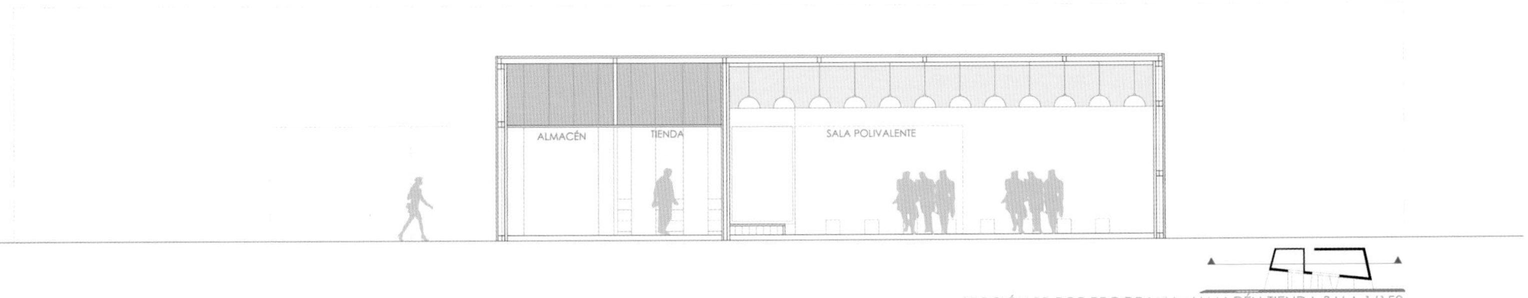

SECCIÓN BB POR PROGRAMA: ALMACÉN-TIENDA-SALA 1/150
IMAGEN INTERIOR DE LA SALA POLIVALENTE

SALA POLIVALENTE

TIENDA

ALMACÉN

FDLM08

CAPITONÉ
CONCURSO PABELLÓN AYUNTAMIENTO
FERIA DEL LIBRO DE MADRID 2008

≡

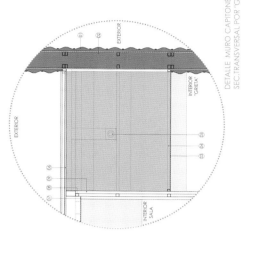

DETALLE MURO CAPITONÉ AZUL
SEC. TRANSVERSAL POR 'GRIETA'
1/50

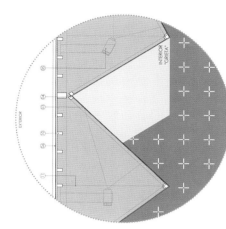

DETALLE LONA PROYECCIÓN
FALSO TECHO 'GRIETA' 1/50

DETALLE SALA POLIVALENTE
1/50

ACCESO

PLANTA 1/50

SALIDA

SALA POLIVALENTE

INSTALACIONES

ALMACÉN

TIENDA

GRIETA DE PASO / PROYECCIÓN IMAGENES / PASEO

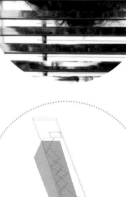

GRIETA DE PASO. PASEO. PROYECCIONES. DESCUBRIR AL ANDAR......

UN MURO DE CAPITONÉ AZUL. IDENTIDAD FERIA/AYUNTAMIENTO.

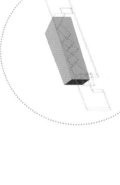

BORRAR LOS LÍMITES DEL PABELLÓN. REFLEJAR LA FERIA, EL RETIRO......

ACCESO/SALIDA A TRAVÉS DE LOS LIBROS. MATERIAL CONSTRUCTIVO.

MEMORIA CONSTRUCTIVA:
01>>TAPIZADO DE CAPITONÉ AZUL REALIZADO EN LONA. 02>>DOBLE SUBESTRUCTURA METÁLICA DEL MURO DE CAPITONÉ ANCLADA AL SUELO Y ARRIOSTRADA CON EL RESTO DEL PABELLÓN. 03>>LONA DE PVC BLANCA. 04>>SUBESTRUCTURA TRANSVERSAL PARA FORMACIÓN DE DIENTE DE SIERRA DE MADERA. 05>>PROYECTOR DE IMÁGENES. 06>>FORMACIÓN DE CUBIERTA DEL PABELLÓN. 07>>FALSO TECHO DE PLADUR LACADO EN NEGRO. 08>>SUBESTRUCTURA VERTICAL METÁLICA DE SEPARACIÓN INTERIOR. 09>>TRASDOSADO DE PLADUR PINTADO EN BLANCO. 10>>ESTRUCTURA HORIZONTAL METÁLICA DE FORMACIÓN DE LA GRIETA ARRIOSTRAMIENTO HORIZONTAL DEL MURO. 11>>PLETINA METÁLICA DE RIGIDIZACIÓN DE LA LONA Y LOS DIENTES DE SIERRA DEL FALSO TECHO DE LA GRIETA. 12>>ILUMINACIÓN SUSPENDIDA SOBRE LA SALA POLIVALENTE. 13>>ILUMINACIÓN PERIMETRAL OCULTA EN EL FALSO TECHO DE LA SALA POLIVALENTE. 14>>ESTRUCTURA TUBULAR METÁLICA DEL VOLUMEN QUE ALBERGA EL PROGRAMA. 15>>CERRAMIENTO EXTERIOR DE CHAPA PLEGADA DE ACERO INOX. SOBRE BASTIDOR METÁLICO.

308

Mobile Unit Poster | *David Garcia Studio*

Participants : David A. Garcia (Architect MAA)
Partner : Alanna Baudinet (Architect)
Project : Open Source Mobile Architectural System In Extreme Environment
Typology : Mobile Building Unit

Location : Antarctica / Construction volume : 8m² / unit
Client : European Commission Culture

MOBILE MEDIA-CENTRIC HABITATION AND WORK UNIT

RADIUS OF OPERATIONS

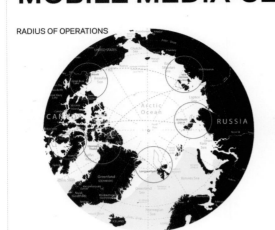

A The proposal for this competition aims to look at the project as a physical and mediatic system. The habitation and working unit is resolved as a modular system, that can be modified in time due to needs and technology advancements or multiplied and linked to create larger units. At the other end of the spectrum, the proposed mediatic system is a network of "cultural beacons" that allow for communication between the arctic societies and the research unit.

B The research unit is designed around an aluminium rectangular frame (2.8 x 2.8 m and 2.3 m height), to which six "façade" elements are attached. These elements are tailored around the necessities for research and habitation in the interior, and shaped aerodynamically on the exterior, using this double shell system to incorporate insulation and house reservoirs.

The suggested scenario shows 13.2 m2 unit, with a facade designed to incorporate sleeping units that transform into desks when folded, including a battery array with in the shell construction. Another façade incorporates toilet and shower with integrated snow smelter, which is filled from the exterior. A pantry and kitchenette façade module holds a galley. Technical shelves and communications are housed in the fourth façade module, which also incorporates a large window for natural light and first aid treatment. The central "roof" canopy has a skylight and the flooring module includes gray water treatment and storage. All these elements are exchangeable, interchangeable and replaceable, due to the fact that they all fit to the same rectangular frame and are removable independently. This allows the unit to be modernised in time, or modify its use to a more specific task. The unit is also designed to grow. By connecting to another unit of the same design, one can modify each unit to house different functions. One unit could concentrate habitation elements, creating a private sphere, and the other could be tailored for work and research activities, doubling the total floor space.

The modules that form each unit are made of an exterior and an interior glass fibre shell filled with insulating foam, creating a sandwich construction. Inside this thick insulating sandwich, different forms of polyurethane containers, which are easily accessible from the inside, hold the fresh and grey water reservoirs, snow smelting systems, which can be filled from the outside. Batteries are stored closed to the floor giving ballast and adding stability when the unit rests on snow, or in an emergency, while floating on water.

The over all outlines of the unit have been contoured to be as aerodynamic as possible while maintaining the maximum internal efficiency regarding availability and use of space. Great care has been taken in allowing for daylight through a generous skylight and windows. Vertical facades are covered with photovoltaic panels, exploiting the mainly horizontal sun rays of the arctic (a potential surface of 25 m2), and together with a deployable wind turbine of 1.800 mm diameter, the unit generates 6 Kwh.

EXAMPLE OF YEAR CALENDAR OF ACTIVITIES AT DIFFERENT COMMUNITIES

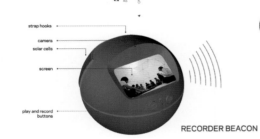

C The cultural "recording beacon" is an extension the mediatic unit. It is designed to stay for a period of time within the cultural groups visited, and to be fully controlled by the user. We propose this system as an anthropological mail service. The beacons are easy to operate and to carry, and charge to mains or on the field, aided by solar cells. The aim is to create a network of cultural sharing, by recording and sending their everyday activities (see potential activity and route diagram) and emitting the video footage to the mediatic unit or other regions (or the net) with the push of a button. Such system would complement the event character of the mediatic unit, allowing the society which is left behind, to continue the aim of culture sharing and preservation. The units could as well be "posted" and exchanged with the neighbouring region, creating a tradition of autonomous artistic and social sharing.

strap hooks
camera
solar cells
screen
play and record buttons

RECORDER BEACON

FACADE MODULE POSSIBILITIES

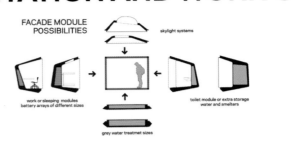

skylight systems

work or sleeping modules
battery arrays of different sizes

toilet module or extra storage
water and smelters

grey water treatmet sizes

FACADE MODULE CONSTRUCTION

main frame

19 inch frames

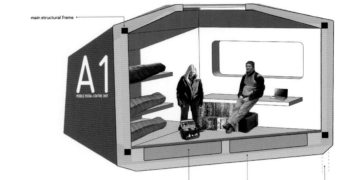

main structural frame

A1
MOBILE MEDIA-CENTRE UNIT

grey water treatment
insulation
axis of attachment (skis)

SECTI

skylight
toilet and shower
battery array

B

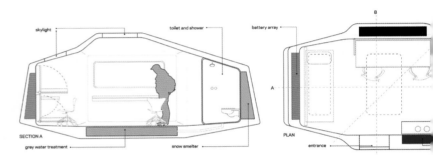

SECTION A

grey water treatment
snow smelter

A

PLAN
entrance

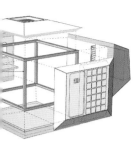

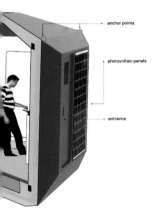

anchor points

photovoltaic panels

entrance

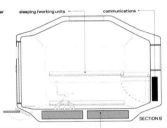

smelter · sleeping /working units · communications

grey water treatment

SECTION B

A1

MOBILE MEDIA-CENTRIC UNIT

SNOW SMELTER

unit on towable skis

SINGLE SELF SUSTAINED UNIT

TWO UNIT SYSTEM: HABITATION AND WORK

THREE UNIT SYSTEM: HABITATION, WORK AND EXHIBITION SPACE

land transport

helicopter transport

sea transport

309

Glowing Cloud | *object-e architecture*

Design : Theodora Christoforidou, Dimitris Gourdoukis, Katerina Tryfonidou, Fotis Vasilakis
Project : Design For An Outdoor Shelter
Typology : Sheltering Structure
Location : Athens, Greece

(1/3)

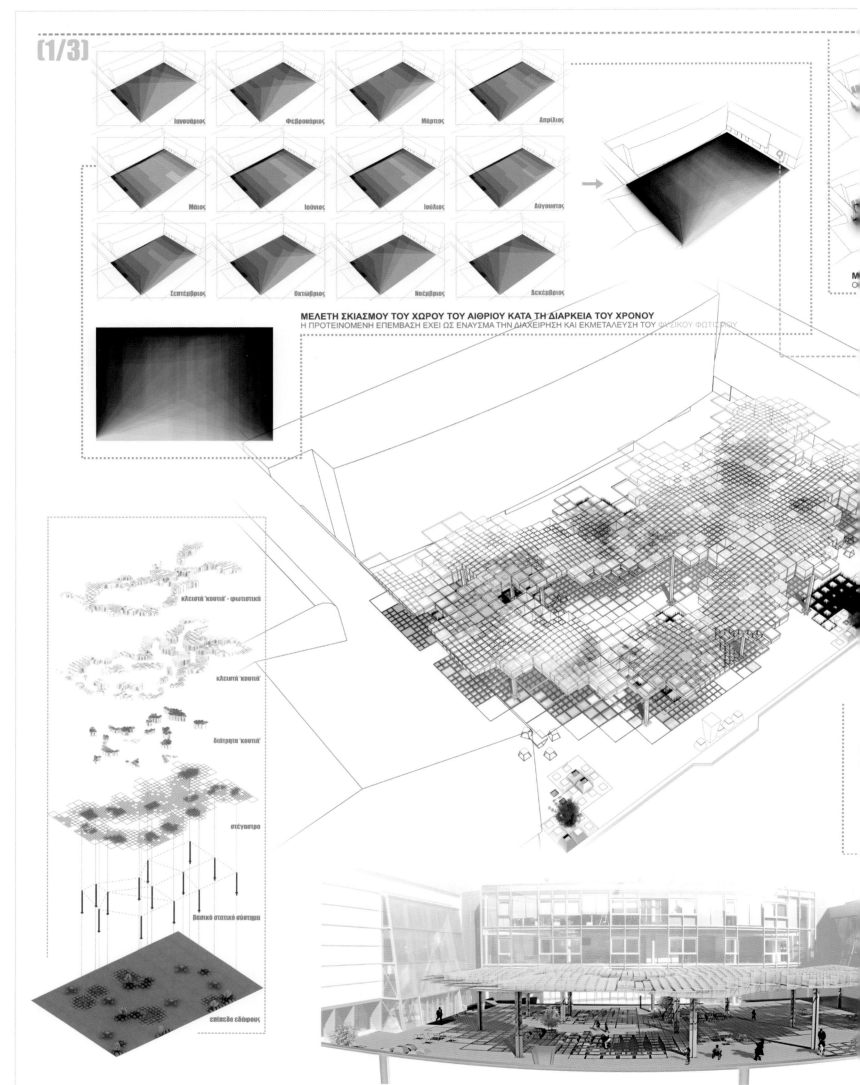

Ιανουάριος | Φεβρουάριος | Μάρτιος | Απρίλιος

Μάιος | Ιούνιος | Ιούλιος | Αύγουστος

Σεπτέμβριος | Οκτώβριος | Νοέμβριος | Δεκέμβριος

ΜΕΛΕΤΗ ΣΚΙΑΣΜΟΥ ΤΟΥ ΧΩΡΟΥ ΤΟΥ ΑΙΘΡΙΟΥ ΚΑΤΑ ΤΗ ΔΙΑΡΚΕΙΑ ΤΟΥ ΧΡΟΝΟΥ
Η ΠΡΟΤΕΙΝΟΜΕΝΗ ΕΠΕΜΒΑΣΗ ΕΧΕΙ ΩΣ ΕΝΑΥΣΜΑ ΤΗΝ ΔΙΑΧΕΙΡΗΣΗ ΚΑΙ ΕΚΜΕΤΑΛΕΥΣΗ ΤΟΥ ΦΥΣΙΚΟΥ ΦΩΤΙΣΜΟΥ

κλειστά 'κουτιά' - φωτιστικά

κλειστά 'κουτιά'

διάτρητα 'κουτιά'

στέγαστρο

βασικό στατικό σύστημα

επίπεδο εδάφους

851

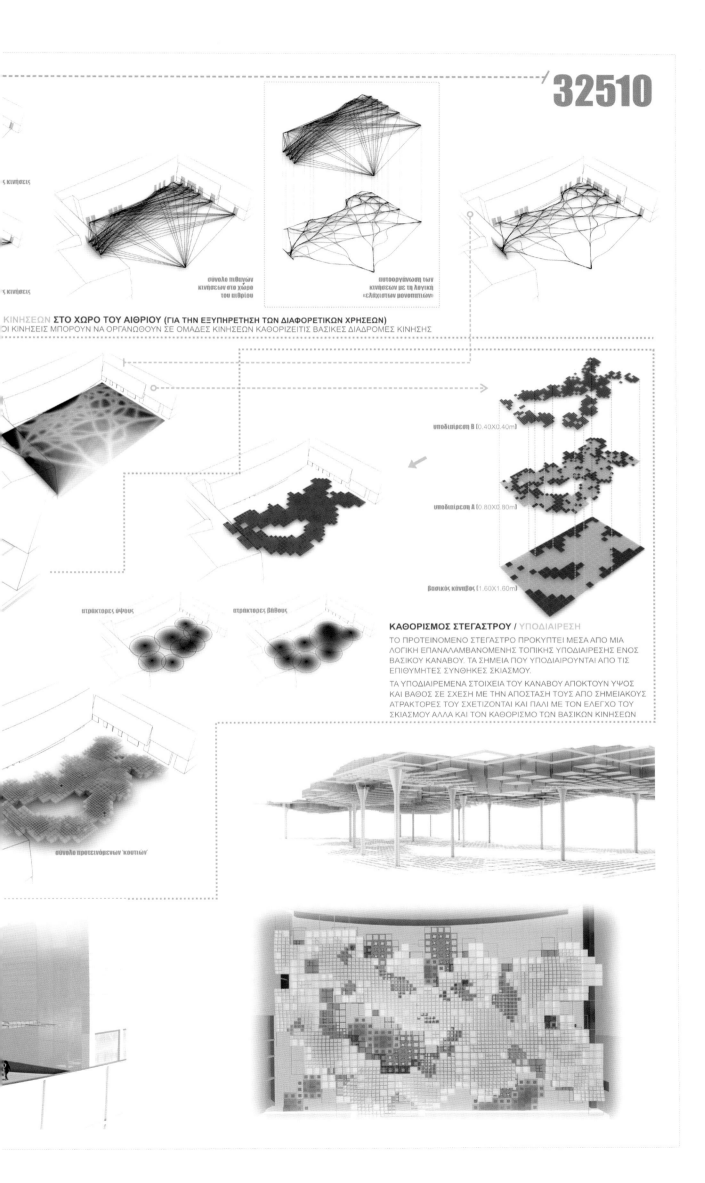

32510

ΚΙΝΗΣΕΩΝ **ΣΤΟ ΧΩΡΟ ΤΟΥ ΑΙΘΡΙΟΥ (ΓΙΑ ΤΗΝ ΕΞΥΠΗΡΕΤΗΣΗ ΤΩΝ ΔΙΑΦΟΡΕΤΙΚΩΝ ΧΡΗΣΕΩΝ)**
ΟΙ ΚΙΝΗΣΕΙΣ ΜΠΟΡΟΥΝ ΝΑ ΟΡΓΑΝΩΘΟΥΝ ΣΕ ΟΜΑΔΕΣ ΚΙΝΗΣΕΩΝ ΚΑΘΟΡΙΖΕΙΤΙΣ ΒΑΣΙΚΕΣ ΔΙΑΔΡΟΜΕΣ ΚΙΝΗΣΗΣ

σύνολο πιθανών
κινήσεων στο χώρο
του αιθρίου

αυτοοργάνωση των
κινήσεων με τη λογική
«ελάχιστων μονοπατιών»

υποδιαίρεση Β (0.40Χ0.40m)

υποδιαίρεση Α (0.80Χ0.80m)

βασικός κάναβος (1.60Χ1.60m)

ΚΑΘΟΡΙΣΜΟΣ ΣΤΕΓΑΣΤΡΟΥ / ΥΠΟΔΙΑΙΡΕΣΗ

ΤΟ ΠΡΟΤΕΙΝΟΜΕΝΟ ΣΤΕΓΑΣΤΡΟ ΠΡΟΚΥΠΤΕΙ ΜΕΣΑ ΑΠΟ ΜΙΑ
ΛΟΓΙΚΗ ΕΠΑΝΑΛΑΜΒΑΝΟΜΕΝΗΣ ΤΟΠΙΚΗΣ ΥΠΟΔΙΑΙΡΕΣΗΣ ΕΝΟΣ
ΒΑΣΙΚΟΥ ΚΑΝΑΒΟΥ. ΤΑ ΣΗΜΕΙΑ ΠΟΥ ΥΠΟΔΙΑΙΡΟΥΝΤΑΙ ΑΠΟ ΤΙΣ
ΕΠΙΘΥΜΗΤΕΣ ΣΥΝΘΗΚΕΣ ΣΚΙΑΣΜΟΥ.

ΤΑ ΥΠΟΔΙΑΙΡΕΜΕΝΑ ΣΤΟΙΧΕΙΑ ΤΟΥ ΚΑΝΑΒΟΥ ΑΠΟΚΤΟΥΝ ΥΨΟΣ
ΚΑΙ ΒΑΘΟΣ ΣΕ ΣΧΕΣΗ ΜΕ ΤΗΝ ΑΠΟΣΤΑΣΗ ΤΟΥΣ ΑΠΟ ΣΗΜΕΙΑΚΟΥΣ
ΑΤΡΑΚΤΟΡΕΣ ΤΟΥ ΣΧΕΤΙΖΟΝΤΑΙ ΚΑΙ ΠΑΛΙ ΜΕ ΤΟΝ ΕΛΕΓΧΟ ΤΟΥ
ΣΚΙΑΣΜΟΥ ΑΛΛΑ ΚΑΙ ΤΟΝ ΚΑΘΟΡΙΣΜΟ ΤΩΝ ΒΑΣΙΚΩΝ ΚΙΝΗΣΕΩΝ

ατράκτορες ύψους

ατράκτορες βάθους

σύνολο προτεινόμενων 'κουτιών'

[2/3]

ΠΡΟΟΠΤΙΚΗ ΑΠΕΙΚΟΝΙΣΗ
ΠΡΟΣΕΓΓΙΣΗ ΤΟΥ ΑΙΘΡΙΟΥ ΑΠΟ ΤΗΝ ΟΔΟ ΠΕΙΡΑΙΩΣ [ΚΛ: 1:100]

ΠΡΟΟΠΤΙΚΗ ΑΠΕΙΚΟΝΙΣΗ
ΠΡΟΣΕΓΓΙΣΗ ΤΟΥ ΑΙΘΡΙΟΥ ΑΠΟ ΤΗ ΟΔΟ ΠΕΙΡΑΙΩΣ [ΝΥΚΤΕΡΙΝΗ ΛΗΨΗ]

ΚΑΤΟΨΗ ΑΙΘΡΙΟΥ / ΔΙΑΜΟΡΦΩΣΗ ΕΔΑΦΟΥΣ [ΚΛ: 1:100]

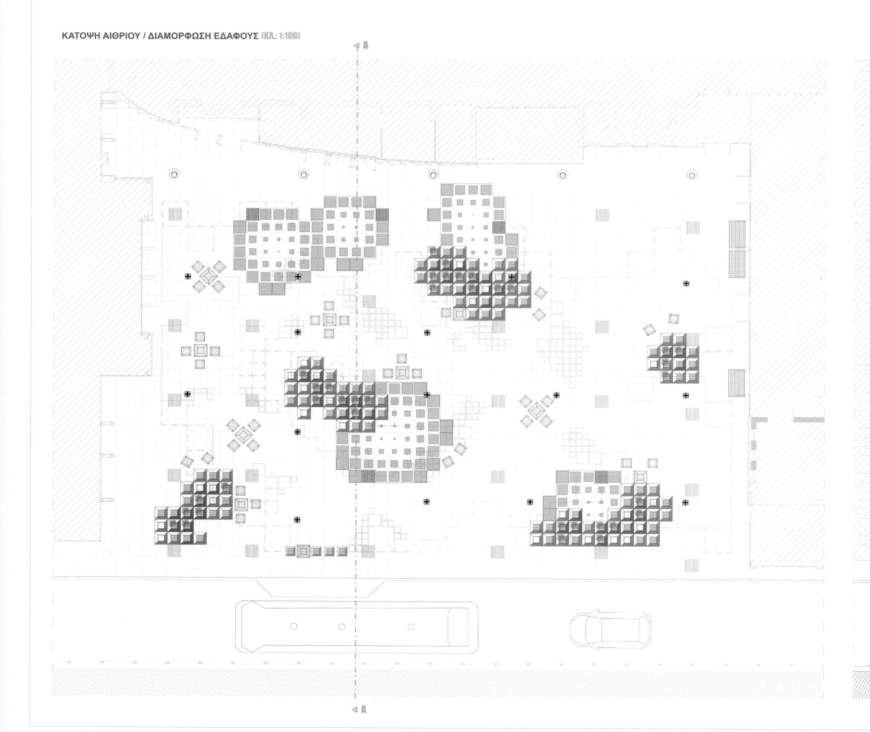

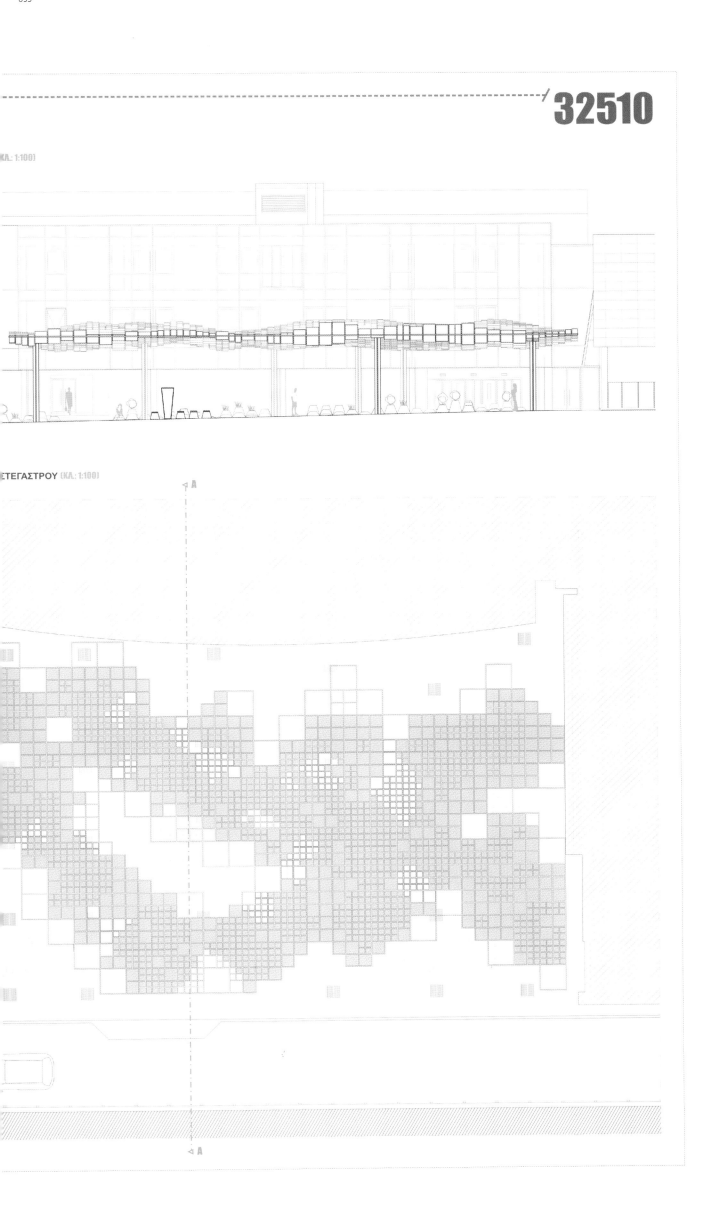

(ΚΛ.: 1:100)

ΕΤΕΓΑΣΤΡΟΥ (ΚΛ.: 1:100)

A

A

A

A

[3/3]

περιοχή δαπέδου με τις
πλάκες σκληρού δαπέδου, το
φυτεμένο χώμα, τα σταθερά
καθιστικά και τις φυτεύσεις

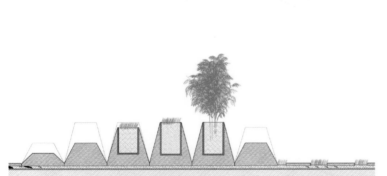

τομή λεπτομέρεια δαπέδου

Μετασχηματιστής

Μεταλλικό σύστημα στήριξης του
πολυκαρβονικού κουτιού

Πλάκα 3x3
LED Luxcon Rebel

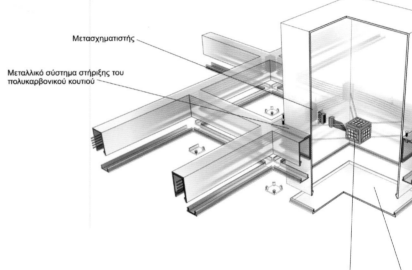

Η αστική επίπλωση είναι μετακινούμενη για να επιτρέπεται
η πλατεία να φιλοξενεί διαφορετικές δραστηριότητες. Τα
τραπέζια μπορουν να διαταχθουν διασπαρμένα με λίγες
καρέκλες γύρω τους για την συνευρεση φίλων, ή να
τοποθετηθούν στην σειρά ή σε σχήμα Π για τις ανάγκες
εκπαιδευτικών προγραμμάτων για παιδιά. Σε συναυλίες τα
τραπέζια απομακρύνονται τελείως και τα καθίσματα
διατάσσονται γύρω από τον χώρο της σκηνής.

Αεροστεγές καπάκι
ημιδιάφανο χυτό πολυκαρβ

διαστάσεις: 40cm x 40cm ή 8
x 80cm, το ύψος κυμαίνεται
40cm εως 1·

0.58

0.58   0.40   0.80   0.40

                0.45

0.40

κινητή αστική επίπλωση   στάση τραμ

32510

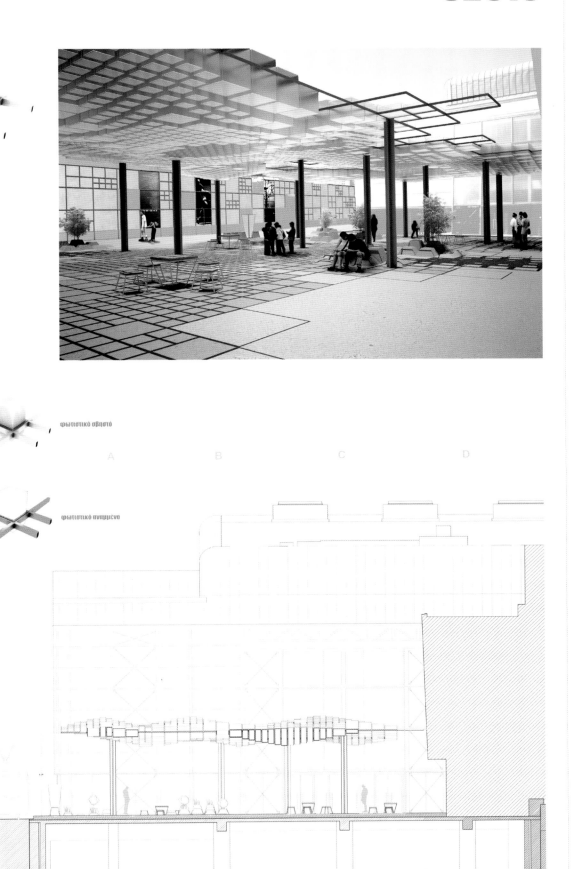

φωτιστικό σβηστό

A   B   C   D

φωτιστικό αναμμένο

ΤΟΜΗ [ΚΛ.: 1:100]

310

Togs | *object-e architecture*

Design : Dimitris Gourdoukis
Project : Design For A Temporary Outdoor Gallery
Typology : Temporary Structure
Location : Denver, USA

TOGS 2 TEMPORARY OUTDOOR GALLERY SPACE

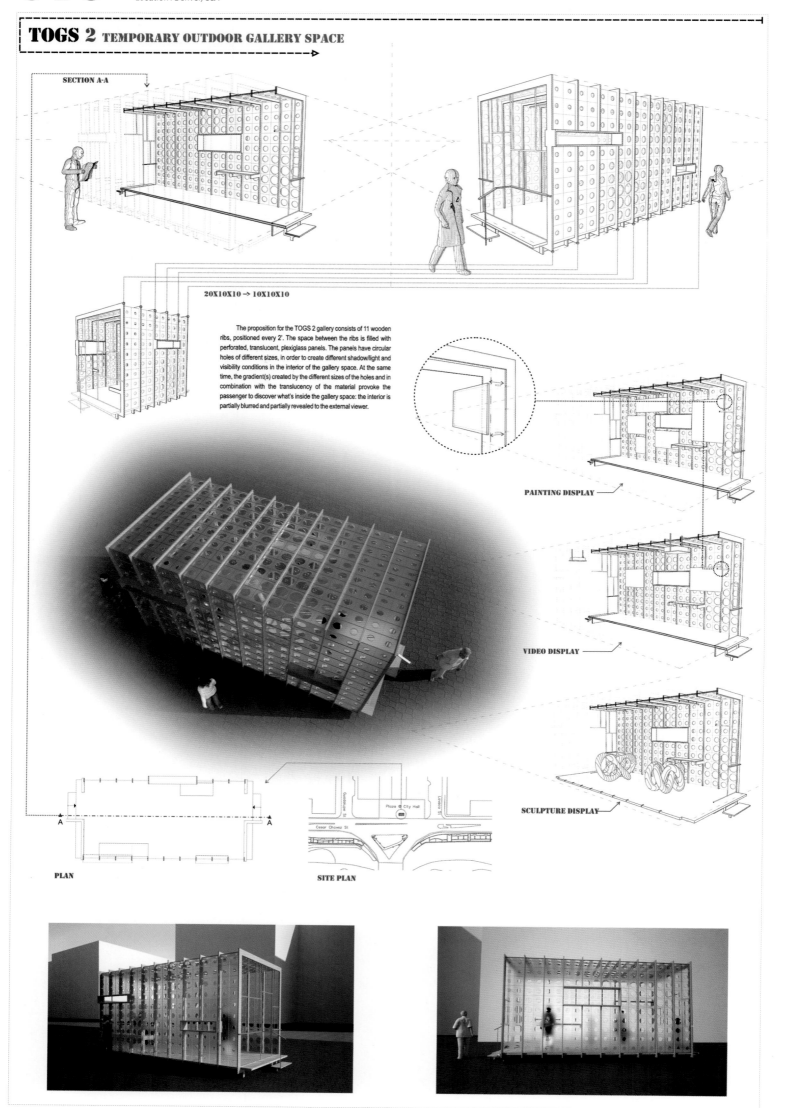

SECTION A-A

20X10X10 → 10X10X10

The proposition for the TOGS 2 gallery consists of 11 wooden ribs, positioned every 2'. The space between the ribs is filled with perforated, translucent, plexiglass panels. The panels have circular holes of different sizes, in order to create different shadow/light and visibility conditions in the interior of the gallery space. At the same time, the gradient(s) created by the different sizes of the holes and in combination with the translucency of the material provoke the passenger to discover what's inside the gallery space: the interior is partially blurred and partially revealed to the external viewer.

PAINTING DISPLAY

VIDEO DISPLAY

SCULPTURE DISPLAY

PLAN

SITE PLAN

London Mosaic | *Arquipelago Studio*

Project Team : Gregory Marinic(principal), Karen Mendoza,
Alejandra Rios, Andrea Barrero
Program : London Olympic Pavilion

311

012741

london
MOSAIC

An Olympic Games Information Pavilion for Trafalgar Square...

Like the city of London itself, the Olympic Games bring people together from around the world to share life and culture. This proposal for the London Olympic Games Information Pavilion reflects the cultural, geographic, and material diversity found within and beyond London.

London will host the most illustrious sporting event in the world for an unprecedented third time. As the largest urban conglomeration in the European Union, the city's cosmopolitan population of over 7.7 million residents reflects larger global diversity. This concept for the London Olympic Games Information Pavilion embeds information derived from a global survey of biological, geological, and geographic generators. This information was studied, diagrammed, and reconsidered for its relevance as a cultural filter serving visitors from around the world.

Conceived as a mobile structure to be deployed first in Trafalgar Square, the pavilion is positioned in the heart of London within one of its most celebrated public spaces. Adapted to the classical formal geometry of its historic environment, this proposal is characterized by a serious of panels and movable partitions. Each partition responds to environmental and human movement, and is engraved with information highlighting London and the Olympic Games, as well as important facts of participating nations. The walls trace a path through Trafalgar Square with interstitial spaces reserved for programmatic elements such as the cafe, shop, projection room, and washrooms.

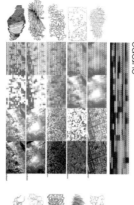

europe

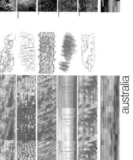

australia

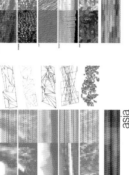

asia

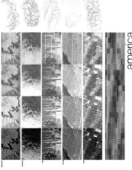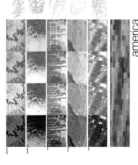

america

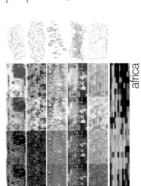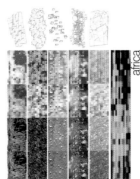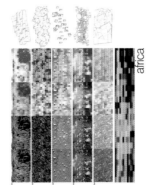

africa

312

Manifold Dubai | PATTERNS

Project Type : Observation Tower
Location : Dubai, UAE
Status : International Competition
Project Team : Marcelo Spina and Georgina Huljich

Principals in Charge : Hironori Kamizono and Geoffrey Elander
Project Designers : Jeeyea Kim and Nathaniel Moore Project Assistants

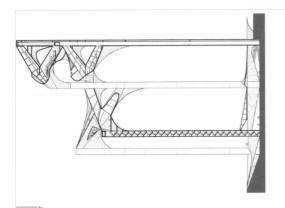

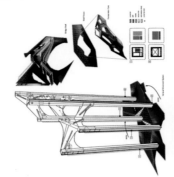

MANIFOLD DUBAI

Project Type: Observation Tower
Location: Dubai, UAE
Status: International Competition Project, 2009
Project Team: Marcelo Spina and Georgina Huljich Principals in charge; Hironori Kamizono and Geoffrey Elander Project Designers; Jeeyea Kim and Nathaniel Moore Project Assistants.

The concept of the tower combines the generic with the highly specific. Generic cores are being locally connected by manifold surfaces in forms of connecting bridges "bridgabells." These shells move diagonally and topologically in between cores, connecting them while stabilizing the cores.

The bridge-shells house the main programmatic spaces of the tower: a nested network of spaces which assemble and connect in oblique ways. Interstitial in nature, these resultant spaces privilege directionality over centrality, while allowing for a series of lounge and seating areas to appear informally along branching trajectories. Given the small envelope area of the shells, the spaces are calibrated for use by small groups of people and they provide natural (cross) ventilation and multiple views.

Five vertical cores constitute the structural spine and movement system of the tower. The cores house the main infrastructure for the tower. Strategically distributed so as to be equidistantly accessible from all occupyeble platforms, three exit stairwells covering the whole extension of the cores provide the necessary means of exiting in case of fire or mechanical malfunction.

HVAC ducts and Electrical systems are also housed within the cores and the serve all occupyeble areas within the tower. Larger zones for cooling units are located within the bridle-shells in service areas directly adjacent to the cores.

Once inside the bridge-shells, mechanical escalators provide the most important means for movement and circulation. They not only connect all the levels but provide a broad array of views and vistas of Dubai breathtaking skyline, from the dessert to the creek, from the ocean coastline and the islands to the high rises.

In addition to the escalators, each level is connected by stepped platforms which are distributed talking full advantage of the slope, hence providing an array of pocket-like spaces perfect for personal enjoyment and panoramic pleasure.

Nest Shelters | *AQSO arquitectos office*

Built Area (GFA) : 90.3 sqm / Site area : 11690 sqm
Client : Soria City Council

Participants : Luis Aguirre Manso, Victoria González Gómez, Noelia Cervero Sánchez
Project : Temporary Pavilions
Typology : Multipurpose Building
Location : Soria, Spain

EE258 EUROPAN9 SORIA 1
REFUGIO NIDO NEST SHELTER

La Soria invisible es una red cambiante, cuyos nodos son sus habitantes, que se desplazan por la ciudad, crean nuevas conexiones, rompen otras... Por eso su representación no es estática, sino que depende de las horas del día, de los días de la semana, y también de la edad y tipo de individuos que la forman. La ciudad física, sus edificios, calles y plazas son el soporte de la ciudad invisible.

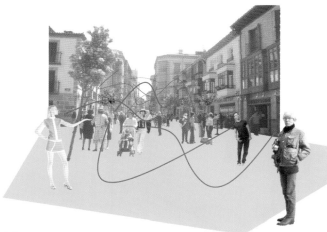

SORIA VISIBLE VISIBLE SORIA

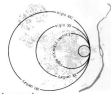

EVOLUCIÓN HISTÓRICA
URBAN SPRAWL

6 de cada 10 viviendas ocupadas
6 out of every 10 dwellings occupied

 = 2.79 pers.

VIVIENDA
HOUSING

19,6%
65 y +

64,6%

16-64

0-15   15,8%

DENSIDAD
DENSITY

La ciudad nace bajo la protección del río Duero, pero posteriormente se extiende hacia el Oeste dándole la espalda. El resultado es un núcleo urbano independiente del río.

● = 200

EDAD DE LA POBLACIÓN
POPULATION BY AGE

El alto porcentaje de vivienda vacía para una población envejecida y sin posibilidades de crecimiento a corto plazo indica que la ciudad no necesita un aumento de infraestructura.

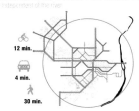

12 min.
4 min.
30 min.

MOVILIDAD
MOBILITY

Se trata de una slow city donde es fácil acceder a cualquier punto del casco urbano y adyacentes.

SORIA

VALLADOLID x8   MADRID x83

TAMAÑO
SIZE

Su reducido tamaño hace posible que un individuo se relacione con gran parte del resto de la población.

El objetivo es revitalizar y ampliar la diversidad de la vida social en torno al río investigando sobre la compatibilidad de usos diversos. La estrategia será deformar la ciudad invisible desplazando parte de los nodos que forman la red social de la ciudad invisible. Esto permite colonizar y reactivar el área del río sin extender la ciudad física mediante refugios nido que cobijan a sus ocupantes.

SORIA INVISIBLE INVISIBLE SORIA

Soria visible
visible Soria

habitantes
inhabitants

relaciones
relationships

Soria invisible
invisible Soria

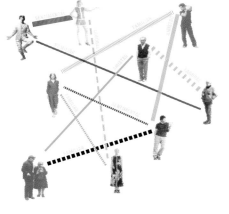

Intentemos dibujar la malla de conexiones que unen a los habitantes de Soria. Clasifiquémoslas, analicemos su densidad y obtendremos el plano de la ciudad invisible subyacente.

DIAGRAMAS DÍAS / HORAS / TIPO RELACIÓN
DIAGRAMS DAYS / HOURS / TYPE OF RELACIONSHIP

Analizando la ciudad invisible diagnosticamos el problema del área del río: falta de actividades permanentes, de flujos sociales que participen de la infraestructura existente y revitalicen la zona.

RED CIUDAD INVISIBLE
INVISIBLE CITY NETWORK

DEFORMACIÓN RED CIUDAD INVISIBLE
DEFORMATION OF INVISIBLE CITY

Colonizar el área del río con la ciudad física no es posible, pero sí lo es mediante la invisible: una trama que se extiende y modifica atrapando el río e incorpora actividades y lugares hasta ahora vinculados únicamente a la ciudad.

SORIA INVISIBLE ⬤ RIO INVISIBLE SORIA ⬤ RIVER

● Área de usos adquiridos.
Cercanos a espacios consolidados en la ciudad o que reciclan usos anteriores

● Área de usos relacionados con ocio

● Área de usos relacionados con cultura

refugios nido
nest-shelters

zona reactivada
revitalized area

VERDE URBANO + ESPACIOS PÚBLICOS
GREEN AREAS + PUBLIC SPACES

USOS
USES

ACTIVIDAD HABITANTES
INHABITANTS' ACTIVITY

Los refugios nido están formados por piezas modulares habitables prefabricadas que ofrecen la posibilidad de combinarlas de manera diferente.

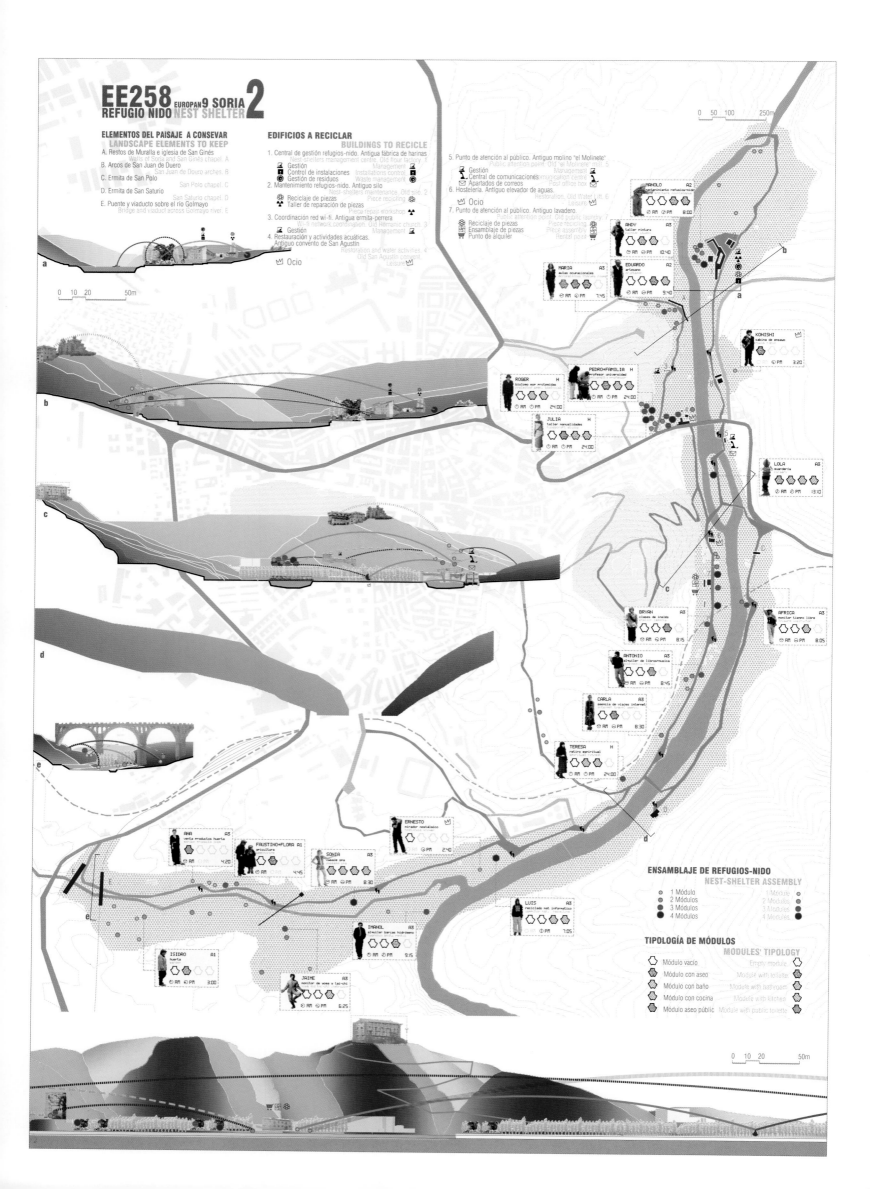

EE258 EUROPAN9 SORIA 3
REFUGIO NIDO NEST SHELTER

Los refugios, agrupados en módulos y generando una geometría orgánica, se relacionan entre sí por el brillo de su material exterior, mientras en interior está moldeado en fibra de vidrio. Cada refugio dispone además de conexión telefónica e internet.

The refuges are grouped by modules, generating an organic geometry. They are related between them by a reflective external material and the inside is moulded in fibreglass. Every refuge has phone line and internet connection.

INCORPORACIÓN DE ELEMENTOS
ELEMENT'S INSERTION

Módulo con cocina
Module with kitchen

Módulo con aseo
Module with toilette

Módulo aseo público
Module with public toilette

Módulo con baño
Module with bathroom

COMBINACIONES DE MÓDULOS
MODULES COMBINATIONS

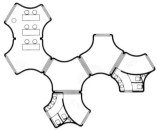

Academia de enseñanza
Academy

Guardería infantil
Nursery

Gimnasio
Gym

0 1 2 m

Lugar de retiro
Spiritual retreat

Apartamento
Apartment

Centro de reuniones / negocios
Business y meetings center

0 1 2 m

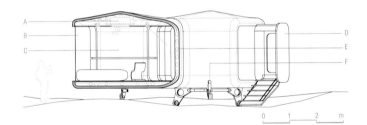

SECCIÓN
SECTION

A. Sistema de climatización.
Air conditioning system. A
B. Doble acristalamiento.
Double glazing. B
C. Interior moldeado de fibra de vidrio.
Fibreglass moulded interior. C
D. Sistema de abertura proyectable.
Projectable door system. D
E. Soportes ajustables.
Adjustable legs. E

0 1 2 m

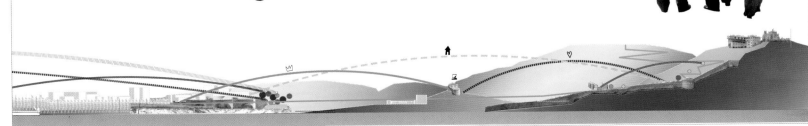

Floor Plan

4

INFORMATION KIOSK

A/V ROOM

V.I.P. DINING

3 ◄ ► 1

GENERAL SEATING

KITCHEN

STORAGE

9'-4"

11'-0"

2

19'-6"   19'-6"

60'-0"

SCALE 3/32" = 1'-0"

Elevations

11'-0"

CERAMICS OF ITALY

1

17'-0"

CERAMICS OF ITALY

2

T.O. ROOF 19'-0"

B.O. CLNG 8'-0"

F.F.L 0'-6"

14'-10"

CERAMICS OF ITALY

3

11'-0"

CERAMICS OF ITALY

4

SCALE 3/32" = 1'-0"

T.O. ROOF 19'-0"

B.O. CLNG 8'-0"

F.F.L 0'-6"

ORGANIZATION PRECEPTS:

A. MAXIMIZE VISIBILITY

B. SATISFY AREA RATIO

C. SIMPLIFY ACCESS

D. CREATE SIGNAGE OPPORTUNITIES

E. DEMONSTRATE TILE PROTOTYPES

F. FUNCTION AS PAVILION HUB

GEOMETRIC RATIONALE

AREA DISTRIBUTION RATIO 80 / 20

1. CENTRAL VOID FOR SEATING

2. EDGE VOIDS FOR ACCESS

3. NET USABLE VOID

---

ame
OL

pants
Pande, Chinmaya Misra

ocation
geles, CA

als List
ing:
gauge steel framing (Cage spacing configured to avoid HSS framing and deputy inspection)
assembly (Type X where necessary)

shes:
ng tiles for walls, soffits (Donated by member sponsors)
g tiles (Donated by member sponsors)
inlay signage systems (Lasercut or CNC routed as necessary)
flooring system (Existing with organizer)
tone/ solid surfacing countertops

ting, Electrical:
sed lighting (Ratio optimized for flourescent/ incandescent/ halogen/ LED energy requirements)
pendant light fixtures
cal outlets, integrated television niches (including data, CAT5 cabling)

on of ramp, ADA access as necessary

tion approach
n offer extensive experience on projects with varied scales and tight fabrication schedules. Our
experience is highly integrated with our design process, using parametric optimization strategies.
e designed and executed similar projects in close coordination with metal, plastics, signage
ators and sub-contractors on similar projects. Our expertise also extends to on-site installation and
abrication review. We can aid the owner with budgeting, negotiation and perform all shop drawing
and technical approvals. We can coordinate closely with a local executive in Orlando, if necessary.
-owner is also available to temporarily relocate during on-site execution and coordination.

kimate budgeting
00 (Excluding sponsor donation)
00 (Approximate contingency)
: $100,000

Concept
mage to the Italian legacy of Mario Radice, Carlo Scarpa and Aldo Rossi, this scheme envisions a
al, yet highly visible pavilion entry. The strategy utilizes the geometric possibilities of each corner
ieve an optimal spatial configuration. By organizing diagonally, the pavilion increases its visibility
as its ability to service a high number of passers by. The layout addresses the dual requirements
ormation accessibility as well as a cafe environment. A simplified zoning closely adheres to the
ed ratio of open to closed space at 80/20. It allows the pavilion to cater to multiple lines of users
ormation, dining and interaction. All usage is defined carefully within a 'voided' envelope. The
sal addresses the essential requirement for a hub, by remaining porous to all users in the Italian
n zone. The scheme also intends to demonstrate the ceramic tile portfolio of member suppliers,
wcasing usage on all surfaces, flooring, wall, soffitt and ceiling. The vertical 'wings' also integrate
for televisions, so the pavilion can function as a presentation booth during the award ceremony.
le options were studied to explore the most optimal distribution of the 600 sqf total built-up area
e booths. The final approach integrated the use of aerial and vertical surface area to enclose a
e without consuming built area. Hence, the concept of a Sculpted Void.

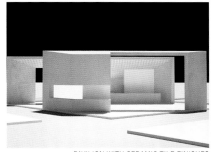

PAVILION WITH CERAMIC TILE FINISHES

INSPIRATION AND PRECEDENTS

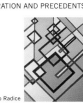

Mario Radice

Carlo Scarpa

Aldo Rossi

ZONING LAYOUT FOR CAFE, INFORMATION, SEATING, V.I.P DINING

VOLUMETRIC AND GEOMETRIC ENVELOPE STUDIES

New Wave: Shelter + Kiosk Design | *CJ Lim / Studio 8 Architects*

Location : Bexhill-on-Sea, UK
Design team : CJ Lim/Studio 8 Architects with Frank Fan, Pascal Bronner
Consultants : Techniker(structural engineers)

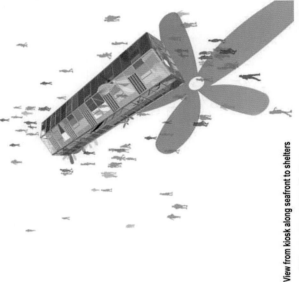

View from kiosk along seafront to shelters

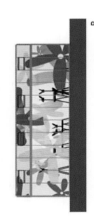

A

B

C

D

E

Roof top Plans + Elevations

A, Shelter 1
B, Shelter 2
C, Shelter 3
D, Shelter 4

E, Kiosk

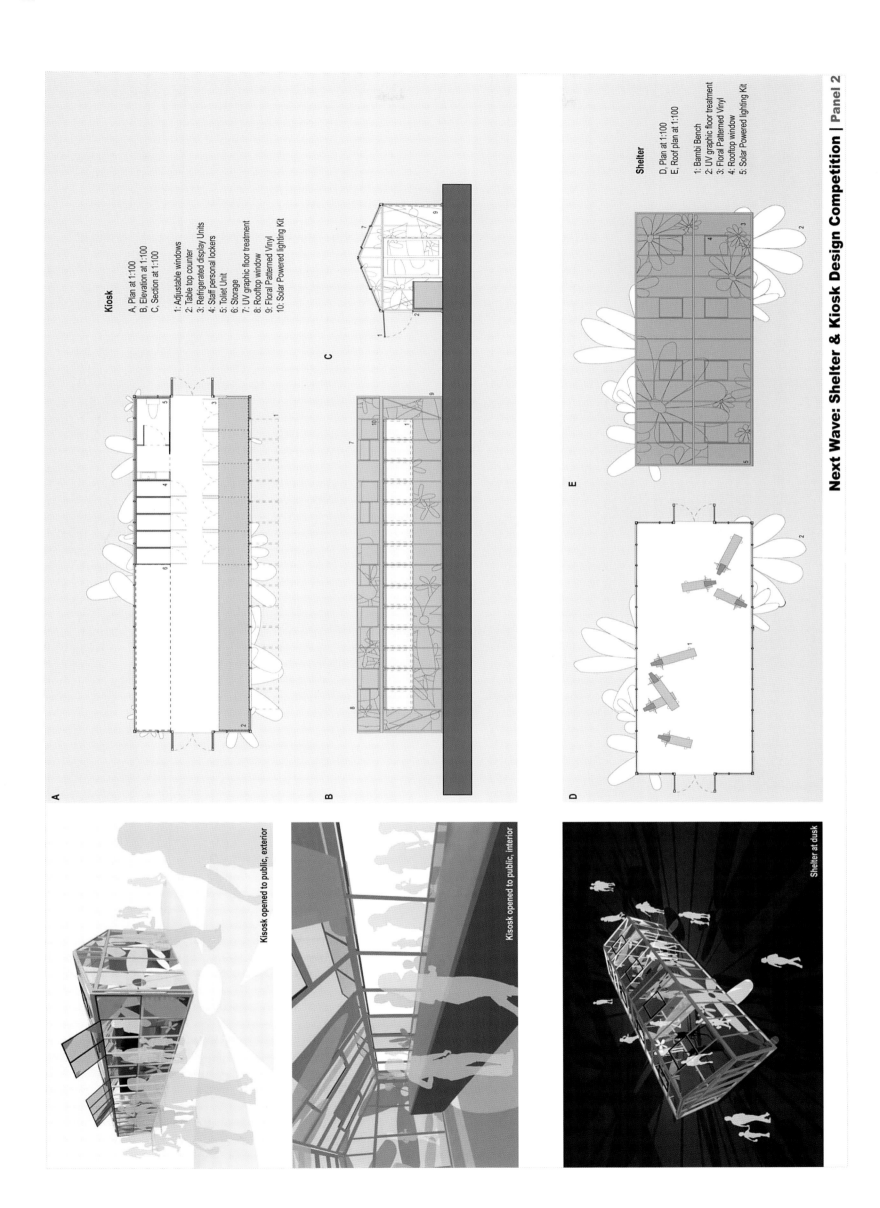

865

Kiosk

A, Plan at 1:100
B, Elevation at 1:100
C, Section at 1:100

1: Adjustable windows
2: Table top counter
3: Refrigerated display Units
4: Staff personal lockers
5: Toilet Unit
6: Storage
7: UV graphic floor treatment
8: Rooftop window
9: Floral Patterned Vinyl
10: Solar Powered lighting Kit

Shelter

D, Plan at 1:100
E, Roof plan at 1:100

1: Bambi Bench
2: UV graphic floor treatment
3: Floral Patterned Vinyl
4: Rooftop window
5: Solar Powered lighting Kit

A

B

C

D

E

Kisosk opened to public, exterior

Kisosk opened to public, interior

Shelter at dusk

Next Wave: Shelter & Kiosk Design Competition | Panel 2

316

Be_Lamina | *LUIS ARREDONDO_ARCHITECT*

Project : Landscape Renovation of the Segura River
Participants : Luis Arredondo
Typology : Landscape
Location : Beniel, Murcia, Spain

Client : Beniel Goberment
Year : 2011

CONCURSO DE IDEAS PARA LA DEFINICIÓN DEL PLAN DIRECTOR ESTRATÉGICO PARA LA **RESTAURACIÓN DEL ENTORNO DEL RÍO SEGURA** CONCU
LEMA BENIEL, APUESTA SEGURA
A SU PASO POR BENIEL LEMA

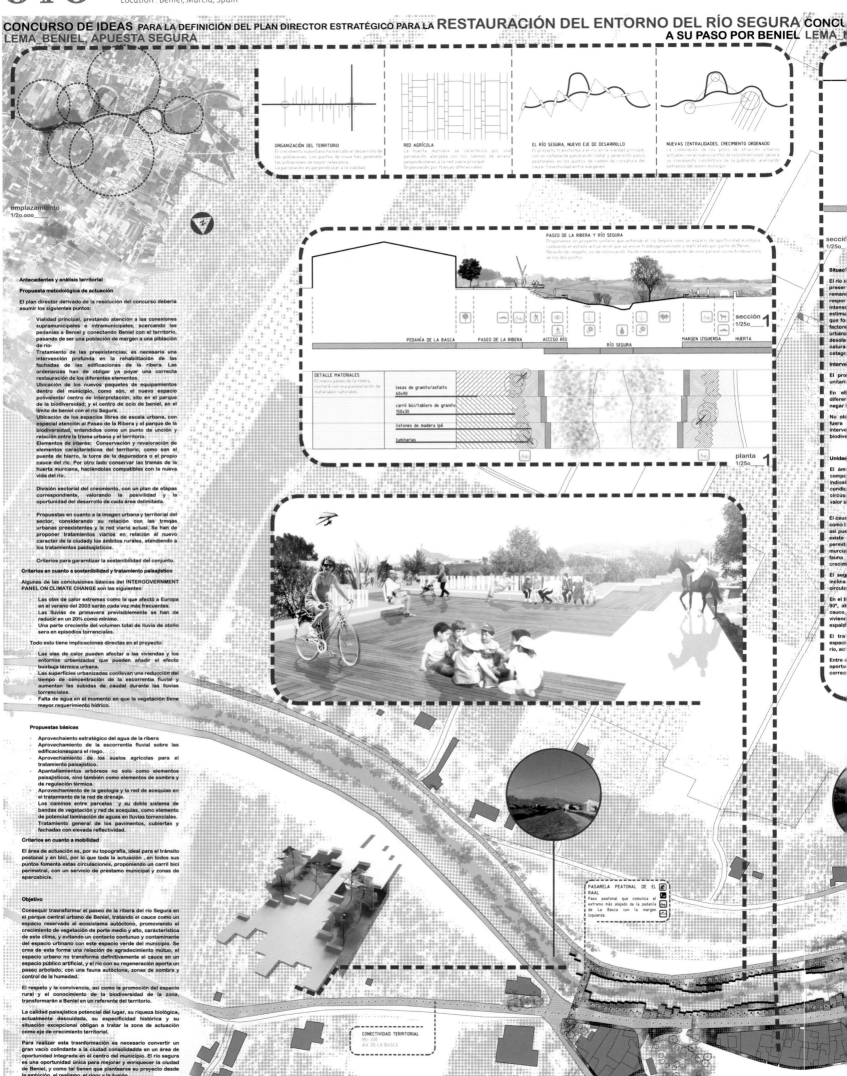

ORGANIZACIÓN DEL TERRITORIO

RED AGRÍCOLA

EL RÍO SEGURA, NUEVO EJE DE DESARROLLO

NUEVAS CENTRALIDADES, CRECIMIENTO ORDENADO

emplazamiento 1/20.000

PASEO DE LA RIBERA Y RÍO SEGURA

sección 1/250

PEDANÍA DE LA BASCA — PASEO DE LA RIBERA — ACCESO RÍO — RÍO SEGURA — MARGEN IZQUIERDA — HUERTA

DETALLE MATERIALES

losas de granito/asfalto 60x90

carril bici/tablero de granito 150x30

listones de madera Ipé

luminarias

planta 1/250

Antecedentes y análisis territorial

Propuesta metodológica de actuación

El plan director derivado de la resolución del concurso debería asumir los siguientes puntos:

- Vialidad principal, prestando atención a las conexiones supramunicipales e intramunicipales, acercando las pedanías a Beniel y conectando Beniel con el territorio, pasando de ser una población de margen a una población de río.
- Tratamiento de las preexistencias; es necesaria una intervención profunda en la rehabilitación de las fachadas de las edificaciones de la ribera. Las ordenanzas han de obligar ya apoyar una correcta restauración de los diferentes elementos.
- Ubicación de los nuevos paquetes de equipamientos dentro del municipio, como son, el nuevo espacio polivalente/ centro de interpretación, sito en el parque de la biodiversidad; y el centro de ocio de beniel, en el límite de beniel con el río Segura.
- Ubicacion de los espacios libres de escala urbana, con especial atención al Paseo de la Ribera y el parque de la biodiversidad, entendidos como un punto de unión y relación entre la trama urbana y el territorio.
- Elementos de interés: Conservación y revaloración de elementos característicos del territorio, como son el puente de hierro, la torre de la depuradora o el propio cauce del río. Por otro lado conservar las tramas de la huerta murciana, haciéndolas compatibles con la nueva vida del río.
- División sectorial del crecimiento, con un plan de etapas correspondiente, valorando la posibilidad y la oportunidad del desarrollo de cada área delimitada.
- Propuestas en cuanto a la imagen urbana y territorial del sector, considerando su relación con las tramas urbanas preexistentes y la red viaria actual. Se han de proponer tratamientos viarios en relación al nuevo caracter de la ciudad los ámbitos rurales, atendiendo a los tratamientos paidsajísticos.

Criterios para garantizar la sostenibilidad del conjunto.

Criterios en cuanto a sostenibilidad y tratamiento paisajístico

Algunas de las conclusiones básicas del INTERGOVERNMENT PANEL ON CLIMATE CHANGE son las siguientes:

- Las olas de calor extremas como la que afectó a Europa en el verano del 2003 serán cada vez más frecuentes.
- Las lluvias de primavera previsiblemente se han de reducir en un 20% como mínimo.
- Una parte creciente del volumen total de lluvia de otoño sera un episodios torrenciales.

Todo esto tiene implicaciones directas en el proyecto:

- Las olas de calor pueden afectar a las viviendas y los entornos urbanizados que pueden añadir el efecto buirbuja térmica urbana.
- Las superficies urbanizadas conllevan una reducción del tiempo de concentración de la escorrentía fluvial y aumentan las subidas de caudal durante las lluvias torrenciales.
- Falta de agua en el momento en que la vegetación tiene mayor requerimiento hídrico.

Propuestas básicas

- Aprovechaiento estratégico del agua de la ribera
- Aprovechamiento de la escorrentía fluvial sobre las edificacionespara el riego.
- Aprovechamiento de los suelos agrícolas para el tratamiento paisajístico.
- Apantallamientos arbóreos no solo como elementos paisajísticos, sino también como elementos de sombra y de regulación térmica.
- Aprovechamiento de la geología y la red de acequias en el tratamiento de la red de drenaje.
- Los caminos entre parcelas y su doble sistema de bandas de vegetación y red de acequias, como elemento de potencial laminación de aguas en lluvias torrenciales.
- Tratamiento general de los pavimentos, cubiertas y fachadas con elevada reflectividad.

Criterios en cuanto a mobilidad

El área de actuación es, por su topografía, ideal para el tránsito peatonal y en bici, por lo que toda la actuación , en todos sus puntos fomenta estas circulaciones, proponiendo un carril bici perimetral, con un servicio de préstamo municipal y zonas de aparcabicis.

Objetivo

Conseguir trasnformar el paseo de la ribera del río Segura en el parque central urbano de Beniel, tratando el cauce como un espacio reservado al ecosistema autóctono, promoviendo el crecimiento de vegetación de porte medio y alto, característica de este clima, y evitando un contacto continuo y contaminante del espacio urbano con este espacio verde del municipio. Se crea de esta forma una relación de agradecimiento mútuo, el espacio urbano no transforma definitivamente el cauce en un espacio público artificial, y el río con su regeneración aporta un paseo arbolado, con una fauna autóctona, zonas de sombra y control de la humedad.

El respeto y la convivencia, así como la promoción del espacio rural y el conocimiento de la biodiversidad de la zona, transformarán a Beniel en un referente del territorio.

La calidad paisajística potencial del lugar, su riqueza biológica, actualmente descuidada, su especificidad histórica y su situación excepcional obligan a tratar la zona de actuación como eje de crecimiento territorial.

Para realizar esta transformación es necesario convertir un gran vacío colindante a la ciudad consolidadda en un área de oportunidad integrada en el centro del municipio. El río segura es una oportunidad única para mejorar y enriquecer la ciudad de Beniel, y como tal tienen que plantearse su proyecto desde la ambición, el realismo, el rigor y la ilusión.

CONECTIVIDAD TERRITORIAL
MU-330
AV. DE LA BASCA

PASARELA PEATONAL DE EL RAAL
Paso peatonal que comunica el extremo más alejado de la pedanía de La Basca con la margen izquierda.

PLANTA GENERAL 1/1000

PASEO DE LA RIBERA, ESPACIO PÚBLICO DE CALIDAD

ILA BASCA   C/DE LA MEDALLA   RÍO SEGURA   ACCESO RÍO   MARGEN IZQUIERDA   C/DEL SEGURA

Vegetación

Franja comprendida entre los 300 m de altitud y la desembocadura del Río Segura. Es el sector de mayor déficit hídrico y con aguas de grado de mineralización medio-alto, lo que supone una barrera infranqueable para muchos de los géneros y especies ripícolas de origen septentrional (*Rosa, Salix, Crataegus, Populus nigra, Clematis vitalba, Lonicera hispanica*, etc.). La vegetación de ribera pasa de estar dominada por especies de óptimo medioeuropeo, a estarlo por una flora termófila subdesértica de óptimo nor teafricano (*Tamarix, Populus alba, Phoenix, Nerium*), con un gran número de especies exclusivas de este sector. La alameda- tarayal constituye la formación riparia característica.

Geoserie riparia termomediterránea semiárida murciano- almeriense y mululiense (*Geosinionicero biflorae-Populeto albae*)

Primera banda de vegetación

Serie riparia de la anea (helófitos). *Sintypho-Schoenoplecteto*

Segunda banda de vegetación

Serie riparia de la alameda-tarayal. *Sinlonicero-Populeto albae*

ALAMEDA - TARAYAL TERMÓFILA	MURTEDA	BALADRAL	TARAYAL TERMÓFILO

mixto en el que la
capas de agua
l principal factor
reo moderado o
desarrollo, por
r de las plantas
ón. Todos estos
de canalización
en un ámbito
ni de evolución
no de segunda

una intervención

n varias áreas
s específicos sin

s con entornos
este sentido, la
n un parque de la
ramunicipal.

puesto que se
idades de paisaje
des tienen unos
nto ajustado a su
neidad como un
to.

ores, que tienen
o de sus cauces,
peta el cauce y
res a 30°, lo que
s de la huerta
aso libre para la
ervada, para el

uros de 45° de
arril paraleo de

n cercana a los
ación natural del
a una fachada de
nvirtiéndolo en la
o de desagüe.

generado unos
l meandro del
tivo.

e un espacio de
x ayudara a una

ZONAS DE SOMBRA EN EL PASEO DE LA RIBERA
La ribera del Segura se convierte en un punto de encuentro.
El carril bici en todo el Paseo y las zonas de estancia cambian el carácter actual del río.
La vegetación crece protegida, aportando al paseo humedad y sombra.

PASARELA PEATONAL DE LA BASCA
Esta pasarela aparece en un antiguo punto de conflicto urbano, cambiando el carácter de incomunicación peatonal previo.

PUENTE DE HIERRO SOBRE EL RÍO SEGURA
Apostamos por su restauración y la restricción del tráfico rodado, convirtiéndolo en un espacio público que permite disfrutar del río.

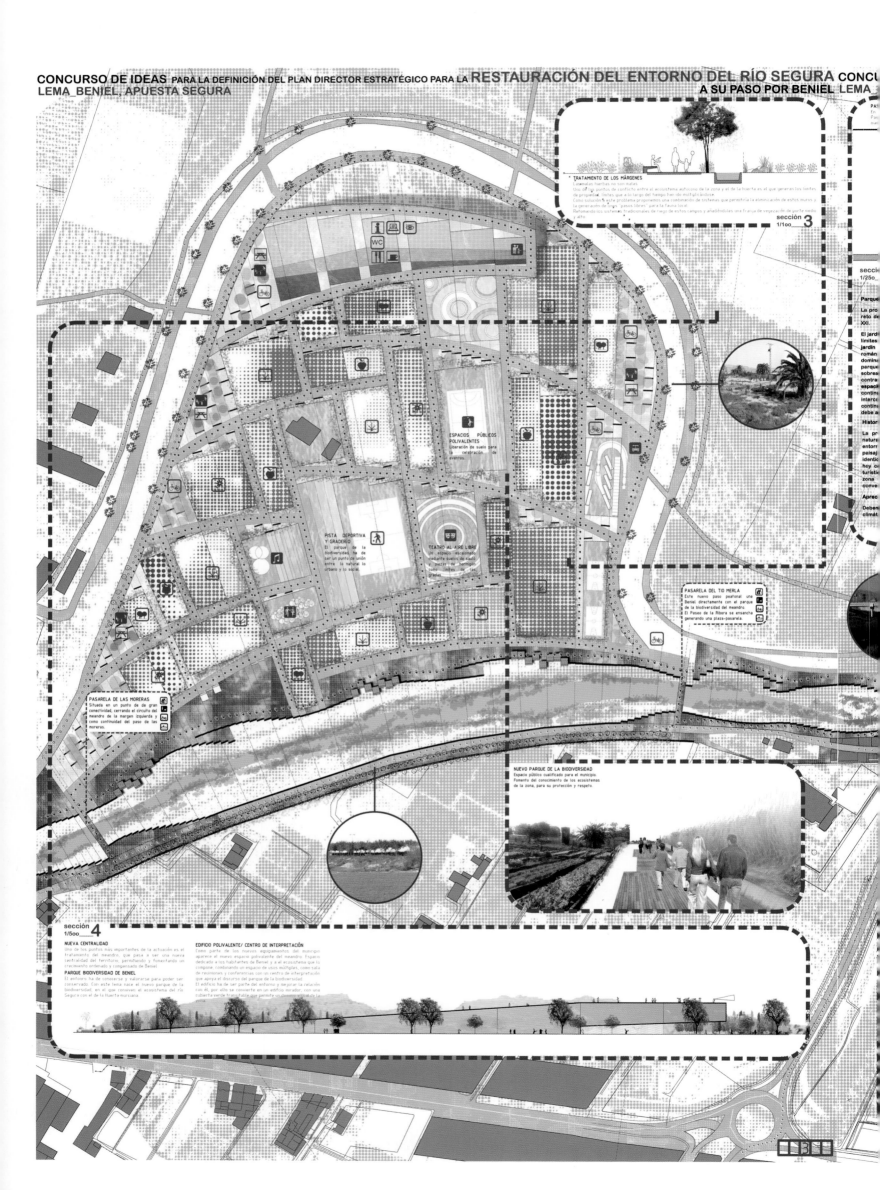

TRATAMIENTO DE LOS MÁRGENES

sección 3
1/1oo

ESPACIOS PÚBLICOS POLIVALENTES
Liberación de suelo para la celebración de eventos.

PISTA DEPORTIVA Y GRADERÍO
El parque de la biodiversidad, ha de ser un punto de unión entre lo natural lo urbano y lo social.

TEATRO AL AIRE LIBRE

PASARELA DEL TIO MERLA
Este nuevo paso peatonal une Beniel directamente con el parque de la biodiversidad del meandro. El Paseo de la Ribera se ensancha generando una plaza-pasarela.

PASARELA DE LAS MORERAS
Situada en un punto de gran conectividad, cerrando el circuito del meandro de la margen izquierda y como continuidad del paso de las moreras.

NUEVO PARQUE DE LA BIODIVERSIDAD.
Espacio público cualificado para el municipio. Fomento del conocimiento de los ecosistemas de la zona, para su protección y respeto.

sección 4
1/5oo

NUEVA CENTRALIDAD
Uno de los puntos más importantes de la actuación es el tratamiento del meandro, que pasa a ser una nueva centralidad del territorio, permitiendo y fomentando un crecimiento ordenado y compensado de Beniel.

PARQUE BIODIVERSIDAD DE BENIEL
El entorno ha de conservarse y valorarse para poder ser conservado. Con este lema nace el nuevo parque de la biodiversidad, en el que conviven el ecosistema del río Segura con el de la huerta murciana.

EDIFICIO POLIVALENTE/ CENTRO DE INTERPRETACIÓN
Como parte de los nuevos equipamientos del municipio aparece el nuevo espacio polivalente del meandro. Espacio dedicado a los habitantes de Beniel y a el ecosistema que lo compone, combinando un espacio de usos múltiples, como sala de reuniones y conferencias con un centro de interpretación que apoya el discurso del parque de la biodiversidad. El edificio ha de ser parte del entorno y mejorar la relación con él, por ello se convierte en un edificio mirador, con una cubierta verde franqueable que permite un recorrido visual de la...

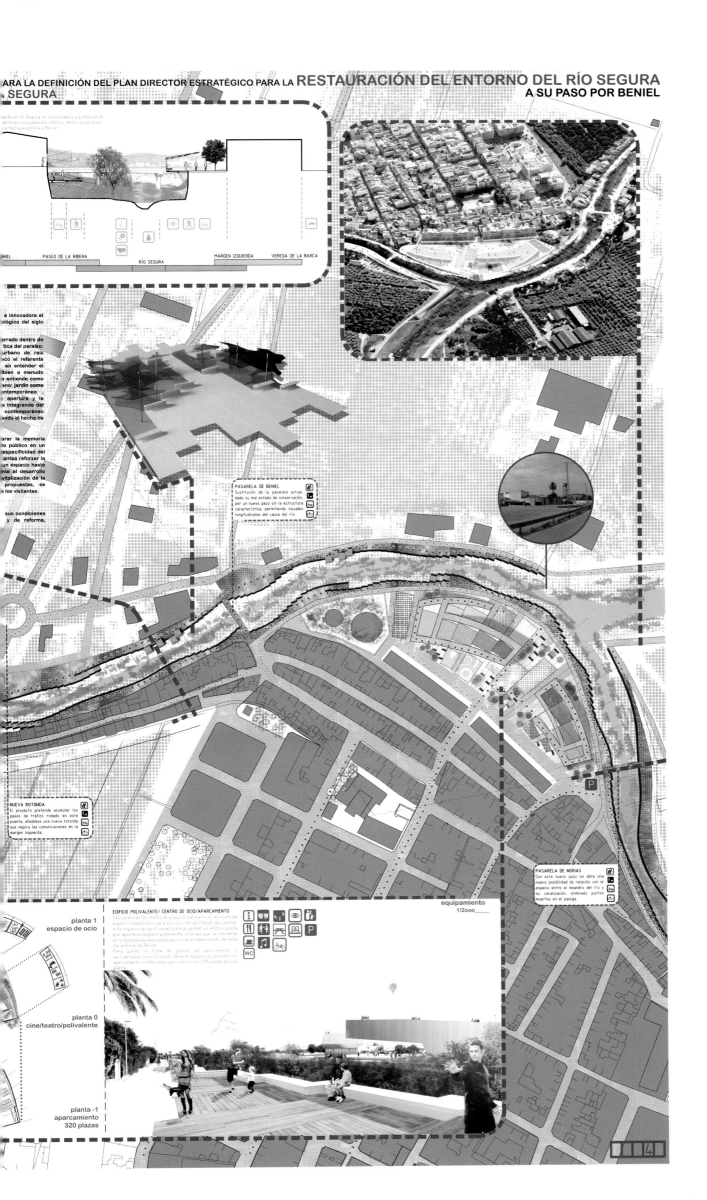

PASEO DE LA RIBERA   RÍO SEGURA   MARGEN IZQUIERDA   VEREDA DE LA BARCA

PASARELA DE BENIEL
Sustitución de la pasarela actual, dado su mal estado de conservación, por un nuevo paso sin la estructura característica, permitiendo visuales longitudinales del cauce del río.

NUEVA ROTONDA
El proyecto pretende acumular los pasos de tráfico rodado en este puente, añadimos una nueva rotonda que mejora las comunicaciones en la margen izquierda.

PASARELA DE NORIAS
Con este nuevo paso se abre una nueva posibilidad de relación con el espacio entre el meandro del río y su canalización, eliminado puntos muertos en el paisaje.

equipamiento
1/2ooo

EDIFICIO POLIVALENTE/ CENTRO DE OCIO/APARCAMIENTO

planta 1
espacio de ocio

planta 0
cine/teatro/polivalente

planta -1
aparcamiento
320 plazas

CONCURSO DE IDEAS PARA LA DEFINICIÓN DEL PLAN DIRECTOR ESTRATÉGICO PARA LA RESTAURACIÓN DEL ENTORNO DEL RÍO SEGURA
LEMA_BENIEL, APUESTA SEGURA
A SU PASO POR BENIEL

RED RECORRIDOS PEATONALES_ NUEVO ESPACIO VERDE CONTINUO
El nuevo Paseo de la Ribera cumple la doble función de generar un recorrido peatonal que une la Basca con Beniel y deleita en su interior el espacio "protegido" del río.

RED CARRIL BICI
La actual situación de dominio del tráfico rodado en la ribera se invierte, proponiendo una circulación restringida a vecinos en la mayor parte posible de zonas.

PASEO DE LA RIBERA   EQUIPAMIENTOS   PARQUE DE LA BIODIVERSIDAD

Historia

La propuesta pretende contribuir a recuperar la memoria natural de la ciudad, convirtiendo el espacio público en un entorno que permite contemplar la calidad y especificidad del paisaje del lugar; no obstante, la propuesta plantea reforzar la identidad de la ciudad ayudándola a integrar un espacio hasta hoy casi olvidado, contribuyendo directamente al desarrollo turístico sostenible e indirectamente a la revitalización de la zona urbana. Las nuevas centralidades propuestas, se convertirán en centros de llegada y acogida de los visitantes.

Apreciación del paisaje

Debemos asumir la calidad del paisaje actual, sus condiciones climáticas y retomar una actitud positiva y de reforma, adaptándose a las condiciones actuales y recuperando paisajes autóctonos.

Además de la necesidad de mantener la biodiversidad específica, es pertinente incorporar la belleza específica del paisaje de huertas. Se trata de evitar convertir los nuevos espacios en parques convencionales, cuya imaginería responde a paradigmas más septentrionales y aprovechar las calidades del paisaje autóctono.

Gestión del agua

La gestión del agua es uno de los temas de mayor importancia para garantizar el éxito de la intervención. El clima de Murcia, asociado a un buen sistema de riego, facilitaría el buen desarrollo de la vegetación, por lo que se conseguirían entornos frondosos en las proximidades del río, generándose microclimas frescos, muy agradables para contrarrestar la sensación de calor especialmente en verano.

El proyecto plantea el agua como posibilitadora de vegetación y como tema de paisaje, a través de su presencia en aljibes, acequias y albercas.

Se propone un sistema integral de gestión del agua, basado tanto en el aprovechamiento de lluvias como en el fomento del autoabastecimiento natural del río. Se propone un sistema de aprovechamiento pasivo de escorrentías pluviales, por medio de una topografía y unos tratamientos materiales que reparten la escorrentía superficial y acumula el agua en franjas drenantes que admitan su inundación puntual, evitando que el agua procedente de las grandes tormentas, especialmente de periodo de retorno superiores a 5 años, se vaya hacia la ciudad consolidada.

Generación de sombras

Dada la potencia del sol en la zona, para favorecer el uso de los diferentes sectores de la intervención se hace imprescindible promover protecciones contra el exceso de insolación en forma de vegetación, estructuras y topografía.

La vegetación se distingue en tres tipos en función del tipo de sombra que genera: sombras en mancha (pulvínulos), sombras en línea (alineaciones), sombras en matriz (plantaciones) y sombras aleatorias (cauce del río).

Tratamiento del río

La restauración fluvial propone un conjunto de actividades encaminadas a devolver al río su estructura y funcionamiento como ecosistema, en concordancia con unos procesos y una dinámica equivalente a las condiciones naturales, o que se pueden considerar como "referencia del buen estado ecológico".

El tratamiento actual del cauce impide y desaconseja un tratamiento de rehabilitación completa, marcándose como camino la total absorción del espacio como parque urbano. Creemos que este camino sería erróneo, ya que un correcto tratamiento de este espacio tendría un valor doble, ya que se aportará un espacio a la ciudad de gran calidad y se le devolverá su calidad al río, generándose una respuesta ambiental directa al municipio.

Conocer el ecosistema, apostar por la biodiversidad, generar un espacio urbano educativo y promover la ecología como factor de ordenación aporta a esta propuesta la calidad de espacio urbano y natural a la vez.

La restauración aporta un mantenimiento de los sistemas biológicos; tiene un valor práctico, ya que controla la erosión, tiene potencial terapéutico y es de gran potencia genético para especies cultivadas; gran importancia económica, ya que fomenta el turismo y revaloriza el municipio; aporta vías de referencia y de investigación científica; la educación acerca de sostenibilidad y ecología queda apoyada por situaciones reales; y tiene, sin duda un valor estético y recreativo.

Tratamiento del suelo

Para las zonas de plantación se establece la necesidad de mejorar el suelo. A este efecto, se propone utilizar gran cantidad de turbas fósiles de explotaciones murcianas existentes, pudiéndose barajar otras alternativas como la plantación de alfalfa regada y abono verde con riego de ácidos húmicos. Así mismo se prevé implementar una cobertura de "mulching" para proteger el suelo y retener humedad.

Para las zonas de uso intensivo, se propone pavimentación pétrea a base de losas de hormigón combinada con sistemas de micro canal, este pavimento en las zonas peatonales del paseo de la ribera se sustituye por madera de ipé, como material natural, con junta abierta en algunos puntos permitiendo relación visual con el cauce del río. Esta misma madera es la que configurará el mobiliario urbano, tanto los bancos perimetrales como las pérgolas.

Para las zonas de uso extensivo se propone una retención superficial por macro porosidad que ayuda a reducir el impacto de las lluvias torrenciales, puesto que el suelo actúa como una gran superficie laminadora aumentando el tiempo de concentración.

PASARELAS Y PUENTES

Como punto esencial de la conectividad a través del río tenemos el sistema de pasos peatonales y de tráfico rodado.

Proponemos una red de pasos peatonales en los puntos de contacto entre tejidos urbanos. Estos pasos se entienden como extensión del Paseo de la Ribera, por lo que, a pesar de su transversalidad, no buscan un protagonismo formal, dejándole este papel principal al "puente de hierro" y al propio río Segura.

Estos pasos peatonales son unas estructuras tensadas, por lo que no requieren de apoyos dentro del cauce del río.

Como límite de estos espacios "mirador" situamos un banco-barandilla, que cualifica el lugar como zona de estar y nuevo mirador. Proponiendo un nuevo punto de vista de Beniel.

La combinación de paseo y pasarelas permite disfrutar del río Segura sin impedir su correcto desarrollo y regeneración. Creando una relación recíproca en la que el respeto de los límites espaciales de la ribera conllevan un aumento de la vegetación, creando un corredor verde real y autóctono.

BENIEL   PASEO DE LA RIBERA   RÍO SEGURA   C/PUERTAS DE BENIEL

sección 6
1/250

ESTADO ACTUAL DEL CAUCE DEL RÍO SEGURA
El cauce esta comprimido entre muros, abandonado a su propia degradación, con una vegetación invasiva que evita el crecimiento de especies autóctonas.
No hay relación entre lo urbano y lo natural.

SECCIÓN PROPUESTA
Limpieza del cauce y replantación de especies autóctonas; se evita el contacto directo de las zonas urbanas con el cauce del río, que pasa a ser un espacio protegido.
Paseo de la Ribera peatonal, contacto respetuoso con el río.

SECTORIZACIÓN DE LA ACTUACIÓN
La actuación se divide en varias fases:
- Paseo de la Ribera (6 sectores) .... 3.325.000 €
incluyendo el tratamiento del cauce
- Pasarelas Peatonales (5 pasarelas) .... 2.100.000€
- Rehabilitación del Puente de Hierro .... 100.000€
- Parque de la Biodiversidad de Beniel
  1.- Parque .... 795.000€
  2.- Zonas equipadas .... 243.000€
  3.- Equipamiento. Centro de interpretación .... 2.150.000€
- Plaza Urbana Beniel
  1.- Urbanización .... 460.000€
  2.- Equipamiento Centro de ocio .... 2.800.000€

APROXIMACIÓN PRESUPUESTO .... 12.973.000€

5

Seoul Market System | *Arquipelago Studio*

Received an Award in the Seoul Public Design Competition 2012
Project Team : Gregory Marinic(Principal), Stephanie Garcia

seoulmarketsystem
Deployable Market Components Adapted to Timeless Nature and Culture

This proposal to enhance the common needs of Seoul's citizens offers a public amenity that can be deployed in customizable configurations that serve various market needs. The Seoul Market System is a component-based system based on five distinct deployable modules. These modules may be deployed individually or in groups depending on needs. As a flexible system, the Seoul Market System offers optimum adaptability to neighborhood flows. The design of the components is based on analysis of cultural and natural generators specific to Korea, particularly its timeless natural environment and ancient culture. A study of formal and material generators was undertaken to determine a configuration that reflects connectivity with place-specific qualities. As a component system, it is lockable and secure. When not in use, the entire system conceals market wares. Along with shelving, storage, electrical services, and display components, the modules also offer public benches. These components are provided in half-circle and linear configurations, offering endless ways to deploy social spaces intermingled within the markets themselves. Like Korean lacquerware and ceramics, the surface is intended to provide durability and will acquire a weather-based patina over time. Solid as well as perforated viewing components are offered in the Seoul Market System. The perforated components are designed to embed a hybrid natural/cultural pattern derived from analysis of conditions inherent to Korea. Seoul Market System activates the streets by providing an integrated network of market and social spaces throughout the city. The system adapts to the needs of citizens and merchants, while simultaneously providing places of curiosity and delight.

CULTURAL DNA->Generators & Transformations

Aerial view of deployed double-system

Market system components deployed at Sungnyemun Gate in central Seoul

A lockable market infrastructure for shopping & socializing

KOREAN PERSIMMON

TEMPLE ARCHITECTURE

ROOF TILE

TEMPLE LANTERNS

FURNITURE

CELADONWARE

318

Baltimore Calling | *Arquipelago Studio*

Project Team : Gregory Marinic(Principal), Carlos Contreras, Jaime Garcia

baltimore *calling.*

Embedding Natural Habitats within Transitional Spaces of the MTA System

This proposal for the Baltimore MTA systems suggest a flexible approach to embedding landscape into urbanism and providing a 'third way' adapted to various conditions, continual change, and unpredictability. The concept, *Baltimore Calling*, offers an insertable light infrastructure that mitigates the adverse effects of MTA Red Line construction from the inside, thus allowing the system as a whole to maintain balance.

_Abandoned Telephone Booth

origins

In the 21st century, methods and means of communication have undergone rapid transformation. A dying icon, the public telephone was once a symbol of modernity and communication. Typically located at a busy downtown street corner or adjacent to bus stops, the telephone booth offered a simple, direct, and affordable way to connect and share information. *Baltimore Calling* recalls the fading memory of this mid-20th century communication device by reinterpreting its form, function, and performance. The project offers a way to simultaneously connect people with information, culture, and nature. Here, the physical dimensions of the classic telephone booth (4' x 4' x 8'), as well as informal geometries of stacked cast-off construction pallets, simultaneously informed the design of site-specific performative architectural installations for Baltimore. Constructs may be temporarily installed at various locations impacted by construction activity throughout the MTA system.

opportunities

Built from unfinished spruce, *Baltimore Calling* has been designed to flexibly adapt to interstitial spaces found within MTA construction zones, rights-of-way, and existing stations. The 'telephone booth' houses a classic telephone, and acts as a 'call center' both literally and figuratively by providing a refuge and a year-round nesting habitat for migratory birds. Seasonally changing and hosting additional native plant material, each installation will continually adapt to and merge with its site over time. As individual installations wear into their sites, these new habitats will collect native vines, tall grasses, mosses, and lichens. Attracting migratory birds, butterflies, and plantlife, the installations will become unexpected amenities for citizens. *Baltimore Calling* has been designed to effortlessly transform over time with zero maintenance. Materially, installations will continually weather from gold-to-amber-to gray, while the habitats themselves will grow into a network of micro-environments that change from season-to-season and year-to-year. Birdhouse, informal telecommunications outpost, or morning glory trellis--such roles suggest only three potentialities for the installations. As a source of both curiosity and delight, *Baltimore Calling* proposes a time-relevant construct that activates, supports, and responds to its immediate environment. The concept offers the potential to make Baltimore a more environmentally-connected place that actively carves out space for natural systems to merge with the city.

_Stacked construction pallets

Hey Dad...I found another one over here!

connections

Baltimore Calling will connect the natural world and humans within an urban context. Just pick up the phone and receive up-to-date information regarding MTA construction delays and transit information, as well as details on area attractions and cultural events. Each phone will offer a touch-tone directory of resources including arts, historical data, neighborhood details, and special events specific to the location of each installation. *Baltimore Calling* telephone users may directly connect to one another, by picking up the phone and selecting a real-time connection with other outposts for immediate updates of MTA conditions elsewhere in the network. *Baltimore Calling* can be assembled on-site with pre-made component parts. The constructs will be built in accordance with sustainable methods using recyclable and renewable materials. Materials will be sourced locally and fabricated in Baltimore. The process will take 1/2 working day to complete at each site.

Baltimore Oriole *(Icterus galbula)*
A small icterid blackbird averages 7 inches long and weighs 1 only ounce. The bird was named for Lord Baltimore since its colors reflect the royal coat-of-arms of the founders of Maryland. Baltimore Calling will create an urban haven and nesting habitat for Baltimore Orioles and other species within interstitial zones impacted by MTA Red Line construction.

OI 001
OSLO

Day One 01

The new Grønmo park represents and applies the steps of a possible overcoming of the consumerist way of life.

From almost an icon for garbage's production and waste, the new meaning and image of the future park will be the path, through recycling, to dematerialisation and production of ideas. In the end it will embody the representation on the Earth of the "utopia" of a **world without objects**.

This visionary approach has the opportunity to become a reality in this very specific location and from this moment in time, as information technologies allow to work and produce out of very few means, generating almost no waste.

Here, the topography and landscape are merged with the recycling and learning facilities and with areas dedicated to new kinds of work and performance.

LUNAR TERRITORY AS A METAPHOR FOR GRØNMO NEW IDENTITY :
A LINK TO ITS FORMER USE AS A LANDFILL, TRANSFORMED IN AN UNIQUE ACTIVE TERRITORY FOR PRODUCTION, LEISURE AND CONTEMPLATION

H.D. WARREN D.D: "LUNAR DAY" FROM THE BOOK "RECREATIONS IN ASTRONOMY", 1879

WORKING ECOLOGY

In the current state of economical crysis, a lot of subjects are reinventing the concepts of work and enterprise. Through self-organization and promoting research and innovation, a parallel, diffusive system of production was born in a wide range of fields: from music to media art, to journalism, to design, to information technology.

Minimal entities working together can develop important cultural enterprises starting from very few means, sharing spaces and producing a network of competences, cooperation, ideas and work.

The Grønmo park will provide general infrastructures and shared facilities which are the basic needs for those kinds of works and become a social tool for cultural production and knowledge exchange. At the same time its venues and exhibitions will be, mainly, produced within the park itself.
The premise is a landscape which is not only a scenography, but a new topography that works as a service platform. It provides electricity (obtained from waste), internet access, flexible spaces to work/study and to perform; tools, archives, shared knowledge and the opportunity to meet, to hybridize processes and media, to understand emerging cultures.

The users will "give back" to Oslo and to the world the possibilities they have got, animating Grønmo and sharing their experience with the visitors of the park. They will be able to give expertise, to teach, organize festivals and events taking place in the park itself during the years. In this way **the park becomes a hub in the recycling and in the creation process**, while the specific location will give a material visibility to workers usually acting too much *behind the curtains.*

The program is a cyclical activity produced and "consumed" in the park itself, an ecosystem of cultural production and exchange. The different areas are activated at different times of the day and of the year, guaranteeing an ever changing combination of uses and processes, attracting a varied public.

This uncommon program for a park, containing working spaces and productive activities, is a medium that provides social integration and new work opportunities, also in connection with the neighborhood, while making Grønmo self-sustainable in terms of cultural offer and entertainment.

New Grønmo will not be used only *"for educational purposes and help visitors to better understand waste and recycling issues"* but to get to understand the possibilities of living/producing with a minimal consumption and to come in close contact with contemporary (cultural and social) issues .

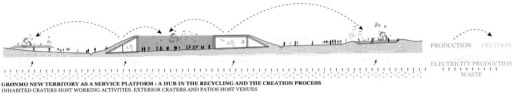

GRØNMO NEW TERRITORY AS A SERVICE PLATFORM : A HUB IN THE RECYCLING AND THE CREATION PROCESS
INHABITED CRATERS HOST WORKING ACTIVITIES. EXTERIOR CRATERS AND PATIOS HOST VENUES

Grønmo as a service platform provides :

Infrastructure

electricity
internet access

Access to technology
and instruments

data
archives
software

Facilities

spaces to work
spaces to expose / perform / communicate
meeting spaces / conference spaces / workshops areas
shared facilities (kitchens / wc / spaces to sleep)

FOR

	Production	Fruition	Leisure
music	electronic / mixing / composing /	conferences	basket
visual art	media art / interactive art / electronic /	festivals	skate park
design	interface / interactive /	exhibitions	green areas
information	journalism / collaborative projects / blogging /	teaching	kids areas
video	making / editing / motion /	consulting	flea market
performance	theatre / ballet / shows /	expertise	bars/cafe
games	coding / modeling / designing /	meetings	fitness
IT	hacking / software programming /	workshops	bike tracks
language	writing / translating / editing /	concerts	walking

THE PROGRAM : A CYCLICAL ACTIVITY PRODUCED AND "CONSUMED" WITHIN THE GRONMO TERRITORY :
AN ECOSYSTEM OF CULTURAL PRODUCTION AND EXCHANGE, INNOVATIVE RESEARCH AND ENTERPRISES

"Every day we crossed that territory, through sandy dunes and rocky hills,

INTERIOR OF THE "CRATERS":
SHARED AND FLEXIBLE SPACES FOR INNOVATIVE CULTURAL PRODUCTION

ART EXHIBITIONS IN EXTERIOR CRATERS, SAND DUNES LANDSCAPE

Day One 02

TOPOGRAPHY FOR LEISURE

While the interiors of the craters serve as shelters for creative and cultural activities, the topography all around is a very innovative scenario for leisure and sport.

The two worlds are in a continuous communication, since creative work cannot exist without places for inspiration and physical activity, while the users of the exteriors spaces are conducted to experiment and get to know the work being done inside the craters. During time the outside areas become also platforms where to exhibit and perform the results of the work done inside the craters, as well as informal meeting places for the users. The single inhabited elements can evolve through time, hosting new technologies and always different types of production following the ever-changing needs. This process is allowed by the "weakness" of the plan, thought to be generic and to act only as an enzymatic element. A flexible system to be colonized and supporting generative processes.

When the landfill system will be dismantled, the outside craters can support new areas for work or just stay as they are, depending on future needs. At the same time the inhabited craters can be demolished or enlarged, adapting to the evolution of the uses.
The program puts different fields in relationship, promoting an uncommon contamination among subjects. At the same time the spaces can be colonized by different activities, the plan never being fixed.

and entering the craters we realized

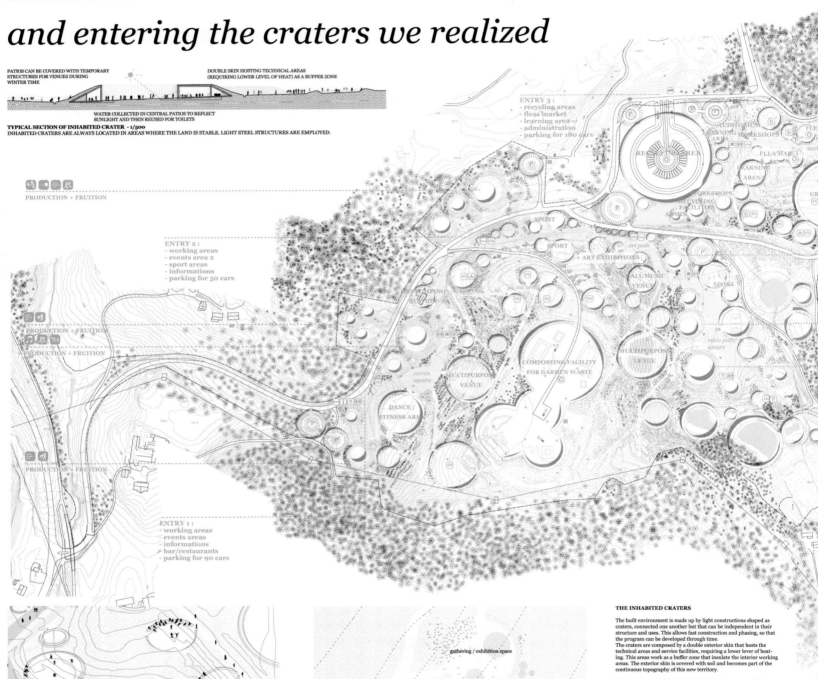

PATIOS CAN BE COVERED WITH TEMPORARY
STRUCTURES FOR VENUES DURING
WINTER TIME

DOUBLE SKIN HOSTING TECHNICAL AREAS
(REQUIRING LOWER LEVEL OF HEAT) AS A BUFFER ZONE

WATER COLLECTED IN CENTRAL PATIOS TO REFLECT
SUNLIGHT AND THEN REUSED FOR TOILETS

TYPICAL SECTION OF INHABITED CRATER - 1/500
INHABITED CRATERS ARE ALWAYS LOCATED IN AREAS WHERE THE LAND IS STABLE. LIGHT STEEL STRUCTURES ARE EMPLOYED.

PRODUCTION + FRUITION

ENTRY 3 :
- recycling areas
- fleas market
- learning area
- administration
- parking for 180 cars

ENTRY 2 :
- working areas
- events area 2
- sport areas
- informations
- parking for 50 cars

PRODUCTION + FRUITION
PRODUCTION + FRUITION

COMPOSTING FACILITY
FOR GARDEN WASTE

ENTRY 1 :
- working areas
- events areas
- informations
- bar/restaurants
- parking for 90 cars

PRODUCTION + FRUITION

THE NEW TOPOGRAPHY:
A CONTINUOUS SYSTEM OF CRATERS, NO BORDERS BETWEEN BUILT ELEMENTS AND LANDSCAPE

gathering / exhibition space

gathering / exhibition space   working areas / open spaces

TYPICAL GROUND LEVEL PLAN OF INHABITED CRATERS - 1/500

THE INHABITED CRATERS

The built environment is made up by light constructions shaped as craters, connected one another but that can be independent in their structure and uses. This allows fast construction and phasing, so that the program can be developed through time.
The craters are composed by a double exterior skin that hosts the technical areas and service facilities, requiring a lower lever of heating. This areas work as a buffer zone that insulate the interior working areas. The exterior skin is covered with soil and becomes part of the continuous topography of this new territory.

The open air area in the centre is a gathering place or an exhibition one, it guarantees a high access to sunlight and presents a micro-climate, repaired from wind and cold air.
Water is collected in this patios in some specific areas, then it's in part recycled for the working areas and in part used to reflect sunlight into the craters.

The patios can be temporarily covered with inflatable structures in order to host some indoor events during the year. They become temporary semi-interior spaces.

OPPORTUNITIES FROM WASTE

The park is also self sufficient in terms of energy as the "fuel" for the whole project comes directly from waste:
The needs for electricity are covered from on-site production through biogas obtained from waste.
At the same time this new territory will also be fed by the surrounding Marka forest, as the pellet extracted from it is used to heat the craters.

People can contribute to the project giving their furniture that would be trashed in order to be used in the new spaces devoted to production, directly linking the reusing/recycling process to the creation one. Biogas (extracted from anaerobic digestion of waste) will become the fuel for buses that will work as shuttles for the park, promoting events and making a "clean" connection and transportation for Grønmo and through Grønmo. During time they can be substituted by electric buses that can be recharged in the park itself.

building a world
bjects."

ENTRY TO MARKA FOREST

A WHOLE NEW TERRITORY...

There are no borders between landscape and built environment as both result in a new artificial inhabited topography whose geology is given by layers of artificial and natural grounds.

The new Grønmo is not just a park but a new territory resembling a lunar landscape. It's mostly made by of a continuity of craters, sometimes inhabited, sometimes pure landscape / land-art elements, hosting outdoor activities.

...RECYCLING THE EXISTING LANDSCAPES.

Upon the main theme of the lunar territory, a sequence of different natures is declined, following the uses and responding to the topography. The idea of nature is far from the idealistic image of "green" that's expected in a conventional park. Here, it is a man made nature, dry and hard, just coming from the actual state of the Grønmo site. Hills of topsoil, mounds of sand and expanses of gravels, followed by rocks and mineral paths, leave place to grass and trees only in some specific areas. This landscape slowly leads to the main entrances of the Marka forest and, being in deep contrast with this one, it will keep the memory of a nature which has been violated by man and that's only now turning into something else. At the same time it follows the idea of a *world without object* where the shape of the landscape itself works as furniture or shelter. **The idea of a "desolate" land creates a connection to its former use as a landfill, while transforming it in a active territory for contemplation, reflection, production, leisure.**

Inhabited craters, hosting working spaces and facilities. They're made of light structures and **built in the areas where the land is stable.** Covered with ground, they are part of the continuous topography of the site.

Exterior craters hosting venues, sport areas, meeting points and various activities. They are made of maximum two meters of ground. Sometimes they're covered with a light roof.

Exterior craters as a protection/insulation for technical activities. Made of ground, max. two metres, they avoid frictions between the maintenance areas (water treatment, gas pumping station...), the recycling areas, the parking areas and the rest of the park.

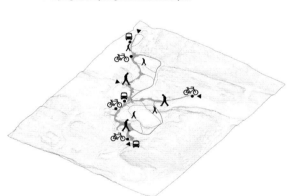

ENTRY 4 :
- working areas
- maintenance
- events area
- informations
- parking for 100 cars

Main pedestrian path. It directly connects the entrances and the main areas and opens in squares and event zones. It's a flat area or a gentle slope topography.

Secondary paths. Destined to leisure and exploration. They cross the different landscapes and are integrated with the context. The paths are all accessible. They are mostly accompanied by bike paths.

Bike sharing points. A system of bike-sharing improves the connection in the park and can be expanded to the neighborhood.

Bus/Shuttle stop. A shuttle connects the city of Oslo with the new territory of Gronmo and makes several stops in connection with the main areas. It'a biogas fueled bus that can work for specific events, advertising, at the same time, the park's activities.

THE LAYOUT OF THE CRATERS
IN RELATIONSHIP TO THE PIPES SYSTEM.

PLAN - 1/2000
100   200

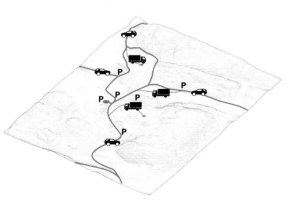

Main Roads. Roads in the park are limited to the minimum.

Secondary roads. For maintenance and technical access only, can only be used by trucks and cars with special permission.

Parking areas are located close to each entry and are in connection with bike sharing points and bus/shuttle stops, in order to promote the use of clean transportation.
A system of **car sharing** will be promoted for the workers coming to Gronmo from different parts of the city.

PRODUCTION + FRUITION
PRODUCTION + FRUITION
PRODUCTION + FRUITION
PRODUCTION + FRUITION
GREEN AREA
NS, ROCKY LANDSCAPE

TERRITORIES OF MEMORY AND INVENTION

The new topography keeps the memory of the process of growth and decay of the site. The idea of nature proposed here is defined and shaped by the culture, the history and the phenomenology of man's inhabitation of the site, but its meaning is subverted from disposal to production.

CRATERS

A land-art archetype (Smithson, Long, Morris, Turrell), the crater represents a spatial condition, (inclusion, protection, discovery, occupation), rather than a shape.

Its minimalist form evolves along human colonization, recalling an anti-romantic view of nature.

MARKA FOREST

Surrounds the Grønmo territory and its presence, rich in trees, vegetation and fauna, is seen as in deep contrast with the new materiality of the site. This opposition reinforce the new site identity and the definition of different uses for the two areas.

SAND DUNES AND GRASS

Shaped by a limestone substrate and covered by a layer of sand. The dunes are planted with dune grass for stabilisation of the sand. They are used in connection with playing areas and in relax/meditation as well as some sport areas.

SAND

The interiors of some craters are covered with sand, and can be easily reshaped for different art exhibition, or used as areas for camping and relax. Those areas are interior to craters used for recreation and are accessible through a network of paths.

LIMESTONE

The limestone base shapes most of the areas. It is sometimes covered with a layer of top soil, and planted with shrubs. It provides conditions for a specialised flora to develop naturally over time. These last "green areas" are located inside several craters.

GRAVELS

The areas covered by a layer of limestone gravel and stones can be used for open air art exhibitions, they are crossed by paths. They are directly recycled from existing materials stocked nowadays in the site, but are adapted to new functions and topography.

ROCKS

Rocky areas are exploration sectors occupied by light installations. Some sectors are colonized by larger scale rocks which avoid the possibility of crossing, they are placed in connection with technical installations which should not be reached by the users of the park.

VOLCANIC SAND

A heavy, glossy, partly magnetic mixture of usually fine sands.

The use of different colors of soil/sands reminds the actual condition of the site where small hills of different earth tones are present.

VOLCANIC BLACK ROCKS

The "black craters" can be connected to areas for contemporary shows of living theatre and dance as well as electronic art shows.

Their almost alien nature becomes a sign for the most innovative performances.

CONCRETE

Concrete surfaces are shaped to be used for sports like skating and BMX or leaved flat for meeting points and squares. Concrete is used in the main path for walking and biking. Those areas are always shaped as topographical elements.

320
Sichuan Earthquake Memorial Landscape | *CJ Lim / Studio 8 Architects*

876

Location : Sichuan, China
Design Team : CJ Lim/Studio 8 Architects with Maxwell Mutanda, Snow Cai
Consultants : Techniker(structural engineers)

5.Flowers Changing Process
充气橙蓬花的变化过程
A. Loading Aid in Chengdu
在成都补给区装载物资
B. Flight to Wenchuan
飞往汶川
C. Docking Over the Ruins
在废墟上空停靠
D. Providing Shelter and Bringing the Community Together
提供庇护所，把社会凝聚在一起。

3.Plan View of Blossom Skyscape
开花星象平面图

4.Detail of Flower in Situ during Reconstruction
重建期间充气橙蓬花在废墟中的细节

Sichuan Earthquake Memorial Landscape Competition
四川地震纪念碑景观设计比赛

A flower is a gift of love, remembrance and expressions of sympathy for the grieving
花是爱的礼物，也是纪念，抒发对死者悲伤的情感。

On 12 May 2008 at CST 14.28, a massive earthquake measuring 8.0 surface wave magnitudes hit Sichuan Province in China. Wenchuan was the epicentre of the earthquake. According to official figures in July, nearly 70,000 are confirmed dead, over 370,000 injured and a staggering number of people are still listed missing.
在2008年5月12号，北京时间14.28，四川汶川发生8.0级大地震，官方数字统计将近37万人被证实死亡。超过37万人受伤。1万多人失踪。

The earthquake has left at least 5 million people homeless – incalculable buildings collapsed to the ground with the city left severely destroyed and almost uninhabitable. Many of the highways and roads into Wenchuan were completely damaged and blocked off. The rough terrain and landslides continuously threatened the progress of search, making emergency rescue missions almost impossible on land. Although aircraft relief operations were deployed to deliver emergency aid, these rescue helicopters had great difficulties in landing.
地震让至少造成最少五百万人无家可归，不计其数的房屋倒塌，损坏，使得无法居住，许多高楼大厦和通往汶川的道路也被破坏。粗糙地形和山体滑坡使得整个搜索和救援任务无法进行。尽管救援飞机运送紧急救助物品，但是降落拉直升飞机带来很大困难。

It has only been about two months since the earthquake hit Sichuan Province – the community is still in mourning, and requires time to assess before starting the process of clearing away the devastation and rebuilding the city. Therefore unlike other remembrance landmarks in the past, this memorial proposal is temporary, functional and flexible intended for multi-locations. Planning and construction of memorial landmark takes time – this proposal can appear over night! The "Thousand Flowers of Sichuan" is a convoy of inflatable canopies that floats over the devastated area like clouds sailing across the skies. These flower-liked shapes perform on the same technical principles as the hot-air balloon – the heated air inside the envelope makes it buoyant. They are constructed out of lightweight materials with a large nylon surface to maximise stability. Each flower envelope range from 15 – 30 m in diameters, and can be folded up into a canvas bag to be loaded manually onto a truck.
距四川地震已经2个月，整个社会还是处在哀悼之中，在清理和重新建造整个城市之前需要时间来恢复和对废墟。因此这个纪念的里程碑和以往的不同，它的设计理念是暂时性，功能性有弹性的，并在许多不同的地方进行，计划和建造此纪念碑需要时间，但是这个方案可以在瞬天就出现。"四川之成千上万朵花了"是一群群充气橙蓬花在受灾区域上像是一朵朵云横跨去天空中，这些花一样形状的橙蓬和气球有着同样的技术概念，受热后橙蓬鼓起产生浮力飞上天空。他们由一种轻质材料构成，并由一个大型足够的里面来乘载起每个花瓣有15–30米的直经构成，并可以折叠起来成为一个帆布包。举手装上卡车。

The Red Cross Society of China has stated that the disaster areas still in need temporary shelters, medical supplies, drinking water and food. From Chengdu, the convoy of inflatable flowers will provide previously unimaginable access and daily deliveries of aid to the most damaged and irregular terrain. The principle advantage of the inflatable flowers, compared to a helicopter, is its ability to hover quietly over sites without causing further risks to unstable grounds. Flat landing surfaces are not required either as the flowers can dock in the sky with only ropes tethered to the ground for stability.
中国红十字社已经在受灾区域开始提供了暂时性的庇护所，医疗供应，水和食物。充气橙蓬花可以每天从成都向灾区提供所需要的物品。和直升飞机比充气橙蓬花的优势在它们可以停留在空中，不会造成进一步的风险。不需要降落到地面，只需在天空中用罗索到地面的来到稳定期内。

Upon arrival to a specific location, aid parcels are gently lowered to the ground. The floating flowers immediately "blossom", extending their petals to give temporary shelters for aid distribution, and canopies of sympathy to survivors who gather amongst the rubbles to remember loved ones lost. The system of loosely connected canopies gives refuge from rain and fierce sunshine to groups of workers and volunteers clearing up the damage. At night, the glowing convoy of flowers can be seen from far and wide, while supplying electricity and light for the night shift workers from its own self-sustainable generators. On the return journey to Chengdu, the floating convoy help to remove large quantities of rubble to an out-of-town designated recycling zone.
抵达后到达特定的位置，援助包裹轻轻地降落到地面，飘动的花即刻"开花"，伸展它们的花瓣为援助分配提供临时性的庇护所，同时给每天同到家园怀念亲人的幸存者一个安慰的屏幕。连接在充气橙蓬花上的充气调节系统会给避难不同的救援人员和志愿者清除到强烈阳光和雨的侵袭。在晚上，可以从很远的地方看见发光的充气橙蓬花，靠自我发电机给夜间值班人员提供了光和电。在回成都的途中，充气橙蓬花可以帮助救援人员把大量的废墟移动到回收站。

The "Thousand Flowers of Sichuan" is a powerful and poetic skyscape of love to remember the passing of many lives. The vibrant colors and forms bring energy and reassurance back into this bleak community – no more dark clouds, only a spring-liked floral sky to inaugurate a new beginning for Wenchuan and the Sichuan Province.
"四川之成千上万朵花"是有诗意有力量的天空中之爱，通过这种警记住怀不幸死去的人们。明亮的颜色和形式给人们带来了力量，毫不畏瞳的阿到曾经暗淡的城市中，没有更多的乌云，只有春天花开的美丽景象。同时他拉汶川县带来了新的开始。

2.Inflatable Flowers Loading Aid Parcels in Chengdu
在成都充气槌蓬花装运急救物品

1.Flowers Blossoming Over the Skyscape of Wenchuan
充气槌蓬花在汶川上空开花

321

Laminar Booth | *Thurlow Small Architecture*

Peepshow Competition Proposal
Location : Calgary, Canada
Design Team : Maia Small, Andrew Thurlow

Fabrication Consultant : Method Designs, ZCorporation
Competition Sponsor : ArtCity

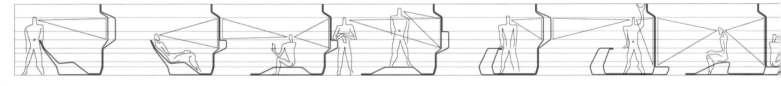

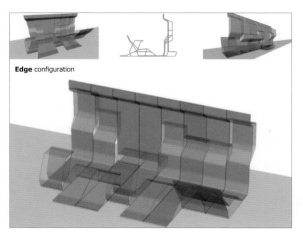

Edge configuration

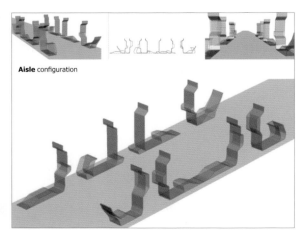

Aisle configuration

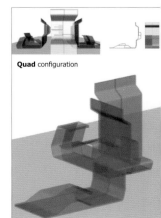

Quad configuration

Peep Show Design Competition
ArtCity 2002   Calgary

Laminar Booth

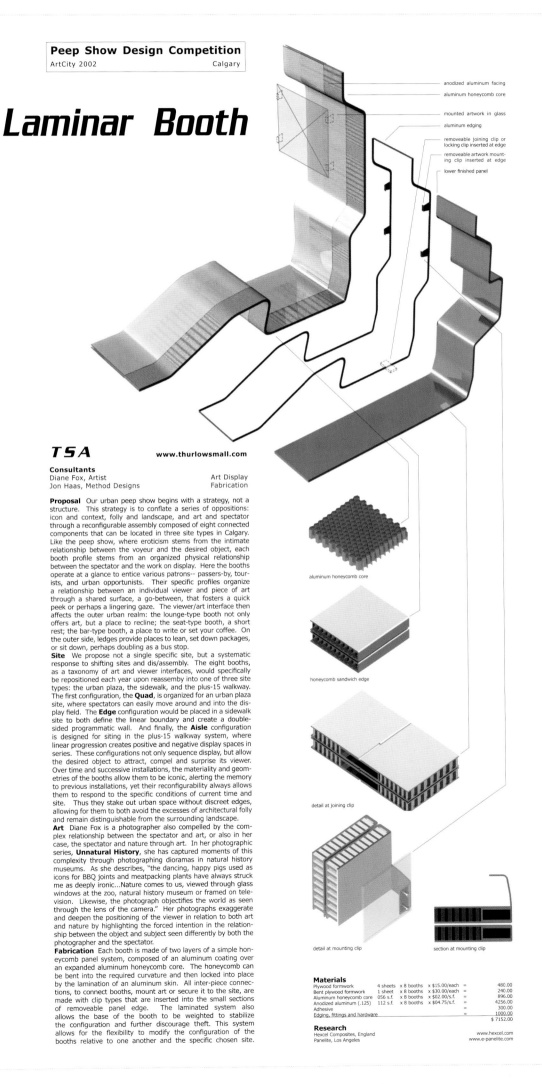

anodized aluminum facing
aluminum honeycomb core
mounted artwork in glass
aluminum edging
removeable joining clip or locking clip inserted at edge
removeable artwork mounting clip inserted at edge
lower finished panel

TSA

www.thurlowsmall.com

Consultants
Diane Fox, Artist   Art Display
Jon Haas, Method Designs   Fabrication

Proposal Our urban peep show begins with a strategy, not a structure. This strategy is to conflate a series of oppositions: icon and context, folly and landscape, and art and spectator through a reconfigurable assembly composed of eight connected components that can be located in three site types in Calgary. Like the peep show, where eroticism stems from the intimate relationship between the voyeur and the desired object, each booth profile stems from an organized physical relationship between the spectator and the work on display. Here the booths operate at a glance to entice various patrons-- passers-by, tourists, and urban opportunists. Their specific profiles organize a relationship between an individual viewer and piece of art through a shared surface, a go-between, that fosters a quick peek or perhaps a lingering gaze. The viewer/art interface then affects the outer urban realm: the lounge-type booth not only offers art, but a place to recline; the seat-type booth, a short rest; the bar-type booth, a place to write or set your coffee. On the outer side, ledges provide places to lean, set down packages, or sit down, perhaps doubling as a bus stop.

Site We propose not a single specific site, but a systematic response to shifting sites and dis/assembly. The eight booths, as a taxonomy of art and viewer interfaces, would specifically be repositioned each year upon reassemby into one of three site types: the urban plaza, the sidewalk, and the plus-15 walkway. The first configuration, the **Quad**, is organized for an urban plaza site, where spectators can easily move around and into the display field. The **Edge** configuration would be placed in a sidewalk site to both define the linear boundary and create a double-sided programmatic wall. And finally, the **Aisle** configuration is designed for siting in the plus-15 walkway system, where linear progression creates positive and negative display spaces in series. These configurations not only sequence display, but allow the desired object to attract, compel and surprise its viewer. Over time and successive installations, the materiality and geometries of the booths allow them to be iconic, alerting the memory to previous installations, yet their reconfigurability always allows them to respond to the specific conditions of current time and site. Thus they stake out urban space without discreet edges, allowing for them to both avoid the excesses of architectural folly and remain distinguishable from the surrounding landscape.

Art Diane Fox is a photographer also compelled by the complex relationship between the spectator and art, or also in her case, the spectator and nature through art. In her photographic series, **Unnatural History**, she has captured moments of this complexity through photographing dioramas in natural history museums. As she describes, "the dancing, happy pigs used as icons for BBQ joints and meatpacking plants have always struck me as deeply ironic...Nature comes to us, viewed through glass windows at the zoo, natural history museum or framed on television. Likewise, the photograph objectifies the world as seen through the lens of the camera." Her photographs exaggerate and deepen the positioning of the viewer in relation to both art and nature by highlighting the forced intention in the relationship between the object and subject seen differently by both the photographer and the spectator.

Fabrication Each booth is made of two layers of a simple honeycomb panel system, composed of an aluminum coating over an expanded aluminum honeycomb core. The honeycomb can be bent into the required curvature and then locked into place by the lamination of an aluminum skin. All inter-piece connections, to connect booths, mount art or secure it to the site, are made with clip types that are inserted into the small sections of removeable panel edge. The laminated system also allows the base of the booth to be weighted to stabilize the configuration and further discourage theft. This system allows for the flexibility to modify the configuration of the booths relative to one another and the specific chosen site.

aluminum honeycomb core

honeycomb sandwich edge

detail at joining clip

detail at mounting clip   section at mounting clip

Materials

Plywood formwork	4 sheets	x 8 booths	x $15.00/each	=	480.00
Bent plywood formwork	1 sheet	x 8 booths	x $30.00/each	=	240.00
Aluminum honeycomb core	056 s.f.	x 8 booths	x $02.00/s.f.	=	896.00
Anodized aluminum (.125)	112 s.f.	x 8 booths	x $04.75/s.f.	=	4256.00
Adhesive				=	300.00
Edging, fittings and hardware				=	1000.00
					$ 7152.00

Research

Hexcel Composites, England   www.hexcel.com
Panelite, Los Angeles   www.e-panelite.com

322

Centro Storico Teramo | *ZO_loft*

Architect : Filomena Acquaviva, Andrea Cingoli, Francesca Fontana,
Michele Manigrasso, Luigi Di Paolo, Roberto Potenza
Client : Comune di Teramo (TE)
Location : Teramo (TE), Italy

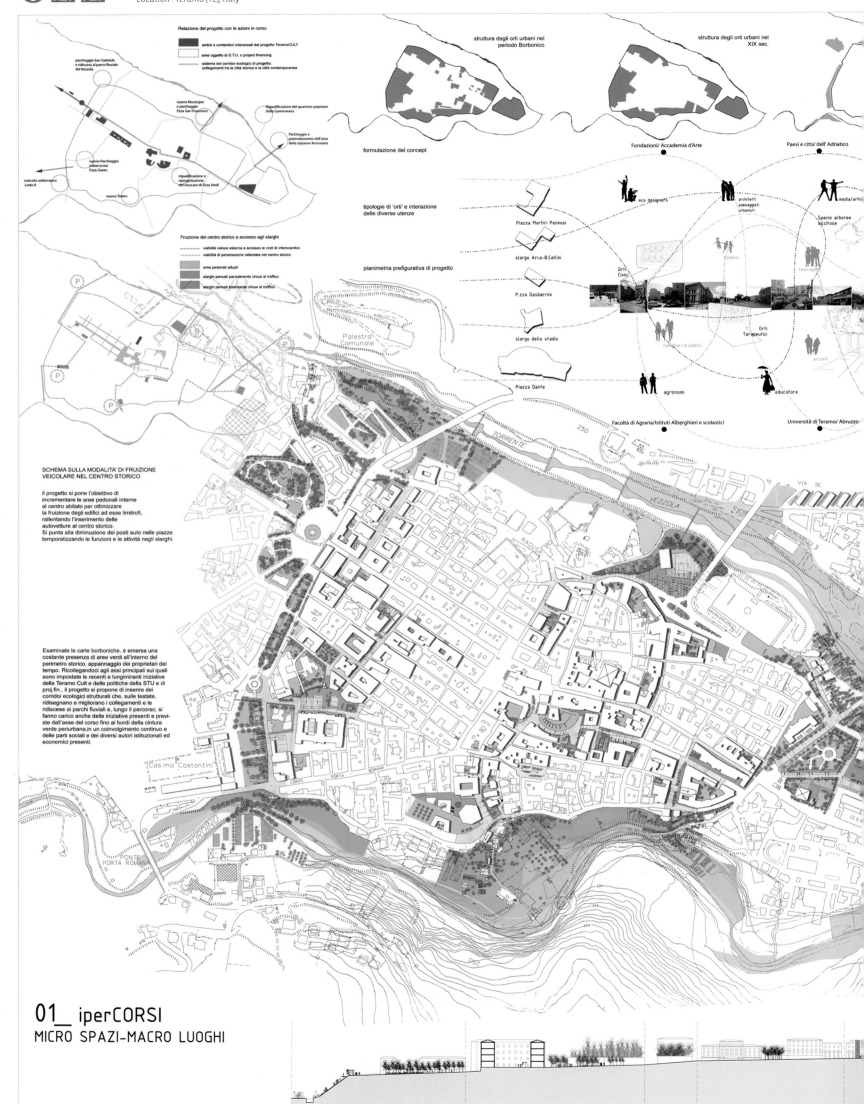

Relazione del progetto con le azioni in corso

ambiti e contenitori interessati dal progetto TeramoCULT

aree oggetto di S.T.U. o project financing

sistema dei corridoi ecologici di progetto; collegamenti tra la città storica e la città contemporanea

parcheggio San Gabriele e ridiscesa al parco fluviale del Vezzola

nuovo Municipio e parcheggio P.zza San Francesco

riqualificazione del quartiere popolare della Gammarana

Parcheggio e potenziamento dell'area della stazione ferroviaria

nuovo Parcheggio sotterraneo P.zza Dante

riqualificazione e riprogettazione dell'innesto di P.zza Verdi

svincolo sotterraneo Lotto 0

nuovo Teatro

Fruizione del centro storico e accesso agli slarghi

viabilità veloce esterna e accesso ai nodi di interscambio

viabilità di penetrazione rallentata nel centro storico

aree pedonali attuali

slarghi pensati parzialmente chiusi al traffico

slarghi pensati totalmente chiusi al traffico

struttura degli orti urbani nel periodo Borbonico

struttura degli orti urbani nel XIX sec.

formulazione del concept

tipologie di 'orti' e interazione delle diverse utenze

planimetria prefigurativa di progetto

Fondazioni/ Accademia d'Arte

Paesi e città dell'Adriatico

Piazza Martiri Pennesi

slargo Arca-B.Cellini

P.zza Gasbarrini

slargo dello stadio

Piazza Dante

eco designers

architetti paesaggisti urbanisti

media/artisti

Specie arboree siccitose

Orti Civici

bambini

teenager

Orti Terapeutici

famiglie/residenti

anziani

agronomi

educatore

Facoltà di Agraria/Istituti Alberghieri e scolastici

Università di Teramo/ Abruzzo

Palestra Comunale

SCHEMA SULLA MODALITA' DI FRUIZIONE VEICOLARE NEL CENTRO STORICO

il progetto si pone l'obiettivo di incrementare le aree pedonali interne al centro abitato per ottimizzare la fruizione degli edifici ad esse limitrofi, rallentando l'inserimento delle autovetture al centro storico.
Si punta alla diminuzione dei posti auto nelle piazze temporalizzando le funzioni e le attività negli slarghi.

Esaminate le carte borboniche, è emersa una costante presenza di aree verdi all'interno del perimetro storico, appannaggio dei proprietari del tempo. Ricollegandoci agli assi principali sui quali sono impostate le recenti e lungimiranti iniziative della Teramo Cult e delle politiche della STU e di proj.fin., il progetto si propone di inserire dei corridoi ecologici strutturati che, sulle testate, ridisegnano e migliorano i collegamenti e le ridiscese ai parchi fluviali e, lungo il percorso, si fanno carico anche delle iniziative presenti e previste dall'asse del corso fino ai bordi della cintura verde periurbana, in un coinvolgimento continuo e delle parti sociali e dei diversi autori istituzionali ed economici presenti.

TORRENTE VEZZOLA

TORDINO

Cas.ma "Costantini"

PONTE PORTA ROMANA

01_ iperCORSI
MICRO SPAZI-MACRO LUOGHI

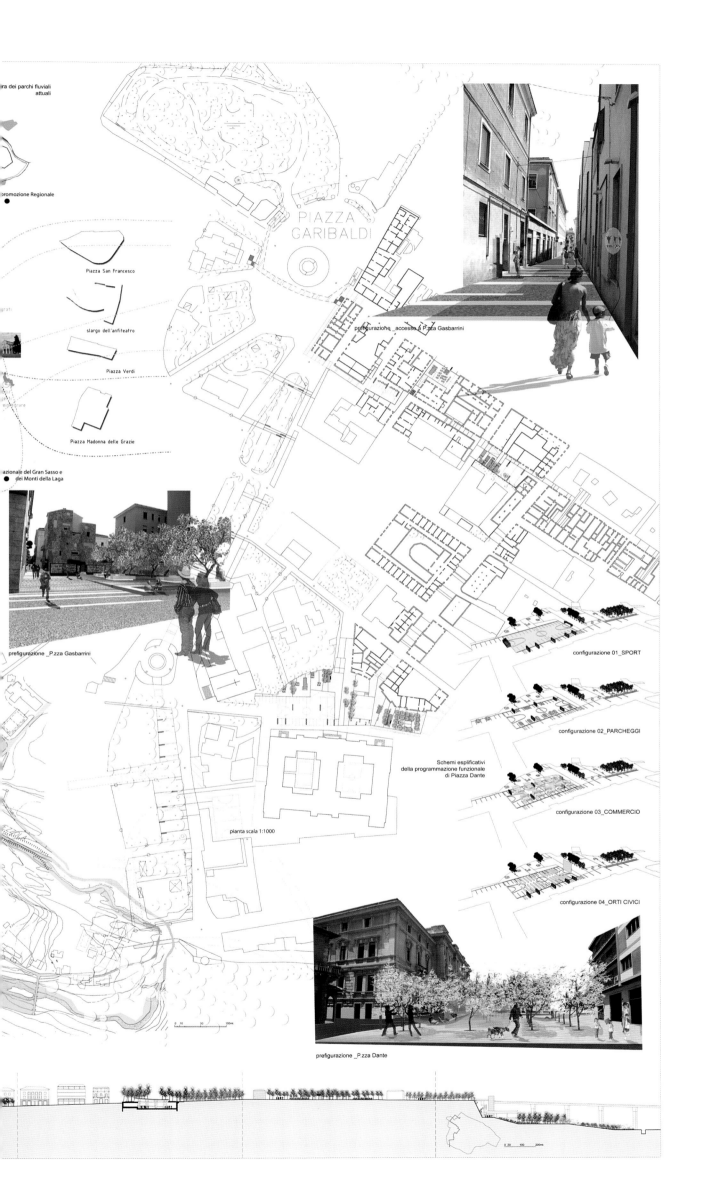

ra dei parchi fluviali
attuali

romozione Regionale ●

Piazza San Francesco

slargo dell'anfiteatro

Piazza Verdi

Piazza Madonna delle Grazie

azionale del Gran Sasso e ● dei Monti della Laga

PIAZZA GARIBALDI

prefigurazione _accesso a P.zza Gasbarrini

prefigurazione _P.zza Gasbarrini

pianta scala 1:1000

configurazione 01_SPORT

configurazione 02_PARCHEGGI

Schemi esplificativi
della programmazione funzionale
di Piazza Dante

configurazione 03_COMMERCIO

configurazione 04_ORTI CIVICI

prefigurazione _P.zza Dante

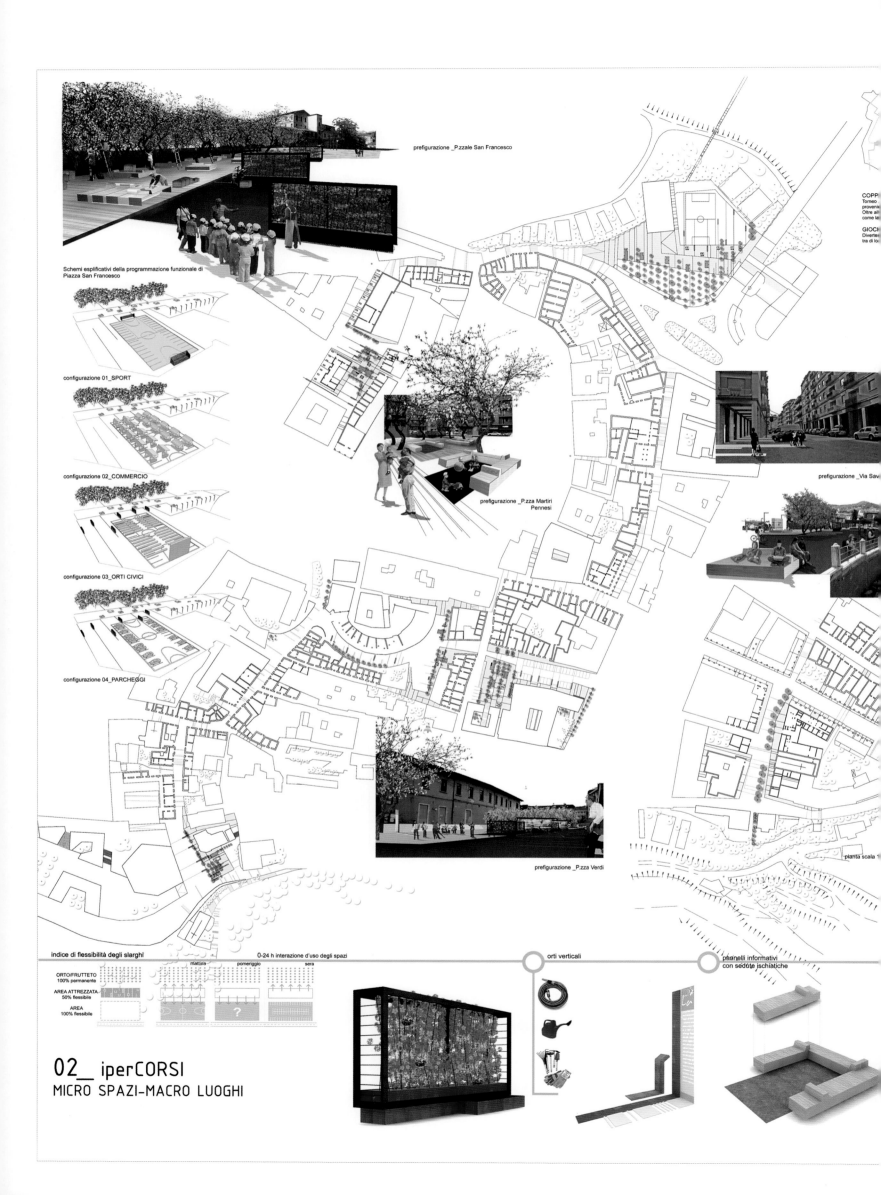

prefigurazione _P.zzale San Francesco

Schemi esplificativi della programmazione funzionale di Piazza San Francesco

configurazione 01_SPORT

configurazione 02_COMMERCIO

configurazione 03_ORTI CIVICI

configurazione 04_PARCHEGGI

prefigurazione _P.zza Martiri Pennesi

prefigurazione _Via Savi

prefigurazione _P.zza Verdi

pianta scala

COPP
Torneo
provenie
Oltre al
come la

GIOCHI
Diverte
tra di lo

indice di flessibilità degli slarghi

ORTO/FRUTTETO
100% permanente

AREA ATTREZZATA
50% flessibile

AREA
100% flessibile

0-24 h interazione d'uso degli spazi

mattina   pomeriggio   sera

orti verticali

pannelli informativi con sedute ischiatiche

02_ iperCORSI
MICRO SPAZI-MACRO LUOGHI

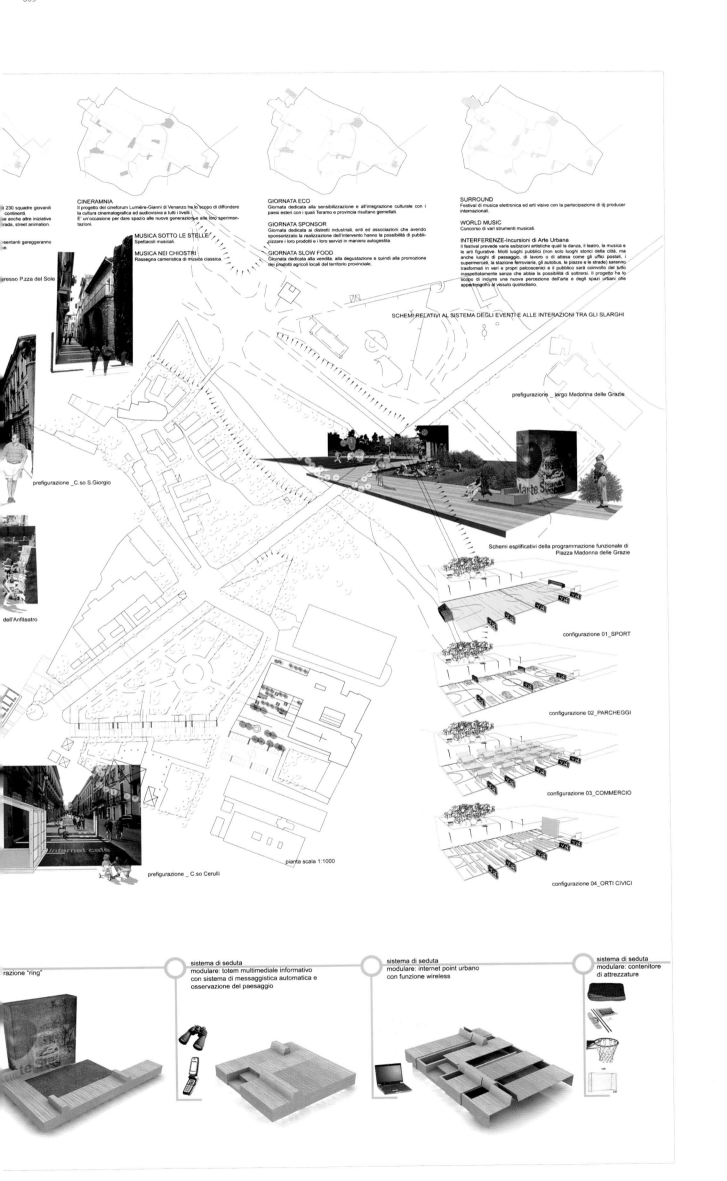

230 squadre giovanili
continenti
e anche altre iniziative
rada, street animation.

sentanti gareggeranno

CINERAMNIA
Il progetto del cineforum Lumière-Gianni di Venanzo ha lo scopo di diffondere la cultura cinematografica ed audiovisiva a tutti i livelli. E' un'occasione per dare spazio alle nuove generazioni e alle loro sperimentazioni.

MUSICA SOTTO LE STELLE
Spettacoli musicali.

MUSICA NEI CHIOSTRI
Rassegna cameristica di musica classica.

GIORNATA ECO
Giornata dedicata alla sensibilizzazione e all'integrazione culturale con i paesi esteri con i quali Teramo e provincia risultano gemellati.

GIORNATA SPONSOR
Giornata dedicata ai distretti industriali, enti ed associazioni che avendo sponsorizzato la realizzazione dell'intervento hanno la possibilità di pubblicizzare i loro prodotti e i loro servizi in maniera autogestita.

GIORNATA SLOW FOOD
Giornata dedicata alla vendita, alla degustazione e quindi alla promozione dei prodotti agricoli locali del territorio provinciale.

SURROUND
Festival di musica elettronica ed arti visive con la partecipazione di dj producer internazionali.

WORLD MUSIC
Concorso di vari strumenti musicali.

INTERFERENZE-Incursioni di Arte Urbana
Il festival prevede varie esibizioni artistiche quali la danza, il teatro, la musica e le arti figurative. Molti luoghi pubblici (non solo luoghi storici della città, ma anche luoghi di passaggio, di lavoro o di attesa come gli uffici postali, i supermercati, la stazione ferroviaria, gli autobus, le piazze e le strade) saranno trasformati in veri e propri palcoscenici e il pubblico sarà coinvolto del tutto inaspettatamente senza che abbia la possibilità di sottrarsi. Il progetto ha lo scopo di indurre una nuova percezione dell'arte e degli spazi urbani che appartengono al vissuto quotidiano.

gresso P.zza del Sole

SCHEMI RELATIVI AL SISTEMA DEGLI EVENTI E ALLE INTERAZIONI TRA GLI SLARGHI

prefigurazione _ largo Madonna delle Grazie

prefigurazione _C.so S.Giorgio

dell'Anfiteatro

Schemi esplificativi della programmazione funzionale di Piazza Madonna delle Grazie

configurazione 01_SPORT

configurazione 02_PARCHEGGI

configurazione 03_COMMERCIO

configurazione 04_ORTI CIVICI

prefigurazione _ C.so Cerulli

pianta scala 1:1000

razione "ring"

sistema di seduta
modulare: totem multimediale informativo con sistema di messaggistica automatica e osservazione del paesaggio

sistema di seduta
modulare: internet point urbano con funzione wireless

sistema di seduta
modulare: contenitore di attrezzature

Gli EcoCULTour sono sistemi ambientali, artistici, culturali, multimediali, che si interfacciano e si inseriscono nel tessuto storico quali corridoi ecologici per il collegamento dei parchi fluviali con il centro città
La nuova delimitazione ricade all'interno della cintura dei parchi periurbani. Il dove il progetto, come da programma, acquista forza proprio nelle relazioni che instaura con il perimetro esterno alle mura e con tutti quegli incubatori culturali e ricettivi caratterizzanti l'offerta terziaria e residenziale dell'area. L'obiettivo è quello di restituire un'esperienza completa di territorio valorizzandone la storia, le tradizioni, i prodotti locali, con attività culturali didattiche e dimostrative costantemente interdisciplinari e motivo di confronto tra le diverse fasce di età

villa comunale

Potenziamento delle relazioni intrinseche dell'area in esame e adozione di tecnologie telematiche d'avanguardistiche per la gestione delle connessioni su più livelli

sistema di irrigazione esistente
diramazioni del sistema di irrigazione previste in polietilene DN 25- 1"

Bluetooth

interrelazioni e rimessa in rete degli incubatori artistici/culturali presenti nell'area con gli ambiti individuati dal progetto

INDICAZIONE QUALITATIVA DELL
PERCENTUALI DI DI FOR
DERIVANTI DALLE AZIONI DI P

DIAGRAMMI DELLE MISURE E AZIONI F

① Il sistema del verde p
sono rimessi in rete con i co
di progetto, implementando
centro verso l'esterno e viceversa
delle piste ciclabili lim

② In previsione di una pa
pedonalizzazione degli s
l'accessibilità
autorizzati nelle aree p
che diventano teatro e incentivo per i

③ Studio delle relazioni tra
rifunzional
e i principali incubatori di serv
operi

Museo ipogeo
Viale dei Tigli
ARCA_Laboratorio per le arti contemporanee
Piazza Dante
10.2008   01.2009
Piazza Cellini e Largo San Matteo

Piazza
Garibaldi

01_ EcoCULTour
MICRO SPAZI-MACRO LUOGHI

fotoinserimento planivolumetria scala 1:500

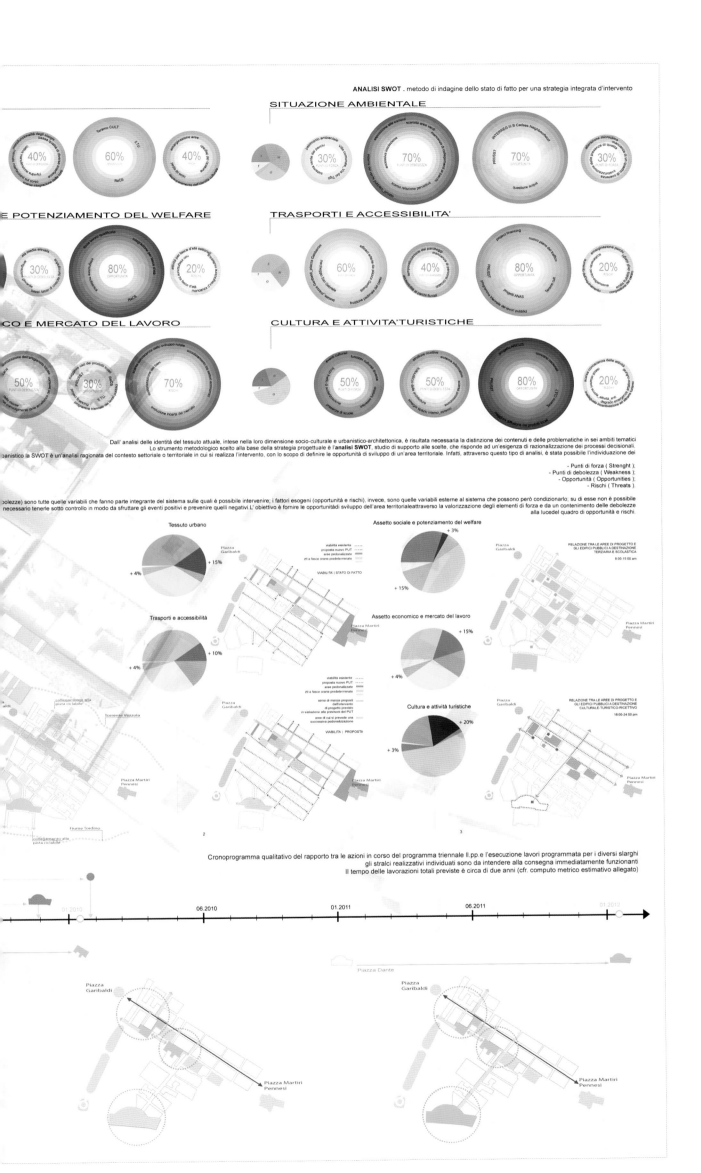

ANALISI SWOT . metodo di indagine dello stato di fatto per una strategia integrata d'intervento

SITUAZIONE AMBIENTALE

E POTENZIAMENTO DEL WELFARE

TRASPORTI E ACCESSIBILITA'

CO E MERCATO DEL LAVORO

CULTURA E ATTIVITA'TURISTICHE

Dall' analisi delle identità del tessuto attuale, intese nella loro dimensione socio-culturale e urbanistico-architettonica, è risultata necessaria la distinzione dei contenuti e delle problematiche in sei ambiti tematici
Lo strumento metodologico scelto alla base della strategia progettuale è l'**analisi SWOT**, studio di supporto alle scelte, che risponde ad un'esigenza di razionalizzazione dei processi decisionali.
banistico la SWOT è un'analisi ragionata del contesto settoriale o territoriale in cui si realizza l'intervento, con lo scopo di definire le opportunità di sviluppo di un'area territoriale. Infatti, attraverso questo tipo di analisi, è stata possibile l'individuazione dei

- Punti di forza (Strenght);
- Punti di debolezza (Weakness);
- Opportunità (Opportunities);
- Rischi (Threats).

oolezze) sono tutte quelle variabili che fanno parte integrante del sistema sulle quali è possibile intervenire; i fattori esogeni (opportunità e rischi), invece, sono quelle variabili esterne al sistema che possono però condizionarlo; su di esse non è possibile
necessario tenerle sotto controllo in modo da sfruttare gli eventi positivi e prevenire quelli negativi.L' obiettivo è fornire le opportunitàdi sviluppo dell'area territorialeattraverso la valorizzazione degli elementi di forza e da un contenimento delle debolezze
alla lucedel quadro di opportunità e rischi.

Cronoprogramma qualitativo del rapporto tra le azioni in corso del programma triennale ll.pp. e l'esecuzione lavori programmata per i diversi slarghi
gli stralci realizzativi individuati sono da intendere alla consegna immediatamente funzionanti
Il tempo delle lavorazioni totali previste è circa di due anni (cfr. computo metrico estimativo allegato)

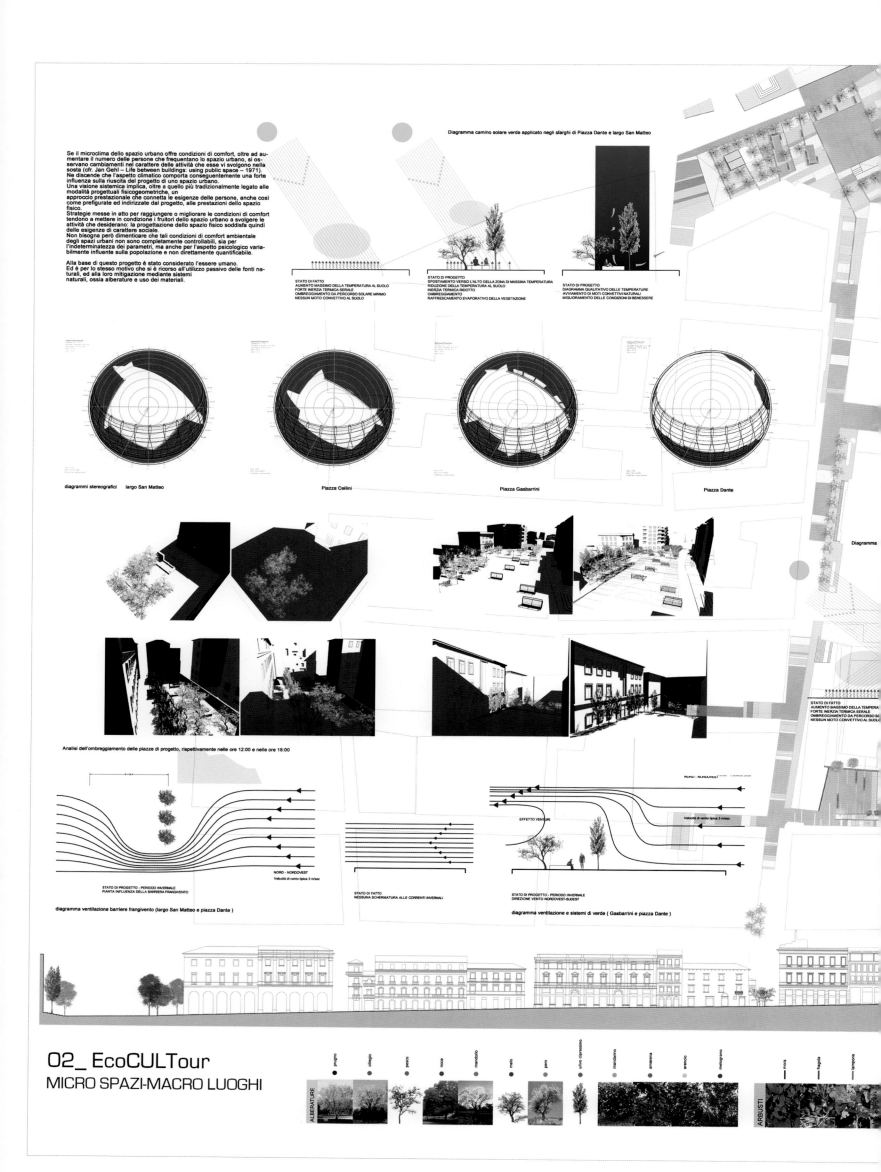

Se il microclima dello spazio urbano offre condizioni di comfort, oltre ad aumentare il numero delle persone che frequentano lo spazio urbano, si osservano cambiamenti nel carattere delle attività che esse vi svolgono nella sosta (cfr. Jan Gehl – Life between buildings: using public space – 1971). Ne discende che l'aspetto climatico comporta conseguentemente una forte influenza sulla riuscita del progetto di uno spazio urbano.

Una visione sistemica implica, oltre a quello più tradizionalmente legato alle modalità progettuali fisicogeometriche, un approccio prestazionale che connetta le esigenze delle persone, anche così come prefigurate ed indirizzate dal progetto, alle prestazioni dello spazio fisico.

Strategie messe in atto per raggiungere o migliorare le condizioni di comfort tendono a mettere in condizione i fruitori dello spazio urbano a svolgere le attività che desiderano: la progettazione dello spazio fisico soddisfa quindi delle esigenze di carattere sociale.

Non bisogna però dimenticare che tali condizioni di comfort ambientale degli spazi urbani non sono completamente controllabili, sia per l'indeterminatezza dei parametri, ma anche per l'aspetto psicologico variabilmente influente sulla popolazione e non direttamente quantificabile.

Alla base di questo progetto è stato considerato l'essere umano. Ed è per lo stesso motivo che si è ricorso all'utilizzo passivo delle fonti naturali, ed alla loro mitigazione mediante sistemi naturali, ossia alberature e uso dei materiali.

Diagramma camino solare verde applicato negli slarghi di Piazza Dante e largo San Matteo

STATO DI FATTO
AUMENTO MASSIMO DELLA TEMPERATURA AL SUOLO
FORTE INERZIA TERMICA SERALE
OMBREGGIAMENTO DEL PERCORSO SOLARE MINIMO
NESSUN MOTO CONVETTIVO AL SUOLO

STATO DI PROGETTO
SPOSTAMENTO VERSO L'ALTO DELLA ZONA DI MASSIMA TEMPERATURA
RIDUZIONE DELLA TEMPERATURA AL SUOLO
INERZIA TERMICA RIDOTTO
OMBREGGIAMENTO
RAFFRESCAMENTO EVAPORATIVO DELLA VEGETAZIONE

STATO DI PROGETTO
DIAGRAMMA QUALITATIVO DELLE TEMPERATURE
AVVIAMENTO DI MOTI CONVETTIVI NATURALI
MIGLIORAMENTO DELLE CONDIZIONI DI BENESSERE

diagrammi stereografici   largo San Matteo

Piazza Cellini

Piazza Gasbarrini

Piazza Dante

Analisi dell'ombreggiamento delle piazze di progetto, rispettivamente nelle ore 12:00 e nelle ore 18:00

NORD - NORDOVEST
Velocità di vento 5pica 3 m/sec

EFFETTO VENTURI

NORD - NORDOVEST
Velocità di vento 5pica 3 m/sec

STATO DI PROGETTO - PERIODO INVERNALE
PIANTA INFLUENZA DELLA BARRIERA FRANGIVENTO

STATO DI FATTO
NESSUNA SCHERMATURA ALLE CORRENTI INVERNALI

STATO DI PROGETTO - PERIODO INVERNALE
DIREZIONE VENTO NORDOVEST-SUDEST

diagramma ventilazione barriere frangivento (largo San Matteo e piazza Dante)

diagramma ventilazione e sistemi di verde (Gasbarrini e piazza Dante)

02_ EcoCULTour
MICRO SPAZI-MACRO LUOGHI

ALBERATURE

ARBUSTI

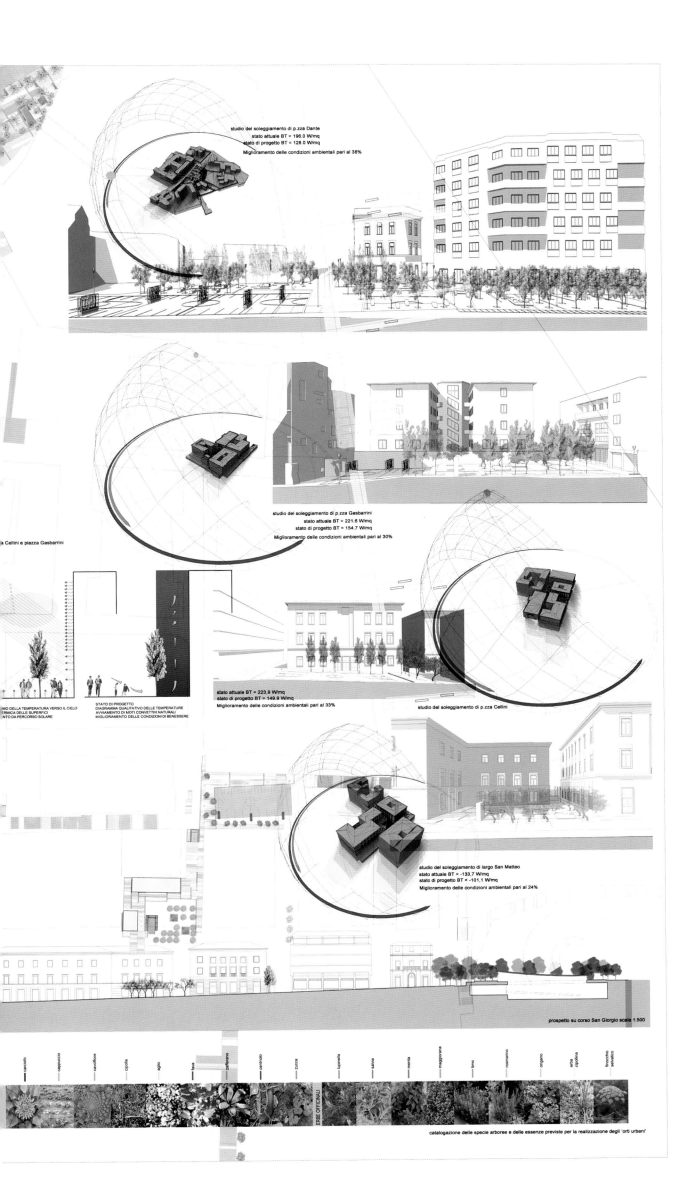

studio del soleggiamento di p.zza Dante
stato attuale BT = 196.0 W/mq
stato di progetto BT = 128.0 W/mq
Miglioramento delle condizioni ambientali pari al 38%

Cellini e piazza Gasbarrini

studio del soleggiamento di p.zza Gasbarrini
stato attuale BT = 221.6 W/mq
stato di progetto BT = 154.7 W/mq
Miglioramento delle condizioni ambientali pari al 30%

MO DELLA TEMPERATURA VERSO IL CIELO
ERMICA DELLE SUPERFICI
NTO DA PERCORSO SOLARE

STATO DI PROGETTO
DIAGRAMMA QUALITATIVO DELLE TEMPERATURE
AVVIAMENTO DI MOTI CONVETTIVI NATURALI
MIGLIORAMENTO DELLE CONDIZIONI DI BENESSERE

stato attuale BT = 223,9 W/mq
stato di progetto BT = 149.9 W/mq
Miglioramento delle condizioni ambientali pari al 33%

studio del soleggiamento di p.zza Cellini

studio del soleggiamento di largo San Matteo
stato attuale BT = -133,7 W/mq
stato di progetto BT = -101,1 W/mq
Miglioramento delle condizioni ambientali pari al 24%

prospetto su corso San Giorgio scala 1:500

catalogazione delle specie arboree e delle essenze previste per la realizzazione degli 'orti urbani'

PIANTA PIAZZA GASBARRINI IN SCALA 1:50

03_ EcoCULTour
MICRO SPAZI-MACRO LUOGHI

PAVIMENTAZIONE

Quarzite indiana beige, mint e grigia;
travertino graffiato;
tot.mq. 580,00

GHIAIA

Ghiaia lavata a diversa granulometria;
mq. 33,00

RING

Sabbia;
Terra rossa;
tot.mq. 31,25

PANCA

SEZIONE LONGITUDINALE SCALA 1:50

ABACO DEI MATERIALI DI PROGETTO

Street print;
mq. 93,00

Uva fragola;

Rose;

Ulivo cipressino;
num. 10

Melo cotogno;
num. 17

STREET PRINT

CORTEN

ORTI VERTICALI

ALBERI

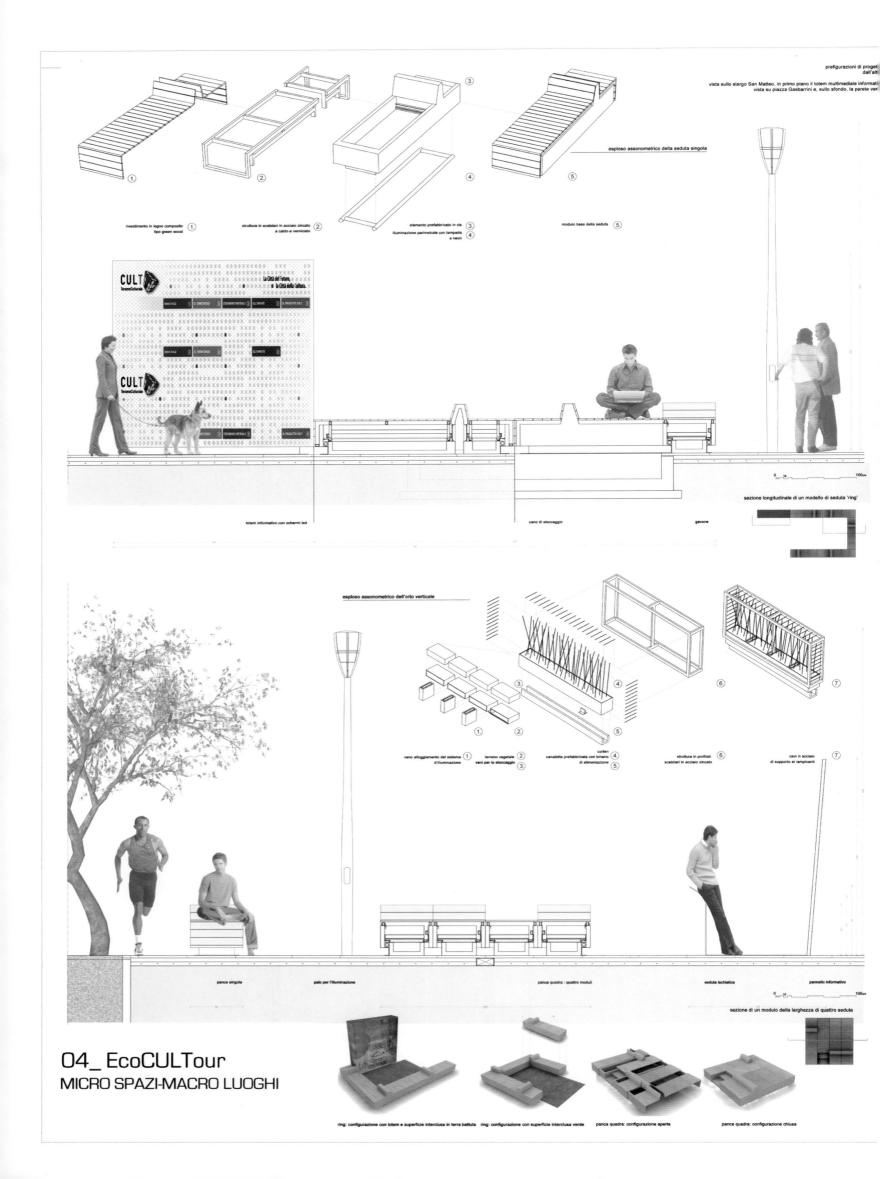

prefigurazioni di progetti
dall'alti

vista sullo slargo San Matteo, in primo piano il totem multimediale informativo
vista su piazza Gasbarrini e, sullo sfondo, la parete ver

esploso assonometrico della seduta singola

rivestimento in legno composito ① tipo green wood

struttura in scatolari in acciaio zincato ② a caldo e verniciato

elemento prefabbricato in cls ③
illuminazione perimetrale con lampada ④ a neon

modulo base della seduta ⑤

sezione longitudinale di un modello di seduta 'ring'

totem informativo con schermi led

vano di stoccaggio

gavone

esploso assonometrico dell'orto verticale

vano alloggiamento del sistema ① d'illuminazione

terreno vegetale ②
vani per lo stoccaggio ③

corten
canaletta prefabbricata con binario ④ di alimentazione ⑤

struttura in profilati ⑥ scatolari in acciaio zincato

cavi in acciaio ⑦ di supporto ai rampicanti

panca singola

palo per l'illuminazione

panca quadra : quattro moduli

seduta ischiatica

pannello informativo

sezione di un modulo della larghezza di quattro sedute

04_ EcoCULTour
MICRO SPAZI-MACRO LUOGHI

ring: configurazione con totem e superficie interclusa in terra battuta   ring: configurazione con superficie interclusa verde   panca quadra: configurazione aperta   panca quadra: configurazione chiusa

323

Centro Storico Sora | *ZO_loft*

Architect : Paolo Emilio Bellisario
Collaborators : Valerio Bracci, Andrea Cingoli, Ilias Fragkakis, Francesca Fontana
Client : Arciconfraternita di Maria SS. Addolorata

Location : Sora (FR), Italy
Design : 2010

Progetto TAV_1

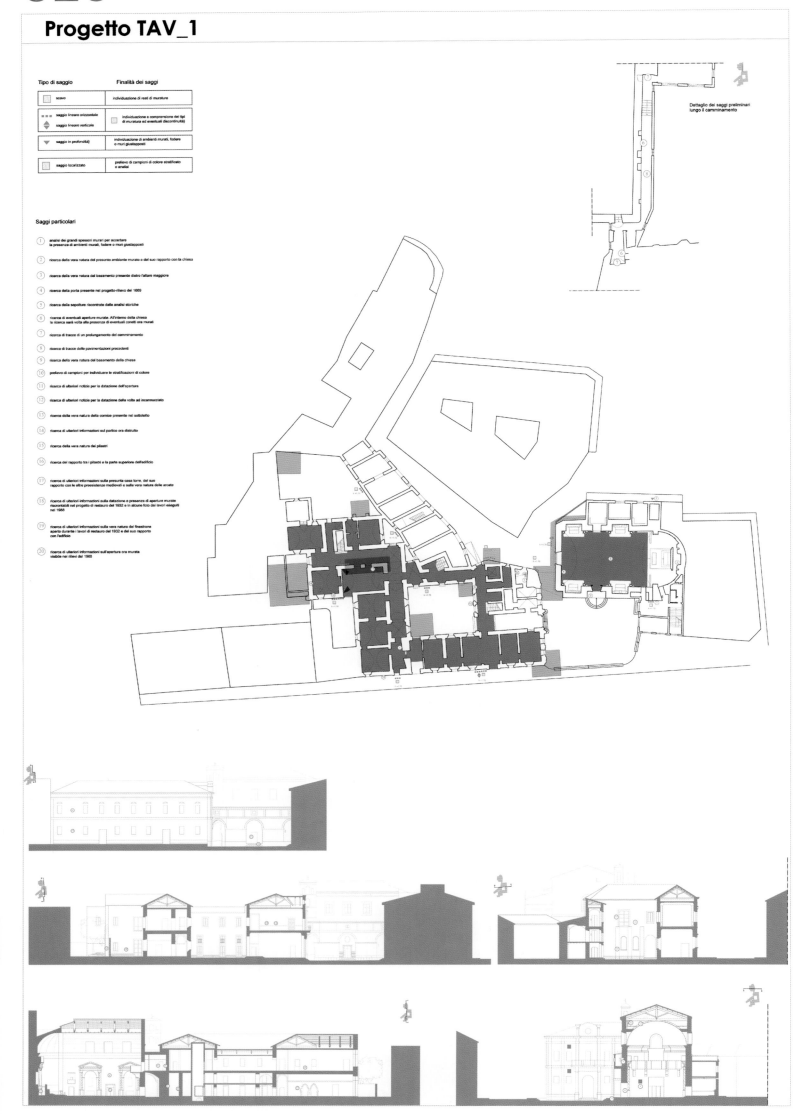

Dettaglio dei saggi preliminari lungo il camminamento

Tipo di saggio — **Finalità dei saggi**

- scavo — individuazione di resti di murature
- saggio lineare orizzontale / saggio lineare verticale — individuazione e comprensione dei tipi di muratura ed eventuali discontinuità
- saggio in profondità — individuazione di ambienti murati, fodere o muri giustapposti
- saggio localizzato — prelievo di campioni di colore stratificato o analisi

Saggi particolari

1. analisi dei grandi spessori murari per accertare la presenza di ambienti murati, fodere o muri giustapposti
2. ricerca della vera natura del presunto ambiente murato e del suo rapporto con la chiesa
3. ricerca della vera natura del basamento presente dietro l'altare maggiore
4. ricerca della porta presente nel progetto-rilievo del 1669
5. ricerca delle sepolture riscontrate dalle analisi storiche
6. ricerca di eventuali aperture murate. All'interno della chiesa la ricerca sarà volta alla presenza di eventuali coretti ora murati
7. ricerca di tracce di un prolungamento del camminamento
8. ricerca di tracce delle pavimentazioni precedenti
9. ricerca della vera natura del basamento della chiesa
10. prelievo di campioni per individuare le stratificazioni di colore
11. ricerca di ulteriori notizie per la datazione dell'apertura
12. ricerca di ulteriori notizie per la datazione della volta ad incannucciato
13. ricerca della vera natura della cornice presente nel sottotetto
14. ricerca di ulteriori informazioni sul portico ora distrutto
15. ricerca della vera natura dei pilastri
16. ricerca del rapporto tra i pilastri e la parte superiore dell'edificio
17. ricerca di ulteriori informazioni sulla presunta casa torre, del suo rapporto con le altre preesistenze medievali e sulla vera natura delle arcate
18. ricerca di ulteriori informazioni sulla datazione e presenza di aperture murate riscontrabili nel progetto di restauro del 1932 e in alcune foto dei lavori eseguiti nel 1988
19. ricerca di ulteriori informazioni sulla vera natura del finestrone aperto durante i lavori di restauro del 1932 e del suo rapporto con l'edificio
20. ricerca di ulteriori informazioni sull'apertura ora murata visibile nei rilievi del 1988

Progetto TAV_2

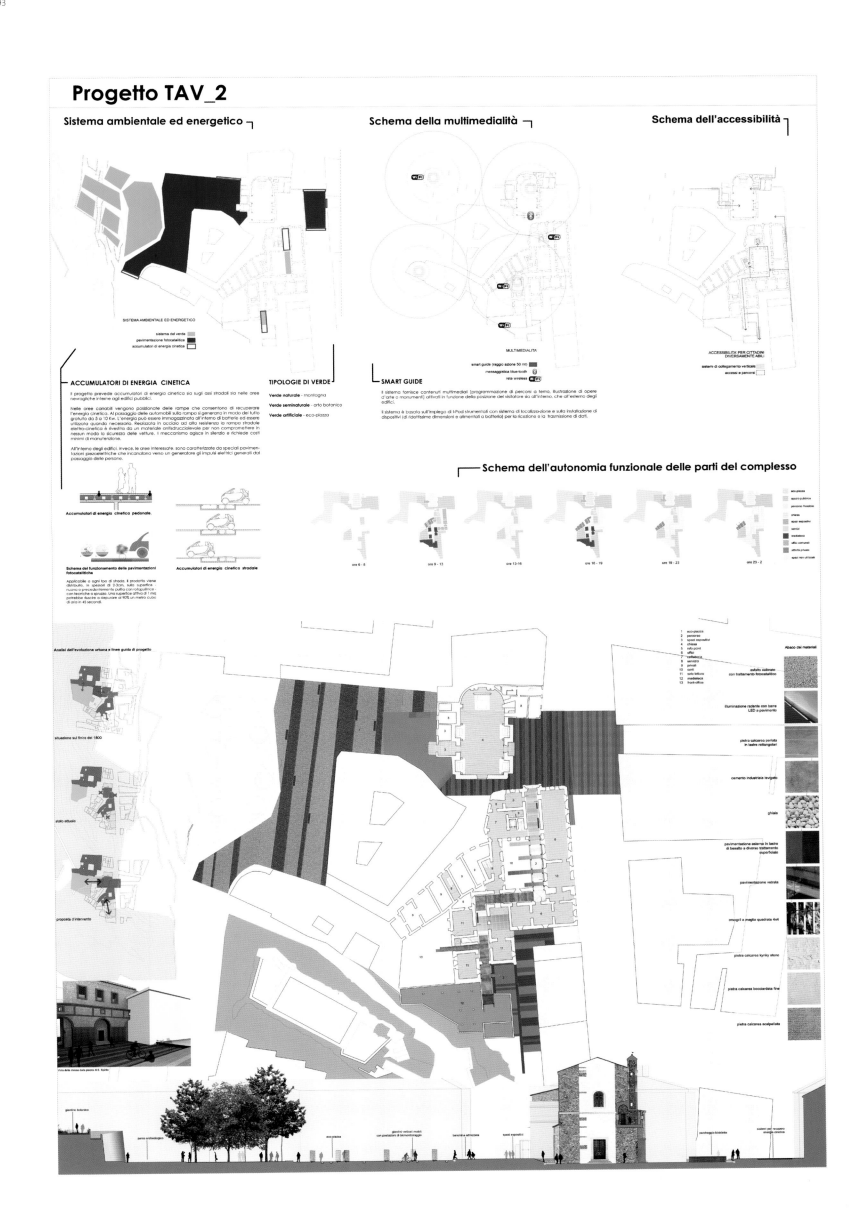

Sistema ambientale ed energetico

Schema della multimedialità

Schema dell'accessibilità

ACCUMULATORI DI ENERGIA CINETICA

TIPOLOGIE DI VERDE

SMART GUIDE

Schema dell'autonomia funzionale delle parti del complesso

Progetto TAV_3

esploso assonometrico del giardino verticale

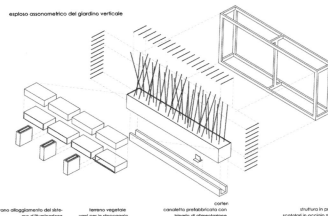

Postazioni mobili di biomonitoraggio ambientale

All'interno dei giardini verticali vengono integrate
essenze che permettono di monitorare
il grado di inquinamento del centro storico

Essenze a basso costo per biomonitoraggio:

1. Hipericum
2. Dacylis
3. Verbascum
4. Picris
5. Daucus
6. Chicorium

vano alloggiamento del sistema d'illuminazione

terreno vegetale
vani per lo stoccaggio

corten
canaletta prefabbricata con
binario di alimentazione

struttura in profilati
scatolari in acciaio zincato

cavi in acciaio
di supporto ai rampicanti

Sezione trasversale tipo degli uffici

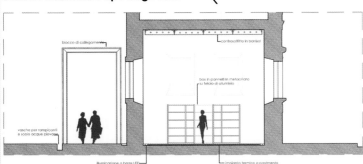

blocco di collegamento

controsoffitto in barrisol

box in pannelli in metacrilato
su telaio di alluminio

vasche per rampicanti
e scolo acque piovane

Illuminazione a barre LED

impianto termico a pavimento

BARRISOL
Fatti su misura, si adeguano ad ogni superficie, forma, situazione,
a lungo.
S'integrano all'architettura, rispondono ai requisiti di benessere e
migliorando la comodità termica ed acustica degli edifici.

• Riciclabili al 100%
• Non tossici (adeguandosi alle normative Europee ed internazionali)

LED
I vantaggi dei LED dal punto di vista illuminotecnico e ambientale sono:
• elevata durata di funzionamento non influenzata dal numero
di accensioni/spegnimenti
• assenza di costi di manutenzione
• elevato rendimento
• luce pulita perché priva di componenti IR e UV
• flessibilità di installazione del punto luce
• funzionamento in sicurezza perché a bassissima tensione
• accensione a freddo (fino a -40 °C) senza problemi
• insensibilità a umidità e vibrazioni
• assenza del mercurio

PANNELLI RADIANTI A PAVIMENTO
Installati su bajanti ad alte prestazioni termiche ed acustiche I
pannelli radianti si possono abbinare alle caldaie a condensazione, assicurando così un notevole risparmio energetico.

box uffici
metacrilato (pannelli 85x40 cm) su struttura in alluminio

vista delle postazioni mobili di biomonitoraggio ambientale

vista del blocco di collegamento

vista del blocco di collegamento

pavimento vetrato

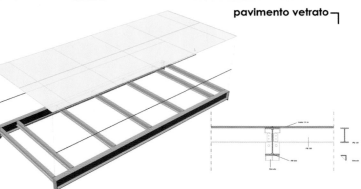

dettaglio del blocco di collegamento

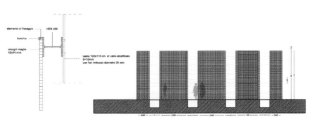

prospetto all 1:100 dei corpi di collegamento

Sezione longitudinale della chiesa

Dettaglio dell'attacco tra la Chiesa
DI S. Spirito e l'edificio del Collegio dopo la riapertura del
camminamento

Vista della facciata della chiesa da Via Loffredo

Il ripristino della spazialità e
della funzione del camminamento consentirà al visitatori
di poter osservare l'interno
della Chiesa di S. Spirito
anche in orari di chiusura di
quest'ultima o durante le
funzioni.
La riapertura del percorso
lascia tuttavia invariata la
completa autonomia dei
due edifici grazie ad una
serie di porte vetrate che
pur interrompendo la continuità visiva creano, lo-
sciano piena autonomia di
gestione dei due edifici.

895

Grundrisse | *MICROCITIES*

Project : Housing Solutions for the Immaterial Worker
1st prize International Competition Think Space / Moral Borders 2011

324

Developers / Owners:

COMPANIES
aiming at a minimization of the costs of immaterial lavor.

Outsource:
design, pr, marketing, accountability, translations, interior architecture, graphic design, writing, engineering, research, advertisement, photography, fashion, audiovisual...
for specific projects

new catalogue edition   consumers tests

sutainibility campaign   stores in Brasil

consumer control software   fall/winter show

kids promotion launch

low fat product image

new market product   new colors line   Taiwan presentation

Users:

IMMATERIAL WORKERS
producing knowledge, communication, creative solutions

Flexibility
individuals performing tasks for different companies, following their needs for a specific project. They can choose working time but must conform to the productive goals of the company, as well as its deadlines

Desires:
single house in the city centre, lowrising, adaptable to his/hers lifestyle's choice and taste.

GRUNDRISSE
HOUSING SOLUTIONS
FOR THE IMMATERIAL WORKER

AN AFFORDABLE DYSTOPIA

For the post-Fordist multitude every qualitative difference between labor time and non-labor time falls short. (P.Virno)

In the post-industrial economy, multinational companies only own the brand and develop the image and philosophy behind the product. Manufacturing is entirely outsourced to partner companies and licence-holders that eventually sell the finished product to the main company at very low prices.

Bringing such a behaviour to its extremes, **companies are able to outsource every aspect of their production to independent workers and make a larger marge of profit even on the immaterial aspects of work.** From marketing to product design and developement, interior design and engineering, the companies do not need any longer to hire personnel but they rather have the tasks done by a vast mass of subjects working flexibly from home on specific projects.

For the immaterial worker the boundaries between life and work are getting completely faded, his work coinciding with his life.
The worker's entire life is now live labor, an "invisible and indivisible commodity". (S.Lotringere). Flexible, skilled and able to communicate through email and smart phones, he is reachable around the clock by the companies and the clients he is working for. He is free of choosing his working time and how to accomplish the tasks, but must conform to the performance's goals identified by the clients or by the companies. Even studying, reading or doing sport become elements connected to his production, since these experiences improve the "knowledge" which informs the immaterial work. (M.Marzano, P.Virno)

Neverending work becomes a moral obligation, a pre-determined path to self improvement as well as a self defense from the social exclusion by unemployment.

GRUNDRISSE is a **basin of «immaterial labor»,** a network of individuals performing on call tasks, adapting their competences for specific projects, assuming their own responsibilities, facing the risks.

GRUNDRISSE is a service company that provides each worker a house where to live and work, rented for only one symbolic euro. Each unit is to be equipped with a technological system of control that keeps the worker in touch with his clients. Some services are integrated, like individual coaching, access to up-to-date technologies, meeting facilities, yoga training, leisure spaces etc., in order to avoid alienation, manage stress, improve the working performance.

GRUNDRISSE's physical expression is a structure composed by different typologies of cells, all made up by one room, where inhabiting and working are completely merged. **The houses are conceived to allow the possibility of working in connection to any other activity and in any possible space.**

The combination of interior styles and furniture organization is infinite, providing to the inhabitant/worker the choice of a customized product that corresponds to his own lifestyle. The exterior image, homogeneously white and «pure», corresponds to the need of a minimalist clever design, well advertised and broadly desired, a conforming good of supposed elitism.

In opposition to the functionalist repetition of the cells in the industrial workers' blocks, houses become here a fashionable individual product for the knowledge urban worker. The fragmentation of the units will prevent social solidarity among the workers while giving them the illusion of an autonomous house in the center of the city: an unfulfilled dream for many other inhabitants.

GRUNDRISSE is a mean of exploitation as well as of social control. It provides the illusion of preventing precarization, keeping the workers always busy for different companies.

The city of Paris is the location for the pilot project. With its ever growing sqm price, the city forces young -knowledge- workers to live in ever smaller units (*studios*), while renting a flat has become harder and harder for precarious individuals or couples, usually unable to provide stabile economic guarantees to the landlords. Providing a house to the flexible workers will be appealing for an ever growing segment of population.

Huge areas of the city, once connected to the main infrastructures (railroads and highways) were populated by industrial structures that today are being delocated outside of what has become part of the city center.

GRUNDRISSE will occupy these sectors of the city, providing a conversion from structures that hosted manual labor into a strip of land destined to the intellectual labor. The direct connection to the infrastructures encourages the worker to travel in many periods of the year, so that he can fast recover from stress-related problems and be even more disconnected from the urban tissue, both physically and socially.

Dismissed industrial area near Paris' Gare de l'Est is now a territory of colonization for immaterial labor.

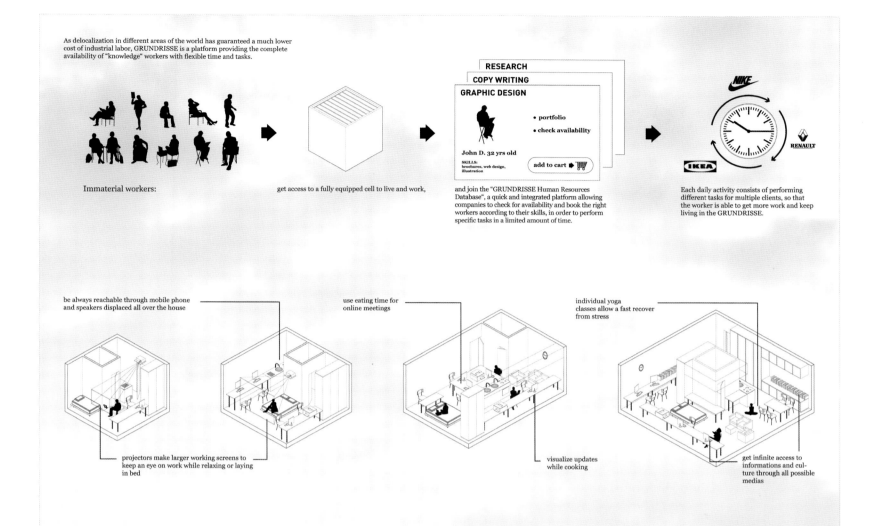

As delocalization in different areas of the world has guaranteed a much lower cost of industrial labor, GRUNDRISSE is a platform providing the complete availability of "knowledge" workers with flexible time and tasks.

RESEARCH

COPY WRITING

GRAPHIC DESIGN

• portfolio

• check availability

John D. 32 yrs old

SKILLS:
brochures, web design,
illustration

add to cart

Immaterial workers:

get access to a fully equipped cell to live and work,

and join the "GRUNDRISSE Human Resources Database", a quick and integrated platform allowing companies to check for availability and book the right workers according to their skills, in order to perform specific tasks in a limited amount of time.

Each daily activity consists of performing different tasks for multiple clients, so that the worker is able to get more work and keep living in the GRUNDRISSE.

be always reachable through mobile phone and speakers displaced all over the house

use eating time for online meetings

individual yoga classes allow a fast recover from stress

projectors make larger working screens to keep an eye on work while relaxing or laying in bed

visualize updates while cooking

get infinite access to informations and culture through all possible medias

GRUNDRISSE

HOUSING SOLUTIONS
FOR THE IMMATERIAL WORKER

325

Sukkah Sill | *Thurlow Small Architecture*

Sukkah Competition Proposal
Location : New York, NY
Design Team : Andrew Thurlow, Jarrod Martin, Christopher Capozzi, Anthony Aversa, Adam Cuomo
Competition Sponsor : Sukkah City NYC 2010

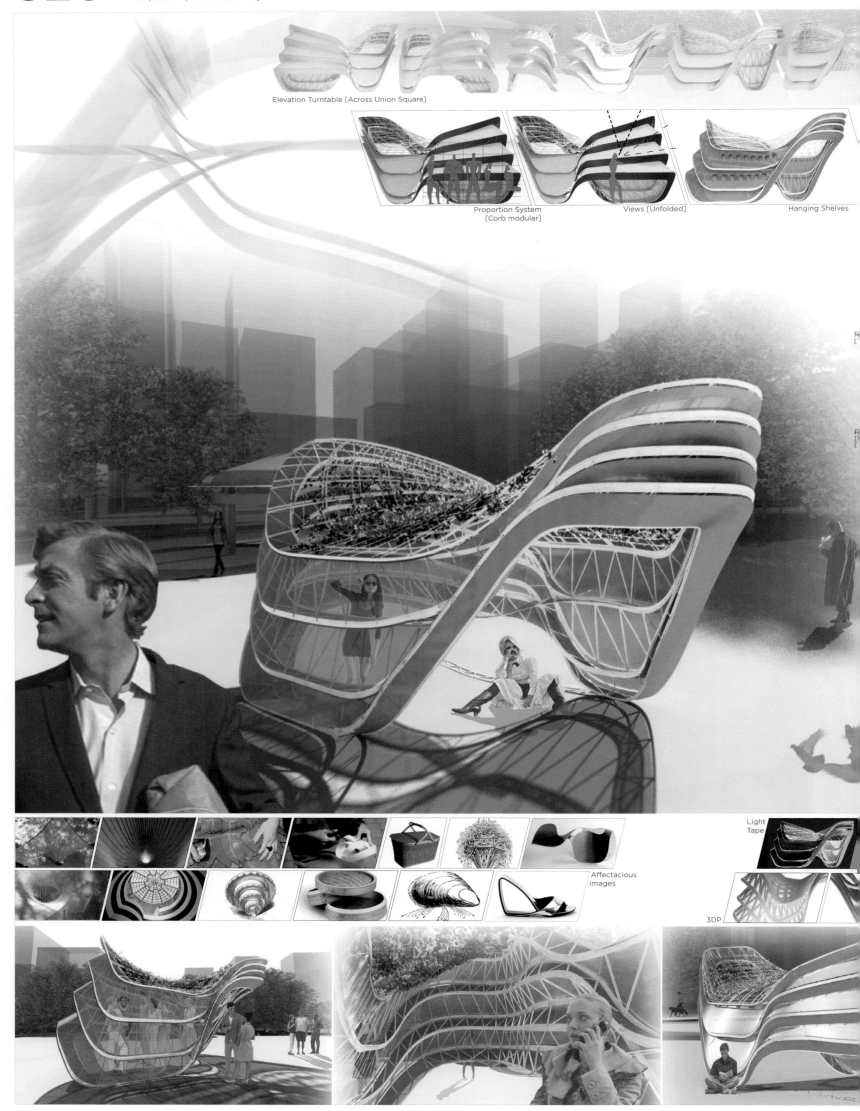

Elevation Turntable [Across Union Square]

Proportion System
[Corb modular]

Views [Unfolded]

Hanging Shelves

Affectacious
Images

Light
Tape

3DP

we all bring something with us, something we need to set down.

Like a sukkah, a sill is less a thing in itself and more a means of support for something else- a space for something to be, a frame for time. In this contradiction of temporary universality rooted in perennial context, the SUKKAHSILL offers a ledge, formed by the accordioning of the enclosure, upon which the exterior environment shows its 'harvest' and the interior offers a mid-day stop, a simple universal place to rest and breathe in the middle of a complex city and a nighttime cocoon for an intimate conversation. Here, for just a moment, there is a protected space and encapsulated view to the sky, above the pressures of the horizon, where we can set down our things, collect ourselves and look up.

The SUKKAHSILL is a lattice made of slats of wood, each with a thin, rectangular profile, connected along their length and at intersections. The two-way gridded roof is woven together like a basket, easily formed by wetting and bending the slats into position using a 1:1 template and pegboard system with removable dowels, similar to how ancient ship builders made wooden ship hulls. The folding structure creates a system of stretched polyamide tully fabric panels that either cover the trusses or provide reveals for views back out onto the city and for glimpses of those inside. The structure creates two and half walls, holds up the permeable roof, and provides an exterior under shelf rack system from which local products, such as potted plants, can be temporarily hung. The interior ledges are just wide enough for a drink, a small package or a short lean. Then, soon, you move on.

SUKKAHSILL

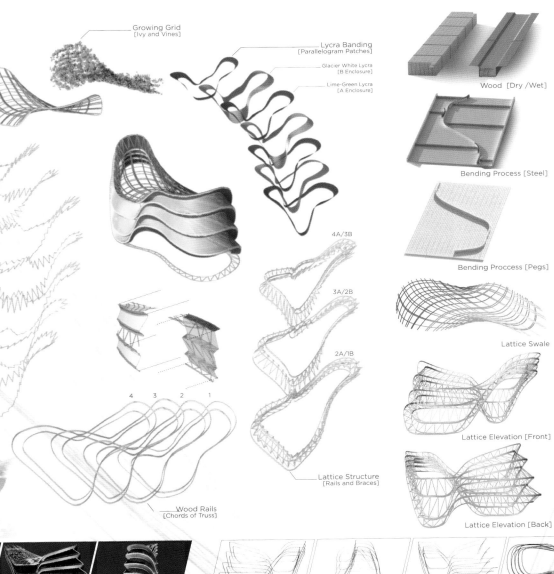

Growing Grid
[Ivy and Vines]

Lycra Banding
[Parallelogram Patches]

Glacier White Lycra
[B Enclosure]

Lime-Green Lycra
[A Enclosure]

Wood [Dry /Wet]

Bending Process [Steel]

Bending Proccess [Pegs]

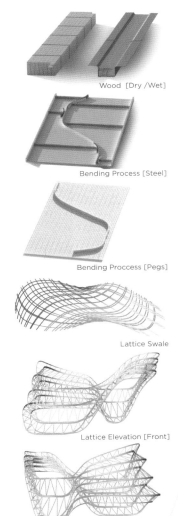

4A/3B

3A/2B

2A/1B

Lattice Swale

Lattice Elevation [Front]

Lattice Elevation [Back]

Lattice Structure
[Rails and Braces]

Wood Rails
[Chords of Truss]

4   3   2   1

Wires

1:1

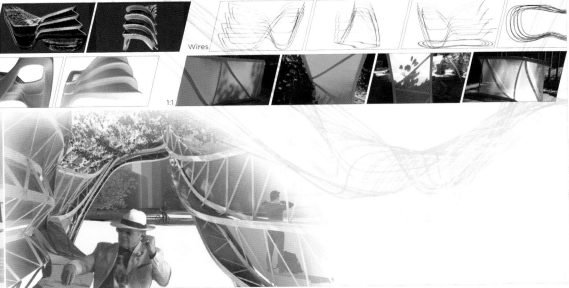

Tr(ee)logy | *CJ Lim / Studio 8 Architects*

Location : London, UK
Design team : CJ Lim/Studio 8 Architects with Martin Tang
Consultants : Techniker(structural engineers)

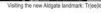
Visiting the new Aldgate landmark: Tr(ee)logy

Passing by the Tr(ee)logy after dinner

Traveling back to the City after visited the Olympic Park

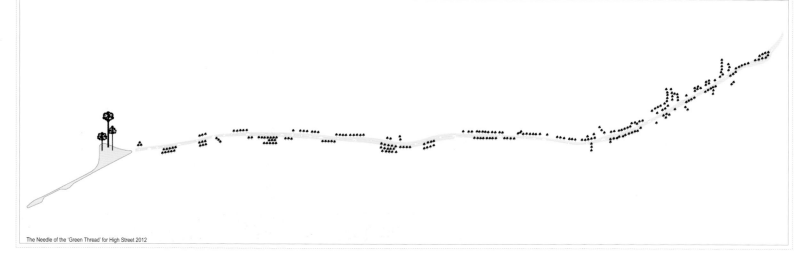
The Needle of the 'Green Thread' for High Street 2012

The Tr(ee)logy

Fair tree! for thy delightful shade
'Tis just that some return be made;
Sure some return is due from me
To thy cool shadows, and to thee.
When thou to birds dost shelter give,
Thou music dost from them receive;
If travellers beneath thee stay
Till storms have worn themselves away,
That time in praising thee they spend
And thy protecting pow'r commend.
The shepherd here, from scorching freed,
Tunes to thy dancing leaves his reed;
Whilst his lov'd nymph, in thanks, bestows
Her flow'ry chaplets on thy boughs.

The Tree
by Anne Kingsmill Finch

The new landmark for Aldgate "Tr(ee)logy" takes its cue from the landscape regeneration along the Green Tread of High Street 2012 – the trees being the metaphor for growth, diversity and sustainability. The Tr(ee)logy (7, 11 and 15 metres in height) reflects the City of London and Aldgates' strong sense of identity and future vision. The structure presents an aura of optimism; its shadows reaches out beyond the island site choreographing the passer-by.

The design comprises three assemblies of profiled cross-laminated timber fretted by water-cutting and secret fixed onto cores of steel. The spaces between the timber plates are filled with panels of non-structural acrylic which are back-lit by LED lighting. The steel cores are bolted onto galvanised screw piles set below pavement levels. The construction process is completely reversible and the sculpture can be dismantled and re-erected elsewhere without damage. The structures are ductile and will bend gradually under accidental impact.

Foundations: The site is heavily congested with existing services below the pavement surface. Temporary screw piles are arranged between these obstructions and rapidly installed by machine. The larger uprights are stabilised with the addition of 'Angel' plates. Electrical services are run to junction boxes and the base-plates prepared.

Construction: The exposed elements of structure are fully pre-fabricated with lifting eyes and the lights tested off-site. The single lorry-load will be delivered over one weekend. A brief road-closure will allow a mobile crane to be set up and the three components installed in quick succession. Services will be linked in and the pavement repaired locally. At the end of the sculptures service the elements will be removed fully intact and the foundation piles left in place or withdrawn. The construction method will ensure minimal environmental impact and negligible disturbance to the surrounding site.

A fine afternoon at the Tr(ee)logy

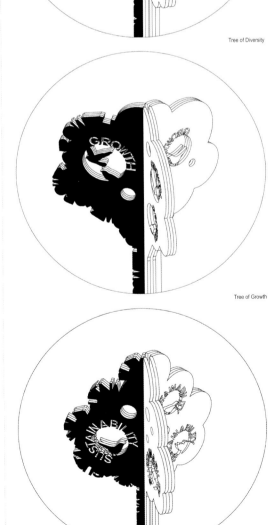

Tree of Diversity

Tree of Growth

Tree of Sustainability

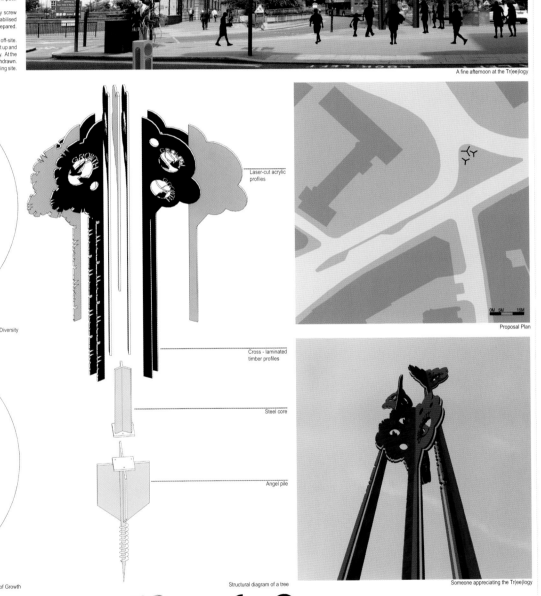

Laser-cut acrylic profiles

Cross - laminated timber profiles

Steel core

Angel pile

Structural diagram of a tree

Proposal Plan

Someone appreciating the Tr(ee)logy

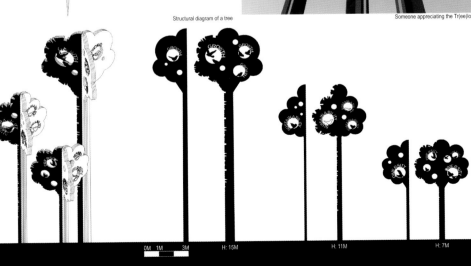

H: 15M   H: 11M   H: 7M

327

Obvita Slide | *Thurlow Small Architecture*

Peepshow Competition Proposal
Location : Calgary, Canada
Design Team : Andrew Thurlow, Maia Small, Snehal Intwala

902

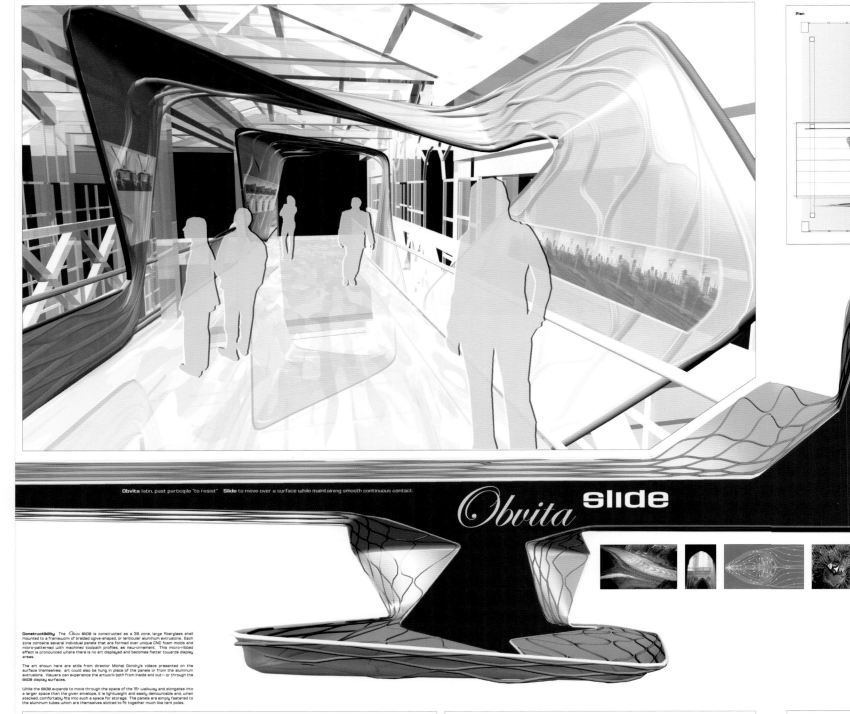

Plan

Obvita latin, past participle "to resist" **Slide** to move over a surface while maintaining smooth continuous contact.

Obvita slide

Constructibility The *Obvita* SIOB is constructed as a 3θ zone, large fiberglass shell mounted to a framework of braided ogive-shaped, or lenticular aluminum extrusions. Each zone contains several individual panels that are formed over unique CNC foam molds and micro-patterned with machined toolpath profiles, as neu-ornament. This micro-ribbed effect is pronounced where there is no art displayed and becomes flatter towards display areas.

The art shown here are stills from director Michel Gondry's videos presented on the surface themselves; art could also be hung in place of the panels or from the aluminum extrusions. Viewers can experience the artwork both from inside and out— or through the SIOB display surfaces.

While the SIOB expands to move through the space of the 15' walkway and elongates into a larger space than the given envelope, it is lightweight and easily demountable and, when stacked, comfortably fits into such a space for storage. The panels are simply fastened to the aluminum tubes which are themselves slotted to fit together much like tent poles.

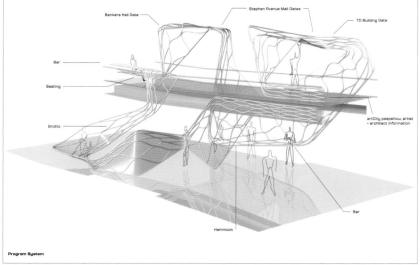

Program System

Bankers Hall Gate
Stephen Avenue Mall Gates
TD Building Gate
Bar
Seating
Grotto
artCity peepshow, artist + architect information
Bar
Hammock

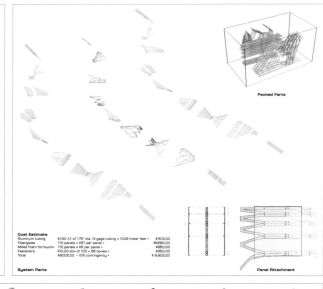

Packed Parts

Cost Estimate

Aluminum tubing	$1.50 /lf of 1.75" dia. 14 gage tubing = 1008 linear feet =	$1512.00
Fiberglass	170 panels = $37 per panel =	$6290.00
Milled foam formwork	170 panels = $5 per panel =	$850.00
Fasteners	$10.00 box of 100 = 35 boxes =	$350.00
Total	$9002.00 + 10% contingency =	$ 9,902.20

System Parts

Panel Attachment

System Taxonomy

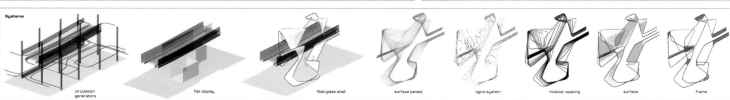

Elevation

Section

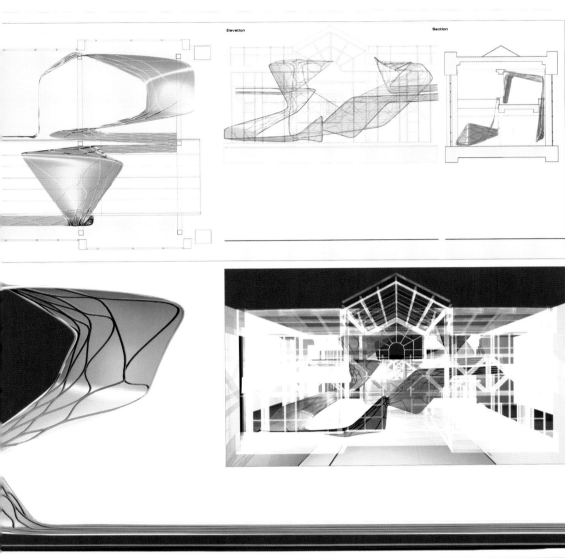

Concept Our proposed art pavilion avoids the enclosed and separate nature of "pavilion," and instead creates pavilion-less-ness: an open, permeable framework. The *Christo* 6808 is a performative envelope that offers three grotto-like territories for grouping and viewing art within the existing 15+ walkway; each space is discreet in scale, delicate, textural and organized nodally along the sinuous, continuous surface structure. The 6808 encourages the adventure of new movement patterns and circulation while broadcasting art by nesting into an existing and familiar space, as a symbiotic organism folds into its pair: the walkway provides security and protection, while the 6808 activates its interior.

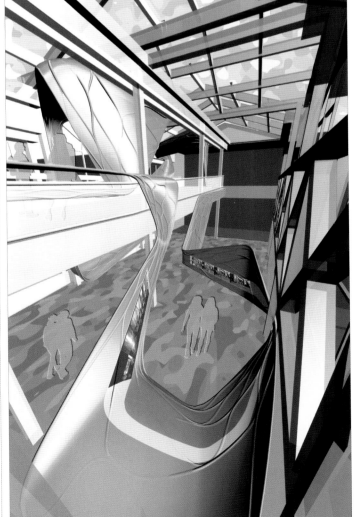

328

Origami Spiral | *Yoshihara | McKee | Architects*

Participants : Sandra McKee, Hiroki Yoshihara, Marcello Pacheco, Yoshinori Nito
Project : A Temporary Summer Gathering Place for 50 or More People,
Providing Shade And Rain Cover with Integrated Performance Area
/Stage for Small Dance Performances, Music Ensembles, Spoken Word Productions

Typology : Temporary Pavilion
Location : Governors' Island, New York City, USA
Construction Volume : maximum Budget $20,000
Client : FIGMENT

ORIGAMI SPIRAL

The origami spiral is a folded cloud-light assembly of extruded polypropylene panels; a mass produced industrial product of eight foot by four foot sheets that is 100 percent recyclable. No tools, machines or specialty expertise is required, simply the art of folding combined with the innovation of rethinking an everyday material.

The origami spiral is a luminous ice cool shelter from the summer sun that expands into the landscape, sheltering and framing the theatrical events that will take place within and against its faceted backdrop.

01

GOVERNORS ISLAND PAVILION, NEW YORK

ORIGAMI SPIRAL

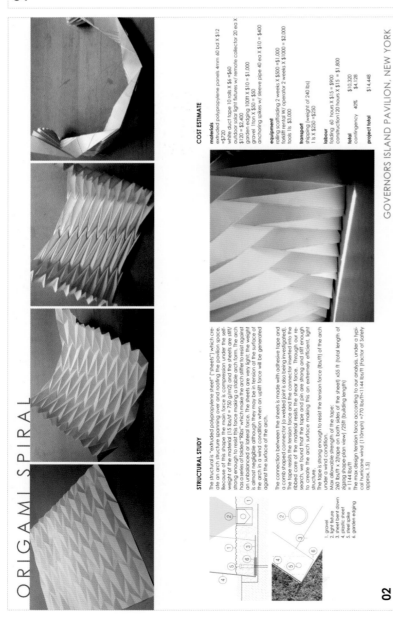

COST ESTIMATE

materials
extruded polypropylene panels 4mm 60 bd X $12
=$720
white duct tape 10 rolls X $6 =$60
outdoor solar light fixtures w/ remote collector 20 ea X
$120 = $2,400
garden edging 100ft X $10 = $1,000
gravel 1 ton X $50 = $50
anchoring spikes w/ sleeve pipe 40 ea X $10 = $400

equipment
rolling scaffolding 2 weeks X $500 =$1,000
forklift rental w/ operator 2 weeks X $1000 = $2,000
tools 1ls $3,000

transport
shipping (weight of 240 lbs)
1 ls X $250 =$250

labour
folding 60 hours X $15 = $900
construction 120 hours X $15 = $1,800

total $10,320
contingency 40% $4,128
project total $14,448

STRUCTURAL STUDY

The structural is "extruded polypropylene sheet" ("sheets") which create an arch structure spanning over and roofing the pavilion space. Because of this shape the main force is compression under the self-weight of the material (15 lbs/f = 750 g/m2) and the sheets are stiff strong enough to resist this force making a stable arch form. The arch has a series of folded "Ribs" which make the arch stiffer to resist against an unbalanced or lateral force. The sheets are very light: the weight is almost negligible although they may be in tension at the surface of the arch in a wind condition when an uplift force will be generated against the surface of the arch.

The connection between the sheets is made with adhesive tape and a comb-shaped connector (a welded joint is also being investigated). The tape resists the tension force and the connector inserted into the ribbed core of the material resists the shear force. Through our research, we found that the tape and pin are strong and stiff enough to create the arch surface making this an extremely efficient, light structure.

The tape is strong enough to resist the tension force (lbs/ft) of the arch under a wind condition.
Max allowable strength of the tape:
260 lbs/ft x 2(tape on both sides of the sheet) x55 ft (total length of zig-zag shape plan view) /25ft (building length)
= 1144 lbs/ft
The max design tension force according to our analysis, under a typical hurricane wind (110mph) =770 lbs/ft<1144 lbs/ft (Factor of Safety approx. 1.5)

1. gravel
2. light fixture
3. sheet bent down
4. plastic sheet
5. steel spike
6. garden edging

02

ORIGAMI SPIRAL

GOVERNORS ISLAND PAVILION, NEW YORK

GOVERNORS ISLAND PAVILION, NEW YORK

RE-SHIP
as a building
the pavilion moves to a new site after folding back into an arch

RE-BUILD/ASSEMBLE
as parts
the pavilion re-taping and replacing any damaged panels

RE-USE
as a standard product
the sheets are used at construction sites as protection after disassembly

RE-CYCLE
as scrap material
the sheets are shipped to the local recycling plant

03

905

100 Armillas | *Atelier do Cardoso*

Project : A Monument to the 100 years of the Portuguese Republic
Project Team : Mafalda Ribeiro Ambrósio + João Gomes Leitão
Colaborator : Manuela Cardial

329

Competition
Project: A monument to the 100 years of the Portuguese Republic.
Title: 100 armillas.
Project team: atelier do cardoso (mafalda ribeiro ambrósio + joão gomes leitão)
Colaborator: Manuela Cardial.
Date: 2010.

100 armillas
Monumento comemorativo do centenário da República Portuguesa

Monumento ao centenário   Moeda de 1 Escudo   Bandeira da República   Estátua da República da autoria de Anjos Teixeira

100 armillas.
Monumento comemorativo do centenário da República Portuguesa.

A esfera armilar, composta por um esqueleto de anéis concêntricos, também designado em latim por "armillas", é um símbolo que nos tem acompanhado ao longo da História, desde a época dos Descobrimentos quando, no reinado de D. Manuel, apareceu representada no centro da bandeira. Este objecto, de enorme significado histórico, está presente em muitos símbolos da República Portuguesa, desde a bandeira às moedas, passando pela própria representação da República na escultura existente na Assembleia da República da autoria de Anjos Teixeira.

Surge então a ideia de projectar uma escultura com um carácter histórico forte e ao mesmo tempo actual e moderno. Cruzando estas duas premissas, chegamos à imagem de uma grande esfera constituída por 100 "armillas". Cada uma representativa de um ano da República Portuguesa.

Estes anéis, com diferentes rotações, formam um padrão que representa a reinterpretação do século XXI da esfera armilar, um conjunto de anéis independentes entre si que se sobrepõem criando zonas de contacto. Metaforicamente, podíamos falar dos 100 anos de República, todos diferentes mas sempre com algo em comum, as ideologias e os princípios que permitiram o seu correcto funcionamento ao longo dos tempos. Em relação à escultura, pode-se dizer que são estes pontos onde o material se cruza, pontos em comum, que permitem que o objecto funcione estruturalmente.

Ao nível urbano, dada a localização estabelecida para este projecto, pareceu-nos interessante o carácter de rótula que o objecto pode estabelecer com a envolvente urbana. Como tal, a escultura apresenta-se como um objecto isolado que, dada a sua forma e dimensão, tem uma forte presença como ícone.

Ao mesmo tempo, dada sua materialidade, a escultura integra-se na envolvente urbana, reflectindo tons e velocidades, funcionando como um captador da mesma, uma escultura que se adapta como se de um camaleão se tratasse, mudando a cada segundo que passa.
Esta característica é observável de dia e de noite. O objecto transforma-se num emissor de luz e sombra, um simbólico farol urbano, para onde se dirigem os olhares. As sombras projectadas no chão, desenhando um padrão em torno da escultura, atingem uma dimensão que lhes confere, por si só, um carácter de projecto urbano.

Memória Técnica.
Os anéis que constituem a esfera são em chapa de aço inoxidável, medem 100mm de largura e 3mm de espessura, com um diâmetro exterior 5 metros. Estes grandes aros estão soldados entre si criando uma estrutura autoportante.

Esta estrutura está apoiada numa base elevada a 15 cm da cota actual da rua. Esta plataforma de forma circular, com diâmetro de 10m e com o centro não alinhado com o da esfera, este pódio assimétrico, não é acessível. Faz parte do monumento, é um plano onde se projectam as sombras, tanto de dia, como de noite. Este plano tem uma estereotomia que representa um desenho de linhas de 10cm, onde estão escritas frases alusivas aos 100 anos da República.

No centro da esfera propomos a colocação de focos de iluminação que permitem que o monumento se ilumine durante a noite, criando assim um interessante jogo de sombra e luz nos pavimentos. Esta iluminação será de cor branca, excepto nos dias comemorativos, em que alternará entre o verde e o vermelho, numa evidente alusão às cores da Bandeira.

Dado que o monumento será implantado na parte superior do túnel da Avenida da República, calculámos o seu peso e verificámos se o mesmo é compatível com os limites de carga suportável, utilizando os cálculos apresentados no projecto do túnel. Com uma localização na Zona I, entre as secções de cálculo 4 e 6, os valores apresentados em tabela referem-se exclusivamente às reacções nos apoios por metro desenvolvido na secção de cálculo 5. Tomando como base os valores da secção 5, verificámos que o valor não majorado das reacções por metro de desenvolvimento é de 935,4 KN/m ou seja 95,38 Toneladas por metro. O peso aproximado do monumento projectado é de 4 toneladas, logo, não excede a sobrecarga para a qual o túnel foi projectado.

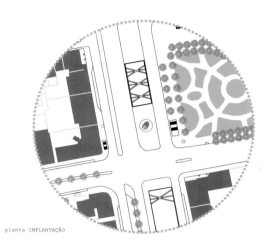

planta IMPLANTAÇÃO

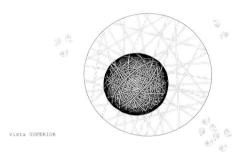

vista SUPERIOR

alçado desde AVENIDA DE BERNA

330

RBR360 | *Horhizon consortium*

Type : Sculpture
Project : Dietmar Koering, Tobias Klein

re-viseted modernism

MF morphogenetic field
RBR:360

frame structure linked to rhizometric tree pattern

design process

1 2 3 4 5

computer aided deformation | original facade | def. vortex | def. vortex size | def. extrude vertices | def. smooth 2 sides

Idea
Adaptability is an ancestral distinction of intelligence, but today's instant variations in rhythm call for something stronger: adaptability of nature! In nature material is used with optimum efficiency. Cells continually adapt to precisely fulfil their function. Through researching organic forms and their production methods the intelligence of the material itself should support the design language, the lightness and stiffness.

360 degree; not only a reference number for a geometrical circle, also a flip around the axe of the body, or the equator.

In Orlando in the sixties a symbolic façade of the "round building", a creative pattern. But the question is if its worth to save a pattern as it is, or to metamorphose it with modern technologies into a new modernist artefact which reflects the history itself. A sculpture with modern technologies and materials, erect as sculpture in the centre of attraction between the Orlando museum of modern art and the science Center. It combines the history of the 60 in 3 ways 3X60ties.

the pattern itself
the science
the art

Like in the evolution through phenotypes, the production is based on a clear code, where the evolution part and the random variation is bounded to the specific landscape and site.

Architectural form and its relationship to nature, environment and society has rich antecedents to the human body.

Material
The main material used for the sculpture is an aramid-fibre-matrix bounded with eco resin through thermosetting, which gives the material the ability to withstand UV, weathering and wind erosion. It is a modern material which can create complex patterns, like the precast concrete in the 60 ties. The main structure will be built through filament winding and resin transfer moulding. This material allows also in computer aided manufacturing an organic design language without additional costing. The thickness of the material will change through the winding system, calculated by software to adapt the stiffness to site + location and natural forces.
The organic structure is covered with a high reflective "lotus-effect" colour. It will be cleaned through natural weather conditions and will reflect the nature itself, which strengthens the idea of a graphical integration to the landscape "feedback from the surroundings".
Today's pursuit to build lightweight for economic, material engineering and environmental reasons is the logical response to today's changing society where flexibility is the prime survival quality.

Materials and technologies have evolved and hence needs the design. In the 60-ties concrete and the concept of pattern making through identical mass fabricated elements dominated the architectural world and was at the time essential to modern architecture. It lead to the development of complex coding and norm systems to ensure the seamless fitting between the different unified components. This ensured a cost optimised building process but undermine in several ways the creative dynamic output of the architecture at the time. Technology has moved on and with it is an understanding of mass customisation that allow the architect to evolve and create intricate ornate works that reflect far better an understanding of natural specification/mutation than before.

Topview

Elevation I

Elevation II

Tetherpoint | *Arquipelago Studio*

Won a Competition for the ACSA and Honorable Mention
in the 'Beauty Pageant' Competition
Project Team : Gregory Marinic(Principal), Ivan Aguirre, Karen Mendoz

331

tetherpoint.
An Adaptive Site-Specific Bicycle Infrastructure for Raleigh

What is that? Well...it's a bike rack!

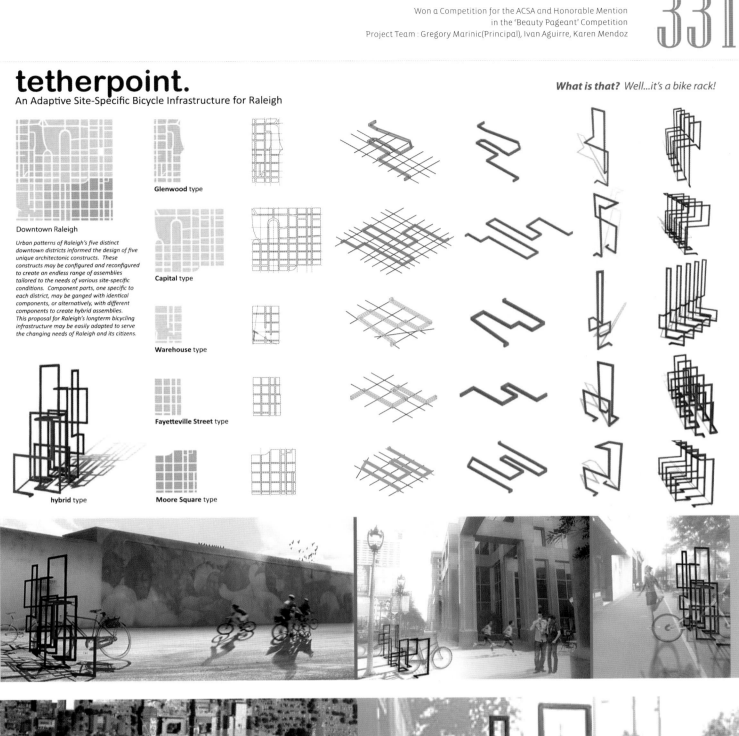

Downtown Raleigh

Urban patterns of Raleigh's five distinct downtown districts informed the design of five unique architectonic constructs. These constructs may be configured and reconfigured to create an endless range of assemblies tailored to the needs of various site-specific conditions. Component parts, one specific to each district, may be ganged with identical components, or alternatively, with different components to create hybrid assemblies. This proposal for Raleigh's longterm bicycling infrastructure may be easily adapted to serve the changing needs of Raleigh and its citizens.

Glenwood type

Capital type

Warehouse type

Fayetteville Street type

Moore Square type

hybrid type

Spirabilis | *Pneumastudio*

Design Proposal : pneumastudio (Cathryn Dwyre and Chris Perry)
Design Team : Cathryn Dwyre, Chris Perry, Justin Snider, Dave Mulder

908

 **spirabilis**

pneumastudio : cathryn dwyre + chris perry

design team : cathryn dwyre, chris perry, justin snider, dave mulder

"Do you know, my friends, that a curious establishment might be founded with rooms of oxygen, where people whose system is weakened could for a few hours live a more active life. Fancy parties where the room was saturated with this heroic fluid, theaters where it would be kept at high pressure; what passion in the souls of the actors and spectators! What fire, what enthusiasm!!" —Jules Verne, Around the Moon

pneumastudio's inspiration for Spirabilis is Diogenes of Apollonia, ca. 5 B.C. who believed air to be the source of all being, the primal force that composed both intelligence and the soul. Nature in the constructed environment can be a bit of a sacred cow tethered to trees, shrubs, and the rolling hill. Rather than "naturalize" the artificial, Spirabilis celebrates artificiality while harnessing the elemental means of sustaining life in a total ecological living system.

Spirabilis utilizes NASA research on Closed Ecological Life Support Systems to prescribe ecological living where hydroponic plants produce the balance of nutrients and oxygen necessary for human life. Tubular algae cultivation provides clean air through micro-controlled output valves as well as lighting and visual effects. The laws of nature are newly shaped, complemented, and extended with technology. Habitation zones, rainwater collecting trees, and conduits of "heroic fluids" are joined with exuberantly growing substances in a new provisional architecture.

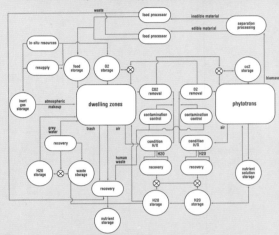

spirabilis, e, adj. spiro,
I. that may be breathed, good to breathe, breathable, respirable.
a. Pass., that serves to sustain life, vital:
b. Act., that can breathe, fitted for breathing, respiratory:

SPIRABILIS : systems flow diagram. This diagram was developed for the SPIRABILIS utilizing research on the design of CELSS (Controlled Ecological Life Support Systems)
Bioscience:Crop Productivity for Earth and Space. Vol 42 No. 7. *Design of a CELSS* by Steven Schwartzkopf, 1992

science + design futurism

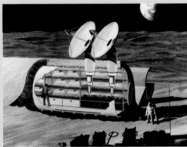

artist's concept of a 1960's NASA proposal for a module-based plant growth unit on Mars

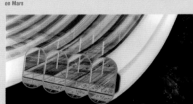

artist's concept of a 1960's NASA proposal for agricultural fields in space

Soviet BIOS-3 phytotron experiment for CELSS wheat farming

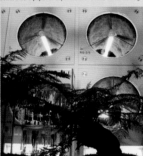

algae farm for oxygen production in space. Sunshine (2007), dir. Danny Boyle

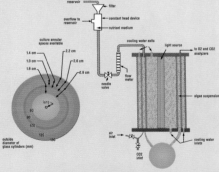

cylindrical algae farm for oxygen production

schematic diagram of algae column culture unit; effect of light intensity and thickness of culture solution on oxygen production by algae. published in Applied Microbiology by R.L. Shuler and W.A. Affens

2001: A Space Odyssey (1968), dir. Stanley Kubrick

House of the Future (1956), Alison and Peter Smithson

building systems

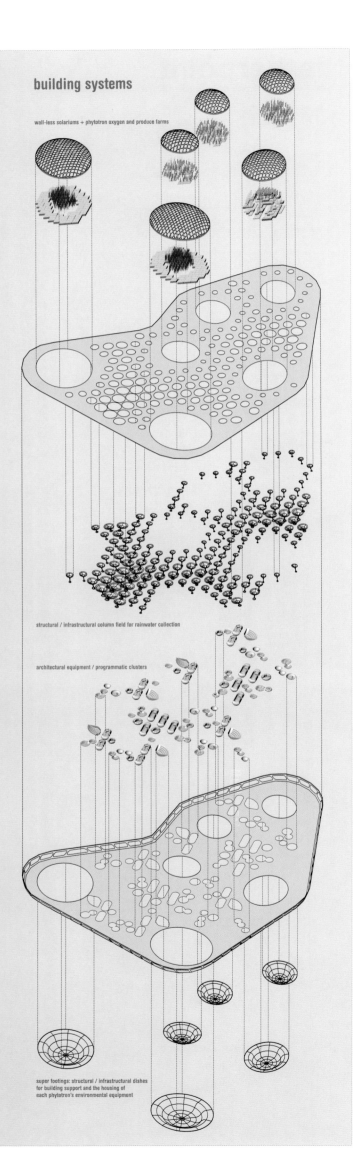

wall-less solariums + phytotron oxygen and produce farms

structural / infrastructural column field for rainwater collection

architectural equipment / programmatic clusters

super footings: structural / infrastructural dishes for building support and the housing of each phytotron's environmental equipment

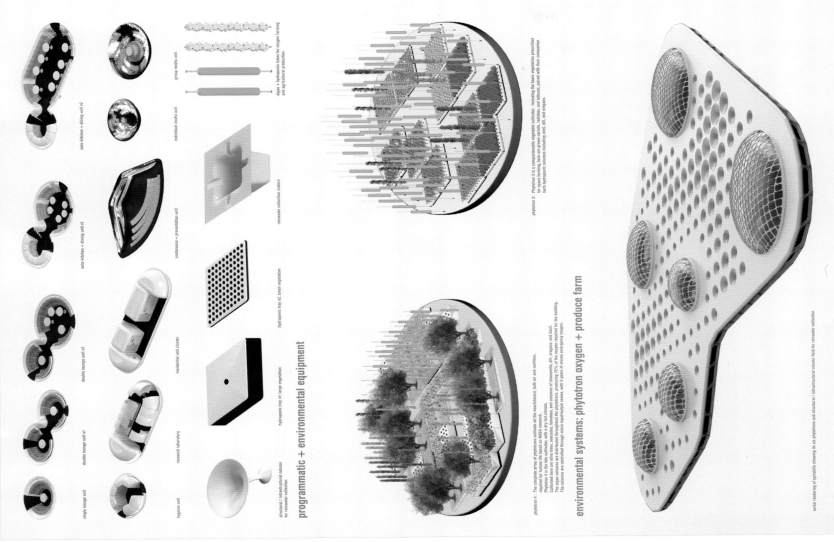

programmatic + environmental equipment

environmental systems: phytotron oxygen + produce farm

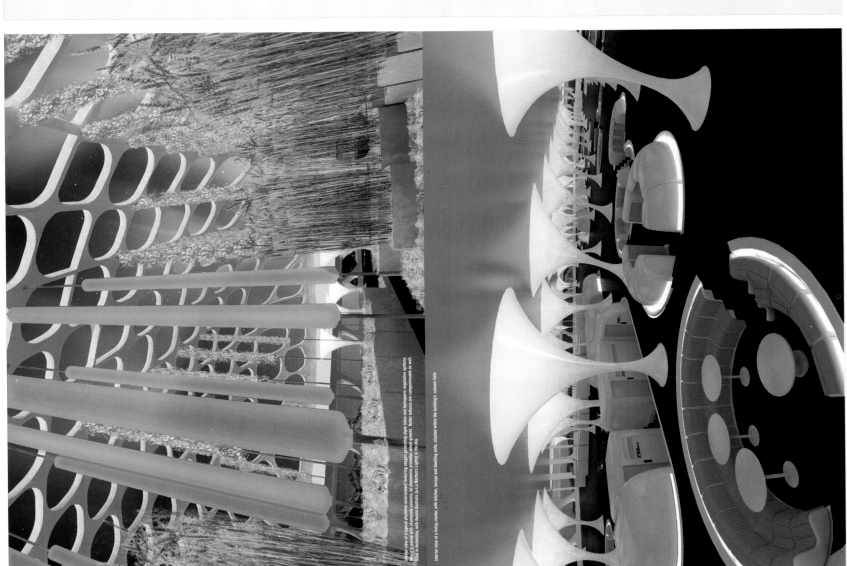

Suckling | *Arquipelago Studio*

Submitted to Drylands Competition
Institution : University of Houston Gerald D. Hines College of Architecture
Project Team : Rigo Moreno, Amanda Kroll, Myles Chumchal
Faculty Advisor : Gregory Marinic

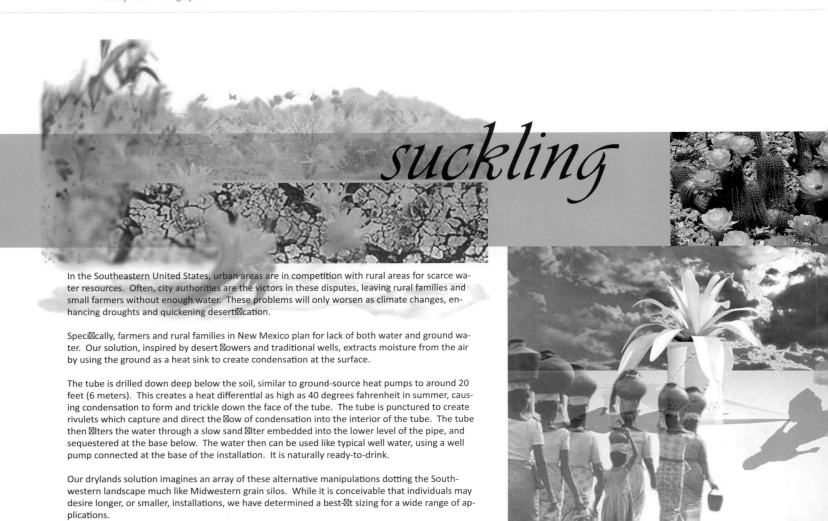

suckling

In the Southeastern United States, urban areas are in competition with rural areas for scarce water resources. Often, city authorities are the victors in these disputes, leaving rural families and small farmers without enough water. These problems will only worsen as climate changes, enhancing droughts and quickening desertification.

Specifically, farmers and rural families in New Mexico plan for lack of both water and ground water. Our solution, inspired by desert flowers and traditional wells, extracts moisture from the air by using the ground as a heat sink to create condensation at the surface.

The tube is drilled down deep below the soil, similar to ground-source heat pumps to around 20 feet (6 meters). This creates a heat differential as high as 40 degrees fahrenheit in summer, causing condensation to form and trickle down the face of the tube. The tube is punctured to create rivulets which capture and direct the flow of condensation into the interior of the tube. The tube then filters the water through a slow sand filter embedded into the lower level of the pipe, and sequestered at the base below. The water then can be used like typical well water, using a well pump connected at the base of the installation. It is naturally ready-to-drink.

Our drylands solution imagines an array of these alternative manipulations dotting the Southwestern landscape much like Midwestern grain silos. While it is conceivable that individuals may desire longer, or smaller, installations, we have determined a best-fit sizing for a wide range of applications.

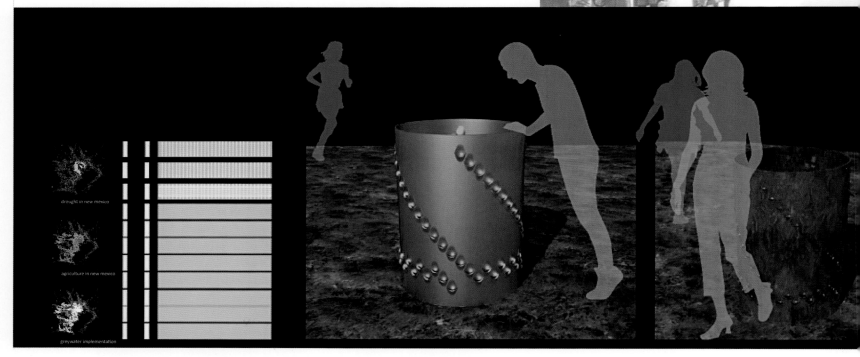

/conduction
/concept
/thermal
/filtration

water pump
rivulets store moisture
water level
fine sand
coarse sand
gravel
water storage

conceptual model
conceptual model
conceptual model

334

Lotto Kiosk | *WWAA*

Designed by : Marcin Mostafa, Natalia Paszkowska,
Andrzej Ryniecki, Andrzej Hunzvi, Iwona Borkowska
Client : Lotto Totalizator Sportowy
Area : 15 sqm / Images : WWAA

Year : Design 2011, Prototype 2010
Animation : Mikołaj Molenda

271129

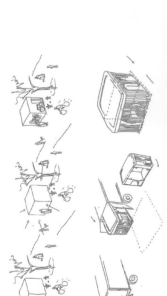

913

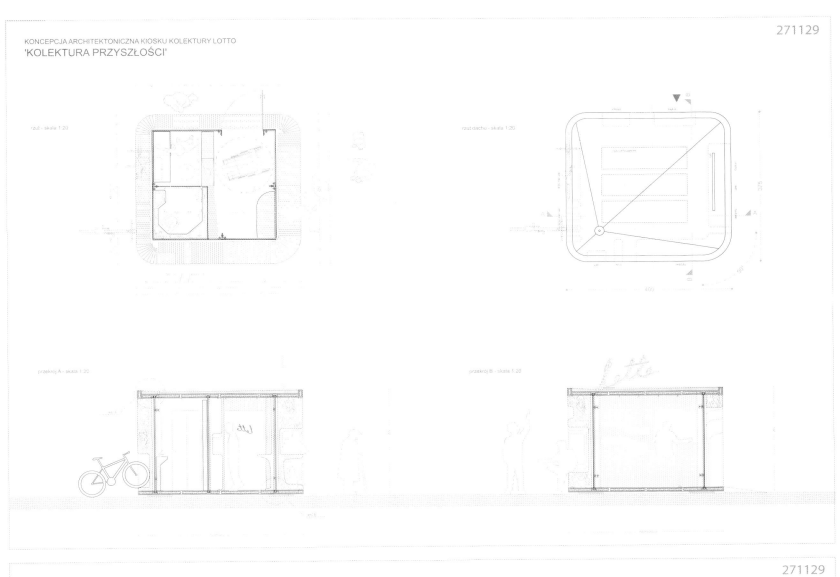

KONCEPCJA ARCHITEKTONICZNA KIOSKU KOLEKTURY LOTTO
'KOLEKTURA PRZYSZŁOŚCI'

rzut - skala 1:20

rzut dachu - skala 1:20

przekrój A - skala 1:20

przekrój B - skala 1:20

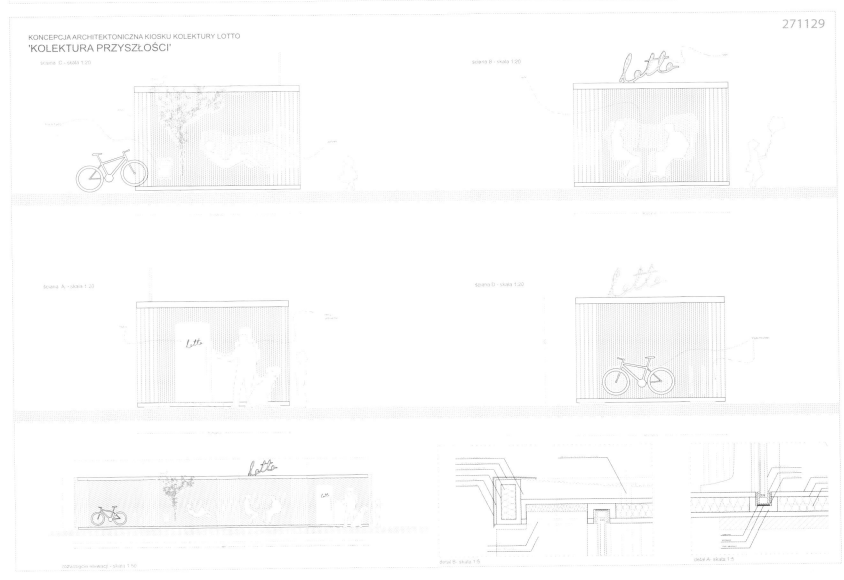

KONCEPCJA ARCHITEKTONICZNA KIOSKU KOLEKTURY LOTTO
'KOLEKTURA PRZYSZŁOŚCI'

ściana C - skala 1:20

ściana B - skala 1:20

ściana A - skala 1:20

ściana D - skala 1:20

rozwinięcie elewacji - skala 1:50

detal B - skala 1:5

detal A - skala 1:5

335 Milano Public Design Festival | *Figura Arquitetos*

Architects : Augusto Ribeiro, Felipe Campolina
Location : Italy
Use : Public equipment
Dimension : 10m²

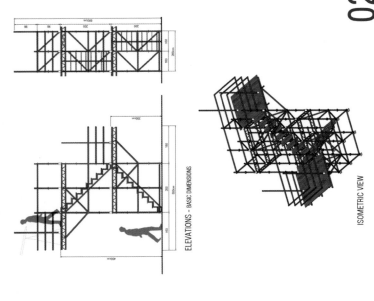

ELEVATIONS - BASIC DIMENSIONS

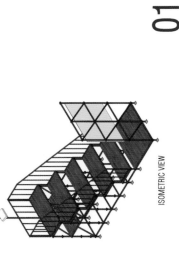

ISOMETRIC VIEW

02

MIRADOR

Structure comprised of tubular metal bars with a diameter of 5cm fixed with metal discs that have flexibility to adapt height and width. The stairs are composed by an independent metal modules attached to the external structure.

The floors of the stairs and the platforms are made of OSB.

For the proposed the structures must be rent from a specializing company during the festival.

Interactive intervention in the city. New ways to see the same place. Ideal for open spaces or near the urban sights in the city.

The estimated cost for implementing the project is $1800,00 euros.

ELEVATIONS - BASIC DIMENSIONS

ISOMETRIC VIEW

01

FREE STAGE

Easy to build using tubular metal structure with a diameter of 5 cm.
The pieces are held with metal discs that adapt to different heights and widths as needed.
The floors and seats are made from OSB. Every structure should be rent from specialized firms during the festival.

The intervention aims to provide days and nights of fun and entertainment in the city during the festival. Movies will be transmitted during the night and during the day, the stage may be a space for dissemination works, exhibitions and space for relax.
Project can be adapted to different places in town, even in film festivals. The grandstand has a capacity of 20 seats.

The estimated cost for implementing the project is $1500,00 euros.

Ullswater Clubhouse | *MSB ARQUITECTOS*

Location : Ullswater, Cumbria, Leeds, UK
Client : Ullswater Club

Participants : Miguel Mallaguerra, Susana Jesus, Bruno Martins, Hugo Aires, Filipe Freitas
Partners : MSB Architects
Project : Clubhouse
Typology : Public Building

336

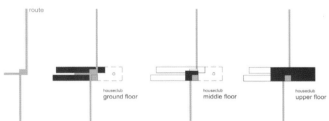

houseclub
ground floor

houseclub
middle floor

houseclub
upper floor

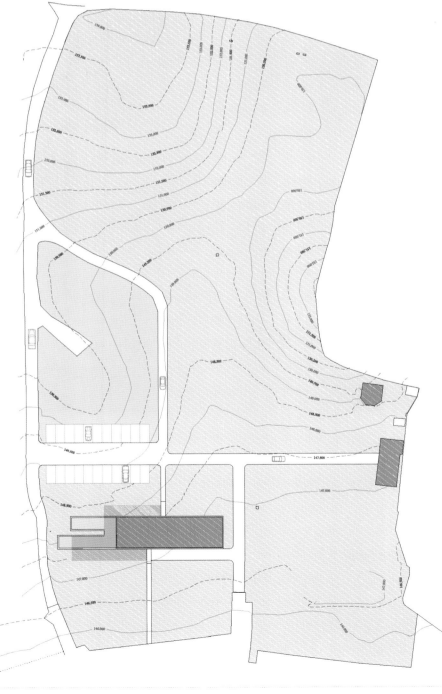

Architectural Ideas Competition

NEW UYC CLUBHOUSE
Ulswater . Cumbria

SITE PLAN | SCALE 1:500

The Ullswater Yacht Club is located on a natural landscape amidst a lake, mountains, trees and fields, framing the setting and giving the place a unique identity. This scenario is reflected in the aesthetics of the new Clubhouse building by its materiality.

This happens not only for visual purposes but also for technical and construction reasons, benefiting from local materials and local labour, thus becoming more economically viable and environmentally sustainable.

The building is essentially organised into two distinct levels. The control room for regattas is located in the transition between these levels. The shower rooms, toilets, storage rooms and reception are found on the ground floor. The program found on this floor is prepared for eventual flooding as the materials permit instant cleaning of the floor slab, walls and ceilings.

At top level, one will find the bar, kitchen and food hall. The bay windows, wrapping around the dining hall, give their users a privileged and ample view over the lake and its boats.

The entire structure is built according to a reinforced concrete system. The quality of the cladding and simplicity of the finishes give the interior spaces its ambience and functional efficiency. Timber and stone are the dominating materials. At lower level the choice of finishes is austere and resistant. At upper level, the materials provide a warmer and more comfortable ambience, however equally as durable.

337

Birnbeck Pier | *Horhizon consortium*

Type : Housing, Civic
Design : Justin C. K Lau, Andrew Yek

03. L I V E W O R K P L A Y

BIRNBECK ISLAND INTERNATIONAL ARCHITECTURAL COMPETITION

The proposal seeks to preserve and enhance fragments of the existing built context which have in recent decades fallen into disrepair as their cultural relevance has eroded. These elements are framed and enclosed within a new airborne structure, the language, scale and geometry of which refers also to a series of radial ground-based residential buildings which step down towards the water's edge.

Linked by the refurbished and enhanced existing pier structure, the ensemble is intended to provide a dynamic and flexible framework which can provide a setting for, and host, a wide range of possibilities for enterprise, innovation and regeneration. It is intended to become a familiar landmark, playing a vital part in the Weston Super Mare of the 21st Century.

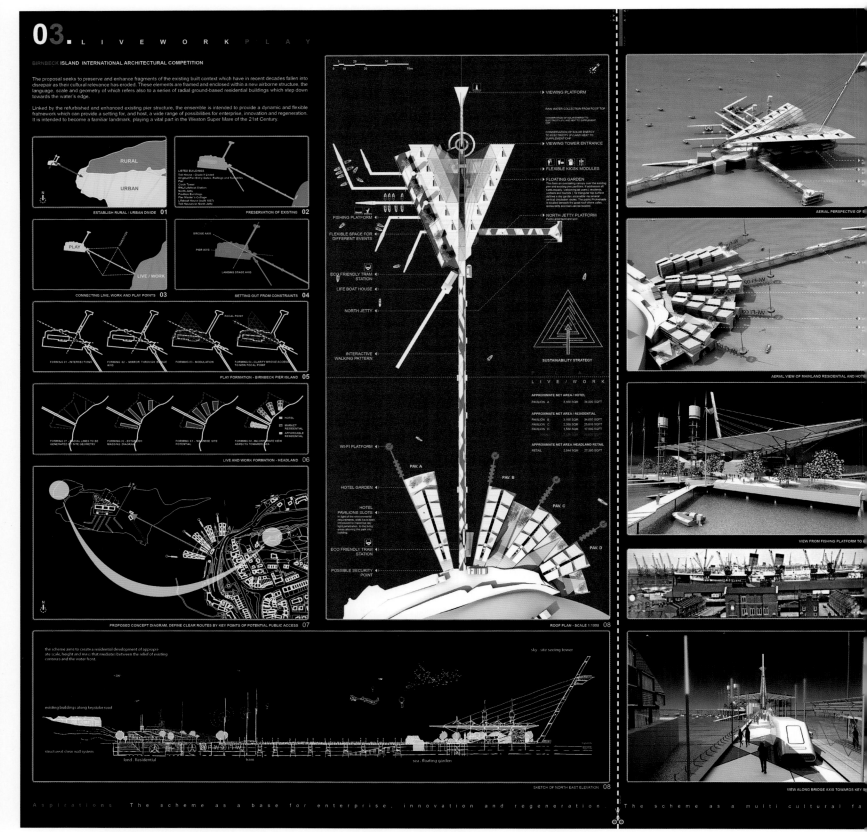

ESTABLISH RURAL / URBAN DIVIDE 01

PRESERVATION OF EXISTING 02

CONNECTING LIVE, WORK AND PLAY POINTS 03

SETTING OUT FROM CONSTRAINTS 04

PLAY FORMATION - BIRNBECK PIER ISLAND 05

LIVE AND WORK FORMATION - HEADLAND 06

PROPOSED CONCEPT DIAGRAM. DEFINE CLEAR ROUTES BY KEY POINTS OF POTENTIAL PUBLIC ACCESS 07

ROOF PLAN - SCALE 1:1000 08

SKETCH OF NORTH EAST ELEVATION 08

AERIAL PERSPECTIVE OF B

AERIAL VIEW OF MAINLAND RESIDENTIAL AND HOTE

VIEW FROM FISHING PLATFORM TO

VIEW ALONG BRIDGE AXIS TOWARDS KEY S

Aspirations   The scheme as a base for enterprise, innovation and regeneration.   The scheme as a multi cultural fa

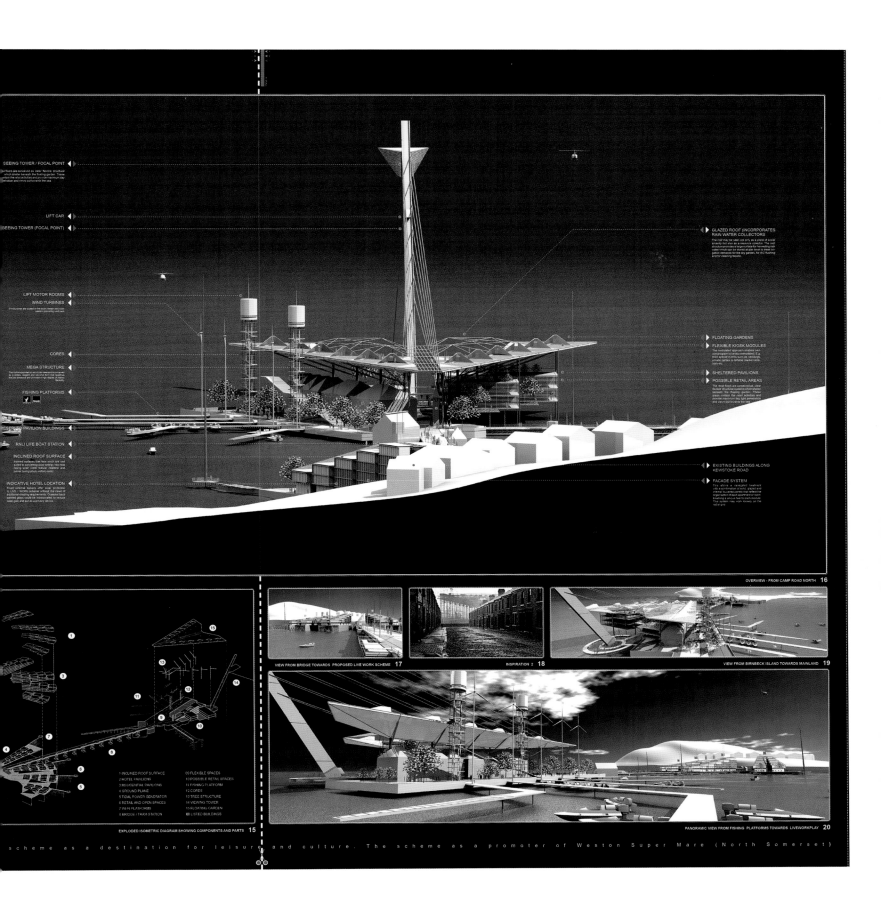

SEEING TOWER / FOCAL POINT

LIFT CAR

SEEING TOWER (FOCAL POINT)

LIFT MOTOR ROOMS
WIND TURBINES

CORES

MEGA STRUCTURE

FISHING PLATFORMS

PAVILION BUILDINGS

RNLI LIFE BOAT STATION

INCLINED ROOF SURFACE

INDICATIVE HOTEL LOCATION

GLAZED ROOF (INCORPORATES RAIN WATER COLLECTORS)

FLOATING GARDENS
FLEXIBLE KIOSK MODULES

SHELTERED PAVILIONS
POSSIBLE RETAIL AREAS

EXISTING BUILDINGS ALONG KEWSTOKE ROAD
FACADE SYSTEM

OVERVIEW - FROM CAMP ROAD NORTH **16**

VIEW FROM BRIDGE TOWARDS PROPOSED LIVE WORK SCHEME **17**

INSPIRATION 2 **18**

VIEW FROM BIRNBECK ISLAND TOWARDS MAINLAND **19**

1 INCLINED ROOF SURFACE
2 HOTEL PAVILIONS
3 RESIDENTIAL PAVILIONS
4 GROUND PLANE
5 TIDAL POWER GENERATOR
6 RETAIL AND OPEN SPACES
7 WHR PLATFORMS
8 BRIDGE / TRAM STATION
09 FLEXIBLE SPACES
10 POSSIBLE RETAIL SPACES
11 FISHING PLATFORM
12 CORES
13 TREE STRUCTURE
14 VIEWING TOWER
15 FLOATING GARDEN
16 LISTED BUILDINGS

EXPLODED ISOMETRIC DIAGRAM SHOWING COMPONENTS AND PARTS **15**

PANORAMIC VIEW FROM FISHING PLATFORMS TOWARDS LIVEWORKPLAY **20**

scheme as a destination for leisure and culture. The scheme as a promoter of Weston Super Mare (North Somerset)

2:pm architectures

2A+P/A

2: pm architectures is a limited liability company based in Bordeaux and Paris. Our company stems from five years of collaboration between partners leading to the set-up of three European workshops, national and international awards, installations, exhibitions and conferences. Our associates have taken advantage of these five years to acquire valuable experience within recognised agencies in Paris, Rennes and Bordeaux to complement degrees in transversal disciplines (architecture, design, art and civil engineering).
2: pm architectures, ever since 2011, shares its Paris Studio with different architects and their Bordeaux studio space with landscapers, urban planners and designers, thus benefiting from dynamic and seamless emulation around the spheres of corresponding know-how. The different companies, while enlisting their views, merging aspirations and exchanging skills, thrive off their alternative dialogue and interconnectedness, hence a strong and productive environment.
2: pm architectures has forged a strong background in architectural theory through their individual courses, as well as participating in and organizing contemporary architecture workshops in France, Greece, Algeria and Morocco. Linking theory with delineation of architectural discipline with a view to the general public by taking part and organizing exhibitions in Paris (Pavillon de l'Arsenal for WildClub) and Bordeaux, (CAPC arc en rêve and the Seven Workshop or 308 for Les vivres de l'art) offers the company ease in public relations.
www.2pmarchitectures.com

2A+P/A is an architectural practice based in Rome. It has been established by Gianfranco Bombaci and Matteo Costanzo, after ten years of experience begun in 1998. The office is involved in architecture, urbanism and landscape design, developing projects such as public building, housing and urban spaces. It's active in the fields of research, through the participation in exhibitions and publishing initiatives. The two partners participated to international design competitions, receiving prizes and honorable mentions, and to several conferences and workshops.

071 France_3

075 Switzerland

162 Dubai

010 France_1

224 Buenosaires

275 Abudhabi

011 France_2

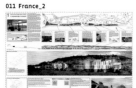

067 Atlanticcity

070 Austria

005 Curtains

013 House of Memory

063 Open Block

065 Urban Block

069 Floating Clouds

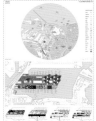

278 Art Wood

3LHD

3LHD is an architectural practice, focused on integrating various disciplines – architecture, urban planning, design and art. 3LHD architects constantly explore new possibilities of interaction between architecture, society and individuals. With contemporary approach, the team of architects resolves all projects in cooperation with many experts from various disciplines.

083 Ujpest Town Center Masterplan

084 Duilovo Waterfront Masterplan

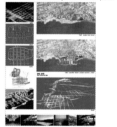

085 Mali Maj

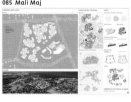

120 Senj Squares

139 Business Centre Sopot

140 Green Pavilion_Restaurant

167 Campus B

AA&U For Architecture, Art and Urbanism

AA + U, For Architecture, Art and Urbanism is an agent for interdisciplinary activities regarding the public domain. It was born out from collaborations of Socrates Stratis with architects and artists. It has a variable size depending on the projects undertaken. The main partner is Socrates Stratis, Dr. architect, urbanist with Riccardo Urbano, architect as the main associate and Maria Loizidou, as partner for visual arts. AA + U considers the projects at urban-architectural scale as an experimental device for creating knowledge which is constantly fed back to the making of projects. It has developed an integrating approach between architecture, art and urbanism in order to tackle issues about public space. The work of AA+U has been exhibited in both 9th and 10thVenice Biennales of Architecture. AA + U has participated in the design and implementation of projects such as residents, parks and public spaces and has won several prizes in local and European architectural competitions.

112 049821

114 394102

154 110 Seconds Sociability

Alessandro Console Studio

Alessandro Console Studio is an idea-based architectural practice. The Studio is involved in architecture, urban planning and landscape design at different levels and scales, developing its ideas and strategies through the participation in architectural competitions, workshops and researches. The field of interest of the Studio ranges between the investigation of the public space and the study of the relationship existing between the concepts of Nature and Artifice. Since its establishing, Alessandro Console Studio has received several awards and honours, among which: the 1st Prize in the 8th Arquine International Competition: "A Site Museum for Tulum", with the project of a hypogeous museum in the major archaeological site of Mexico; the Merit Award in the second stage of the International Architectural Competition for HKDI, with the project of the new Hong Kong Design Institute; has been selected as Finalist for the second stage of the International Design Competition for Central Open Space in MAC, with the project of the major green area in Sejong, new administrative city of the Republic of Korea.
www.alessandroconsole.com

001 [tamor]

017 I Portici

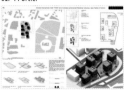

168 Bezalel

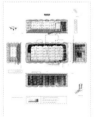

203 Walk(in) the Line

232 Busan Opera Housei

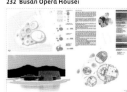

277 Ploughed Fields

AQSO arquitectos office

AQSO is a multidisciplinary office composed of an international group of professionals dedicated to contemporary architecture, urban planning and cultural research. Their philosophy combines a rigorous and pragmatic approach with an innovative attitude. Based in Spain and China, the office approaches every project with an ambitious methodology that investigates and analyzes social, economic, technical and sustainable issues. Their ability covers a wide range of types and scales, from public, commercial and residential buildings to town planning and urbanism. AQSO understands architecture as a multidisciplinary process, a comprehensive approach beyond living spaces, a method in cooperation with different professionals and consultants to become the coherent nexus between imagination and reality. Their team has the international vision, experience, flexibility and ability to materialize each project from concept to site supervision. The office is founded by Luis Aguirre and is an international partnership. The practice relies on a multicultural team of experienced architects working on an open cross-disciplinary collaboration platform. AQSO has been awarded for several international design competitions including Europan 9 and the Self-sufficient IaaC contest. The firm has received several prizes for public and restricted architectural competitions in Spain and China, where the company is based.
www.aqso.net

053 Harvest home

155 Ramp up the 'Mun

244 Open Arte-fact

245 Atienza Music Hall

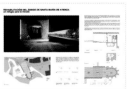

258 Wavescape

313 Nest Shelters

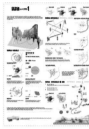

arenas basabe palacios arquitectos

ARPHENOTYPE

Arquipelago Studio

Atelier do Cardoso

ENRIQUE ARENAS LAORGA (1974), architect graduated at ETSAM (Madrid). He has developed projects in very different areas: rehabilitations, housing, institutional and events. He has held lectures at several academic institutions, and is now researcher at ETSAM. He teaches at IED Madrid.
LUIS BASABE MONTALVO (1975), architect graduated at the TU Graz. Since 2003 he teaches design studio at ETSAM, where he is also working on his PhD. He was guest researcher and faculty at various Universities: RWTH Aachen (Germany), Cambridge (UK) and CEPT Ahmedabad (India).
LUIS PALACIOS LABRADOR (1983), architect graduated at ETSAM (Madrid, 2009) and Master in Advanced Innovation and Technology (ETSAM, 2011). He was active member of the Housing Research Group at ETSAM, where he develops his PhD and teaches Design Studio since 2009. He has held lectures and workshops in India and UK.
arenasbasabe@gmail.com

Member of .horhizon.com
Dietmar Köring is an architect, researcher, and educator living in Cologne. He currently teaches Digital Design at TU Braunschweig and Technology and Design at CIAD / Cologne Institute for Architecture and Design. In 2011 he was Guest Professor for Virtual Realities and Design at TU Innsbruck and research assistance for Smart Grids Project at the University Cologne. He is the owner of the architectural research office Arphenotype, where he focuses on blurring the boundaries of different artistic disciplines. His research was awarded by the Jaap Bakema Fellowship / NAI in 09/10. Dietmar's work has been internationally published and exhibited, including Heide Museum of contemporary Arts, GermanTechnology Museum Berlin, Sueddeutsche, Heute Journal, Das Parlament and other. He has given internationally lectures and workshops. Dietmar is co-founder of the narrative research network horhizon.
http://www.Arphenotype.com

Arquipelago is a contemporary and progressive practice developing projects in architecture, interiors, urban design, and identity. Believing that buildings and spatial experiences are embedded with information, the practice seeks new directions that investigate sustainable solutions informed by site-specificity, materials innovation, and regionalism. With offices in New York and Houston, the practice operates through design, research, teaching, and speculation. Arquipelago is multi-cultural and multi-perspectival.

Maintaining a careful balance between art and architecture, Arquipelago crafts environments that actively blend buildings, interiors, and landscapes. The practice engages with context through a 21st century lens, merging rational and technological order with notions of the ephemeral. Central to Arquipelago's work is an interest in identifying and visualizing temporal conditions within the built and natural worlds. Shifting between micro and macro views of context, information is translated into layered mappings that guide the conceptual development of a project. Timelessness and weathering are equally considered in the design of total environments adapted to context, culture, climate, and ecology.
www.arquipelagostudio.com

Atelier do Cardoso is a young office which has its origins in Lisbon, Portugal in 2005. The two members of the team Mafalda Ribeiro Ambrósio and Joao Gomes Leitao met at the Lusíada University of Lisbon. They were graduated in 2004 and 2003 respectively.
The architect's training has been a journey through Portugal and Spain. Followed a different path in diverse architectural offices. At the some time design competitions become a platform for experimentation and exploration of new ideas.
Right now they live and work in Madrid. Spain.
www.atelierdocardoso.com

008 Fancy Fences

012 Garten> HOF

081 Tranversal Processes

186 Lucia

187 Un Cadavre Exquis

304 Anthropometric Pavilion

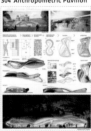

304 Trac 2

306 Palaste Elaste

311 London Mosaic

317 Seoul Market System

318 Baltimore Calling

331 Tetherpoint

333 Suckling

100 Town@Country : London Farm Tower

226 Reappropriation

248 Lamina

279 Fields of Dreams_Bat Yam

280 Diasporic Landscapes

030 Baobab House

329 100 Armillas

Axi:Ome

ax·i·om (ăk'sē-əm) noun: self-evident or universally recognized truth; a maxim + form·me (for 'm['e]) verb: to compose or to assemble = ax·i·o·me (ăk'sē-əm 'm['e])] Axi:Ome, derives from the crossing of two Latin words axiom and forme. We engage architecture as research; a mode of representation directly interfaced into social, cultural and economic influences. For us, originality pertains to authenticity where each project is a thesis of situations. We are aware of the representations we employ and how they inform the work. Architects are on the edge of performance and material opportunities with the developing digital operations that allow for increased participation in the building process. We encourage technological conditions that enable freedom within our design choices, and we believe that original work in today's climate involves a spirit of collaboration where unique opportunities preside over individual authorship. Our design practice is at a critical juncture between speculative and built works. This transition propels our research into the territory of negotiating client and economic feasibility. We develop design process within formal manipulation of materials and space, an unfolding dialogue between two and three dimensional representations, a concern for environmental and experiential enjoyment of place, and an orchestrated balance between new methods of fabrication and industry standards.
www.axi-ome.net

46 Orchid Tower

B+U, llp

BplusU's mission is to constantly push the boundaries of architecture and urban design. Using technology and research in combination with hands-on design, the firm's projects are often informed by the mapping and transforming of imperceptible forces, including sono¬grams. BplusU has developed analytic and generative software that has allowed it to implement its theories into a three-dimensional form. BplusU is on a continuous mission to research and experiment with new technologies, building materials and construction techniques by virtue of 3D technology and manufacturing techniques often employed outside of the architectural profession.
Headquartered in Los Angeles, California and established in 2000 by architects Herwig Baumgartner and Scott Uriu, each partners with over 15 years of professional experience, BplusU is a full-service architecture firm that has worked on projects both nationwide and abroad. The architects' work has comprised cultural locations (includ¬ing museums, concert halls and exhibition spaces), educational and transportation facilities, master planning and urban design, offices and mixed-use developments, restaurants, and residential work.
www. bplusu.com

216 NTC Art Museum

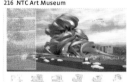

222 Performing Arts Cente

b4architects

The group was founded in Rome in 2003, as a free relationship between architects that work in a synergic way, joining several knowledge. From 2008 the active partners are Gianluca Evels and Stefania Papitto.
Measuring us from urban and landscape design until interior design and restoration, in a process that involve specific competences, always respecting the environmental characteristics. We are interested in producing works that contribute to the debate of the complexity of modern life. Our approach to any project is to involve all parties in a creative collaboration to define the objectives of the project with a balanced combination within critical readings of the local context and the 'outsider' perspective of us. The work on pre-existent spaces and the interior design projects try to explain all the available elements in a new synthesis: the traces of the history of the building, the expectations of the client, psycho-sensorial aspects of the architecture united in a continuous spatial and visual tale. We also dedicate to further activities, like some different experiences at the
www.b4architects.com

018 Nesting Thought

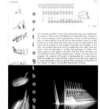

122 A101 Urban Block

166 Watermark Shaping

169 Kinder Garten

262 Kube kong

BKK-3

Architecture is developing concepts of abstract thinking about objects.
Form and content are closely interwoven so that a social, emotional and sustainable architecture is created. The basic structures develop from contents like function, sociology, technic, economy and ecology. The intelligent superposition of the content also brings an added value that is greater than the sum of the individual points. When searching for the right solution the dead ends can also be explored. Sometimes productive waste is necessary to get to the goal.
BKK-3 is also known for the interactive involvement of users into the planning process. The award-winning Co-housing project MISS SARGFABRIK is a model for the comprehensive development and support of our projects.
www.bkk-3.com

016 Intercultural Quarter

072 Green City Graz

271 New Apostolic Church

blank studio architecture

blank studio was created to honor the capacity for architecture to challenge, inspire and elevate design awareness in an environment that is directed toward increasingly simplistic and synthetic solutions. The design process centers upon investigation and synthesis, the experiential use of pace, an authentic expression of materiality, and the engagement of the senses. Within this inclusive method of design, blank studio endeavors through its work, to transcend meaninglessness and create that which is a testimony to the potential of the designed environment. In addition to realized projects, blank studio actively participates in the theoretical realm as well, through teaching and by taking part in various local and international design competitions. As an emerging concern in our natural and built environments today, explorations into sustainable technology and practices inform much of the current work of blank studio.
www.blankspaces.net

055 'T' House

056 Littles Road Residence

Brisac Gonzalez Architects

Brisac Gonzalez is a multi-lingual and multi-national London based architecture firm established in 1999 by Cecile Brisac and Edgar Gonzalez.

The practice has won numerous awards and competitions across the world, and is currently working on projects in the UK, Scandinavia, France, and Russia. By working on a variety of building types in numerous locations we continuously enrich the knowledge in our practice and the buildings we produce.

We are concerned with all things architectural in the broadest sense, be it urban or interior design, cultural and commercial buildings, as well as sociological matters. We work by collaborating with our clients and challenging the conventional to create outstanding architecture, better places to live and work, and greater value in the built environment.

Instead of producing repetitive designs, our work evolves from rigorous working methods that include collaborations with specialist consultants, comprehensive research of our project's sites, extensive use of three-dimensional studies, and most importantly responding to our clients needs.

Projects such as the Museum of World Culture in Gothenburg and Le Prisme, a multi-purpose concert hall in France brought Brisac Gonzalez to the attention of a wide field of clients and gave the office international acclaim.

www.brisacgonzalez.com

241 Music School and Performance Hall

242 Opera and Culture House

246 Music of Rock Music

Carloslampreia[x]arquitectos

Carlos Lampreia, architect (1990), is project teacher at FAA-Universidade Lusíada de Lisboa since 1994, studied at OPorto Architecture School and at Lisbon Technical University FA-UTL. Master in architecture theory and researching to Phd about, strategy, place and material, concerning architecture and arts. His Lisbon based office, carloslampreia[x] arquitectos, works on an experimental way with young architects and students towards architectural materialisation, participating both in international competitions and individual private requests.

carloslampreiaxarquitectos.blogspot.com

066 Alesund Fjord New Waterfront

CHA:COL

CHINMAYA+APURVA:COLLABORATIVE CHA:COL was established by partners Chinmaya and Apurva in 2006 as a multi-disciplinary design firm based in Los Angeles. The primary interest in creating this design studio was collaboration. Absorbing influences and ideas from all disciplines, CHA:COL hopes to stay independent of ideological predilections.

Our architectural experience working for firms and as a studio, includes commercial, residential and institutional projects around the world. They have ranged in scale and program from large museums and mixed-use commercial centers to single-family residential projects and product design.

Before forming CHA:COL, Chinmaya Misra graduated from SCI_Arc in 2001 and till recently at Jerde Partnership, Apurva Pande graduated from UCLA in 2002 and worked till recently at the office of Frank Gehry.

chacol.net

156 Woven Horizon

157 Bracketing the Ravine

223 Connective Tissue

314 Sculpting the void

CJ Lim / Studio 8 Architects

CJ Lim is the founder of Studio 8 Architects, and the Professor of Architecture and Cultural Design at the Bartlett University College London.

His design focuses on innovative interpretations of cultural, social and environmental sustainability programmes. His recent award winning eco-cities are for the Chinese and Korean Governments. CJ is listed in Debrett's People of Today and the International Who's Who for his architecture and academic contributions. The Guardian and the Independent newspapers, and Iakov Chernikhov Foundation Moscow have included CJ in their talent listings. In 2006, the Royal Academy of Arts London awarded CJ the Grand Architecture Prize, the prestigious award with past winners including Lord Rogers and Lord Foster.

His most celebrated architecture, "Virtually Venice", investigated East-West cultures and identities – commissioned by the British Council UK for the Venice Architecture Biennale. Monographs publications include "441/10...we'll reconfigure your space when you're ready" (1996), "Sins + Other Spatial Relatives" (2001), "How Green is Your Garden?" (2003), "Museums [work in process]" (2004), "NeoArchitecture: Studio 8 Architects" (2005), "Virtually Venice" (2006), and "Smartcities + Eco-warriors" (2010).

www.cjlim-studio8.com

004 The Tomato Exchange

127 Newark Gateway Project

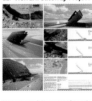

198 MoCCA(Museum of Comic + Cartoon)

264 Liantang/Heung Yuen Wai Boundary Control Point

300 Mersey Observatory

315 New Wave: Shelter + Kiosk Design

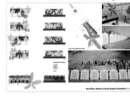

320 Sichuan Earthquake Memorial Landsca

326 Tr(ee)logy

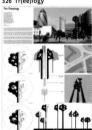

Dai Nagasaka

...orn in Kanagawa, 1960. Graduated from
...yoto Institute of Technology, 1982.
...Worked at Atelier ɸ, 1985. Assistant profes-
...or, Kyoto Institute of Technology, 1989.
...stablished Méga, 1990.Associate profes-
...or, Nara Women's University, 2003. Profes-
...or, Kyoto Institute of Technology, 2008
...wards, Kajima Prize, SD Review, 1990.
...rand Prize, Environment & Art Design
...ompetition '92, 1992. Minister's Prize of
...he ministry of construction, "Furusato no
...iaodukuri" Competition, 1996. Selected
...rchitectural Design 2003. Selected Archi-
...ectural Design 2006. Excellent Prize, 54th
...anagawa Architectural Competition,
...009. Excellent Prize, 55th Kanagawa
...rchitectural Competition, 2010. Selected
...rchitectural Design 2011. 36th Hokkaido
...rchitectural Encouragement Prize.

...9 Fireproof Cider Box House

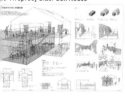

8 Recycled Urban Space

David Garcia Studio

The Studio, founded by David Garcia,
is based in Copenhagen, Denmark. We
cooperate with experts and respected
scientists on a multitude of international
projects.
The Studio is an experimental architectural platform focusing on extreme
environments. Projects span through
various scales and spheres of action,
often challenging the status quo through
inventiveness and a cross-disciplinary approach. Collaborative work with the scientific community and technical institutions
is part of every project we undertake.
We truly believe that what exists is only
a small part of what is possible, and we
design driven by this principle.
www.davidgarciastudio.com

148 Unesco Delta City Competition Poster

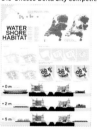

209 Jossingfjord Competition P2-P6

225 Zoo as Network

295 Urban Sky Link Poster

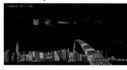

296 Reflections Poster

308 Mobile Unit Poster

Donner Sorcinelli Architecture

Donner Sorcinelli Architecture is an international architectural design office based
in Italy, dedicated to create innovative
projects. Founded by architects Luca Donner and Francesca Sorcinelli, the Studio
pays particular attention to the theme of
sustainable and affordable architecture
in all its variants, based on experimentation and research in various fields like
Architecture, Planning, Landscape, Interiors and Design. The research into new
architecture typologies and solutions,
applied to this themes is represented
through various projects developed by
the DoSo in a number of countries such as
South Korea, USA, Canada, Italy, Finland,
UAE and Saudi Arabia.
www.doso.it

024 Butterfly House

165 Urban Block

178 New School Campus and Primary

261 Tourist Facilities

294 Swiss Pavillion Expo 2015

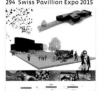

301 Panoramic Tower and Congress Building

DORELL.GHOTMEH.TANE / ARCHITECTS

DORELL.GHOTMEH.TANE / ARCHITECTS is
an international partnership founded in
January 2006 in Paris and practicing Architecture, Urbanism and Space Design. It
is lead by three multinational architects:
Dan Dorell (Italy), Lina Ghotmeh (Lebanon), Tsuyoshi Tane (Japan). The architects
have built their professional experience
through their work with international
practices among which Ateliers Jean Nouvel, Paris / David Ajaye Associates, London
/ Foster and Partners, London / Henning
Larsens Tegnestue A/S, Copenhagen and
Renzo Piano Building Workshop, Paris.
Today, DGT is one of the leading practices
of the new generation of architects. It
has won the international competition of
the Estonian National Museum, currently
under construction (Estonia, 2013) and is
leading a series of cutting edge yet phe-
nomenally sensitive projects including the
R Project (France, 2012), ELKhoury's apartment complex (Lebanon, 2012), the Saito
Kinen Opera scenography (Japan, 2011).
The practice counts a multicultural team
of 14 architects and collaborates with
professionals of interdisciplinary fields.
www.dgtarchitects.com

214 Wonder Ground

215 The House of Arts

Fake Industries, Architectural Agonism

Cristina Goberna & Urtzi Grau
Fake Industries Architectural Agonism
(FKAA) is an architectural office that
explores the potential of copies to expand
the limits of discipline rejecting originality
as essential architectural value, and
investigating positive disagreement
as engine for the advancement in the
discipline. FKAA is an entity of variable
boundaries – with headquarters in New
York and Barcelona – orchestrated by Cristina Goberna and Urtzi Grau, professors
of studio design at the Graduate School of
Architecture, Planning and Preservation,
Columbia University and Cooper Union
School of Architecture.

Fake Industries
The world is full of architecture, more or
less interesting; we do not wish to add any
more. The last four hundred years of architectural excess produced enough undiscovered public architectural knowledge
to nurture, at least, our practice; the last
twenty, a hangover of creative-shapes-
on-steroids we are trying to recover from.
F**k originality. Rather, copies allow us to
explore all the potential left unexplored
by other's rush. Knowledge can be public,
yet undiscovered, if independently created fragments are logically related but
never retrieved, brought together, or
re-conceptualized. And that is what we do.
Don't ask us for new stuff, we copy.

Architectural Agonism
Friction in architectural discourse is not
only desirable but necessary for the development of the field. The lack of consensus
should be taken as an engine for the
creation of knowledge and Agonism, in its
opposition to Antagonism, as a positive
approach to discussions and the creation
of polemics in the field. We are interested
in the production of strong positions that
activate and extend public architectural
polemics.

www.fakeindustries.org

095 Roundabout Prophylaxis

211 Roundabout Science Lab

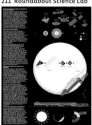

Figura Arquitetos office

Figura is a company formed by a highly skilled team with experience in architecture, design and computer graphics. Our commitment to quality and innovation enables us to collaborate with our clients broadly and reliably for the creation of a wide variety of visual and architectural solutions. We have been providing our services for some years, working in partnership with local and foreign clients, due to our reputation for excellence in this area.

We see the 3D visualization as a fundamental and integral part of architecture, design and advertising.It is an essential tool for communicating the desired intent, ranging from a simple design process, to a final presentation of an enterprise, contributing then to the success of marketing strategies.

www.figura.arq.br

057 Ecobitat

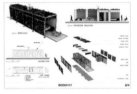

058 A New Way to Inhabit

060 Chalés LN

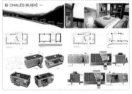

176 Prêmio Masisa de Arquitetura

177 Sede do TRT Go

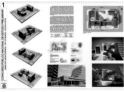

franz zt gmbh

franz zt gmbh was established in 2009 by robert diem (1976) and erwin stättner (1973)

In the beginning, there is often a competition. it's a chance for interesting projects and begins with the search for the best solution for complex tasks.

In between, the concept needs to be developed. The complex tasks need to be solved appropriately, whether they are intelligent, unexpected, charming or sexy. in the further process, it is important to have a strong concept to deal with laws, requirements, cost,

deadlines or breakdowns at the construction site the realized project and the satisfaction of the user is what counts in the end.

www.franz-architekten.at

043 Pol2 housing

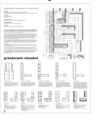

150 SHB Company Building

171 S87 Kindergarten

181 WU University of Economics

183 Wifi Technology-Centre

192 BHW Education Campus

193 LPS Liese Prokop Secondary School

194 PHY Technical Schoo

195 SZI Center for Special Pedagogics

219 DGL Sportshall

297 STM Foot Bridge Margaretengürtel

Geotectura

GEOTECTURA means merging land and architecture together with ecological values, cost effective technologies, psychological considerations and social responsibility.

GEOTECTURA is an award winning architectural studio founded by architect Dr. Joseph (Yossi) Cory. Our work was published and exhibited worldwide. We use in the office green design techniques combined with social awareness and creativity.

Specializing in innovative design GEO-TECTURA is committed to explore new sustainable horizons by preserving and restoring the balance between natural and built environment. Our projects are based on multi-disciplinary research and the office uses an open source design approach to optimize the best result for each challenge through the collaboration with designers from various fields such as science, architecture, art, landscape architecture, sociology and psychology.

www.geotectura.com

117 The Eco Nest

201 The 3Spheres Museum

gutiérrez-delafuente arquitectos

The gutiérrez-delafuente arquitectos office was founded in 2006 in Madrid by Natalia Gutiérrez Sánchez (Madrid, 1980) and Julio de la Fuente Martínez (Madrid, 1980). The founders are graduate architects of Escuela Técnica Superior de Arquitectura de Madrid (ETSAM) and have continued their training in Madrid and Ateliers Jean Nouvel office in Paris.

Natalia Gutiérrez is currently a Member of the Ethics Committee of Madrid Architects Association COAM.

They have won prizes in numerous national and international competitions, including two in Europan 09, Europan 10, Europan 11, IQ Wohnquartiere and the Multipurpose Centre Valle de Salazar.

They have been published in numerous magazines, exhibited in Spain, Germany and Austria as well as having several models exhibited in The Architectural Gallery of the magazine El Croquis.

Gutiérrez-delafuente focuses its research activity in contemporary urban mutation processes such as the reconversion of abandoned brownfields and industrial areas, or the phenomenon of shrinking cities.

At present they are building several singular projects in Spain and Germany, and also working in Austria.

www.gutierrez-delafuente.com

090 Vivaigle

091 Leo Major

092 Desmaterialitations

093 Local land art identity

Horhizon consortium

Horhizon is a design and research network established in 2008 in London to challenge the academic boundaries in architecture, spatial design, installation art, animation and films. Currently with 9 international members who are architects, educators, writers, artists, and film makers, actively involved in conducting experimental research through academic projects, exhibitions and publications. Ethos @ manifesto

Horhizon is an ongoing line at which the earthy establishments and the sky-high ambition meet. It has no limit to a person's mental perception, experiences, or interest. Horhizon broadens our outlook, perspective, perception; range of experience, range of interests, scope, and prospect. Rhizome, in botany, is a horizontal stem of a plant that is usually found underground, sparkling out roots and shoots from its nodes. The rhizome is a key metaphor in the philosophy of Gilles Deleuze and Felix Guattari. Horhizon therefore considers itself as a living body of interconnected relationships of located nodes in which its quality to evolve, to mutate, to grow is determined by its members.

The horizon is a symbol for romantic distance to all sites of our view. The observer is in the system surrounded by never ending space. The first step as point of departure to a never reachable arrival. With every movement the horizon starts to shift. It represents an evolution of wandering, flying in a state of flux. Reflected is disorientation. This disorientation links up to the otherness of being. Each being in this space has its own view, its own horizon. But it is not loneliness which drives us. It is the gift to observe nature and other beings. Through communication we are wired to those beings. Like a rizometric structure it forms a new organism, a living web. No politics, a system with strong will to survive. In addition it blends together. It opens the horizon. Once spread over all continents there is only one "HoRhizon" which can be seen everywhere. A rizometric structure with exchange of information is the only way to see behind the horizon; we will fly back to the Garden of Eden and realizing that we are already there; home. Out of space this big blue cloud as location. The new HoRhizon is born. This result achieved through adaptation of the already known networks which melt together into this new organism. The final goal: communication and exchange of information in real-time. This generated information as access able gift to mankind; not object based and without payable value. HoRhizon as free server for development of radical constructivism. It is alive. The information alters its location non-stop. A free will which generates the counterpart to our coded body with set lifetime.

The new being is not mortal anymore. A explosion on a dune at exodus of life, this generated reborn matter as attractor for what mankind call "mind". The HoRhizon erased the "I"; the new term "US". We are there. This space has to be adjusted to new circumstance. Acting as new drug which is spread out from the silverscreen. Welcome to the HoRhizon.
www.horhizon.com

7 Linzertus

9 Urban Sardinops

0 Paraparvulos

1 Youth Burgos

7 Capitoné

041 Strawberry Fields Forever

042 D3 housing

087 D3 Natural Systems competition

088 Farmer's market

089 Unesco_ competition

111 Scape or no One – Doing Nothing – Nowhere

143 Ephemeral Structures

144 Kingscross Gasholder

145 Narrating Embodiment

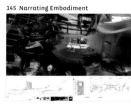

189 Encapsulated Fields

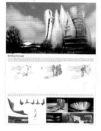

190 Istanbul Disaster Prevention

243 Moulin Rouge

284 Cityscape 1

330 RBR360

337 Birnbeck pier

HTDSTUDIO DESIGNOFFICE™

HTDSTUDIO DESIGNOFFICE is an internationally recognized, research and design based practice with a mission to bring innovative design excellence to architectural, interior, urban and sustainable design projects. HTDSTUDIO's work has appeared in publications and exhibitions around the world. Our clients include Third Eye View Studio, Aristeia International Inc., Brooklyn New School, The City of Newark, Financial Women's Association, FLATT Media Group, Nonprofit Finance Fund, the Permanent Mission of Namibia to the UN, and numerous organizations, corporations and private clients in the U.S., Europe, Asia, the Middle East and Caribbean.
www.htdstudio.net

230 Mercedes Benz Business Center

231 Small Hospitals Big Idea Competition

Ian Caine + Derek Hoeferlin

Ian Caine and Derek Hoeferlin are registered architects and urbanists in Boston and St. Louis, USA. Formed in 2009, their award winning collaboration researches and designs projects that engage architecture, landscape and urbanism within larger systemic contexts. They are currently focused on climate change and infrastructure. Caine and Hoeferlin co-designed one of the six first place entries in the Rising Tides competition in San Francisco; were named finalists in the Build a Better Burb competition in Long Island, New York; and, have been published internationally and featured on the Discovery Channel. Caine holds a Bachelor of Arts in Political Science and Master of Architecture from Washington University in St. Louis, where he was a member of the design faculty. Caine is currently pursuing a post-professional degree in urban design at the Massachusetts Institute of Technology. His research examines relationships between physical infrastructure and public space. Hoeferlin holds Masters of Architecture from Tulane and Yale Universities and is currently an Assistant Professor at Washington University in St. Louis. His research geo-spatially compares global deltas and watersheds to inform future adaptive design strategies.

101 The 21st Century Right of Way

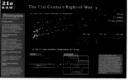

102 The 100 Year Plan

103 The Tsunami + Coral Reef Research Network

IaN+

IaN+ is multi-disciplinary agency aims at being a place where theory and practice of architecture overlap and meet. The studio was set up in 1997 and materializes around the core of its three members with diverse professional formation and experience: Carmelo Baglivo, Luca Galofaro, for design project and theory and Stefania Manna for engineering.
They have been participating to many national and international architectural competitions, gaining prizes and mentions as In 2006, the Italian Architecture Gold Medal for the first realized work with the "Tor Vergata" University scientific research building.
www.ianplus.it

159 Cheongna City Tower

160 Maribor

221 Serlachius

Interface Studio Architects

We believe that creativity and innovation are triggered by limitations. We resist smoothing over the process of design into a streamlined approach that leads to specific stylistic or material tendencies. Rather, we pursue an open-source, inclusive trajectory that collapses often contradictory goals into the process and encourages a dramatic range of expression. Our work is urban - it attempts to broker complex and contested relationships in different ways relative to different contexts.
www.is-architects.com

158 Higher Ground

263 025397

J. MAYER H. Architects

Founded in 1996 in Berlin, Germany, J. MAYER H. studio, focuses on works at the intersection of architecture, communication and new technology. Recent projects include the Town Hall in Ostfildern, Germany, Potsdam Docklands Masterplan 2002, a student center at Karlsruhe University and the redevelopment of the Plaza de la Encarnacion in Sevilla, Spain. From urban planning schemes and buildings to installation work and objects with new materials, the relationship between the human body, technology and nature form the background for a new production of space. Juergen Mayer H. is the founder and principal of this crossdisciplinairy studio. He studied at Stuttgart University, The Cooper Union and Princeton Universtiy. His work has been published and exhibited worldwide and is part of numerous collections including MoMA New York and SF MoMA. He has taught at Princeton University, University of the Arts Berlin, Harvard University, Kunsthochschule Berlin, Architectural Association in London and is currently teaching at Columbia University, New York.
www.jmayerh.de

128 Quartier M Düsseldorf

Jägnefält Milton

Jagnefalt Milton was founded 2009 in Stockholm, Sweden by Carl Jagnefalt and Konrad Miltonafter winning the Galway Centre Pier competition. The office has since then continued tosucefully compete in international competitions but are also designing a number of buildings inSweden.
Carl Jagnefalt previously worked at Joli Ark and White Architects in Stockholm. He studied atE.S.L.A.P, Paris and at the Royal Institute of Technology in Stockholm.
Konrad Milton previously worked at OMA in Rotterdam and X-Architects in Dubai. He studied at ETH, Zurich and at the Royal Institute of Technology in Stockholm.
www.jagnefaltmilton.com

130 Second Act

131 Sky Pier

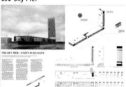

132 Villa Sapmi

kadawittfeldarchitektur

his is kadawittfeldarchitektur'. Founded
1999 in Aachen by Klaus Kada and
erhard
ittfeld, today we represent much more
an pure architectural form. The inter-
sciplinary approach of our work fuses
rchitecture, interior architecture, and
esign, on the one hand, and interfaces
oth urban planning and urban projects
the other - to reflect the wide range of
ur creative work today.
adawittfeldarchitektur creates an
added-value" space. Our young creative
am generates added-value space:
e-space, communications-space,
omestic-space, and work-space. Our way
handling volume, material, supporting
ructure and utilization yearns to be
tegrated into the urban fabric. We seek
counterbalance the heterogeneity of
e city face, and the homogeneity of
e diversified city space with the goal of
ntemporaneity and sustainability, with
oth spectator and user in mind.
adawittfeldarchitektur is individuality.
gether with our clients we search out
ptimum conditions: future-oriented, in
terplay between tradition and technol-
y, spanning the past and present,
oligated to the environment.
adawittfeldarchitektur is strategic
anning. Good architecture is brought
life not only by a creative idea, but
so by good details. Thanks to extensive
pertise with the most diverse projects,
e represent top-notch competence, on-
dget and on-schedule.
ww.kwa.ac

188 Student Service Center

205 Brüder Grimm Museum

3 DHPG Haus

4 MVRegensburg

5 Mönchengladbach Arcaden

7 Thyssen Krupp

Katsuhiro Miyamoto & Associates

Katsuhiro Miyamoto was born in Hyogo,
1961. Graduated in Architecture from University of Tokyo, 1984. Completed the Master Course at University of Tokyo, 1987. Lecturer, Department of Architecture,Osaka
University of Arts, 1995. Associate
Professor, Department of Architecture,
Osaka University of Arts, 1999. Reorgan-
ized to Katsuhiro Miyamoto & Associates,
2002. Associate Professor, Department of
Environmental Design,Osaka University
of Arts, 2005. Professor, Graduate School
of Engine ering and Urban Research
Plaza,Osaka Ciy University, 2008. Lecturer
at Tokyo University of Science.
www.kmaa.jp

033 Northern Style Housing Complex in Aomori

034 Chushinji Temple Priests' Quarters

206 Water and Sculpture Hills ICHIHARA

Keiichi Hayashi Architect

Keiichi Hayashi was born in Osaka, 1967.
1991 Graduated from Metal Engineering,
Kansai University, 1991. 1993 Graduated
from Architecture, Kansai University,
1993. 1997 Established Keiichi Hayashi
Architect, 1997.
It is important for me to make architecture using basic materials and uncom-
plicated construction methods. I try to
create a system that is based on pure
architecture but becomes complex when
people use it.
www.haya-at.com

054 Living with Dog

Kevin Kennon Architects

Kevin Kennon is the recipient of two
NYS/AIA Design Awards, 7 NYC/AIA
Design Awards, the I.D. Magazine Award,
the American Architecture Award, the
Architectural League Young Architects
Award and the Progressive Architecture
Award. He has been a visiting professor
of design at Yale University, Princeton
University, the Cooper Union and an
Adjunct Professor of Design at Columbia
University. He is a founding principal of
United Architects, which was selected as a
finalist for the World Trade Center Design
Competition by the Lower Manhattan De-
velopment Corporation. He also designed
and built the temporary public viewing
platform at Ground Zero.
Kevin Kennon has over 24 years experience practicing architecture. In 2002, he
founded Kevin Kennon Architects, after
leaving as a design partner at Kohn,
Pedersen & Fox Associates, P.C.
www.kkarchitect.com

040 Minneapolis House

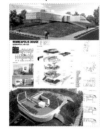

142 Tian Fang Tower

KLAIR Architecture

Coming from two different cultures, our courses meet and complete each other in our career. Our respective urban experiences, from Seoul to Paris, passing by other fascinating cities in constant mutations where we stayed, feed our thought. It is at ecdm, where we both worked as project architect, that we collaborated for the first time. Around motivating projects, a look, a reactivity and a desire to make a team are formed. Dialogue and complementarity that underpin our creative approach allowed us to design projects with simplicity and critical thinking, without formal prerogatives, oraesthetic imperatives associated with different trends. We are also conscious of our role as "social actor" and we are committed to accompany the client to carry out to success each operation. Our architectural and societal concerns also converge to broad principles, joining us around a taste for both innovation and creative research, for the practice on construction site and for the design study phase : - Making contextual and prospective works, - Translate programmatic data in a spatial and functional interpretation, strong and legible, - Privilege the introduction of nature in urban areas, - Bring a sensitive and unique dimension to each project.
www.klair.fr

044 Modular City

045 COM

121 DER

172 GEN

210 POZ

Kokaistudios

Kokaistudios is an award winning multi-disciplinary design firm founded in 2000 in Venice by Italian architects Filippo Gabbiani & Andrea Destefanis. Founded with the dream to create a collaborative office of young and talented architects devoted to researching and formulating the design solutions to the demands of tomorrow and capable of working on a worldwide basis;the firm has grown after 10 years into a team of 30 people headquartered in Shanghai, China.
With our focus of offering total design solutions, Kokaistudios has completed over 140 projects spanning the range of architecture, heritage renovation, and interior design. The firm has received numerous awards including the Asia Pacific Region of 2011 International Property Awards, Commercial Space in IAI Award 2010, MIPIM Asia Award 2010 and 2011, "40 under 40 Award" from Perspective Magazine. In addition to these awards Kokaistudios has also received 2 UNESCO Asia Pacific Heritage Awards for the Bund 18 and HuaiHai Lu 796 projects in Shanghai where Kokaistudios is responsible for the entire architectural and interior design projects. .
Our goal remains firmly on a worldwide basis challenging, interesting and innovative projects, and to offering our clients creative solutions and the highest levels of service.
www.kokaistudios.com

141 Wanda Wuhan Phase One of Donghu CBD Competition

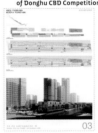

KWK PROMES

Robert Konieczny (born in 1969), founded KWK Promes together with Marlena Wolnik in 1999. At present he ramains a single owner (Marlena Wolnik finished collaboration in 2004). KWK Promes received many national and international awards for completed and unrealized projects. His Broken House created together with Marlena Wolnik is recognized as one of the icons of Polish architecture. For the same project he was nominated to European Prize of the Miesa van der Rohe Foundation. He was nominated to more times for the Komoda House (together with Marlena Wolnik) in 2004 and for the Aatrial Housein 2006. The last one was named the House of the Year by winning a contest by a prestigious portal World Architecture News (Konieczny was the first Pole, to be qualified to the contest). In 2007 KWK Promes was on the Wallpaper's list of the 101 most exciting architectural offices in the world (the only one from Poland). In 2007 a Spanish publishing house Scalae numbered KWK Promes among the 44 best young architects in the world. Besides that, during the second International Competition for young Architects Leonardo 2007 organized in Minsk KWK Promes received a gold medal for the Hidden House, a Grand Prix for the Aatrial House for the best completed project, and a special prize of the Russian Architect Association. In 2008 Robert Konieczny was the prizewinner of the Europe 40 under 40 - Europe's Emerging Young Architects and Designers awarded by The European Centre for Architecture Art Design and Urban Studies and The Chicago Athenaeum. At the same time the Aatrial House and the Hidden House were named the best buildings in the world of 2008 (The International Architecture Awards 2008). In 2008 the OUTrial and Safe Houses were also nominated to the European Mies'a van der Rohe Prize (altogether there were 5 nominations to the European edition). In 2011 Robert Konieczny was awarded with the Annual Prize of the Minister of Culture and National Heritage.
kwkpromes.pl

212 Museum of Contemporary in Wrocław, Poland

213 National Museum Przelomy

Lapo Ruffi Architetto

Lapo Ruffi (1971), architect. He has dedicated himself to architecture and design since 1998. In 2002, he opens his own office, LRA, working in planning research and experimentation with projects of various natures and scales: urban projects to single-family houses, interior design to furnishings. In 2007, his work is published in the book 1000x European Architecture and exhibited in the exposition FlorenceEXIT | Segnali e fermenti di una nuova generazione di architetti and at the Festival della Creatività in Florence. In 2008, he was the winner of the international competition Europan 9 in Pistoia, Italy; he was invited to exhibit at RIZOMA_Biennale dei giovani architetti italiani and was included in the anthology Young Blood 2007_Annual dei talenti italiani premiati nel mondo. In 2010, he was the winner of the international competition Europan 10 in Montreux, Switzerland. He lives and works in Pistoia.
ec2.it/laporuffiarchitetto

068 Calamari Union

080 Synapsiedlung

Leon11

Leon11 is a networking of architects and designers based on patterns of thought, proposing and developing the collective work as a new way to understand the artistic and architectural production. Since its founding in Madrid in 2005, the intensity and quality of production of labor has increased, collaborated with many architects and artists renowned nationally and internationally, which has given us the opportunity to understand the artistic production a combination of "Experience" and "Creativity" and basing our theoretical manifesto on responses related to the "Innovation of the reality." Leon11 team currently consists of eighteen persons from different disciplines (architects, illustrators, graphic designers, sculptors, video production, etc.) with international and concerns plural formations, promoting collaborative working methodologies that foster innovation and exploring new research proposals, creative and architectural.
Members are part of ZOOHAUS Leon11, multidisciplinary working group, a networking platform for creation from the network: an open-space tool, communicative and creative enabler-promoter for the development of new artistic, social and technical.
www.leon11.com

082 Inhabiting the sky

238 The Kaohsiung Maritime Cultural & Pop Music Center

238 Square in the Sky

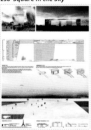

290 The Golden Lane

Lima Urban Lab

LUIS ARREDONDO _ARCHITECT

Marchi_Architectes

MICROCITIES

Pablo Díaz - Graduate of Architecture and urbanism at the University Ricardo Palma (Lima). Has been a design professor at the University Ricardo Palma (1998 -2005). He currently is a principal professor and advisor in the School of Architecture of the University San Martin de Porres. He has been involved in the design workshop of the Lima Urban Laboratory.

Diego Rodríguez - Graduate of Architecture and urbanism at the University Ricardo Palma (Lima).He has been a design professor at the Faculty of Architecture at the University Ricardo Palma. Currently is a design and architecture theory professor in the school of architecture at the University San Martin de Porres (USMP).
www.lul-lab.com

048 Urban House by Eternit

138 Lugar de la Memoria

270 Creating a Digital Culture

272 Machu Picchu Rain Forest Resort
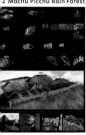

Our work follows two different lines, often cross-linked.
The first one is our research line focused in the social area, looking for new systems of relating and grouping. We understand public spaces as a frame of creation for the new society. Inside this line we create a fusion of projects purely architectonical with a highlighted sculptural/artistic aspect, endeavoring to benefit the resulted project with both fields.
Our second line of working is based in the production of ideas, concepts and models in a purposeful limitless context, looking for new challenges, new programs and new solutions to our society demands. Combination of these two lines generates a huge range of different ways understanding research as a target, and the participation in competitions as the path to follow. We are focused in the social aspect of our work, the public space as a core of the action, not as an observer, and architecture as a tool to humanize the city.
www.arredondoarquitecto.com

046 Amel101

047 Bandact

048 Zigzag

049 Replica

050 Concavo_Convexo

---

185 Continuitat Ritmica

247 Sekretu Bat Orion

268 CM_Lamina

316 Be_Lamina

Sensitive to the spirit of a place, the firm Marchi_Architectes, one of the prizewinners of Les Nouveaux albums des jeunes architectes et des paysagistes (NAJAP) of this year delivery by the Minister of Culture and Communication of France, conceives of architecture as a reconciliation with nature. Adélaïde and Nicola draw on the richness of their travels and encounters as well as the reality of the profession as the framework for the act of construction. They are uniquely influenced by their Erasmus earned at the Porto School of Architecture (Portugal) in 1996 and instruction by Alvaro Siza, Pritzker 1992. Adélaïde Marchi (born in 1973, graduate of the École Nationale Supérieure d'Architecture de Paris la Seine) and Nicola Marchi (born in 1968, graduate of the Milan Polytechnic) founded Marchi_ Architectes in 2004. Upon their return from Paris, Adélaïde Marchi plunged straight into the profession at Brunet & Saunier, where she earned her spurs. This was the source for her knowledge of "pragmatic evidence of a worksite, management of skills and people, budgetary constraint by developer". As for Nicola, he works for the firms of Édouard François, Manuelle Gautrand and Christian de Portzamparc. Nicola Marchi's degree in architecture was directed by Edouardo Souto de Moura (Pritzker 2011).
www.anmarchi.com

052 Kuelap

153 eVolo 06
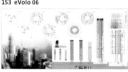

175 Courbevoie

251 Geneve

298 The Living Bridge

Microcities practise and research focuses on the collision between work, politics, popular culture and leisure time, resulting into projects which are clear and specific, while still keeping within the richness and the metaphor of all the explored fields. Their main interest lies in questioning and stressing common habits and conditions through pragmatic projects, theoretical speculation, or even utopian visions.
In their works outside and inside are not separated by a boundary but more often by a blurred territory, an interstitial space which undermines antinomies such as public and private, home and community, mineral and natural. The line between exterior and interior becomes an "ambiguous" moment of in-between: it defines a limit, but also an open environment for human unusual occupations, both private and collective.
At the heart of Microcities' practice is the idea of calling into question the context we live in, turning it into a true design tool, in order to subvert conventional typologies and explore new ways of living. The professional activity is constantly verified and substantiated by a research conducted through teaching (common space/leisure time) and through frequent writings on art, architecture, media and technology.
microcities.net

079 Symbiosis
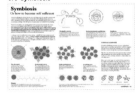

276 Alice in Wonderwall

319 Day One

324 Grundrisse

Modostudio

modostudio is a multi-disciplinary practice of architecture, urban planning and industrial design. Profiting from the diversified skills of the founding partners and the continual collaboration with experts from various fields, modostudio combines architectural theory, research, innovation and experimentation with high technical knowledge and professionalism.
Established at the end of 2006 by three principal architects, Fabio Cibinel, Roberto Laurenti, and Giorgio Martocchia, after many years of collaborating with internationally acclaimed architects like Massimiliano Fuksas, Piero Sartogo, Erik Van Egeraat and Kas Oosterhuis, modostudio in a short time was awarded and shortlisted in many international architectural competitions.
modostudio partners have been teaching architecture at Cornell University in 2008. They currently teach architectural design at IED - European Institute of Design and sustainable design at Inarch postgraduate master.
www.modostudio.eu

179 Escuela de Ciencias de la Salud

202 Elisabeth and Helmut UHL Foundation

073 Ciudad Del Medio Ambiente

074 Le Cret-Du-Locle

116 Ex Fonderie Riunite

125 Lpailuohjeilma

164 Edil Tomarchio

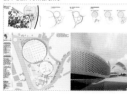

MOTOElastico

MOTOElastico[Simone Carena | Marco Bruno] is an architecture office based in Italy and Korea, directed by the Italian architects Simone Carena and Marco Bruno. MOTOElastico is a multidisciplinary design firm: its activity ranges from urban development to architecture, interior and furniture design. MOTOElastico provides a full design service, from concept development to construction supervision, carefully fitting each project into the local potentials and know-how.
Globalized contemporary architecture tends to produce similar designs all over the world. International offices import a 'colonial' style that lacks local identity. MOTOElastico is trying to give each project a sensible character in order to produce unique landmarks deeply rooted in the local culture. The Italian lifestyle design finds its sources in the local differences of a multicultural peninsula, the pride of local taste and subsequent competitiveness of neighboring visions. Italian History is made of centuries of creative adaptation: taking something foreign and transforming into something new and strongly "Italian". Observation and transformation are the keys to this process.
MOTOElastico comes from the 10 years experience of the Studio Elastico (Torino based office founded in 1995 by S. Carena, S. Pujatti and A. Del Maschio) and from a 5 years presence in Korea.
Each project used valuable insights from all founders and members of Studio Elastico and precious cooperation with local designers: details of each project can be found in the index.
For Industrial design MOTOElastico cooperates with Elasticodisegno.
www.elasticodisegno.it

031 Plug-in Hanok

253 Big Leaves Dream Carriers

292 Prancing Zebra

MSB ARQUITECTOS

MSB – ARQUITECTURA E PLANEAMENTO, LDA was established in 2004, in Funchal, by architects Miguel Mallaguerra, Susana Jesus and Bruno Martins. The MSBs are experienced in producing projects and studies directed to the areas of architecture, urban planning and interior design. The works produced inside this young workgroup reveal the fascination by contemporaneous architecture accompanying its time, having developed over recent years a number of projects in the area of Housing, Hospitality, equipment and Urban Development, noted for its quality recognized by the victories achieved in national and international competitions. The office maintains an open philosophy to the world, both in its communication policy, but also in how it works with its partners inside and outside of Portugal, privileging the work in multidisciplinary teams, and promoting ideas as the crucial factor in their projects.

235 Busan Opera House

265 Metro Station 20

267 Airbaltic Terminal

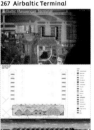

336 Ullswater Clubhouse

NABITO ARCHITECTS

NAbito (Alessandra Faticanti 1975, Roberto Ferlito 1973) is a multidisciplinary team based in Barcelona and active on the mediteranean territories like Italy Spain and France looking for similarities and differences. His attempt is to redefine a different process of elaboration for a new contemporary culture, from the social and economic point of view. The goal of nabito arquitectura is to develop a cultural mix related and in communication with parallels realities. Nabito Won the important european award "Nouveaux albums des jeunes architectes Paris 2006", given by the ministry of culture. They won several competitions in Europe starting to build his first buildings.
www.nabit.it

035 The Node

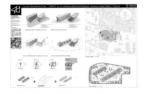

036 Stairscraper an Horizontal Skyscraper

037 Torre Familia

115 Cfpos Belgrade

119 Kites for Europe

NICE ARCHITECTS

nodo17-architects

Nice Architects loves to produce surprising ideas, optimistic visions and lifefull strategies in architecture,
urban & landscape design and related fields.
PEOPLE _ M.arch., MI. TOMAS ZACEK (* 1979)
Schools: Faculty of architecture STU Bratislava – PhD. (Current study)
Faculty of architecture STU Bratislava – M.arch.
Faculty of building constructions STU Bratislava – MI.
Works: Aurex (SVK), Mitchell & associates (IRL), Dominique Perrault (FR),
BIG (DK), Willy Muller (ESP), Nice Architects (SVK)
_ M.arch. IGOR ZACEK (* 1982)
Schools: Faculty of architecture STU Bratislava – M.arch.
Department of civic design, University of Liverpool
Works: Aurex (SVK), Venhoeven CS (NL), Nice Architects (SVK)
_ B.arch. SONA POHLOVA (* 1984)
Schools: Faculty of architecture STU Bratislava – B.arch.
Arquitectura La Salle, Universitat Ramon Llull, Barcelona
Works: Aurex (SVK), Vallo-Sadovsky architects (SVK), Barbarela studio (ESP), Nice Architects (SVK)
www.nicearchitects.sk

Manuel Pérez Romero (1972) studied architecture (1998) in E.T.S.A., Las Palmas (Canary Islands); Torino Polytechnic, (Italy), Milano Polytechnic, (Italy), Westminster University (London, UK), ETSA Madrid Polytechnic (PhD). Actually he is making a research for his Thesis, about the implementation of the probable in the time oriented processes.
He is a Lecturer of Design Projects at E.T.S.A.G. in Alcalá de Henares since the year 2001, and he has been Lecturer of Design Projects at E.T.S.A. Madrid, (2000-2001) and actually, also a professor of Construction System and Workshop at IE School of Architecture.
He founded the partnership nodo17 architects (2002), and has been awarded in many national and international competitions. More than 100 publications in differents magazines and books.
Recently, the corean editorial Damdi Publishing Co., has published a 250 pages monographic "mook" (magazine + book) about nodo17 work. (DD collection, Design Documents Series, number 33, 2009).
He has registered the brand "Reverse Town Planning" (Urbanismo Inverso) for a new methodology for the Urban Remodelling.
www.nodo17.com

138 Sustainable Intersacalar Node

236 I-Opera

239 Hotel Music Skin

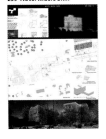

240 Auditorium Poliedro

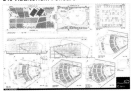

113 Reykjavik,island

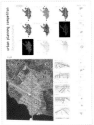

281 Medzijarky

282 Garden

283 Sun Square

059 Houseboat

061 Danubiana House

062 Eco Capsula

064 Vila Bahamy

020 Valley House

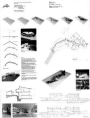

007 From Flower to Flower

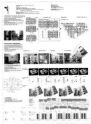

014 Granero House

015 Living-Dike House

019 North Face

object-e architecture

Object-e architecture is a platform, created by Dimitris Gourdoukis in 2006, in order to explore new territories in architecture with the aid of computational tools and techniques. Object-e started as an exploration of new directions for design through computation; where computation is understood as the explicitly or implicitly coded digital processes that are aiming not in the computerization and optimization of existing practices, but in the invention of new ones. Through time, object-e moved beyond the borders of computation and engaged design at large, trying to graft computation with the social, political and ecological issues that architecture is facing today. Object-e is based on several collaborations with people coming from different backgrounds, with different design intentions and agendas. The outcome of this process, being in most cases collaborative, is therefore defying any concept of style; identity is formed through difference and constant transformation.
object-e.net

051 Inflateit

094 FLOW

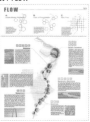

096 inje(un)ction

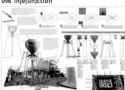

097 Para*site

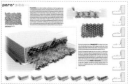

309 Glowing Cloud

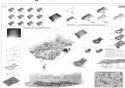

310 Togs

OCDC

OCDC (Organized Crime Design Collective) is a research-based office located in Downtown Los Angeles' Little Tokyo district. To explore how we can popularize architecture in our world of possibility, we look for design values that are participatory in the loop of contemporary life by examining design models that can be fully integrated within the world of consumption. We combine the concerns of hyper-ergonomic desires with stimulative visual communication, moving architectural practice through a thought process that promotes the beauty of materialization. Our projects strive to capture and reveal the experience of contextual fluidity between nature, culture and technology.
www.ocdc.info

022 Bubble House

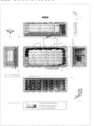

023 Car Park Housing

026 Dingbat Trio

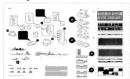

028 Upcycle House

136 Parachute Pavilion

249 Jumbo Jet Theater

OFIS arhitekti

... architectural office based in ljubljana formed by rok oman and spela videcnik in 1998.
ofis work negotiates between architectural projects in different scales (from 30m2 to 50.000 m2), performing arts and set design.
Rok Oman - (born 1970) studied architecture at the ljubljana school of architecture (grad.oct.1998) and at the architectural association in london (grad.feb.2000).
Špela Videčnik - (born 1971) studied architecture at the ljubljana school of architecture (grad.oct.1997) and at the architectural association in london (grad. feb. 2000).
www.ofis-a.si

151 City Municipality Ljubljana

174 Kindergarten Ribnica

PATTERNS

PATTERNS is a design research architectural practice based in Los Angeles and operating globally. Founded in 1999 and headed by Co-principals Marcelo Spina and Georgina Huljich, PATTERNS work has gained international recognition for its innovative approach to design and architecture that fuses advanced computation with an extensive understanding of form, tectonics and materials. PATTERNS's vision is to generate innovative spatial forms that actively engage, enhance and influences the body, constantly challenging its relationship to the built environment akin to the complexity of contemporary life.
www.p-a-t-t-e-r-n-s.net

220 Vestbanen Kulturatrium

237 Stranded Shells · New Busan Opera Hous

266 LTHYW

312 Manifold Dubai

Paul Preissner

Paul Preissner is an architect and educator, establishing Paul Preissner Architects in 2006. He was awarded the second place in the South Korean competition for the Jeongok Museum of Pre-History in 2006, and his work was showcased in a solo show at the Museum of Contemporary Art in Chicago entitled "Spotted" in 2009. His work is part of the permanent collections of the Art Institute of Chicago and has been well published, most notably in Architectural Record, Architectural Design, Archis/Volume, Indian Architect and Builder, and in recent books Hatch (Laurence King), Digital Architecture Now (Thames and Hudson) and Digital Diagram II (Archiworld). He is an Assistant Professor at the University of Illinois-Chicago and lives with his wife and their dog in Chicago.
www.paulpreissner.com

00 Museum of Polish History

27 Jeongok Museum of Pre-History

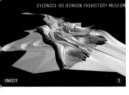

33 Busan Opera House

Pneumastudio

An interdisciplinary design practice situated between the fields of architecture and landscape architecture, pneumastudio was formed in 2011 and premiered its work in two exhibitions that same year, the first of which was held at the Design Museum in Barcelona and the second at GLOBAL Design / New York University's Gallatin School of Individualized Study. pneumastudio was featured in the book Bracket 2: Goes Soft published by Actar in 2012.
Cathryn Dwyre holds a Masters Degree in Landscape Architecture from the University of Pennsylvania. She is the Managing Editor of Dirt co-published by the MIT Press and University of Pennsylvania in Spring 2012. Chris Perry holds a Masters Degree in Architecture from Columbia University and is Assistant Professor at the Rensselaer School of Architecture, where he is also the Director of the Post-Professional Program. Prior to joining the faculty at Rensselaer he was the Louis Kahn Visiting Assistant Professor at the Yale School of Architecture.
Pneumastudio operates within an expanded field of design practice and draws upon technological advancements in a variety of disciplines external to both architecture and landscape architecture, including robotics, information design, ecology, the environmental sciences, and product design.
www.pneumastudio.org

332 Spirabilis

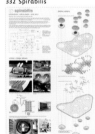

Posad

Posad is an Urban Design office based in The Hague, the Netherlands. Posad works on strategic designs with various scale levels, from region to street.
Posad offers more than a design, as designs are often quickly befallen by the realities of social and economic change, and the demands of a growing number of stakeholders in the planning process.
We offer future proof strategies to improve the milieu, scaling from region to street. This strategy provides a firm foundation for a range of solutions to the challenges of urban design. It distinguishes characteristic features and qualities of locations, while simultaneously identifying necessary conditions for change.
Regardless of scale, any design is influenced by the challenges of the physical and social context. Posad operates throughout a broad range of scales ranging from region, to city, to street and vice versa.
The systematic application of these varying scales reveals relationships and opportunities, resulting in a future proof design.
We believe that realizing the best plans is the product of a collaborative effort. In the end, our designs address those matters that, while appearing simple, are essential and often overlooked. It is our goal to develop attractive designs that improve the comfort and durability of our living environments.
We strive to offer a result that goes beyond the design brief. By implementing an integral working process derived from proven strategic methodologies, we add value and distinction in design.
www.posad.nl

105 Between the Lines

107 Brik

108 Own Harvest

PRAUD

109 Golden Grip

110 Mirakelsteeg

PRAUD is a Boston based firm formed in 2010 by Rafael Luna and Dongwoo Yim. As a research and design firm, PRAUD focuses on a contemporary approach to understanding the effects of urbanity and developing architectural process. PRAUD's research takes into account various scales in architecture and urbanism with key topics such as hybridity, urbanity, density, and transformation. Our architectural dialog is a synthetic gesture between contemporary vocabulary in architecture and urban research. Dongwoo Yimprincipal(founding partner) received a Master of Architecture in Urban Design at Graduate School of Design (GSD), Harvard University, and bachelor's degree in Seoul National University. Dongwoo has professional experiences in various countries such as S. Korea (Junglim Architecture, Space Group), Japan (Maki & Assoc.), The Netherlands (West 8), and US (Machado-Silvetti Assoc.)His research focuses on integral urbanism and architectural typologies that catalyze urban transformation in large scale, and his publication "Pyongyang, and Pyongyang After" was published in May, 2011. He is a part-time faculty at Rhode Island School of Design. Rafael Lunaprincipal(founding partner) received a Master of Architecture from Massachusetts Institute of Technology, Rafael has professional experiences in various countries such as Japan (Toyo Ito Associates), UK (KPF), France (Ateliers Jean Nouvel), and US (Martha Schwartz Partners, Sasaki Associates, dECOI Architects, and Machado-Silvetti Assoc.)His research focuses on hybrid architectural typologies and density. He is currently working on developing the topic more through PRAUD's new publication "I Want To Be Metropolitan," which is due to be completed at the beginning of 2012.
praud.info

197 Extension of Serlachius Museum Gösta

228 Hotel Liesma

234 Busan Opera House

REC ARQUITECTURA

remote-controlled

scandurrastudio

Sinestezia

Our job comes from the openness to every signal around the project and the range of possibilities in order to be consistent with all the elements involved, getting the innovations and proposals into feasible projects. The course of Rec's proposals is founded in five main principles:
The office focuses on: research, teaching, private and public commissions, international scenarios, theories, sustainability [passive systems], construction, cutting edge design tools, lectures, workshop and above all, VIABILITY on each project; professional expertise interested in developing art and craft.
Understanding "less is more" in...." how to do more with less" Essays and theories manifested on "REC" buildings are: "From the evolution of species to the Peacock Tail" / "Holistic Zero Energy" / "The revolution of the 4th screen" / "Promoter-interpreter or Architect-composer" / "New groups or New elements" / "Design with chaotic infrastructure" / "Programmatic Innovations" / "Materials with local identity rather than Aesthetics" / "Kitchen recipes come to an end" / "The user as spectacle vs Star architects" / "Viable technology" / "Building as infrastructure" / "Formwork as infrastructure in stock to become formwork again". "Rec arquitectura" has been mentioned in specialized magazines such as "Architectural Record" in October 2010 as one of the most influential emergent architectural offices with a prominent trajectory.
www.recarquitectura.com

260 Kujira

293 Venice

303 Glowworm

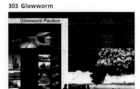

Studio is located Muenster, Germany. Works regarding space-encompassing artistic research. Since 2002 Professor chair of –their depiction" at the Peter Behrens School of Architecture, Duesseldorf, Germany.
Since 2005 Professor at the Texas A&M University, Faculty of Architecture, College Station, USA
www.remote-controlled.de

039 HDW-01

Scandurrastudio tackles themes liked to the contemporary city and its transformations. Projects of design become opportunities for study of the meaning of the project. The studio's activity covers different scales of intervention, from strategies of territorial planning to urban, architectural, interior and exhibit design, as well as the artistic direction of corporate image and production at an international level.
The studio's work is rooted in the belief that architecture, and more precisely the architecture of space, plays a fundamental role in the lives of human beings and their relationship with the world, and has an enormous power to define the individual. In this way questions and problems are accumulated that become a critical resource with which to tackle the opportunities for design.
scandurrastudio.com

270 Lamina

285 Las

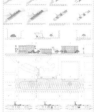

Architectural Studio Sinestezia was founded by Ana Zatezalo Schenk in 2005, with headquarters in Paris and an office in Belgrade. With each project, Sinestezia is trying to affirm contemporary architectural expression, where form and design departs from the usual experience, the ordinary.
The in Sinestezia have experience that stretches across the Europe, Americas and Asia as well as across fields of Master Planning, Housing, Public buildings and Interiors. With such a combination of different professional experience and aspirations we recognize the importance encouraging and developing specialties of each member of our team. Therefore, we became full members of internationally recognized organizations in the field of management and environment such us U Green Building Council and Fidic.
sinestezia.com

106 Veloville-Roule À Reims

029 Europan Rioja

129 Amsterdam

204 JVC

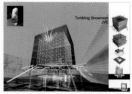

256 Expo 2012 'Ocean Partner'

Slot.

The design process of Slot is characterized by a consequent methodological investigation on the context. Since its foundation in 2008, Slot has specifically focused on the exploration of cultural and urban aspects and their artistic translation into formal concepts, proofed by awards and honorific mentions in design competitions around the globe.
In April of 2009, Slot won the first prize in an open competition for the Mexican Pavilion at the Universal Expo Shanghai 2010, the winning project out of more than 300 participants; during the same year, Slot is considered as Mexico's emergent office with the most promising international projection by Arquine magazine (no. 49). In 2009, Slot received a special mention in the International Competition for a Sustainability Center on Afsluitdijk, The Netherlands. Slot is considered one of the top 50 design offices throughout the American continents, by Arquine magazine (no. 50) in 2010.
Slot is currently involved in a number of projects of different scales in Mexico, Europe and Asia. They include urban design proposals, single and collective dwelling projects, as well as public and cultural developments for governments and private investors. Just recently, Slot signed a contract of collaboration with the De Tao Masters Academy in Beijing, which includes teaching Master Studio Classes and further project collaborations.
www.slot-studio.com

025 California Senior Housing

076 Mexico 2030

124 International Business Center

126 Masterplan Vienna

196 Architecture Faculty

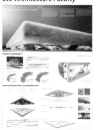

199 Art Gallery Maribor

229 House of John Paul II "Do not Fear"

255 Expo Yeosu 2012 Korea

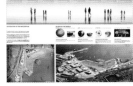

291 Hong Kong Boundary Crossing

299 Mexican Pavilion

StudioNOWA

NOWA was established in 2005, but it has been working since the year 2000 thanks to the commitment of the Architect Marco Navarra, who, with his work started in 1995, has received many prices and awards, also international, either for his works, or for the competitions he has been selected for.
The office works in many fields, from architectural integrated planning to works supervision, from feasibility studies to environmental consulting and landscape consulting. The office also deals with organizing workshops, setting up exhibitions, and curatorship of books and catalogues.
At present, the office is carrying out some planning works, both public and private. The work team consists of three partners and six collaborators, among which four architects, a secretary and a person in charge for the Calls for Proposals.
The operative and administrative location develops on a 250-square-meter area and it is equipped with 12-computer positions connected to a LAN system and an AIR-PORT system, it has a lab for the models and many support equipment for the fast development of activities.
www.studionowa.com

032 Treinuno

173 Cricket

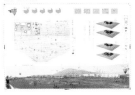

Takashi Nishibori

Jiro Endo(BA) - Graduate Musashino Institute of Art, Tokyo 1991, and, studied at Berlage Institute, Amsterdam, worked in Tokyo. Co-founder of architecture practice "intentionallies" in 1995 and, "guesthousetokyo" in 1998 in Tokyo. Established "Newguesthouse" and International music festival "Soi-music" in 2003, and, moved practice in Bangkok since 2009. Taught in Sri lanka, and, has been taught at School of Architecture and Design, King Mongkut's University of Technology, Thonburi, Bangkok since 2010. Exhibited work at "Sharjah biennial 8 at UAE 2007" as a member of Soi-project, and, co-designer of Thailand's largest outdoor music festival "Big Mountain Music Festival".
Takashi Nishibori(BSc, AADlp) : Graduate AA school, London 2002, worked in London, Shanghai and Bangkok, taught in London, and, has been taught at School of Architecture and Design, King Mongkut's University of Technology, Thonburi, Bangkok since 2005. Recently, practice in Bangkok, exhibited work at "Setouchi International Art Festival 2010" in Japan, and, co-designer of Thailand's largest outdoor music festival "Big Mountain Music Festival".
Nuttiya Prapasotsil[Mew] (BA) : Graduate School of Architecture and Design, King Mongkut's University of Technology, Thonburi, Bangkok 2011, currently practice in Bangkok.
Nada Inthaphunt : Study in final year at School of Architecture and Design, King Mongkut's University of Technology, Thonburi, Bangkok

152 TsuTsuTsu-Village

Vallo Sadovsky Architects

Vallo & Sadovsky Architects was founded in 2004 by architects Matus Vallo and Oliver Sadovsky. Based in Bratislava, Slovakia, the practice focuses on architecture, town planning and interior design as well as on smaller scale projects comprising furniture and exhibition design. Through gained experience abroad, the young practice has developed a good base knowledge for mastering all stages of architectural design. VSA have a strong understanding of the social aspect of architecture and developed a clear belief that architecture in general can affect people's everyday life.
www.vallosadovsky.sk

118 Community Centre Dobriš

161 Mixed-Use Building Konventná Street

Thurlow Small Architecture

Founded in 2001 by Maia Small, AIA and Andrew Thurlow. Thurlow Small Architecture offers architecture, interiors, and urban design services in Rhode Island and Massachusetts. TSA is a registered WBE/DBE.

Andrew Thurlow is a partner at Thurlow Small Architecture and a tenured Associate Professor in Architecture at the Roger Williams University School of Architecture, Art & Historic Preservation, where he founded and runs the Digital Manufacturing Laboratory. His current professional and academic interests focus on the reciprocities between digital technologies and architectural design, with specific emphasis on integrated workflow models of parametric modeling and robotic prototyping.

Maia Small, AIA is a partner at Thurlow Small Architecture, Inc., an architecture and urban design office begun in 2001 that operates in the local networks of Rhode Island and the global discourse of architecture and landscape urbanism. Along with being a registered and experienced architect, her area of expertise is in urban environments and infrastructure.
www.thurlowsmall.com

002 400,000 Houses

003 AIDS Mobile Unit

021 Y-Wing Housing

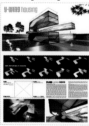

077 Gabion Field

254 Yeosu Pavilion Competition

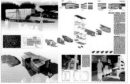

286 Bastion Lattice

288 The Green Ray

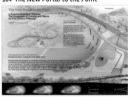

302 Tea House

321 Laminar Booth

325 Sukkah Sill

327 Obvita Slide

why-architecture

wHY Architecture is a collaborative workshop for creativity in architecture and design that brings a fresh and unfettered approach to each project. Each new project is considered unique and succinct, and is approached with no pre-determined style or set vocabulary. wHY Architecture brings their teamwork approach to all projects and injects new ideas and solutions in architecture so that it is executed with the highest degree of quality and intelligence in construction.
www.why-architecture.com

104 The New Portal to the Point

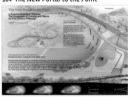

217 Quebec

WWAA

Architects Marcin Mosrafa and Natalia Paszkowska are founding partners of WWAA. They co-operated as students of Warsaw Technical Uni. on school projects and have been working together since 2003, with focus on projects for architectural contests, of which majority they won or were awarded prizes. WWAA undertakes actions in many scales ranging from graphics, every-day use objects to furniture, urban objects, interiors, houses, office buildings as well as public buildings.

Since 2010 we have been tightly cooperating on several projects with a renown Slovakian, now based in Warsaw, stage designer Boris Kudicka. Marcin Mostafa and Natalia Paszkowska have been cooperating since 2005. They have entered for the Expo 2010 competition together with their friend Wkjtek Kakowski. In 2008 they won together with Jan Sukiennik competition for cultural centre in Warwaw.
www.wwaa.pl

257 Thematic Pavilion Expo 2012 Yeosu

259 Polish Pavilion Expo 2010 Shanghai

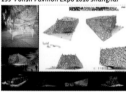

334 Lotto Kiosk

335 2009 Milano Public Design Festival

XCOOP

More than architecture. - The world economical recession instigates strategies for re-thinking situations and confronting prevailing realities:

XCOOP® is a think tank, that through its flexible and permeable approach, analyses contemporary living and provides creative solutions within a wide range of professions.

XCOOP® engages professionals exhibiting strong skills in their particular area of expertise and involves them in a virtual brainstorm through an untiring network exchange.

XCOOP® aims at transforming and improving our surroundings by involving the right mix of professionals to maximize quality and by applying the right ambition into everyday life.

XCOOP® values human initiative, promotes exchange and information, and strives into approving local resources and efficiency.
www.xcoop.org

006 De Laanwoningen in Haagwijk

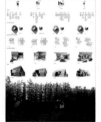

123 Alibaba

XML Architecture Research Urbanism

XML is a contemporary cultural practice specialized in Architecture, Research and Urbanism. XML is interested in developing architectures that both reflect and provoke contemporary ways of life. By understanding program organization as a key strategy within each project XML aims for establishing new relations between buildings and society, the projects of the office are fuelled by a reflection on the contemporary city as source of cultural production.

From its base in Amsterdam XML has been involved in worldwide cross-disciplinary projects with an emphasis on cultural analysis. The work of XML is characterized by a research driven approach. XML continuously works on a wide rage of scales, ranging from a series of spatial scenario's for the Netherlands in 2040 for the Goverment Chief Architect, to a design for a multi use building at the heart of Amsterdam, and researching and designing the interior architecture of the plenary hall of parliaments.

www.x-m-l.org

86 TALLINN - GREEN CEMENT

307 New Serlachius Museum

69 El Cementerio de la Cornisa

Yoshihara | McKee | Architects

Our partnership was established in 1996 with offices in New York and Tokyo. Our projects range in type and size from small residential works to large scale urban interventions. This wide variety of projects has allowed us to work with many types of programs and clients. We have developed innovative uses of under-utilized materials for private residences as well as large scale institutions that chance the urban character of the city.

Our working relationship started during the construction of the Tokyo International Forum, a cultural complex in Tokyo. Since that time we have been working and traveling together, between offices in New York and Tokyo. Through our work we strive to understand the differences and similarities of perception, materiality and space between western and eastern culture.

We approach each project as a unique opportunity to collaborate on issues of culture, the environment, and materiality. Every project is different and provides new challenges. We provide full architectural services from feasibility studies through to the final commissioning of the project, with the understanding that construction administration is a vital stage in implementing the design.

We continue to test our architectural ideas in the theoretical world of competitions, and we also enjoy the process of seeing our projects being built.

www.yoshiharamckee.com

218 Fútbol Para la Oportunidad Social

328 Origami Spiral

ZALEWSKI ARCHITECTURE GROUP

ZALEWSKI ARCHITECTURE GROUP is an architectural office residing in Gliwice (Poland) established in 2005 by Krzysztof Zalewski. The office specializes in individual projects adapted to particular needs of each and every client. ZAG architects have vast experience in designing various buildings: commercial, administrative and office buildings, hotels, healthcare facilities, industrial objects and residential) buildings.

ZAG team was awarded in numerous local and nationwide contests and it has built reputation and recognition for working not only with individual clients but also with state institutions and well-known natiohal companies.

"For us architecture is a part of cultural environment surrounding a man. It refers to the past and to the present. It is continuously transformed by the time - defined by the user's present needs and designed to realize its future functions. Our aim is to create architecture that corresponds with the time in which it is created, the localization in which it is set, and with the user for whom it should serve."

www.zalewskiag.com

027 Housing Estate in Zabrze

163 FIS-SST Office Building

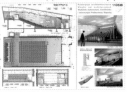

180 Lecture Halls A, B, C at Silesian University of Technology

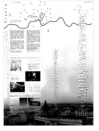

287 Cracow Triennial of Architecture

ZO_loft

With the addiction of dissimilar competence, individuality and personality mixed with an ongoing research and experiences ZO_loft was born, offering a mobile, dynamic, and flexible architecture, design and urban space.

ZO_loft proposes to discover and use inexpensive and sustainable technologies and materials, while analizing recovery and recycling processes, investigating in life-style and activities of our fellow human, providing easy marketing strategies and better understanding the differing consumpion needs of the populations in general.

Planning and managing the changement ZO_loft is following its aims by reinventing or hybridizing functions, contaminating or showing an apparent funcional disgregation.

What we do - architecture, industrial design, interior design, technical consulting, product development ed engineering, exhibitions and events setting, communication scheming, temporary performance and installations, marketing management e communication scheming, rendering *and 3D modeling.*

http://www.zo-loft.com

098 Arbatax Waterfront

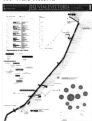

099 Viale Vittoria

182 Campus Folcara

184 Campus USI / SUPSI Lugano

272 Piazza Dante

273 Piazza Duomo

274 Piazza Gregis

322 Centro Storico Teramo

323 Centro Storico Sora